From Peril to Partnership

From Peril to Partnership

US Security Assistance and the Bid to Stabilize Colombia and Mexico

Paul J. Angelo

A Council on Foreign Relations Book

OXFORD
UNIVERSITY PRESS

Oxford University Press is a department of the University of Oxford. It furthers the University's objective of excellence in research, scholarship, and education by publishing worldwide. Oxford is a registered trade mark of Oxford University Press in the UK and certain other countries.

Published in the United States of America by Oxford University Press
198 Madison Avenue, New York, NY 10016, United States of America.

Library of Congress Cataloging-in-Publication Data
Names: Angelo, Paul J., author.
Title: From peril to partnership : US security assistance and the bid to stabilize Colombia and Mexico / Paul J. Angelo.
Description: New York, NY : Oxford University Press, 2024. |
Includes bibliographical references and index.
Identifiers: LCCN 2023009079 (print) | LCCN 2023009080 (ebook) |
ISBN 9780197688106 (hardback) | ISBN 9780197688120 |
ISBN 9780197688113 (epub) | ISBN 9780197688137
Subjects: LCSH: Military assistance, American—Colombia. | Military assistance, American—Mexico. | Internal security—Colombia. | Internal security—Mexico. | Drug control—Colombia. | Drug control—Mexico. |
Plan Colombia (U.S.) | Merida Initiative (U.S.)
Classification: LCC E183.8.C7 A64 2023 (print) | LCC E183.8.C7 (ebook) |
DDC 327.730861—dc23/eng/20230324
LC record available at https://lccn.loc.gov/2023009079
LC ebook record available at https://lccn.loc.gov/2023009080

DOI: 10.1093/oso/9780197688106.001.0001

Printed by Sheridan Books, Inc., United States of America

The Council on Foreign Relations (CFR) is an independent, nonpartisan membership organization, think tank, and publisher dedicated to being a resource for its members, government officials, business executives, journalists, educators and students, civic and religious leaders, and other interested citizens in order to help them better understand the world and the foreign policy choices facing the United States and other countries. Founded in 1921, CFR carries out its mission by maintaining a diverse membership, including special programs to promote interest and develop expertise in the next generation of foreign policy leaders; convening meetings at its headquarters in New York and in Washington, DC, and other cities where senior government officials, members of Congress, global leaders, and prominent thinkers come together with CFR members to discuss and debate major international issues; supporting a Studies Program that fosters independent research, enabling CFR scholars to produce articles, reports, and books and hold roundtables that analyze foreign policy issues and make concrete policy recommendations; publishing *Foreign Affairs*, the preeminent journal of international affairs and US foreign policy; sponsoring Independent Task Forces that produce reports with both findings and policy prescriptions on the most important foreign policy topics; and providing up-to-date information and analysis about world events and American foreign policy on its website, www.cfr.org.

The Council on Foreign Relations takes no institutional positions on policy issues and has no affiliation with the US government. All views expressed in its publications and on its website are the sole responsibility of the author or authors.

In memory of Grandma Liz (1932-2022), Kevin Middlebrook (1950-2022), Malcolm Deas (1941-2023), and Mario Scafuro (1954-2023)

Contents

Acknowledgments

This book represents the culmination of more than twenty years of academic, professional, and personal experience in US–Latin American security relations. The final product would not have been as complete or as accurate without the input of thousands of people spanning three continents. I remain humbled by the generosity, candor, and humor of the many individuals who supported me along the way.

I am especially grateful to my colleagues, mentors, and managers in government service. From the Pentagon's counternarcotics office and the US Southern Command to US embassies in Colombia and Honduras and the US Naval Academy, the teams on which I worked encouraged and challenged me—reminding me time and again that foreign policy decision-making is seldom black and white. Likewise, I am inspired by the example of service given by so many of the people I met on my journey—be they representatives of the US Department of Defense, partner governments, academia, journalism, or the human rights movement. I hope the words in this book do justice to the nuanced and purposeful thinking they embody.

I reserve special gratitude, as well, for the hundreds of people who sat for interviews with me during fieldwork trips to Colombia and Mexico. I did my best to meet people where they were intellectually, emotionally, and even geographically—and along the way had riveting conversations with sources in an array of locations: coffee shops, dog parks, a water taxi, billiards halls, government offices, and remote jungle outposts. Several interviewees opened their homes to me. Honoring the trust they displayed as we discussed sensitive issues, ones that could put their personal safety at risk, is a responsibility I take seriously. I have identified interviewees only when they specifically requested it. The anonymity of the many other people who contributed to this book's content reflects the ongoing challenges they face in advancing security, justice, and peace in the Americas. I was careful to ensure that the book's conclusions faithfully represent their collective wisdom, but whatever the shortcomings in these pages, they are mine alone.

To bring this project to fruition, I found an exceptional partner in Oxford University Press. My editor, David McBride, was supportive, insightful, and patient during more than two years of collaboration, and I cannot thank him enough. Likewise, Sarah Ebel's diligence and responsiveness were critical in getting this book to print. Mahalakshmi Balamurugan also proved a most thorough and communicative production manager, and Rudy Leon was helpful in bringing together my index.

The Council on Foreign Relations (CFR), under the leadership of Richard Haass, put tremendous faith in this project. As with much of what CFR produces, the final product was a team effort. James Lindsay, Shannon O'Neil, and Patricia Lee Dorff deserve a special mention for pushing me at every turn to refine my language, challenge my assumptions, and identify the policy relevance of my project. Their vision helped ensure that this book serves to inform academic debates and policy discussions alike. I owe so much to my two research associates, David Gevarter and Caroline Kapp. They were fabulous colleagues and intellectual partners without whom this book would have been impossible. Helen Glenn Court, my independent copyeditor, helped pick up where David and Caroline left off, and her detail orientation was only outmatched by her enthusiasm and good nature. Jacquelyn Bengfort expertly corrected the final draft manuscript and caught every misapplied preposition. Thank you.

Other CFR colleagues who contributed in big and small ways include Ramila Jacovich, Dominic Bocci, Steven Cook, Alice Hill, Liz Economy, Charlie Kupchan, Sergio Infante, Inu Manak, Stewart Patrick, Paul Stares, Amy Baker, Jean-Michel Oriol, Shira Shwartz, Chris Tuttle, Marcelo Agudo, Janine Hill, Victoria Alekhine, Patrick Costello, Meghan Sullivan, Anya Schmemann, Jenny Malamo, Megan Daley, Susan Nelson, Katharine Ferguson, Hunter Hallman, Hassanatu Savage, Sara Shah, José Pablo Ampudia, Felipe Deidan, Fabiana Avendaño, Andrés Villar, Kara Molnar, Samuel Lynch, Luciany Capra, Leticia Chacón, Gabriela Saenz, and Lauren Overton. I also appreciated the chance to talk through security assistance with CFR's resident experts, its military and intelligence fellows: Myles Caggins, Jon Eberlan, Walker Field, Rob Francis, Doug Jackson, Mark Kappelmann, Bill Patterson, Roy Pettis, Sean Reagan, James Ryans, and Jay Vann.

The Smith Richardson Foundation generously supported this project through a grant awarded as part of the Strategy and Policy Fellows program, enabling me to convene a group of experts to review select chapters of my draft manuscript. I am ever thankful to Frank Mora for bringing his expertise to those sessions as moderator. Other contributors who provided oral and written feedback include Rodrigo Aguilar, Cynthia Arnson, Liliana Ayalde, Raúl Benítez-Manaut, Guadalupe Correa-Cabrera, Richard Downie, Gabriel Farfán-Mares, Maggie Feldman-Piltch, Barbara Fick, Brian Fonseca, Luigi Einaudi, Vanda Felbab-Brown, Juan Carlos Gómez, Caryn Hollis, Adam Isacson, Daniel Mahanty, Kristina Mani, P. Michael McKinley, Johanna Mendelson-Foreman, Keith Mines, Mark Morris, James Nealon, Pat Paterson,

Anne Patterson, Randy Pestana, Annie Pforzheimer, John Polga-Hecimovich, Celina Realuyo, Dan Restrepo, Gimena Sánchez-Garzoli, Andrew Shapiro, Arturo Sotomayor, David Spencer, and Mark Wilkins. I am also grateful to Juan Pablo Cortés, the talented illustrator who designed the cover art. He represents a new generation of creatives in Honduras pushing boundaries and imparting hope.

My youthful interest in Latin America became a lifelong passion thanks to the inspired work and mentorship of Rebecca Bill Chavez, Jim Stavridis, Mike LaRosa, Kevin Middlebrook, and Malcolm Deas. This cohort indulged my curiosity and afforded me the intellectual tools needed to complete an undertaking of this magnitude. I am forever in their debt.

At the US Naval Academy, University of Oxford, and University College London, other leading influences, some of whom provided feedback on earlier drafts of this book, include Sean Fahey, Josh Hollands, Dan Masterson, Iwan Morgan, Craig Mullaney, Jenny Pearce, Eduardo Posada-Carbó, Tim Power, Kate Saunders-Hastings, Sharon Voros, and Stephen and Alexandra Wrage. My colleagues from the US Naval Academy's Languages and Cultures Department, the William J. Perry Center for Hemispheric Defense Studies, and the US Navy Foreign Area Officer community also demonstrated unparalleled support at different stages of the project.

So many friends and loved ones listened to me discuss (and fret over) this project for years, providing advice and perspective when I needed them most. I am especially appreciative of Ali Kalaji, Lisa Munde, Stephanie Junger-Moat, Leo Arango, Yasir Arce Molinares, Chris Musangi, Javier Arrieta, Mauricio Artiñano, Terry and Brian Babcock-Lumish, Ricardo Burgos, Gwen Burnyeat, Michael Camilleri, Jud Campbell, Augie Domínguez, Will Freeman, Bridget Friese, Carolina González, Glen Goodman, Jarahn Hillsman, Trang Ho, Olga Illera, Helen and Robert Knox, Michelle Kotek, Kristina Leszczak, Evelyn Pérez-Verdía, Celi Pitt, Jorge Rincón, Delphine Schrank, Lev Sviridov, Stewart Tuttle, Doug Wilson, Hakan Yilmaz, and Nick Zimmerman.

Finally, I owe so much to my family, especially my parents—Sandra and Mario Scafuro and Carmen and Diane Angelo. They may not have always understood my path—one that took me far away from them for long periods of time—but they always encouraged my ambitions and supported my decisions. Likewise, my late grandparents, Elizabeth Julian and Carmen Angelo, imparted the skills on which I drew every day of the writing and production process. The work ethic and concern for the world I inherited from them are reflected in these pages. This book is as much theirs as it is mine.

List of Acronyms and Abbreviations

	English	Spanish
ABD	Air Bridge Denial	
ACI	Andean Counterdrug Initiative	
ACP	Andean Counterdrug Program	
AFEUR	Urban Counterterrorism Special Forces Group	Agrupación de Fuerzas Especiales Antiterroristas Urbanas (Colombia)
AFI	Federal Investigative Agency	Agencia Federal de Investigación (Mexico)
AI	Integrated Action	Acción Integral (Colombia)
ANAP	National Academy for Penitentiary Administration	Academia Nacional de Administración Penitenciaria (Mexico)
ANDI	National Association of Businesspersons	Asociación Nacional de Empresarios de Colombia
AUC	United Self-Defense Forces of Colombia	Autodefensas Unidas de Colombia
BACRIM	criminal bands	bandas criminales (Colombia)
CARSI	Central America Regional Security Initiative	
CCAI	Center for Integrated Action Coordination	Centro de Coordinación de Acción Integral (Colombia)
CEDEF	Committee for the Design of the Army of the Future	Comité de Diseño del Ejército del Futuro (Colombia)
CETI	Strategic Committee for Transformation and Innovation	Comité Estratégico de Transformación e Innovación (Colombia)
CIA	Central Intelligence Agency	
CISEN	Investigation and National Security Center	Centro de Investigación y Seguridad Nacional (Mexico)
CNDH	National Commission for Human Rights	Comisión Nacional de Derechos Humanos (Mexico)
CNMH	National Center for Historical Memory	Centro Nacional para la Memoria Histórica (Colombia)
CNS	National Commission of Security	Comisión Nacional de Seguridad (Mexico)
COTEF	Command for the Transformation of the Army of the Future	Comando de Transformación del Ejército del Futuro
CREI	Committee for Strategic Review and Innovation	Comité de Revisión Estratégica e Innovación (Colombia)
CSDI	Colombian Strategic Development Initiative	

	English	Spanish
DAS	Administrative Security Department	Departamento Administrativo de Seguridad (Colombia)
DDR	disarmament, demobilization, and reintegration	
DEA	Drug Enforcement Administration	
DFS	Federal Directorate of Security	Dirección Federal de Seguridad (Mexico)
DIILS	Defense Institute for International Legal Studies	
DIRI	Defense Institution Reform Initiative	
DNI	National Intelligence Directorate	Dirección Nacional de Inteligencia (Colombia)
DRMR	Defense Resource Management Reform	
DSCA	Defense Security Cooperation Agency	
DSCU	Defense Security Cooperation University	
DTO	drug-trafficking organization	
ELN	National Liberation Army	Ejército de Liberación Nacional (Colombia)
ENSI	National Poll about Insecurity	Encuesta Nacional sobre Inseguridad (Colombia)
ENVIPE	National Survey on Victimization and Perception of Public Security	Encuesta Nacional de Victimización y Percepción sobre Seguridad (Mexico)
ESF	Economic Support Fund	
ESMAD	Mobile Antiriot Squad	Esquadrón Móvil Antidisturbios (Colombia)
EU	European Union	
EUM	end-use monitoring	
EZLN	Zapatista National Liberation Army	Ejército Zapatista de Liberación Nacional (Mexico)
FARC	Revolutionary Armed Forces of Colombia	Fuerzas Armadas Revolucionarias de Colombia
FASP	Public Security Support Fund	Fondo de Aportaciones para la Seguridad Pública (Mexico)
FBI	Federal Bureau of Investigation	
FGN	Attorney General's Office	Fiscalía General de la Nación (Colombia)
FGR	National Prosecutor's Office	Fiscalía General de la República (Mexico)
FICOSEC	Trust for Competitiveness and Citizen Security	Fideicomiso para la Competitividad y Seguridad Ciudadana (Mexico)

	English	Spanish
FMF	Foreign Military Financing	
FORTASEG	Subsidy for the Strengthening of Performance in Public Security	Fortalecimiento del Desempeño en Materia de Seguridad Pública (Mexico)
FUDRA	Rapid Deployment Force	Fuerza de Despliegue Rápido (Colombia)
GAFE	Airmobile Special Forces Group	Grupo Aeromóvil de Fuerzas Especiales (Mexico)
GAULA	Groups of Unified Action for Anti-Kidnapping	Grupos de Acción Unificada por la Libertad Personal (Colombia)
GDP	gross domestic product	
GIEI	Interdisciplinary Group of Independent Experts	Grupo Interdisciplinario de Expertos Independientes (Mexico)
IACHR	Inter-American Commission on Human Rights	
IACtHR	Inter-American Court of Human Rights	
ICESI	Citizens' Institute for Studies on Insecurity	Instituto Ciudadano de Estudios sobre la Inseguridad (Mexico)
IMET	International Military Education and Training	
INCD	National Institute to Combat Drugs	Instituto Nacional para el Combate a las Drogas (Mexico)
INCLE	International Narcotics Control and Law Enforcement	
INEGI	National Institute of Statistics and Geography	Instituto Nacional de Estadística y Geografía (Mexico)
INPEC	National Penitentiary and Prison Institute	Instituto Nacional Penitenciario y Carcelario (Colombia)
ISEA	International School of Education and Advising	
ISG	Institute for Security Governance	
JEP	Special Peace Jurisdiction	Jurisdicción Especial para la Paz (Colombia)
LC23S	23 September Communist League	Liga Comunista 23 de Septiembre (Mexico)
M-19	19th of April Movement	Movimiento 19 de Abril (Colombia)
MAP	Military Assistance Program	
MAR	Revolutionary Action Movement	Movimiento de Acción Revolucionaria (Mexico)
MORENA	National Regeneration Movement Party	Movimiento de Regeneración Nacional (Mexico)
MSSD	most similar systems design	

	English	Spanish
MTT	mobile training team	
NADR	Nonproliferation, Antiterrorism, Demining, and Related	
NAFTA	North American Free Trade Agreement	
NATO	North Atlantic Treaty Organization	
NORTHCOM	US Northern Command	
OADPRS	Prevention and Social Readaptation Agency	Órgano Administrativo Desconcentrado Prevención y Readaptación Social (Mexico)
OECD	Organization for Economic Co-operation and Development	
OHCHR	Office of the United Nations High Commissioner for Human Rights	
PAN	National Action Party	Partido Acción Nacional (Mexico)
PDLP	Party of the Poor	Partido de los Pobres (Mexico)
PETEF	Strategic Transformation Plan for an Army of the Future	Plan Estratégico de Transformación Ejército del Futuro (Colombia)
PFM	Federal Ministerial Police	Policía Federal Ministerial (Mexico)
PFP	Federal Preventive Police	Policía Federal Preventiva (Mexico)
PGN	Inspector General's Office	Procuraduría General de la Nación (Colombia)
PGR	Attorney General's Office	Procuraduría General de la República (Mexico)
PJF	Federal Judicial Police	Policía Judicial Federal (Mexico)
PNCT	National Territorial Consolidation Plan	Plan Nacional de Consolidación Territorial (Colombia)
PRD	Democratic Revolutionary Party	Partido de la Revolución Democrática (Mexico)
PRI	Institutional Revolutionary Party	Partido Revolucionario Institucional (Mexico)
PSI	party system institutionalization	
SEDENA	Secretariat of National Defense	Secretaría de Defensa Nacional (Mexico)
SEGOB	Secretariat of the Interior	Secretaría de Gobernación (Mexico)
SEMAR	Secretariat of the Navy	Secretaría de Marina (Mexico)
SETEC	Secretariat for Justice Sector Reform	Secretaría Técnica (Mexico)

	English	Spanish
SIEDCO	Statistical Information System for Delinquency, Coexistence, and Operations	Sistema de Información Estadístico, Delincuencial, Contravencional y Operativo (Colombia)
SOUTHCOM	US Southern Command	
SSP	Secretariat of Public Security	Secretaría de Seguridad Pública (Mexico)
SSPC	Secretariat of Security and Civilian Protection	Secretaría de Seguridad y Protección Ciudadana (Mexico)
SSR	security sector reform	
STCSN	Technical Secretary of the National Security Council	Secretariado Técnico del Consejo de Seguridad Nacional (Mexico)
SUBSEMUN	Municipal Public Security Subsidy	Subsidio de Seguridad Pública Municipal (Mexico)
UP	Patriotic Union	Unión Patriótica (Colombia)
USAID	US Agency for International Development	
USCAP	US-Colombia Action Plan	
USMCA	United States–Mexico–Canada Agreement	

Forged under Fire: US Partnership with Colombia and Mexico

Latin America's appetite for the *narconovela*, the television genre that depicts the drama of the drug trade, peaked around the time that Colombia's infamous Norte del Valle Cartel disintegrated and just as Mexico's top cartels came to dominate the production and transshipment of the region's drug products. With the soaring drug violence of the 1990s, the worst in Colombia's history, in the rearview mirror, the country's entertainment industry in the mid-2000s launched wildly successful soap operas depicting life on the wrong side of the law. *Mafia Dolls* (*Las muñecas de la mafia*), *The Snitch Cartel* (*El Cartel de los Sapos*), and *Pablo Escobar: The Drug Lord* (*Pablo Escobar: el patrón del mal*) portrayed the intrigue, glamor, violence, and chaos of Colombia's most notorious cartels and armed groups—and the international tentacles of Latin America's drug trade. But these shows were more than entertainment. Their timing and global reach were such that the Mexican market, itself beleaguered by rising drug violence, could take stock of the lessons of Colombia's tragedy.[1] *Narconovelas* were at once a reminder of just how bad things had been and a sensationalist warning of the perils of mismanaging security.

In the mid-2010s, Netflix capitalized on this successful template and revived these dramas for an English-speaking audience, one far removed from the violence perpetrated by Latin America's drug gangs but all too familiar with their illicit exports. The United States has long been the premier market for illicit narcotics globally, but until *Narcos* was released in 2015 Americans' exposure to the international consequences of their appetite for drugs was limited to a handful of popular books—Mark Bowden's *Killing Pablo* and Michael Levine's *Deep Cover*—and blockbuster films such as *Scarface*, *Traffic*, and *Blow*. Although these projects profiled Latin America's most treacherous personalities, seldom were the stories told through the lens of the Latin Americans who lived and died for the drug trade. *Narcos* attempted to rectify this oversight by giving voice to drug barons, their families, and public officials in Colombia and Mexico. However, season after season the real protagonist of the series was the US Department of Justice's Drug Enforcement

From Peril to Partnership. Paul J. Angelo, Oxford University Press. © Oxford University Press 2024.
DOI: 10.1093/oso/9780197688106.003.0001

Administration (DEA), embodied by actor portrayals of real-life agents Javier Peña, Steve Murphy, and Kiki Camarena.

Inevitably, *Narcos* draws comparisons between Colombia's and Mexico's experiences in the drug wars and the United States' role in helping wage them, something this book also does. However, that the show is set more than thirty years in the past hides the ultimate lesson: the Colombia of Pablo Escobar is long gone, but the Mexico of Miguel Ángel Félix Gallardo is still in full swing. Indeed, *Narcos'* portrayal of Latin America's governance problems ignores the nuance so essential to understanding why Colombia was able to subdue its worst offenders while improving security for its citizens and why Mexico has failed to dismantle its cartels and reduce crime and violence. Central to that story are the institutions that have received as little attention in academia as they do in popular culture: Colombia's and Mexico's state security forces.

Police officers, detectives, soldiers, and sailors are at once heroes and villains in the saga to bring security and the law to vast regions of Latin America's most violent countries. On the one hand, they answered a call to service at great risk to their lives and the lives of their families in taking on cartels, paramilitary groups, and insurgencies resolved to subvert and even overthrow the democratic political order. Some analysts have described that brand of commitment in a country like Colombia as nothing short of quixotic, bordering on reckless and even suicidal.[2]

The same forces tasked with bringing safety and order, however, have themselves betrayed the Colombian and Mexican people from time to time in gross violations of human rights and major acts of corruption. In some instances, they have served as invaluable points of entry for organized crime groups seeking to suborn the state, eroding the credibility and legitimacy of the police and military to act on behalf of and in service to citizens.

Yet when the viability of the state was called into question during escalating drug violence in both Colombia and Mexico, the security forces were in no uncertain terms the one thing standing in the way of a complete collapse of government. This book is the story of how they helped prevent such disasters and, just as important, how civilian officials simultaneously aimed to limit the actions of the police and militaries by holding them accountable to democratic norms.

But as *Narcos'* US protagonists suggest, Colombia and Mexico were not alone in their struggle. The US government played a major role in taking on criminals and helping refashion, and even forge, new state security forces. The DEA was an important but not solitary actor in this scenario. In both Latin American countries, the United States pursued a whole-of-government approach to facilitate institutional reform in the security and justice sectors—that is, its Congress and a broad spectrum of executive agencies rallied behind two of the most significant US foreign assistance commitments in the post–Cold War era. To the extent that this book is about Colombia's and Mexico's security forces, it is also a portrait of how Washington leveraged its long-standing relations with counterparts in Bogotá and Mexico City to help build more effective and accountable police and military institutions in those countries.

Plan Colombia (2000–11) and the Mérida Initiative (2007–16), as US assistance efforts in Colombia and Mexico became respectively known, were multibillion-dollar programs intended to enhance security provision, fortify justice, and deepen democratic governance. Both programs lasted approximately a decade, and the primary beneficiaries in Colombia and Mexico included law enforcement agencies such as police and criminal investigative units; armed forces including the army, air force, navy, and marines; prosecutorial offices and public defenders; and even civil society organizations that helped address the causes of crime and violence and worked to hold governments accountable for transgressions committed by state officials. US security assistance to Colombia and Mexico recognized state security forces not only as partners but also as potential sources of insecurity engaged in predatory practices that eroded public trust. Thus the United States supported partner efforts to implement security sector reform. More professional, capable, and democratic government institutions, it was thought, would be more effective in disrupting criminal activities while restoring credibility and legitimacy to the state.

For the United States, Plan Colombia and the Mérida Initiative were each a means to an end: a reduction in drug trafficking, the stabilization of volatile and violent neighbors, and the defense of democratic partners in the Western Hemisphere. But security assistance also carried tremendous political symbolism, elevating Colombia and Mexico as top US foreign policy priorities, even while US national attention was focused mostly on the Middle East and Central Asia.[3] US partnership with Colombia and Mexico eventually took on political symbolism and strategic value for the United States, too, especially with the rise of leftist leaders in Latin America in the early 2000s who sought greater distance and autonomy from Washington. In this way, partnership via Plan Colombia and the Mérida Initiative—the "means"—became a highly relevant end state in its own right.

For some officials and institutions in the recipient countries, US security assistance was seen as a lifeline—an expression of diplomatic, economic, and political partnership at times when the state was under assault.[4] The United States became an essential facilitator of institutional transformation by providing expertise, training, equipment, and intelligence. It also provided the Colombian and Mexican security sectors with access to security hardware and technology that had previously been off limits, invariably provoking a pivot in the way US partners waged their campaigns against nonstate armed groups. And although US contributions were considerable, the Colombian and Mexican governments were every bit as committed to the effort, outspending the United States on revitalizing their security sectors by at least a factor of four in Colombia and of ten in Mexico.

Despite comparable agendas and similar programs implemented via Plan Colombia and the Mérida Initiative, the desired outcomes materialized far more in Colombia than in Mexico. Whereas Colombia saw crime and terrorism drop considerably and public support for the police and military soar, Mexico's security sector demonstrated little progress in restraining violent offenders and saw an erosion of its credibility as corruption and human rights abuses increased. This book seeks to explain this difference. To date, much of the academic literature about security assistance centers on the donor country—in these cases, the United States—and far too little on domestic conditions in recipient countries that enable or impede positive outcomes for security sector reform. *From Peril to Partnership*, on the other hand, puts Colombian and Mexican institutions at the center of the analysis and, in doing so, deepens the understanding of what factors underpin the success or failure of security assistance. Ultimately, it concludes that private sector support, continuity in security strategy, and security sector centralization led to more favorable outcomes in Colombia than in Mexico.

What Is Security Assistance?

Security assistance refers to financial resources, services, hardware, and education and training contributed to a foreign government for enhancing that nation's security in ways that help meet a donor government's strategic objectives. For the United States, the primary goal is to advance US national and international security by empowering allies and partners to confront shared challenges to peace and stability.[5] It is at once a technical and political tool of statecraft. Such assistance entails arms transfers, training and equipping combat forces, law enforcement support, defense institution reform and capacity-building, humanitarian assistance, and educational activities.[6] The United States has a long tradition of providing aid to allied militaries, dating as far back as the Spanish-American War, but in recent decades security assistance has become central to a "lighter-footprint approach" to stabilize fragile partner states without directly committing US troops.[7] The provision of arms, technology, training, and technical support to a foreign police or military force is a responsibility of the secretary of state, as enshrined in the Foreign Assistance Act of 1961 and the Arms Export Control Act of 1976. But in the period following the attacks of September 11, 2001, Congress approved expanded authorities for the Department of Defense to implement an increasing share of security assistance programming globally with the aim of building more capable counterterrorism partners during wartime.[8] The Pentagon refers to these activities as "security cooperation," but they are, in fact, an integral part of the US security assistance architecture. Collectively, US security assistance to and cooperation with partner governments between fiscal years 2006 and 2016 topped out at more than $204.6 billion and made up about 27 percent of total foreign aid, second only to socioeconomic development funding and signaling the prominence of security assistance as a preferred US foreign policy tool.[9]

Congress plays an essential role in structuring security assistance and in providing oversight of its administration through two main funding authorities, Title 22 and Title 10.[10] Title 22 funds are appropriated to the Department of State to fund the department's activities related to arms and materiel sales and donations, peacekeeping operations, development strategies, nonproliferation and antiterrorism efforts, and international narcotics and law enforcement support. Even though the Department of State retains ultimate authority over the distribution of such resources, it consults and frequently allocates Title 22 funds to the Department of Defense for management and implementation of the purchase and sale of military hardware to foreign governments, the transfer of excess defense articles to them, and military-to-military training missions. Title 10 funds, on the other hand, are reserved exclusively for the Department of Defense and cover programs associated with security cooperation with foreign forces, including train-and-equip programs, capacity-building of partner forces, exercise and operational support, institutional reform, counternarcotics, and humanitarian assistance. The executive departments in Washington manage and allocate Title 22 and Title 10 funds, but the associated programming is implemented principally by US diplomats, military personnel, and contractors attached to US embassies abroad and the Pentagon's geographic combatant commands.[11]

Although the State and Defense Departments control the lion's share of US security assistance resources, the Department of Justice, the US Agency for International Development (USAID), the Department of Homeland Security, and the intelligence community also participate in supplemental activities that support the overall objective. After all, holistic approaches that combine a donor government's instruments of national power reflect the wisdom of decades of Washington's involvement in military campaigns and development work abroad. Given the complexity of this ecosystem, the US government has repeatedly attempted to streamline coordination across executive departments and agencies. In 2013, the Barack Obama administration (2009–17) signed Presidential Policy Directive 23, encouraging greater interagency collaboration and calling for an overhaul of US security assistance planning and assessment procedures. In the years that followed, the US government created budgets that pooled resources across agencies and provided more flexible access to funds to address emergent threats more effectively. Unfortunately, understaffing at the Department of State and the resulting bureaucratic inertia constrained progress on improving coordination.[12] Additionally, in 2017, Congress consolidated budget lines for Department of Defense security assistance activities in the annual National Defense Authorization Act, creating a new Section 333 under Title 10 authority. However, no matter the growing legislative interest in exerting oversight of US security assistance, these programs designed to build partner capacity were partially redundant with those already covered under the Department of State's foreign military financing authorities, failing to accomplish meaningful differentiation across executive departments, let alone the intended State-Defense integration.

Interagency coordination is not the only or even principal challenge for US security assistance today. Despite the US government's repeated reliance on security assistance as a tool for global stability, such assistance all too often falls victim to a one-size-fits-all model that fails to account for the differences between security sectors in different countries and the unique political dynamics in countries on the receiving end of the aid. Critics argue that "under the current security assistance system, the returns on America's security investments are limited, inconsistent, and not strategic."[13] In addition to failing to tailor security assistance to match the specific circumstances of recipient governments, the architects of US security assistance also rely too heavily on ad hoc implementation, the US armed services seeing large-scale advisory duties as tangential to their primary mission and thus devoting too few resources for effective program execution.[14] Furthermore, security assistance as practiced today risks militarizing US foreign policy given the outsized voice of the Pentagon in formulating and implementing it, and regardless of the implementing department or agency, security assistance activities too often fall short on the systematic evaluation of program efficacy.

Worryingly, the bureaucratic setup risks perpetuating a status quo that empowers nondemocratic partners and undermines human rights given that US security assistance providers have occasionally prioritized battlefield accomplishments at the expense of accountability for crimes and abuses committed by US partners.[15] This is especially problematic, as former Secretary of Defense Robert Gates emphasizes, in that "the effectiveness and credibility of the United States will only be as good as the effectiveness, credibility, and sustainability of its local partners."[16] In one recent high-profile incident, Saudi Arabian citizens who would later go on to participate in the 2018 killing of journalist Jamal Khashoggi received State Department–approved paramilitary training in the United States.[17]

The 2019 Global Fragility Act was branded as a new strategy for preventing conflict and promoting stability through partnership with foreign governments in ways that seek to rectify the shortcomings of previous interventions, including addressing human rights abuses, corruption, and impunity. As of 2022, however, Washington had identified only nine focal countries and was dragging its feet on devising and then implementing ten-year plans for each of them, as stipulated by the law.[18]

As Washington wrestles with this task and seeks to make good on the promise of security assistance to enhance global stability, policymakers and practitioners can draw valuable lessons from Colombia and Mexico by evaluating conditions in recipient countries that affected the efficacy of US-funded programs and reforms. Armed with a greater appreciation of how local dynamics improve chances of success, Washington could then include tailored incentives for deeper cooperation with host nation institutions while disempowering or disincentivizing those officials or institutions that stand in the way of progress. Colombia and Mexico are particularly instructive because US security assistance efforts in those countries were unique when compared globally; they not only prioritized the operational effectiveness of partner forces but also emphasized democratic accountability. Plan Colombia and the Mérida Initiative are among the most comprehensive experiences in security assistance this century and are thus a critical consideration for improving the design of future US involvement with foreign security sectors.

What Is Security Sector Reform?

When the United States provides security assistance to a partner government, restoring or building the credibility of a state security sector can help delegitimize and dismantle rival armed groups and stabilize a volatile scenario. Further, when security assistance is directed in ways that seek to modify oversight and accountability of military and law enforcement organizations in accordance with democratic principles, donor countries such as the United States become parties to a process known as security sector reform. Unlike traditional train-and-equip missions characteristic of US security assistance in many countries, security sector reform demands improved governance of the security sector. The US government's focus on delivering not just effectiveness but also democratic legitimacy within Colombian and Mexican security institutions rendered Plan Colombia and the Mérida Initiative two of the most high-profile instances of US-backed security sector reform globally.[19]

The security sector reform concept originally took hold in the wake of the Cold War, a period of global democratization and economic liberalization that was accompanied by an increase in nonstate violence and organized criminal activity.[20] Threats to citizen security posed by common crime and the fear of crime shifted global attention from state-on-state violence to insecurity fueled by economic marginalization and social exclusion and perpetrated by nonstate domestic and transnational actors.[21] The notion of "human security," which prioritizes the safety and well-being of individuals and communities, prescribes that there can be no security without development.[22] Thus security sector reform arose as a response from donor countries to support conflict prevention and peacebuilding in other countries through "security and development policy . . . [to strengthen] the governance of security institutions; and . . . [to build] capable and professional security forces that are accountable to civil authorities."[23] Sarah Meharg and Aleisha Arnusch define the ultimate objective of security sector reform as the provision of "safety, security, and justice to [a] civilian population within the context of the *rule of law*."[24] By definition, security sector reform seeks to inculcate among security sector officials respect for democracy, for the independence of the law, and for its equal application to citizens and state agents alike.[25] As the theory suggests, a security sector that can provide for citizen security by employing its capacity for violence discerningly and proportionately while remaining answerable to the law contributes to a public order that maximizes the citizenry's exercise of democratic rights. After all, good security sector governance is associated with lower risk of civil war or the recurrence of internal armed conflict, the prevention of human rights abuses that fuel societal grievances, and improved public perceptions of state legitimacy.[26]

Accounting for the centrality of the rule of law to such endeavors, security sector reform seeks to advance democratic consolidation, and international donors such as the United States, the European Union, and the United Nations lend their support by sharing experience and expertise, providing financial resources, and verifying progress. The range of activities undertaken in the name of security sector reform is diverse. According to the US government,

> Security sector reform is an umbrella term that might include integrated activities in support of: defense and armed forces reform; civilian management and

oversight; justice; police, corrections; intelligence reform; national security planning and strategy support; border management; disarmament, demobilization, and reintegration; and/or reduction of armed violence.[27]

By nature, many of these activities are contentious—both for donor governments and in the recipient countries. Early theorists Thomas Hobbes and John Locke insisted that the state derives its power from its capacity to ensure the safety and security of its citizens, for those protections are at the heart of why citizens submit some of their freedoms to government in the first place.[28] Max Weber referred to this principle as "the monopoly of the legitimated use of force," noting that the state achieves legitimacy to the extent that it serves as the sole source of societal violence, administered principally by police and military forces to establish order as a collective benefit to its citizenry.[29] Not surprisingly, when a foreign government administers assistance to this end, its involvement is inherently sensitive because the kinds of support or reforms laid out by donor governments could upset the balance of political power in recipient countries.[30] Further, for the United States, security assistance entails political conditionality, or incentives and disincentives to improve partner government conduct on issues such as human rights, democratic governance, corruption, and nuclear proliferation. As Tommy Ross and Melissa Dalton describe, US officials have disproportionately focused on punitive measures that too often upset interlocutors in partner governments and strain US diplomatic relations while undermining possibilities for cooperation.[31]

For these reasons, the use of the term *security sector reform*, which itself suggests a vulnerability in partner governments, has fallen out of fashion in Washington in favor of *building partner capacity* and *defense institution-building* in the post-9/11 period.[32] The authors of the Presidential Policy Directive on Security Sector Assistance admitted that a principal reason US policymakers have been reluctant to use the term *security sector reform* is that it is less palatable to political leaders in partner nations. This does not mean, however, that the United States ever abandoned the underlying principles and objectives of security sector reform in its assistance.[33] If anything, the last decade has seen more attention and more resources devoted to advancing mechanisms of civilian control of the armed forces, accountability for abuses and crimes committed by security sector personnel, and bureaucratic professionalization among partner forces. Although these accountability objectives are seldom the top priority in US security assistance, they nonetheless are an important consideration in the design of US interventions, as reflected in the creation of new US institutions with governance objectives in mind. Today the Department of Defense's Defense Security Cooperation University oversees the International School of Education and Advising, which unites the Institute for Security Governance and the Defense Institute for International Legal Studies, and six regional centers that advise and train partner governments in best practices for defense institutional reform. What is more, since 2020 the Pentagon has invested unprecedented resources to train and develop its own security cooperation workforce, an effort to monitor and evaluate the accomplishment of US objectives systematically and to institutionalize lessons learned in security assistance implementation.[34]

Despite the importance of pro-democracy initiatives in Colombia and Mexico, political sensitivities surrounding the use of the term *security sector reform* were also present in the two countries. In Colombia, the Ministry of Defense billed Plan Colombia as a "transformation" process. One military official stressed that security sector reform wrongly implies that the security forces' way of doing business previously was "dirty and needed to be scrapped."[35] Another understood it as a "forced imposition from the outside," which was "never the case in Colombia."[36] In Mexico, public officials and security leaders seldom branded security sector reform as such, even though Mexico went even further than Colombia by creating entirely new security forces during the years of the Mérida Initiative. And though Mexican authorities and analysts interviewed for this book tended not to push back on the semantics as did some of their Colombian counterparts, reform measures were introduced in a piecemeal and incremental fashion, devoid of the pomp and circumstance as well as concerted public scrutiny of a wholesale sectoral reform. One former US official clarified Washington's security assistance motivations in saying that "security sector reform was not the point of all this, but it was the point of some of it, and Washington was delighted when its efforts started bearing fruits."[37] To this end, although the US experience in Colombia and Mexico is instructive in identifying trends, opportunities, and pitfalls in the administration of US security assistance across the board—and even of US-sponsored security sector reform—recognizing the political limits of US strategies and agenda-setting in partner security sectors is fundamental to the success or failure of a given intervention and, more broadly speaking, reinforces the principal conclusions of this book.

US Security Assistance to Help Stabilize Colombia and Mexico

To identify conditions that facilitate successful security assistance, including progress on security sector reform, this book analyzes variation on security sector governance in Colombia and Mexico, the central dependent variable in the literature on security assistance and security sector reform. Security sector governance is not a discrete, dichotomous variable. It should instead be understood as falling along a spectrum between good governance and bad governance.[38] Albrecht Schnabel describes good security sector governance as consisting of an "effective, affordable, and efficient security sector" that exhibits civilian democratic control and oversight by government ministries, legislatures, and civil society.[39] Similarly, Ursula Schröder identifies the two dimensions of security sector governance as the "quality of security provision," referring to the delivery of security to the citizens of a state, and the "quality of security sector governance," or the quality of the governing bodies and mechanisms that oversee the security sector.[40] Echoing this theoretical basis, the two criteria by which this book evaluates security sector governance are effectiveness, or the ability of security institutions to fulfill their designated function (provide security), and democratic accountability to civilian authorities and to the law, or the ability of oversight bodies to govern the security sector efficiently and transparently. Good security sector governance is "the goal," and security sector reform, including efforts encouraged by international security assistance, is a "way of getting there."[41]

The US record on advancing security sector governance in other countries is mixed.[42] Despite billions of dollars spent on improving the effectiveness and accountability of Iraqi security forces, many of them collapsed when the Islamic State waged a conquest of northern Iraq in 2014. However, policymakers routinely underscore significant progress in lesser-known missions such as in Kosovo, the Philippines, El Salvador, and Liberia. In a systematic analysis of twenty security cooperation programs intended to build partner capacity in weak or failing states, Kathleen McInnis and Nathan Lucas find that the most successful programs were those intended to build alliances and interpersonal and institutional linkages; less successful were those aimed at expanding international participation in military coalitions and bolstering partner forces to mitigate or end conflict.[43] Likewise, Steven Childs notes that security assistance geared toward education and training is more positively correlated with stability than hardware transfers.[44] Christopher Paul and his colleagues find that recipient countries with higher indicators for political and economic development better absorb US security assistance and better manage associated programs over time.[45] However, these authors stress the importance of a healthy civilian bureaucracy in the security sector as the foundation for deeper institutional reforms, effectively making the case for a two-pronged approach that addresses not only the technical capabilities of a partner force but also its management and oversight.

Most recently, differing approaches and outcomes surrounding US security assistance in Afghanistan and Ukraine illustrate the varied US record, underscoring the timeliness and importance of this book's analysis. The rapid surrender of Afghanistan to the Taliban in 2021 emphasized what many US defense officials already knew to be true: US efforts to train and equip Afghan forces failed. The more than $85 billion the US government poured into Afghanistan over two decades had a nearly negligible impact on the effectiveness, never mind the will to fight, of Afghan security forces. Furthermore, troves of weapons, ammunition, and supplies paid for by the United States are today in the hands of US adversaries in the Taliban.[46] The US strategic plan in Afghanistan was to build Afghan forces, allow those forces to lead operations with US support, and eventually hand the warfighting over completely to those forces to maintain the country's stability on their own. Yet because of the mismatch between US transfers of sophisticated warfighting technology and the limited ability of Afghan soldiers to adopt such equipment, US units on the ground too often opted for unilateral action, cutting their Afghan partners out of the planning and putting them in the backseat during operations. Faced with routine combat and terrorist attacks, US troops could not help but operate as an occupying force engaged in crisis management, relegating their partner nation training responsibilities to a secondary priority and affecting the ability of US security assistance to achieve its stated objectives.[47]

In contrast, the Ukrainian government's ability to mount a credible and relatively successful response to Russia's 2022 invasion demonstrates the promise of sustained US security assistance and patient diplomatic engagement. In the wake of the 2014 Russian invasion of Crimea, the US government authorized nonlethal security assistance and advisory support to facilitate the transformation of Ukrainian forces into a military capable of defending its national territory. But ever fearful of provoking Moscow, Washington did not commit its combat troops to Ukraine and only slowly introduced lethal defensive equipment to aid packages, commensurate with the Ukrainian forces' ability to adopt new material and technology. The caution, scale, and sustainability of US security assistance to Ukraine from 2014 forward helped build trust between the two countries and ever-growing proficiency in the Ukrainian forces—conditions that made possible the rapid expansion of security assistance starting in 2022 that helped rebuff the Russian advance on Kyiv.[48]

As these two examples reveal, part of the reason success is so elusive is that security assistance design is often plagued by extrinsic and intrinsic tensions. In some cases, the US government's objective is simply to build a relationship with a foreign security sector to prevent that government from aligning with Washington's strategic competitors (that is, China and Russia), whereas elsewhere capacity enhancement and governance reform are at the core of security assistance programs.[49] Typically, problems arise when relationship-building goals block long-term reform or when the multiplicity of goals hinders genuine efforts to evaluate the overall efficacy of security assistance.[50] These trends are also consistent with democracy promotion efforts writ large.[51] Promoting democratic values is often at odds with other strategic priorities like regime stability, in which case US decision makers tend to prioritize national security objectives at the expense of their ideals.[52] This was repeatedly the case in the post-9/11 period, when the US government unsuccessfully set out to harmonize foreign policy objectives like democratization, regional security, and economic stability through military interventions in the Middle East.[53] For the United States, foreign assistance missions in practice have tended to be tactical rather than strategic—more focused on compliance with US prescriptions than on changing political and institutional cultures in partner nations. Similarly, the programs that make up foreign aid at times include inherent contradictions. Despite consensus that local ownership of a security strategy and grassroots involvement in its design are critical facilitators of success, security assistance is by nature a donor-controlled and top-down institution-building activity. In short, security assistance generates a classic principal-agent problem, in which the ambitions of the United States and of the recipients of its aid are often misaligned.[54]

Accounting for these inconsistencies on the donor side, it is not surprising that the literature on security assistance and security sector reform has largely ignored the agency of recipient governments and civil societies undergoing and implementing reforms.[55] In fact, Ursula Schröder and Fairlie Chappuis identify "local agency and domestic power constellations" as the frontier of the field's research agenda, and Paul Jackson, among other scholars, offers the term "second-generation" security sector reform as a new conceptual approach that addresses the interplay between donor governments and local power relations.[56] Only a handful of scholars have begun to explore the conditions in recipient countries that complement donor-led prescriptions and help boost the effectiveness and accountability of security sectors. Louis-Alexandre Berg, for one, focuses on the cohesion of ruling party political networks and the constraints on a government's existing revenue base as critical to how receptive it is to foreign aid.[57] Others, such as Denis Kocak and Johannes Kode, hold that partisan division affords military and law enforcement actors opportunities to maintain and strengthen their internal role as arbiters of disputes between opposing political forces, undermining good security sector governance.[58] Jonathan Powell and his colleagues find that maintaining moderate to high defense budgets and authorizing the acquisition of new military technologies are ways to reduce the risk that security forces challenge or undermine civilian democratic rule.[59] But other authors, such as Sarah Meharg, Aleisha Arnusch, and Felix Heiduk, suggest that local structural impediments like food crises, high poverty and unemployment rates, the excessive availability of small arms, and land disputes are sometimes too great and can stymie the effectiveness of programs aimed at improving the performance of security forces.[60]

Further, the success of security sector reform initiatives is often constrained by the differing strategic objectives of the donor and recipient governments: the notion of what effective security provision looks like often varies across social and cultural contexts.[61] When considerable asymmetry exists between the donor and recipient objectives, carrots and sticks are unlikely to induce major institutional change. Embracing the Weberian principle, the US government too often assumes that its partner governments want to defeat their rivals. However, existing conflict and power structures in recipient countries sometimes make the elimination of nonstate armed groups undesirable, especially where public officials are highly prone to corruption. The continued existence of a national security threat helps national leaders justify major expenditures on security forces, including their own praetorian guards. In a bid to consolidate power, sustaining a low level of conflict, at least one that does not threaten to upend the political order, ensures that resources continue to flow and that political authorities can continue to shore up their clientelistic, corrupt, or even partisan bases of support. In Somalia, state-aligned militia groups strengthened authoritarian forms of rule, monopolized local economies, and engaged in predatory and violent behavior—all while being embraced by subnational authorities, the national government, and on occasion international interveners.[62]

Where academics and policymakers agree is in the importance of political will and local ownership in the recipient country to make good on the intended investments in reform.[63] Such was the case in 2014 when President Obama launched the Security Governance Initiative, which targeted six African countries based on their perceived ability to absorb US security assistance in ways that would lead to positive outcomes for security sector reform. But because political will is so difficult to operationalize and even detect, Paul Jackson notes that researchers tend "to *over*estimate the transformative abilities of powerful external actors" but overlook the hard politics of finding "entry points, and those who would be sympathetic" to the aims of security assistance and security sector reform in the recipient country.[64] This is consistent with Louis-Alexandre Berg's contention that the intensity and coherence of international assistance matter but that the significance of security assistance depends on political openings dictated by elite interests in recipient countries.[65] Jahara Matisek and William Reno agree, finding that "acting on the nuances of a complicated political context is an information-intensive exercise and requires adjusting [security assistance] to fit specific contexts."[66] For this reason, this book dissects the role of domestic stakeholders in supporting or undermining improved security sector governance and seeks to answer how the United States can take advantage of opportunities in the negotiation and design of security assistance while safeguarding against potential spoilers. Acknowledging and accounting for the agency of officials, institutions, and citizens in recipient countries is at the heart of getting security assistance right.

Book Outline

Plan Colombia and the Mérida Initiative infused billions of US dollars into the Colombian and Mexican security sectors, respectively, over more than a decade to professionalize law enforcement, military, and judicial agencies struggling to contain formidable threats to citizen security. A commitment to enhancing the security sector's respect for democratic governance, rule of law, and human rights underpinned US strategies in both countries. Despite similar challenges and program designs, however, Plan Colombia resulted in a professional and increasingly accountable security sector that, though not without its problems, has proven capable of delivering enhanced citizen security. The Mérida Initiative failed to do the same in Mexico. This book seeks to distinguish the domestic variables in Colombia and Mexico that enabled or impeded the success of security assistance.

Chapter 1 details US security assistance to Latin America in the twenty-first century and underscores why security assistance activities in Colombia and Mexico are suitable for comparison. Chapters 2 and 3 survey the history of US ties to the security sectors in Colombia and Mexico and lay out the programmatic components and focal areas for improving security sector governance in both countries. Chapter 4 offers a thorough evaluation of the degree to which security assistance and associated domestic programs in Colombia and Mexico accomplished the intended objectives for two dimensions: effectiveness and accountability of the security sector. For this assessment, this book considers indicators such as victimization by crime, violence, and terrorism; territorial control by state institutions; public opinion; alleged human rights violations; impunity rates; and drug seizure data, among others.

After identifying a discrepancy in outcomes, the book pivots to the three principal independent variables that contributed to such disparate results, explored in chapters 5, 6, and 7. This discussion identifies business elites, political parties, and security sector bureaucracy as consequential determinants of the success of a given reform effort.

First, the book argues that Plan Colombia was uniquely successful because of the significant financial contributions from national business elites to fund a reformed security sector. Given that national budgets ensure the sustainability of reforms after the drawdown of international donations, a government's ability to implement enduring programs hinges on the buy-in of national business elites. The case of Mexico, in which business elites did not support the security sector to the extent that their Colombian counterparts did, demonstrates that the absence of big business participation in security sector reform can have an adverse effect on the outcome.

Second, because the most auspicious cases typically feature multiyear and even multidecade investments, democratic governments with major political divides are vulnerable to incomplete implementation of reforms. Colombia achieved stability of strategic vision on improving security sector governance over more than a decade because of national interparty consensus. In Mexico, however, security became a polarizing partisan issue, and thus reform efforts were vulnerable to modification and reorientation when the executive changed party hands in 2012 and then again in 2018. Simply put, political polarization undermined the continuity of reform efforts in Mexico.

Third, earlier reforms to centralize the security bureaucracy in Colombia, which thereby subordinated the Colombian National Police to the Ministry of Defense, streamlined the adoption of US-sponsored reforms, practices, and equipment. Conversely, in Mexico, the proliferation of security institutions and the dispersal of authority encouraged by the country's decentralized, federal system undermined the Mérida Initiative's objectives. Analysis of these two examples leads to the conclusion that a centralized security bureaucracy that links national-level security providers to local communities appears better equipped to neutralize spoilers than a decentralized bureaucracy.

Next, chapter 8 explores the degree to which improvements in Colombia and Mexico were sustainable over time, highlighting the evolving nature of US relations with the security sectors in both countries following the drawdown of security assistance. Here the book identifies some of the long-term advantages that security partnership with the United States bestowed on Colombia and Mexico and the challenges that continue to undermine regional security. The book concludes with an overview of the relevance of the three independent variables for donor governments in designing future interventions, highlighting the implications of this paired comparison for the broader literature on security assistance and security sector reform.

The analysis in this book underscores the importance of individualized approaches to security assistance design, a conclusion that if not stated explicitly was implied by nearly every analyst, policymaker, or practitioner in Colombia, Mexico, and the United States consulted for this project. Throughout, this book aims to profile their collective expertise while deconstructing their efforts to build effective and accountable security sectors and thus to bring order, democracy, and stability to Colombia and Mexico.

Notes

1. Sánchez, 2006.
2. Rosenberg, 1992.
3. Senior Obama administration official, personal communication, Washington, DC, October 28, 2021.
4. Senior US development official, personal communication, Tegucigalpa, Honduras, August 25, 2016.
5. Bergmann & Schmitt, 2021.
6. Epstein & Rosen, 2018, p. 1.
7. Kleinfeld, 2016, p. 1. Joseph L. Votel and Eero R. Keravuori (2018, p. 40) refer to the "by-with-through" approach that came to characterize US stabilization strategy in the Middle East in the 2010s: operations "led *by* our partners, state or nonstate, *with* enabling support from the United States or US-led coalitions, and *through* US authorities and partner agreements."
8. Specifically for Colombia, Congress passed the FY 2002 Emergency Supplemental Appropriations Act to enable a unified campaign against narcotics trafficking and terrorist organizations, synchronizing separate defense funding lines to tackle a common threat. Congress also enacted in 2005 Section 1206 funds, a $350 million annual authority for the Pentagon to assist partners in counterterrorism efforts. This flexible account allowed the Department of Defense to supplement the activities approved by the Department of State under foreign military financing appropriations but without the same level of oversight and scrutiny. Likewise, Section 333 of the 2017 National Defense Authorization Act awarded a new line of funding to the Department of Defense to build the capacity of partner nation security forces.
9. Reveron, 2010, p. 32. Unless otherwise specified, all dollars are US currency.
10. McCallister et al., 2020, pp. 1-7–1-12.
11. Kelly et al., 2010, pp. xii–xiii. The principal agencies responsible for security cooperation are the Defense Security Cooperation Agency, the geographic combatant commands, the Joint Staff, security cooperation organizations typically housed at US diplomatic missions, and the military departments.
12. Mehta, 2016.
13. Bergmann & Schmitt, 2021.

14. Baginski et al., 2009, p. 8.
15. Omelicheva, 2017.
16. Gates, 2010, p. 2.
17. Mazzetti & Bergman, 2021.
18. US Department of State, 2020; Yayboke et al., 2021.
19. Liberia, Kosovo, and Haiti are often cited as the most prominent instances of US-supported security sector reform, but none of these countries received nearly as much in terms of resources and high-level attention from the US government as Colombia and Mexico did. Other countries and international organizations, like the United Nations, have supported security sector reform in Mali, South Sudan, Libya, Somalia, and Yemen, among others.
20. Bailey & Dammert, 2006, p. 1; Sedra, 2016, p. 20.
21. UNDP, 1994, p. 23; Neild, 1999, p. 1. Given the complexity of security threats, the line between citizen security and national security has become blurred (Ospina Restrepo, 2010, p. 140). In the Latin American context, threats to citizen security and domestic threats to national security, often posed by nonstate armed groups, are often one and the same, and given that regional governments tend to conflate national security and citizen security concerns, the author treats state strategies to address the former as a component of the latter (Acero Velásquez, 2004, p. 169).
22. OECD, 2010, p. 6; Paris, 2001.
23. OECD, 2011, p. 13.
24. Meharg & Arnusch, 2012, p. 3 (emphasis in the original).
25. Bleiker & Krupanski, 2012; Donais, 2017.
26. Berg, 2022, p. 6.
27. USAID et al., 2009, p. 3.
28. Hobbes, 1651/2012; Locke, 1690/1980.
29. Weber, 1919/2004. Put succinctly, "citizenship involves an exchange: more security in return for less freedom of action," and even today, citizen security continues to be one of the most significant challenges of government and, by extension, one of the biggest obstacles to democratic consolidation (Whitehead, 2002, p. 167). For the remainder of this book, the Weberian principle is referred to as the *monopoly of force*.
30. The United States Institute of Peace handbook on stabilization and reconstruction refers to this notion as political primacy, or the basic premise that everything is political, and encourages donor governments to employ a "conflict lens" that understands rewards and punishments, and winners and losers in the conduct of stabilization missions (Cole et al., 2009, pp. 3–15).
31. Ross & Dalton, 2020.
32. Blair, 2017; Giraldo, 2017, pp. 75–76.
33. Hanlon & Shultz, 2016, p. 9.
34. Gould, 2022. The State Department also requested additional funding from Congress to boost its staff and hire more experts to improve security assistance coordination with the Pentagon. State's political-military workforce numbers in the low hundreds, whereas the Defense Department's security cooperation workforce is composed of some twenty thousand civilian and uniformed members.
35. Retired Colombian Army colonel, personal communication, Bogotá, Colombia, 2017. One security analyst concluded, "Transformation really is security sector reform. The Colombian Army is reforming military schools, introducing new doctrine, reallocating

resources, tightening budgets, and forging joint operations" (government security analyst, personal communication, Bogotá, Colombia, October 26, 2017). García Covarrubias distinguishes between adaptation, modernization, and transformation as stages on a scale of military reform and notes that "for the moment in [Latin America, the term *transformation*] is most synonymous with a process of change, reform, modernization, or restructuring" (2007, p. 18).

36. Colombian Navy lieutenant, personal communication, Bogotá, Colombia, October 31, 2017.
37. Former senior US diplomat, email correspondence, September 28, 2021.
38. Schröder, 2010.
39. Schröder, 2010, p. 8.
40. Schröder, 2010, p. 14.
41. Myrttinen, 2019, p. 14.
42. Sandor Fabian (2021) concludes that US programming has achieved its goal of instilling foreign soldiers with democratic values that they then transmitted to national forces. In a survey of 350 military personnel, Fabian finds that US-trained soldiers had, on average, a greater respect for democratic norms than those who did not receive US training. Despite these findings, Fabian acknowledges the shortcomings of US military assistance and the numerous times it has bolstered future authoritarians and warlords.
43. McInnis & Lucas, 2015.
44. Childs, 2019.
45. Paul et al., 2015.
46. Whitlock, 2021.
47. Atwell & Bailey, 2021. In contrast, the United States remained in a "supporting role" in Colombia. As Keith Mines notes, "it was a classic case where patience, a blend of soft and hard power, and national determination on both sides combined" to yield a successful end state (2021, p. xxi).
48. Bergmann, 2022.
49. Marcella, 1982, p. 43.
50. Kleinfeld, 2016, p. 3.
51. For more information on the positive relationship between democracy promotion and democratization, see Agné, 2012; Elliott, 2016; Linz & Stepan, 1996; K. E. Smith, 2001. For a more skeptical take, see Grugel, 2002; Leininger, 2010; Pridham, 1994; Pridham & Vanhanen, 2002; Selim, 2015.
52. Grimm & Leininger, 2012, p. 408; Whitehead, 2001.
53. Nuñez, 2002; Shaw, 2007; S. Smith, 2003.
54. Downes, 2021; Gwinn, 2022.
55. Donais, 2018; Jackson & Bakrania, 2018.
56. Schröder & Chappuis, 2014, p. 133; Jackson, 2018. Nicolas Lemay-Hébert (2013) refers to this neglect of politics as the "empty-shell" approach, which risks producing a security sector that favors local elites but lacks legitimacy among the broader population.
57. Berg (2022) emphasizes that domestic political contestation is at the heart of institutional change and can enable or hamper the influence of external actors. As his detailed case studies demonstrate, even the most intensive and coherent efforts on the part of donors have failed to inculcate improved security governance.
58. Kocak & Kode, 2014.

59. Powell et al., 2018.
60. Meharg & Arnusch, 2012; Heiduk, 2014.
61. Brooks & Stanley, 2007.
62. Felbab-Brown, 2020.
63. Cole et al., 2009; Detzner, 2017; Dursun-Özkanca, 2021; Egnell & Haldén, 2009; Jackson, 2011; Kurtenbach, 2018.
64. Jackson, 2018, p. 5.
65. Berg, 2022, p. 239.
66. Matisek & Reno, 2019, p. 9.

1

The Security Sector in Latin America

Comparing US Security Assistance to Colombia and Mexico

Following decades of authoritarian governance, in some cases military dictatorships, Latin America saw a wave of democratization in the 1980s and 1990s. By the early 2000s, countries that had been embroiled in brutal internal armed conflicts and fallen victim to state oppression had mostly brokered peace. In a study of nineteen countries in the region, seventeen enjoyed free and fair elections and constitutional rule, even though the quality of democracy varied from country to country.[1] Latin America became the most democratic region in the world outside Europe and North America, and widespread enthusiasm for democracy as the preferred system of government heightened expectations for the region's democratic consolidation.[2]

Unfortunately, repeated economic crises, rampant inequality, and weak institutions created incentives for crime and corruption, and in the twenty-first century Latin America endured an unrelenting surge in insecurity. Whereas earlier violence had largely been associated with the ideological conflicts of the Cold War, economic opportunities presented by the illegal drug trade underpin this new wave of criminality. Cartels and gangs have preyed on marginalized communities to increase their commercial output, diversify their illicit activities, and expand their geographic footprint. From Argentina to Mexico, competition between these groups and governmental efforts to dismantle them have fueled violence. According to Latinobarometer polling starting in 2008, insecurity has repeatedly ranked as a leading concern for the nascent democracies in the Americas.[3] The Latin America and Caribbean region quickly earned a reputation as the world's most murderous, the Igarapé Institute finding that, despite being home to a mere 8 percent of the world's population, Latin America and the Caribbean register some 33 percent of the world's homicides.[4]

Against this backdrop, the security sector in Latin America has played an ever more prominent role in a bid to address nonstate security threats and preserve the democratic order. The mandates of police forces today encompass a

From Peril to Partnership. Paul J. Angelo, Oxford University Press. © Oxford University Press 2024.
DOI: 10.1093/oso/9780197688106.003.0002

wide range of tasks and responsibilities, including citizen coexistence, community conflict resolution, crime prevention, drug crop eradication, and capture-or-kill raids against gangs and organized crime groups. However, inexperienced and corrupt judicial officials have failed to hold those who break the law to account, and regionally, a mere twenty of every hundred murders lead to a conviction, significantly less than the global average of forty-three.[5] In an extreme case, the impunity rate for all crimes in Mexico is an estimated 99 percent. In effect, the law fails to deter perpetrators. Meanwhile, military forces, especially military police units, have increasingly supplemented civilian police forces or national gendarmeries on the streets to contend with the rising sophistication and militarization of organized crime in the region.[6] The perceived incompetence of civilian police forces in containing violent crime, the public's esteem of the armed forces in relation to other institutions, and the popularity of *mano dura* (heavy-handed) public security strategies have contributed to an outsized reliance on the military in the provision of domestic security. In the words of Gustavo Flores-Macías and Jessica Zarkin, Latin America in recent decades has almost universally undergone a militarization of its law enforcement agencies and a constabularization of its armed forces.[7]

Further, to compensate for capacity deficiencies across civilian government institutions, the region's security forces, which are often among the few state institutions with a nationwide footprint and typically enjoy large and inviolable budgets, have adopted responsibilities not usually associated with police and military forces. In addition to fighting crime, they administer social services, function as agents of infrastructure development, coordinate disaster relief, and enforce national borders. This growing domestic role has resulted in the delivery of important state services. In many countries, however, the overreliance on police and military forces to address social needs has come at a significant cost to the security institutions themselves. Given the growth of protest movements across the region in the late 2010s, police and military forces not specifically trained for public order missions have also been called on to participate in crowd and riot control, leading to an uptick in accusations of rights abuses by security force personnel. Likewise, in 2020, governments across Latin America directed the police and military to enforce unpopular lockdowns aimed at preventing the transmission of the coronavirus disease.

Beyond filling gaps left by other state service providers, in some Latin American countries, the military also remains an arbiter of political power, reflecting unfulfilled promises of democratization and civilian control of the armed forces. In Venezuela and Brazil, active-duty and retired military officers have occupied senior cabinet positions; in Honduras, Bolivia, and

Peru, police and military leaders have facilitated or countenanced the removal of heads of state in acts they believed consistent with their responsibilities to uphold the constitutional order.

Even though in most cases the security sector forfeited its role in governance during the region's transition to democracy, the military's removal from direct rule was "conditional and partial."[8] Across Latin America, police and military leaders succeeded in securing a compulsory advisory role to elected politicians, allowing the forces themselves to set security agendas and strategies. They also shielded uniformed personnel from accountability for atrocities committed during periods of military rule.[9] In some countries, the security forces retain judicial autonomy to punish their own members in specialized judicial procedures that often result in impunity for crimes committed against civilians.[10] To this day, security forces continue to influence politics by controlling state intelligence agencies and civilian officials' access to privileged information.

The tension between effectiveness and accountability of government institutions is inherent in any democracy, but in societies beleaguered by authoritarian or praetorian traditions, effective security strategies often occur at the expense of democratic norms.[11] Meanwhile, real-world security challenges, especially those posed by nonstate armed groups, have forced regional police and militaries to adapt their tactics and approaches in fulfilling their protective and defensive roles against citizen security threats. These difficulties have proven particularly burdensome for countries along drug and migration corridors such as Colombia, Mexico, Honduras, and Haiti. Not coincidentally, these cases are among the most prominent regional examples of attempted security sector reform in the twenty-first century. Yet many principal objectives of these reform efforts remain unaccomplished.[12] Unresolved tasks for the consolidation of democratic security sector governance include reevaluating institutional doctrine and use-of-force guidelines, cultivating effective civilian public agencies to alleviate the logistical and reputational costs associated with the security sector's participation in nonsecurity tasks, empowering independent oversight authorities, and synchronizing capabilities and equipment acquisitions with operational needs.[13]

US Security Assistance: A Regional Perspective from Latin America

To encourage and facilitate such reforms, Latin American governments have relied on the help of other countries and international organizations for funding and technical expertise. The US government is a leading provider of such security assistance. Robust US support for regional militaries dates to the early twentieth century but escalated considerably during the Cold War, when Washington trained and equipped troops for counterinsurgency operations against left-wing guerrilla groups. Yet, as the Cold War ended, US security assistance to Latin America once again increased during the late 1990s in response to the growing menace of the global drug trade and regional trafficking groups. Despite the dismantling of Colombia's Medellín and Cali cartels by the early 2000s, new and often nimbler drug-trafficking organizations cropped up in Colombia, Mexico, and Central America. Washington partnered with regional military and police forces to eradicate coca, opium, and marijuana crops; monitor aerial and maritime drug activities; interdict drug shipments on the high seas and at ports of entry; and bring criminal leaders to justice through special operations missions and extradition treaties. US support for these tactics accelerated with the war on terrorism during the administrations of Presidents George W. Bush (2001– 2009) and Barack Obama. Terrorist organizations across the world finance their violent activities through proceeds from the drug trade, prompting the US government to provide considerable security assistance to partner police and military forces taking on nonstate armed groups at odds with US interests.

In this most recent phase, US security assistance to Latin America has generally focused on two core goals: curbing the flow of illicit goods across borders and reducing the incidence of predatory and violent crime in vulnerable communities. Eduardo Moncada differentiates between these competencies as control policies and prevention policies.[14] Control stipulates the use of security forces and the criminal justice system to prosecute individuals and social groups that perpetrate crime and cause insecurity, whereas prevention entails deterrence strategies to stop crime and violence before they occur. By putting drug traffickers behind bars, restricting profits from the drug trade, and raising the cost of doing business through vigilance, Washington and its regional partners opted for a control strategy that attempted to make it more difficult for criminals to access lethal weapons, perpetrate violence, and subvert state institutions. By increasing security provision, social inclusion, and economic opportunities to populations that often suffered the worst effects of criminality, officials in Washington and regional capitals aimed to prevent victimization of citizens, deny criminal groups new recruits, and stem displacement and migration. These dual objectives were not weighted equally across Latin America because control policies took precedence wherever criminals posed an existential threat to the state through revolutionary activity or widespread corruption, but US programming supported both tactics throughout the region in the early twenty-first century.

Control-oriented activities were in part more prominent, including in the two cases addressed in this book, because they represented continuity with earlier US counterdrug strategies in the Americas. As far back as the 1980s, the US government waged what was primarily a supply-side drug war—that is, taking militarized actions in other countries to interrupt drug production.[15] President George H. W. Bush (1989–93) set this precedent in 1989 when he signed National Security Directive 18, authorizing more than $250 million in military, intelligence, and police assistance to destroy poppy, coca, and cannabis fields in Latin America and to interdict drug shipments bound for the United States. Although the success of this strategy has long been the subject of debate in the United States and Latin America, US policymakers, buoyed by high-profile killings and arrests of drug kingpins, continued to provide resources and training to regional military and police forces, who served as proxies for US law enforcement goals south of the border. Even though so-called decapitation strategies that removed cartel leadership often only spawned new groups seeking to fill a power vacuum in the criminal underworld, the punitive aspect of these policies and other supply-side strategies proved popular among the US public. Most Americans favored sending US troops to help the Colombian military capture drug traffickers in 1990 and continued to believe drug shipment interdiction to be the most effective counterdrug strategy in 2001.[16]

Aerial crop eradication, or spraying coca fields with the herbicide glyphosate from propeller planes, became another central component of US counternarcotics support activity, particularly in Colombia.[17] It was a small-footprint, high-impact tactic to reduce the yield of precursor material used for cocaine production, but spraying coca crops never yielded a long-term victory over the supply of cocaine. No matter how effective spraying coca crops was at reducing cultivation, the street value of cocaine in the United States never spiked in response, meaning that the supply continued to meet user demand, and the United States remained the top consumer of cocaine for decades. The recognition that aerial crop eradication was a limited tool spurred the implementation of more diverse security assistance programming to the region and led to a greater emphasis on reducing consumer demand in the United States. But even as attitudes in the United States and Latin America shifted in favor of legalization of some drugs, the US government continued to pursue an aggressive counternarcotics strategy—and increasingly a counterterrorism one—in Latin America, which focused on building the operational capabilities of police and military forces and the technical capacity of judicial officials to capture and incarcerate drug criminals.[18]

Some of the principal activities and programs associated with US security assistance included the transfer of military hardware and weapons, the provision and sale of maritime and aviation platforms, and their associated maintenance and operations training. Washington also facilitated the construction of new bases, training schools, and intelligence centers, from which it operated unmanned aerial vehicles to improve geospatial imagery. Likewise, the US government maintained forward operating locations, or rented space on host nation military bases or airports, to house US military personnel and aircraft essential for the conduct of regional counternarcotics operations. These facilities—located in Honduras, El Salvador, Ecuador, Aruba, and Curaçao—became especially important to the US government after the closure of Howard Air Force Base in Panama in 1999, serving as outposts to collaborate with partner nations. And Latin American military and police officers became top beneficiaries of US-based training and professional education courses at institutions such as the Western Hemisphere Institute for Security Cooperation, the William J. Perry Center for Hemispheric Defense Studies, and the International Law Enforcement Academy.

The US State and Defense Departments also helped set up and train specialized and elite military and police units to conduct high-risk operations against illegal armed groups, and the Department of Justice created Foreign-Deployed Advisory Support Teams and Sensitive Investigative Units to support the activities of these elite units, vet their leaders, and build judicial cases against drug-trafficking organizations. Finally, human rights training became a central component of all US security assistance activities in Latin America. US executive departments, conscious of the misalignment between US democratic values and previous support for autocratic governments in the region, ensured that police and military recipients of US instruction, intelligence, and equipment transfers received mandatory human rights training. Washington established a comprehensive, albeit imperfect, human rights certification process for the release of security assistance to partner military and police forces and engaged in routine high-level human rights dialogues with political and security sector leaders in recipient countries. Indeed, the US Southern Command (SOUTHCOM), the Department of Defense's organization responsible for security policy implementation in much of Latin America, is the only US combatant command to establish a human rights office to advance respectful and proportional conduct among partner security forces as they interact with their citizens.

US security assistance has varied in scope and scale across the region, but the two most prominent beneficiaries in Latin America in the twenty-first century are Colombia and Mexico. Washington has devoted the bulk of its resources to these two countries for several reasons. For one, insurgent groups, drug cartels, and gangs grew increasingly brazen in taking on Colombian and Mexican security forces, and the United States, the principal driver of demand for drugs from the region, acknowledged its responsibility by helping embattled democratic partners address the blight of violence and criminality. From a practical angle, Colombia has long been the world's top supplier of cocaine and shares a border with Venezuela, a country that has become a top security concern for the United States for its drug-trafficking and terrorism activities. Mexico became the most important drug transshipment country and a top supplier of illicit opioids to the US market starting in the early 2000s, and its geographic position as a neighbor fueled concerns about spillover violence into US border states. Partnership with the governments of these two countries gave US authorities their best chance at waging a successful supply-side campaign while mitigating drug-related fallout at home. Furthermore, although much of Latin America became dominated by left and center-left political movements that rejected US security assistance as an imperialist imposition, successive Colombian and Mexican presidents, who were centrist or conservative in ideology, did not seek alienation from Washington and pursued friendlier diplomatic and security relations with the US government. The pink tide, as the rise of anti-US leftist governments became known, reduced the United States' hard- and soft-power influence in much of Latin America, but Colombia and Mexico presented opportunities to continue waging a supply-side war on drugs while helping advance pro-market economic ties and liberal democratic values in a region that was becoming increasingly protectionist, authoritarian, and diplomatically unaligned with the United States.

In Colombia and Mexico, Washington went beyond the traditional train-and-equip approach common during the Cold War and during the early 2000s frequently implemented in the Middle East, North Africa, and Central Asia. Rendering security forces effective at combating insurgents and drug cartels in Colombia and Mexico was only half of the equation. Enhancing democratic accountability to include respect for human rights and the constitutional order was an important component of Washington's agenda in both countries and consistent with the broader objective of democracy promotion in the Americas.[19] The release of security assistance was conditioned on progress on defending human rights and on delivering justice for abuses committed by state security forces. For Colombia, this took the form of an annual certification process conducted by the State Department; for Mexico, it required a comprehensive annual report to Congress, authored by the State Department but infused with input from civil society organizations.

In both cases, the United States withheld or delayed security assistance over human rights concerns, a rebuke taken seriously by recipient governments and especially by their security sectors. In Colombia and Mexico, the US government rigorously applied the Leahy Laws, which prohibit US security assistance to foreign security forces implicated in gross violations of human rights.[20] Finally, to reduce impunity for state-perpetrated abuses and other crimes, the Departments of State and Justice and the US Agency for International Development (USAID) provided technical expertise to judicial institutions in Colombia and Mexico and helped usher in major judicial reforms with the aim of improving efficiency and deepening democratic practice. In no other country in the world was US security assistance so generous and simultaneously so focused on the security sector's compliance with democratic norms as in Colombia and Mexico.

When taken globally, of the top ten beneficiaries of US security assistance in the post-9/11 period, Colombia and Mexico stand out for their relative degree of democratic consolidation. Outside countries where the US government was actively involved in combat, such as Afghanistan, Iraq, and Libya, other top recipients of US military and police aid included Israel, Egypt, Ukraine, Pakistan, Jordan, Lebanon, and Tunisia—countries in which the encouragement of democratic norms among security forces is more often than not occluded by sensitive strategic objectives such as rebuffing territorial aggression, keeping the peace in places known for cross-border animosity, or combating militant Islamic terrorism.[21] In all these cases, US aid to the security sector was sustained for more than a decade and exceeded $250 million total per country. Yet many leading recipients feature undemocratic political systems and even legal pluralism, or the existence of parallel governmental and informal legal systems that are at odds with each other. Additionally, among other democratic beneficiaries of substantial US security assistance, such as the Philippines, Indonesia, and Liberia, the resources expended over comparable time frames pale in comparison, totaling less than half the price tag of Plan Colombia and the Mérida Initiative.[22] As far as twenty-first-century security assistance is concerned, Plan Colombia and the Mérida Initiative are unique with respect to their scope and scale of engagement.[23]

A Paired Comparison of Colombia and Mexico

During the administration of Colombian President Andrés Pastrana (1998–2002), the US government answered a Colombian government appeal for international support by providing significant training and equipment contributions to the Colombian military and police, starting in 2000. Although Pastrana's original program was conceived as an economic and political development strategy to address the root causes of drug violence and the persistence of guerrilla insurgencies, Washington insisted that improved state capacity to provide security was the essential foundation for other development goals. It subsequently awarded upward of 75 percent of its bilateral assistance to Colombia's security sector.[24] With the infusion of $1.3 billion into security and justice institutions, Colombia became the largest recipient of US security assistance outside the Middle East and the third largest worldwide. Plan Colombia, which was extended under a variety of US funding authorities until 2011, focused on improving the operational effectiveness of the Colombian military and police to combat drug-trafficking organizations, to enhance the Colombian government's ability to extend justice and the rule of law throughout its national territory, and to "make governance more transparent, participatory, and accountable."[25] By 2011, Washington had contributed more than $8 billion to the Colombian government to this end.[26]

Although several analyses posit that Plan Colombia fell short of its counterdrug and human rights objectives, to date no exhaustive, comprehensive analysis of security sector reform in Colombia has been undertaken.[27] The literature on Plan Colombia has only superficially addressed the relationship between US security assistance, the professionalism of the country's security forces, and democratic consolidation, even though by many accounts Plan Colombia was efficacious.[28] As Karen DeYoung notes, "Three administrations and $10 billion later, what is known as 'Plan Colombia' is widely considered one of the most successful US assistance efforts in history."[29] General David Petraeus and Michael O'Hanlon herald Plan Colombia as a unique triumph for US foreign policy in the post-9/11 period.[30]

According to the US Embassy in Bogotá, President Álvaro Uribe (2002–10) oversaw a significant period of reform, and in 2004 the government extended the presence of the National Police to all the country's 1,099 municipalities, many of which had been devoid of government services and investments due to a lack of security: "Attacks conducted by illegally armed groups against rural towns decreased by 91% from 2002 to 2005. Between 2002 and 2008, Colombia saw a decrease in homicides by 44%, kidnappings by 88%, terrorist attacks by 79%, and attacks on the country's infrastructure by 60%."[31] Although the data presented are certainly incomplete, they do paint a picture of considerable progress. US policymakers—Democrats and Republicans alike—routinely cite these improvements as evidence of positive foreign policy intervention. In 2016, Secretary of State John Kerry remarked,

> The key to Plan Colombia's success was its comprehensive vision of how security is established and maintained. Law and order is only part of the equation. With support from the United States, Colombians moved ahead on multiple fronts to improve governance. . . . Just as important, the government came to terms with the fact that human rights abuses were committed not solely by rebel groups, but also by its own forces—and that those abuses, too, must be stopped.

Inspired by these accomplishments, the administration of President George W. Bush endeavored to replicate the Plan Colombia model in Mexico, another Latin American partner in the war on drugs that faced crippling rates of crime and violence by the mid-2000s.[32] Following the declaration of a war on the country's drug cartels by newly elected President Felipe Calderón (2006–12), the US Congress approved funding for Mexico and Central America under the Mérida Initiative in 2007. The initiative was a multiyear strategy to combat narcotics trafficking, money laundering, and transnational organized crime through $1.4 billion geared at Mexico's struggling security sector. The Department of State listed the program's principal objectives as providing "equipment and training to support law enforcement operations and technical assistance for long-term reform and oversight of security agencies."[33] From its inception, the Mérida Initiative pushed US government aid commitments to the Mexican security and justice agencies upward of $3 billion. This high level of support was sustained through fiscal year (FY) 2017, when the Donald Trump administration (2017–21) reoriented Washington's priorities in the US-Mexico security relationship (see chapter 8). Although some programming associated with the Mérida Initiative persisted beyond 2017, the analysis in this book primarily covers the period from FY 2008 to FY 2017.

Unlike its Colombian equivalent, the Mexican security sector struggled to institutionalize the Mérida Initiative reforms encouraged by the US government and implemented by its own. During a congressional hearing nearly five years into the assistance plan's implementation, the US House of Representatives Western Hemisphere Subcommittee chair, Representative Connie Mack (Republican-Florida), described the Mérida Initiative as a complete failure.[34] From 2007 to 2015, more than 164,000 Mexicans were murdered, a vast majority at the hands of cartel and gang violence, and despite unprecedented strides in US-Mexican partnership on a common security framework, levels of crime and violence rose in the decade after the agreement was signed.[35] In 2019, the Mexican government registered more annual homicides than at any point since the Mexican Revolution. Likewise, media coverage of a string of high-profile security and justice failures made it difficult for either government to defend the Mérida Initiative's record. As addressed in chapter 4, the missing students from Ayotzinapa, the extrajudicial killings by the Mexican Army in Tlatlaya, and the escape of Joaquín "El Chapo" Guzmán from a maximum-security prison underscored the Mexican state's inability to crack down on human rights abuses, impunity, and corruption—in other words, its failure to deliver a reformed security sector. Against this backdrop, one observer described the legacy of the Mérida Initiative's approach to insecurity: "While drugs continued to flow north and US government weapons and cash laundered . . . flowed south, the Calderón security strategy remained basically unchanged over the years. Its effect was a catastrophic expansion of violence and a crime-solving rate of nearly zero."[36] Indeed, the poet Javier Sicilia solemnly declared "a crisis of civilization in Mexico"—one that generous amounts of security assistance and an attempt at security sector reform failed to contain.[37]

Most Similar Systems: Colombia and Mexico

Despite the difference in outcomes, US security assistance and security sector reform in Colombia and Mexico match on many relevant contextual variables, allowing for meaningful comparison. This quality makes the two countries good candidates for the most similar systems design (MSSD), which, like John Stuart Mill's method of difference, requires that comparative cases be as similar in as many ways as possible to control for extraneous variance.[38] According to Adam Przeworski and Henry Teune, intersystemic differences constitute explanatory factors for variation on the dependent variable—in this case, security sector governance—in an MSSD study.[39] The MSSD is appropriate for comparisons that produce different outcomes despite similar contexts and thus helps researchers eliminate potential sufficient causes, or those causes that when present meet the threshold for producing a given outcome. In this tradition, Arend Lijphart recommends matching cases with comparable contexts so that background variables may serve as controls.[40] Although it is impossible to keep all potential explanatory factors constant, this logic remains useful for qualitative studies that permit researchers to address causal complexity thoroughly.[41]

Moreover, the inductive reasoning associated with small-*N* studies, those for which the number of cases under consideration is low, is invaluable for concept formation and hypothesis generation for undertheorized phenomena; having more variables than cases is not a problem if seen through this lens.[42] A paired comparison thus tends to generate probabilistic, partial, conditional, and provisional theories, but for some concepts conclusions of this sort are an acceptable and a best compromise.[43] More specifically, qualitative comparison is a useful methodological approach for understanding "long-term, complex, dynamic, and partially open-ended" processes such as democratization and security sector reform.[44]

In this vein, Colombia and Mexico exhibit comparable criminal threats, political systems, and capacity challenges in the security sector—all variables that are central to the comparative analysis of this study. In addition, the US government identified analogous strategic priorities with respect to Colombia and Mexico. Plan Colombia and the Mérida Initiative benefited from similar US programming and funding lines, time horizons, and established security ties between the US government and the Colombian and Mexican security sectors preceding the uptick in assistance. Indeed, the only major work to compare US security policies in Colombia and Mexico acknowledges this confluence of objectives in its title—*One Goal, Two Struggles: Confronting Crime and Violence in Colombia and Mexico*.[45]

The first noteworthy similarity pertains to the challenges that nonstate armed groups pose in both countries. Colombia and Mexico are two former Spanish colonies characterized, before the surge in US security assistance, by failing security sectors overwhelmed by internal organized crime threats. Both feature "cartel-state conflict—sustained armed confrontation between sophisticated and well-armed drug trafficking organizations (DTOs) and state forces."[46] In fact, some of the same illicit trafficking networks operate in both countries. Washington's announcement of concerted foreign policy plans to help revamp the Colombian and Mexican security sectors occurred when insecurity and state incapacity had reached such staggeringly high levels that some analysts considered the two countries to be on the brink of state failure.[47] In both instances, illegal armed actors used drug profits to control territory, arbitrate community justice, enforce some version of the law, co-opt public officials and political parties, and establish governance institutions in parallel to those of the state. Although public support for these criminal organizations is low in both countries, the groups have succeeded in wielding considerable influence at the local and even regional levels, where they administer clientelistic networks through a mix of incentives, such as protection and economic kickbacks, and disincentives, such as violence. In Colombia and Mexico, improving the performance of the security sector meant not only expanding operations throughout the national territory but also reaching populations with a tenuous connection to the state.

Second, both Colombia and Mexico exemplify a "vulnerable democratic environment," which Querine Hanlon and Richard Shultz describe as a political setting in which multiparty electoral democracies exhibit an inability to fully deliver civil liberties, rule of law, and civilian oversight of security forces.[48] Although there are unique postconflict considerations in Colombia and distinctive postauthoritarian considerations in Mexico with regard to security sector reform, the two countries, alongside Costa Rica, are credited with having the longest-running civilian-led governance in Latin America—a region where military regimes took power in nearly every country during the second half of the twentieth century. The countries' militaries have remained largely apolitical in the modern era, but in both cases security forces are a central authority in state construction, especially outside metropolitan areas. Accordingly, Laurence Whitehead identifies Colombia and Mexico as an ideal paired comparison for democratization studies because democratization emerged out of "liberalizing reforms within a long-standing civilian constitutional tradition of restricted or controlled electoral contestation."[49] Furthermore, Colombia and Mexico are large, industrialized nations with upper-middle-income economies and long histories of electoral politics.[50] Regionalism, rooted in patronage and clientelism, has become a defining feature of both electoral systems, although the political power of subnational authorities is more formalized and historically more entrenched in Mexico's federalist model than in Colombia's more centralized political system.[51]

Third, the Colombian and Mexican security sectors confronted similar capacity challenges that prompted security sector reform in the first place. Police forces in both countries historically had reputations for ineptitude and corruption, and their inability to perform basic police functions such as aiding stranded motorists or securing the scene of a crime contributed to low public approval ratings. Illegal armed groups often derailed government security policies by bribing police units. Similarly, in modern history, on occasion the police in Colombia and Mexico have been co-opted by political parties, rendering them biased in favor of certain parties over others and thereby undermining the rule of law. In contrast, the armed forces remained at the margins of national politics for decades, securing a high degree of institutional autonomy in exchange for their subordination to civilian authorities.[52] This separation from politics contributed to a public perception in both countries of the military as considerably more trustworthy than other state institutions. For this reason, citizens have customarily preferred the armed forces to the police in addressing the most formidable challenges to public order.

Nevertheless, a tradition of internal autonomy in turn rendered civilian oversight of the security sector minimal. Improving mechanisms of accountability became a focus of Plan Colombia and the Mérida Initiative, especially because Washington could not justify expenditures on corruptible institutions in partner nations without devising mechanisms to ensure that US funds were administered and absorbed transparently. Beyond their organizational accountability in the security forces, Colombia and Mexico also underwent major reforms to their judicial institutions in recent decades, shedding the inquisitorial model of criminal justice and transitioning to an accusatorial one to improve the efficacy of investigative agencies and courts. Although Plan Colombia and the Mérida Initiative were oriented from the outset to support principally military and police forces, US government agencies pursued complementary efforts to support judicial reform in a bid to help reduce impunity for crime.

Fourth, the ambition and design of US security assistance in Plan Colombia and the Mérida Initiative were largely consistent.[53] As explored in depth in chapter 3, the same US executive departments and agencies were responsible for security assistance—State, Defense, Justice, and USAID—and the primary US funding lines included foreign military financing, International Military Education and Training, and international narcotics control and law enforcement. Although Colombian and Mexican partner institutions were organizationally and culturally distinct, US objectives, conditions, and strategies did not vary significantly. Moreover, US policymakers recognized the transnational nature of Colombia's and Mexico's security threats and therefore enhanced funding and training to the security sectors in neighboring countries to deter the displacement of criminal groups across borders. The Andean Regional Initiative (ARI) and the Central America Regional Security Initiative (CARSI), although modest in relation to the resources contributed to Colombia and Mexico, were efforts to support police and military forces in places like Ecuador and Peru, and Guatemala and Honduras, respectively, as improved security provision in Colombia and Mexico risked the relocation of nonstate armed groups to more vulnerable or corruptible countries.[54]

Last, noteworthy US involvement in the security sectors in Colombia and Mexico preceded Plan Colombia and the Mérida Initiative for at least a decade in both cases, which proved crucial to the formulation of robust security assistance strategies. Even though this lengthy involvement in Colombia and Mexico generated skepticism among some members of the US Congress, who questioned why so much previous investment had accomplished so little in the war on drugs, familiarity with the challenges and deep cross-national relationships ultimately paved the way for broad bipartisan support.[55] When Presidents Bill Clinton (1993–2001) and George W. Bush presented, respectively, Plan Colombia and the Mérida Initiative to Congress, many members on Capitol Hill had links to the beneficiary institutions of the partner governments, having visited the countries on official visits and routinely tracked indicators of each country's performance in fighting the drug war. Their exposure to the issues of bilateral concern led to broad support for deeper security ties with Colombia and Mexico. Plan Colombia, a component of the Military Construction Appropriations bill H.R. 4425, passed with a 306–110 vote in the House of Representatives and a 96–4 vote in the Senate. Similarly, the Supplemental Appropriations bill H.R. 2642, which contained appropriations for the Mérida Initiative, passed with a House vote of 409–2 and in the Senate with a vote of 92–6.[56]

The Limits of Comparing Plan Colombia and the Mérida Initiative

However similar Colombia and Mexico appear at the macro level, the differences between the two countries and between the two security assistance initiatives are important ones. In fact, these differences help draw more nuanced conclusions about security assistance and security sector reform and help clarify the disparity in outcomes. The three independent variables profiled in chapters 5, 6, and 7 represent the most consequential differences as far as security sector governance is concerned, but other major differences mentioned here also had some bearing on the success of US security assistance and thus provide opportunities for future comparative work on Colombia and Mexico.

One of the most significant departures between the two cases pertains to state capacity to respond to public demands, including for security provision. Although both Colombia and Mexico are democracies, their political institutions developed in different ways. Colombia's democracy, however weak or besieged, witnessed decades of sustained interparty electoral competition prior to Plan Colombia. Parties vied for political power in routine elections and benefited from regional and local electoral bases. The main problem of governance in Colombia has been the total absence of state authority in the country's rural regions, along its borders, and in marginalized urban neighborhoods. Large swaths of Colombian national territory historically remained beyond the reach of political authorities. The lack of institutions capable of collecting taxes, arbitrating legal disputes, enforcing the law, and protecting citizens from crime and violence nationwide is precisely what gave rise to nonstate armed groups seeking to fill a governance void. Colombia's difficult physical geography and a tradition of centralized political power provided additional incentives for illegal activities in these regions.[57]

Conversely, the Mexican state's authority, no matter how corrupt or weak, was rarely absent.[58] As a senior Mexican diplomat remarked, "In Mexico, the state has always been very present. Mexican villages have schools, clinics, highways, and commercial spaces. There may have been gaps in terms of the provision of security, but the state is present in terms of social and physical infrastructure."[59] Unlike in Colombia, interparty electoral competition was essentially nonexistent for much of the country's history, but political patronage as a governance model ensured the tentacles of the state reached even Mexico's most remote populations. The Institutional Revolutionary Party (Partido Revolucionario Institucional, or PRI) dominated politics for seventy-one years, routinely silencing opposition through corrupt electoral practices, co-optation of would-be dissenters, and repression of opponents—all while ensuring the government collected taxes, albeit irregularly, and reinvested in communities via party-driven clientelism.[60]

The presence of the Mexican state throughout the national territory is in part why Mexico averted the proliferation of large-scale, national-level armed insurgencies that came to dominate Colombian politics from the 1960s forward, another dissimilarity with consequences for the outcomes assessed in this book.[61] Despite comparable practices (such as control of territory; supplanting state authority; and kidnappings, assassinations, and massacres), Colombia's insurgent and paramilitary groups are distinct from Mexico's drug gangs. Colombia's nonstate perpetrators of violence have operated as political actors, unlike Mexico's financially motivated cartels.[62] The post–Cold War survival of guerrilla insurgencies, such as the Revolutionary Armed Forces of Colombia (Fuerzas Armadas Revolucionarias de Colombia, or FARC) and the National Liberation Army (Ejército de Liberación Nacional, or ELN), necessitated a standing counterinsurgency mission for the Colombian security sector that overlayed other public order operations in a way that Mexico has generally avoided. Colombia also boasted nine peace processes in the period between the 1980s and the 2016 FARC peace deal, including the demobilization and reintegration of the United Self-Defense Forces of Colombia (Autodefensas Unidas de Colombia, or AUC) paramilitary group during Plan Colombia.[63] As exemplified by the 2016 FARC peace accord, political accommodation of demobilized opponents of the state has become a defining feature of Colombian political life. But for those insurgent groups that remain at war, the Colombian security sector's operational footing is unmistakably a counterinsurgent one. From a US perspective, Colombia became a laboratory for how Washington could export a model of "clear, hold, build" counterinsurgency that it was practicing in Afghanistan and Iraq, and successive political leaders in Colombia, especially the popular President Uribe, were eager to receive US assistance and to adopt US counterinsurgency and counterterrorism tactics for fighting nonstate armed groups.[64]

Such considerations were not a prominent part of the operational strategy Washington encouraged in Mexico, and Mexican authorities were at least initially more constrained to treat the threat posed by drug cartels as a matter of public order and primarily a responsibility of law enforcement. Whereas Colombia's anachronistic insurgencies were led by politically driven and aging fighters, Mexico's cartels were an ascendent force with a steady supply of weapons and recruits and enough revenues to suborn the state when necessary. At the outset of the Mérida Initiative, Mexican authorities were just coming to terms with a newly confrontational and rapidly evolving criminal threat. This difference and thus the difference in threat perception help account for the gulf in security and defense spending between the two countries. Colombia, knowing full well what resources were needed to defeat the FARC and ELN on the battlefield, consistently spent more than 3 percent of its GDP on defense expenditures. However, Mexico never exceeded the 0.5 percent threshold during the Mérida Initiative, despite the growing reliance on the military in the implementation of security strategy.[65] The lack of consensus on how to deal with the cartels (see chapter 6) constrained President Calderón, whose hotly contested election in 2006 tempered the popularity of his administration's policies from the outset and denied him the mandate to pursue a better financed strategy akin to Colombia's contributions during Plan Colombia. In short, the extent to which Mexico's organized crime groups—such as the Sinaloa Cartel, Gulf Cartel, and the Zetas—could wage war, corrupt, and penetrate society was not fully known until after Mexican authorities began confronting them.

Some scholars refer to the situation in Mexico as a criminal insurgency, which suggests that criminals fight to remove the influence of the state in their zones of control but do not attempt to overthrow the state.[66] However, it is not clear that the government's strategy focused on political control in contested areas, especially given that the problem was so often not one of state absence but of the corruption of local officials by organized crime. One observer remarked, "The Mexican army does not have a hearts and minds mindset and is uncomfortable operating domestically, being seen as a political actor; it is focused on eliminating the enemy and occasionally providing humanitarian relief."[67] John Bailey concludes, "In summary, Colombia is a case of a complicated internal war in which drug production and trafficking play a significant role; Mexico is a case of hyper-violent criminal organizations that use terrorist-like methods to challenge the government and society."[68]

In fact, when US Secretary of State Hillary Clinton commented in 2010 that parts of Mexico resembled Colombia twenty years prior, Mexican authorities, forever cautious of US interventionism, protested the unwelcome comparison.

That US military advisors could enter Mexico in large numbers in the same way they did under Plan Colombia was an alarming prospect for nationalist Mexicans, which is in large part why the Bush administration backtracked on its initial branding of the Mérida Initiative as Plan Mexico.[69] Although some Mexican politicians agreed with Clinton's comparison, Calderón's spokesperson, Alejandro Poiré, rejected her remarks.[70] From that moment forward, the Obama administration abandoned any hyperbolic rhetoric suggesting the Colombianization of Mexico.[71] Although this reluctance to draw parallels between Colombia and Mexico may be rooted in political sensitivities, this anecdote serves as an instructive reminder of the inherent dissimilarities between the Colombian and Mexican situations.[72]

These contrasting sensitivities point to another principal difference: national attitudes toward the United States. Whereas the Colombian government has long considered the US government an ally and the Colombian people generally hold a positive view of the United States, Mexican leaders, with some notable exceptions, have historically viewed the United States with deep suspicion. The US and Colombian security forces enjoy a trusted relationship that started during the Korean War and was revived during the 1980s to combat the Medellín and Cali cartels. Juan Gabriel Tokatlian describes this relationship as Bogotá's "spoiled subordination" to Washington, citing the Colombian government's perennial aspiration to curry US favor by aligning its policies with those of the United States.[73] Conversely, the Mexican military and police tend to distrust the US government, and at Mexican military schools curricula historically depicted the United States as Mexico's top adversary. Even into the early years of the North American Free Trade Agreement (NAFTA), a symbol of growing cooperation between the United States and Mexico, Mexican authorities consistently pursued autonomy from the United States. From 1993 to 1995, in an attempt to chart its own strategy, Mexico refused all US counterdrug assistance outright.[74] Nationalism and anti-US sentiment run deep in the Mexican national psyche, dating back to the 1845 US annexation of Texas and the subsequent Mexican-American War—so much so that some analysts consider the relatively positive counterdrug relationship between the United States and Mexico altogether surprising.[75] According to one analyst, the country's nationalist approach to security has led to a nationalist military culture.[76]

Geographic proximity played a role not only in these contrasting perceptions of the US government but also in the contrasting tenor of bilateral relations. Mexico's 1,981-mile border with the United States has long meant that a wide array of issues dominates the bilateral agenda. The free flow of goods and services, undocumented migration, and illicit trafficking are among the most pressing areas of interest for both governments.[77] Insecurity related to organized crime is just one of a host of mutual concerns. However, the bilateral relationship with Colombia was defined for decades almost entirely by the drug war. Colombia's geographic distance from the United States rendered foreign policy issues such as trade and immigration as optional agenda items for Washington. This geographic distinction is also evident in Washington's distribution of bureaucratic responsibility for the two countries. Whereas the Department of Defense's SOUTHCOM in Miami, Florida, implements security and defense policies for Colombia and the rest of Latin America and the Caribbean, responsibility for Mexico falls to the US Northern Command (NORTHCOM) in Colorado Springs, Colorado. And whereas SOUTHCOM's focus is largely one of security cooperation with regional partners, NORTHCOM's mission centers on homeland defense.

On this final point, the US security assistance architecture was not identical between Colombia and Mexico, no matter the broad similarities between Plan Colombia and the Mérida Initiative. From a planning standpoint, the Department of State retained leadership of both efforts in Washington. Additionally, the decision to fund both Plan Colombia and the Mérida Initiative through supplemental appropriations reduced the prospect of bureaucratic competition within the US government because no single executive department was required to commit its funds to finance the new programs. However, the Department of Defense had an outsized presence in Colombia relative to Mexico given the overall emphasis on military-to-military programs.[78] At its peak, the tally of US military personnel in Colombia for training and maintenance reached eight hundred, with an additional six hundred civilians fulfilling Defense and State contracts. Yet in Mexico, sensitivities regarding Mexican sovereignty limited the US military footprint, which peaked at a mere forty-nine individuals in 2015, many of whom were engaged in routine diplomatic work in a country with more than twice the population of Colombia.[79] Meanwhile, the US law enforcement presence in Mexico reached upward of five hundred agents at the height of the Mérida Initiative, underscoring the relative emphasis on policing operations in resolving Mexico's security crisis.[80]

To this end, the relative influence of the Drug Enforcement Administration (DEA) in setting the tone for the bilateral security relationship was greater in Mexico. Mexican cartels were perceived as a matter for law enforcement agencies that the military would supplement in areas of the country where police capacity was low, and among US agencies, the DEA, not the Department of Defense, was traditionally the top purveyor of surveillance technology and tactical intelligence to Mexican authorities.[81] In the decades preceding the

Mérida Initiative, the DEA achieved a remarkable level of autonomy within Mexico's borders, training foreign police officials, recruiting informants, and conducting undercover operations. In Colombia, although the DEA was central to the dismantling of the Medellín and Cali cartels, the agency came to play a secondary role to the Department of Defense, especially as Colombian guerrilla and paramilitary groups (as opposed to cartels) became the top drug-trafficking organizations in the country by the early 2000s.

In Colombia, where Washington's ambition was to shore up the credibility of its host nation counterparts as a means of eroding support for nonstate armed groups, the strategy and rhetoric of US officials, including those at the DEA, sought to avoid embarrassing the Colombian government. Arrests and extraditions of drug traffickers were framed as incremental progress, and instances of corruption that came to light were presented as opportunities to reform institutions that were never questioned as being anything but democratic. On the other hand, the DEA's messaging about Mexican institutions had become antagonistic over time, especially after the murder of DEA Special Agent Enrique Camarena in 1985. As María Celia Toro notes, the DEA made a habit of publicizing governmental corruption in Mexico, leaking information to the press that incriminated Mexican authorities (with or without any credible basis) and discrediting their institutional counterparts.[82]

During the Mérida Initiative, at a time when top-line US messaging encouraged "partnership" and "shared responsibility" for the drug war, the DEA's activities in Mexico were frequently at odds with this spirit of cooperation, undercutting Mexican institutions in the pursuit of quick wins (arrests, interrogations, and extraditions) often implicating Mexican public officials.[83] As one US official noted, "When you let loose US agencies on a country, they find what they want, and in Mexico, the DEA didn't coordinate well with other players in the interagency or with their Mexican counterparts."[84] As Simon Reich and Mark Aspinwall find, the DEA's unilateral actions often humiliated the Mexican government and tended to elicit defensive reactions from Mexican authorities rather than cooperative ones.[85] Further, the DEA's operational focus on capturing cartel leaders resulted in record cartel arrests during the early years of the Mérida Initiative while contributing to the atomization of organized crime.[86] The proliferation of smaller organized crime cells made little difference in terms of drug production and transport but did make it more difficult for US and Mexican authorities to dismantle criminal organizations at a time that both governments sought to demonstrate progress on the security front.

One thematic area on which US executive agencies, including the DEA, could all agree in Mexico was on justice reform, which became a central component of the Mérida Initiative in a way that it was not in Plan Colombia. This became especially true when the Obama administration made combating impunity a main objective of US support to Mexico, which had begun a decade-long transition toward an accusatorial-style justice system starting in 2008. In Colombia as well as in Mexico, inquisitorial justice systems, which are not rooted in the presumption of innocence, rendered judicial procedures long and inefficient, contributing to a significant case backlog. Plea bargains were not authorized in criminal codes to settle disputes, and because judges wielded considerable authority to accuse, prosecute, and sentence defendants, they became highly susceptible to intimidation and bribery.[87] Unlike Mexico, where the transition to an accusatory system happened in tandem with the Mérida Initiative, Colombia began its own transition nearly a decade before Plan Colombia with the rewrite of its constitution in 1991. The 1992 criminal code established a new Attorney General's Office (Fiscalía General de la Nación, or FGN) with the power to indict and issue preventive detention while investigating criminal cases.[88] Additional legislation, such as Law 600 of 2000 and Legislative Act 03 of 2002, governed other aspects of the new system, and Plan Colombia contained some resources aimed at strengthening the continuing transition to an accusatory system, including technical expertise for holding oral trials and delivering effective investigations.

As discussed in chapter 4, this difference in sequencing likely affected popular perceptions of government efficacy. In Colombia, the courts had years of working within the accusatorial justice system when the security forces began to mount major offensives that resulted in more arrests. However, as Mexican authorities captured record numbers of criminals, the country's lawyers, prosecutors, and judges faced two major challenges: they were learning on the job and in a high-risk environment how to build and try cases, and the new justice system's focus on conditional release of suspects on bail or bond ended up putting many criminals back out on the streets to commit additional offenses before their trial dates. Although this book does not systematically evaluate the performance of Colombia's and Mexico's judiciaries, the differences noted here affected the design and outcomes of Plan Colombia and the Mérida Initiative and underscore the responsibility that both the security sector and justice sector bear for improving security outcomes.

Security forces across Latin America underwent a considerable shift both organizationally and operationally as the region transitioned from authoritarianism to democracy and as the top security concerns shifted from communism to drug trafficking. But in the 1990s and early 2000s, many military and police forces, which had previously been arbiters of political power, never fully relinquished their prerogatives and exceptionalism among institutions as nascent democratic governments sought to deliver representative governance and enhance transparency and the rule of law. Security sector reform, facilitated by international security assistance, gained momentum as the consensus solution for building more professional and democratic security forces across the region, especially in countries facing a dramatic rise in crime and violence due to the proliferation of illicit economies. Yet, as of 2022, this promise and, more broadly speaking, democratic consolidation remained unfulfilled, and regional military and police forces have grown more comfortable performing roles not traditionally associated with democratic security forces, including overtly political ones, than at any point since the transition to democracy.

Colombia and Mexico are the two most prominent Latin American beneficiaries of security assistance during this period and received the most concerted and sustained support from the United States to build more effective and accountable security institutions. The similarities between Plan Colombia and the Mérida Initiative make these instances of security assistance and security sector reform compelling cases for comparison, but as the remaining chapters of this book reveal, the disparity in results between the two countries warrants a deeper exploration of the factors that contributed to relative success in Colombia and overall failure in Mexico—for both modifying approaches in those two countries and applying lessons elsewhere across the globe.

Notes

1. Smith & Ziegler, 2008.
2. LAPOP, n.d.
3. “Informes Anuales,” 2008.
4. Igarapé Institute, 2021.
5. Woody, 2019.
6. Military police are a branch of the military, usually the army, responsible for the enforcement of the armed forces laws and regulations against criminal activity by military or civilian personnel, typically on military installations. They differ from civilian police forces or national gendarmeries, which have prescribed law enforcement duties among the civilian population.
7. Flores-Macías & Zarkin, 2019.
8. Krujit & Koonings, 2013, pp. 17–18. Patrick Paterson (2022) offers a framework for positive civil-military relations in democratic societies.
9. Agüero, 1992.
10. Michael Webb (2005) articulates a dichotomy of military autonomy, insisting that not all autonomy is incompatible with democracy. Whereas political autonomy has a negative

effect on democratic consolidation, professional autonomy over day-to-day administrative and operational functioning enhances the institution's effectiveness, cohesion, and professionalization.

11. Dammert, 2013, pp. 82–88; Mainwaring, 2003, p. 4.
12. Mani, 2011; Sotomayor, 2014.
13. Tomesani, 2018.
14. Moncada, 2016, p. 10.
15. Crandall, 2020, p. 178.
16. Falco, 1996; Pew Research Center, 2001; Morin, 1990.
17. Other top coca-growing countries, such as Peru and Bolivia, never adopted aerial spraying programs, instead opting for localized eradication tactics, or those that use glyphosate or manual weeding of specific crop plots, and alternative crop development, which seeks to replace coca with productive and licit crops. Daniel Mejía (2016) presents a cost-benefit analysis of Plan Colombia eradication efforts that recommends a moratorium on aerial spraying campaigns against coca production.
18. Isacson et al., 2013, pp. 2–5.
19. On a practical level, Washington justified an accountability narrative for two reasons: one, US taxpayers had long demanded that US funding not be used in ways that undermine or even facilitate human rights abuses, and, two, state-perpetrated atrocities in Colombia and Mexico eroded support for US partner security forces, rendering them less effective in tackling terrorists and criminal groups and restoring citizen security. Furthermore, the signing of the Inter-American Democratic Charter in 2001, which reinforced the commitment of thirty-four countries of the Western Hemisphere to promote democracy and defend it when it is under threat, provided a legal requirement for US policies toward the region to reinforce the rule of law and democratic governance.
20. These amendments to the Foreign Assistance Act of 1961 and the annual Department of Defense appropriations bills stipulate a prohibition on the furnishing of assistance to any foreign security force unit where there is credible information that members of the unit have committed gross violations of human rights and have not been held to account. A digital database of all foreign military and police recipients of US security assistance, managed by the Department of State, facilitates human rights vetting requirements that support the implementation of the Leahy amendments. For additional information, see Serafino et al., 2014.
21. US Department of State, 2021b; "Peace and Security Sectors," 2021.
22. Because security assistance and security sector reform pertain to the state's monopoly of force, the analytic approach most appropriate for evaluating success or failure is at the macro level. Eduardo Moncada (2016, pp. 6–9) highlights subnational approaches in his work on urban violence because they permit greater appreciation for the linkage dynamics among local actors, but US security assistance has mostly been framed, funded, and implemented by national-level officials and agencies. Thus this book focuses on central governments and their linkages to international actors pushing a reform agenda.
23. Muggah & Szabo de Carvalho, 2014, p. 14. James Rochlin makes a convincing argument for comparing Colombia and Mexico and dissects the social forces historically that precipitated a "revolution in military affairs" in both countries (2007, p. 2). Some comparative politics scholars may question why Brazil was not included as a case for comparison given the prevalence of drug-related violence there. Unlike Colombia and Mexico, however, Brazil is

not a major drug producer and is not geographically located along a drug corridor leading to the United States, rendering it a lower priority for US authorities—a reality reflected in the minimal US security assistance devoted to it.

24. Ramírez Lemus et al., 2004, p. 108. Pastrana originally billed his quest to attract foreign investment as a "Marshall Plan" for Colombia (Rojas, 2015, p. 28). Other countries, particularly in Europe, supported Pastrana's development focus, but when the US government made clear that its hefty support of Plan Colombia was contingent on a strategy that focused on security, Pastrana conceded to the Clinton administration, and much of the originally pledged European support dissipated.
25. US Department of State, 2016a.
26. Following major battlefield victories against Colombia's most lethal insurgencies, the Obama administration sought to deemphasize security assistance, and Plan Colombia ceased to appear in budget requests and administration policy documents after 2011 (Rosen, 2014, p. 4). By this juncture, Washington had reduced its assistance to levels consistent with other partner governments across the globe, as policymakers on both sides of the relationship expressed satisfaction with the strength of the country's security institutions and progress in reducing coca yield (Beittel, 2012, p. 27). Pablo Rojas Mejía (2016) finds that Plan Colombia reduced the net supply of cocaine by more than 50 percent, even slightly affecting the street price of cocaine in the United States for the first time ever.
27. Hylton, 2010; Isacson, 2011; Lindsay-Poland, 2018; Oehme, 2010; Rosen, 2014; Tate, 2015. The indicators of analysis for most of the existing work on Plan Colombia focus on counterdrug measures, not on measures of institutional change.
28. Benítez Manaut, 2014; Ramírez de Rincón, 2014.
29. DeYoung, 2016.
30. Petraeus & O'Hanlon, 2013.
31. US Department of State, 2016a.
32. Cepeda & Tascón, 2015, pp. 149–155.
33. US Department of State, 2009.
34. Graham, 2011.
35. Ashby, 2015; Breslow, 2015.
36. Hernandez, 2012.
37. Córdoba et al., 2018.
38. Mill, 1843/1882, p. 455.
39. Przeworski & Teune, 1970, pp. 32–34.
40. Lijphart, 1971, p. 690.
41. Anckar, 2008, pp. 390–395.
42. Collier et al., 2010, p. 10.
43. Coppedge, 2012, pp. 5, 129–141.
44. Whitehead, 2002, p. 204.
45. Arnson et al., 2014.
46. Lessing, 2017, p. 2.
47. Friedman, 2008; Mason, 2001. Erika Rodríguez Pinzón (2016, pp. 22–23) explains how the Colombian government used the state failure discourse to paint state institutions as the real victims of the Colombian conflict in a convincing bid to attract international attention and aid. Ana María Forero Ángel (2017) explores the legacy of this narrative in the construction

of institutional identity in the Colombian military. On state failure in Colombia and Mexico, see Kenny et al., 2012.

48. Hanlon & Shultz, 2016, p. 6. Enrique Arias and Daniel Goldstein refer to these states as "violent democracies" (2010). The literature on state-building holds that conflict is a principal driver of state capacity and institution-building, which makes the "vulnerable democratic" context an especially fruitful research area (Hanlon & Shultz, 2016; Thies, 2005; Tilly, 1975). As Paul Jackson and Shivit Bakrania find, "emerging policy themes of urbanizations, counterterrorism and organized crime are almost absent" from the existing literature on security sector reform, making the case selection of this book a novel contribution (2018, p. 14).
49. Whitehead, 2002, p. 202. Laurence Whitehead identifies the parallel processes of democratization in Colombia and Mexico as sufficiently similar but unique within Latin America to warrant a paired comparison.
50. "World Economic Outlook Database," 2016. In 1999, the Colombian gross domestic product (GDP) totaled $252.7 billion. In 2007, just prior to the signing of the Mérida Initiative, the Mexican GDP topped out at $1.69 trillion. Although Mexico's economy is significantly larger than Colombia's, the per capita GDP has consistently ranked the two economies as upper middle-income countries.
51. Kaufman & Trejo, 1997; Ocampo, 2015; Reding, 1995. The Colombian experience as a decentralized unitary state that features limited autonomy for subnational governments dates to the Colombian Constitution of 1991. Conversely, Mexico's federalist system was introduced in the Constitution of 1824 and was reiterated in the Constitution of 1917, which remains in effect.
52. Camp, 2005, pp. 1–3; Freeman & Sierra, 2004, p. 268; Ramírez Lemus et al., 2004, p. 123; Rath, 2013. The autonomy of the Colombian Armed Forces dates to the 1940s and 1950s—a period of intense partisan violence in Colombian history known as La Violencia. The widespread perception of the military's neutrality during that period, when the armed forces reluctantly assumed power at the request of the Liberal and Conservative Parties, convinced civilian reformers in the aftermath of La Violencia to grant the armed forces authority to design and implement national security policy without much civilian oversight. This autonomy was reinforced throughout the Cold War, as the military retained extraordinary powers during states of emergency. In Mexico, the PRI, which governed Mexico for seventy-one years, struck an agreement with the military in the years following the Mexican Revolution that afforded the armed forces significant prerogatives in exchange for noninterference in political affairs (Rath, 2013). The Mexican Congress has traditionally exerted little control over military budgets and acquisitions, and military courts have historically handled offenses against military discipline and crimes committed by military members. Further, the armed forces retain autonomy over their budgets and have privileged access to national security decision-making (academic security analyst, personal communication, Mexico City, September 11, 2017).
53. Mines, 2020, p. 11.
54. Initial Mérida Initiative appropriations included CARSI funding, but for FY 2010, Congress treated CARSI appropriations as a separate program.
55. Feeley, 2013b; Hanson Bond, 2016; Traficant, 1998; Vacius & Isacson, 2000.
56. For congressional deliberations surrounding Plan Colombia, see Rojas, 2015, pp. 40–52.
57. McDougall, 2009.

58. Paul et al., 2014, p. 41.
59. Former Mexican Ambassador to the United States, personal communication, Mexico City, August 25, 2017.
60. Anderson & Cockcroft, 1965; McCormick, 2016; Reding & Whalen, 1993. In 1929, General Plutarco Calles founded the Mexican Revolutionary Party (Partido Revolucionario Mexicano), which in 1946 was rebranded as the PRI.
61. Mexico has a long history of local armed insurgencies, most recently the Zapatista National Liberation Army (Ejército Zapatista de Liberación Nacional, or EZLN) in the state of Chiapas, but seldom did these outbreaks of revolutionary activity gain national traction as the Colombian insurgencies did throughout the 1980s and 1990s.
62. Benítez Manaut, 2014, p. 58; Idler, 2019. The 2018 election cycle in Mexico was marred by a triplication of political killings from the 2015 elections, reflecting a growing involvement of cartels in the political realm (Sieff, 2018).
63. The disarmament, demobilization, and reintegration (DDR) of the AUC (2003–2006), sanctioned by the Justice and Peace Law (Ley 975 de 2005, Ley de Justicia y Paz), occurred amid security sector reform, leading to a reduction of arms available to criminal actors and likely contributing to the drops in violence seen in chapter 4. The process led to the collective demobilization of some thirty-two thousand paramilitary fighters. Despite ample recidivism among ex-combatants, many of whom joined new criminal bands (*bandas criminales*, or BACRIM), tens of thousands of demobilized fighters abided by the terms of DDR and pursued legal livelihoods (Ávila & Valencia, 2018; McDermott, 2014; Salazar, 2011). Mexico, on the other hand, experienced no such détente with any of the country's criminal groups during security sector reform.
64. Hylton, 2010, pp. 107–110. This is an operational approach that emphasizes extirpating an insurgent threat from a geographic area, ensuring that the threat does not return by establishing state presence, and thereafter investing in development projects that incorporate civilian populations into national politics and commercial activity (GAO, 2008; Ucko, 2013). The philosophy underpinned US counterinsurgency strategy in Afghanistan, Iraq, and Syria.
65. As Craig Deare notes, Mexican politicians have struggled to find the right balance on the size and strength of the armed forces given both the history of territorial conquest by the United States and the low risk of territorial defense needs in the modern era (2021, p. 2.).
66. Paul et al., 2014, p. 18.
67. J. Furszyfer, personal communication, Mexico City, September 5, 2017.
68. Bailey, 2011b.
69. Zepeda & Rosen, 2014, p. 42.
70. Wilson & Kornblut, 2010. Mexican Senator Alejandro González (PT-Durango) remarked, "We are on our way to Colombianization" (Wilson & Kornblut, 2010).
71. Casas-Zamora & Cárdenas, 2010.
72. María Llorente and Jeremy McDermott (2014) caution against holding Plan Colombia up as a model for Mexico.
73. Tokatlian, 2000.
74. In financial terms, the capacity of the Mexican government to fund and direct its own reforms, with a GDP more than three times that of Colombia, was greater than that of the Colombian government ("World Bank Open Data," 2018). Mexican Congressman Waldo Fernández asserted that, without wanting "to appear ungrateful for US assistance," Mexico

really did not need money or equipment under the Mérida Initiative, but US technical support was essential (W. Fernández González, personal communication, Monterrey, Mexico, February 7, 2018).

75. Freeman & Sierra, 2004, p. 265.
76. Benítez Manaut & Deare, 2021, p. 4.
77. Shannon O'Neil, for one, interprets these strong and diversified linkages between the United States and Mexico as a favorable context for US democracy promotion: "Despite frequent misunderstandings our long shared history, intertwined economies, and strong personal and community links provide the constant multilayered interaction necessary to work together toward the complex goal of strengthening democracy" (2013, p. 8).
78. As Thomas Pickering (2009) notes, the whole-of-government approach to implement Plan Colombia was a novelty relative to other foreign policy objectives. Traditionally, interagency initiatives "remained under the watchful eye of the National Security Advisor," with the Cuban missile crisis and the Balkan wars as the exceptions. Pickering remarks, "What made Plan Colombia interesting and different was that, while it was set up as an interagency project, its leadership was lodged at the Department of State." The initial task force team included representatives from the National Security Council, Department of State, Department of Defense, the Joint Chiefs of Staff, USAID, the White House Office of National Drug Control Policy, and the Department of Justice.
79. Defense Manpower Data Center, 2015.
80. Reich & Aspinwall, 2013.
81. Toro, 1999.
82. Toro, 1999.
83. This is not the first time in history that US executive departments and agencies in Mexico differed on drug policy strategies. Carlos Pérez Ricart (2020) notes that in the earliest years of the DEA's operation in Mexico "struggles between the State Department personnel at the embassy and DEA personnel were constant and had the unintended consequence of developing a fragmented foreign policy with a lack of internal coherency." Tensions among the DEA, other agencies in the US government, and Mexican authorities came to a head in 2020 when US authorities charged and arrested former Mexican Secretary of National Defense General Salvador Cienfuegos Zepeda for his suspected links to organized crime. Despite considerable evidence against the retired general, US Attorney General William Barr wasted no time in dropping the charges and authorizing Cienfuegos's release back to Mexico in a bid to preserve a cooperative relationship with the Mexican government, much to the disappointment of investigators who had spent years building an air-tight case. One veteran DEA agent remarked, "If we had to pay a price in Mexico to finally prosecute someone like Cienfuegos, we were all willing to pay it because it would have made a difference. But instead, we paid the price and got nothing" (Golden, 2022).
84. Former senior US diplomat, email correspondence, September 28, 2021. John Feeley and James D. Nealon (2022) suggest that the DEA's tendency toward noncompliance does not represent disloyalty but instead a distinct bureaucratic culture. They explain, "Most DEA agents have been US street cops. Most Department of Justice officials sent overseas have served as assistant US attorneys or are career Department of Justice staff—folks for whom judicial independence, the sanctity of an investigation, and the sacrosanct pursuit of a conviction in a US court trump all other considerations. This makes for an extremely bad fit

when joining a diplomatic organization, where relationships and policy goals are measured in shades of frustrating gray, and where the ambassador is, by presidential order, the boss."

85. Reich & Aspinwall, 2013. Simon Reich and Mark Aspinwall note that US unilateralism around drug policy in Mexico initiates a cycle in which Mexico reacts defensively on the grounds that its sovereignty has been violated and thereafter introduces "strangulation strategies," or defensive regulations that limit US freedom of movement in Mexico. As explored in chapter 8, this occurred most markedly following the arrest of retired General Cienfuegos in 2020 in Los Angeles, which prompted the Mexican government to usher in a law restricting counterdrug cooperation and the autonomy of foreign agents, especially the DEA, on Mexican soil.
86. US Drug Enforcement Administration, 2009.
87. Villegas & Revelo, 2010.
88. Nagle, 2012, p. 5.

2
The Origins of Plan Colombia and the Mérida Initiative

Although Washington's diplomatic relations with Colombia and Mexico varied historically, its security ties with both countries were marked by steadily expanding cooperation throughout the twentieth century. During World War II, the governments of Colombia and Mexico, which had both previously fallen victim to US territorial expansionism, set aside their suspicions toward the regional hegemon and rallied behind the US and Allied cause.[1] The superpower status of the United States after the war provided further incentives for cooperation, and the US government marshaled consensus on containing communism in the Western Hemisphere through emerging multilateral forums such as the Inter-American Defense Board in 1942, the Inter-American Treaty of Reciprocal Assistance (Rio Treaty) in 1947, and the Organization of American States in 1948. The reinvigoration of President Richard Nixon's (1969–74) war on drugs during the presidency of Ronald Reagan (1981–89) led to an expansion of defense and law enforcement collaboration with friendly governments in the Americas. As the counterdrug fight took center stage in the United States in the 1980s, a growing chorus of US policymakers insisted on the national security dangers posed by illicit narcotics, effectively securitizing the political debate over how to reduce international trafficking and domestic consumption of drugs.[2] Meanwhile, Colombia and Mexico, which figured as critical source and transit countries for marijuana, cocaine, and heroin, became ground zero for US counterdrug efforts regionally, providing the need for enhanced bilateral relations to tackle organized crime and violence.

US security assistance to Colombia and Mexico surged in the 2000s as the Department of Defense identified in its 2001 *Quadrennial Defense Review Report* "threats emanating from the territories of weak and failing states" as a top priority in the Western Hemisphere.[3] On the eve of both Plan Colombia and the Mérida Initiative, popular characterizations of the countries' security crises included references to state failure or collapse, putting Colombia and Mexico in the same category as far more fragile governments such as Somalia,

From Peril to Partnership. Paul J. Angelo, Oxford University Press. © Oxford University Press 2024.
DOI: 10.1093/oso/9780197688106.003.0003

Yemen, and Syria. In retrospect, these exaggerated depictions of Colombia in 2000 and Mexico in 2007 underestimated the resilience of Colombian and Mexican institutions but nonetheless laid bare the very real crisis of legitimacy that security forces in both countries faced. The prioritization of Colombia and Mexico as recipients of US security assistance was an outgrowth of that immediate threat calculation, but more broadly, Plan Colombia and the Mérida Initiative were the fruit of decades of steadily expanding security cooperation between Washington and its allies in Bogotá and Mexico City.

US-Colombian Security Relations Prior to Plan Colombia

As early as the 1930s, the US government actively sought to cultivate a security relationship with the Colombian government when it opened the US Naval Mission office in Bogotá.[4] A stable—if restricted—democracy with Caribbean and Pacific coastlines, Colombia presented unique opportunities for US investors, and the country's geographic proximity to Panama made Colombia essential to the defense of sea lanes flowing into the Panama Canal. US-Colombian links expanded during World War II, when the Colombian government supported US plans to protect the canal from sabotage and eventually joined the Allies in 1943, following German submarine attacks on Colombian cargo vessels.

Although the Colombian Navy collaborated with its US counterparts in limited antisubmarine operations during World War II, it was not until a decade later during the Korean War that US-Colombian relations flourished. The prospect of global communist expansion distressed Colombian elites, especially considering mounting discontent over land tenure in the Colombian countryside. Consequently, the country's political leaders sought to shore up international support and legitimacy by partaking in the UN mission to rebuff communist expansionism from North Korea.[5] Eager to upgrade its armament and equipment, the Colombian military was the only Latin American force to contribute troops, more than four thousand, and a naval frigate to the multilateral military coalition on the Korean Peninsula. This experience exposed the Colombian military to US training practices, synchronized the forces' weapons systems with those of the United States, and strengthened the anticommunist convictions of the military's leaders.[6] The exchange also aligned US and Colombian strategic visions for hemispheric security, which aimed to prevent the spread of Soviet influence throughout the region. These ties proved advantageous for the Colombian security forces in the decades that followed, especially as US alarmism over communist agitation in Latin America surged following the 1959 Cuban Revolution.[7]

One Colombian military officer concluded that starting in the 1950s the Colombian military divided into two factions: those who practiced the doctrine of active defense as learned in Korea and trained for a conventional interstate war, and those who practiced the doctrine of counterinsurgency, which France was implementing at the time to suppress rebellion in Algeria.[8] Neither faction necessarily prevailed in the decades that followed, and the Colombian military continued to train for both missions. Although the organization of the military and its core competencies still reflected the Korea-era biases, the country's domestic political reality required that the military's doctrine and operational activity remain centered on internal security. Indeed, throughout the 1950s, armed conflict between the country's Liberal and Conservative Parties culminated in a period of civil unrest known as La Violencia. During the brief but consequential rule of Army General Gustavo Rojas Pinilla (1953–57), Colombia's main political parties ceded political control to the military's high command to quell partisan violence, which claimed the lives of more than two hundred thousand Colombians in less than a decade of fighting. Seeking to depoliticize the military and the police, which had become aligned with the Conservative Party and perpetrated some of the worst violence in the countryside, Rojas Pinilla issued a decree to reorganize the security forces during his first week of rule. The reform granted the Ministry of War (Ministerio de Guerra, later the Ministerio de Defensa Nacional, or the Ministry of National Defense) administrative and operational jurisdiction over the National Police force and reaffirmed the ministry's control of the armed forces—a configuration that persists today. The change ensured that the country's security institutions would serve the interests of the state over party allegiances and streamlined the sector's focus on tackling the wanton banditry and gruesome violence devastating Colombia's rural regions.[9]

The Liberal and Conservative leadership eventually agreed to end hostilities and restore civilian rule in 1957 in a power-sharing arrangement called the National Front (Frente Nacional). Remarkably, the Colombian military relinquished political power in exchange for considerable autonomy over its internal matters and, more broadly, state security policies. However, this transition did not fully put an end to political discontent or violence.[10] The accord, which stipulated that the Liberal and Conservative Parties would alternate control of the presidency and legislature every four years and ensure partisan parity for public jobs even at the municipal level, closed opportunities for alternative political movements to achieve national power. As in much of Latin America, communist groups, excluded from political life, began to organize militarily in the countryside with the aim of seizing power by force. Colombia's most enduring guerrilla insurgencies—the Revolutionary Armed Forces of Colombia (Fuerzas Armadas Revolucionarias de Colombia, or FARC), the National Liberation Army (Ejército de Liberación Nacional, or ELN), and the 19th of April Movement (Movimiento 19 de Abril, or M-19)—emerged in the 1960s and 1970s as leftist armed groups excluded from the political sphere. Not surprisingly, Colombia became an important theater for US security aid and partnership to combat endemic communist insurgencies.[11]

Against the backdrop of the Cold War, the US government endeavored to make Colombia a "showcase for capitalist development and modernization" under President John F. Kennedy's (1961–63) regional initiative, the Alliance for Progress. The country received $833 million in loans and more US Military Assistance Program (MAP) funding than any other Latin American country in the 1960s.[12] In 1961, the first of several dozen US mobile training teams (MTTs) arrived in Colombia to assist the military and police in improving their intelligence capabilities, conducting psychological operations, and monitoring guerrilla movements from helicopters.[13] Awash in international assistance, the Colombian Armed Forces expanded markedly from 1960 to 1966, growing from 20,800 service members to 53,500.[14] The Colombian military and police also worked more closely together under the leadership of General Alberto Ruiz Novoa, who reoriented the security forces to sponsor economic and social development projects through a US-supported program called Plan Lazo.[15] The strategy featured rehabilitation commissions that coordinated relief efforts for areas struck by natural disaster, assisted displaced people in finding work, resolved land title issues, and provided medical attention to needy populations.[16] As rebel groups expanded their territorial footprint, "winning hearts and minds" became a vital mission for the Colombian security sector. In 1964, the Ministry of Defense issued the Joint Counterinsurgency Plan, which built on the principles of Plan Lazo and formalized the military's counterguerrilla doctrine.[17] However, tensions between General Ruiz Novoa and President Guillermo León Valencia, rooted in differences over the military's expansion into social development projects in the countryside, led to the general's dismissal in 1965, and by the 1970s, new uniformed leaders oversaw a reorientation of the Colombian military away from the objectives of Plan Lazo, stunting the program's initial promise.

The principal antagonists in Colombia's armed conflict transformed when insurgents and other criminal organizations gained strength and resources from their expanding involvement in drug trafficking. Beginning in the 1970s, Colombia's geographic location, fertile soil, and weak government institutions facilitated the country's first large-scale marijuana and cocaine production. Not long after, the prohibitionist polices of the US and Colombian governments encouraged those involved in the illicit drug trade to invest heavily in measures to protect their drug crops and transit routes, giving rise to heavily armed drug-trafficking organizations. As the drug trade became immensely profitable, the 1980s saw the rapid expansion of the illegal industry and the outbreak of the country's fierce cartel wars, pitting drug syndicates against each other and against the Colombian state. At the height of their power, the Medellín and Cali cartels ruthlessly murdered and kidnapped thousands of Colombians, including politicians, police officers, and journalists. Intent on demonstrating their political reach, they indiscriminately bombed public spaces in an intimidation campaign that eventually succeeded in strong-arming politicians to ban the extradition of drug criminals to the United States by enshrining it in the 1991 Constitution.

President Reagan, facing a growing crisis of US domestic drug abuse and concerned about the vulnerability of Colombia's government to nonstate threats, took increased interest in the country during this period. What followed was a notable expansion of US security assistance, especially as Colombia became the top cocaine producer in the world. In 1984, the Reagan administration released more than $50 million in arms to the Colombian security forces and increased training for military personnel, 4,844 of whom received instruction between 1984 and 1990.[18] Security ties between the governments were especially robust during the administration of Colombian President César Gaviria Trujillo (1990–94), whose tenure coincided with Colombia's inauspicious distinction as the world's most dangerous country.[19] In particular, the US Army's 7th Special Forces Group grew in prominence as a purveyor of training for foreign internal defense missions. Whereas the Drug Enforcement Administration (DEA) helped Colombia with intelligence, analysis, investigations, arrests, and search warrants, the US Army focused on the patrolling, marksmanship, land navigation, mountaineering, and mission planning that permitted Colombian police forces to carry out operations against drug traffickers.[20]

Even as the relationship between the two nations strengthened, US assistance at this juncture failed to address the underlying issues. Alarmingly high crime rates and pervasive police corruption had led to a crisis in public trust.[21] By the early 1990s, the cartels had managed to infiltrate Colombia's long-standing democratic institutions through threats and bribery. The Colombian National Police, even its Elite Force (Cuerpo Élite), were among the most vulnerable to these tactics, and Human Rights Watch singled out the police in a 1993 report for waging a "social cleansing" campaign against street people, drug addicts, thieves, and LGBTQ + individuals.[22]

Acknowledging just how compromised its partners in the Colombian security forces were, the United States reoriented its aid to support security sector reform. From 1993 to 1998, the US government laid the groundwork for its later intervention—Plan Colombia—by supporting a major overhaul of the National Police under Colombian Law 62 of 1993 (Ley 62 de 1993).[23] With National Police General Rosso José Serrano at the helm, the police force implemented its own Cultural Transformation Program (Programa de Transformación Cultural) from 1995 to 1998, carried out a highly publicized purge, improved processes for background checks on police units, and expanded benefits and promotion opportunities for personnel to improve retention and curb corruption.[24] Serrano's efforts and commitment so impressed US policymakers that, even "at a time when US officials trusted no one else in Colombia," Serrano continued to work closely with US agencies in toppling the cartels.[25] Nevertheless, Serrano's and the United States' focus on militarizing the campaign against the cartels had the paradoxical effect of creating distance between the police and the citizenry when the National Police were aiming to boost their image among the public.[26]

The US government and the Colombian National Police targeted cartel command and control by adopting a kingpin strategy focused on arresting or killing cartel leaders.[27] A specialized Colombian military-police unit (Bloque de Búsqueda)—supported by US Special Forces, the DEA, and the Central Intelligence Agency (CIA)—killed Colombia's most wanted drug trafficker, Pablo Escobar, in 1993, and by 1995 Colombian authorities had captured the seven leaders of the Cali Cartel. These successes boosted the morale of the National Police and vindicated those who had pushed for institutional reform.

However, what was initially seen as a triumph of the Colombian state actually led to an equally dark period in its war on criminality. Following the dissolution of the Cali Cartel, the violence did not disappear. In fact, the kingpin approach inadvertently generated a power vacuum in the drug industry—a circumstance that spawned some three hundred mini-cartels by the early 2000s.[28] As Colombia's cartels atomized, guerrilla and paramilitary groups also wrested control of the farming, preparation, and transport of coca leaves and paste, facilitating the armed factions' expansion in territory and size throughout the decade.[29] As the security situation deteriorated, Bogotá's ability to counter the growing influence of these groups was in serious doubt. Whereas combating cartels was primarily the responsibility of the National Police, the task of countering armed militias fell to the armed forces. The military was poorly organized, demoralized, and ill equipped.[30] The strengthening of illegal armed actors came at a time when the military, although numerically its largest in history, had neglected to train and equip soldiers for the battlefield reality within the country.[31] Defense leaders failed to build on the counterinsurgency lessons of the 1960s and in the decades that followed largely maintained an organization that was structurally prepared for regular warfare, lacking the nimbleness needed to take on ever-growing nonstate armed groups.[32] Further, the military did not enjoy as robust a relationship with the US government as the National Police did. Despite earlier cooperation with US counterparts, a rise in human rights abuses committed by the Colombian Armed Forces alarmed US policymakers, leading to the suspension of US military aid to the country in the early 1990s.

From 1996 to 1998, the military suffered crushing defeats on the battlefield and even on their own turf as the FARC besieged military bases, resulting in the surrender of hundreds of soldiers around the country.[33] These setbacks coincided with an unexpected souring of US-Colombian relations as evidence surfaced implicating the 1994 campaign of the then president of Colombia, Ernesto Samper Pizano (1994–98), in the receipt of drug money from the Cali Cartel during his election campaign.[34] The Republican majority in the US Congress insisted on a hard-line counterdrug stance, forcing the hand of President Clinton, a Democrat. In 1995, the US government decertified the Samper administration as a partner in the war on drugs, even going as far as to revoke Samper's US travel visa. This drastic measure, reserved for the most noncompliant drug-supplying countries in the world, resulted in the suspension of all nonsecurity assistance to Colombia and undermined the authority of the Colombian state at a time when guerrilla and paramilitary groups were gaining impressive strength.[35]

Despite this reversal in relations, some counterdrug money continued to flow to Colombia as the Andean country came to dominate the chain of cocaine production and distribution. During the 1990s, the US government spent an estimated $1 billion to fight drug cultivation and trafficking in Colombia.[36] Even the Colombian military, which had not traditionally benefited from counterdrug support, received excess defense articles from Operation Desert Shield—the US response to the 1990 Iraqi invasion of Kuwait—and technical advice in establishing counterdrug riverine forces.[37] Although the Samper administration failed to convince Washington to resume more collaborative diplomatic ties during his tenure, the Colombian president tried to mend his relationship with the United States—and a disapproving Colombian military high command—by supporting counterdrug legislation, implementing a maritime agreement to pursue drug-trafficking suspects at sea, increasing the Ministry of Defense's budget, and revamping military promotion criteria.[38]

The departure of Samper from office in 1998 offered a welcome respite from the frustration, and at times hostility, that had come to define US-Colombian relations in the mid-1990s. Samper's successor as president, Andrés Pastrana, successfully campaigned for office on two vital issues: opening a peace dialogue with the FARC, which had grown in strength during the 1990s as it increased its involvement in the drug trade, and improving relations with international benefactors, especially the United States.

US Security Assistance via Plan Colombia

In 1998, Pastrana confronted emboldened insurgents, an unprecedented economic crisis, and a humanitarian disaster provoked by one of the most damaging earthquakes in the country's history. The FARC, which had amassed an armed force of twenty thousand insurgents, had captured more than five hundred Colombian soldiers and police and boasted an armed presence in every one of Colombia's mainland departments. Even though the Colombian Army led an internal review of its own capability deficiencies in 1998, resulting in an initial restructuring of the armed forces with the aim of protecting the civilian population, the inability of the security sector to control public order nationally became ever more apparent with the growing influence of the far-right United Self-Defense Forces of Colombia (Autodefensas Unidas de Colombia, or AUC) paramilitary group.[39] Pastrana originally issued a document titled "Plan Colombia" in December 1998, calling for public, private, and international investment to help resolve the country's high rates of violence and drug production. The strategy consisted of five components: a peace process with the FARC, economic growth, counterdrug suppression, justice and human rights reform, and democracy promotion and social development. Cognizant that a monopoly of the legitimate use of force underpinned the accomplishment of these larger objectives, Pastrana insisted that reforming the Colombian security sector was the only way out of Colombia's morass. For this, he concluded, Colombia needed US support.[40]

Although Colombia's security problems were not an immediate concern for the average US citizen, policymakers in Washington found ample justification for major investments to fortify and help reform the Colombian security forces.[41] Most important, by 2000, transnational drug trafficking had become a matter of US national security, and President Clinton believed Colombia to be an essential arena in which to prove that he and his party were "tough on drugs."[42] In the run-up to the 2000 US presidential race, the Democratic Party faced criticism from Republicans for having paid too little attention to the menace of drug abuse—a potential electoral liability for Vice President Al Gore, who stood as the party's nominee for the election. The Democrats found a forceful response in Plan Colombia. In "A National Strategy for a Global Age," a policy manifesto published in December 2000, the White House asserted that "the most effective counterdrug operations are mounted at the source where illegal drugs are grown and produced," and it set the goal of reducing illegal drug access in the United States by 50 percent by 2007.[43]

As Winifred Tate notes, counternarcotics aid and militarization became a solution to the Clinton administration's political vulnerability, and boosting immediate assistance to the Colombian military rather than to the Colombian police, whom Republicans in Congress had long championed, allowed the Democrats to contrast themselves with their political rivals.[44] President Clinton proclaimed that Plan Colombia was a "visionary and audacious effort to deepen democracy, extend prosperity, end the prolonged internal armed conflict, and combat the production and trafficking of drugs that, similar to narco-terrorism, had cut short so many lives and obstructed for so long progress in Colombia."[45] However, in its quest to help the Colombian government regain its sovereignty, the US government would need to take an uncomfortable step: deepening its partnership with a security sector embroiled in accusations of corruption and human rights abuses.

Republicans in Congress were also wary of President Pastrana's initial peace bid and balked at his demilitarization of the *despeje*, a tract of territory ceded to the FARC as a condition of the negotiations. But when President Clinton's State Department committed to redoubling drug crop eradication in the heart of the FARC's zones of influence, Republican support for Plan Colombia followed as the party found its own rationalizations for supporting militarization of the counterdrug fight in Colombia.[46] President Pastrana's message that Colombia, a country three hours by air south of Miami, was on the verge of collapse into a narco-state necessitated a strong response from the United States.[47] In fact, multiple strategic justifications for generous security assistance in Plan Colombia enabled institutional alliances to coalesce around the issue of helping Colombia improve security by professionalizing its security forces.[48] Plan Colombia was "a domestic counternarcotics policy intended to address the Clinton administration's moral crisis, a peace policy to support negotiations with the guerrilla forces, a counterinsurgency policy that would strengthen the security forces, and an economic development policy to spur development in remote regions," all at once.[49] In 2000, President Clinton, backed by bipartisan consensus in Congress, launched US contributions to Plan Colombia, committing $1.3 billion in security and development assistance. For many US lawmakers, as well, Plan Colombia presented an opportunity for Washington to award profitable government contracts to US-based military hardware and technology companies, and contractors lobbied hard to generate support for military assistance to Colombia on Capitol Hill.[50]

A focus on the supply side of the drug trade, rather than on domestic US consumption, enabled US politicians to shift responsibility for the nation's drug problem to an external actor. Further, to avoid becoming mired in a Vietnam-like escalation and to prevent backlash at home, US officials sought to minimize US casualties by enlisting the Colombian security forces to fight the war against transnational drug-trafficking organizations.[51] Regardless, this strategy entailed an expansion of Department of Defense personnel in the country to monitor the introduction of new technologies, the application of new training, and the implementation of institutional reforms. Plan Colombia's emphasis on the security forces also meant an upswell in funding for the US government's geographic combatant command in the area, SOUTHCOM.[52] A geographically focused entity with jurisdiction over the US military's Latin American and Caribbean operations, SOUTHCOM readily accepted the influx of resources, and the Department of Defense averted major post–Cold War budget reductions by embracing the counterdrug mission.[53]

Department of Defense involvement was subject to strict restrictions by Congress, however. US law prohibited the participation of US service members in combat operations in Colombia, and the Plan Colombia appropriations bills capped the number of US personnel authorized in the country at any given time to a maximum of four hundred military advisors and four hundred civilian contractors.[54] In 2004, US President George W. Bush later revised these limits, in part to protect one of Washington's other interests in the country—Colombian oil reserves.[55] In 2001, 170 guerrilla bombings on the Caño Limón-Coveñas pipeline in the north of the country forced a shutdown in the flow of oil for much of the year, prompting the US government to surge special forces advisors to the area to help train new Colombian Army units devoted to protecting energy infrastructure.[56] The global war on terrorism enabled Washington to expand its counterterrorism footing across the world, allowing the Bush administration to cleverly portray persistent attacks against Colombia's oil pipelines by the FARC and ELN as a direct terrorist threat to US interests.[57] This enlargement of both mission and personnel took place at a time when US and Colombian relations with the oil-producing government of Venezuelan President Hugo Chávez had deteriorated.[58] US authorities were heartened by the conservative, pro-US administration in Bogotá, and ensuring that Colombia could thrive economically by protecting its principal extractive industries became yet another rationalization for enhanced US-Colombian security ties.

For their part, leaders at the US Department of State, Department of Justice, and Agency for International Development (USAID)—the other principal actors involved in administering security assistance—offered equally compelling justifications for their embrace of Plan Colombia in its early years. Senior Foreign Service officers at the Department of State noted the perceived success of US security policy in El Salvador in the 1980s as a conflict resolution tactic and argued that the department could play a similarly supportive role in ongoing peace negotiations in Colombia.[59] Thomas Pickering, the undersecretary of state for political affairs at the time, and retired General Barry McCaffrey, President Clinton's drug czar, jointly spearheaded an interagency decision-making and policy implementation process that prioritized collegiality and coordination. Owing to his military background, McCaffrey's deep connections at the Pentagon helped ensure the Department of Defense's deference to the White House and State Department for negotiating and coordinating security assistance to Colombia.[60]

The Department of Justice and its subsidiary, the DEA, also welcomed a deeper relationship with the Colombian Ministry of Justice to facilitate extraditions of drug traffickers and eventually provide technical advice on judicial reform. Pastrana's conciliatory tone with the United States and commitment to bringing drug traffickers to justice reassured Clinton's Department of Justice that Colombian political leadership was amenable to resuming extradition talks. USAID was originally expected to assume a prominent role in the implementation of Plan Colombia; the agency's lines of engagement in Latin America include drug crop substitution, rule-of-law construction, and conflict resolution programs. Nonetheless, the US Congress, which initially funded only those programs that had a direct nexus with drug suppression, emphasized the chemical spraying of Colombia's coca crops in lieu of manual and voluntary eradication, resulting in a smaller USAID mission at the outset of the bilateral initiative.[61] Consequently, Washington's soft-power objectives, implemented by USAID's traditional bureaus and even the more expeditionary Office of Transition Initiatives, received only modest resources, had a limited reach, and produced variable results in the first years of Plan Colombia.[62] Additionally, the security situation in the country made the implementation of USAID programs difficult at this early stage. Returning the monopoly of force to the Colombian state via its security forces was the resolute focus of US security assistance—a strategy that demanded, in the minds of those on Capitol Hill, a most aggressive approach.

In this vein, Plan Colombia was a continuation but also an expansion of previous practice: the US government doubled down on its support for the Colombian security forces as a way of stabilizing the country and accomplishing US strategic objectives, but the magnitude of resources expended and the buy-in from across the political spectrum and the executive departments marked a new era in US-Colombia security relations.

US-Mexican Security Relations Prior to the Mérida Initiative

Like Plan Colombia, robust US security assistance under the Mérida Initiative in Mexico was the culmination of decades of expanding bilateral cooperation on security matters. However, close security relations were not always a given. For the first century following Mexico's formal independence from Spain in 1821, the United States and Mexico maintained a tense relationship that featured frequent border conflicts. This period included the secession of Texas and its subsequent annexation by the United States and the Mexican-American War (1846–48), which saw US troops occupy the Mexican capital and resulted in the US annexation of more than half of all Mexican territory.

President Franklin D. Roosevelt (1933–45), however, ensured more productive relations with Mexico with the introduction of the Good Neighbor Policy, which renounced the United States' self-proclaimed right to military intervention in the hemisphere as enshrined in the Monroe Doctrine. This positive turn improved the willingness of Mexican authorities to coordinate with the US government on common matters of security.[63] Roosevelt wagered that improved hemispheric relations would help consolidate alliances and ensure economic opportunities in the event of war in Europe. Further, the country's long border with Mexico required the two countries to cooperate on bilateral issues ranging from agricultural practices and petroleum access to contraband and banditry.[64]

Notably, the 1940s witnessed increased military-to-military cooperation, as the Mexican government joined the Allied effort in 1942. In addition to the establishment of the Joint US-Mexico Defense Commission in 1942, resulting in enhanced intelligence sharing with the United States, the Mexican military sent a flight squadron to support the US effort in the Pacific theater. At least 250,000 Mexican citizens living in the United States also donned US uniforms and deployed with the US Armed Forces during World War II.[65] Mexico's mineral wealth supplied the US arms industry with much-needed silver, copper, lead, zinc, and iron during the war years. In 1941, the Mexican and US governments even settled an economic dispute that resulted from Mexico's 1938 nationalization of the oil industry, thereby providing the northern neighbor with expanded access to petroleum.[66] Like Colombia's participation in the Korean War, Mexico's involvement in World War II enabled a modest process of military modernization through US military training, opening the door to future forms of military-to-military cooperation.[67]

Starting as early as the Mexican Revolution (1910–20), the Mexican military was undergoing a largely internally driven reform process that rendered the force an attractive partner for the US Department of War (consolidated with the military service branches and renamed the Department of Defense in 1947).[68] The regular army that remained in the 1920s was composed of "a diverse coalition of armed peasants, ranchers, middle-class professionals, *caudillos*, former federal soldiers, cowboys, miners, and a smattering of urban workers"—an often unwieldy group that consumed 50 percent of the federal budget, engaged in sporadic revolts, and lacked the discipline expected of professional armies.[69] After 1935, however, President Lázaro Cárdenas (1934–40) embarked on a reformist campaign to improve the image and effectiveness of the military by encouraging physical fitness, punishing soldiers for unbecoming social vices, and normalizing military family life by introducing a system of social insurance and housing.

Mexican involvement in World War II permitted the government to drive ahead with additional organizational reforms, including mandatory conscription until 1948. Between 1941 and 1945, the Mexican military, eager to obtain modern weapons and training, welcomed increased security cooperation with the United States—a stark departure from the anti-US sentiment of the institution's old guard.[70] The Mexican government was reluctant, however, to permit the establishment of US military bases in the country. The Institutional Revolutionary Party (Partido Revolucionario Institucional, or PRI), still consolidating its political power inside Mexico, feared that the Mexican military's greater exposure to the highly autonomous officers of the US military might ultimately undermine the party's efforts to disempower the army's political wing. Indeed, following the war and during the administration of President Miguel Alemán (1946–52), the PRI government firmly established civilian control of the force by relieving the military's General Staff, the group of officers leading the administrative and operational aspects of the organization, asserting presidential prerogative in selecting the institution's leadership, and revamping and depoliticizing the curriculum at the Military College.[71] As was the case in Colombia following Rojas Pinilla's brief and exceptional rule, Mexico's civilian authorities had successfully subordinated the military to their command by the 1950s.[72]

US-Mexican counternarcotics collaboration dates to this era as well.[73] Building on the regulatory and prohibitionist strategies of the early twentieth century in the United States, punitive counterdrug policies appeared on both sides of the border in the 1940s.[74] To some extent, Mexican authorities buckled under US pressure to militarize their counternarcotics strategy starting in the 1940s, but the repressive stance against drug use was also consistent with conservative social values in Mexico that reflected little tolerance for the use of psychoactive substances. Moreover, the PRI embraced the opportunity presented by hard-line counterdrug policies to expand its bureaucratic footprint and advance a process of nationalization and centralization in Mexico's geographic periphery.[75] As Carlos Pérez Ricart notes, "The punitive paradigm [sponsored by the United States] could not have been applied in Mexico had Mexican policymakers not seen the competitive advantages offered to them by the policies proposed, and if those policies had not reflected traditional Mexican attitudes."[76]

These attitudes prompted the founding of new security institutions with a counternarcotics mandate. In 1947, the Mexican government created, with US assistance, the Federal Directorate of Security (Dirección Federal de Seguridad, or DFS), similar in design and authority to the US government's Federal Bureau of Investigation (FBI). The DFS, often in coordination with the Mexican Army and sometimes with the advisory input of the FBI, was charged with pursuing criminal groups that specialized in producing and transporting marijuana and opium products.[77] In short order, drug contraband became a defining issue of bilateral security ties.

The Mexican government's efforts to centralize some of the country's law enforcement and intelligence capabilities were welcomed by their FBI and CIA counterparts, who supported the budding agencies well into the 1950s. Thus the US government anticipated the backing of the Mexican government following the outbreak of the Cold War and the division of the world into US and Soviet spheres of influence.[78] However, the Mexican ruling party, the PRI—itself a product of social revolution—disappointed the US government when it offered its unconditional recognition of the Cuban Revolution and the island nation's new communist government, leading to a period of cool relations between Washington and Mexico City.

Even so, domestic developments in Mexico in the 1960s gradually led to greater ideological parity between the neighboring countries. As Marxist political groups such as the 23 September Communist League (Liga Comunista 23 de Septiembre, or LC23S) and the Revolutionary Action Movement (Movimiento de Acción Revolucionaria, or MAR) gained traction in Mexico, PRI authorities grew concerned about internal challenges to their autocratic rule. As in Colombia, the security sector assumed a more active role in repressing left-wing movements, some of which developed into small-scale insurgencies like the Party of the Poor (Partido de los Pobres, or PDLP).[79]

The abusive tactics of this period and the resulting human rights violations became colloquially known as the dirty war (*guerra sucia*) period. Notably, unlike in Colombia and other countries that confronted insurgencies during this period, Mexican insurgencies did not receive material support or training from the Cuban government, making repression of the radical left in Mexico more achievable.[80] Even though the US government did not provide significant resources to Mexico's security forces during this period, shared anticommunist sentiment ensured that both countries worked, albeit mostly in isolation, toward the same goal of containing revolutionary fervor on the North American continent.[81]

The 1960s also marked the growing involvement of the Mexican military in counterdrug missions, especially the eradication of marijuana and poppy crops.[82] In 1969, the Nixon administration embarked on a massive border-crossing drug interdiction program known as Operation Intercept, pressuring the Mexican government to enhance its own counterdrug measures.[83] Operation Intercept stipulated a thorough inspection of every northbound plane, person, and vehicle entering the United States, effectively slowing all commercial activity along the border and creating pressure on the Mexican government, which faced the prospect of declining tourism and slowing exports. The "exercise in international extortion" worked for the new US president, and Mexican government begrudgingly agreed to pursue drug traffickers with greater vigor in exchange for more relaxed border enforcement. Mexico City also enlisted the support of its military to destroy drug crops in a US-Mexican aerial spraying campaign called Operation Condor.[84] Although the military, which was historically oriented toward external defense, cautiously took on these operations, this new role exposed an institution that prided itself on its professionalism to the corrupting influence of criminal enterprises, with predictably devastating results. Military zone commanders often took a cut from the profits of gangs that farmed drug crops in the commanders' areas of responsibility, and police forces, which controlled highway checkpoints and border crossings, were known to accept bribes in exchange for allowing product to pass onward to the United States.[85] By the 1980s, drug corruption in the ranks of the military had become so grave that the institution's leadership increased counterdrug intelligence, expanded phone surveillance, and rotated zone commanders with greater frequency to target corrupt soldiers.[86]

This operational vulnerability appears to have had surprisingly little initial impact on US-Mexican security relations. US officials celebrated in classified cables the Mexican military's eradication and interdiction successes against heroin trafficking and lauded the senior-level appointments of officers perceived to be vehemently antidrug.[87] Eventually, though, the infiltration of

Mexican police forces by drug traffickers undermined Mexico's credibility and precipitated a major diplomatic impasse. The US government suspected several high-ranking individuals in the Mexican government, even a director of the DFS, of close ties to drug gangs. After the 1985 murder of DEA agent Enrique Camarena Salazar by drug operatives linked to Mexican security officials, the US government publicly called into question the commitment of the Mexican security sector to confront the drug issue.[88]

Mexican authorities reacted by reorganizing the country's principal counterdrug agencies. The government quickly moved to abolish the DFS and founded a new federal force with technical advice from the DEA called the Investigation and National Security Center (Centro de Investigación y Seguridad Nacional, or CISEN).[89] Mexican President Miguel de la Madrid (1982–88) strengthened the Mexican Army's counterdrug capabilities as well by establishing in 1986 the Rapid Response Force, later renamed the Airmobile Special Forces Group (Grupo Aeromóvil de Fuerzas Especiales, or GAFE), which was equipped to deploy on short notice to suppress outbreaks of drug-related violence.[90] The Carlos Salinas de Gotari (1988–94) administration, for its part, shared President Reagan's conviction that drug trafficking was a national security threat. By the turn of the decade, the Mexican government had dispatched more than twenty-five thousand military troops in domestic counterdrug missions.[91] Nonetheless, US intelligence officials remained apprehensive about how the Mexican military's obsolete equipment, lack of logistical control, corruption, and inadequate training would inevitably hamper the forces' ability to deliver operational results.[92]

Bilateral concerns about the drug problem persisted into the early 1990s as traffickers increasingly used Mexican terrain to smuggle Colombian cocaine into the United States. The Central America–Mexico corridor, a region already rife with contraband and trafficking networks, became the preferred path for Colombia's cartels, especially as the United States became more effective at intercepting drugs along Caribbean corridors.[93] Mexican drug gangs became more centralized as well, and for a time ceased fighting among each other and instead worked together to devise a coordinated plan to negotiate state protection for their illegal activities. Some of these gangs formally joined forces, consolidating their armed power in the form of new Mexican cartels. Cartel leaders represented much larger criminal confederations and sent designated interlocutors to represent their interests to corrupt government officials, offering kickbacks for a blind eye from security forces toward trafficking activities. Successive directors of the Federal Judicial Police (Policía Judicial Federal, or PJF) obliged, providing these services to Mexico's budding cartels in exchange for handsome financial rewards. As in Colombia, police agencies in Mexico have long been highly susceptible to nefarious moonlighting, and some police officers lend their expertise and intelligence to the country's armed gangs and cartels in their off-duty hours.[94] In the early 1990s, organized crime syndicates in Mexico reportedly paid more than $500 million annually in bribes, more than double the budget of the Mexican Attorney General's Office (Procuraduría General de la República, or PGR).[95]

The relative peace that intercartel collaboration had achieved, however, was short lived, and the organizations ultimately splintered into warring bands that vied for control over lucrative transit routes. In 1993, such competition resulted in sporadic and sensational outbursts of violence, particularly in border cities, and the 1994 emergence of the Zapatista National Liberation Army (Ejército Zapatista de Liberación Nacional, or EZLN) insurgency in the southern Mexican state of Chiapas added to deteriorating security in the country.

The wave of public disorder exacerbated the already uneasy US-Mexican relationship. The United States, having entered into the North Atlantic Free Trade Agreement (NAFTA) with Canada and Mexico in 1994, grew anxious about collapsing trade barriers that facilitated greater cross-border traffic even as its neighbor to the south appeared not to take seriously its responsibility in combating the drug trade.[96] Relations became unambiguously tense when Mexican authorities admitted in 1997 that the country's Commissioner of the National Institute to Combat Drugs (Instituto Nacional para el Combate a las Drogas, or INCD), General Jesús Gutiérrez Rebello, had long-standing ties to drug cartels.[97] Fierce debate over decertification of Mexico as a drug war ally ensued in the US Congress, which ultimately rejected the proposed sanctions. To salvage the bilateral relationship, President Clinton's executive agencies doubled down on cooperation with Mexican President Ernesto Zedillo (1994–2000) to root out endemic security sector corruption once and for all.[98] The Zedillo administration's attempt to address the corrupting influence of the cartels resulted in a concerted effort to arrest the leadership of the Gulf of Mexico and Tijuana cartels, leading to an all-out war between the cartels and the security forces.[99]

Institutional reforms in the security sector complemented the government's punitive measures against corrupt officials and the cartels. Although the federal government had less leverage to impose reform on state and municipal police forces due in part to a devolution of autonomy to municipal governments starting in 1983, the Zedillo administration initially purged more than 1,800 PJF agents, reducing the force by half.[100] In 1998, in the face of flagging public trust, the government dissolved the PJF altogether, founded the Federal Preventive Police (Policía Federal Preventiva, or PFP), and increased the responsibilities of state governments in the realm of public security.[101] Zedillo's successor, President Vicente Fox (2000–2006)—notably, the first non-PRI president since 1929—also attempted to professionalize and centralize law enforcement by creating the Federal Investigative Agency (Agencia Federal de Investigación, or AFI), which assumed the functions previously ascribed to the PJF. However, the AFI also succumbed to widespread corruption. By 2005, the Mexican Attorney General's Office reported that one-fifth of the AFI's officers faced investigations into criminal activity; in response to renewed public criticism of the federal force, the government once again reorganized the AFI and rebranded it as the Federal Ministerial Police (Policía Federal Ministerial, or PFM) in 2009.[102]

In this time frame, Mexico also transitioned from a one-party autocracy under the PRI to a multiparty democracy. Nevertheless, the gradual political opening in the 1990s resulted in further politicization of the state and municipal police forces, which were typically led by partisan appointees of governors and mayors. With the introduction of new political parties and genuine electoral competition at subnational levels, political power became more diffuse. What followed was an increasing lack of coordination among authorities at each level of government on how to address a much-needed law enforcement reform, in turn opening the door to an even greater public security role for the armed forces.[103] In 1995, the Secretariat of National Defense (Secretaría de Defensa Nacional, or SEDENA), which comprised of the army and the air force, promulgated a development plan that helped guide the transformation and modernization process. In the plan, the military willingly accepted a larger mandate in counternarcotics and in supporting law enforcement missions.[104]

This early reform effort also included restructuring of the army into smaller, mobile units; revamping the military intelligence apparatus; creating a command to coordinate joint operations between SEDENA and the Secretariat of the Navy (Secretaría de Marina, or SEMAR); developing new special forces squadrons to address local insurgencies; and introducing new technology, equipment, and weapons.[105] In some ways, SEDENA was reacting to a growing dissatisfaction within the army over the institution's handling of the EZLN insurgency, command structure, promotions, and technical competence.[106] Desperate for a viable security partner across the border, the US Department of Defense signaled its support for the reform, and after a series of unprecedented high-level defense summits, including the first visit to Mexico by a secretary of defense (William J. Perry), Washington accelerated security assistance for the Mexican military like never before.[107]

From 1996 to 2000, the United States doubled the number of Mexican trainees at US military schools, and the sale of US-manufactured body armor, armored vehicles, and night-vision equipment to SEDENA spiked.[108] Washington also transferred tens of millions of dollars in excess defense articles to the Mexican military, including seventy-three Vietnam-era UH-1 helicopters. However, Mexican defense officials did not see the donation as worthy of gratitude. The transfer of outmoded helicopters, many with debilitating maintenance problems, irritated the Mexican Army's high command. The turnover in the US secretary of defense position from William Perry to William Cohen also affected the growing sense of interpersonal trust between senior US and Mexican defense officials. Accordingly, US accusations that SEDENA had deployed the helicopters in counterinsurgency missions, a violation of the terms of their transfer, offended Mexican authorities. The ensuing fallout highlighted the tension underlying the bilateral security relationship and the sensitivity of the Mexican government to perceived US condescension.[109] In protest, the Mexican government decommissioned the helicopters from its arsenal in October 1999 and returned the donated aircraft to the United States. In doing so, Mexican authorities made it clear that security cooperation with Washington would occur only if the United States were prepared to treat its neighbor as an equal.

Despite these misgivings, cooperative security relations steadily expanded in the early years of the 2000s, as cross-border security remained at the forefront of the bilateral agenda.[110] Following the 9/11 attacks on New York and Washington, the NAFTA community assumed a newfound importance for the Bush administration. The specter of terrorist violence on US soil resulted in an unprecedented urgency to deny would-be terrorists entry into US territory via the Mexican border. Mexican notions of national security were thus forever changed after the US declaration of a global war on terrorism. Given US concerns about terrorist interest in exploiting the porous US-Mexico border and widespread corruption on the Mexican side of the border, Mexican authorities recognized that they could no longer devise security policies independent of the threat perceptions—and preferences—of their northern neighbor.[111] In April 2002, the inauguration of the Department of Defense's NORTHCOM, the military command with a mandate to implement regional US defense strategy in North America, signaled the emphasis on continental and border security and US hopes for a growing security partnership with Mexico.[112]

To the satisfaction of US policymakers and in parallel with increased border security measures, President Fox pursued a more confrontational strategy against drug-trafficking organizations.[113] Mexican military units also participated in US-sponsored exercises and implemented a military education curriculum using US training philosophies and textbooks.[114] In 2005, the three NAFTA governments signed the Security and Prosperity Partnership of North America agreement, synchronizing regional strategies for counterterrorism, border security, and the protection of strategic resources.[115] The accord also established a series of thematic working groups for the signatories' executive ministries, which increased opportunities for dialogue between US and Mexican leaders. It was out of this pact that the Bush administration sought to design, in coordination with the Mexican government, a more narrowly focused plan to extend "the perimeter of the US homeland security area to the Mexico-Guatemala border."[116] Under the auspices of Washington's desired arrangement, the enforcement of US entry restrictions would no longer only take place in California or Texas but also in places like Campeche, Chiapas, and Tabasco. Doing so would enlarge the United States' protective buffer while standardizing security practices between the US and Mexican governments.

Although President Fox remained reticent about the idea during his last year in office, his successor, Felipe Calderón, assumed the presidency with a weak mandate and a desire to consolidate domestic and international support for his government.[117] In him, the United States found a partner who was eager to enhance the bilateral agenda in this fashion.[118] President Calderón's receptiveness to greater collaboration with the United States coincided with an increasingly tense security situation in Mexico. By 2006, an escalation of cartel violence had made international headlines, and Mexican border cities like Tijuana and Ciudad Juárez became contested turf for the country's principal drug clans.[119] On December 10, 2006, the newly inaugurated president sent 6,500 troops into his home state of Michoacán to quell a spate of violence that had left dozens of people dead in a series of mass killings perpetrated by drug gangs. The unmistakable aim of this deployment was to curb the destabilizing impact and social ramifications of wanton drug violence, amounting to what became known as the beginning of Mexico's own war on drugs.[120]

National political leaders recognized the urgency of addressing the security sector's incapacity to stem growing violence.[121] Of Mexico's 2,438 municipalities, four hundred had no functioning municipal police, and 90 percent of the country's law enforcement agencies had fewer than one hundred members and offered salaries of less than $350 per month—more than ten times lower than the average US police officer at the time.[122] The Mexican government's inability to contain the cartels subjected the Calderón administration to international criticism and domestic demands for change. A creeping sense of political isolation, combined with a belief that the United States and Mexico shared responsibility for the drug trade, pushed the Mexican executive to seek help from Washington.[123] As US Assistant Secretary of State Thomas Shannon noted, "Never before has a president committed Mexico's military to help and assist police in this kind of battle, and never before has a Mexican president approached the United States, in the manner that President Calderón has, to make the request for assistance that he has."[124]

US Security Assistance via the Mérida Initiative

In 2007, these overtures and long-standing US hopes for improved security cooperation culminated in the signing of the Mérida Initiative, the bilateral security agreement named in honor of the seminal meeting between Presidents Bush and Calderón in the Mexican city of Mérida.[125] At the heart of the agreement was a commitment to shared responsibility to address common security threats between neighboring countries.[126] The pact naturally entailed counterdrug and border security programs, but more broadly the US government committed to helping the Calderón administration build and reform military, law enforcement, and judicial bodies to address the root causes of crime and violence in Mexico.[127] As Alejandro Poiré, one of the Calderón administration's architects of the Mérida Initiative, explained, "Our strategy was based on three elements: weakening organized delinquency through judicial reform, institutional reconstruction in the security sector, and the reconstruction of the country's social fabric through prevention. . . . It required a certain closeness to the US government."[128] To this end, the Bush administration's initial conception of the plan involved a $1.4 billion request from Congress. Roughly 60 percent of the initiative funded immediate counternarcotics, counterterrorism, and border security measures, but the remainder focused on long-term programming for security sector reform, institution-building, and rule-of-law construction.[129]

With this unprecedented opportunity, US policymakers and the myriad actors of the interagency process examined how best to support Mexican authorities. Lawmakers continued to see US drug policy through a securitized lens, and Plan Colombia provided the Bush and Obama administrations with a template for expanding the counternarcotics and public security relationship with Mexico.[130] However, US policymakers believed that every effort should be made to avoid the perception that the bilateral strategy was mere militarization, which was a frequent criticism of Plan Colombia.[131] To Calderón and Washington alike, it was important to deny Calderón's domestic and regional opponents, including a growing contingent of leftist and anti-US

Latin American heads of state, the chance to criticize the reform initiative as a US imposition on Latin America.[132]

Unlike in Colombia, counterinsurgency and counterterrorism concerns—at least as they pertained to domestic actors in Mexico—were not a central component of cooperation. Policymakers perceived military operations as quick fixes to a dire situation but not a long-term solution to Mexico's woes. Even so, early support decidedly favored the Mexican military. Given the historical unreliability of Mexican police forces, partnership with the armed forces had clear benefits. Compared with the Federal Police (Policía Federal), the army and navy could match the drug cartels in terms of firepower and tactics. Further, given the military's greater professionalism and higher salaries and benefits packages, the Mexican public trusted soldiers to be not only more proficient but also more immune to infiltration by drug gangs than the country's other security forces—so much so that SEDENA formalized processes of coordination and assistance to police forces in the counterdrug fight with the creation of the Federal Support Military Corps (Cuerpo de Fuerzas de Apoyo Federal) in 2007.[133] Although the Mexican government pursued limited military deployments to contain internal violence from 2003 to 2005, President Calderón deployed a previously unthinkable fifty thousand military troops in domestic security roles during his six-year tenure.[134] US authorities encouraged the same kingpin strategy that decapitated the Medellín and Cali cartels in Colombia, and President Calderón and his party's leaders—who even before Calderón's election reached out to President Bush to propose deeper security ties to go after cartel leaders—welcomed US intelligence assistance for this purpose.[135]

The Mérida Initiative involved donations and purchases of new helicopters, light planes, and high-tech intelligence capabilities from US suppliers.[136] In the words of President Fox, the Mexican Army in the early 2000s was "very, very poor," possessing outmoded planes, weapons, and arms that "couldn't even fight the Nicaraguan Army."[137] However, all that changed during the Mérida Initiative, under which Mexican defense buying increased dramatically.[138] Although Mexican law prohibits US military personnel from "operating" in Mexican national territory, US defense contractors, retired military officers, and private security companies participated in extensive training of Mexican agencies, and US Special Forces sent training teams to help improve the readiness of the Mexican Army, Marine Corps, and Federal Police starting in 2008.[139] In addition, Secretary of Defense Robert Gates visited Mexico in April 2008, the first such high-level visit from the Pentagon since 1995. On his trip, Gates took advantage of the occasion to reiterate US support, indicating that the Department of Defense in particular was committed to its Mexican partners.[140]

Much as they did in their deliberations over Plan Colombia, members of the US Congress identified in the Mérida Initiative solutions and prospective opportunities for their constituents despite their initial concerns about the Bush administration's reluctance to consult Capitol Hill during the bilateral negotiations.[141] The strategy offered Republicans and Democrats a chance to demonstrate that Washington took the concerns and fears of US voters and businesses in border states seriously. Cross-border tourism and manufacturing industries were especially vulnerable to a deterioration in public security, and a large Mexican-American population with strong ties to family members in Mexico made US inaction untenable. In 2009, the National Sheriffs' Association even requested that Congress double Mérida Initiative funding, and state governors and political representatives from the southwest border states doggedly pressed national leaders to respond to growing insecurity.[142] Moreover, the early emphasis of the Mérida Initiative on military and security hardware afforded US defense companies opportunities to compete for contracts to sell new aircraft, body scanners, and X-ray technology.[143] From 2008 to 2010, US assistance included the purchase of $590.5 million in surveillance aircraft and Black Hawk helicopters alone—a transfer of equipment that ensured continued business for US manufacturers who signed maintenance and training contracts that lasted well into the 2010s.

In addition to the White House, Congress, and the Department of Defense, other executive branch departments and agencies seized on the Mérida Initiative to boost relationships with Mexican counterparts. The Department of State oversaw the administration of all security assistance, including that of the Department of Defense, but also insisted that it could play a role in training civilian law enforcement agencies by sponsoring polygraph capabilities and vetting criteria, including background checks, drug testing, and financial disclosures.[144] Corruption and human rights abuses had been longstanding concerns in Washington, which welcomed the opportunity to address these challenges under the new partnership framework.[145]

For their part, senior leaders at the Department of Justice and USAID believed that the Mérida Initiative could help strengthen Mexican justice institutions and synchronize US and Mexican best practices for investigations and trials. The Office of Overseas Prosecutorial Development, Assistance, and Training organized training pipelines for Mexican federal prosecutors, USAID provided investigative advice to prosecutors at the state level, and the Bureau of International Narcotics and Law Enforcement Affairs set up mock courtrooms at police facilities to give officers training in testifying as witnesses.[146] President Calderón's plan for justice reform, approved in 2008, even pushed the Mexican Technical Secretariat for Justice Sector Reform

(Secretaría Técnica) to seek US help in revamping Mexico's courts, law school curricula, and criminal code.[147] The ten-year judicial reform process would, in the later years of the Mérida Initiative, consume the bulk of US resources as institution-building and rule-of-law consolidation became the emphases of US assistance after an initial period of hardware transfers.[148]

The Mérida Initiative grew out of an often cautious yet ever-expanding bilateral security relationship. Although historically the United States and Mexico did not show the same closeness as the United States and Colombia, a common understanding of the need to share responsibility for issues affecting both sides of the border prevailed in the early 2000s. As it did in Colombia, the US government opted for generous security assistance to enable a struggling partner to reform poorly equipped and unsuitable security institutions in the face of forbidding nonstate threats. As was true of Plan Colombia, the myriad opportunities inherent in a deeper partnership with Mexico encouraged diverse US policymaking actors to coalesce around the Mérida Initiative and to throw their weight behind US security assistance as the primary pillar of renewed engagement.[149] Divergent approaches by US interagency actors and differences in the political circumstances faced by Colombia and Mexico, however, resulted in uneven implementation of US security assistance between the two countries, producing the disparate outcomes that are the focus of the following chapters of this book.

Notes

1. The Mexican-American War (1846–48) resulted in the United States' eventual annexation of Texas and all Mexican territory north of the Rio Grande. Likewise, following the outbreak of the Mexican Revolution in 1910, the US Army sought to secure the porous border from incursions by Mexican rebels and federal forces, even launching occasional raids into Mexican territory through 1919. In Colombia, the United States supported an insurrectionist movement in the Panama province in 1903, sending a US Navy gunboat to the aid of the separatists. On declaring independence from Colombia, authorities from the nascent Republic of Panama granted the United States a perpetual lease on the economically vital Panama Canal Zone in exchange for $10 million plus $250,000 annually in rent.
2. The concept of *securitization* refers to how speech acts and political rhetoric can shape public perception of an issue as a threat to security, regardless of whether it actually constitutes a threat to international security (Buzan et al., 1998). In 1986, the Ronald Reagan administration issued National Security Decision Directive 221, declaring drugs a US national security threat (Reagan, 1986), and in 1988, Reagan founded the Office of National Drug Control Policy, which coordinated national strategies to combat drugs and thus solidified the governing philosophy that drugs were a pressing matter of national security.

3. US Department of Defense, 2001, p. 5.
4. Coleman, 2008, pp. 5–7. On the origins and early structure of the Colombian military, see Vargas, 2002.
5. Angelo & Illera Correal, 2020, p. 19.
6. Forero Ángel, 2017, pp. 94–98; Rodríguez Hernández, 2005; Scheina, 2003, pp. 75–103.
7. Randall, 1992, pp. 201–219.
8. Colombian Army captain, personal communication, Bogotá, Colombia, October 27, 2017.
9. The apolitical posture of the Colombian Ministry of Defense is central to the organization's identity. For much of the institution's early history, there was a permanent tension between the search for a professionalized, competent military, the military's partisan usefulness, and the tendency to employ the military as an impartial guarantor of constitutionality and legality (Vargas, 2002, p. 103). Today, however, "the soldiers, regardless of their ranks, construct strategies on the battlefield that guarantee their survival, while the senior ranks give birth to narratives that guarantee the survival of the imagined tradition of the institution as one that is neutral, apolitical, and a friend of the Colombian people" (Forero Ángel, 2017, p. 14).
10. Leal Buitrago, 1994, pp. 133–137; Vargas, 2002, p. 145.
11. Pécaut, 2008, pp. 33–39. On the National Front era and the political exclusion of communist movements, see Karl, 2017, pp. 182–218.
12. Crandall, 2002, p. 24.
13. Crandall, 2002, p. 24.
14. Maullin, 1973, p. 73.
15. According to Francisco Leal Buitrago (1994, p. 140), some Colombian military professionals considered Plan Lazo a uniquely Colombian innovation. In doing so, it is plausible that they sought to distance themselves from concurrent yet ill-starred US counterguerrilla campaigns in Southeast Asia.
16. Briscoe, 2006.
17. Leal Buitrago, 1994, p. 148; Valencia Tovar, 2006, p. 51.
18. Stokes, 2004, p. 71.
19. Tokatlian, 1994.
20. Higgins, 2022, pp. 191–192.
21. Casas Dupuy, 2005, p. 5.
22. Durán-Martínez, 2017, p. 79; Human Rights Watch, 1993.
23. Torres Velasco, 1994, pp. 192–202.
24. Durán-Martínez, 2017, p. 81; Tate, 2013, p. 219. The transformation of the National Police in the 1990s occurred in two distinct phases. Starting in 1993, the reform endeavored to professionalize, decentralize, and civilianize the police force by implementing more community-based security strategies. However, Serrano's appointment as director general of the institution in 1994 triggered phase two, reorienting the force away from this model and instead pursuing a more militarized approach to combating the Medellín and Cali cartels.
25. Darling, 2000.
26. Llorente, 2006.
27. The US government pursued a similar strategy to similar effect against cartels in Mexico and terrorist organizations in North Africa, the Middle East, and Afghanistan. Empirically, the kingpin strategy has seldom resulted in an elimination of terrorist groups or criminal organizations.

28. Rosen, 2014, p. 15.
29. Llorente & McDermott, 2014, p. 23. Although some guerrilla groups demobilized during the 1980s, the FARC, ELN, and some smaller insurgencies outlasted the Cold War and, in fact, expanded. The FARC used drug profits to facilitate its expansion from 3,600 members in 1986 to more than seventeen thousand insurgent fighters in 2001 (Rosen, 2014, p. 17). On the FARC's ascendancy, see Steele, 2017; Pécaut, 2008.
30. Forero Ángel, 2017, p. 119. On the state of military affairs in Colombia at this juncture, see Leal Buitrago, 2006a, pp. 150–151.
31. Angelo & Illera Correal, 2020, p. 21.
32. Leal Buitrago, 1994, p. 155. According to Alberto Patiño Villa (2010, p. 203), Colombia historically lacked the capacity and the force size to defend its national territory, which is why it often resorted to diplomatic and legal resolutions to border disputes.
33. Pastrana Arango, 2005, p. 83.
34. The scandal, known as the 8,000 Process (Proceso 8.000), also tied twenty-one members of Congress, hundreds of police officers, private companies, and national-level government authorities to the Cali Cartel (Durán-Martínez, 2017, p. 80).
35. Rosen, 2014, p. 24.
36. Rosen, 2014, pp. 11–13. The Air Bridge Denial program sponsored by the US Department of Defense in the 1990s targeted planes carrying coca paste from Bolivia and Peru to Colombian cocaine laboratories. The relative success of this initiative had the unintended effect of driving coca paste production northward to Colombian territory to minimize the risk of detection and seizure. Colombia became the world's top coca and cocaine producer (Higgins, 2022, p. 194).
37. Retired US Army colonel, personal communication, Tegucigalpa, Honduras, May 20, 2016.
38. Leal Buitrago, 2006a, pp. 146–147; GAO, 1998, p. 3.
39. Cristo, 2016, p. 52; Garrido, 2001, p. 33; retired Colombian Navy commander, personal communication, Mayport, Florida, August 10, 2022. The AUC often acted as an appendage of local state authorities who ensured a degree of state protection for the group. In exchange, AUC fronts provided security against insurgent attacks and often supported the campaigns of local political candidates with campaign contributions and through the violent intimidation of the electorate. AUC leader Salvatore Mancuso explained: "[The AUC] taught the population [of 35 percent of the country] how to vote because there was no presence of the state and we, the AUC, supplanted official authorities" (Caracol Radio, 2005).
40. Cristo, 2016, p. 70. The Colombian government's aims were institutional strengthening and economic development in the most conflict-affected regions of the country with support from the United States, the European Union, and international lending and development banks. Some European countries opposed the initiative once the US government declared its preference for militarization of the counterdrug fight. European leaders argued that such a strategy altered the military balance between the government and the FARC in the midst of peace negotiations, which began in 1998. In the end, the only international benefactor that delivered fully on Pastrana's request was the United States (Cristo, 2016, pp. 63–66). On the delicate balance between pursuing peace and security sector reform and the military's displeasure with Pastrana's peace bid, see Pastrana Arango, 2005, pp. 198–200.
41. Romero, 2004, p. 85.
42. Hurst, 2002, p. 3.

43. Clinton, 2000, p. 26. The US drug control strategy focuses on drug supply reduction through drug crop eradication in source countries and interdiction in transit countries and demand reduction through educational initiatives, penalization of domestic drug possession, and rehabilitation of drug users in the United States.
44. Tate, 2015, p. 31; GAO, 1998, p. 18. Colombian Army Generals Jorge Enrique Mora and Fernando Tapias Stahelin were initially unenthusiastic about the military's assumption of a counternarcotics role. The Colombian Army was focused on "winning hearts and minds and did not want to be seen as an oppressor of peasants" (retired US Army colonel, personal communication, Tegucigalpa, Honduras, May 20, 2016).
45. Pastrana Arango, 2005, p. 14.
46. Méndez, 2017, p. 97.
47. Cristo, 2016, p. 66.
48. González, 2014.
49. Tate, 2015, p. 137.
50. Lindsay-Poland, 2018, p. 11; Tate, 2013, p. 227. Winifred Tate explores in detail the deliberations surrounding the purchase of helicopters for the Colombian military and police and the influence of "material politics" on congressional decision-making (2013, p. 227). John Lindsay-Poland also suggests that constructing military facilities and providing US equipment via Plan Colombia was "a circular business" in which US investments benefited the US government and private firms (2018, p. 85).
51. Hurst, 2002, p. 3.
52. Tate, 2015, p. 141.
53. Retired US Army colonel, personal communication, Tegucigalpa, Honduras, May 20, 2016.
54. Vaicius, 2003.
55. Leal Buitrago, 2006a, p. 235; Lindsay-Poland, 2018, p. 57; Murillo, 2004, pp. 137–138.
56. Isacson, 2007.
57. Forero, 2002b; Fulo Regilme, 2018. On February 4, 2002, HR 4775 Supplemental Appropriations Act for Further Recovery from and Response to Terrorist Attacks on the United States was signed into law and gave the Colombian government authority to use Plan Colombia contributions to fight insurgents, especially those endangering oil infrastructure (Rosen, 2014, p. 50). The National Defense Authorization Act of 2005 rectified these personnel limitations, raising the military cap from four hundred to eight hundred and the civilian contractor cap from four hundred to six hundred.
58. Romero, 2004, p. 59.
59. Tate, 2015, pp. 145–148.
60. A. Patterson, email correspondence, September 10, 2021. The Plan Colombia Interagency Task Force included representatives from International Narcotics and Law Enforcement (Department of State), Western Hemisphere Affairs (Department of State), USAID, Department of Justice, Department of Defense, and the Central Intelligence Agency. For one observer, Plan Colombia was "where the US government discovered the interagency process and found that collaboration is only possible to the extent that leadership encourages it" (senior US development official, personal communication, Tegucigalpa, Honduras, August 25, 2016). On the effects of departmental cultures on policy formulation in state-building, see Waldman, 2014.
61. Tate, 2015, pp. 155–158. This arrangement shifted in the later years of Plan Colombia. When institution-building and alternative development became central objectives of US

support after 2006, USAID became the lead agency to coordinate US Embassy activities in areas of the country reclaimed by the Colombian state.

62. Rojas, 2015, pp. 93–116.
63. The Monroe Doctrine refers to a US policy initiated under President James Monroe (1817–25) that rejected European expansionism and colonization in the Western Hemisphere. A reinterpretation of the doctrine occurred under President Theodore Roosevelt (1901–1909), who issued the Roosevelt Corollary in 1904. This policy clarified the United States' perceived right to intervene militarily in Latin America and the Caribbean to address "chronic wrongdoing, or an impotence which results in a general loosening of the ties of civilized society" (Roosevelt, 1904).
64. Jones, 1939.
65. Mitchell, 2018, p. 109.
66. Paz, 1997, pp. 74–102.
67. Turbiville, 2010, p. 6.
68. The US Departments of War and State supported providing Mexico the means to defend itself against external aggression (Paz, 1997, p. 48).
69. Rath, 2018. A *caudillo* refers to a personalist leader or strongman wielding military and political power in the Iberian and Ibero-American contexts.
70. Paz, 1997, pp. 6–7.
71. Rath, 2018. Before President Alemán, Mexican presidential candidates were traditionally selected from the military's high command. In 1946, then President and former General Manuel Ávila Camacho selected Alemán, a university professor, career bureaucrat, and civilian, to succeed him (Camp, 2005, p. 25). Ávila Camacho was the last presidential selectee to come from the ranks of the military.
72. Rath, 2013.
73. Astorga, 2005.
74. For a history of US regulatory and prohibitionist polices, see Crandall, 2020, pp. 88–109.
75. Pérez Ricart, 2017, pp. 33–52.
76. Pérez Ricart, 2017, pp. 47–48.
77. Kenny & Serrano, 2012, p. 32.
78. Navarro, 2010, pp. 121–149.
79. Alan Knight (2010, pp. 264–265) highlights the irony of the PRI's revolutionary slogans and decades of polices that promoted regressive capitalism and growing inequality. Although a number of social and agrarian movements challenged the regime's "public transcript" in the 1960s, the PRI, with the help of the army, won the war of ideas and successfully contained armed revolutionary threats to the regime.
80. Castañeda, 1994.
81. Ojeda, 1976, p. 93. Washington recognized the importance of Mexican nationalism as both a foreign policy stance and as a factor in sustaining public support for the PRI's political regime domestically (Loaeza, 2013, p. 38).
82. The initial involvement of the Mexican military in these roles occurred during a 1948 operation known as the Great Campaign (gran campaña), subsiding for a time until the 1960s. Nevertheless, given that the military's slow growth occurred in a fashion incompatible with the growth of militaries in neighboring countries (including the United States), the second half of the twentieth century made it clear that external security was not the principal focus of the country's military (Sánchez Lara, 2017, p. 49).

83. Weintraub, 2010, p. 68.
84. Liddy, 1991, p. 135. The US and Mexican governments launched the program in 1975, and it lasted until the mid-1980s, when both governments cited diminishing effectiveness and ecological concerns over the use of herbicides (Weintraub, 2010, p. 78). Washington was also concerned about corruption in the Mexican security forces responsible for the aerial spraying (Watt and Zepeda, 2012, pp. 48–54).
85. Camp, 2005, p. 117; Kenny & Serrano, 2012, p. 34.
86. Camp, 1992, p. 59.
87. Defense Intelligence Agency, 1977.
88. Murphy, 1988. Camarena was responsible for uncovering a multibillion-dollar drug operation that involved Mexican police, army, and government officials. In 1990, the DEA, leery of providing actionable intelligence to its Mexican counterparts, kidnapped on Mexican soil one of the suspected perpetrators of Camarena's torture and murder—a further setback for bilateral cooperation (Weintraub, 2010, pp. 78–79).
89. The responsibilities of CISEN included the formulation of strategic, tactical, and operational intelligence to prevent, contain, and neutralize risks to the constitutional order and territorial integrity of the Mexican state. However, CISEN also suffered from debilitating corruption within its ranks starting in 1987, when the Juárez Cartel infiltrated the organization's leadership (Watt & Zepeda, 2012, p. 98). Since the 2005 passage of the National Security Law (Ley de Seguridad Nacional), CISEN served as the top intelligence agency for the executive branch (Sánchez Lara, 2017, p. 56). However, in one of his first acts as president in late 2018, Andrés Manuel López Obrador replaced the CISEN with a new National Intelligence Center (Centro de Inteligencia Nacional, or CNI), aligning it with the new Secretariat of Security and Civilian Protection (Secretaría de Seguridad y Protección Ciudadana) (Rennemo, 2020). For a summary of reforms adopted by the Mexican government in the security realm in the 1990s, see Chabat, 2010, pp. 25–27. For a history of the CISEN, see Herrera-Lasso M., 2010.
90. Turbiville, 2010, p. 15.
91. Kenny & Serrano, 2012, p. 38.
92. US Army Intelligence and Threat Analysis Center, 1993, p. 5.
93. Schaefer et al., 2009, p. 22; Yashar, 2018.
94. Kenny & Serrano, 2012, p. 57.
95. Kenny & Serrano, 2012, p. 41. Mexico's Secretary of Public Security Genaro García Luna estimated in 2010 that cartels collectively paid more than $1 billion a year in bribes to the country's municipal police (Keefe, 2012). García Luna, a close ally of President Calderón, has himself dodged accusations of corruption and collusion with the Sinaloa Cartel throughout his long career in the federal police forces (Wolf & Celorio Morayta, 2011, pp. 697–698). In 2019, he was arrested in the United States on charges of drug trafficking and accepting millions of dollars in bribes, to which he pled not guilty in October 2020. The Calderón administration, for its part, repeatedly faced criticism that it was engaged in the nationwide protection of the Sinaloa Cartel, as purportedly evidenced by its preference to repress other criminal organizations more resolutely (Martin, 2013, p. 42).
96. Ashby, 2014; US Department of State, 1995, p. 11.
97. Preston, 1997. General Jesús Gutiérrez Rebollo was convicted and sentenced to thirty-five years in prison for protecting drug trafficker Amado Carrillo (Weintraub, 2010, p. 80).

98. Durán-Martínez, 2017, p. 98. To foster greater understanding and coordination between Mexico and the United States on the drug issue, the two governments created bilateral forums like the Plenary Group on Law Enforcement and the High-Level Contact Group for Drug Control. In 1998, those efforts culminated in the publication of the *US-Mexico Bi-National Drug Strategy* (Domínguez & Fernández de Castro, 2013, pp. 45–46).
99. Domínguez & Fernández de Castro, 2013, p. 44.
100. Rodríguez, 1993.
101. O'Neil, 2013, p. 268.
102. Cook, 2007, p. 9.
103. Kenny & Serrano, 2012, p. 58.
104. Turbiville, 2010, p. 15; US Department of State, 1995, p. 13.
105. Turbiville, 2010, pp. 16–17.
106. Camp, 2005, p. 38. Many officers in the army and presidential guard resented the promotion of soldiers who had not participated in the campaign against the EZLN (Piñyero, 2001, p. 13).
107. The Mexican military's historical tendency to keep the US military at a comfortable distance is due to a long-standing calculation that the two biggest risks to Mexican national security were the direct political intervention of Washington in Mexican domestic issues and the deployment of US military troops into Mexico's borderlands (Martínez Álvarez & Garza Elizondo, 2013, p. 98).
108. Turbiville, 2010, pp. 22–24.
109. Turbiville, 2010, p. 24.
110. The Mexican government's international security strategy in the 1990s featured the following: a rejection of alliances with any US rival, a rejection of foreign policy interests that the US government could construe as a threat, a commitment to a reduced military capability so as not to threaten the United States, the build-up of military capability to combat drug trafficking, a preference for US weapons suppliers, and extensive cooperation with the US government on international security matters (Domínguez & Fernández de Castro, 2013, pp. 36–37).
111. Martínez Álvarez & Garza Elizondo, 2013, p. 94.
112. Ruiz Pérez, 2011, pp. 322–323.
113. Chabat, 2010, pp. 27–28; Deare, 2017, pp. 211–215.
114. Camp, 2005, p. 13.
115. Carlsen, 2018, p. 85; Watt & Zepeda, 2012, p. 193.
116. Benítez Manaut, 2009, p. 226; Carlsen, 2018, p. 85.
117. The results of the 2006 presidential election were controversial because the National Action Party (Partido Acción National, or PAN) candidate, Felipe Calderón, defeated runner-up Andrés Manuel López Obrador by just 0.6 percent of the vote and achieved only 35.9 percent of the total vote (Deare, 2017, p. 274). Although the Federal Electoral Tribunal recognized Calderón's victory as legitimate, Calderón entered office in December 2006 with a weak mandate, and many Mexicans perceived his early policy decisions, including militarization of the drug war and the Mérida Initiative, as ploys to boost his legitimacy (academic security analyst, personal communication, Mexico City, September 11, 2017; Wolf & Celorio Morayta, 2011, p. 672). However, as one researcher declared, "The decision to deploy the military was too important to minimize by saying it was a way to consolidate power after a heated and contested election. Calderón was shocked and nervous about

the threat the drug traffickers posed to the state. When the narco-traffickers fled to the mountains after the military intervened in Michoacán, the public applauded him, and he felt that the militarization strategy was mostly working" (M. C. Toro, personal communication, Mexico City, September 7, 2017).

118. Lakhani & Tirado, 2016; Olson, 2017.
119. The "real beginning" of the Mexican drug war was in 2004, after Mexican authorities captured the Gulf Cartel's leader, Osiel Cárdenas (Martin, 2013, p. 39). As the Gulf Cartel underwent internal reorganization, the Sinaloa Cartel attempted to seize the Nuevo Laredo *plaza*, or smuggling corridor, only to be repelled by the Gulf Cartel's armed wing known as Los Zetas.
120. Chabat, 2010, p. 30.
121. Deare, 2017, p. 276.
122. Benítez Manaut, 2013, p. 156.
123. Olson, 2017.
124. US House of Representatives, 2007, p. 20.
125. The Mérida Initiative was originally labeled the Joint Strategy to Combat Organized Crime (Martin, 2013, p. 40).
126. Wolf & Celorio Morayta, 2011, p. 670. "Shared responsibility" illuminates the degree of agency exhibited by Mexico in the formulation of the plan, as the United States accepted co-responsibility for drug violence in Mexico (Lozano Vázquez, 2016, p. 216).
127. Calderón, 2007.
128. A. Poiré, personal communication, Mexico City, September 14, 2017.
129. Olson, 2017.
130. Arteaga, 2009; Carlsen, 2010.
131. Turbiville, 2010, pp. 32–33.
132. Roberts & Walser, 2007.
133. Paul et al., 2014, pp. 31–32; Weintraub, 2010, p. 70.
134. From 2002 to 2006, the Attorney General of Mexico, Army General Rafael Marcial Macedo de la Concha, facilitated the first major joint operations between military and federal police forces against drug-trafficking targets (such as Directiva Azteca XXI, Operación México Seguro) (academic security analyst, personal communication, Mexico City, September 11, 2017). The Calderón administration thereafter laid the groundwork for a process of law enforcement and justice sector reform, with the eventual goal of transferring domestic policing roles to better trained civilian police forces.
135. Cook, 2007, p. 3; Deare, 2021, p. 7.
136. Carlsen, 2018, p. 88.
137. Deare, 2021, p. 6.
138. Partlow, 2015.
139. Mexican Army officers even began training in counterinsurgency tactics and traveled to Iraq to observe the implementation of US tactics in the field (Carlsen, 2018, p. 87). However, because of traditional Mexican sensitivities to impingements on sovereignty, NORTHCOM's MTTs passed largely under the radar. One observer noted that US military personnel were not even allowed to leave the bases where they were working alongside their Mexican counterparts so as to avoid public scrutiny of their embedded presence (retired US Army colonel, personal communication, Tegucigalpa, Honduras, May 20, 2016).

140. Turbiville, 2010, pp. 31–32.
141. US House of Representatives, 2007, pp. 1–2.
142. Turbiville, 2010, p. 34.
143. Olson, 2017.
144. US House of Representatives, 2007, p. 15.
145. US Department of State, 2008.
146. Former senior US diplomat, email correspondence, September 28, 2021.
147. USAID, 2018b.
148. One observer who worked on the implementation of the Mérida Initiative noted that the US government used security hardware transfers as a way of "buying entrée" into institutions that were skeptical of the United States. Foreign military sales and foreign military funding programs in Mexico later "opened the door" to training and education programs that focused on developing the human capital of the Mexican security forces (former senior US diplomat, email correspondence, September 28, 2021).
149. Ashby, 2014, pp. 182–224.

3
Structuring Security Assistance in Colombia and Mexico

Plan Colombia and the Mérida Initiative were US whole-of-government approaches to help boost the effectiveness and accountability of the Colombian and Mexican security sectors, respectively. Although militaries were the early beneficiaries of US aid in both cases, US commitments shifted to civilian institutional capacity-building and state consolidation by the late 2000s in Colombia, and law enforcement and justice institutions received the bulk of Washington's attention in Mexico with the arrival of President Obama to the White House in 2009. In this way, Plan Colombia and the Mérida Initiative evolved to address the outstanding security challenges and governance deficiencies specific to the Colombian and Mexican contexts. The US bureaucratic departments, the lines of funding, the beneficiary institutions, and the reform objectives were fundamentally consistent across the two cases, and in both instances, US interventions directly benefited state institutions contending with the threat posed by domestic, nonstate, illegal armed groups. Given these commonalities and the macrocontextual similarities noted in chapter 2, Colombia and Mexico are good candidates for comparative analysis as it relates to security assistance and security sector reform.

That said, US and Mexican authorities made deliberate strides to distinguish the Mérida Initiative from Plan Colombia to account for nuances of each bilateral relationship and in the countries' respective security threats. Both security assistance initiatives emerged out of a similar desire among US policymakers to address external security crises that had far-reaching transnational consequences. Yet Plan Colombia and the Mérida Initiative bent to the distinct preferences of policymakers in the United States and constituent, partisan, and organizational differences in the recipient countries, affecting the degree to which security assistance led to improved outcomes for effectiveness and accountability in partner security sectors. Likewise, even though the institutional actors on the US side were largely consistent between the two security assistance interventions, their priorities were not necessarily consistent across time and space. Although the programming presented in this chapter could suggest a consolidated front for

From Peril to Partnership. Paul J. Angelo, Oxford University Press. © Oxford University Press 2024.
DOI: 10.1093/oso/9780197688106.003.0004

security assistance implementation, it is worth noting that the evolution of US strategy in both countries was the product of continuous debate and negotiation among the US executive agencies and on Capitol Hill.

Plan Colombia

Congress passed legislation in support of Plan Colombia in 2000 as part of the Military Construction Appropriations Act of 2001 (P.L. 106-246) by providing $1.3 billion for counternarcotics and institutional modernization in Colombia and its neighboring countries.[1] Although Plan Colombia was never formally authorized as a multiyear assistance strategy, US legislators supported annual funding requests from the executive branch under its heading through fiscal year (FY) 2011. US security assistance continued to flow to Colombia well after 2011, and political leaders in both countries still often referred to continuing security cooperation broadly as Plan Colombia. As the fruits of Colombia's security strategy became increasingly evident, even resulting in a peace process with the Revolutionary Armed Forces of Colombia (Fuerzas Armadas Revolucionarias de Colombia, or FARC) from 2012 to 2016, the US government encouraged greater self-sufficiency among Colombian security institutions, off-loading its defense commitments in Colombia by emphasizing *nationalization*, or the process by which the Colombian government assumed financial responsibility for equipment maintenance and acquisitions previously provided by Washington.[2] The United States would continue to support Colombian security institutions, especially on counternarcotics objectives, but the major push to reform and modernize the country's military and police had concluded by the second decade of the 2000s. FY 2012 thus saw a considerable reduction in US security assistance to Colombia; for the first time in a decade, annual aid dropped below $300 million, a threshold at which it stabilized for the remainder of the decade. Although later chapters of this book address the sustainability of US security assistance and its perceived accomplishments and failures in Colombia through 2022, the 2000 to 2011 period is a useful time frame for empirical comparison with the Mérida Initiative in Mexico.

Given the range of implementing actors involved in security assistance, Washington financed the aid package, totaling nearly $8.4 billion between 2000 and 2011, in a piecemeal manner and relied on eight distinct lines of accounting (Beittel, 2012, p. 38). Table 3.1 presents a yearly breakdown of funding for Plan Colombia and reflects greater specialization over time. After the expiration of Clinton-era funding, the George W. Bush administration incorporated institutional reform programming in Colombia—in addition to coca eradication, interdiction, and alternative development programs—via

Table 3.1. US Assistance for Plan Colombia in Millions of US Dollars

Fiscal Year	ACI/ ACP	ESF	FMF	IMET	INCLE	NADR	Air Wing	Defense	Total
2000	60.1						38.0	128.5	226.6
P.L. 106-246	832.0							100.7	932.7
2001	48.0						38.0	190.2	932.7
2002	379.9					25.0	38.2	117.3	560.4
2003	580.2		17.1	1.2		3.3	41.5	164.8	808.1
2004	473.9		98.5	1.7		0.2	45.0	178.2	797.5
2005	462.8		99.2	1.7		5.1	45.0	155.3	769.1
2006	464.8		89.1	1.7			45.0	140.5	741.1
2007	465.0		85.5	1.6		4.1	37.0	129.4	722.6
2008	244.6	194.4	55.1	1.4	41.9	3.7	39.0	119.9	700.0
2009	230.1	196.5	53.0	1.4	45.0	3.2	12.4	129.9	669.5
2010		201.8	55.0	1.7	243.9	4.8	12.9	129.4	649.5
2011		184.4	47.9	1.7	204.0	4.8	3.6	110.4	556.8
Total	4,241.4	777.1	600.4	14.1	534.8	84.2	395.6	1,792.0	8,410.1

Source: Beittel, 2012, p. 38.
Note: ACI/ACP = Andean Counterdrug Initiative/Program; ESF = Economic Support Fund; FMF = foreign military financing; IMET = International Military Education and Training; INCLE = International Narcotics Control and Law Enforcement; NADR = nonproliferation, antiterrorism, demining, and related

a regional plan called the Andean Counterdrug Program (ACP), initially known as the Andean Counterdrug Initiative (ACI). Also leveraged were the Department of State's Air Wing account and Sections 1004, 1033, and 1204 of the National Defense Authorization Act, dedicated to counternarcotics, law enforcement support, and security cooperation, respectively. Other governmental funds such as foreign military financing (FMF) and the International Military Education and Training program supported the acquisition of military hardware and implementation of advanced professional training respectively, and the US government drew from the Nonproliferation, Anti-Terrorism, Demining, and Related Programs budget to finance counterterrorism initiatives following the declaration of the global war on terrorism.

Equipment Modernization, Enhanced Training, and Operational Changes

As John Bailey notes, Plan Colombia developed in two phases.[3] From 2000 to 2006, assistance focused on modernizing and enhancing the security forces' operational posture to beat back insurgent groups and drug traffickers. The centerpiece of the early assistance package was funding for the "Push into Southern Colombia" initiative, delivering equipment, training, and aircraft to bring Colombian soldiers to the highly conflictive and coca-rich regions of the country. Following major improvements in the provision of security and starting in 2006, US commitments coincided with the Colombian government's increased emphasis on defense institution-building and the consolidation of the gains achieved during the first phase. Washington advised Bogotá in producing the 2007 National Consolidation Plan, which US policymakers embraced as an opportunity to redirect US assistance, and a US Embassy effort known as the Colombia Strategic Development Initiative (CSDI) aligned US contributions with Colombian-led programs to expand security, justice, and other provisions of services across the national territory. Starting in 2008, the Bush administration reassigned alternative development and institutional capacity-building programs to the Economic Support Fund (ESF), and in 2010, the Obama administration shifted ACP funds into the international narcotics control and law enforcement (INCLE) accounting line.

Throughout Plan Colombia, US executive departments lent support to a variety of Colombian institutions, but considering Washington's militarized approach to counternarcotics, the Colombian Ministry of Defense received the bulk of assistance. Although the Colombian National Police had been Washington's preferred partner from the beginning of the drug war, the Colombian Army's leadership recognized Plan Colombia as an opportunity to deepen its involvement in the counterdrug fight and thus benefit from greater US resources and more specialized training. The military communicated early on in Plan Colombia's negotiation its willingness to assume a greater role in taking on drug traffickers, and to this end, Plan Colombia focused on developing the capabilities of the Colombian Army's Aviation Brigade and a newly founded Counternarcotics Brigade.[4] Prior to the creation of these new elite counterdrug units, the paucity of officers and noncommissioned officers in Colombian Army battalions made it difficult for US trainers to build up a cadre of professional soldiers who could thereafter replicate the training in their own ranks. The new organizational model expanded billets for senior leaders within army units and improved unit-level retention of new skills and operational practices.[5]

Other important changes included delivering night-vision technology to the forces, enabling operations around the clock, and buying and maintaining 289 helicopters from 2000 to 2011.[6] Improved air mobility led to the creation of rapid-reaction units in both the army and National Police, shifting the advantage in the Colombian conflict to the Colombian government.[7] The construction of a joint military intelligence center in the heart of insurgent-dominated territory at the Tres Esquinas base also improved the security sector's ability to respond in real time to criminal activity and threats to citizen safety. By 2003, the mobile police force, the Carabineros, reestablished a police presence in the 169 municipalities that had lacked it a year earlier.[8] The National Police received considerable assistance in the conduct of a drug-crop eradication program, which entailed aerial and manual operations, and during the Bush years, the Colombian Army benefited from supplies and training that bolstered the security of the country's oil infrastructure. These last two lines of effort specifically addressed US strategic priorities in Colombia: drugs and terrorism. In addition, US advisors helped the armed forces establish joint commands, such as the Joint Task Force Omega (Fuerza de Tarea Conjunta Omega) to target the FARC's stronghold in the Meta, Guaviare, and Caquetá departments, and the Joint Special Forces Command to participate in hostage rescue operations and the pursuit of insurgent leaders.[9] In addition, specialized army units such as the Lanceros, modeled after the US Army Rangers, became top beneficiaries of US resources after 2003, when the US government trained them to track and rescue three US Embassy contractors kidnapped by the FARC.[10]

The Colombian Air Force also took advantage of new reconnaissance aircraft and geospatial technology, and the Colombian Navy acquired two maritime surveillance aircraft, hundreds of riverine and coastal patrol craft, and night-vision and communications equipment through US equipment transfers and purchases.[11] Ground-based radar sites at Leticia, Marandúa, San José de Guaviare, and Tres Esquinas and maritime radar enhancements at bases in Riohacha, Cartagena, and San Andrés gave the Colombian government an upper hand against trafficking groups.[12] Improved intelligence techniques and surveillance equipment proved a major advancement for the Colombian security sector, and the Department of Defense helped Colombia construct additional intelligence fusion centers across the country, which emphasized the recruitment of informants and geospatial tracking of guerrilla movements.[13] In 2006, Washington also provided laser-guided munitions to target guerrilla commanders—a tactic that revolutionized the way the Colombian government pursued its enemies and contributed to some of the Colombian military's most propitious raids on FARC camps.[14]

Organizational Reform and Institutional Capacity-Building

These operational changes were accompanied by organizational reforms. In 2010, the Colombian government upgraded the ministry's planning and budgeting programs through the Defense Resource Management Reform, sponsored and advised by the US Department of Defense. This effort institutionalized processes such as estimating future defense costs, linking strategic planning to budgets, and improving investment planning to meet the security needs of the Colombian people.[15] Whereas the Colombian Ministry of Defense at the outset of Plan Colombia often lacked the financial resources to plan for multiyear investments, ministry leaders by the end of the Uribe administration were already beginning to align strategies, equipment life cycles, and desired capabilities with projected budgets decades into the future.

Beyond the Pentagon, other US executive departments contributed to professionalization objectives through specialized training. The State Department's Bureau of International Narcotics and Law Enforcement Affairs provided considerable resources to this end, seeking to build the capacity of its Colombian police partners to eradicate coca, destroy drug labs, interdict cocaine, and investigate criminals. Although the Department of Justice played a noteworthy role in administering Plan Colombia aid to advance judicial reform, its Drug Enforcement Administration (DEA) also worked closely with the National Police to carry out counternarcotics operations within its own funding stream independently of Plan Colombia.[16] Although its law enforcement mission primarily targets specific narcotics production and trafficking operations, the DEA has a long history of promoting institutional reforms in Colombia with the goal of creating more effective, transparent local partners for counterdrug activities, chief among which was the creation of elite counternarcotics units within the Colombian police.[17] DEA activities concurrent with Plan Colombia included working with US special forces to train elite police units, helping plan Colombian-led drug eradication missions, orchestrating interdictions of smuggling operations, providing real-time data on criminal activity to the National Police, and coordinating extraditions of drug kingpins to the United States.[18]

At the beginning of Plan Colombia, a major criticism of the US decision to provide hardware and training to military and militarized police forces in Colombia was the perception that Washington was involving itself in another Vietnam-style counterinsurgency campaign.[19] To prevent that, policymakers placed strict requirements on the disbursal of security assistance, agreeing to fund capabilities and operational units with an explicit counterdrug focus. In practical terms, that also meant that the US Embassy in Bogotá could share actionable intelligence on guerrilla movements or operations only to the extent that the guerrilla fronts in question were actively engaged in drug trafficking. Although the lines were often blurred as the FARC, National Liberation Army (Ejército de Liberación Nacional, or ELN), and United Self-Defense Forces of Colombia (Autodefensas Unidas de Colombia, or AUC) became increasingly involved in the drug supply chain, the US government at first sought to distance itself as much as possible from involvement in Colombia's long-running politically based armed conflict and aimed to focus on confronting violence and criminal activities directly related to drugs.

It was not until the 9/11 terrorist attacks in 2001 and the collapse of peace talks with the FARC in 2002 that the US government began to signal its support for a military defeat of Colombian insurgents using resources from the United States. US public support of the war on terrorism empowered the US government to tackle terrorist groups and their sources of financing worldwide. The FARC, ELN, and the AUC were all considered foreign terrorist organizations by the Department of State, so when President Bush published his 2002 National Security Strategy, the text read, "In Colombia, we recognize the link between terrorist and extremist groups that challenge the security of the state, and drug trafficking activities that help finance the operations of such groups."[20] Endorsing this characterization, Congress swiftly approved the request for "expanded authority" to use counterdrug funds for counterterrorism missions in Colombia to "provide the means for more effective intelligence gathering and fusion, and to provide the flexibility to the Department of State when the distinction between counternarcotics and counterterrorism are [*sic*] not clear cut."[21] At this point, counterterrorism and, by virtue of the FARC's and ELN's tactics and the Colombian Army's footing, counterinsurgency became viable missions for Washington's support to Colombia, a welcome development for Colombia's public officials and security forces.

Indeed, the 9/11 attacks in the United States offered Colombian politicians an opportunity to elevate Colombia's decades-old struggle to the international political agenda and, by doing so, obtain external assistance for a broader vision of security sector reform.[22] Until Plan Colombia, the Colombian military's combat units favored an antisubversive footing that manifested as long deployments to remote parts of the country in pursuit of military victories against insurgents. The Colombian military struggled to conduct preventive operations that would deter insurgents or deny them the ability to perpetrate attacks on population centers, governmental infrastructure, and the security forces. Furthermore, in the early years of the plan, US security assistance did not entail the adoption of new warfighting modalities among the military's rank and file given that only specialized units enjoyed US counterdrug funding and training. However, a post-9/11 windfall of US aid, training, and advisory support enabled the historic reconfiguration of the military into a force also equipped for counterterror operations. The institutional focus now also prioritized flexibility, rapid reaction, and superior intelligence to disrupt terrorist incidents before they occurred.[23]

The intersection of US and Colombian counterterrorism interests resulted in the inauguration of several specialized and highly mobile military and police units. In addition to the Army's Counernarcotics Brigade, the Colombian Ministry of Defense founded the Rapid Deployment Force (Fuerza de Despliegue Rápido, or FUDRA), Groups of Unified Action for Anti-Kidnapping (Grupos de Acción Unificada por la Libertad Personal, or GAULA), and the Urban Counterterrorism Special Forces Groups (Agrupación de Fuerzas Especiales Antiterroristas Urbanas, or AFEUR) all during the first years of the assistance plan.[24] These more agile and well-trained teams allowed the Colombian government, previously lacking in access to the FARC heartland in the southern and central parts of the country, to capitalize on new aviation assets and take the fight directly to the insurgents. Armed confrontations between the FARC and the Colombian security forces increased from 150 annually in the late 1980s to some four hundred annually throughout the 1990s to more than 1,200 in 2003.[25] Although Colombian leadership was at the forefront of the development of new units, Plan Colombia provided them with the material support and strategic direction to confront the country's principal armed groups head-on.[26] Additionally, the Colombian government instituted a program called Soldiers from My Hometown (Soldados de Mi Pueblo) that permitted conscripted soldiers to perform military service in their home communities, an effort to boost the army's legitimacy among local populations by providing a more familiar, human face to its operations.[27]

Plan Colombia assistance to Colombian institutions beyond the Ministry of Defense principally benefited the Human Rights Ombudsman (Defensoría del Pueblo), the Attorney General's Office (Fiscalía General de la Nación, or FGN), and the Ministry of Justice and Law (known during the Uribe administration as the Ministry of the Interior and Justice), including the National Penitentiary and Prison Institute (Instituto Nacional Penitenciario y Carcelario, or INPEC).[28] The main objectives of this additional US support included the consolidation of the rule of law, especially in areas of the country reclaimed from illegal armed groups, and judicial reform.[29] The Department of State, Department of Justice, Department of Treasury, and US Agency for International Development (USAID) served as the managing agencies, and USAID in particular played a critical role in expanding the reach of the Colombian judicial system to remote regions of Colombia. During Plan Colombia, Washington focused its efforts with two justice sector goals in mind: helping Colombia transition toward a more effective and efficient model of justice and creating community conflict resolution mechanisms to reduce judicial caseload.[30] Plan Colombia assistance additionally targeted the root causes of Colombia's conflict such as underdevelopment and exclusion, and major USAID programs aimed to build community resilience through alternative development investments for coca growers and humanitarian and economic relief for internally displaced populations.

Safeguarding Colombian civil society was also a priority under Plan Colombia given the heightened vulnerability of human rights defenders, environmentalists, and labor unionists to attacks by the country's myriad armed actors. This became especially true as Washington and Bogotá engaged in free-trade deliberations starting in 2004, prompting intense scrutiny on Capitol Hill of Colombia's ability to protect labor and human rights activists. USAID funded protective measures, including communications equipment and bulletproof vests, for more than 4,500 human rights workers from 2000 to 2008 and contributed to the construction of courtrooms and community conflict resolution centers, known as Justice Houses (Casas de Justicia).[31] The US Embassy also dedicated resources to educating legal professionals about the 2003 criminal procedure code modernization and the transition from an inquisitorial to an accusatorial justice system.[32] US agencies were generally reluctant to involve themselves too deeply in the reform of the Colombian penitentiary system, which was plagued by corruption and incompetence. Nevertheless, US support in the early years of Plan Colombia led to the construction of the first maximum-security prisons in Colombia to meet international incarceration standards, an achievement that US and Colombian authorities alike hoped would reduce recidivism and deny the most powerful lawbreakers the ability to direct their criminal organizations from within the penal system.[33]

As many of these measures began to take effect, the tide in Colombia's war on insurgents and drug traffickers turned decidedly in the government's favor. Following major operational changes, organizational reforms, and a windfall of resources to build institutional capacity across the security sector, the Colombian government was capturing or killing leaders of illegal armed groups in record numbers and, as described in chapter 4, regained the trust of its people and its allies abroad as reliable providers of security in the country. Its primary mission accomplished, Washington's annual security assistance tapered off as President Juan Manuel Santos (2010–18) took office and opted for a different approach to neutralizing the dangerous behavior of nonstate armed groups.[34] For the first time since the Pastrana administration at the turn of the millennium, a sitting Colombian president recognized the political nature of the Colombian armed conflict and abandoned rhetoric that dismissed the FARC and ELN as terrorists and bandits. This dramatic shift ultimately enticed the insurgent groups to entertain peace negotiations. After all, the military and the FARC had reached a battlefield stalemate by 2010, and although the FARC retained zones of influence in rural areas, the insurgent group possessed a much-reduced offensive capability.[35] When the Santos administration and the FARC agreed to a framework for peace in 2012, Colombia's security sector reform effort, which had run a course of more than a decade, took a backseat to this more pressing political objective.[36]

The Obama administration cautiously supported President Santos's peace bid, eventually sending seasoned diplomat Bernard Aronson as US Special Envoy to the Colombian Peace Process in early 2015. As President Santos rallied international support for a negotiated peace with the FARC, culminating in 2017 with collective demobilization, Santos and his Ministry of Defense sought to avoid aggressive moves or major security sector investments that would undermine the trust required to convince the FARC to disarm.[37] The peace process signaled a philosophical shift in the security sector—one that emphasized preparing the country's major security and justice institutions for postconflict roles. As discussed in chapter 8, the FARC's dissolution did not actually spell the end of the Colombian armed conflict, which persisted as of 2022 with outbreaks of insurgent violence from FARC dissident groups and the ELN. Moreover, drug gangs continue to occupy the coca-rich areas of the country vacated by the FARC. However, the strategic focus of the Colombian military and thus the scope of US security assistance decidedly shifted around 2011 and certainly by 2016. And the once-vertical relationship between the United States and Colombia had, at least in rhetorical terms, become a strategic partnership of equals.[38]

The Mérida Initiative

The United States sought to nurture a similar partnership with Mexico by rendering generous security assistance to help the Mexican government contend with wanton drug violence south of the US border. However, the apolitical nature of Mexico's principal security threats and its historical sensitivities to perceived violations of sovereignty resulted in an aid architecture different from Plan Colombia's. Originally announced in October 2007, the Mérida Initiative received congressional approval in June 2008, when the House Committee on Foreign Affairs passed Bill HR 6028, authorizing roughly $1.6 billion for engagement through FY 2010. The Bush administration requested an additional $500 million for Mexico in a 2008 supplemental appropriations request, thereby rendering Mexico the top recipient of US assistance in Latin America and displacing Colombia for the first time since 1999.[39] Despite this commitment, the initial assistance, which included major equipment transfers, faced a number of administrative hurdles; a Government Accountability Office report noted difficulties in tracking the successful administration of funds and on-time delivery of the equipment purchased and donated.[40] In some cases, these inefficiencies resulted in program implementation delays of up to three or four years. By July 2010, $669 million of the $1.3 billion appropriated for Mexico in 2007 had been obligated by the Department of State, but only $121 million had actually been spent.[41] Yet, as the Calderón administration came to a close in 2012, Washington had accelerated the delivery of roughly $873.7 million in equipment and more than $146 million in training to the Mexican security sector.[42] Although US red tape had significantly delayed projected contributions via the Mérida Initiative, by the close of 2017, Washington managed to contribute nearly $3 billion in security assistance to Mexican partner institutions.

Congress was equally thorough in determining the level and composition of the Mérida Initiative funding as in Plan Colombia, earmarking funds to prioritize specific programs, particularly those pertaining to institutional reform and human rights.[43] Like Plan Colombia, the Mérida Initiative relied on multiple sources of funding to reflect the varied priorities. The preferred lines of accounting were development assistance, ESF, and INCLE. Comparatively, foreign military financing overall totaled $150 million less than the allowance earmarked in Plan Colombia and was not offset by larger defense contributions through other funding lines, as it was in Colombia, suggesting that Washington deemphasized military contributions to Mexico. In fact, starting in FY 2012, the State Department determined that FMF would continue to flow to Mexico but no longer as a formal element of the Mérida Initiative, which came to center on law enforcement. Post-2012 FMF figures nonetheless were part of Washington's broader institutional modernization and reform strategy in Mexico and thus are included in the assistance totals presented in table 3.2.[44]

Table 3.2. US Assistance for Mérida Initiative in Millions of US Dollars

Fiscal Year	Dev. Asst.	ESF	FMF	IMET	INCLE	NADR	Total
2007	9.3	9.0		0.1	36.7	0.2	55.1
2008	8.2	34.7	116.5	0.4	263.5	1.3	424.6
2009	11.2	15.0	39.0	0.8	406.0	3.8	475.8
2010	10.0	15.0	265.2	1.0	365.0	3.9	660.1
2011	25.0	18.0	8.0	1.0	117.0	5.7	174.7
2012	34.4	33.3	7.0	1.0	248.5	5.4	328.6
2013	26.2	32.1	6.6	1.2	190.1	3.8	260.0
2014		46.8	6.6	1.4	143.1	3.9	201.8
2015		46.1	4.7	1.5	110.0	2.9	165.2
2016	10.5	39.0	7.0	1.5	100.0	2.2	160.2
Total	133.8	289.0	460.6	9.85	1,979.9	33.1	2,906.3

Source: US Department of State, 2016b; Ribando Seelke & Finklea, 2017.
Note: ESF = Economic Support Fund; FMF = foreign military financing; IMET = International Military Education and Training; INCLE = International Narcotics Control and Law Enforcement; NADR = nonproliferation, antiterrorism, demining, and related. This table provides an overview of US security assistance from the inception of the Mérida Initiative through the end of the Obama administration. Starting in 2017, US security assistance to Mexico continued with an annual appropriation of around $150 million but for the first time faced criticism and even derision by newly elected presidents in both countries. Although Mérida-era programs continued to operate from 2017 to 2022, rhetorical and programmatic pivots, explored in chapter 8, spelled the end of the cooperative spirit envisioned by the Mérida Initiative's architects.

Hardware Acquisitions, Border Security, and Information-Sharing

Like Plan Colombia, the Mérida Initiative focused initially on improving the effectiveness of the security sector to provide for citizen security and fight organized crime through US equipment transfers and training of the Mexican security forces. The major beneficiaries of this initial package were the Secretariat of National Defense (Secretaría de Defensa Nacional, or SEDENA) and the Secretariat of the Navy (Secretaría de Marina, or SEMAR), because Calderón had delegated responsibility for public security in much of the country to the armed forces until he could raise a newly fashioned and professional Federal Police force, the main branch of the Secretariat of Public Security (Secretaría de Seguridad Pública, or SSP).[45] To this end, the US government delivered nine new UH-60M Blackhawk helicopters to Mexico (three to SEMAR and six to the SSP), eight Bell 412 helicopters to SEDENA, and four maritime surveillance aircraft to SEMAR.[46] Because Mexico's drug gangs and cartels were not as readily identifiable as Colombian insurgent and paramilitary groups, whose members wore uniforms and operated as military fronts in Colombia's rural regions, new helicopters did not have as obvious a role in Mexico, where criminal groups have tended to blend in among the general population. Thus aviation assets were not as central to US assistance in Mexico as in Colombia. However, these relatively modest acquisitions under the Mérida Initiative enabled more frequent counternarcotics and law enforcement operations, further extending the reach and extent of the rule of law by moving personnel to distant and inaccessible regions.[47]

Although by pure numbers, the aerial mobility contribution in Mexico was minor relative to the aviation donations to Colombia, the training and maintenance associated with the transfer of US defense equipment necessitated the adoption of new norms and "ways of going about business" in the recipient institutions.[48] For instance, the Mexican Army, which historically relied on an arsenal of older French, German, and Italian military hardware, increased its acquisition of US weaponry "100-fold" during the Felipe Calderón and Enrique Peña Nieto (2012–18) administrations.[49] New materiel facilitated increased touch points between Mexican military personnel and their US counterparts, who delivered robust training to Mexico on the use of US-made aircraft and weaponry. Closer collaboration also led to an expansion of personnel exchanges, with SEDENA and SEMAR officers being posted to NORTHCOM and other US military installations, and a noteworthy increase in bilateral cooperative counternarcotics operations.[50] Emboldened by new equipment and a mandate to take on a growing share of the country's public order missions, the Mexican armed forces, encouraged by the United States, also sought to guard against accusations of improper conduct or abuses against the Mexican citizenry. In this vein, SEDENA gestured to the human rights community, which was uncomfortable with Mexico's increasing militarization, by inaugurating the Civil-Military Liaison Unit to strengthen lines of communication between the army and civil society.[51]

Improving the intelligence collection and border security capabilities of the Mexican security forces were additional objectives for US policymakers, especially because Mexican authorities were historically hesitant to share sensitive information with Washington; many Mexican officials believed that closer collaboration could be perceived as a betrayal of national sovereignty.[52] However, the Mérida Initiative included NORTHCOM support for the establishment of an intelligence fusion center that collated inputs from SEDENA and SEMAR.[53] A major accomplishment in this regard was the founding of the Naval Intelligence Unit (Unidad de Inteligencia Naval) in 2008, which weathered repeated diplomatic rows between the United States and Mexico and as of 2022 remained the most trusted Mexican intelligence service from the perspective of partner US agencies.[54] The unit's organization and training benefited from investments from the United States, United Kingdom, France, and Spain; also, unlike SEDENA's intelligence arm, SEMAR's team boasted both uniformed and civilian personnel, affording it greater access to diverse intelligence sources and a nuanced perspective in the production of intelligence reports.

Additionally, more than $20 million was earmarked for the installation of a secure communications system between national security agencies on both sides of the border, and upward of $30 million was immediately spent on X-ray scanners and customs inspections equipment.[55] The Department of State funded the purchase of computer equipment and software to integrate Mexican law enforcement intelligence into a unified database called Platform Mexico (Plataforma México), enabling unprecedented integration among military and law enforcement forces that traditionally shied away from co-operation among each other and with US agencies.[56] Department of State officials also expended resources to help Mexican immigration authorities consolidate their databases to facilitate greater information-sharing between the two countries. The United States also partly financed the new Binational Intelligence Office, which for the first time gave US intelligence officials a physical foothold in Mexico City and facilitated their collection on drug traffickers and other transnational crime outfits.[57]

Law Enforcement and Justice Sector Reform

The Federal Police, which was intended to be the principal beneficiary of municipal data registered in Platform Mexico, also received US resources, surveillance equipment, and technical advice to establish a central command and control facility and a new training academy in San Luis Potosí.[58] The US government focused on course development and technical training; the Mexican federal government provided the bulk of funding for facilities construction and staff salaries. Unlike in Plan Colombia, assistance through the Mérida Initiative did not include funding for the eradication of marijuana and opium, due to the Mexican government's insistence that it would tackle drug-crop cultivation using its own resources; instead, US authorities opted for interdiction support to deny traffickers the ability to move their product toward the US border.[59] For this, the Department of State donated forensic equipment and canine teams to help Mexican police seize illegal drugs and weapons.[60] The Mérida Initiative also provided funding for the Clandestine Laboratory Initiative, a joint project between State and the DEA that targeted laboratories in Mexico specifically producing synthetic drugs such as fentanyl and methamphetamine.[61] The DEA similarly delivered training for "clandestine drug lab detection units" within the Mexican police, and some $4.6 million under the Mérida Initiative was allocated to furnish handheld drug detectors and protective equipment for these units.[62]

Although a lesser priority of the original agreement as conceived during the Bush administration, law enforcement and justice reform became the principal US lines of effort under President Obama, who inherited the initiative when he entered office in 2009.[63] The original announcement of the Mérida Initiative—and its budget—lasted only through 2010, but the Obama administration refashioned US commitments under the banner "Beyond Mérida," requesting $310 million in 2011 and $282 million in 2012.[64] The revamped approach embraced four main pillars to address the underlying causes of the security crisis: disrupting organized crime, institutionalizing rule of law, creating a twenty-first-century border, and building resilient communities.[65] As Washington moved away from military hardware and technology and instead focused on building institutional capacity, the major beneficiaries included the SSP; the National Commission of Security (Comisión Nacional de Seguridad, or CNS); the Attorney General's Office (Procuraduría General de la República, or PGR); the Public Ministry (Ministerio Público); civil society organizations; and the Prevention and Social Readaptation Agency (Órgano Administrativo Desconcentrado de Prevención y Readaptación Social, or OADPRS).[66] One US official described the division of labor within the US government at this juncture: "The State Department ran the capacity-building show, while the DEA ran the operational show. The Mérida Initiative ceased to be a military program."[67]

The Bureau of International Narcotics and Law Enforcement Affairs saw in the revamped Mérida Initiative an opportunity to focus on the SSP's capacity through equipment and technology donations, to train municipal police forces in border districts at the International Law Enforcement Academies in El Salvador and New Mexico, and to advise the Mexican executive branch on streamlining coordination among police forces. With US assistance, President Calderón established guidelines and processes for the recruitment, selection, training, promotion, and retirement of Federal Police personnel. By 2013, the US government had trained more than nineteen thousand federal law enforcement officers.[68] It also helped shift the Mexican authorities' focus to financial intelligence through the introduction of new training and software; in 2015, the US and Mexican governments approved a $75 million program to develop an automated, interagency biometrics system to collate information on criminals. The Department of State and USAID also prioritized crime and violence prevention programs in the communities most vulnerable to criminal activity. The same agencies committed resources to bridge the divide between the Mexican government and civil society by helping Mexican authorities administer protection mechanisms for vulnerable human rights defenders and by hosting forums to facilitate discussion between government and civil society actors.[69] In 2017 alone, USAID granted $25 million to help Mexican authorities design a national human rights strategy.[70]

Further, the justice sector reform introduced by President Calderón in 2008 provided the Department of Justice and USAID with opportunities to grant technical assistance and training to Mexico's judges, prosecutors, and lawyers under the auspices of the Mérida Initiative. The new accusatorial justice system demanded that justice officials gather evidence to build cases against suspected criminals, guarantee the rights of the accused (presumption of innocence, due process, limitations on preventive detention), and incorporate police into the administration of justice by awarding them investigative functions.[71] Thus after 2010, US interagency work focused on training police and judicial authorities on how to secure crime scenes, protect evidence, conduct investigations, and prosecute cases. The Department of Justice guided the design and implementation of a national training program for nine thousand prosecutors and investigators called Project Diamante, and more than thirty thousand justice professionals in the new criminal justice system benefited from USAID training programs overall.[72] Additional support even reached the Mexican Senate, which relied on USAID to assist in drafting legislation to create new standards for the legal profession in Mexico, and the Attorney General's Office received more than $60 million to digitalize records and modernize its forensics processing systems.[73] The introduction of alternative dispute resolution, as well, sought to increase the flexibility and efficiency of the justice sector, reducing massive judicial case backlogs. The State Department also helped bolster the sector's transparency by equipping more than 120 courtrooms in twenty-one Mexican states with audio and video recording equipment to record oral proceedings, which replaced the closed-door sessions of the previous criminal justice system.[74]

Given the role of state and local justice institutions in processing some 90 percent of criminal offenses in Mexico, Washington channeled many of its resources for justice sector reform into subnational institutions—a departure from the focus on federal security forces for security sector reform.[75] USAID sponsored programs to build analytical capacity for state and federal judicial institutions alike to demonstrate progress on issues like high pretrial detention rates and funded fifteen projects valued at $49 million to promote ethical behavior and transparency in procurement processes.[76] As security forces became more proficient at conducting arrests, prison populations expanded, and the Mexican judiciary traditionally held those suspected of involvement in organized crime for at least forty days without access to legal counsel, something permitted under the legal practice of *arraigo*. Although the new justice system continued to implement *arraigo*, its usage dropped considerably.[77] Also, as in Colombia, to improve conditions for inmates and prevent criminal recidivism, the US Embassy helped at least ninety-eight correctional facilities meet security and humanitarian standards to secure both international accreditation and certified correctional instructors from the Mexican National Academy for Penitentiary Administration (Academia Nacional de Administración Penitenciaria, or ANAP).[78] Summing all these activities starting with the initial Mérida allocations in 2007, Washington committed a total of more than $406 million to Mexico's criminal justice transformation.

After a decade of intensive US security assistance, the State Department pointed to the unprecedented intelligence and law enforcement cooperation, the creation of national training standards for law enforcement and judicial officials, and the international accreditation of Mexican institutions as some of the principal accomplishments of the Mérida Initiative.[79] However, unlike in Colombia, public security had grown more precarious rather than less over the years of the Mérida Initiative's implementation, with record homicide tallies and a soaring sense of insecurity among Mexico's citizens. Meanwhile, political changes in the United States and Mexico ushered in a pivot in bilateral relations that hampered the goodwill and mutual respect that were hallmarks of the Mérida Initiative. When President Trump took office, his rhetoric and executive orders relating to the US-Mexico relationship departed from the institutional capacity-building objectives of previous US administrations, prioritizing combating drug production, improving drug interdiction, and stemming undocumented migration. His uncharitable description of Mexican migrants during his presidential campaign and his blatant distrust of Mexican authorities further derailed deeper cooperation initiatives.

Likewise, President Andrés Manuel López Obrador (2018–present) came to power in part by pledging to demilitarize the government's strategy against criminal organizations, preferring to address the socioeconomic causes of criminal activity. In early 2019, he even went as far as to proclaim that "[the Mérida Initiative] hasn't worked" and that Mexico did not "want cooperation in the use of force" but rather for development.[80] Indeed, the new administration in Mexico City shied away from the targeted crime prevention efforts that USAID had long supported and replaced them with broad social programs,

Table 3.3. US Interagency Actors and Colombian and Mexican Beneficiary Institutions

Plan Colombia		Merida Initiative	
United States	**Colombia**	**United States**	**Mexico**
Department of Defense	Ministry of Defense	Department of Defense	Secretariat of National Defense and Secretariat of the Navy
Department of State	Ministry of Justice, Attorney General's Office, and Inspector General's Office	Department of State	Attorney General's Office, National Prosecutor's Office (formerly Public Ministry), and state judiciaries
Department of Justice (including Drug Enforcement Administration)	National Penitentiary and Prison Institute	Department of Justice (including Drug Enforcement Administration)	State and municipal police forces
US Agency for International Development	Human Rights Ombudsman	US Agency for International Development	Secretariat of Public Security and Secretariat of the Interior
Office of National Drug Control Policy	Social Action/ Integrated Action	Office of National Drug Control Policy	Prevention and Social Readaptation Agency
Central Intelligence Agency/ Director of National Intelligence	Administrative Security Department (replaced by National Intelligence Directorate)	Central Intelligence Agency/ Director of National Intelligence	Investigation and National Security Center and Naval Intelligence Unit
	Civil Society	Department of Homeland Security	Mexican National Migration Institute
			Civil Society

Source: Author's tabulation.

sidelined hallmark programs of the Mérida Initiative, and instead inaugurated a new federal policing force, the National Guard (Guardia Nacional).[81] Although the National Guard continued to rely on the military for its own staffing and recruitment, the institutional reconfiguration frustrated the US executive departments and agencies that had invested so much in existing police programming. López Obrador's election marked not only a reorientation of the bilateral security relationship but also an admission on the Mexican side of the border that the country's US-backed security strategy had fallen short of its goals.

Violent crime rates in Mexico soared by 2015, plateauing in 2020. Despite a brief improvement in public perception of the country's security situation, most indicators of criminality surged during the later years of the Peña Nieto administration and into López Obrador's tenure, discussed further in chapter 4. In contrast to the progress in Colombia, Mexico and its US bureaucratic partners had little evidence to demonstrate that a decade of major investment in security sector reform had resulted in greater safety for most Mexicans. Recognizing this failure, Mexico's foreign secretary, Marcelo Ebrard, declared in 2021 that "the Mérida Initiative is dead . . . we are now in another era."[82]

Notes

1. The Plan Colombia legislation initially included seven spending conditions, most focused on human rights. In 2000, President Clinton waived six of the seven criteria in a bid to expedite assistance to Bogotá.
2. By 2008, Washington began to express frustration with the sluggish pace of Colombian "nationalization" of equipment, maintenance, operations, and funding of US-sponsored programs (GAO, 2008, pp. 62–70). It reoriented aid, in part, to communicate to the Colombian government that the US taxpayers would not fund all programs indefinitely. On CSDI, see Rojas, 2015, pp. 190–197.
3. Bailey, 2011b.
4. GAO, 2008, p. 27. Prior to Plan Colombia, the US military limited its engagement with the Colombian Army to four annual mobile training teams sent to the 12th and 24th Brigades based in the coca-rich south of the country. However, in 2000, the 24th Brigade became implicated in accusations of human rights abuses, whereupon US aid was suspended. Starting in 1999, the US Army helped build a new 935-person counterdrug battalion, which passed US vetting standards and allowed for the resumption of aid (retired US Army colonel, personal communication, Tegucigalpa, Honduras, May 20, 2016).
5. Higgins, 2022, p. 195.
6. Bailey, 2011b; A. Dávila Ladrón de Guevara, personal communication, Bogotá, Colombia, November 15, 2017. The leadership of the Colombian Army was historically at odds with the Colombian Air Force concerning logistical requirements such as flight hours, crew rest, and landing conditions and long wanted to be in control of their own aviation assets (retired US Army colonel, personal communication, Tegucigalpa, Honduras, May 20, 2016).
7. Demobilized FARC military strategist, personal communication, Antioquia, Colombia, November 2, 2017.
8. GAO, 2008, p. 28. The National Police also underwent a major structural and oversight reform in 2003 following scandals surrounding cases of illicit enrichment by police officers and the mismanagement of US-donated funds (Casas Dupuy, 2005).
9. GAO, 2008, pp. 34–35. The cultural shift toward jointness was not without dramatic consequences for the armed forces given that fourteen generals retired on the announcement of joint commands because they rejected the notion of taking orders from someone of a different service (D. Hernández, personal communication, Medellín, Colombia, November 7, 2017).

10. Retired US Army colonel, personal communication, Tegucigalpa, Honduras, May 20, 2016. On the role of the US military in the founding of the Lanceros during the Cold War, see Rodríguez Hernández, 2005, pp. 75–82. In one of the most brazen rescues, the Colombian military successfully retrieved Ingrid Betancourt, a former Colombian presidential candidate; three US Embassy contractors; and eleven Colombian soldiers and police officers without firing a single shot (Santos, 2009, pp. 241–263). This was a mortal blow to the morale of the FARC, which had in the months prior to the rescue operation seen a number of high-profile deaths and desertions within their ranks.
11. GAO, 2008, pp. 36–38.
12. Rochlin, 2007, p. 51.
13. Lindsay-Poland, 2018, p. 88. President Uribe expanded the government's human intelligence capabilities by raising a network of 1.5 million government informants and by equipping highway travelers with panic buttons linked to satellites to report insurgent activity. Real-time intelligence helped prevent attacks on Colombian government infrastructure and military bases and allowed for the deployment of rapid-reaction forces. Raids on guerrilla units surged from 477 in 2002 to 1,784 in 2004 (Rochlin, 2007, pp. 53–54).
14. Controversially, the Uribe administration ordered the bombing of a FARC camp in Ecuadorian territory in 2008, resulting in the death of FARC Secretariat Commander Raúl Reyes. This incident generated a diplomatic row involving Colombia, Ecuador, and Venezuela over the violation of Ecuador's national sovereignty.
15. Miklaucic & Pinzón, 2017, p. 280.
16. Jayamaha et al., 2010, p. 51.
17. Nadelmann, 1987, p. 11. Although the creation of elite units typically improves performance for operational metrics such as the number of insurgent leaders removed from battle and the number of drug labs destroyed, Washington's focus on elite units risks neglecting other units responsible for the day-to-day operations of security institutions, stunting the broader objective of institutional reform.
18. Jayamaha et al., 2010, pp. 54–60.
19. Schemo, 1997.
20. The White House, 2002, p. 10.
21. US House of Representatives, 2002, p. 63.
22. The first consideration of the guerrilla threat as a terrorist one in Colombia dates to Decree 1923 of 1978, the now infamous Security Statute of the administration of President Julio César Turbay (1978–82). This measure, according to César Niño González (2016, p. 54), transformed the cohabitation of the state, society, and the insurgency into a scenario in which violent actions inflicted by insurgents represented domestic terrorism, a phenomenon detached from the international context of the Cold War.
23. Borrero Mansilla, 2006, p. 130; Boyle, 2010; Niño González, 2016, p. 57.
24. Niño González, 2016, p. 59.
25. Rochlin, 2007, p. 31.
26. In 1998, the Colombian military's leadership defined the four lines of effort that made up security sector reform: strengthening the force through changes in command, control, and structure; transformation of military training; more efficient logistical support; and the modernization of communications systems (Rojas, 2015, pp. 68–69).
27. Palma, 2019.

28. President Uribe merged the Ministries of the Interior (Ministerio del Interior) and of Justice (Ministerio de Justicia) into a single body in 2002, but in 2011, President Santos removed the functions of the Minister of the Interior and renamed the resulting body the Ministry of Justice and Law (Ministerio de Justicia y del Derecho).
29. GAO, 2008, p. 46.
30. Rojas, 2015, p. 111. On the transition to an accusatorial system in Colombia, see García Villegas, 2006.
31. GAO, 2008, p. 57.
32. US Department of State, 2018a.
33. Pachico, 2011b. A former INPEC official recalled that Plan Colombia helped fund the implementation of a quality control system to ensure that Colombia's maximum-security prisons met international norms (V. M. Tique, personal communication, Bogotá, Colombia, December 15, 2017). The first prison to receive international certification was finished in 2000, and by 2018, the Colombian government had financed ten additional prisons built on that model. Unfortunately, the prison system's budget languished. The number of apprehended criminals increased by more than 100 percent from 2005 to 2010, but INPEC's budget grew at a fixed pace of just 3 percent each year.
34. Botero Suárez, 2017, p. 4.
35. J. A. Salgado Restrepo, personal communication, Medellín, Colombia, November 7, 2017.
36. On signing the peace accord in September 2016, the Obama administration dedicated $450 million for FY 2017 to support the implementation of the deal in a gesture known as Peace Colombia.
37. Correa Castañeda, 2006, p. 215. Unlike in the Central American peace processes, the composition, structure, and doctrine of the Colombian military were not up for negotiation in the FARC peace talks.
38. The White House, 2013.
39. Turbiville, 2010, p. 35. This assistance package represented more security assistance in one year than the total assistance rendered in the twelve years preceding the Mérida Initiative (Benítez Manaut, 2009, p. 230).
40. GAO, 2010, p. 15.
41. GAO, 2010, p. 11.
42. Ribando Seelke & Finklea, 2017, p. 13. One US official working in Mexico from 2010 to 2015 noted President Calderón's frustration with the torpor of US assistance. Despite a promised windfall of assistance, Calderón was flummoxed at the unwelcome lull after the initial delivery of military hardware (US State Department official, personal communication, Tegucigalpa, Honduras, May 27, 2016). On the US official's arrival in Mexico in March 2010, Washington charged his office with spending $800 million by December of that year, but even as his team met the spending deadline, the Regional Procurement Support Office, unaccustomed to such a massive assistance package, could not work quickly enough to disburse the funds and fulfill the requests.
43. Ribando Seelke & Finklea, 2017, p. 11.
44. Ribando Seelke & Finklea, 2017, p. 11.
45. The Federal Preventive Police (Policía Federal Preventiva, or PFP) were rebranded as simply the Federal Police with the Federal Police Law (Ley de Policía Federal), which took effect in June 2009 (Chabat, 2010, p. 33). Some analysts maintain that the Federal Police, equipped with repressive gear and tactics, represent a step further in the direction of militarization

of the internal security sphere in Mexico (Alvarado Mendoza & Zaverucha, 2010, p. 255; Moloeznik, 2006). Additionally, SEMAR expanded its maritime policing capability and boosted recruitment of marines to handle this role, eclipsing the use of the PFP and later the Federal Police in maritime domain (Guevara Moyano, 2011, pp. 30–31).

46. US Department of State, 2018b.
47. US Department of State, 2018b. The Mexican government benefited from more generous financial resources to purchase its own equipment than the Colombian government did at the outset of Plan Colombia—which helps explain why materiel donations were not as large a component. Between 2014 and 2015, SEDENA purchased twenty-one additional Blackhawk helicopters and more than three thousand Humvees from the United States (Lindsay-Poland, 2015). In the same period, SEMAR purchased five Blackhawk helicopters and four King Air 350ER aircraft to assist in surveillance operations.
48. Retired US Army colonel, personal communication, Tegucigalpa, Honduras, May 20, 2016.
49. Beckhusen, 2015. The surge in purchases of US-grade equipment, weaponry, and aircraft during the Calderón administration retooled the Mexican security sector away from European providers and guaranteed the renewal of acquisitions, maintenance, and training contracts with the US defense industry for decades (Partlow, 2015).
50. Office of National Drug Control Policy, 2016.
51. Guevara Moyano, 2011, p. 14.
52. Benítez Manaut, 2014, p. 63.
53. Washington invited Mexican military leaders to observe intelligence fusion techniques in Afghanistan, sparking interest in the establishment of such capabilities in Mexico. However, when cartels infiltrated some of the SEDENA staff at the Mexican operations center and it was dismantled, SEMAR intelligence officers founded their own intelligence fusion unit (senior Obama administration official, personal communication, Washington, DC, October 28, 2021).
54. Larson, 2021.
55. Benítez Manaut, 2009, pp. 231–232.
56. Cook & Ribando Seelke, 2008, p. 3.
57. Cruz, 2020, p. 190.
58. The Calderón administration complemented these contributions by expanding the force size to nearly forty thousand police officers, increasing federal police salaries, and enforcing more rigorous recruitment standards (such as polygraphs, background checks, financial review, and competency tests) (Wolf & Celorio Morayta, 2011, p. 696).
59. Woody, 2017. Roughly 10 percent of Mérida Initiative funding during the Obama administration went directly to counternarcotics ends; the rest of the programming addressed anticorruption, police training, and judicial reform (US State Department official, personal communication, Tegucigalpa, Honduras, May 27, 2016).
60. Ribando Seelke & Finklea, 2017, p. 14.
61. US Department of State, 2018b, p. 222.
62. GAO, 2019a, p. 22.
63. Fonseca, 2016.
64. Bailey, 2011b.
65. Ribando Seelke & Finklea, 2017, p. 10. The original four goals of the Mérida Initiative were to break the power and impunity of organized crime; assist the Mexican government in strengthening border, air, and maritime controls; improve the capacity of the justice system;

and curtail gang activity while diminishing the demand for drugs (GAO, 2010). However, the Obama administration adjusted the ambition of the bilateral assistance package to target specific structural drivers of criminality in Mexico (Finkenbusch, 2016).

66. President Peña Nieto subordinated the SSP to the Secretariat of the Interior (Secretaría de Gobernación, or SEGOB) and renamed it the CNS in 2013. The CNS fell under the Federal Public Administration (Administración Pública Federal), charged with the maintenance of peace and security in public spaces, until López Obrador disbanded it and established the Secretariat of Security and Civilian Protection (Secretaría de Seguridad y Protección Ciudadana, or SSPC) in its place.
67. Former senior US diplomat, personal communication, Mexico City, December 3, 2021.
68. Bolaños, 2016, p. 107; Feeley, 2013b.
69. USAID, 2018a.
70. Ribando Seelke & Finklea, 2017, p. 29.
71. Shirk, 2010.
72. Ribando Seelke & Finklea, 2017; USAID, 2018a, p. 18. One major criticism of support for justice sector reform is that the US Embassy overemphasized the retraining of judges but failed to reorient the practices of the public ministries and the police, which represent the initial steps in the chain of custody of evidence (researcher from Mexican Institute of Human Rights and Democracy, personal communication, Mexico City, January 18, 2018).
73. Benítez Manaut, 2009, p. 233; USAID, 2018b.
74. Ribando Seelke & Finklea, 2017, p. 18.
75. Ingram & Shirk, 2012, p. 120.
76. GAO, 2019a.
77. Ribando Seelke & Finklea, 2017, p. 17.
78. Senior Calderón administration security official, personal communication, Mexico City, January 26, 2018; Ocampomi, 2021; US Department of State, 2018b. Between December 2006 and March 2010, 121,199 individuals with links to organized crime were arrested in Mexico, and the surge in arrests demanded greater capacity in the prison system (Moloeznik, 2013, p. 71).
79. Rosen & Ribando Seelke, 2020, p. 2.
80. Sheridan, 2019.
81. Rosen & Ribando Seelke, 2020, p. 2.
82. Sheridan & Sief, 2021.

4

Evaluating Security Sector Reform in Colombia and Mexico

This chapter evaluates the success of reorganizations and reforms undertaken during Plan Colombia and the Mérida Initiative through the two dimensions of security sector governance: effectiveness and accountability. Context-relevant indicators help assess these two aspects in Colombia and Mexico over more than ten years of sustained security assistance in each case. In Colombia, effectiveness significantly improved across the security sector. But the accountability of the sector to independent, civilian authorities—albeit better than in the 1990s—remained uneven and continued to present challenges for democratic governance. In Mexico, most indicators of effectiveness and accountability reflected minimal positive change and, in some instances, showed major deterioration despite the introduction of reforms. Explaining this disparity in outcomes between the two cases is the focus of the remaining chapters.

Assessment Indicators in Colombia and Mexico

Assessment frameworks for security sector reform include general recommendations for evaluating progress, but the most authoritative models deliberately exclude comprehensive lists of specific assessment indicators because the evaluation of reforms should be, above all, contextual.[1] The Organization for Economic Co-operation and Development (OECD) handbook on security sector reform, produced by its Development Assistance Committee, puts it this way:

> Some readers may therefore be disappointed to find that this toolkit does not contain lists of standard indicators. The reason is that standard indicators are inadvisable because they are not context-specific, are unlikely to be locally owned, and because security sector reform is too complex to be measured with a simple list of indicators.[2]

From Peril to Partnership. Paul J. Angelo, Oxford University Press. © Oxford University Press 2024.
DOI: 10.1093/oso/9780197688106.003.0005

For example, the homicide rate would be an inappropriate indicator of security sector reform in a country with a low incidence of murder but high rates of corruption among security forces. It is, however, a critical indicator in Mexico and Colombia, where homicide figures are historically both high and a persistent concern for citizens.

Determining the efficacy of reforms within police and military forces poses further challenges because relevant, reliable data are oftentimes unavailable or incomplete. Donor and recipient governments alike often neglect the need for baseline surveys and do not systematically evaluate their investments. This holds true for the US government.[3] The State Department has repeatedly faced criticism for its presentation of input ("advice and resources given") and output ("goods, products, and services provided") indicators as evidence of the success of security assistance in Latin America.[4] Instead, indicators of outcomes relating to improvements in security sector governance, such as improved professional standards of conduct among the security forces, increased geographic coverage of security services, and positive citizen perception of security and the security sector, would serve as a better measure of the success of reforms.[5]

In cases of security assistance spanning decades, meaningful baseline statistics are also frequently unavailable because of underdeveloped data collection methods at the outset of the interventions. Not until the 1990s and early 2000s, for instance, did national governments and international organizations begin to conduct victimization surveys in much of the developing world, and even then the most ambitious surveys were not completed annually.[6]

Further, selecting indicators and determining how to measure trends are often politicized activities. Evidence suggests that changes in the Colombian government's statistical compilation practices led to an underestimation of kidnappings committed during the Uribe administration by nearly 40 percent—a move that publicly played to the government's narrative of dramatically improved security.[7] Ironically, other critics claim that the country's security forces inflated crime and violence statistics during the Pastrana administration, overestimating figures to attract more international aid.[8] Similarly, the nonprofit México Evalúa reported in 2016 that state attorneys general offices across the country manipulated data to suggest a decrease in high-impact crimes.[9] Some Mexican state governments also underreported homicides and reclassified violent crimes as nonviolent or unintentional offenses, complicating efforts to establish reliable statistics for casualties in the war on drugs.[10]

Finally, inconsistencies in data collection and computation methodologies make comparing longitudinal data difficult given that the responsibility for collecting and compiling data changes hands over the years.[11] Deciphering and documenting the underlying political interests at play is therefore an essential task for researchers attempting to present conclusions based on available data.[12] In short, a wholly quantitative study would fail to fully describe either successes or failures.

In this chapter, qualitative data collected through interviews with government and civil society representatives inform conclusions about security assistance effectiveness and the broader political and security context. Additionally, because the purpose of security sector reform is, after all, improving security for the citizenry, the public experience of security is central to indicator selection. Public opinion is a crucial indicator in that it shapes national debate and public policies, affects the discretion and ease of operation of criminal groups, and can mobilize and empower civil society.[13] For this reason, measures focused on public opinion and on the performance of the security sector in reducing rates of victimization by crime among the general population are grounds for comparison of security sector governance across time and space.

Different indicators are useful for assessing the effectiveness and accountability elements of a security sector. Effectiveness refers to the ability of security institutions to fulfill their designated functions and institutional missions. These functions and missions vary between countries depending on the constitutional and operational mandates of relevant institutions, but broadly speaking, more effective security sectors are those that reduce the incidence of crime and violence through security provision that makes use of rules-based professional practices and premier technologies. Relevant indicators typically include operational accomplishments, public perceptions of fairness and effectiveness, and absolute and relative measures of crime and violence, as seen in tables 4.A.1 and 4.A.2.[14] Police and military forces, the principal institutions relevant to this book, typically have different institutional features and social obligations. However, in both Colombia and Mexico, where their operational mandates were occasionally blurred, their efforts jointly affected outcomes related to crime and violence. This book differentiates between police and military performance where appropriate but evaluates effectiveness at the macro level.

On the other hand, accountability describes the ability of a democratic government to exert oversight—having laws, rules, policies, practices, and institutions in place that hold members of the security sector responsible for their actions and transparent in their methods.[15] This is particularly true in the delivery of justice for crimes or abuses committed by members of the security sector. Undemocratic governments often lack transparency and equal treatment under the law when it comes to the security sector. In democratic societies, however, the accountability of police and military forces is typically enforced by civilian control of these institutions, represented by civilian ministers, legislative inquiries, and civilian criminal justice jurisdiction over crimes and abuses committed by uniformed members.[16] In Colombia and Mexico, where security forces have historically enjoyed a high degree of autonomy, however, civilian oversight is not a given. Considering the political sensitivity of accountability and the secrecy with which security forces tend to guard their internal processes, deciphering the level of impunity within the security sector can be challenging. For measures of accountability, this study considers the indicators presented in tables 4.A.3 and 4.A.4, including numbers of public complaints filed against security forces, sentencing for extrajudicial murders, and public perceptions of corruption in the security sector. Additionally, identifying the security sector's relations with civilian authorities in the executive, legislative, and judicial branches adds additional texture to determine the ease with which civilian authorities exert their prescribed oversight.

Plan Colombia and Security Sector Reform

As discussed in chapter 2, the Colombian security sector in the late 1990s found itself unable to provide for its own basic security requirements, let alone the security of most Colombian citizens. The Revolutionary Armed Forces of Colombia (Fuerzas Armadas Revolucionarias de Colombia, or FARC) killed or kidnapped thousands of military and police personnel in attacks on government installations from 1997 to 2000. One former FARC insurgent proudly proclaimed, "The security forces were confined to their bases, so we had to go to them to engage them in conflict. They were very vulnerable."[17] FARC assaults on remote military outposts such as Las Delicias, Patascoy, El Billar, Miraflores, and Mitú became synonymous with the growing power of Colombia's nonstate armed groups—and the concomitant weakness of the Colombian security forces. In 1999, US Ambassador to Colombia Myles Frechette acknowledged, "The Colombian military is basically a barracks military, not one that is organized to go after guerrillas. They have some brave and capable people, but they are strictly a reaction force, and not a very mobile one at that."[18] Some battered army units relied on paramilitary groups to prevent insurgents from occupying tracts of territory devoid of state authority, but these private armies were themselves responsible for major abuses against the civilian population.[19] The National Police, for its part, had undergone a limited reform in the early 1990s but lacked a presence in at least fifty municipalities across the country in 2001, effectively ceding control to illegal armed groups or transient military units.[20] Moreover, the police did not consolidate efforts to record crime statistics until 2003 with the nationwide rollout of the Statistical Information System for Delinquency, Coexistence, and Operations (Sistema de Información Estadístico, Delincuencial, Contravencional y Operativo, or SIEDCO).

At the outset of Plan Colombia, Colombia's cities were among the most dangerous in the world, and the country had earned a reputation as the world's kidnapping capital. But more than a decade of security sector reform helped Bogotá improve security provision across the country. By 2011, most indicators of crime and violence had fallen sharply—even in many rural areas that for decades had been abandoned by the state or ravaged by conflict. Additionally, Colombia's security institutions grew more accountable for crimes and abuses committed, and the programming associated with Plan Colombia facilitated enhanced security sector governance for most applicable measures.

Effectiveness

The Colombian case shows steady and sometimes dramatic improvements for indicators of effectiveness, and most observers, even vehement critics of the Colombian security sector, reported more proficient security institutions at the conclusion of Plan Colombia.[21] Violent crimes such as homicide and kidnapping declined steeply, and acts of terrorism and subversion by illegal armed groups dropped notably. From 2000 to 2011, the homicide rate in Colombia more than halved, from seventy-one per hundred thousand inhabitants to thirty-five. Kidnappings per hundred thousand inhabitants dropped from a high of 8.8 to 0.7 over the same period. Violence related to the country's armed conflict also tapered off but only after an intensification that coincided with the Colombian military's Plan Patriota offensive against the FARC from 2003 to 2006. Although the incidence of homicide countrywide decreased, some regions (Valle del Cauca, Casanare, Chocó, and Guajira departments) where combat operations were ongoing experienced spikes, and during the first years of the Uribe administration, assassinations of city mayors increased from previous years before falling by more than two-thirds in 2004.[22]

During the period of heightened conflict, Colombian authorities also captured record numbers of members of nonstate armed groups, and the country's main insurgencies saw their force sizes dwindle as many of the rank and file voluntarily demobilized in government-sponsored reinsertion programs, which reported record defections from the FARC and National Liberation Army (Ejército de Liberación Nacional, or ELN) in the years following Plan Patriota. As recruitment became more difficult, Colombia's principal nonstate armed groups also found their ability to extend their geographic influence across the country severely reduced. Indicators depicting the national reach of these organizations, such as the acreage of drug crops or the civilian population zones affected by combat, reflect a considerably smaller territorial footprint by 2011.[23] Terrorist attacks on civilian populations and infrastructure also dropped significantly, especially those waged in the vicinity of the Caño Limón-Coveñas oil pipeline. The 490-mile pipeline, which traverses thirty-three municipalities, faced more than nine hundred attacks in the fifteen years preceding Plan Colombia and 170 attacks in 2001 alone—a number that steadily decreased to seventeen in 2004.[24] The offensive footing of the Colombian military put illegal armed groups on the run, denying paramilitary and insurgent groups haven and logistical support in population centers. One demobilized FARC combatant remarked, "When we sensed that the tide had changed, we moved out of the cities to safe zones beyond the government's reach."[25] This perspective points to an increasing monopoly of force by the government, at least in the more densely populated parts of the country.

Given that the reduction of cocaine production and trafficking was the primary interest of the US government in Colombia, the capacity of Colombia's security forces to eradicate coca, destroy drug labs, and interdict illicit narcotics and precursor chemicals became an important measure of success in Plan Colombia. In 2000, an estimated 163,000 hectares—just over four hundred thousand acres—of coca were grown in Colombia. By 2011, this figure had decreased to sixty-four thousand hectares (see figure 4.1).[26] Government seizures of processed cocaine also increased, skyrocketing from a low of 57,000 kilograms seized in 2001 to a peak of 203,000 in 2009 (see figure 4.2).[27] The Colombian military and police—equipped with new, more sophisticated aircraft and maritime patrol boats—benefited from greater mobility and more detailed intelligence, enabling a significant expansion of counterdrug capacity during the years of Plan Colombia. Colombia's improved performance on this front did not appreciably affect cocaine consumption or pricing in the United States, though, especially as coca cultivation ballooned elsewhere in the Andes. Further, Colombia's insurgents and cartels began diversifying their criminal income through illegal mining and extortion in the later years of Plan Colombia, partly in response to the government's dogged pursuit of drug traffickers.[28] As of 2022, Colombia remained the world's principal source of cocaine, suggesting that repressive counterdrug policies alone will

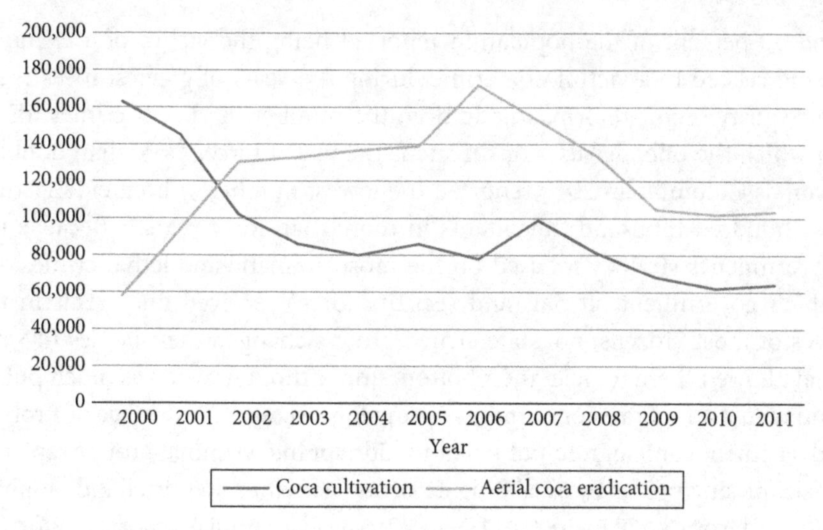

Figure 4.1. Coca Cultivation and Aerial Eradication in Colombia (Hectares)
Source: UNODC, 2012; UNODC, 2005.

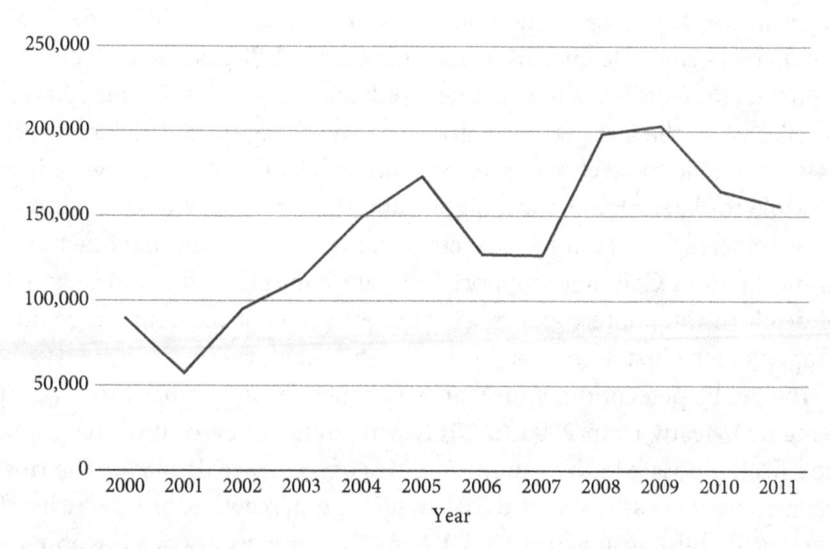

Figure 4.2. Cocaine Hydrochloride Seizures in Colombia (Kilograms)
Source: GAO, 2019b; UNODC, 2012.

not put an end to illicit drug production.[29] And recent Drug Enforcement Administration (DEA) reporting indicates that by the late 2010s, coca cultivation and cocaine production were once again on the rise.

Despite lower figures for the most extreme acts of violence and crime by the end of Plan Colombia, citizen security remained a major concern for Colombians. Crime victimization remained relatively steady: between 30 and 40 percent of the population reported being the victim of a crime or being related to a victim of a crime during the years of greatest investment in security sector reform. In addition, the number of violent crimes, those in which the offender uses or threatens the use of force, more than doubled even as Colombia in 2017 reported the lowest number of homicide victims per hundred thousand inhabitants in more than forty years.[30] Because the government's strategy focused on the most dramatic and lethal crimes, for which government officials and security forces received due credit in the eyes of most citizens, nonstate armed groups changed their tactics in ways that allowed them to meet their bottom line without drawing as much public and media attention. For example, opting for discretion in the face of a robust government campaign to put a halt to kidnapping, criminal groups replaced their missing profits by escalating extortion activities. Reported kidnappings dropped from 3,572 in 2000 to 199 in 2016, yet Colombia's reported extortion rate more than tripled over the same period. Victimization rates did not fluctuate significantly, but the profile of crimes committed did. The Colombian government, for its part, attempted to shine a positive light on the higher numbers. Former Defense Minister Luis Carlos Villegas noted, "People are reporting more, which shows greater confidence in our institutions. And this is reflected in the fact that the authorities, including the judicial authorities, have been able to react better, to be more efficient."[31] Even though it is impossible to determine by how significant a margin Colombians had previously underreported crimes, academic studies on homicide and other causes of mortality in Colombia support Villegas's conjecture: the underreporting of death in the poorest and most remote regions of the country gradually dropped in the first decades of the twenty-first century.[32]

The public perception of insecurity declined during Uribe's first term and remained steady from 2005 to 2011, with some 40 percent of the population feeling unsafe in their municipalities of residence. However, the rise in pedestrian crimes in the mid-2010s saw the perception of insecurity rise once again, hitting 50 percent in 2016. As Colombians worried less about the country's armed conflict given the FARC's and ELN's weakening, insecurity and delinquency replaced armed conflict and the war on terrorism as the country's principal concerns. This shift also likely reflects changes in criminal activity from attention-grabbing crimes such as kidnappings, many of which occurred on highways or in remote rural areas, to the more discreet tactic of telephone extortion of urban businesses.[33] In addition, the increased accessibility of high-value items such as mobile telephones rendered urban dwellers more susceptible to sidewalk assaults and pickpocketing, fueling perceptions of danger.[34] A creeping preoccupation with personal safety also contributed to an explosion of registered private security firms in Colombia, from 760 in 1996 to more than six thousand in 2017.[35] Although many of these companies specialized in the sale of security and surveillance technology to customers, at least one analyst surmised that this proliferation helped create "a situation that makes one think that there is actually a crisis in the fulfillment of the state's role with respect to one of its inherent functions," even if other factors underpinned the private security bonanza, including the increased attainability of private security precautions for a growing middle class.[36]

The major security sector institutions fared better in the public eye during Plan Colombia than this sense of insecurity suggests.[37] Whereas a mere 40 percent of Colombians expressed a degree of trust in the Colombian Armed Forces in 1998, 60 percent did by the middle of Uribe's presidency. The military's takeover of the Comuna 13 neighborhood of Medellín from urban guerrilla groups in 2003 and the dismantling of FARC fronts near Bogotá were especially salient victories that fueled urban public support for the security forces.[38] A popular program known as Live Colombia and Travel across Her (Vive Colombia, Viaja por Ella) provided government security escorts to tourist caravans on Colombian highways during holiday seasons, restoring citizen faith in the military and police and promoting national pride. Unquestionably, major battlefield victories over the FARC from 2006 to 2008, which the Uribe administration skillfully publicized, further bolstered the military's positive image. From 2008 to 2015, one pollster consistently reported public approval of the military above 70 percent, even surging to 90 percent in 2008.[39]

One of the secrets to this newfound operational prowess was the armed forces' interoperability. In 2003, the Colombian Army, Navy, and Air Force established Joint Task Force Omega with US support to pursue the FARC in the group's traditional zones of influence. The integration of air, ground, and riverine assets under a single commander delivered some of Colombia's most propitious victories against insurgents and set a precedent for joint action that has become standard practice in the Ministry of Defense.[40] The planning of joint army-police operations—a practice dating back decades but one that became more prominent during the offensives of the Plan Colombia era—enabled the government to arrest perpetrators and secure suspected crime scenes on the spot. The Prosecutor General's Office and Human Rights Ombudsman retained responsibility for inspecting crime scenes and conducting investigations, but in remote and inaccessible areas of the country, police officers trained to protect valuable evidence from tampering or the elements often proved critical to building successful cases against criminals.[41]

These operational modifications as well as the expansion of the National Police's presence throughout the national territory paid off, with public trust in the National Police increasing from a low of 32.1 percent in 1998 to 52.3 percent in 2005.[42] In 2011, more than 69 percent of Colombians reported having a favorable opinion of the police.[43] These advances are particularly noteworthy given the increased contact that Colombian security forces had with the citizenry during the early 2000s. The number of police per hundred thousand inhabitants increased from 241 to 343 from 1999 to 2011, above the UN prescription of three hundred, and in 2016 the number of uniformed police and military members per hundred thousand inhabitants reached 997. When the FARC peace accord was signed in 2016, Colombia reported the highest number of security force personnel per capita in all Latin America.[44] This numerical increase was also accompanied by greater professionalism. In 2000, drafted soldiers, who served only twelve to eighteen months, made up roughly 70 percent of the Colombian military. But many troops would never see combat: those who were high school graduates, around 19 percent of the total force size, were automatically exempt from combat duty.[45] By December 2001, the government changed its conscription criteria to accommodate more battle-ready troops, and the number of combat-exempt soldiers dropped from thirty-five thousand in 1998 to less than three thousand. Meanwhile, the number of professional soldiers increased from twenty-one thousand to fifty-three thousand, and the number of combat-trained draftees from forty-seven thousand to sixty-one thousand.[46]

Bogotá also began to take crime and violence prevention initiatives seriously over the first decade of the 2000s. During the second half of the Uribe administration, the Ministry of Defense, at the time under the leadership of the future president, Juan Manuel Santos, embraced a prominent role within a broader whole-of-government effort to address the needs of Colombia's most conflictive regions. This pivot was originally conceived as a strategy for social inclusion of internally displaced populations, former combatants, and child soldiers into society but quickly expanded to focal areas like rural development and access to justice.[47] Integrated Action (Acción Integral, or AI), a presidential initiative and component of the Democratic Security Policy (see chapter 5), incorporated fourteen governmental institutions in the delivery of services to more than fifty priority municipalities.[48] AI's top lines of effort included social policies to reduce community vulnerability to recruitment by nonstate armed groups, educational reform, territorial control through security and justice initiatives, and economic development. In conjunction with government employees of a parallel civilian organization focused on economic and social development known as Social Action (Acción

Social), the military and police provided humanitarian relief, infrastructure improvements, and medical services in communities historically bereft of central government presence and investment. Centers for Integrated Action Coordination (Centro de Coordinación de Acción Integral, or CCAI) which operated as regional hubs in outlying areas, adopted methodologies to prioritize community-based interventions and conducted routine monitoring and evaluation of AI investments.[49]

The significance of this mission for the security forces even led to the creation of an entire directorate led by a flag officer in the Ministry of Defense. For many military commanders, AI was both a moral and practical course of action: the military was the only government entity that could reach some of Colombia's most vulnerable populations, and its interface with communities affected by armed conflict represented an opportunity to "win hearts and minds" while gaining valuable information against insurgent groups.[50] AI, later referred to as the National Territorial Consolidation Plan (Plan Nacional de Consolidación Territorial, or PNCT), was a strategy that combined "security, counternarcotics, and development in a sequenced approach targeting remote, but strategically important, areas where illegal armed groups continue to operate."[51]

This new paradigm, which one military officer described as "a shift from total spectrum to total dimension warfare," also marked an important transformation in Colombia's security sector reform: the military and police willingly became purveyors of diverse services to Colombia's most disadvantaged populations.[52] From 2004 to 2010, the geographic coverage of AI activities increased from 46 to 69 percent of the country's municipalities, whereas red zones, those in which the military was actively involved in combat, decreased from 15 to 6 percent.[53] In the regions of the country where the Colombian government most heavily invested in AI activities, such as the Macarena mountain range, illicit crop acreage plummeted, school enrollment spiked, health outcomes improved, and homicides dropped.[54] Yet the sustainability of these gains varied from region to region. Rebecca Bill Chavez recalls that "a robust civilian surge did not follow the armed forces into the Macarena region," and soldiers continued to lead development projects for the local population.[55] All too often, civilian executive agencies, citing budgetary constraints, did not deliver as expected in priority zones, leaving the military and police to fill gaps and meet local expectations long after the establishment of CCAIs.

Even though the Ministry of Defense saw dramatic improvements in effectiveness and popular approval, Colombians still viewed related institutions less favorably than the security forces.[56] Despite criminal justice reforms, the country's major justice institutions registered unimpressive approval among the

Colombian population.[57] Whereas 41.3 percent of the population approved of the justice system's performance in 2005, 32.2 percent did in 2011 and 30.9 percent in 2015.[58] Judicial reform contributed to only a slight rise in the number of judges per hundred thousand inhabitants, and case backlog remained a debilitating problem, even though productivity increased by an average of 389 cases per judge per year.[59] Colombian citizens reported only 24 percent of crimes to authorities, reflecting a widespread lack of confidence in the effectiveness of the justice system. Of those crimes, 58.3 percent advanced beyond a formal inquiry or investigation in 2016, a noteworthy improvement from the 17.2 percent of cases that advanced in 2005 (see table 4.A.1).[60] Even under the new system, legal experts cited generous statutes of limitations to explain the system's torpor at investigating, hearing, and prosecuting cases. As of 2022, judges still took most cases to trial several years after the commission of the crimes in question.[61] Although Colombia's Constitutional Court "is the envy of the rest of Latin America for its quality and independence," levels of impunity from criminal prosecution in the lower courts remained extremely high.[62]

Overall, the security sector made strides in its effectiveness from 1999 to 2011. Security sector reform contributed to improved public perceptions about the major agencies of the sector. Not only did Colombians perceive their country as safer, albeit cautiously, but observers from abroad did also. Hotel occupancy, a common measure for tourism and, by extension, international perceptions of security, reached a high of 57 percent in 2019.[63] This improved national image also paved the way for a growing international recognition of the Colombian security sector's adaptability, professionalism, and proficiency. Indeed, the Colombian military and police have since deployed to Central America, Mexico, the Caribbean, and Afghanistan under a security cooperation program known as the US-Colombia Action Plan (USCAP), which pairs Colombian advisors with local security forces to devise strategies against transnational threats.[64] Between 2009 and 2013, Colombia provided training to 21,949 individuals from forty-seven countries in skills such as interdiction, police testimony, intelligence operations, and counterdrug raids.[65] In 2017, Colombia became Latin America's first and only North Atlantic Treaty Organization (NATO) partner, a rare, privileged place among the world's democratic militaries. On the heels of this announcement, Colombian military leaders insisted that their postconflict preparations and legacy of transformation would situate the country's security sector as Latin America's leader in defense and security matters by 2030.[66] The confidence that this ethos transmits is a far cry from the battered and bungling posture of the Colombian security sector in the 1990s and unquestionably embodies the promise of security sector reform.

Accountability

Despite great strides in the effectiveness of the security sector, the Colombian government's efforts to improve accountability produced mixed results. The justice sector still struggled to enforce the law writ large, including for crimes committed by military and police personnel. Additionally, the Colombian Congress, even with its constitutionally prescribed oversight role, did not fully embrace its prerogative as a check on the country's security agencies. In this context, the security sector's accountability, though improved, remained a major challenge for the security sector's credibility in the years that followed the drawdown of major US security assistance.

The 1991 Constitution, an effort to democratize Colombian society, led to an initial wave of reforms that reined in the military's traditional autonomy and enforced greater checks on its authority.[67] The minister of defense, a position previously occupied by a general, instead became a civilian appointee, and the ministry's civil service was expanded, generating nonuniformed expertise in security matters while increasing promotion opportunities for civilian employees. The Administrative Security Department (Departamento Administrativo de Seguridad, or DAS) intelligence service benefited from civilian leadership for the first time as well. Further, the new constitution created the Attorney General's Office (Fiscalía General de la Nación, or FGN) and a human rights ombudsman to serve as checks on executive abuses or overreach, including from within the security forces. The Inspector General's Office (Procuraduría General de la Nación, or PGN) also launched a security division to guard against abuse and corruption by monitoring the activities of the country's security forces. During the 1990s, a National Commission for Police Matters liaised with civil society to process complaints filed against police officers and supervise relevant investigations independently from the rest of the force. Although the commission was disbanded in 1997 based on the belief that it was performing tasks already part of other agencies' mandates, the rest of these institutions collectively became important watchdogs to enforce greater security sector accountability during Plan Colombia.[68]

Having independent oversight infrastructure in place was alone insufficient to temper the excesses of historically self-governing security forces. In the years immediately following the reforms, the Colombian military and police were responsible for worrisome abuses. In 1992, state security forces and associated paramilitary groups perpetrated the majority of politically motivated killings within the country. Moreover, the constitution retained clauses affirming the jurisdiction of military courts over crimes committed by members of the armed forces and even the National Police. Military courts seldom produced credible inquiries or fair trials, allowing ethically and legally compromised officials to remain in their posts.[69] A 1997 ruling of the Constitutional Court put an end to military jurisdiction over serious crimes, including crimes against humanity. But additional reforms to promote accountability would eventually require top-level political direction, beginning in earnest under the Pastrana administration, and new legislation.

One of the ways the executive and legislative branches in Colombia can take the security sector to task is by conditioning budgetary appropriations. However, given the gravity of the security challenges at the outset of Plan Colombia and the resources necessary to deliver security sector reform, the security sector benefited from large budget increases without conditions year after year, complementing the billions of dollars in technology, equipment, and training provided by Washington. Funding for the Colombian Armed Forces and National Police more than doubled as the Ministry of Defense's force grew from 231,000 personnel in 1999 to more than 481,000 in 2016.[70] But although this expanding budget funded specialized and technical training for a more capable military with better readiness and mobility, it rendered the security forces essential in ways that challenged efforts to exact more accountability.

As Bogotá devoted the necessary resources to sustain a larger force size, President Uribe and his cabinet placed extraordinary pressure on the military and police to produce results, but rather than drawing on the existing oversight infrastructure, officials relied on public displays of disapproval to correct bad behavior. Uribe's approach sometimes entailed ridicule in the media and undesirable reassignments for officers responsible for battlefield defeats or blunders. In issuing orders, he occasionally skipped the military chain of command and sometimes even the minister of defense by dealing directly with subordinate military commanders in the field. Marta Lucía Ramírez, Uribe's first minister of defense, also embarrassed the military by intentionally exposing a large military contracting scandal during her first months in the post, making public the "mafia that had infiltrated the highest ranks of the institution."[71]

These incidents put military and police leaders on the spot and reinforced subordination and compliance. Yet the personalized and even performative nature of this censure tended not to eliminate bad behavior within the ranks. Instead, it pushed some military and police personnel to go to greater lengths in covering their tracks when committing abuses or crimes. Further, given the centrality of security to Pastrana's, Uribe's, and Santos's governing strategies, Colombian presidents could not afford to publicly antagonize the military and police over every act of corruption or abuse, meaning that presidential oversight was limited. In the words of one Colombian officer, the executive came to be seen less as a check on the Ministry of Defense and more as "a defender of its institutional privileges" against the backdrop of an internal armed conflict.[72]

The Colombian Congress, for its part, tended to cede its oversight authority to the executive branch in matters of defense, and the legislature only sporadically took major steps to curtail the autonomy of the security services.[73] Most notably, the Senate inaugurated a new Committee to Monitor Intelligence and Counterintelligence Activities (Comisión de Inteligencia y Contrainteligencia) in 2013, following repeated scandals implicating the DAS in wiretapping the communications of members of the Supreme Court and civil society.[74] This response was the exception, though, not the norm. As former Vice Minister of Defense Jorge Mario Eastman noted, "The main prerequisite of Congress is to oversee the external debt. They get involved when we ask for money to buy weapons systems abroad. But they don't really say no."[75] In fact, from 1998 to 2018, a majority of congressional deliberations undertaken by the second committees of the Colombian Congress—those responsible for security and defense matters—focused on celebrations, honors, and monuments.[76] Colombian legislators routinely made use of the right to solicit information from the Ministry of Defense and to call representatives from the ministry to give congressional testimony, but even when the legislature advanced proceedings against defense ministers for scandals within the security sector, as in 2005 and 2007, the motions of censure failed to garner enough support to dismiss the ministers.

One area where the Ministry of Defense eventually improved its transparency was in publicizing information about spending via a US-Colombian collaboration known as the Force-Oriented Cost Information System, which helped Colombia's legislature better understand the security sector's spending priorities and intentions. However, during the peak years of Plan Colombia, the second committees were mostly interested in abiding by legislative procedure rather than deliberating over security matters.[77] Given the broad interparty consensus on security (see chapter 6), committees were, in the words of one analyst, "very much a rubber stamp" for the implementation of the executive's security strategy. Many legislators avoided scrutinizing the security sector because doing so did not translate into votes for reelection: military and police officers cannot vote, and challenging a security strategy that was so popular was, electorally speaking, unwise.[78]

Even though the legislature approves all promotions to the rank of admiral or general, debate about security in the legislative chambers during the peak years of Plan Colombia was minimal.[79] Seldom did legislators examine problems in the implementation of security policy, shortcomings in mission accomplishment, poorly conceived operations, or statistics relating to the handling of military abuses by the judicial branch.[80] They rarely if ever questioned the suitability of the executive's recommendations for promotion, abdicating their authority to exert influence over the security sector's leadership and thus performance.[81] Even as recently as 2017, one police officer noted that the Colombian Congress made only a few cosmetic changes to the draft document of a new police code, which greatly expanded the authority of police officers—in effect, granting the National Police carte blanche to devise and implement its own citizen security policy.[82] Legislative scrutiny also rarely extended to the human rights record of the Colombian Armed Forces. In fact, a coalition of conservative parties in the 2016 Congress unsuccessfully attempted to enlarge the role of the country's military justice system by affording it expanded jurisdiction over atrocities committed by military members, potentially reversing the 1997 ruling by the Constitutional Court.

Even though criminal courts retained jurisdiction in cases of human rights abuses and crimes against humanity committed by the military throughout the duration of Plan Colombia, the impunity rate for extrajudicial murders attributed to state agents remained at 98 percent in 2011.[83] Most worryingly, the Colombian government's initial approach to dealing with the excesses of the security sector on the human rights front was one of "rejecting the gravity of the phenomenon and hiding it; while presenting the victims [of these abuses] as delinquents or terrorists."[84] Even with increased attention to the security forces' worst excesses, as evidenced by mandatory human rights and international humanitarian law training for all uniformed members of the Ministry of Defense during Plan Colombia, human rights protections and justice for human rights abuses were lacking. A newfound restraint in the use of lethal force significantly decreased the risk of deadly contact with the security forces, but even so, the early years of security sector reform coincided with a rise in abuses against the civilian population, mostly committed by the army.

As of 2022, the extent of these excesses was only just coming to light.[85] Notably, major domestic and international scrutiny emerged from a 2008 scandal that implicated army officers and soldiers in the murder of civilians whose corpses were presented as insurgents killed in combat. These executions, which the military tallied to bloat its operational accomplishments, became known as false positives (*falsos positivos*), and senior army leadership, having covered up or ignored the practice, rewarded units with promotions, increased pay, and time off.[86] In 2005, Defense Minister Camilo Ospina issued Directive No. 29, prescribing financial rewards for the capture or killing of members of illegal armed groups. In the years that followed, accusations of military executions of civilians more than doubled, peaking in 2007 at 1,119.[87] Table 4.1 depicts the grim results of the decision to incentivize body counts.

From 2008 to 2018, the Attorney General's Office opened more than 4,750 investigations into suspected false positives and extrajudicial murders, but the lethargy of the courts delayed the delivery of justice in all but some eight hundred cases.[88] According to a 2015 report from the FGN, 5,137 officials potentially participated in extrajudicial murders since 1986, of which 923 were convicted at the time of the report's release; 862 members of the army received prison sentences.[89] Starting in 2020, the Special Jurisdiction for Peace (Jurisdicción Especial para la Paz, or JEP), which evolved out of the 2016 FARC peace accord, began to process 6,402 false positive cases spanning from 2002 to 2008.[90] In 2021, the JEP called eleven retired and active generals to provide testimony and even secured an appearance from former President Santos, who had been defense minister during the worst state-perpetrated violence and who asked for forgiveness from the victims' families. General Mario Montoya Uribe, a former commander of the armed forces accused of overseeing the alleged abduction and execution of as many as 104 civilians, declared himself innocent and blamed the massacres on inadequate training. As of 2022, however, Colombia's Truth Commission determined the false positives committed under Montoya's leadership to be crimes against humanity committed as official policy of the state.[91] Although Colombia's justice system has finally advanced investigations and convictions

Table 4.1. Reported Combat Kills and Extrajudicial Murder Investigations in Colombia

Year	Deaths Reported	Investigations	Percentage
2002	1,775	167	9.4
2003	2,113	220	10.4
2004	2,282	346	15.2
2005	2,067	349	16.9
2006	2,236	694	31.0
2007	2,703	934	34.6
2008	1,559	378	24.2
2009	635	60	9.4
2010	555	59	10.6
2011	406	52	12.8
Total	16,331	3,259	20.0

Source: Rojas & Benavides, 2017, pp. 65–66.
Note: Deaths also include insurgent and paramilitary fighters killed.

for these abuses, the torpor with which the Colombian government reacted to these accusations reveals a major deficiency in the security sector's accountability mechanisms.[92] Indeed, in 2016, the Inter-American Commission on Human Rights (IACHR) referred several cases of extrajudicial murder to the Inter-American Court of Human Rights (IACtHR), citing the Colombian government's failure to comply with a series of recommendations to expedite justice for false positives.

Yet even as violations of international humanitarian law and extrajudicial murders peaked from 2003 to 2007, the number of formal complaints that members of the public made against the security forces remained low. Given that abuses predominantly occurred in rural areas of the country where the Colombian military was typically the only permanent interface citizens had with the state, the communities most affected by violations of human rights lacked independent mechanisms to denounce abuses. Only later in Plan Colombia did accusations against security sector actors increase to levels more congruent with the kinds of accusations that evolved out of the false positives scandal, implying greater access to justice institutions and greater confidence to criticize publicly the security sector. One possible explanation for this shift is the sustained attention to outlying communities in routine and emergency municipal security consultations, presided over by the president or minister of defense, and the rapid growth of Justice Houses, which serve as "decentralized service units, information centers, and alternative dispute resolution mechanisms."[93]

Even though accountability for previous crimes remained elusive, steps were taken to prevent future abuses. In a promising turn of events, the false positives scandal led to the creation of new human rights organizational infrastructure. In 2010, Congress passed Law 1407 (Ley 1407 de 2010, Código Penal Militar), which reiterated the requirement that all human rights abuses and violations of international humanitarian law be processed in civilian courts. In 2011, the Colombian executive branch implemented new coordination mechanisms between the Ministry of Defense, the Human Rights Ombudsman, and the Attorney General's Office for the handling of suspected violations of human rights.[94] The Colombian Army also established in 2009 the Graduate School of Human Rights and International Humanitarian Law (Escuela de Graduados en Derechos Humanos y Derecho Internacional Humanitario).[95] This heightened awareness of human rights appeared to have had an influence on the conduct of the military and police in combat operations, as the number of accusations of extrajudicial murders dropped from thousands a year to double digits annually from 2009 to 2021. Even members of the FARC noticed a change in the way soldiers conducted themselves in combat. As one former FARC leader explained, "The false positives scandal was a mortal blow for the army because it caught the attention of the world. It was politically and psychologically problematic for the middle ranks operating on the ground, as they were afraid of inflicting civilian casualties. This affected their combat posture."[96] The sustainability of these changes after the drawdown of Plan Colombia, however, was a different question altogether, and a spate of high-profile accusations of police violence in 2021—a topic discussed at greater length in chapter 8—left some observers wondering whether the Colombian security sector had truly learned its lesson. But in the early years of the Santos administration, consensus domestically and internationally was that the Colombian military's and police's human rights doctrine was there to stay. One human rights official noted that Colombia was held to a very high human rights standard because the country's armed conflict required the application of international humanitarian law, "an amplifier of credibility" for the military because it provided an objective, external standard by which the institution's conduct could be evaluated.[97] And over time, the Colombian security sector demonstrated measurable improvements. On the other hand, the absence of an armed conflict in Mexico inhibited the development of similar legal standards to limit the use of violence by state security forces.

US pressure over human rights concerns proved crucial in making the topic more of a priority in the Colombian security sector. Compliance with human rights standards and improving the accountability of the security forces were consistent demands of US legislators in exchange for robust security assistance. Part of the monitoring and oversight of the Colombian military and police was inherent in the US contracting process. Transfers of equipment and technology from the United States to Colombia required an agreement between the two governments on how Colombian units intended to use the materiel, and the US Embassy employed hundreds of officials in the annual verification of transferred defense articles in an end-use monitoring program. More broadly, though, Washington administered a formal process of annual human rights conditionality dating back to 2000.[98] Under the agreement, the Department of State was required to annually certify that the Colombian government was meeting an acceptable standard of human rights based on its commitment to dismissing military and police members who commit abuses, investigating accusations of abuse and corruption by deploying Judge Advocate General officers to field units, delivering justice for military human rights violations in civilian courts, and severing ties between the security forces and paramilitary groups.[99] The US Congress waived this requirement in 2000, the first year of Plan Colombia, on national security grounds, but every year after Colombia received a positive certification, even though some international civil society organizations challenged the notion of any real progress.[100] Winifred Tate, for one, critiques the US government for merely creating new beneficiaries of aid or shifting resources to "clean" units instead of suspending security assistance when allegations of human rights violations surfaced.[101] Although the wholesale termination of security assistance would have prevented any unintentional complicity of the US government with Colombia's human rights abuses, it would have also removed Washington's most significant lever to help shape security outcomes and advance accountability within the ranks, simultaneously failing to resolve the human rights crisis.

Some activists, however, gave Washington credit for placing such considerable emphasis on human rights in the delivery of security assistance to Colombia. Colombian politicians and uniformed leaders, aware of the close US policymaker scrutiny they faced, took vetting of the security forces seriously and have historically taken actions to appease their US benefactors on the human rights front.[102] In fact, when Senator Patrick Leahy (Democrat-Vermont) became the chair of the Senate Appropriations Committee in 2006, Colombia's certification for human rights became a topic of persistent debate on Capitol Hill. The senator, who had previously spearheaded the regulations that govern vetting for beneficiaries of US security assistance, stipulated the release of aid in 2007 and 2008 on the Colombian government's delivery of justice in cases of military and police abuse.[103] Ultimately, the aid was not withheld, but the delay in delivering new equipment sent a strong signal to the Colombian military that, no matter its operational successes, its relationship with its closest partner was not unconditional, especially as accusations of false positives mounted.

Civil society organizations were another major check on the security sector, but given high rates of impunity for crime in Colombia, many leading activists felt exposed and vulnerable to manipulation and intimidation over the years of security sector reform. Homicides of members of vulnerable professions (unionists, local public officials, and journalists) dropped notably starting in 2002, indicating an increased capacity to protect such populations from armed threats through state-provided security details and a permanent presence of the security forces throughout the national territory.[104] However, civil society activism became especially challenging during the Uribe years, when the state's intelligence services reportedly "set out to destroy the human rights movement."[105] As one human rights defender insisted, "Uribe publicly accused us of abetting terrorism, infiltrated our organizations, intercepted our communications, issued death threats, and canceled our travel visas. Ours was a fight for survival, and our activism took a backseat."[106] The stigmatization of the profession in Colombia became so acute that in 2017 conservative voices in its Congress vehemently opposed the candidacy of human rights defenders to staff the JEP on the grounds that human rights defenders could not be impartial.[107]

Protecting civil society groups and investigative journalists remained a leading challenge for the Colombian government well beyond Plan Colombia—a reality that became apparent in the years following the 2016 peace accord, during which hundreds of social leaders and human rights defenders were murdered for their activism. In 2016, 77 percent of Colombians expressed doubt that the Colombian government was doing enough to protect human rights, and from 2009 to 2022, the annual number of human rights defenders threatened, attacked, and murdered rose.[108] Although the murder rate for members of the press dropped considerably during Plan Colombia and thereafter, threats and even armed attacks against the country's journalists, who are among the sole voices to contest official narratives and report from distant conflict zones, continued.[109] Against a backdrop of reduced yet persistent human rights abuses, slow and inconsistent delivery of justice, and the continued vulnerability of civil society in Colombia, the country's record on improving the security sector's accountability was decidedly mixed by the end of formal Plan Colombia programming in 2011. The military and police remained subordinate to civilian authorities, but all too often those officials failed to exert their prescribed oversight roles or vitalize existing oversight infrastructure. Thus domestic and international pressure over rights abuses was a primary mechanism through which accountability was addressed, giving birth to security assistance conditions, new use-of-force conduct in operations, better training with a human rights focus, and eventually convictions for the security sector's most egregious transgressions.

The Mérida Initiative and Security Sector Reform

Mexico, although characterized by familiar challenges, reflects different trends altogether. While the Institutional Revolutionary Party (Partido Revolucionario Institucional, or PRI) was at the helm of national politics until 2000, the party's leaders traditionally tolerated the activities of criminal organizations in exchange for nonviolence.[110] The security forces and justice system, rather than independently pursuing criminal actors, often acquiesced to this arrangement at the direction of political authorities, keeping violence levels low for decades.[111] This period in Mexican history is popularly known as the Pax PRIista, and save occasional outbursts of intercartel fighting, the government was largely able to keep a lid on insecurity without the state's coercive apparatus.[112]

The transition to democracy led to the collapse of these clientelistic arrangements, and party competition and the decentralization of political authority after the National Action Party's (Partido Acción Nacional, or PAN) 2000 presidential victory contributed to conflict over drug routes, or *plazas*, among the country's criminal groups. As Mónica Serrano highlights, "the weakening of presidential authority created a vacuum that was rapidly filled by both legitimate and illegitimate actors, including criminal groups."[113] It was in this context that the security and justice institutions confronted a real test of their abilities to meet the safety and justice requirements of the Mexican people rather than the dictatorial interests of a single-party regime.[114] However, as the Mexican state transitioned from authoritarianism to democracy, from collusion to confrontation with organized crime, the police and courts proved ill equipped to contend with the new wave of insecurity unleashed by a growing and increasingly atomized criminal threat.[115]

The reconfiguration of the criminal ecosystem also coincided with global shifts in narcotics trafficking. Colombian cartels, which had long controlled the drug supply chain of cocaine to the US market, found their international reach reduced due to the dogged pursuit and increased prosecution by Colombian and US law enforcement authorities in the Caribbean. In this unstable terrain, Mexican drug-trafficking organizations identified an opportunity for consolidation and control of the trade making use of trafficking routes in Central America and Mexico. In the late 1990s and early 2000s, these groups unleashed a violent campaign to exterminate or subdue competing drug clans in Mexican territory. The opening of the cocaine transshipment economy in Mexico raised the stakes for Mexican criminal groups, as profits surged five- to tenfold, and greater control of cocaine distribution enabled Mexican cartels to bribe police, military, and political officials at every level of government.[116] A windfall of profits also boosted the coercive capacity of the country's largest cartels, and criminal competition resulted in violence in border towns such as Tijuana, Nuevo Laredo, and Ciudad Juárez.

By 2006, the internal dynamic in Mexico had changed so dramatically that powerful and heavily armed drug cartels had begun to confront the state directly. The country's police forces were inept and in complete disarray, and the army was in crisis, having seen more than a hundred thousand desertions during President Fox's term.[117] By the time Felipe Calderón took office, it was clear that the only way to address citizen insecurity was by reforming the country's security institutions. One observer pondered, "The only tool left for the government to use against the cartels was the army. How do you reform the only institution that is capable of bringing the state back from the brink while accelerating its operations?"[118]

The security sector reform effort undertaken by Calderón and supported by the Mérida Initiative entailed an unprecedented reconceptualization of Mexico's security and justice bodies. But despite massive investments and a newfound strategic direction, Mexico's reforms improved neither the effectiveness nor the accountability of the security sector over more than a decade of attempted modernization and reorganization. The indicators in table 4.A.2 suggest a decline in public trust in the major institutions of the security sector and a worsening of crime data and victimization. The number of abuses ascribed to state agents skyrocketed. Even though the Mexican justice system transitioned to an accusatorial system starting in 2008, the inability of justice officials to hold state actors to account, let alone tackle a near-absolute impunity rate, left many Mexicans feeling pessimistic about the reforms—and about the future of their country writ large.[119]

Effectiveness

During the Mérida Initiative, rates for most crimes in Mexico increased noticeably, peaking around 2010 and 2011 and then dropping only to rise again by 2016. Alarmingly, Mexico witnessed a surge in violent crimes such as homicide and kidnapping after President Calderón declared war on drug cartels, which themselves became embroiled in a violent turf war from 2008 to 2012. This upward trend continued even after the end of the most intense cartel fighting. In 2019, Mexico's homicide rate reached its highest level since the tumultuous years of the Mexican Revolution a century earlier. From 2007 to 2017, Mexico's reported homicide rate tripled from 7.84 per hundred thousand inhabitants to 22.5. This contrasts with Colombia, where murders and terrorism increased at the outset of Plan Colombia but then steadily reduced over the course of security sector reform. In fact, in the years following the period of analysis, Mexico reported record rates of homicide even as kidnappings and extortions also rose—suggesting the overall inadequacy of the Mérida Initiative and associated security programs in addressing Mexico's violent crime problem.[120]

As in Colombia, when Mexican authorities intensified their campaign against cartels, illicit businesses became riskier and costlier, affecting the geographic reach and overall intensity of organized crime activity. High-profile massacres, which had become commonplace in heavily populated urban centers during the most intense years of the cartel wars, were rare by 2016. According to the Mexico Peace Index, the number of states with particularly visible and violent organized crime activity dropped from twelve in 2007 to three in 2016.[121]

Even so, cartels retained significant social and political influence in some regions, and from 2007 to 2017 organized crime groups increased poppy cultivation in areas of the country beyond the reach of government security forces by a factor of six (see figure 4.3). In 2017, poppy cultivation in Mexico reached some forty-four thousand hectares. The Mexican government stepped up efforts to interdict the ever-increasing supply of heroin in the country, but these interdictions only represented a small fraction of the heroin produced (see figure 4.4). For example, in 2018, Mexican forces captured some 589 kilograms—about 1,300 pounds—of heroin. For the same year, the US Office of National Drug Control Policy estimated that Mexico produced some 106 metric tons—or 230,000 pounds—of potential pure heroin.[122]

Mexico's heroin production and interdiction statistics do not tell the whole story, however. Mexico is also a critical transit country for cocaine exported from South America, and during the later years of the Mérida Initiative, cocaine seizures by Mexico's army dropped noticeably—at a time when cocaine hauls in neighboring transit countries remained high.[123] Furthermore, during the 2010s, the synthetic opioid fentanyl, which is a hundred times more potent than heroin, rose in popularity in the United States, and Mexico became an important transshipment and even production country for the drug.[124] Much

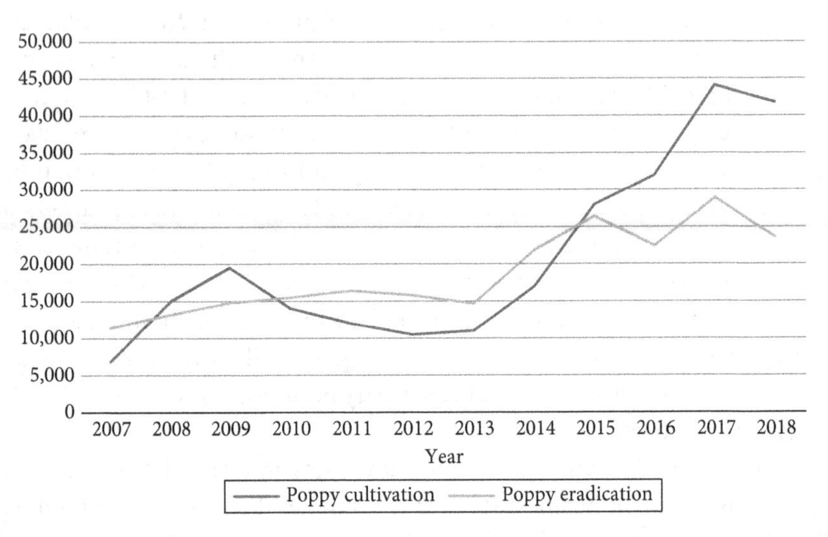

Figure 4.3. Poppy Cultivation and Eradication in Mexico (Hectares)
Source: Rosen & Ribando Seelke, 2020; UNODC, 2016; Frissard, 2020.

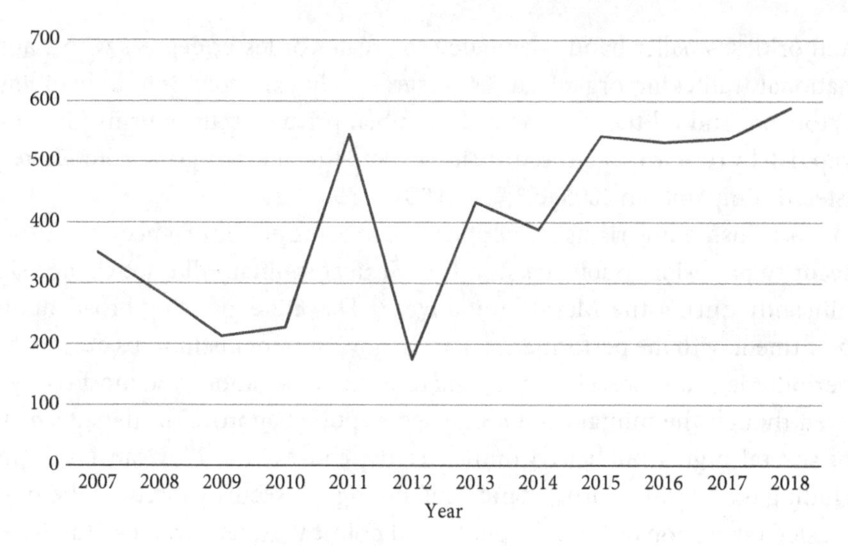

Figure 4.4. Heroin Interdiction in Mexico (Kilograms)
Source: México Unido Contra La Delinuencia, 2021.

to the disappointment of US authorities, Secretariat of National Defense (Secretaría de Defensa Nacional, or SEDENA) leadership was slow to admit that Mexico even has a homegrown fentanyl industry.[125] Mexican authorities' fentanyl seizures steadily increased by the late 2010s in response to increased US pressure. Mexican forces interdicted only about 16 kilograms of fentanyl in 2015, rising to 341 kilograms in 2018—a rather unremarkable result given the suspected pervasiveness of the drug in the country.[126]

More crime also translated into increased victimization in Mexico during the Mérida Initiative. Whereas in the mid-2000s the number of crime victims per hundred thousand inhabitants remained steady (just above ten thousand), that figure nearly tripled by 2016, 46 percent of Mexicans having fallen victim to crime or being related to a victim of crime. In 2016, more than 74 percent of Mexicans reported feeling unsafe in their states of residence, relative to 59 percent in 2007, and the perception of insecurity rose from almost 40 percent in 2008 to just over 48 percent in 2017. The percentage of the population that identified insecurity and delinquency as the country's most important problems corresponded with this mounting sense of insecurity over time. According to a 2016 government poll, 59 percent of the population perceived insecurity to be a paramount concern to other social problems, including unemployment, poverty, health, and corruption.[127] Even with a reduction in violence perpetrated by organized crime since 2012, petty crimes in cities rose, driving a sense of anxiety over personal safety.[128] "Local crime has become more predatory in nature. As the balance of power tipped away from state authorities, smaller bands—affiliated to greater or lesser degrees with transnational trafficking organizations—aggressively expanded into kidnapping, extortion, and oil theft."[129] As in Colombia, private security firms filled the gaps left by overwhelmed security forces, and the industry grew from 173 registered companies in 2005 to 3,977 in 2016.[130]

Notwithstanding rising crime and an increasing public reliance on nonstate security provision, public trust in the Mexican military did not change significantly during the Mérida Initiative.[131] Despite expressing broad disappointment with the performance of most government institutions during this period, Mexicans perceived the armed forces to be among the most trusted, even though the military did see drops in public approval in the aftermath of several highly publicized human rights abuses. The Mexican Navy (including the Marine Corps) stands out among the security forces as the most trusted institution by both the public and political leaders, who have assigned the most sensitive and daring operations to navy units. One human rights defender suggested that the military owed its popularity to savvy public relations campaigns that routinely profile the armed forces' operational achievements on television and radio outlets, whereas another analyst asserted that the military's ability to remain above partisan politics has given it a reputation as an impartial force in an increasingly polarized political climate.[132] Yet from the perspective of at least one US official who was one of the architects of the Mérida Initiative, the Mexican military became more proficient at targeting and detaining drug kingpins, something not reflected in crime statistics but that still helped boost the armed forces' image.[133]

Unlike in Colombia, interoperability among the security forces remained low, and lack of trust between the army and the navy was persistent. Both institutions proved reluctant to share intelligence and conduct joint missions with each other, let alone coordinate their public security work with law enforcement institutions due to the belief that sensitive information would end up in the hands of criminals. This latter hesitancy appears not to be unfounded, though, as opinion polls recorded a notable decline in public trust in the police over the years of security sector reform.[134] Moreover, across the security sector, the level of professionalism and restraint when dealing with suspected criminals and members of the public plummeted. In addition, a lack of publicly available information about the murder of civilians by the security forces potentially shielded the military forces from more pointed criticism and public rebuke. The number of civilians killed in relation to the number injured during confrontations with the armed forces and Federal Police, a figure known as the lethality index, rose noticeably after 2007, so much so that Mexican authorities ceased reporting this data in 2014.[135] This reversal in transparency was as clear a sign as any that the trajectory of security sector reform was in the wrong direction.

As the quality of security services deteriorated, recruitment for the security sector became difficult. Before Calderón's reforms, police were only paid on average $600 per month, $250 short of what was deemed adequate for meeting basic necessities.[136] In addition, a faster pace of public security operations caused by greater cartel activity required an increase in force size, but the number of security force personnel in relation to the population of Mexico remained considerably lower than in countries of comparable size and insecurity. Proportionally, the Colombian public security forces reported more than twice the personnel of the Mexican forces in 2016. In Mexico, higher standards accompanied some new recruitment strategies for the federal and state police forces during the Mérida Initiative, but more stringent entry requirements also limited the pool of qualified candidates. As a result, the number of police per hundred thousand inhabitants actually decreased following Calderón's initial reforms.[137] In response to these personnel shortfalls and in an effort to stamp out corruption, some Mexican police agencies began admitting more women, a reconfiguration that resulted in improved public trust in municipal police and a reduction in bribery accusations in places like Mexico City.[138] One researcher, however, highlighted that even though background checks and polygraphs have been applied to police forces across the country and especially at the federal level, the Mexican government has been unable to muster the political will to organize an independent police evaluation body.[139] This gap in oversight afforded some members of the police the ability to kidnap and kill alongside the cartels with impunity, worsening the country's crisis of forced disappearances.[140]

Calderón achieved a noteworthy restructuring of the national police forces by disbanding the Federal Investigative Agency and Federal Preventive Police and then creating two new forces: the Federal Ministerial Police (Policía Federal Ministerial, or PFM), tasked with fighting corruption and organized crime and housed in the Attorney General's Office (Procuraduría General de la República, or PGR), and the new autonomous Federal Police under the Secretariat of Public Security (Secretaría de Seguridad Pública, or SSP), responsible for arrests and investigations into federal crimes. Although for some crimes these two bodies had overlapping and even conflicting responsibilities, Calderón's new national-level police forces enjoyed budget increases, new technology and information-sharing capabilities, and new personnel standards to include clear protocols for promotion, discharge, vetting, discipline, and professional development.[141] However, the focus on recruiting the best and the brightest for the SSP denied the PFM large numbers of talented new recruits, even though the government's overall investigative capacity expanded and eventually improved case processing times.[142] Further, with Genaro García Luna at the helm of the SSP, the institution's spending increased twelvefold from 2008 to 2012, and new recruitment criteria attracted more highly educated candidates to join the force. The government intelligence agency known as the Investigation and National Security Center (Centro de Investigación y Seguridad Nacional, or CISEN), the US Federal Bureau of Investigation, and the American Association of Police Polygraphists all advised on the introduction of stringent vetting and background check practices. From 2006 to 2010, the federal police forces grew from just under thirteen thousand officers (12,907) to more than thirty-five thousand.[143] But for all these changes, public trust in the police only improved modestly from 2007 to 2016, and a series of high-profile incidents implicating Federal Police officers in shoot-outs, murders, and kidnappings prevented efforts to improve the image and professionalism of national law enforcement. Although the Federal Police were perceived as less corrupt than other police forces, they lagged far behind the armed forces in their perceived effectiveness.

Some police forces in the country made strides in improving gender inclusivity and attempted to foster better relations with the citizenry through community policing initiatives. Yet these accomplishments, which were typically contained to a small geographic area, had a negligible effect on the overall experience of citizen security in Mexico. Ironically, efforts to expand these models or to impose a national standard for community policing among municipal forces were met with fierce resistance from critics who argued that such changes could actually derail successful local models of policing, which derive their legitimacy in part from their local origins and identity.[144] In an act of compromise, the Peña Nieto administration respected the autonomy of subnational governments to raise and train their own police forces while reorienting federal funding and incentives toward crime prevention and social readaptation programs. In 2013, the newly inaugurated president, who had campaigned so pointedly against Mexico's drug war, pivoted toward prevention to distinguish his security strategy from the militarized approach of his predecessor; thus he assigned an annual budget of $20 million to implement crime and violence prevention strategies at the municipal level, coordinated by the newly created federal Subsecretariat for Prevention and Citizen Participation (Subsecretaría de Prevención y Participación Ciudadana).

However, the influence of partisan politics on national security decision-making, a topic explored at length in chapter 6, led to the politicization of resource distribution in the prevention program. Rather than focusing on the most at-risk municipalities in the country, the PRI's leaders, in a bid to shore up their bases of clientelistic support, ensured that Subsecretariat monies were spread across the national territory to more than a hundred municipalities.[145] Furthermore, the federal incentives scheme did not involve some of the most important municipal actors in the implementation of prevention strategies. The Subsecretariat only committed resources to local organizations engaged in prevention if they could match federal contributions—a requirement that in turn excluded most municipal civil society groups given the lack of sufficient finances to meet the government's entry threshold.[146] One former employee of the Subsecretariat reported, "There was no evidence in the country that a national initiative can have results at the local level without involving all of the local actors. . . . The prevention office was just paying lip service to a problem."[147] The disbursal of resources without any evidence-based impact analysis debilitated the first federal program to take prevention seriously, and corruption at the state level resulted in gross mismanagement of funds. Given these challenges, the prevention office achieved very little during its short time in existence, and the Subsecretariat's budget plummeted to zero by 2017.[148] The former director general for interagency coordination of the Subsecretariat, Eunice Rendón, lamented, "Prevention never became a state policy. It remained a presidential policy initiative, and people did not take it seriously."[149]

As in Colombia, the Mexican Armed Forces boast a long tradition of community-oriented services provision, but the Secretariat of National Defense and Secretariat of the Navy (Secretaría de Marina, or SEMAR) engaged in civic action in a more ad hoc fashion than their Colombian counterparts did over the periods of analysis. Roderic Camp notes that the Mexican military's deployment to outlying communities to deliver health services, education, infrastructure improvements, and food aid did not originate as a counterinsurgency measure but as a component of the military's revolutionary tradition.[150] As far back as 1921, the government justified the military's involvement in development whenever such activities had some connection, however vague, to military objectives. The armed forces have historically used their humanitarian and disaster relief work to demonstrate efficiency while boosting their public image. Nevertheless, SEDENA never systematically monitored or evaluated its interventions. Likewise, violence prevention was not the specific rationale for the military's civic action. Thus unlike Colombia's Integrated Action, the Mexican military's development-oriented work did not reflect reform as much as continuity, no matter the need for a differentiated approach focused on prevention.

Additionally, just as crime prevention strategies underwhelmed, reforms to the judiciary did not bring major improvements in delivering justice for crimes already committed. As in Colombia, trust in the justice system in

Mexico declined after the transition to the accusatorial legal model. Whereas 50.6 percent of the population expressed some confidence in Mexican justice in 2006, by 2017 only 36.5 percent did.[151] As one researcher stressed, "Prosecutors are entirely dependent on the political agendas of state governors. There has never been a transition to democracy in these institutions, and their structures and values are autocratic. Many also have strong ties to organized crime."[152] Mexicans expressed an increasingly negative perception of judicial independence even as the legal system transitioned from closed hearings to oral, transparent trials and corrupt federal prosecutors were purged during the Calderón administration.

During the final years of the Mérida Initiative, justice remained out of reach for most Mexicans. The national average of magistrates and judges per state in 2016 was 3.5 per hundred thousand inhabitants, less than half that in Colombia.[153] The international average is 16.2. The inability of the courts to process evidence and issue verdicts in a timely and transparent matter contributed to low reporting rates for crime and thus to rampant impunity. A 2016 report revealed especially dire statistics: only seven of every hundred crimes were reported to the authorities.[154] This resonates with similar data made available by the 2015 results of a government poll, which found that at least 93.7 percent of all crimes committed in Mexico went unreported, a number known as the *cifra negra*, or "dark figure" of crime.[155] The report also pointed out that the overall number of reported crimes resulting in convictions was at 4.4 percent.[156] When evaluated nationally and by region, the official impunity figure, taken alongside the *cifra negra*, suggested that nearly 99 percent of the crimes committed in 2016 went unpunished.

The reform of the Mexican criminal code relieved some pressure on the penitentiary system, as the number of pretrial detainees steadily decreased after 2007. In 2011, the Mexican Congress introduced pretrial release measures for detainees who could post bond, but as of 2015, more than 50 percent of all detainees had still not faced trial.[157] In 2016, overcrowding in prisons lingered around 30 percent, double the worldwide average.[158] Further, a 2011 report by the National Commission for Human Rights (Comisión Nacional de Derechos Humanos, or CNDH) concluded that crime syndicates controlled 60 percent of the country's penitentiary facilities.[159] The increase in jailbreaks is the most visible indicator of the level of control exerted by organized crime, as the number of escaped prisoners increased tenfold from 2007 to 2011.[160] According to one account, overwhelmed, underappreciated, and poorly compensated prison staff lack the incentives and support necessary to put their own lives at risk, resulting in a system that "exacerbates social conflicts and damages [all Mexicans]."[161]

As this panorama suggests, the effectiveness of the Mexican security sector shifted very little over the period of analysis. Rates for most crimes surged, public perceptions of security deteriorated, preventive measures failed to figure into the national agenda in any meaningful way, and the sweeping judicial reform did not furnish a reduction in impunity or greater efficiency. By some estimations, Mexico's security sector was more disorganized in 2017 than it was at the outset of the Mérida Initiative, and security, at least in the minds of most Mexicans, had only worsened. As of 2021, one-quarter of Mexicans reported being a victim of police corruption, nearly a third reported crime victimization, and more than half felt unsafe in their neighborhoods.[162] A US official familiar with Mexico's insecurity summarized the challenges this way: "The security sector in Mexico is broken. There is no joint staff, no civilian minister of defense, no integrated ministry for coordination among the forces. . . . The leadership of the sector is in a turf war for influence—all while the Mexican people suffer."[163]

Accountability

Unlike Colombia's, Mexico's transition to democracy was drawn out and delayed many of the structural reforms that would have engendered greater institutional oversight of the security sector. Colombia's 1991 Constitution, resulting from a political compromise with demobilized insurgent groups, overhauled the institutional architecture of the Colombian government. Mexican political liberalization was more incremental and involved the gradual introduction of mechanisms to check the autonomy of the security sector.[164] Despite the judicial reform from 2008 to 2016, Mexican courts struggled to curb the excesses of the country's security forces, and executive and legislative bodies did not assert oversight privileges in ways that curbed the autonomy of the military and police. One researcher highlighted, "The reforms that are occurring are structural but do not have a democratic component because there still isn't an institution that is above the rest and monitors corruption. Mexico is responding to a crisis, not conducting security sector reform."[165]

These inadequacies were sustained against a backdrop of generous and largely unrestricted spending on security and justice institutions starting in 2007. The major ministries and agencies of the Mexican security sector benefited from a windfall of national resources throughout the Mérida Initiative despite no concurrent increase in financial oversight. Moreover, unlike in the Colombian case, spending on the military and police significantly outpaced the budget expansion for the justice sector, supporting a perception that Mexican authorities emphasized the capture of criminals over the delivery of justice. According to Eduardo Bohórquez, head of the nongovernmental organization Transparencia México, the repressive apparatus of the state grew during the Calderón and Peña Nieto administrations, and enough judicial infrastructure to accommodate greater case volumes was in place. However, the Attorney General's Office and its team of prosecutors underwent adaptation to the new accusatorial system just as the demands being placed on the justice sector increased.[166] This shake-up sustained high levels of impunity for crimes, including those ascribed to state security forces. Additionally, the Mexican government never committed to a full overhaul of the PGR when it enacted a 2014 constitutional reform that replaced the PGR with a new National Prosecutor's Office (Fiscalía General de la República, or FGR). The Mexican Congress neglected to pass the constitutional and legislative reforms needed to establish and staff an independent FGR, instead automatically transferring PGR personnel to the FGR without retraining them for their new roles in a new institution.[167]

As in Colombia, the legislature scarcely exerted oversight of the security sector.[168] The two houses of Congress operated committees to investigate and check the autonomy of federal agencies, but for the armed forces and Federal Police, congressional debate extended to matters of security policy only, not appropriations or contracting.[169] The military budget increased year after year from 2007 to 2016, yet the security committees in Congress never published findings linking the budget increases to improvements in citizen security.[170] Congress also avoided sanctioning security forces accused of corruption or human rights abuses through institutional audits or investigations.[171] One analyst noted, "The Committee on Public Security (Comisión de Seguridad Pública) serves a mere supervisory function. It rarely has an active role in policy formulation, and it only meets to discuss how bills are to be presented to the Senate floor."[172] Another proclaimed, "The Bicameral Security Committee does not have any real power. There is zero accountability. Article 27 of the Constitution asserts that state security requests must first be presented to the Committee and then forwarded to the president for approval, but that just does not happen."[173] Furthermore, the military often conceals intelligence, personnel information, and operational details from legislators and the public on national security grounds, even though Mexico's Transparency Law (Ley Federal de Transparencia y Acceso a la Información Pública de 2015) is "on paper one of the most advanced in the world."[174] In 2013, army leaders even refused to release information about its purchase contracts for boots, citing a fear that making such information public would allow criminals to determine the total force size.

Considering this lack of transparency, security sector reform did not result in improvements in the public's perception of the accountability of the security forces. Despite high approval of the military among the population, which remained mostly unaffected, the public perception of corruption in SEDENA and SEMAR increased from 2011 to 2016 and remained steady for the Federal Police.[175] Not surprisingly, subnational police forces also suffered from low credibility. An estimated 62 percent of police forces nationwide had links to drug-trafficking organizations, and an astounding 57 percent of weapons issued to the police were used in illegal activities.[176]

The high perception of corruption may also relate to the fact that several human rights cases from the 2010s involving the military and police remained unresolved as of 2022. In fact, public complaints filed against members of the security forces for suspected human rights violations rose from just under three thousand (2,843) in 2007 to more than seven thousand by 2015. Between 2006 and 2009, SEDENA saw a 1,000 percent increase in human rights complaints.[177] Reports of torture by the security forces increased by 600 percent between 2003 and 2013, and kidnappings and disappearances implicating members of the military rose since their expanding involvement in the drug war starting in 2006.[178] One of the most high-profile incidents occurred in Ayotzinapa in the dangerous state of Guerrero on September 26, 2014, when six students from a teacher's training school were killed and another forty-three disappeared as they traveled to Mexico City to attend a protest. The armed forces continually claimed to have had no information about the abduction or subsequent massacre. But a 2022 investigation by the Interdisciplinary Group of Independent Experts (Grupo Interdisciplinario de Expertos Independientes, or GIEI) uncovered evidence that the military had been conducting surveillance of the students prior to and during the abduction. Had such information been shared promptly, the armed forces' communications intercepts could have been used to locate the students.[179] One survivor maintains that municipal police forces, the mayor of the town of Iguala, and the army all colluded with a drug cartel to murder and dispose of the student's bodies.[180] The Ayotzinapa tragedy attracted intense scrutiny of the security forces—and the political actors who defend them—in a way that resembled the aftermath of the 1968 Tlatelolco Massacre, in which the Mexican military killed as many as three hundred civilians in a Mexico City protest.[181] As of 2022, the Iguala police chief had been sentenced to prison, and after considerable delay, authorities finally arrested retired General José Rodríguez Pérez, commander of the local 27th Army Infantry Battalion when the tragic events occurred. Likewise, federal authorities opened a trial against Mexico's former attorney general and issued more than eighty arrest warrants in relation to the case.

Although composite numbers of extrajudicial murders at the hands of state actors remain publicly unavailable, several incidents are well known. Two notable cases occurred in Tlatlava, State of Mexico, where soldiers killed twenty-two civilians in 2014, and Tanhuato, Michoacán, where the Federal Police executed the same number in 2016. The UN Special Rapporteur on Extrajudicial, Summary, or Arbitrary Executions summarized in 2016 that "extrajudicial killings and excessive use of force by security officers persisted."[182] In 2016, the CNDH registered some ten thousand formal accusations of abuse by the army since 2006, finding that in more than one hundred cases military personnel committed serious human rights violations.[183] Laura Carlsen asserts, "The pattern that emerged clearly showed that human rights violations are a strategic and structural part of Mexico's security policy."[184] This became even more apparent in 2021, when Mexican authorities charged thirty marines for alleged participation in a string of forced disappearances in Nuevo Laredo, Tamaulipas, dating to 2018. This case stands out because it implicates SEMAR, the more trusted military force, but it also sheds light on what has long been considered a routine practice for wayward military units: minimizing public scrutiny by disappearing victims of extrajudicial murder.[185] Further, in a country where more than seventy-nine thousand people have gone missing since 2006, it is plausible that the tally of military and police abuses in the country is even higher than these infamous cases suggest.

One area in which the Mexican government made some progress was in complying with a 2011 Supreme Court ruling that required military members suspected of human rights violations to be tried in civilian courts. Starting as early as 2004, the Supreme Court began a process of reinterpretation of Article 57 of the Code of Military Justice, which protected the military's prerogative to try its personnel outside civilian courts thanks to a legal mechanism known as the *fuero militar*. The court's thinking evolved on this issue partially because of extensive mobilization by civil society.[186] But the real impetus for change came in the wake of the IACtHR's rulings in the cases of Castañeda Gutman and Radilla Pacheco, which laid blame on the Mexican military in two instances of forced disappearance. For one researcher, they represented a "before and after" in the Mexican human rights community, and in 2014, the legislature revamped the Code of Military Justice, stipulating that abuses committed by members of the military against civilians be processed by the civilian criminal justice system to prevent bias.[187]

Although the military code retained jurisdiction over cases involving abuses committed by military members against other military members and still reserved vast powers of search and seizure for military prosecutors and judges, the removal of the *fuero* has been one of the unmistakably positive advances made with respect to the security sector's accountability.[188] But as a practical matter, the removal of the *fuero* did not immediately result in reductions in impunity or heavier sentences.[189] One analyst stated that "the modifications to the *fuero* exist only on paper; it is still nearly impossible to prosecute members of the military for the abuses they committed."[190] This assertion is supported by the fact that civilian judges have tended to be as lenient in sentencing in military-related human rights cases as was the military justice system.[191] Federal prosecutors opened 217 investigations into alleged homicides by security forces between December 2012 and January 2018, obtaining convictions in only four cases.[192]

In accordance with a 2011 Mexican constitutional reform on human rights, the Mexican government increased the mandatory training of military and police forces on human rights protections.[193] Yet even though the Mexican government reported record numbers of abuse complaints in 2015, the 275,000-strong army was still dismissing on average fewer than one hundred soldiers per year for improper conduct.[194] Additionally, the security forces' purported intimidation of civil society remained a primary concern for human rights activists. From 2015 to 2016, the military and police services conducted more than nine hundred arbitrary detentions of human rights defenders.[195] These figures are consistent with public perceptions. In 2014, 57.8 percent of Mexicans considered grave human rights violations by the police and army in Mexico to be frequent.[196] Attacks on and murders of human rights defenders and journalists nationwide also increased during the Peña Nieto presidency, and in 2017, Mexico became the most dangerous country in the world to practice journalism outside of a war zone.[197] Media self-censorship in states wracked by violence and crime has been pervasive, and in this context nongovernmental actors who expose uncomfortable and unfavorable truths about the government, and especially its security forces, do so only at great risk to their lives.[198] Alarmingly, a civil society investigation revealed through leaked documents that the federal government or army allegedly continued to use spyware to hack into the cell phones of journalists and activists investigating human rights abuses as recently as 2021.[199]

As in Colombia, human rights protections in Mexico took center stage in discussions surrounding US assistance via the Mérida Initiative, but US pressure in Mexico was not as significant a factor in changing the security sector's approach to human rights as it was in Colombia. This result was likely due to the difference in US influence relative to Colombia and Mexico. US assistance represented nearly a third of Colombia's defense and security budget in 2000, but Mérida funding never exceeded a tenth of Mexican expenditures.[200] By the conclusion of both Plan Colombia and the Mérida Initiative, Colombia had received nearly three times more security assistance from the United States than Mexico had—at least seven times more on a per capita basis.[201] One observer noted, "We got what we wanted in Colombia more often because we meant more to them. The balance of power in Mexico was completely different, and at times we 'needed' them to accept the money more than they needed it [to advance our policy objectives]."[202]

Yet Sergio Aguayo, one of the country's leading human rights defenders, insisted, "The human rights protocols related to [Mérida Initiative aid] are ill-defined and ambiguous. . . . The US government puts money toward a reform that all parties know will not work, and Mexico accepts the money knowing that it will not necessarily be successful in improving human rights."[203] This ambiguity is in part a result of a compromise made between the US and Mexican governments. Unlike in Colombia, where annual certification was a requirement for the release of security assistance, President Calderón rejected US proposals to "certify" Mexico's performance with respect to human rights protections, citing concerns over sovereignty violations. Instead, Washington and Mexico City established a series of human rights dialogues that involved civil society actors and representatives of the security sector in the publication of an annual report to inform US decision-making on the release of funds to Mexico.[204] The practice of convening roundtables subsided after the early years of the Mérida Initiative, but civil society organizations continued to submit monthly reports to the Department of State over the duration of the Mérida Initiative. Separately, vetting under the Leahy Amendment's reporting requirements still applied to Mexican security force units receiving US funding and training, and each year the Department of State conditioned 15 percent of Mérida Initiative funds on Mexico's compliance with international human rights standards.[205]

In September 2010, the Department of State blocked $26 million until the Mexican government made progress on increasing transparency and decreasing impunity within the security sector. Similarly, in 2015, Washington withheld a nominal yet symbolic $5 million in aid following the Ayotzinapa massacre.[206] Executive Director of the Americas Division of Human Rights Watch José Miguel Vivanco remarked, "This is unprecedented. [The Department of State] has been systematically reluctant to use the leverage provided by law. What they have tended to emphasize is keeping the bilateral relationship as the principal objective, and human rights normally takes a back seat."[207] The revocation of security assistance sent a strong message to Mexican leaders that the eyes of the international community were fixed squarely on the government's willingness to deliver justice in extreme cases of violence and abuse. One observer, in fact, asserted that the US Embassy's signaling that the Mexican security forces were failing to meet international human rights obligations began to affect public opinion, which had the real potential "to force the hand of the political class toward compliance."[208]

This cautious optimism appears not to have come to fruition, though, given that Mexico's human rights crisis grew progressively worse during the final years of the Mérida Initiative. Overall, the Mexican government made minor progress in cultivating the accountability of the security sector. The main accomplishment of the reforms enacted over the decade of analysis was the reassignment of jurisdiction for human rights abuses committed by the military to the civilian criminal courts. But corruption, inexperience with the new justice system, and unprofessional investigative practices slowed the momentum in processing rising numbers of criminal cases nationwide and investigations into alleged human rights violations by security sector personnel.[209] These deficiencies and a culture of secrecy in the security sector fed staggering levels of impunity, and absent any real consequences for crime and abuse, some security officials continued to use intimidation tactics against civil society and the media. Predictably, violence and corruption were the most important themes of the 2018 presidential race, and although outsider Andrés Manuel López Obrador was most vocal in calling for a radical purge and reform of the national security infrastructure, his competitors coincided with him in raising the profile of accountability as a top electoral issue.[210]

In both elements of security sector governance, effectiveness and accountability, the Colombian security sector improved demonstrably, and by the conclusion of Plan Colombia, the security sector showed an enhanced ability to provide for citizen security, even though its answerability to the law and to civilian oversight remained inconsistent. Following 2011, the Colombian legal system managed to sanction errant and abusive elements of the security sector, but persistent threats to civil society activism warranted caution concerning the security sector's overall accountability. The Colombian case is a moderate success when understood within the broader literature on security assistance and security sector reform. In Mexico, on the other hand, the security sector was barely more effective at delivering citizen security in 2017 than it was in 2007, and the judiciary and legislature proved unable or unwilling to assert their authority over the country's military and police forces. Civil society, as well, faced increasing limits on its ability to hold the security sector to account and, as in Colombia, would benefit from greater protections provided by the Mexican government. Simply put, Mexico's attempt to reorganize, modernize, and professionalize the security sector disappointed, reflecting the limits of even generous security assistance.

Table 4.A.1. Indicators of Effectiveness, Colombian Security Sector

Indicator	1999	2000	2005	2010	2011	2016	2021
Public trust in armed forces[1]	40.0 (1998)[a]	51.3[a]	63.1[a]	55.2[a]	56.6[a]	Female: 49.7 Male: 59.7 Total: 54.8[b]	48.0[a]
Public trust in police[1]	32.1 (1998)[a]	41.2[a]	52.3[a]	46.8[a]	42.0[a]	Female: 38.8 Male: 31.1 Total: 34.9[b]	37.0[a]
Public trust in judiciary[1]	29.0 (1998)[a]	37.9[a]	41.3[a]	34.0[a]	32.2[a]	Female: 28.7 Male: 26.8 Total: 27.7[b]	23.0[a]
Public trust in PGN	—	—	58.6[b]	58.9[b]	59.5[b]	Female: 29.3 Male: 33.0 Total: 31.2[b]	34.0[c]
Public trust in FGN	—	—	61.6[b]	61.9[b]	61.7[b]	—	27.0[c]
Perceives country to be insecure (%)	—	—	41.7[b]	39.3[b]	40.4[b]	51.2[b]	51.5[b]
Feels insecurity or delinquency are country's most important problem (%)	—	—	4.9[a]	12.9[a]	14.5[a]	18.4[b]	13.0[c]
Feels armed conflict or war on terrorism are country's most important problem (%)[2]	—	—	44.1[b]	28.0[b]	28.5[b]	17.0[a]	—
Colombia Peace Index score[3]	—	—	2.8 (2007)[e]	2.7[e]	2.7[e]	2.8[e]	2.7[e]
Victimized by at least one crime or related to a victim of a crime (%)	34.5 (1998)[a]	34.0 (2001)[a]	36.7[a]	31.5[a]	37.7[a]	34.0[a]	—
Reported homicides per 100K inhabitants	64.7[f]	71.0[f]	42.9[f]	38.9[f]	35.0[f]	25.2[f]	26.8[g]
Reported kidnappings per 100K inhabitants[4]	8.0[g]	8.8[g]	1.9[h]	0.6[h]	0.7[h]	0.4[g]	0.3[g]
Estimated kidnappings per 100K inhabitants	8.4[i]	8.8[i]	3.0[i]	2.7[i]	0.7[j]	0.4[j]	—
Estimated extortions per 100K inhabitants[4]	2.8[g]	2.9[g]	4.2[g]	2.9[g]	3.9[g]	10.1[g]	15.7[k]
Violent crimes per 100K inhabitants[5]	184.5[g]	176.4[g]	144.7[g]	235.1[g]	240.6[g]	454.8[g]	—
Acts of terrorism against civilian population and private sector interests	1,194[g]	1,549[g]	612[g]	472[g]	571[g]	224[g]	232[g]
Acts of subversion against police personnel and facilities	437[g]	414[g]	195[g]	131[g]	152[g]	56[g]	338 (2020)[g]

Registered victims of conflict	332,932[l]	681,095[l]	530,049[l]	218,161[l]	258,926[l]	105,910[l]	148,287[l]
Victims of terrorist acts[6]	2,815[l]	3,517[l]	1,953[l]	1,524[l]	3,523[l]	925[l]	486[m]
Victims of internal forced displacement	275,868[l]	603,231[l]	479,475[l]	196,470[l]	233,696[l]	96,953[l]	73,971[n]
Victims of forced disappearance	8,499[l]	11,726[l]	6,962[l]	1,400[l]	1,275[l]	70[l]	16[o]
Number of victims of antipersonnel mines	82[l]	157[l]	914[l]	933[l]	760[l]	77[l]	152[p]
Members of illegal armed groups arrested[7]	1,236[g]	1,556[g]	8,093[g]	1,737[g]	1,976[g]	1,237[g]	—
Individual members of illegal armed groups demobilized	68[g]	173[g]	2,564[g]	2,446[g]	1,528[g]	934[g]	144[o]
Security force personnel per 100K inhabitants based on World Bank reporting	636.8[g]	579.4[g]	863.9[g]	927.7[g]	970.7[g]	996.9[g]	857.3[g]
National police per 100K inhabitants[8]	241.7[g]	235.5[g]	296.6[h]	337.1[h]	343.4[h]	376.6[g]	334.5[g]
Females in national police (%)	—	—	6.7[h]	4.8[h]	5.5[h]	9.0[g]	18.1 (2022)[g]
Females in armed forces (%)	7.4[g]	—	—	—	10.6 (2013)[g]	3.0[h]	—
Estimated total crimes formally reported to government authorities (%)	20–27 (1985–2003)[f]	—	—	—	18.5 (2013)[f]	24.0 (2017)[q]	27.1 (2020)[r]
Reported crimes that never advanced beyond formal inquiry or investigation (%)	—	—	82.8[s]	86.9[s]	83.6[s]	58.3[s]	—
Magistrates and judges per 100K inhabitants	—	—	8.9[h]	10.0[h]	10.0[h]	11.4 (2015)[h]	5.7 (2017)[h]
Prisoners untried or in pretrial detention (%)	42.7[s]	40.8[s]	38.5[h]	30.7[h]	27.2[h]	32.6[s]	33.9 (2018)[h]
Penitentiary overpopulation beyond facility capacity	43.2[s]	35.6[s]	42.2[s]	24.3[s]	32.2[s]	56.5[s]	44.9[h]
Penitentiary officers per 100 inmates	—	—	13.4[h]	17.0[h]	15.8[h]	—	30 (2017)[h]
Hectares of coca cultivation	160,120[s]	163,290[s]	85,750[s]	61,811[s]	63,765[s]	146,140[s]	143,000 (2020)[t]

(*continued*)

Table 4.A.1. Continued

Indicator	1999	2000	2005	2010	2011	2016	2021
Hectares of poppy cultivation	—	4,273 (2001)[s]	1,950[s]	341[s]	338[s]	462[s]	600 (2019)[u]
Potential pure cocaine production (metric tons)	—	700 (2001)[v]	645 (2004)[w]	329[x]	273[x]	775[x]	936 (2019)[m]
Cocaine seizure at US southwest border (kilograms)	—	—	22,653[w]	13,797[x]	14,591[x]	10,700[x]	10,653 (2019)[x]

Source: Author's tabulation.
Notes: For detailed sourcing, see table 4.A.5.

1. A lot or some trust expressed.
2. 2021 figure unavailable due to data reporting changes.
3. Scale 1 (most peaceful) to 5 (least peaceful).
4. Based on World Bank population reporting.
5. Based on World Bank population reporting; defined as crimes committed with a firearm; 2021 figure unavailable due to data reporting changes.
6. 2021 figure covers victims of explosive artifacts, including those affected by antipersonnel mines.
7. Public reporting in 2021 referred to members of illegal armed groups "neutralized," encompassing arrests, demobilizations, and deaths.
8. UN reports changes in definition or counting rules.

Table 4.A.2. Indicators of Effectiveness, Mexican Security Sector

Indicator	2007	2008	2011	2015	2016	2021
Public trust in armed forces[1]	64.3[a]	57.4[a]	54.9[a]	58.7[a]	64.8 (2017)[b]	SEMAR: 90.2 SEDENA: 87.8[c]
Public trust in the police[2]	32.6[a]	23.4[a]	18.9[a]	24.0[a]	31.4 (2017)[b]	22.0[a]
Public trust in Federal Police/National Guard[3]	37.0[d]	33.0[e]	55.4[f]	56.2[g]	65.1[h]	82.7[c]
Public trust in state judicial/ministerial police[2]	16.0[d]	14.0[e]	38.2[f]	42.4[g]	55.5[h]	57.7[c]
Public trust in preventative municipal police/local police[2]	24.0[d]	25.0[e]	36.0[f]	36.0[g]	50.2[h]	55.1[c]
Public trust in transit police[2]	14.0[d]	14.0[e]	32.9[f]	31.3[g]	43.6[h]	47.2[c]
Public trust in judicial power[2]	31.7[a]	25.1[a]	25.6[a]	23.9[a]	36.5 (2017)[b]	24.0[a]
Public trust in public ministry[2]	22.0[d]	22.0[e]	36.9[f]	41.5[g]	49.9[h]	57.7[c]
Civilians killed in relation to number injured during confrontations with armed forces[4]	1.6[i]	2.8[i]	9.4[i]	7.7 (2013)[i]	11.6 (2014)[i]	—
Civilians killed in relation to number injured during confrontations with Federal Police[4]	—	2.7[i]	4.7[i]	20.0 (2013)[i]	4.6 (2014)[i]	—
Feels unsafe in neighborhood (%)	45.2 (2006)[b]	39.9[b]	43.1 (2012)[b]	51.6 (2014)[b]	48.1 (2017)[b]	52.0[b]
Feels that insecurity and delinquency are country's most important problem	12.9[a]	32.6[a]	38.5[a]	27.3[a]	30.0[a]	58.9[c]
Feels unsafe in states of residence	59.0[d]	65.0[e]	66.6[f]	72.4[h]	74.3[j]	75.6[c]
Mexico Peace Index Score[5]	2.1[k]	2.3[k]	2.6[k]	2.2[k]	2.3[k]	3.6[k]
Crime victims per 100K inhabitants	10,482[d]	12,000[e]	24,499[f]	28,202[g]	28,788[j]	23,520 (2020)[c]
Victimized by at least one crime or related to a victim of a crime or both (%)	39.1[a]	42.2[a]	41.5[a]	57.2[a]	46.0[a]	28.4 (2020)[c]
Reported homicide per 100K inhabitants	7.8[l]	12.2[l]	22.6[l]	16.4[l]	16.2 (2016), 22.5 (2017)[m]	26.6[k]
Reported kidnappings per 100K Inhabitants	0.4[k]	0.8[k]	1.1[k]	0.9[k]	0.9[n]	0.4[n]

(continued)

Table 4.A.2. Continued

Indicator	2007	2008	2011	2015	2016	2021
Estimated kidnappings per 100K inhabitants	1.3[k]	2.7[k]	4.6[k]	3.4[k]	3.6[k]	4.8[k]
Estimated extortions per 100K inhabitants	30.5[k]	46.9[k]	43.8[k]	52.7[k]	52.4[k]	73.5[k]
Organized crime offenses per 100K inhabitants	106.0[k]	115.4[k]	85.3[k]	63.3[k]	63.1[k]	63.8[k]
Violent crimes per 100K inhabitants[6]	4,134[k]	4,258[k]	4,510[k]	3,272[k]	2,972[k]	3,180[o]
Armed forces personnel per 100K inhabitants[7]	255.8[p]	268.2[p]	276.9[p]	266.9[p]	263.6[p]	—
Police per 100K inhabitants[8]	20.2[l]	29.4[l]	358.3[l]	301.0[l]	231.0[o]	—
Females in Federal Police forces (%)	—	—	10.9[l]	13.6[l]	—	16.8 (2020)[r]
Females in state police forces (%)	—	—	18.4[q]	20.2[q]	—	24.1 (2019)[s]
Females in armed forces (%)	3.3 (2006)[t]	—	5.0[f]	—	5.8[t]	11.7[t]
Total crimes formally reported to government authorities (%)	21.0[c]	22.0[e]	—	—	—	10.1 (2020)[c]
Total crimes that result in a formal inquiry or investigation by authorities (%)	13.0[c]	15.0[e]	8.4[f]	6.3[g]	6.4[i]	6.7 (2020)[c]
"The dark figure of crime" (*cifra negra*)[9]	87.0[c]	85.0[e]	91.6[f]	93.7[g]	93.6[i]	93.3 (2020)[c]
Magistrates and judges per 100K inhabitants	—	—	4.0[l]	4.4[l]	—	2.2[k]
Prisoners untried or in pretrial detention (%)	70.7[l]	67.3[l]	56.9[l]	50.6[l]	—	24.1 (2020)[l]
Penitentiary overpopulation beyond facility capacity	28.2[u]	28.2[u]	22.7[u]	25.4[u]	-2.8[u]	2.9[v]
Penitentiary officers per 100 inmates	—	—	19.5[l]	16.7[l]	—	18.7 (2020)[r]
Hectares of poppy cultivation	6,900[l]	15,000[l]	12,000[l]	26,100[l]	24,800[p]	21,500 (2020)[w]
States with organized crime score exceeding 4 on scale of 5[10]	9[k]	12[k]	5[k]	2[k]	3[k]	2[k]

Methamphetamine seizures at US border (kilograms)	1,860[x]	2,201[x]	10,969 (2013)[x]	16,351[x]	21,081[x]	68,355 (2019)[x]
Potential pure heroin production (metric tons)	18[x]	38[x]	42 (2014)[y]	70[z]	81[z]	78 (2019)[z]
Heroin seizure at US southwest border (kilograms)	404[x]	556[x]	1,855 (2012)[y]	2,140[z]	1,690[z]	2,580 (2019)[z]

Source: Author's tabulation.

Notes: For detailed sourcing, see table 4.A.6.

1. A lot or some trust expressed by respondents. Data from Latinobarometro (a) puts the trust in the armed forces at 48 percent in 2020, but polls conducted by the Mexican government's National Institute of Statistics and Geography (Instituto Nacional de Estadística y Geografia, or INEGI) contradict this percentage by a significant margin.
2. A lot or some trust expressed.
3. A lot or some trust expressed. The Federal Police disappeared in 2019 with the enactment of the National Guard Law. Its responsibilities and personnel were transferred to the National Guard.
4. Mexican government ceased reporting "lethality index" in 2014.
5. Scale 1 (most peaceful) to 5 (least peaceful).
6. Based on World Bank population reporting.
7. Based on World Bank population reporting. 2021 was excluded due to inconsistent reporting about the number of SEDENA and SEMAR personnel transferred to the National Guard.
8. 2007 and 2008 reflect Federal Preventative Police; 2011, 2015, and 2016 reflect the total number of police nationwide. 2021 was excluded due to the introduction of SEDENA and SEMAR personnel into the National Guard, which replaced the Federal Police.
9. The amount of unreported or undiscovered crime.
10. Scale 1 (most peaceful) to 5 (least peaceful) (out of thirty-two states).

Table 4.A.3. Indicators of Accountability, Colombian Security Sector

Indicator	1999	2000	2005	2010	2011	2016	2021
Number of public complaints filed against members of the security forces for supposed human rights violations[1]	MOD: 1,273 Other: 32 INPEC: 348[y]	—	MOD: 48 Other: 0 INPEC: 25[y]	MOD: 337 Other: 13 INPEC: 33y	MOD: 389 Other: 19 INPEC: 46[y]	MOD: 817 Other: 439 INPEC: 416[y]	—
Deceased persons as a result of contact or confrontation with the security forces	—	997 (2003)[g]	1,025[g]	446[g]	324[g]	238[g]	—
Violations of international humanitarian law[2]	1,837[z]	2,487[z]	1,355[z]	909[z]	1,389[z]	—	1,472[z]
Open extrajudicial execution investigations	—	—	—	2,336[aa]	1,622[aa]	2,316[aa]	2,535[bb]
Sentences for extrajudicial execution investigations[3]	—	—	—	103[aa]	148[aa]	133[aa]	—
Extrajudicial execution complaints filed against the army	75[cc]	194[cc]	450[cc]	53[cc]	—	—	—
Municipal security consultations[4]	—	0 (2003)[g]	0[g]	6,141[g]	6,821[g]	6,467[g]	—
Justice Houses (community conflict resolution)	—	24 (2002)[s]	40[s]	59[s]	77[s]	105[s]	114[s]
Human rights defenders murdered	—	—	32 (2009)[s]	32[s]	49[s]	51[s]	145[dd]
Human rights defenders attacked but not murdered	—	—	17 (2009)[s]	10[s]	50[s]	32[s]	44 (2018/19)[s]
Human rights defenders threatened	—	—	99 (2009)[s]	109[s]	140[s]	225[s]	1,351 (2018/19)[s]
Journalists murdered	7[ee]	8[e]	2[ee]	2[ee]	1[ee]	0[ee]	1[ff]
Business professional's perception of judicial independence[5]	—	—	3.2[gg]	3.5[gg]	3.5[gg]	2.9[gg]	2.9 (2019)[gg]
Uniformed personnel receiving training in human rights[6]	—	—	—	118,735 (2009)[g]	346,724 (2013)[g]	250,000[g]	488,181[k]
Spending on armed forces and police as percentage of GDP	3.8[hh]	3.0[hh]	3.4[hh]	3.6[hh]	3.1[hh]	3.4[hh]	3.4 (2020)[hh]

Source: Author's tabulation.
Note: For detailed sourcing, see table 4.A.5.

1. *Other* refers to state security agencies that are not part of the Ministry of Defense (MOD).
2. Committed by all armed actors.
3. 2021 data unavailable due to change in judicial processing with the Special Jurisdiction for Peace.
4. Local government and citizenry present.
5. Scale 1 (least independent) to 7 (most independent).
6. 2021 figure dates from June 2020 through May 2021.

Table 4.A.4. Indicators of Accountability, Mexican Security Sector

Indicator	2007	2008	2011	2015	2016	2021
Public complaints filed against members of the security forces for human rights violations[1]	2,843[u]	3,476[u]	4,378[u]	7,881[u]	7,658[u]	—
Public perception of corruption in the armed forces[2]	—	—	Navy: 15.8 Army 22.5[f]	Navy: 17.3 Army: 25.1[g]	Navy: 19.7 Army: 25.1[h]	Navy: 19.4 Army: 24.8[c]
Public perception of corruption in the Federal Police/National Guard[3]	—	—	57.0[f]	54.6[g]	55.3[h]	26.2[c]
Public perception of corruption in the state judicial ministerial police[2]	—	—	69.7[f]	62.4[g]	63.3[h]	59.8[c]
Public perception of corruption in the preventative municipal police[2]	—	—	71.6[f]	66.5[g]	66.7[h]	65.5[c]
Public perception of corruption in the transit police[2]	—	—	83.1[f]	77.9[g]	76.1[h]	73.9[c]
Public perception of corruption among judges (%)[2]	—	—	66.3[f]	65.6[g]	65.1[h]	65.4[c]
Public perception of corruption in the public ministry[2]	—	—	69.7[f]	64.8[g]	65.8[h]	62.4[c]
Public perception of corruption in the PGR/FGR	—	—	—	59.2[g]	59.6[h]	54.8[c]
Human rights defenders murdered	3[aa]	6[aa]	20[aa]	18[aa]	36[aa]	25[aa]
Aggressions against human rights defenders	—	—	224[aa]	971[aa]	938[aa]	1,659 (2020)[aa]
Arbitrary detentions of human rights defenders	23[aa]	262[aa]	90[aa]	570[aa]	375[aa]	249[aa]
Journalists murdered	11[bb]	13[bb]	10[bb]	11[bb]	13[bb]	7[cc]
Business professional's perception of judicial independence[4]	3.6[dd]	3.4[dd]	3.2[dd]	3.1[dd]	3.1[dd]	—
SEDENA personnel receiving training in human rights[5]	48,197[t]	—	196,316[t]	64,517[t]	208,004[t]	—
SEDENA personnel dismissed for improper conduct	118[t]	89[t]	123[t]	87[t]	69[t]	—
Spending on armed forces as percentage of GDP	0.5[p]	0.4[p]	0.6[p]	0.7[p]	0.6[p]	0.6 (2020)[ee]
Federal spending on public security as percentage of GDP[6]	0.2[gg]	0.3[gg]	0.8[gg]	0.9[gg]	0.8[gg]	1.0[ff]

Source: Author's tabulation.
Note: For detailed sourcing, see table 4.A.6.
1. Annual public reporting for complaints stopped in 2018.
2. Perceived as corrupt or somewhat corrupt.
3. Perceived as corrupt or somewhat corrupt. The Federal Police disappeared in 2019 with the enactment of the National Guard Law. Its responsibilities and personnel were transferred to the National Guard.
4. Scale 1 (least independent) to 7 (most independent).
5. Numbers reflect fiscal year totals (not based on calendar year); includes international humanitarian law training.
6. Encompasses budgets for all secretariats and agencies that have a role in public security, including armed forces.

Table 4.A.5. Index: Colombia

Letter	Source
a	Latinobarometer, www.latinobarometro.org
b	LAPOP, https://www.vanderbilt.edu/lapop/index.php
c	Invamer 2021, https://www.valoraanalitik.com/wp-content/uploads/2021/05/2021-05-Invamer-Poll.pdf
d	LaFM, https://www.lafm.com.co/colombia/la-gran-encuesta-asunto-del-pais-que-mas-le-preocupa-los-colombianos
e	Global Peace Index, http://maps.visionofhumanity.org/#/page/indexes/global-peace-index
f	ECSC 2017, https://formularios.dane.gov.co/Anda_4_1/index.php/catalog/532/overview
g	Ministerio de Defensa, https://www.policia.gov.co/dijin
h	UNODC, https://data.unodc.org/#state:0
i	Centro Nacional de Memoria Histórica, http://www.centrodememoriahistorica.gov.co/informes
j	País Libre, http://www.elpais.com.co/judicial/en-el-2012-fueron-secuestradas-305-personas-en-colombia-segun-la-fundacion-pais-libre.html
k	Ministro de Defensa 2020-21, https://www.mindefensa.gov.co/irj/go/km/docs/pccshrcontent/Recursos%20MDN/Plantillas%20Documentos/Ministerio/CentroDocumentos/InformesAlCongreso/Recursos/memorias2020-2021.pdf
l	Red Nacional de Información, https://rni.unidadvictimas.gov.co/
m	ICRC 2022, https://www.icrc.org/es/document/balance-humanitario-colombia-2022-dih
n	OCHA 2021, https://reliefweb.int/report/colombia/colombia-impacto-y-tendencias-humanitarias-entre-enero-diciembre-de-2021-08-de
o	Datos Abiertos 2022, https://www.datos.gov.co/Inclusi-n-Social-y-Reconciliaci-n/Sistema-de-Informaci-n-de-Eventos-de-Violencia-del/c59y-p4sz/data
p	Gobierno de Colombia 2022, http://www.accioncontraminas.gov.co/Estadisticas/estadisticas-de-victimas
q	Ethos: Descifrando el Gasto Público en Seguridad, https://ethos.org.mx/es/ethos-publications/reporte-ethos-descifrando-gasto-seguridad/
r	ESCS 2020, https://www.dane.gov.co/files/investigaciones/poblacion/convivencia/2020/Bol_ECSC_2020.pdf
s	Ministerio de Justicia, http://www.minjusticia.gov.co/
t	UNODC 2020, https://www.unodc.org/documents/crop-monitoring/Colombia/Colombia_Monitoreo_de_territorios_afectados_por_cultivos_ilicitos_2020.pdf
u	Semana 2022, https://www.semana.com/mejor-colombia/articulo/en-la-gastronomia-y-la-industria-nacional-de-farmacos-estarian-las-oportunidades-para-explorar-usos-licitos-de-la-amapola-como-lo-han-hecho-paises-europeos/202104/
v	DEA 2007, https://www.justice.gov/archive/ndic/pubs21/21137/21137p.pdf
w	DEA 2010, https://www.justice.gov/archive/ndic/pubs38/38661/38661p.pdf
x	DEA 2020, https://www.dea.gov/sites/default/files/2021-02/DIR-008-21%20 2020%20National%20Drug%20Threat%20Assessment_WEB.pdf

Table 4.A.5. Continued

Letter	Source
y	Defensoría del Pueblo, http://www.defensoria.gov.co/es/public/Defensor/454/Informes-al-congreso.htm
z	CINEP, http://www.cinep.org.co/
aa	OHCHR, http://www.hchr.org.co/index.php/informes-y-documentos/informes-anuales
bb	US Department of State, https://www.state.gov/wp-content/uploads/2022/03/313615_COLOMBIA-2021-HUMAN-RIGHTS-REPORT.pdf
cc	CCEEU, http://coeuropa.org.co/
dd	Defensoría del Pueblo, https://www.defensoria.gov.co/es/nube/comunicados/10697/Un-total-de-145-l%C3%ADderes-sociales-y-defensores-de-derechos-humanos-fueron-asesinados-en-2021.htm
ee	Semana 2022, http://especiales.semana.com/periodistas-asesinados/
ff	CPJ, https://cpj.org/data/killed/americas/colombia/?status=Killed&motiveConfirmed%5B%5D=Confirmed&type%5B%5D=Journalist&cc_fips%5B%5D=CO&start_year=2021&end_year=2022&group_by=location
gg	World Economic Forum, https://www.weforum.org/
hh	World Bank, https://data.worldbank.org/

Source: Author's tabulation.

Table 4.A.6. Index: Mexico

Letter	Source
a	Latinobarometer, www.latinobarometro.org
b	LAPOP, https://www.vanderbilt.edu/lapop/index.php
c	ENVIPE 2021, https://www.inegi.org.mx/contenidos/programas/envipe/2021/doc/envipe2021_presentacion_nacional.pdf
d	ENSI 2008, https://drcureces.files.wordpress.com/2009/12/icesi-5a-encuesta-nacional-sobre-inseguridad.pdf
e	ENSI 2009, http://internet.contenidos.inegi.org.mx/contenidos/Productos/prod_serv/contenidos/espanol/bvinegi/productos/metodologias/est/io_ENSI-6_2009.pdf
f	ENVIPE 2012, http://internet.contenidos.inegi.org.mx/contenidos/Productos/prod_serv/contenidos/espanol/bvinegi/productos/metodologias/ENVIPE2012/
g	ENVIPE 2015, http://www.beta.inegi.org.mx/contenidos/proyectos/enchogares/regulares/envipe/2016/doc/envipe2016_presentacion_nacional.pdf
h	ENVIPE 2016, http://www.beta.inegi.org.mx/contenidos/proyectos/enchogares/regulares/envipe/2016/doc/envipe2016_presentacion_nacional.pdf
i	MUCD, http://www.mucd.org.mx/
j	ENVIPE 2017, http://www.beta.inegi.org.mx/proyectos/enchogares/regulares/envipe/2017/

(*continued*)

Table 4.A.6. Continued

Letter	Source
k	Mexico Peace Index, http://visionofhumanity.org/app/uploads/2017/04/Mexico-Peace-Index-2016_English.pdf
l	UNODC, https://data.unodc.org/#state:0
m	InSight Crime, https://www.insightcrime.org/news/analysis/insight-crime-2016-homicide-round-up/
n	SESNSP 2017, http://secretariadoejecutivo.gob.mx/docs/pdfs/
o	IEP 2022, https://www.visionofhumanity.org/wp-content/uploads/2022/05/ESP-MPI-2022-web.pdf
p	World Bank, https://data.worldbank.org/
q	INEGI Censo Nacional, http://www.beta.inegi.org.mx/proyectos/ccpv/2010/
r	CNSPF 2020, https://www.inegi.org.mx/contenidos/programas/cnspf/2021/doc/cnspf_2021_resultados.pdf
s	CNGSPSPE 2020, https://www.inegi.org.mx/contenidos/programas/cngspspe/2020/doc/cngspspe_2020_resultados.pdf
t	SEDENA, https://www.gob.mx/sedena
u	CNDH, http://www.cndh.org.mx/Informes_Anuales_Actividades
v	Animal Politico, https://www.animalpolitico.com/2022/01/2021-tercer-ano-aumento-poblacion-prision/#:~:text=Los%20datos%20oficiales%20de%202021,de%206%20mil%20374%20internos.
w	UNODC 2018–19, https://www.unodc.org/documents/mexicoandcentralamerica/2021/Mexico_Monitoreo_Plantios_Amapola_2018-2019.pdf
x	DEA 2010, https://www.justice.gov/archive/ndic/pubs38/38661/38661p.pdf
y	DEA 2015, https://www.dea.gov/sites/default/files/2018-07/2015%20NDTA%20Report.pdf
z	DEA 2020, https://www.dea.gov/sites/default/files/2021-02/DIR-008-21%202020%20National%20Drug%20Threat%20Assessment_WEB.pdf
aa	Comité Cerezo, https://www.comitecerezo.org/spip.php?article2867&lang=es#Sexto-informe-de-violaciones-de-derechos-humanos-contra-personas-defensoras-nbsp
bb	Sin Embargo, http://www.sinembargo.mx/20-12-2017/3360109
cc	International Press Institute, https://ipi.media/deaths/?topic=0&country=mexico&years=2021&
dd	World Economic Forum, https://www.weforum.org/
ee	Banco Mundial (World Bank), https://datos.bancomundial.org/indicador/ms.mil.xpnd.gd.zs?locations=MX
ff	Pajaro Politico, https://www.animalpolitico.com/el-blog-de-causa-en-comun/presupuesto-2021-cuanto-para-seguridad/#_ftn8
gg	Centro de Estudios de Finanzas Públicas, http://www.cefp.gob.mx/new/index.html

Source: Author's tabulation.

Notes

1. Ball et al., 2003; "Exploring the transition," 2016; Popovic, 2008; *Swedish contact group security sector reform assessment framework*, 2010; OECD, 2011, pp. 41–62.
2. OECD, 2011, p. 10.4.
3. Goldenberg et al., 2016; Wolf & Celorio Morayta, 2011, p. 678.
4. Meyer, 2019, p. 18; OECD, 2011, p. 10.16.
5. Mertens & Wilson, 2012. Donna Mertens and Amy Wilson present a template for program evaluation that distinguishes between outputs (evidence of service delivery), outcomes (medium-term changes accomplished within five years of investment), and impact (long-term changes accomplished seven to ten years after investments).
6. UNODC, 2019.
7. Bermúdez Liévano, 2013; Gurney, 2015. During the Pastrana administration, a committee comprised of representatives from the Attorney General's Office, the Colombian intelligence community, the army, the president's office, and civil society reviewed and tabulated the country's official kidnapping figures. However, in 2003, the Uribe administration disbanded the committee and officially registered only those kidnappings processed by the Attorney General's Office. This resulted in discrepancies between official numbers and those compiled by the country's National Center for Historical Memory (Centro Nacional para la Memoria Histórica, or CNMH). From 2002 to 2010, official statistics reflect a tally of 9,382 kidnappings in the country, whereas the CNMH reports 15,537 during the same period.
8. Rodríguez, 2013.
9. Lastiri, 2016.
10. Moloeznik, 2013, p. 66.
11. At the outset of the Mérida Initiative, the National Poll on Insecurity (Encuesta Nacional sobre Inseguridad, or ENSI) published by the Citizens' Institute for Studies on Insecurity (Instituto Ciudadano de Estudios sobre la Inseguridad, or ICESI), an independent civil society organization, was the standard public opinion poll on perceptions of security and crime ("El ICESI, una 'respuesta al dramático problema,'" 2002). However, in 2010, the Mexican Congress determined that annual public opinion surveys about insecurity should be organized by the government's National Institute of Statistics and Geography (Instituto Nacional de Estadística y Geografía, or INEGI), giving birth to the National Survey on Victimization and Perception of Public Security (Encuesta Nacional de Victimización y Percepción sobre Seguridad, or ENVIPE) (Instituto Nacional de Estadística y Geografía, 2011, p. 1).
12. In this study, the sensitivity of some subjects, particularly as they relate to human rights abuses, complicated efforts to secure accurate and complete data. Some Colombian and Mexican government representatives rejected requests for data, whereas others provided incomplete responses. These gaps are reflected in tables 4.A.1 through 4.A.4 as not available (—).
13. Schedler, 2015, pp. 13–14. Responses by organized crime groups to state security strategies are also likely to have a major effect on performance indicators but are difficult to measure given the clandestine nature of crime. For example, Benjamin Lessing finds that abatement of cartel violence in the 1990s in Mexico depended not so much on the actual repression of criminal organizations as on an increased capacity to repress, which acted as a deterrent to further antistate violence by cartels. By offering cartel leaders incentives against violence

while posturing with a greater repressive capacity, governments can help rein in rampant insecurity. He explains: "Backed into a corner, cartels fight; given an attractive alternative to conduct their business in less violent ways, most do" (Lessing, 2017, p. 5).

14. Although more than fifty indicators, both categorical and numerical, were considered for the book, data were not available for many. The indicators included represent the most complete data for security sector reform in Colombia and Mexico and cover the first two years of robust US assistance, the last two years of such US assistance, a single year halfway through the bilateral assistance plan, The tables also include updated figures for the year 2021 to facilitate analysis of the sustainability of improvements. Unless otherwise indicated, respondents as listed in the tables of this chapter refer to participants in governmental and nongovernmental polling.
15. Berg defines security governance as "the laws, rules, policies, and practices through which political leaders exercise authority over security forces" (2022, p. 24).
16. The US Armed Forces retain judicial autonomy through the Uniform Code of Military Justice, a prerogative set by Congress. Military courts are expected to adjudicate cases "without partiality, favor, or affection," and the military's commitment to this principle has scarcely been called into question in modern history, even though President Donald Trump generated controversy by overturning a ruling with which he disagreed (Dunlap, 2019).
17. Demobilized FARC member, personal communication, Córdoba, Colombia, December 8, 2017.
18. Rohter, 1999.
19. Evans, 2005; Ocampo, 2015. "It was a pacification strategy, and it worked. Sometimes the army did not conduct operations because it did not want to follow judicial protocol, so it was easier to leave those tasks to the AUC," said one business leader (representative of the Colombian business community, personal communication, Bogotá, Colombia, December 14, 2017).
20. Cortés et al., 2012, p. 22.
21. The sustainability of improvements fluctuated after 2011, particularly once the Colombian government finalized peace negotiations with the FARC. The removal of the FARC from the criminal underworld generated a power vacuum that spawned a worrisome cycle of violence among the country's five largest illegal armed groups. Further, despite a noteworthy drop in the homicide rate, instances of massacres, targeted assassinations of social leaders, and armed confrontations were on the rise in 2022.
22. Rangel, 2005, pp. 54–56; Martínez Cárdenas et al., 2015, p. 166.
23. Miguel García Sánchez (2014) reports a negative correlation between the local incidence of illicit drug trafficking and citizen trust in government.
24. Veillette, 2005, p. 11.
25. Demobilized FARC military strategist, personal communication, Antioquia, Colombia, November 2, 2017.
26. During Plan Colombia, aerial spraying of glyphosate was the primary eradication method for destroying coca crops. The method was banned by President Santos in 2015 because of the purported health risks posed to inhabitants of the sprayed areas, the potential for human error—and destruction of licit agricultural crops—and other environmental damage. Since then, manual eradication—the destruction of coca crops by hand—has been the primary method Colombian forces have employed.
27. UNODC, 2005, 2012.

28. Otis, 2014, pp. 10–11.
29. Mejía, 2016.
30. Diaz & Jiménez, 2018.
31. Gill, 2017.
32. Vallejo et al., 2018.
33. Mejia, 2010.
34. Montenegro, 2017.
35. "La tecnología supervigilancia," 2018.
36. Paz, 2014.
37. One prominent human rights defender argues that the security forces are attuned to public opinion and fear losing legitimacy among the citizenry. "Public opinion," he says, "has been a force for change in the army" (F. González, personal communication, Bogotá, Colombia, October 27, 2017).
38. Castellanos, 2006, pp. 311–333; Leal Buitrago, 2006a, pp. 231, 243.
39. Invamer, 2021.
40. Corporación Observatorio para la Paz, 2009, pp. 181–195. One observer explained it this way: "When Plan Colombia resources began arriving, the Pentagon imposed a new strategy on the Colombian military: go into the mountain and eat shit for six months. This new practice required a cultural shift, as previously the army's doctrine did not call for long, isolating deployments. The military felt like it had to comply and produce real results" (academic security analyst, personal communication, Bogotá, Colombia, November 20, 2017).
41. Colombian National Police captain, personal communication, Bogotá, Colombia, November 15, 2017.
42. In 2010, the National Police implemented a program that prioritized police patrols based on the geography of crime hotspots. Plan Cuadrantes was implemented in eight major cities and registered a 22 percent reduction in homicides in the beneficiary communities in just one year of operation (García et al., 2013).
43. Invamer, 2021. In early 2016, the Colombian media uncovered a cadet prostitution network in which senior police leaders paired officer candidates with senior government officials. This became known as the Community of the Ring scandal, and the then director of the National Police, General Rodolfo Palomino, resigned amid his suspected involvement ("Un texto para comprender," 2016).
44. Donadio & Kussrow, 2016.
45. Rabasa & Chalk, 2001, p. 104. General Jorge Enrique Mora undertook the first major personnel restructuring in the Colombian military to increase the number of professional, nondraftee soldiers by 150 percent and to improve the training for draftees. His effort, dubbed Plan 10.000, was the first major impetus on the part of the military to create and enforce a high standard of military recruitment (Colombian Army captain, personal communication, Bogotá, Colombia, October 27, 2017).
46. DeShazo et al., 2009, p. 14.
47. Ramírez de Rincón, 2014.
48. The theory of Integrated Action dates to the 1950s and is a strategy of civil-military cooperation to complement foreign doctrines such as psychological operations and "political war" (Castillo Castañeda & Niño González, 2016, p. 132). Under President Uribe's Democratic Security Policy, the Office of the Presidency extended these principles to territories and civilian populations recently "pacified" by the Colombian state and set up Centers for

Integrated Action Coordination (Centro de Coordinación de Acción Integral, or CCAI) to attend to the most pressing needs of the communities. On the security sector's pacification and stabilization strategy during the Uribe presidency, see Brett, 2018; Delgado, 2015.

49. Colombian Navy lieutenant, personal communication, Bogotá, Colombia, October 31, 2017.
50. Government security analyst, personal communication, Bogotá, Colombia, October 26, 2017.
51. Beittel, 2012, p. 35.
52. Colombian Army captain, personal communication, Bogotá, Colombia, October 27, 2017.
53. Cristo, 2016, p. 233.
54. Mejía, 2016, p. 13; Santos, 2009, pp. 156–158.
55. Marczak et al., 2022, p. 66.
56. For a survey of the cost effectiveness of the judicial branch in Colombia, see Clavijo, 2011.
57. US Office on Colombia, 2012.
58. "Latinobarómetro," 2017.
59. Avila Ceballos, 2015; Restrepo, 2009.
60. Ministerio de Justicia, 2018.
61. Erazo, 2012. Although many challenges remain, Colombia's justice system in 2022 had improved significantly since the 1980s and 1990s, when the Colombian Congress permitted the creation of what were called faceless courts, allowing judges, prosecutors, and witnesses to conceal their identities and thereby protect themselves from defendants in cases of drug trafficking, rebellion, and terrorism (Alquila Lawrence, 1997). Recent examples of the robustness of Colombian courts include the extradition of paramilitary commanders, the Constitutional Court's enforcement of presidential term limits, the prosecution of politicians involved with the narcotics trade and paramilitary groups, and the implementation of recommendations made by the IACHR (Barbosa Castillo, 2016, p. 73).
62. Shifter, 2009, pp. 71–72. On impunity in Colombia, see Rojas Betancourth, 2005.
63. Valora Analitik, 2022.
64. Baires, 2017; Eijking, 2019; Niño González, 2016, pp. 65–71. Arlene Tickner and Mateo Morales Callejas (2015) contest the appraisal of Colombia as a country with enough of a track record of progress and exportable know-how, contending that Colombia's positioning as a security exporter can be traced in large part to the discursive practices in Washington and Bogotá that celebrate the country as a "success story."
65. Tickner, 2014.
66. Cadavid, 2017, p. 10.
67. Porch, 2008, p. 132. Francisco Leal Buitrago (2006a, pp. 97–109) notes that the new constitution itself did not make substantial changes to the country's security forces but instead that President Gaviria's administration introduced a reform agenda that centralized and civilianized the administration of security policy.
68. Barbosa Castillo, 2016, p. 58; government security analyst, personal communication, Bogotá, Colombia, October 26, 2017.
69. Human Rights Watch, 1993.
70. World Bank Open Data, 2018.
71. M. Romero, personal communication, Bogotá, Colombia, December 14, 2017. The military high command did succeed in convincing President Uribe to replace Minister Ramírez in 2003 after repeated scuffles between her and the military's top brass (Marks, 2005, p. 90).

72. Colombian Army colonel, personal communication, Bogotá, Colombia November 20, 2017.
73. In 1999, just prior to Plan Colombia, the Colombian Congress extended extraordinary powers to President Pastrana for a period of six months to commence restructuring of the armed forces without legislative oversight (Rojas, 2015, p. 69).
74. Comisión legal de seguimiento, 2014. The DAS was replaced in 2011 by the National Intelligence Directorate (Dirección Nacional de Inteligencia, or DNI). Skinner and Shedd note that during Plan Colombia military intelligence improved dramatically, but not enough attention was paid to improving coordination between the Ministry of Defense and the DNI, stunting progress on dismantling organized crime networks and on addressing corruption and human rights abuses (Marczak et al., 2022, pp. 78–79).
75. Porch, 2008, pp. 134–135.
76. Pachón Buitrago, 2020, p. 18.
77. Miklaucic & Pinzón, 2017, p. 282.
78. Folke Bernadotte Academy researcher, telephone conversation, November 9, 2017.
79. Colombian National Police captain, personal communication, Bogotá, Colombia, November 24, 2017.
80. Bernal Pulido & Correa Henao, 2016, p. 229. In 2019, the Colombian Senate approved the promotion of General Nicacio Martínez Espinel, the commander of the Colombian Army, from three to four stars despite protests over his service from 2004 to 2006 as the executive officer of a brigade implicated in at least twenty-three extrajudicial murder accusations (Manetto, 2019).
81. Ideas for Peace Foundation researcher, personal communication, Bogotá, Colombia, October 25, 2017.
82. Colombian National Police captain, personal communication, Bogotá, Colombia, October 27, 2017.
83. Centro de Investigación y Educación Popular, 2011, p. 7. Diana Rojas (2015, p. 84) considers US pressure to reform the Military Penal Code (Código Penal Militar) an important factor in the transfer of jurisdiction. In fact, its passage in 2000 was one of the conditions for Congress to approve Plan Colombia, even though the move was resisted by the Colombian military's high command (US Department of State, 1998). However, Barbosa Castillo notes, "In Colombia, more than the influence of international decisions, it has been the internal reflection about democratic values and about justice that has given rise to significant changes in the Military Justice System" (2016, p. 57). On the deliberations surrounding the transfer of jurisdiction to the civilian justice system, see Kyle & Reiter, 2013, pp. 395–397; Leal Buitrago, 2006a, pp. 208–209.
84. Rojas & Benavides, 2017, p. 53. One observer noted that in Colombia when human rights violations by the military increased, the societal grievances against the security sector in part enabled increased recruitment for the FARC (human rights defender, telephone conversation, February 8, 2023).
85. "Colombia: JEP cita a Marcos Pinto y a Édgar Rodríguez," 2021.
86. Lindsay-Poland, 2018, p. 157.
87. Colombia Reports, 2017.
88. ISSAT, 2017.
89. Colombia Reports, 2017. Accusations of extrajudicial homicides by the army are the highest, representing 89.2 percent of all suspected cases (Coordinación Colombia-Europa-Estados Unidos, 2012, p. 85).

90. From 2015 to 2017, the military purged for misconduct more than 3,600 officers and noncommissioned officers, which represented about 1.5 percent of the total force size (academic security analyst, personal communication, Bogotá, Colombia, November 20, 2017). According to one security analyst, Colombian General Alberto José Mejía Ferrero polygraphed an entire brigade in 2017 and quietly forced out the soldiers who could not pass the test (government security analyst, personal communication, Bogotá, Colombia, October 26, 2017).
91. Bermúdez Liévano, 2022. In February 2022, four months before the Truth Commission unveiled its report, the Iván Duque administration (2018–2022) released a report documenting the security forces' view on the false positives scandal, which holds that the human rights violations in question were "individual acts" committed by wayward service members, not state policy.
92. "Víctimas de falsos positivos," 2021.
93. Méndez, 2015.
94. "Gobierno presenta 15 medidas," 2011.
95. ISSAT, 2017.
96. Demobilized FARC military strategist, personal communication, Antioquia, Colombia, November 2, 2017.
97. Human rights defender, telephone conversation, February 8, 2023.
98. On US human rights conditionality, see Tate, 2015, pp. 70–71.
99. At least one critic insists that the use of paramilitary forces as state proxies in a counterinsurgency campaign was the direct result of demands for transparency generated by US human rights conditions (Tate, 2015, pp. 11–12).
100. Fellowship for Reconciliation and US Office on Colombia, 2010.
101. Tate 2011, pp. 337, 341.
102. A. Isacson, personal communication, Washington, DC, October 12, 2017.
103. Consolidated Appropriations Act, 2008, 2007.
104. Logros de la Política de Consolidación, 2008, p. 10.
105. M. Romero, personal communication, Bogotá, Colombia, December 14, 2017.
106. José Alvear Restrepo Law Association representative, personal communication, Bogotá, Colombia, December 15, 2017.
107. Gómez, 2020.
108. Latin American Public Opinion Project, n.d.; Ministerio de Justicia, 2018.
109. AJ+, 2015.
110. Martin, 2013.
111. Kenny et al., 2012; Kleinfeld, 2018, p. 41.
112. Bolaños, 2016, p. 99. According to at least one analyst, the PRI even encouraged the military to participate in the country's illicit economies, as "a weak, rich, happy military was unlikely to unleash a coup" (Kleinfeld, 2018, p. 41).
113. Serrano, 2018, p. 54.
114. Bolaños, 2016, p. 100.
115. Jones, 2016, p. 76.
116. Serrano, 2018, pp. 56–57.
117. Kenny et al., 2012, p. 68.
118. L. D. Vázquez Valencia, personal communication, Mexico City, September 5, 2017.

119. As true of most indicators in Mexico, impunity varies by region. The Center for Studies about Impunity and Justice (Centro de Estudios sobre Impunidad y Justicia) publishes an annual report focused on regional variation (Índice Global de la Impunidad, 2017).
120. Ángel, 2019; "Why Mexico's murder rate is soaring," 2018. The number of reported kidnappings diverges dramatically from the actual estimate of kidnapping victims, demonstrating the confusion of sorting crime statistics in Mexico. Cecilia Farfán-Méndez notes that underreporting is the biggest problem in the design of effective crime reduction strategies (cited in Olson et al., 2018). In the violent state of Guerrero, for instance, a mere 2 percent of crimes are reported to authorities and mostly only for the purposes of insurance claims, even though the Mexican government notes rampant extortion in the region.
121. Vision of Humanity, 2017.
122. Rosen & Ribando Seelke, 2020.
123. Riesenfeld, 2015.
124. In 2021, some 75 percent of the 107,622 overdose deaths in the United States were attributable to opioids such as fentanyl (National Center for Health Statistics, 2022).
125. "Mexico sees fentanyl seizures up 465%," 2020.
126. México Unido Contra la Delincuencia, 2021.
127. Instituto Nacional de Estadística y Geografía, 2016a.
128. Instituto Nacional de Estadística y Geografía, 2016b; Markovits, 2016. This trend may also reflect a surge in violence associated with domestic drug dealing in Mexico (Weintraub, 2010, pp. 69–71). Drug consumption in Mexico increased dramatically from 2003 to 2017 (Rivera, 2017; Durán-Martínez, 2017, p. 101).
129. Lettieri, 2018.
130. Instituto Nacional de Estadística y Geografía, 2011; Markovits, 2016.
131. Sonja Wolff and Gonzalo Celorio Morayta contend that militarization of the drug war fulfilled its original purpose to rally public opinion around the military, which proved essential to sustaining the president's popularity and legitimacy, even though it was a "spectacular failure" in preventing drug trafficking (2011, p. 706).
132. Researcher at the Miguel Agustín Pro Juárez Human Rights Center, personal communication, Mexico City, September 14, 2017; J. Furszyfer, personal communication, Mexico City, 5 September 2017. Spending on advertising, recruitment, and public relations by SEDENA in 2013 was 22,900 percent more than the figure for 2004; likewise, SEMAR's spending on public relations surged 10,000 percent during the same period (Centro Miguel Agustín Pro Juárez de Derechos Humanos, 2015).
133. Senior Obama administration official, personal communication, Washington, DC, October 28, 2021.
134. Instituto Nacional de Estadística y Geografía, 2016a; Latin American Public Opinion Project, n.d., Linobarómetro, n.d.
135. Schmitt & Ahmed, 2016.
136. O'Neil, 2013, p. 267.
137. E. Rendón, personal communication, Mexico City, January 3, 2018. The problem in Mexico, according to one analyst, is not the quantity of police but rather the lack of professionalization (academic security analyst, personal communication, Bogotá, Colombia, November 20, 2017).
138. Kahn, 2013.
139. G. Fondevila, personal communication, Mexico City, September 6, 2017.

140. El Universal, 2021.
141. Naimark-Rowse & Markowitz, 2018, p. 6.
142. Sabet, 2011, pp. 257–258.
143. Naimark-Rowse & Markowitz, 2018, p. 11.
144. Researcher at the Miguel Agustín Pro Juárez Human Rights Center, personal communication, Mexico City, September 14, 2017.
145. E. Rendón, personal communication, Mexico City, January 3, 2018.
146. S. Ley, personal communication, Mexico City, January 9, 2018.
147. A. Mendoza Bautista, personal communication, Mexico City, January 18, 2018.
148. E. Rendón, personal communication, Mexico City, January 3, 2018.
149. E. Rendón, personal communication, Mexico City, January 3, 2018.
150. Camp 2005, p. 101.
151. Latin American Public Opinion Project, n.d. Curiously, government polling indicates a reverse trend, with support for the judiciary, the Public Ministry, and the Attorney General's Office peaking in 2017, but this seems suspect considering the harsh criticism leveled by most of the author's interviewees (indicators 7 and 8, table 4.A.2) (Instituto Nacional de Estadística y Geografía, 2016a).
152. K. Ansolabehere, personal communication, Mexico City, September 4, 2017.
153. *Global Impunity Index Mexico*, 2016, p. 14.
154. *Global Impunity Index Mexico*, 2016, p. 14.
155. Instituto Nacional de Estadística y Geografía, 2016a. On the perceived futility of citizen denunciations in Mexico, see Schedler, 2015, pp. 195–199.
156. *Global Impunity Index Mexico*, 2016, p. 14. Only ten states have an impunity level better than the national average, and twenty-four states are within 10 percent from the lowest ranking state, according to the Global Impunity Index.
157. Ross, 2015.
158. *Global Impunity Index Mexico*, 2016, p. 14.
159. ISSAT, 2015; "Murders, corruption and crime," 2017.
160. Guerrero, 2013, p. 130.
161. Aguayo et al., 2021, p. 122.
162. LAPOP, 2022, p. 108.
163. US defense official, personal communication, Mexico City, September 8, 2017.
164. J. J. Romero, personal communication, Mexico City, December 21, 2017. The autonomy of the military was particularly acute during the Fox administration. Fox attempted to appoint a cabinet coordinator, Rubén Aguilar, through whom he anticipated issuing orders to SEDENA and SEMAR, but leaders in both institutions insisted that they were only constitutionally bound to take orders directly from the president (Mexican Institute of Human Rights and Democracy researcher, personal communication, Mexico City, January 18, 2018).
165. J. Furszyfer, personal communication, Mexico City, September 5, 2017.
166. E. Bohórquez, telephone conversation, April 6, 2018. In Ciudad Juárez, the municipal police detained on average six hundred individuals per month during 2017, but the district attorney's office only managed to process between seventy and eighty cases per month. Of those cases, only ten on average resulted in formal case proceedings, and only three on average resulted in a sentencing (Citizen's Observatory for Prevention, Security, and Justice representative, personal communication, Ciudad Juárez, Mexico, January 15, 2018).

167. Suárez-Enríquez & Indacochea, 2018, p. 12. For technical data about the early results of the transition to an accusatorial justice system nationwide, see México Evalúa, 2017.
168. Loeza Reyes & Pérez-Levesque, 2010, p. 139.
169. E. Bohórquez, telephone conversation, April 6, 2018. Historically, the legislature's defense-related committees have included military officers seconded to Congress and military retirees to mediate between the president and legislators (Deare, 2021, pp. 3–4).
170. Mexican Institute of Human Rights and Democracy researcher, personal communication, Mexico City, January 18, 2018.
171. G. Fondevila, personal communication, Mexico City, September 6, 2017. SEDENA retains a corporate structure and operates its own banking system and productive industries, such as livestock, to raise funds for its operating budget. This leads to a "certain informality about raising money" to sponsor reforms (US defense official, personal communication, Mexico City, September 19, 2017). In 2013, SEDENA justified its expansion into the construction industry, completing contracts worth more than $250 million, on the pretext that in many regions it was too violent or dangerous for construction companies to operate (Aranda, 2016).
172. Government political analyst, personal communication, Mexico City, January 29, 2018.
173. J. J. Romero, personal communication, Mexico City, December 21, 2017.
174. E. Bohórquez, telephone conversation, April 5, 2018; researcher at the Miguel Agustín Pro Juárez Human Rights Center, personal communication, Mexico City, September 14, 2017; México Evalúa, 2017, p. 11.
175. The perceived corruption indices included in table 4.A.4 refer to the percentage of respondents who believed that the institutions referenced were "corrupt" or "somewhat corrupt" (Bajraktari et al., 2006; Center for Democracy and Governance, 1998; Kinzelbach & Cole, 2007).
176. Watt & Zepeda, 2012, p. 202.
177. Moloeznik, 2013, p. 78. Multiple interviewees consulted for this book reported that many human rights complaints during this period were actually not instances of human rights abuse but rather acts of corruption.
178. Lakhani & Tirado, 2016.
179. Diaz, 2022.
180. "Testimonio, Sobreviviente de la masacre a estudiantes de Ayotzinapa," 2014.
181. As Roderic Camp summarizes, "The consequences [of Tlatelolco] can be broadly categorized: altered views of the military toward civilian leadership, altered views of the political leadership toward the military, the views of younger officers toward older officers within the military, and changed views of the role of the military in Mexican society" (1992, p. 28).
182. Heyns, 2016, p. 1.
183. Human Rights Watch, 2018. Congressman Waldo Fernández González holds that the military is not nearly as abusive as the media presents it to be. He stated that only 0.03 percent of all military operations in the country result in a reported abuse and that the military's leadership needs to do a better job of defending the institution and boosting its public image (W. Fernández González, personal communication, Monterrey, Mexico, February 7, 2018).
184. Carlsen 2018, p. 76.
185. Villegas, 2018b.

186. Researcher at the Miguel Agustín Pro Juárez Human Rights Center, personal communication, Mexico City, September 14, 2017. One expert commented that the *fuero* took so long to challenge because there was a tacit pact between the military leadership and civilian politicians to preserve the status quo. Politicians in Mexico benefit from judicial protections via a constitutionally prescribed *fuero* as well, and the people protected by it were leery of generating national debate about the *fuero militar* for fear that it might call into question their own privilege (E. Bohórquez, telephone conversation, April 6, 2018).
187. K. Ansolabehere, personal communication, Mexico City, September 4, 2017.
188. Calderón and the military's leadership agreed from the outset that human rights corrections needed to be a part of the institutional reform of the military and agreed to carry out the recommendations of the IACtHR and administer reparations for a number of high-profile cases (A. Poiré, personal communication, Mexico City, September 14, 2017).
189. Mexican Institute of Human Rights and Democracy researcher, personal communication, Mexico City, January 18, 2018.
190. A. Isacson, personal communication, Washington, DC, October 12, 2017.
191. Kyle & Reiter, 2013, p. 400. One human rights advisor to the Mexican government recounted a high-profile case of extrajudicial murder in which a prominent national businessperson, sympathetic to the army, paid the fees for a high-powered legal team to defend the accused soldiers, facilitating impunity for the crime based on procedural errors (human rights defender, telephone conversation, February 8, 2023).
192. Wilkinson, 2018.
193. A. L. Fernández Aguilar, personal communication, Monterrey, Mexico, February 6, 2018; García Castillo, 2015.
194. More than one thousand army members, some of whom present conduct trouble or face investigations into their involvement in abuses, desert the ranks of the institution annually ("Secretaría de la Defensa Nacional," n.d.).
195. Comité Cerezo, 2017. State–civil society relations vary dramatically across the national territory and, in some regions, are characterized by a high degree of cooperation and even goodwill (Shirk et al., 2014).
196. Schedler, 2015, p. 183.
197. Cosgrove, 2017. The Mexican media does not have a long tradition of criticizing security sector actors, especially the military. The first instances of major criticism of the military dates to SEDENA's suppression of the Zapatista National Liberation Army (Ejército de Liberación Nacional, or EZLN) rebellion in Chiapas in 1994 and 1995, when the media published commentary critical of the military's excesses and actively sought out victims of army abuses (Camp, 2005, p. 39).
198. ISSAT, 2015; Reyna García, 2018.
199. Stevenson, 2022.
200. For a breakdown of US security assistance relative to Mexican defense spending and detailed information about US funding lines, see Aguayo et al., 2021, pp. 377–393.
201. Author's calculations.
202. Former senior US diplomat, email correspondence, September 28, 2021.
203. S. Aguayo, personal communication, Mexico City, September 13, 2017.
204. Finkenbusch, 2017. Prior to the Mérida Initiative, SOUTHCOM hosted a conference with Colombian and Mexican military officers to discuss the human rights certification process

in Colombia as a template for Mexico, but the Mexican participants made clear that similar measures were completely unacceptable to Mexico (human rights defender, telephone conversation, February 8, 2023). The US Congress initially proposed retaining the right to withhold 25 percent of the Mérida funds if the Mexican government failed to deliver on the following four human rights conditions: the establishment of a commission to process complaints filed against police, an independent monitoring mechanism, the investigation of all military and police involved in human rights abuses by civilian judicial authorities, and the prohibition of torture to obtain confessions (Wolf & Celorio Morayta, 2011, p. 673). However, the reaction of Mexican authorities against "interventionist" maneuvers succeeded in limiting the scope of US human rights conditions (Velásquez & Schiavon, 2009, p. 94). The Mexican government argued that the US government's contribution of $400 million, less than 10 percent of Mexico's own expenditures in the counterdrug fight, was too little to warrant such an audacious demand (Weintraub, 2010, p. 74).

205. In contrast to Colombia, where the US Embassy refused to work with units found to have committed human rights abuses, in Mexico the Department of State pushed for a remediation process by which "tainted units" could deliver justice for abuses and thereafter reestablish ties with Washington (retired US Army colonel, personal communication, Washington, DC, October 12, 2017).
206. Calderón responded to the first retention of funds by submitting legislation to strengthen the National Commission for Human Rights and to transfer jurisdiction of military abuses of human rights to civilian courts (D. V. Negroponte, 2013, p. 158).
207. Malkin & Ahmed, 2017.
208. L. D. Vázquez Valencia, personal communication, Mexico City, September 5, 2017.
209. On failed proposals to reform the security forces during the Calderón administration, see Piñyero, 2010, pp. 164–165.
210. "Corrupción y seguridad," 2018.

5

Bringing in Big Business

The Role of the Private Sector

In countries where the state is unable to establish order in economically vital spaces, business leaders tend to protect their interests by either propping up private security forces or supporting the creation of more professional police and military forces.[1] When governments and big business historically operate in isolation from one another, the probability of collaboration on security policy remains low given the scant trust between the two parties and the absence of forums for negotiation. Conversely, collaborative government-business relations typically result in a united front that reinforces shared policy preferences to confront insecurity.[2] In Colombia and Mexico, wherever US security assistance was complemented by private sector contributions to the overall security strategy, state capacity for security provision improved. On the other hand, when the private sector ignored or resisted a more active role in underwriting security sector reform and related citizen security strategies, the state's ability to curb violent crime remained low.

Gustavo Flores-Macías reinforces these conclusions in his important work on elite taxation in Latin America.[3] He argues that security crises can create windows of opportunity for the taxation of financial elites, especially when elites lack access to acceptable substitutes for the public good in question (security provision). However, "the resulting tax arrangement will depend on the strength of business-government linkages," with shared ideology and mechanisms for cooperation positively affecting elite willingness to assume a greater tax burden.[4] In places where links between big business and government authorities are weak, though, elite taxation and associated efforts at state-building tend to fail.

This chapter offers ample support for Flores-Macías's theory and also identifies two other decisive variables with consequences for improved security sector governance: the nature and locus of the security threat and elite perceptions of insecurity. When violent actors cannot be placated or managed

From Peril to Partnership. Paul J. Angelo, Oxford University Press. © Oxford University Press 2024.
DOI: 10.1093/oso/9780197688106.003.0006

and when elites' financial interests and personal safety are at risk, heightened elite perceptions of insecurity drive solutions that favor security sector reform, especially where business-government ties are strong. Conversely, when elites identify alternatives to overcoming security threats with force and when they experience relative insulation from societal violence, elite prescriptions for resolving public safety challenges tend not to favor robust investments in state security forces.

The level of cohesion among economic and political elites at the national level differed at the outset of Plan Colombia and of the Mérida Initiative, resulting in differing levels of private sector support for public security strategies.[5] Whereas in Colombia public-private cooperation on reforming security forces was the next step in an already close relationship between business and political elites, in Mexico overlap was modest between business and political elites. In Mexico, business leaders did not have a long tradition of entering national politics, which undermined big business faith in reforms introduced at the federal level. Furthermore, business leaders in Colombia and Mexico differed in their perception of security sector reform as the best way of providing for citizen security and the importance of citizen security for business operations, opting instead for private security provision or accommodation of criminal groups in Mexico.[6] Collectively, these factors were consequential for security outcomes in both countries.

In Colombia, at the heart of this fusion of interests between business and politics is the critical juncture of the failed peace process with the Revolutionary Armed Forces of Colombia (Fuerzas Armadas Revolucionarias de Colombia, or FARC) in 2002, which convinced economic and political elites alike that institutional reform and modernization were the only feasible solution to Colombia's security crisis and the only way to overcome an ideologically driven and uncompromising enemy. As a result, wealthy Colombians acquiesced and paid a security tax to help underwrite security sector reform, thereby creating greater incentives for public oversight of the government's security strategy. In Mexico, big business distrusted the federal government and only casually participated in its security strategy. This is partially attributable to the relative insulation of big business from the worst effects of the country's criminality, rendering private sector leaders reluctant to become too closely associated with the anticrime activities of the national executive and the Mérida Initiative. Because the private sector was not an active participant in setting the federal security agenda, it lacked specific mechanisms to hold the government accountable for worsening security. The Mexican case features some degree of subnational variation, however. As this chapter details, municipally led reforms in Ciudad Juárez and Monterrey enjoyed the support of regional business elites, whose financial interests and lives were increasingly at risk due to an uptick in violent criminal activity. Consequently, they assumed a leading role in financing and designing security interventions that improved security indicators at the municipal and state levels.

Insecurity and the Colombian Private Sector

Colombia reached a breaking point in its security crisis between 1997 and 1998. The growing armed power and geographic reach of insurgent and criminal groups undermined the state's authority and exposed increasing numbers of Colombian citizens to wanton violence. The class antagonism embraced by the FARC's leaders ensured that the group's principal targets for kidnapping, terrorist acts, and extortion were members of the financial elite. As the FARC gained strength and grew more brazen in their assaults on civilian populations, the group's strategy shifted to targeting urban areas to focus on killing and kidnapping wealthy and influential people; doing so gave the guerrilla group an air of national relevance they had not previously enjoyed and fueled fears among elites for their personal safety.[7] Between 1996 and 2002, the number of kidnappings increased by 85.7 percent, and any previous complacence among the country's wealthiest citizens became untenable as more of them fell victim to guerrilla violence.[8] The effect of guerrilla activity on Colombia's top earners during this period drove defensive reactions ranging from financial accommodation to complicity with right-wing paramilitarism.[9] As one US official remarked,

> Colombia is a rich country. Elites generally tolerated narco-traffickers like Pablo Escobar until he came into direct competition with traditional elite interests. It was only when the FARC started kidnapping on the highway to Villavicencio and bombed El Nogal [social club] that they finally realized that placating criminals does not work. They knew they had to push back—and they did.[10]

Despite the significant financial burden generated by conflict—including high-risk insurance premiums, increased transaction and operating costs, and damaged infrastructure—urban elites previously perceived the decades-long conflict to be an unfortunate but manageable aspect of doing business in Colombia.[11] However, as FARC activities increasingly targeted cities, Colombia's wealthiest citizens grew more concerned about personal safety in the late 1990s, suggesting that it was not just the nature of the threat but also its changing locus that boosted elite support for dealing with insecurity.

When President Pastrana placed peace at the center of his political agenda starting in 1998, in large part as a response to the pressure of Colombian civil society organizations, the private sector wagered that a negotiated solution would be good for their safety and business interests and supported his bid.[12] Cattle ranchers offered to donate land to peasants as part of a settlement, and the commercial sector purchased government-issued "peace bonds" (Bonos en Solidaridad para la Paz) to collect revenues for social and military investment.[13] Pastrana's concurrent effort to solicit international financing to strengthen state institutions via Plan Colombia further reassured big business and solidified the president's support base within the country's top economic echelon.[14]

Despite this momentum, the faith of the Pastrana administration and the Colombian private sector in the possibility of a negotiated peace was put to the test by continued FARC assaults on Colombians.[15] In April 2000, the FARC forcibly collected a tax on asset holders of more than $1 million in areas under the group's influence; armed blockades of government highways restricted the distribution of goods to more than a hundred municipalities in the country; and airplane hijackings and mass kidnappings did little to convince the private sector that peace talks were leading to improved security.[16] The kidnapping of the daughter of the head of the Bogotá industry association further tested the patience of Colombian business leaders.[17] In a 1999 public opinion poll of 498 business executives, a majority preferred establishing an authoritarian government with extraordinary powers to dismantle the FARC militarily if the peace talks failed, and a Gallup poll of more than five hundred private sector leaders showed that favorable views of the peace process dropped from 70 percent to 11 percent from March to December 2000.[18] By the time the FARC negotiations collapsed on February 20, 2002, the private sector was eager to tack in a new direction in pursuit of improved security.

As the FARC fortified its battleground footing and expanded its criminal activities, "they showed us all that they were not negotiating in good faith," one observer remarked. The insurgent intransigence "left the government with the *mano dura* (hard-handed) option only," and most Colombians who had initially supported the peace process endorsed this strategic pivot.[19] The absence of alternatives for dealing with guerrilla-perpetrated violence drove consensus among political and financial elites: security sector reform as the only viable solution to resolving the country's violence.[20] Luz Estella Nagle asserts, "While Colombians [had] not forgotten that the military is guilty of many sins, Colombians [were] willing to support a better trained and much better equipped military to rescue their nation from chaos."[21]

Fortunately, Pastrana had decided early on to modernize and professionalize the armed forces in tandem with peace talks, improving tactics and operational capacity before the end of negotiations. When he ordered the military to retake a forty-two-thousand-square-kilometer demilitarized zone called the *despeje* from FARC insurgents the day talks broke down in 2002, Plan Colombia was already in its second year of implementation, and the armed forces boasted new special forces training, helicopters, advanced intelligence, and, most important, a strong operational mandate.[22] That security sector reform would be a principal component of Pastrana's Plan Colombia was welcomed, but US authorities stressed to Pastrana early on that international support alone would not be enough. Colombia needed to boost its contributions to the fight and assume local ownership of the effort. US Senators John McCain (Republican-Arizona), Chris Dodd (Democrat-Connecticut), and Fred Thompson (Republican-Tennessee) on a visit to Colombia in 2001 made the US position clear: Colombia and the United States shared responsibility for the regional drug problem, but Bogotá devoted far too little of its budget to tackling drug production and the country's grave security situation.[23] If Colombia wanted a continuing commitment from Washington, Colombians were going to have to increase their own security and defense expenditures.

Financing Colombia's Security Strategy: The Democratic Security Tax

One of the Colombian government's historical weaknesses has been its inability to introduce taxes and enforce tax collection. Nazih Richani explains that since Colombia's independence "large landowners, cattle ranchers and the agribusiness elite conspired to resist the growth of state power," restricting the tax base of the central government.[24] What resulted was an arrangement in which Colombian elites usually succeeded in securing tax exemptions for the wealthy and toleration of systemic tax evasion across society.[25] The reluctance of the wealthy to pay higher taxes was so acute that in the 1990s Colombia had the second-smallest tax revenue per capita in South America.[26]

However, the security crisis in the early 2000s created the right set of incentives to prompt an increase in citizen contributions.[27] The government, in the face of mounting debt, could no longer afford to mortgage the security effort on loans and bond sales and turned to taxes to relieve stress on the rising fiscal burden.[28] An economic recession in 1999 left the country without access to international credit markets, necessitating an increase in taxation as part of the economic restructuring encouraged by the International Monetary Fund.[29] This was the impetus that thrust President Álvaro Uribe, who campaigned on a militarized security strategy, onto the scene in 2002 and allowed him to usher in one of his signature policies: the Democratic Security Tax (Impuesto de la Seguridad Democrática).

In hopes of averting prolonged confrontation with private sector leaders and their well-positioned allies in Congress over the terms of the security tax, Uribe implemented extraordinary decree measures just days after taking office.[30] On declaring a State of Internal Unrest (Estado de Conmoción Interior) for three months, the newly inaugurated president introduced a special tax to address declining security.[31] The Democratic Security Tax, earmarked for defense and security expenditures, applied to high-net-worth citizens, and total sums of revenue represented about 1 percent of the country's gross domestic product (GDP) and 20 percent of the security sector's budget.[32] The new tax, enacted in 2002 and renewed on three occasions during the Uribe presidency, facilitated a 120 percent increase in the security sector's expenditures and amounted to roughly 5 percent of the government's tax revenue in the first decade of the 2000s.[33]

The government assessed the first tax at a rate of 1.2 percent in 2002 against individuals with assets higher than 169.5 million Colombian pesos ($65,000) to finance the professionalization of the armed forces.[34] The following year, the Congress approved a second tax of 0.3 percent on assets surpassing 3 billion Colombian pesos ($1 million) to facilitate recruitment for the security forces from 2004 to 2006.[35] The third round, passed in 2006, mimicked the second in targeting the same echelon of wealthy citizens but increased the rate to 1.2 percent; these funds helped finance the security sector's "consolidation" strategy and the acquisition of new aircraft and maritime equipment from 2007 to 2010. Finally, in 2009, the legislature backed one last round at a rate of 2.4 percent (the 3 billion pesos were valued at $1.4 million in 2011) through 2014.[36]

Spending priorities for the new tax revenue were outlined in a 2003 presidential declaration as the Democratic Security Policy (Política de Defensa y Seguridad Democrática), identifying insurgent groups as the principal threat to Colombia's national interest and setting goals for a whole-of-government approach to protect the population by denying sanctuary for illegal armed actors.[37] The policy promised to reduce kidnappings, expand demobilization and reintegration programs for insurgents, improve rural infrastructure, and attack the command structure of illegal armed groups.[38] In this vein, the strategy called for sweeping and coordinated reforms in the administration of the Ministry of Defense's finances, acquisitions, public relations, and operational planning and improvements to the criminal justice system to hold offenders accountable. It identified strategic objectives for each governmental entity, such as strengthening the military's and police's reputations and authority in regions long deprived of the state's presence, and it imposed internal mechanisms of accountability—and data collection requirements—for the accomplishment of reform goals. And, in 2003, Uribe launched a presidential office to coordinate the activities of government stakeholders in his development and civic action plans, which were central to the government's Democratic Security Policy.

The ambition of the Democratic Security Policy was only outmatched by its price tag: a figure that totaled some $1 billion a year for each year of the Uribe administration.[39] Before the tax, roughly 92 percent of the government's defense budget was committed to existing operating costs, but after 2003, investment expenditures more than doubled, with revenues from the security tax making up some 20 percent of the national defense and security budget.[40]

Private Sector Compliance with Security Taxation

As Flores-Macías finds, three factors in particular contributed to the willingness of Colombian business elites to finance the modernization and professionalization of Colombia's security forces: the combination of fiscal and security crises, improving perceptions of the government's provision of public safety, and unity among business and government elites.[41] Central to the successful imposition of taxes was a growing faith among financial elites that Plan Colombia was rendering government forces sufficiently capable of providing security for Colombia's citizenry and businesses, which had increasingly become accustomed to financing their own protection through private security firms. Indeed, Washington's reputational gamble on supporting Colombia paid off by 2002 as newly inaugurated military brigades and aviation squadrons put the guerrillas on the run after years of humiliating attacks and ambushes on the military and police. Big business in Colombia finally started to view government strategies as the solution to the country's security dilemma.

Business leaders reported no formal consultation between the government and the private sector's leading associations regarding the initial security tax, but the Uribe administration made private assurances to the business sector's top executives about the tax's renewal after 2002 and secured support from leading business groups to corral the backing of top industry executives.[42] Many business owners accepted the second tax in 2003 without much pushback.[43] By that stage, the security forces had demonstrated a winning strategy that financial elites were eager to endorse.[44] As the former president of a business association from one of the country's principal productive industries acknowledged, "I believed that the money was being wisely spent toward [the strengthening of the security forces], and the results convinced me of it."[45]

Even progressive members of the president's opposition supported the tax, which they saw as an opportunity to increase the tax burden of the wealthy. Yet the country's wealthiest citizens actually saw the levy as a compromise to avoid more far-reaching tax reform.[46] To this end, Uribe routinely defended financial elites against an increase in other income taxes and instead used existing budgets by freezing public-sector wages and pensions. His administration also transparently and publicly defended its imposition of the security tax in the first place through high-profile dialogues and investment summits to reassure high-income citizens that the government was making good use of their taxes.[47] Elite faith in the results increased as the result of a surge in foreign direct investment, which grew by a factor of seven between 2002 and 2006 in large part due to improved security. This helped the government justify its repeated appeals to financial elites to fund the war effort.[48] In particular, Colombians who had moved abroad because of the violence in earlier decades also began to repatriate some of their wealth to Colombia and invest in the country, helping spur a stock market boom that began in 2004 and saw an eightfold increase in the market by 2010.

The intersection of elite interests in Colombia was another essential factor in the passage of the Democratic Security Tax. Big business in Colombia historically maintained a cohesive and privileged bloc that has successfully defended elite prerogatives in the political sphere—including as they pertained to the security tax.[49] Financial elites felt represented in government because so many from within their ranks and in their families entered government service. Luis Carlos Villegas, President Santos's minister of defense from 2015 to 2018, illustrates the strength of these linkages. Having started his career in the Ministry of Foreign Relations (Ministerio de Relaciones Exteriores), he later served as governor, secretary general of the National Coffee-Grower's Federation (Federación Nacional de Cafeteros), president of the National Association of Colombian Businesspersons (Asociación Nacional de Empresarios de Colombia, or ANDI), peace negotiator, ambassador, and defense minister. Overlap of this kind also meant that political officeholders and business leaders socialized in the same spaces and understood the interests and pressures facing each group.[50] Hence an important factor that permitted financial elites to accept higher taxation for security sector reform was the tight-knit and cohesive nature of elite circles, which convinced big-business owners that their political counterparts would make good on investments while protecting class interests.[51]

President Uribe's unique status among the political elite made the introduction of the Democratic Security Tax even more palatable to the private sector.[52] As a large landowner and former Liberal Party politician whose family had been directly victimized by the FARC, Uribe understood the conflict in a way that few from the upper echelons of the Bogotá elite did. Furthermore, he was from a region of the country, Antioquia, where business-minded elites typically resisted encroachments by the central government, making his tax appeal all the more novel and unlikely. His security-first platform united the interests of distinct elements of the private sector—from coastal ranchers and interior coffee growers to manufacturing and energy executives. Moreover, Uribe appointed to his cabinet several prominent members of the urban business community, including Juan Manuel Santos, who helped assuage the concerns of the commercial and industrial sectors about the rise of a geographic "outsider" to the presidency.[53]

The application of the Democratic Security Tax also gave rise to the Ethics and Transparency Commission (Comisión de Transparencia y Ética), which granted financial elites a forum through which they monitored state expenditure on security matters and could hold the government responsible for ineffective or misguided spending and strategy.[54] The private sector's support was grounded in its ability to exert control over or monitor processes of policy implementation—in this case, security sector reform.[55] Private sector support was thus a boost not only for the effectiveness of the security sector but also for its accountability. In fact, because elite-financed resources were at stake, Bogotá even expressed a limited willingness to tackle corruption in the security sector—long seen as a contentious move—by strengthening the mandate of the attorney general to go after crooked members of the military and police.[56] Such measures encouraged top contributors to the Democratic Security Policy to maintain their public support for the tax for the duration of the Uribe administration.[57]

As the following section explores, no such consensus among financial elites ever materialized surrounding the issue of insecurity in Mexico at the national level, limiting big business's involvement in helping the government set a successful security agenda.

Insecurity and the Mexican Private Sector

In contrast to the chaos in Colombia on the eve of Plan Colombia, insecurity in Mexico had not reached a critical threshold nationally by the early stages of Calderón's war on the cartels, and the country's private sector was not sufficiently affected by crime and violence to help shape and fund federal security strategies in a coordinated way. Perhaps surprisingly, Mexico registered its lowest homicide rate on record in 2007, the first full year of the Calderón administration.

Big Business's Indifference to Federal Security Strategies

When Calderón called for sweeping reforms in the country's security institutions at the beginning of his administration, many financial elites, although frustrated by high levels of corruption within the security sector, did not perceive force modernization and professionalization as a pressing national priority—at least not one that would require greater contributions from the country's business sector.[58] Unlike in Colombia, where violence was widespread and affected vast stretches of territory, violence in Mexico was concentrated in a few states and municipalities. Even some of the country's top security analysts understood Mexico's security crisis during the Calderón administration not as a national problem but as a collection of local crises.[59] In Colombia, the challenge posed by insurgents was seen as a politico-military threat that only a stronger state could combat, whereas the insecurity posed by Mexico's cartels proved to be mostly localized and apolitical.[60] Rafael Fernández de Castro notes that for many years it was difficult for the Mexican public to accept that a national problem of insecurity even existed because the government had created a narrative that most of the victims of the country's violence were themselves involved in organized crime.[61]

As crime against innocent bystanders skyrocketed by the early 2010s, popular demonstrations against crime, violence, and human rights abuses became prevalent in many cities across the country. In some regions, vigilante citizens, frustrated by government inaction, took matters into their own hands and established private armies. In 2012, the emergence of self-defense forces in the states of Michoacán and Guerrero to defend against pervasive extortion garnered significant media coverage in a way that both alarmed and embarrassed Mexican authorities.[62] More than five years into the Mérida Initiative and Calderón's security sector reform efforts, insecurity was on the rise. The outbreak of criminal violence in the country's agricultural south occurred on the heels of an extraordinary surge in insecurity in industrial border cities such as Ciudad Juárez and Monterrey from 2008 to 2012. As civil society pressure mounted, even some of the country's top business owners began to coordinate with human rights groups and NGOs to implement local violence reduction initiatives.[63] Despite the involvement of the private sector in these few municipal security strategies, mechanisms linking the private sector to the federal government's security sector reform never emerged, limiting the leverage of big business over the government's management of the reform. In Mexico, unlike in Colombia, there was "zero talk of a security tax."[64] Raúl Benítez Manaut clarifies, "In Mexico, police reform was implemented while crime and homicides were on the rise and created fear in the general population, which led to the strategies' rejection by the majority of elites."[65]

Moreover, the US government did not appear to make forceful demands of Mexican financial elites in the negotiation of the Mérida Initiative as it had done in the early stages of Plan Colombia. After all, Mexico's security and defense budget was already increasing, and concerns about infringing on Mexican sovereignty tempered Washington's negotiating posture during both the Bush and Obama administrations.[66] The delayed delivery of critical Mérida hardware and resources also constrained the Calderón administration in the early years of the force modernization process and made it more difficult to deliver operational results that would have convinced financial elites that state security institutions were capable of delivering and sustaining enhanced security, especially relative to the early operational successes of Plan Colombia that were facilitated by expedited supply chain contracting on the US side.[67]

Similarly, in Colombia, a watershed crisis—the 2002 failure of Colombia's peace talks with the FARC—convinced elites that meaningful alternatives to militarized responses to insecurity were no longer in play. In Mexico, however, many private sector leaders still believed that insecurity and violence could be managed—either through clandestine payments to violent actors or by negotiating the protection of criminal networks through corrupt government officials.[68] Business leaders from across the country were not interested in funding or overseeing security sector reform so long as the security situation did not pose them any major problems.

The Peña Nieto administration did not prioritize courting the private sector to help fund its security policies either. In fact, the former director of the Colombian National Police, Óscar Naranjo (2007–12), arrived in Mexico in 2012 to advise Monterrey's private sector on a local security strategy and then provide recommendations to incoming President Peña Nieto. In both instances, he expressly argued in favor of the imposition of a security tax.[69] These overtures were met with little success nationally, however, given that no bona fide crisis to engage the private sector ever materialized. This became especially true as crime rates tapered off during the first years of the Peña Nieto administration, convincing many that the worst of the country's violence had passed. Once crime and violence spiked again in 2016, the administration's political capital was severely diminished, undermining its ability to reorient security sector reform and solicit greater support from big business to that end.

One analyst explained, "There is not enough public outrage over insecurity, and the public has become inured to high levels of violence. Also, violence is targeted, and it rarely touches elite circles."[70] Implicit in this argument is a sense that business leaders would help fund security sector reform only if they could identify a direct benefit to their personal safety or investments. In the words of one researcher, and as reflected in the case of Colombia, "Business leaders only started caring [about security] when they became victims."[71]

Organized crime last targeted Mexican financial elites on a large scale in the 1990s. Then, the 1994 kidnappings of well-known executives Ángel Losada Moreno and Alfredo Harp Helú shocked the country's wealthiest citizens into investing heavily in private security measures such as bodyguards and armored vehicles. Since this period of security privatization, high-net-worth Mexicans have seldom been major targets for criminal groups.[72] Further, the Mexican private sector typically relies on municipal police forces to protect businesses and operations, encouraging close personal relationships between financial elites and local government and eliminating the perceived need to contribute to federal security initiatives.[73] In this context, elite groups, already insulated from the most damaging effects of criminal violence, had little personal incentive to contribute to massive public-sector security programs, especially federally managed ones.

A pervasive distrust among the wealthy of the government's ability to manage tax revenues transparently and effectively also reinforced elite reluctance to support a security tax. In Mexico, the business class typically resists the levying of new taxes because it has little faith in the government's ability to make transparent use of public revenue, pushing politicians to look for ways to expand budgets without raising taxes.[74] According to one researcher, Mexican business elites are more concerned about the impact of corruption on profits than they are about the effects of insecurity, which is why anti-corruption watchdog organizations attract generous donations from big business.[75] This reflects a long-standing tension in Mexico's elite circles: unlike their counterparts in Colombia, Mexican political and financial elites infrequently mingle, and in many cases, their ambitions are at odds.[76] As Roderic Camp emphasizes, "Mexico is clearly not characterized by an overlapping power elite," and the cooperative spirit that took hold in Colombia never prevailed in Mexico.[77] In a study of power elite circles, Camp finds that only one leading Mexican political figure out of more than two hundred from 1970 to 2000 occupied influential roles in both political and economic spheres.[78] In fact, despite a growing participation of technocratic and business-minded individuals in government during the Calderón administration, the generation of Mexican politicians that dominated politics in the 2010s was predominantly middle class in origin.[79]

Top private sector executives also complained that federal tax revenues seldom trickle back into the communities or territories that contribute the most or where investment is most needed. This is largely a function of peculiar governmental budgeting rules. Mexican municipalities receive 72 percent of their revenue from federal transfers and do not have the legal authority to raise funds except via payroll taxes, unlike in Colombia, where cities increased tax revenues to fund local crime prevention.[80] The funds to finance public security services at the state level are pooled by the federal government into a special budgetary item known as the Fund of Shares for Public Security in the States and Federal District (Fondo de Aportaciones para la Seguridad Pública de los Estados y del Distrito Federal, or FASP), allowing for political patronage in distributive priorities. Financial elites resented the way federal politicians distributed funds to expand their clientelistic networks rather than prioritizing recipient states by demonstrated need.[81]

Still, insecurity convinced high-income Mexicans to subsidize some limited federal efforts—a scenario that led to sporadic private sector involvement in security programs. Yet often when the Mexican private sector did contribute to reforms, investments undermined accountability. For example, in Tamaulipas in 2016, business donors paid 800 Mexican pesos ($40) a day per soldier for hundreds of extra army soldiers deployed in the state at the request of regional landowners. Instead of being used to pay the salaries and per diem of the military from a central account, however, these transactions took place directly between the Secretariat of National Defense (Secretaría de Defensa Nacional, or SEDENA) leaders and local business owners, paving the way for influence peddling and bribery.[82] In other instances, local business leaders and politicians collaborated with federal security forces ad hoc to build physical infrastructure such as barracks and training facilities in places of intensifying conflict, such as Coahuila and Guanajuato.[83] At the federal level, private sector contributions focused principally on expanding benefits to security force personnel. The banking sector raised nearly $100 million over a little more than a decade for a program called Sponsor Them (Bécalos), providing academic scholarships for children of military and Federal Police personnel, and banks extended larger mortgage credit lines to military members.[84] Although these investments showed budding elite interest in security, they were poorly coordinated with broader governmental strategies and were only a small contribution given the country's vast wealth and the magnitude of the security problem. Moreover, one analyst noted that the informality of many private sector investments left security forces feeling indebted to private donors, not to the state.[85] Alejandro Poiré, Calderón's national security spokesperson and secretary of the interior, insisted that "Public monies should finance military infrastructure projects through annual budget appropriations, not informal deals brokered with local elites. Where is the accountability?"[86]

The lack of a security tax is not solely to blame for the failure of Mexico's security strategy. However, in Colombia, taxation created mechanisms of broader private sector participation in government strategy and of accountability. According to Poiré, it was not so much that the private sector in Mexico was uninterested in security policy but that financial elites lacked a mechanism to hold the government accountable for failures.[87] He remarked,

> The private sector is the most interested party in ensuring the success of a security policy, which is why economic elites did not question an annually expanding security budget during the Calderón administration . . . but because of lax participation on part of the citizenry, the Mexican government has never produced a diagnosis of the security threat and has not introduced meaningful evaluation mechanisms.

Andreas Schedler also describes how both the Calderón and Peña Nieto administrations deliberately sidelined citizens, including the private sector, in the formulation of security strategy.[88] Calderón's administration framed the problem as one of rival drug gangs fighting among each other, a challenge for which the government perceived military and police repression to be the only viable solution. The tactic was one of externalization, which understood delinquents not as Mexican citizens but as wayward individuals operating outside the concept of the nation. Conversely, President Peña Nieto's discourse about Mexico's levels of violence denied the existence of a national security crisis and sought to minimize the severity of the problem.[89] Despite rhetorical differences, the message to the Mexican citizenry—including business elites—was the same: "We, the government, will handle this; you can all relax."[90]

Subnational Change Agents: The Private Sector in Ciudad Juárez and Monterrey

Although security sector reform in Mexico at the federal level failed to draw significant backing from the country's economic elite, two subnational cases—Ciudad Juárez and Monterrey—stand out for strong ties between financial elites and local government efforts to reform the security sector, contrasting with national trends.[91] In both cases, state and municipal governments enacted sweeping structural changes to the local security sector by strengthening security and law enforcement institutions, and to do so, they relied on significant resources from a willing class of financial elites. Successes in these two metropolitan areas lend further support to the argument that big business buy-in can be consequential for the outcomes of security sector reform.

Ciudad Juárez

Ciudad Juárez shares a border with El Paso, Texas—which ranked in 2018 among the top ten safest cities in the United States.[92] The answer to how Ciudad Juárez became the most dangerous city in not only Mexico but also the world from 2008 to 2012 is linked to the city's location along a principal drug-smuggling corridor into the United States.[93] The city, which hosts four border crossings into the United States, has historically served as an important hub for the Mexican economy thanks to the proliferation of duty-free manufacturing plants called *maquiladoras*, which have contributed to steady economic and population growth since the 1960s.[94] However, the surge in cross-border movement of goods and people also gave rise to increased drug trafficking, and, under the leadership of Amado Carrillo Fuentes, the Juárez Cartel, founded in the 1970s, consolidated its regional power and came to control one of the primary transportation routes, worth billions of dollars of illegal shipments annually.

The group's monopoly of the Juárez *plaza*, or drug-trafficking route, was not safe for long, especially following the 1997 death of its leader.[95] From 1994 to the mid-2000s, violence in the city increased as rival drug gangs challenged the power of the Juárez Cartel. The effect on most citizens, however, remained low as outbursts of violence occurred in marginalized neighborhoods and remote parts of the city; public perceptions of security also remained favorable, evidenced by a bustling local economy and robust cross-border tourism.[96]

Circumstances changed in 2007, when an armed faction of the Sinaloa Cartel descended on Ciudad Juárez to confront their local rivals and seize control of the *plaza*. The homicide rate in Ciudad Juárez skyrocketed to 224 murders per hundred thousand inhabitants in 2010 from some thirty-five in 2004, and on average, organized crime groups perpetrated ten kidnappings a day in 2010.[97] In addition to a violent turf war in which innocent people often became collateral damage, the crime syndicates engaged in rampant extortion, which before 2007 was virtually unknown in the city. By 2010, roughly eight thousand businesses had fallen victim to routine extortion, forcing many in the private sector to close or relocate their operations.[98]

President Calderón responded to local calls for assistance by deploying the army and Federal Police to Ciudad Juárez, amassing more than ten thousand federal security agents in the city by the end of 2010. This strategy, known as Joint Operation Juárez (Operación Conjunta Juárez), was intended to overwhelm the dueling cartels with federal presence and firepower but ended up complicating matters on the ground.[99] Conflicts involving municipal, state, and federal authorities disturbed the local government's tenuous pact with the Juárez Cartel and fueled violence between state authorities and organized crime.[100] One observer noted that the Sinaloa Cartel, considered the largest and most powerful drug-trafficking organization in the Western Hemisphere, had infiltrated the Federal Police, yet the municipal police collaborated with the Juárez Cartel—a scenario that occasionally pitted state agents against one another in armed confrontations.[101] Between 2007 and 2011, Ciudad Juárez reported more than nine thousand murders, peaking at 3,116 in 2010 alone.[102] This wave of violence also contributed to an economic recession in the city, as the decline in tourism hit small- and medium-sized businesses especially hard.[103] The federal-led war on drugs also exposed the local population to abuses and corruption by federal forces: the Federal Police even orchestrated a spate of kidnappings for their financial gain and later blamed innocent members of the community, including municipal police officers, for the crimes.[104]

It was clear that federal efforts to improve security were failing. By 2010, the explosion of a car bomb and the murder of three employees of the US Consulate demonstrated that "no one was immune from the savage violence."[105] That year, the population's resentment of the federal government was so unmistakable that recurring protests against the federal presence prompted the withdrawal of the army from the city.[106] To improve relations with local citizens, the Calderón administration complemented its continued deployment of the Federal Police, which helped dispel any perception of militarization, with a campaign to help "repair the social fabric"; and the government launched a $270 million bid to conduct preemptive interventions in the city's most troubled and marginalized neighborhoods.[107] The We Are All Juárez (Todos Somos Juárez) campaign became the first major federal impetus for municipal crime and violence prevention in Mexico.[108] The initiative entailed state and municipal police reforms, educational improvements, public infrastructure projects, and economic stimulation. Central to the strategy was the involvement of civil society and especially the local private sector.

The federal government looked to existing community mechanisms in Ciudad Juárez to channel expanded investment into preventive measures. To this end, the Calderón administration benefited from an established relationship between local government and the business community to work collaboratively on security matters. Starting in 2007, a group of the city's top community leaders—many entrepreneurs fed up with a slumping economy and rampant crime that affected their business operations—founded a public safety forum called the Security and Justice Roundtable (Mesa de Seguridad y Justicia) to relay the community's concerns to the municipal and state governments.[109] The roundtable, convened monthly, was an innovative measure to bring together the city's top stakeholders—including politicians, police, human rights organizations, and businesses—to strategize for improved security. As one business leader described it, "The roundtable set up different committees based on different criminal trends and assigned relevant authorities to each committee. This was novel because for the first time many public officials were being introduced to their counterparts in other government agencies and were encouraged to work hand in hand."[110] According to a US Embassy official, "Policing is about communication and about sharing information. If police are part of an ecosystem with businesses and moms, the police will be more effective, and the roundtable became a lesson not just in communication but in empathy."[111]

Nevertheless, this approach to managing community-based problems confronted a major weakness: a lack of resources. The roundtable did not have a large operating budget of its own, and local authorities depended on a transfer of revenue from federal and state governments to fund the proposed initiatives. But a spike in extreme violence in early 2010 made implementing security reforms more urgent than ever before. The massacre of fifteen young people in January 2010 at a party in the Villas de Salvárcar neighborhood was a tipping point for local business owners, teachers, and human rights defenders, and the event unified civil society in a quest to deliver effective solutions to the city's ever-worsening insecurity.[112]

Given the local government's marginal budget for public security, the city's business sector, largely made up of automotive and electronics companies with similar operating models and shared priorities, responded to the crisis in 2010 by establishing a public–private partnership, the Trust for Competitiveness and Citizen Security (Fideicomiso para la Competitividad y Seguridad Ciudadana, or FICOSEC), to boost private sector contributions to local strategies for tackling insecurity.[113] At the petition of the Juárez business community, which had historically featured strong linkages with local and state governments, the state legislature introduced in 2011 an additional 0.05 percent payroll tax on all business owners in the state of Chihuahua, earmarking any revenue associated with the tax for crime prevention programs and security sector reform.[114] The FICOSEC tax was an unprecedented request by a business community in Mexico to raise its own tax burden. Further, the FICOSEC operating model confers control over the spending priorities on the trust, which consults the roundtable to define the community's needs. FICOSEC funds are, in essence, public resources administered by a council of private citizens.[115]

In FICOSEC's first five years of operation, the government collected more than $4 million annually, which financed new schools and drug rehabilitation centers, youth sports leagues, vocational training, and the certification of municipal and transit police.[116] FICOSEC also underwrote programs to complement investments from the federal government via We Are All Juárez, demonstrating an impressive and unprecedented synergy between civil society and the federal, state, and municipal governments. The roundtable and FICOSEC succeeded in pressuring state government authorities to apply lengthier sentences for kidnapping and murder, and the security tax was instrumental in subsidizing higher salaries, advanced training, and career benefits for the municipal police force and the district attorney's office.[117] Some of the most meaningful contributions included courses in crime scene investigation for state and municipal police officers and the recently reformed State Attorney General's Office (Fiscalía General del Estado de Chihuahua). Perhaps most important, FICOSEC founded a public security observatory that collects community data, analyzes local crime trends, and evaluates the effectiveness of anticrime strategies in the city.

One of the private sector's priorities was the reform of the municipal police force, long perceived as guilty of collusion with organized crime. The appointment of Julián Leyzaola (2011–13), a retired army lieutenant colonel, as the Ciudad Juárez police chief signaled a major change in the security sector. On assuming command, Leyzaola purged thousands of corrupt and incompetent municipal police officers from the force, purchased new patrol vehicles and weapons, and broke with the past by changing the color of its uniforms from gray to blue.[118] During Leyzaola's tenure, FICOSEC sponsored audits of the local force and background checks and polygraph tests of police personnel. Leyzaola's successors continued the reform initiative through 2016, improving training, extending life insurance benefits to police officers, and cracking down on drug traffickers.[119] The newly minted municipal police assumed an aggressive posture toward organized crime, and from 2011 to 2015, the force arrested record numbers of gang and cartel members.[120]

Gradually, the city's security initiatives began to bear impressive results, and crime rates declined starting in 2012. Following a slight decrease in cartel-related violence, the withdrawal of the army and a reduction in the presence of the Federal Police—two institutions widely regarded in Ciudad Juárez as abusive and corrupt—likely contributed to a decline of certain types of crime. By 2015, homicides in Ciudad Juárez had fallen from highs of more than three thousand per year to just 256.[121] The kidnapping rate, which peaked at nine per hundred thousand inhabitants in 2009, also dropped to below one per hundred thousand in 2014.[122] Nevertheless, rising national crime rates in Mexico during 2019 and 2020 spelled a return to more violent days for Mexico's border cities, reflecting the fragility of security gains amid ongoing turf wars among cartels.

Although residents of Ciudad Juárez continue to debate why violence dropped off, security analysts celebrate the efforts of the private sector as having a profound effect.[123] The consensus-driven work of FICOSEC and the Security and Justice Roundtable helped set the security agenda and held the federal, state, and municipal governments accountable for their relevant investments.[124] Notably, the private sector's leadership remained committed to crime prevention even after the crime reduction. Former FICOSEC Director Arturo Luján Olivas summarized it this way: "Although FICOSEC is nationally regarded as a success story and I am proud of the public-private partnership, crime rates are still not at what I would consider an acceptable level."[125] He and other civic leaders insisted that the positive results on the security front also overshadowed a growing problem with corruption in the municipal government, including among the police, which surfaced as a new priority for the roundtable.[126] Although challenges remain, Ciudad Juárez serves as a powerful example for Mexican municipalities contending with wanton crime and violence and, more broadly, a convincing point of reference for private sector involvement in security sector reform.[127]

Monterrey

The business community of the state of Nuevo León, concentrated in the greater Monterrey metropolitan area, also demonstrated the importance of private sector commitment to improved security.[128] Monterrey has been Mexico's most important industrial city for much of the country's modern history and is an epicenter of the automobile parts, steel, cement, and beverage industries. In the 2010s, it was the third largest metropolitan area and the second wealthiest city in Mexico. The same year, Monterrey's GDP per capita was the highest in the country, with projections for 2025 ranking the city as the wealthiest in all Latin America.[129] Like Ciudad Juárez, Monterrey's proximity to the US border has proven both a blessing and a curse given that the access to the US market has attracted producers of both licit and illicit goods. However, whereas Ciudad Juárez was valuable trafficking terrain dating back to the 1970s, Monterrey figured prominently in the criminal geography of the country only starting in the mid-2000s. Indeed, Monterrey was traditionally a safe haven where criminals often relocated their families to protect them from the bloodshed of the cartel wars. Not until 2008 did drug traffickers begin to see the city as a business opportunity, when the leaders of the Beltrán Leyva Cartel, former associates of the Sinaloa Cartel, began to infiltrate local government, feed the region's domestic drug market, and extort local businesses. To help them with their takeover of Nuevo León, Beltrán Leyva made an alliance with the violent Los Zetas Cartel.[130]

Originally part of the Gulf Cartel, Los Zetas had made inroads into the north of the country and began courting youth gangs, which boasted more than twenty-six thousand members in Monterrey in 2008, to supply the local drug market.[131] The shifting alliances among the criminal underworld ultimately resulted in a formal divorce between the Los Zetas and the Gulf cartels in 2010. When the Los Zetas and the Beltrán Leyva leaders formed a pact, Monterrey became ground zero for a bloody rivalry between the Los Zetas and their former associates in the Gulf Cartel. In 2010, the number of homicides in Nuevo León tripled from the year before, rising to 828.[132]

The year 2011 was a watershed for the city of Monterrey as acts of violence became ever more astonishing and deadly. Gun battles raged in the city's wealthiest neighborhoods, criminals draped mutilated corpses from city bridges, and seventy-eight security officials were killed in the first six months.[133] On August 25, eight arsonists working at the behest of the Los Zetas Cartel committed the most dramatic act of violence in a long string of assaults when they set ablaze a casino, leaving fifty-two dead. Between 2009 and 2011, homicides rose by 700 percent, and massacres, kidnappings, and carjacking became daily occurrences.[134] As in Ciudad Juárez, the city's business community, afflicted by high rates of extortion and concerned for the safety of their families and employees, demanded that the government retake the city from the clutches of organized crime. One of the principal impediments to doing so, however, was the widespread infiltration of the state and municipal police by the Los Zetas Cartel.[135] In Monterrey, the unreliable police force was an existential threat to the city's business class.

Monterrey's financial elites supported the reform of local security forces because organized crime had pushed elites to a breaking point.[136] Prior to the 2010s, the city's private sector mostly turned a blind eye to the influx of drug wealth in the city because it was good for local businesses, but subjected to the extreme violence associated with the drug trade, business owners quickly reversed course.[137] Nuevo León traditionally benefited from an active civil society, and the business community in particular has a long tradition of collaboration to manage community issues via an informal forum called the Group of the Ten (Grupo de los Diez), a consortium of the ten wealthiest companies in the state.[138] When the Mexican Marine Corps and Federal Police arrived to impose order in Nuevo León, the leaders of the Group of the Ten, who were well aware of the excesses of the federal security forces in Ciudad Juárez, sought alternatives to federal occupation.[139] A long-term federal presence in the city was not an option for Monterrey's financial elites. So, in coordination with Governor Rodrigo Medina de la Cruz (2009–15), the private sector hired experts to diagnose the security deficiencies of the state, devise realistic solutions, and recruit skilled personnel countrywide for the formation of a new state police force.[140]

Governor Medina, of the then opposition Institutional Revolutionary Party (Partido Revolucionario Institucional, or PRI), was especially supportive of the effort to raise a new professional police force in Nuevo León because the state's top business leaders, many of whom were ruling National Action Party (Partido Acción Nacional, or PAN) voters, had a direct line to President Calderón.[141] Had Medina obstructed efforts to reform the local police, a surge of federal troops to the state would have been inevitable, making the PRI look vulnerable on the issue of security just prior to the 2012 federal elections.[142] From 2010 to 2011, the Group of the Ten also convinced the federal government to initiate a widespread purge of state and municipal police in Monterrey in a comprehensive accreditation process. Likewise, the business group volunteered to pay a temporary payroll tax to finance the creation of a new state police force. The resulting collaboration became known as the Alliance for Security (Alianza por la Seguridad). During this period, the state government, private sector, and civil society funded and organized two forums to structure security strategies and reforms: the Civic Council (Consejo Cívico) and the Citizen's Council for Public Security of Nuevo León (Consejo Ciudadano de Seguridad Pública de Nuevo León, or CCSPNL). It was through these bodies that the state's principal stakeholders provided the capital and human resources to set a state security agenda, create a culture of legality among the citizenry, and stand up a more professional police force.[143] With a rise in payroll taxation, new contributions boosted state security and justice spending from just over $350 million in 2012 to nearly $500 million in 2017.[144]

Thanks to the state's business donors and some federal subsidies, the new Civil Force (Fuerza Civil), inaugurated in September 2011, boasted higher recruitment standards, specialized training, and a relatively generous operating budget.[145] Officers received at the outset a starting salary of 15,000 Mexican pesos ($1,175) per month—double the average Mexican police officer's salary—and lived in military-style barracks, concentrating the officers in a single living space and thus making it more difficult for organized crime to corrupt individual officers.[146] Crime data for the city suggest that, in large measure, the reform effort worked soon after the Civil Force entered into operation. In 2011, criminals carjacked an average of forty-five vehicles a day, a figure that dropped to an average of four per day in 2013.[147] By 2015, the number of kidnappings reached a low of twenty-one for the year, and the number of homicides nearly halved from peak levels, registering at 451 for 2015.[148] Further, even though extortion rates increased, the perception of insecurity also plunged: the number of poll respondents in the state who felt unsafe in their communities dropped from a high of 49 percent in 2011 to a low of 20 percent in 2014.[149]

The Civil Force is not a community police force equipped to address the social and community causes of violent crime, which was the focus of FICOSEC's early work in Ciudad Juárez. Instead, it was created to address the kinds of violence that occurred from 2009 to 2013 and captured international headlines, including roadblocks, kidnappings, massacres, and sensationalist homicides.[150] One US diplomat noted in an interview that the private sector's contributions to the establishment of the Civil Force afforded business leaders an outsized voice in its orientation, even giving the institution an "air of privatization."[151] Although the Civil Force, like the Ciudad Juárez municipal police, helped reduce crime rates and incidents of public shootouts, it has been only a partial success and has been less able to meet the evolving needs of the population as the character of criminal and violent activity has shifted. For instance, in 2018, the state saw a high incidence of forced disappearances, especially among women and the Central American migrant population near the US border, in large part because the Civil Force simply did not have a clear strategy for addressing that kind of violence.[152] Moreover, many business leaders expressed frustration with the government's overreliance on the private sector to fulfill core responsibilities of the government. In 2013, the state legislature of Nuevo León sought to build on the momentum of the previous security tax and raised a long-standing payroll tax from 2 to 3 percent to facilitate the expansion of the Civil Force to at least seven thousand officers by 2015—a move resisted by several of Monterrey's wealthiest residents, who insisted that the government use existing tax revenue more efficiently.[153]

As crime rates in Monterrey dropped, the need to build a force of fifteen thousand, as originally projected, seemed unnecessary to many. By the end of Medina's term in 2015, the Civil Force struggled to reach even five thousand officers.[154] The steep cost of maintaining the police deterred further expansion, and the election of Jaime "El Bronco" Rodríguez as the new state governor in 2015 ushered in a new posture with regard to security.[155] Alarmingly, the new administration let reforms lapse and appointed close associates without security credentials to key positions.[156] Moreover, although violence subsided in Nuevo León, the neighboring state of Tamaulipas experienced a surge in criminal activity, and some analysts contend that the reduction in violence in Monterrey may not have had to do as much with the effective institutional reform as it did with the displacement of violence to other communities.[157]

Starting in 2018, several observers even called into question the sustainability of the reforms and security advances, as crime was on the rise once again.[158] Recognizing a new wave of violence and mounting abuses committed by Civil Force officers, Senator Samuel García began in 2019 to promote an effort to "restore the origin, esprit, and strategies [that inspired the Civil Force] and revitalize" the institution. Yet as of 2022, his hope for a new wave of security sector reform in Nuevo León still failed to garner the necessary support—perhaps critically from the region's private sector.[159]

Factors such as the nature and locus of the security threat, the relative impact of violence on elite businesses and personal safety, and the cohesion of elite circles affected the degree to which financial elites agreed with, and thus endorsed, government prescriptions for reducing violence. Private sector elites in Colombia and Mexico held different views regarding insecurity in their countries and the best overall strategy for confronting violence, affecting the willingness of big business to rally behind security sector reform. Between the two cases, elites harbored different class attitudes to the reform priorities espoused in Plan Colombia and the Mérida Initiative, which in turn affected the prioritization and accountability of each country's reform effort.

As Arturo Ramírez Verdugo and Reyes Ruiz González contend, "Full implementation of the measures to revert insecurity is expensive . . . and imposes such severe stress on local budgets so as to eventually require increases in taxes and reduction in other expenditures for at least the ensuing three to five years."[160] One of the factors that made all the difference at the national level in Colombia and at the subnational level in Mexico was the creation of a formal mechanism, a security tax, to channel private sector contributions toward and to regulate governmental spending on security sector reform. Representing a boost for both the effectiveness and accountability of the security sector, the examples in this chapter exemplify the power of security taxes to maintain continuity of effort, ensure greater transparency, and engender better security sector governance.

The Colombian case validates the position that an engaged private sector can be a critical facilitator of security sector reform. The subnational cases of Ciudad Juárez and Monterrey in Mexico offer additional support for this theory and help demonstrate the significance of elite experiences and perceptions of insecurity on elite willingness to back security sector reform. Whereas all three cases reflect high cohesion in elite networks and runaway violence that affected elite interests at the outset of institutional reform initiatives, the largely criminal nature of the security threat and its evolving locus in the Mexican subnational cases—away from elite victimization—changed elite calculations about the return on their investment in security sector reform in the long run. In Ciudad Juárez, big business continued to support the contributions to the security sector through FICOSEC even as the worst of the state's violence subsided because of the broader community's continuing concerns about corruption and risks associated with police infiltration by organized crime. However, some signature programs for monitoring local police lapsed while reforms to the police stalled, and over time the Security and Justice Roundtable's activities reflected a greater focus on societal violence prevention, broadening the base to more nonstate beneficiaries.[161] In Monterrey, as violent crime dropped, so too did private sector interest in fulfilling the initial ambition to build a much larger Civil Force. For a time, violence either moved or was managed, and it was only when homicides soared in 2022, once again putting elite interests at risk, that the state government redoubled its efforts to grow the police force.[162] Alternatively, in Colombia the persistence of ideologically motivated insurgents who targeted elites and would only submit in the face of overwhelming force fueled elite concerns and thus sustained elite preferences for building on the progress of the Democratic Security Policy and Plan Colombia with robust financing for the country's military and police.

Notes

1. Moncada, 2016, pp. 95, 185. The term *big business* refers to the top economic echelon consisting of large profit-making corporations that act as an interest group in the public policymaking process.
2. Cammett, 2007; Maxfield & Schneider, 1997; Moncada, 2016; Walton, 1977.
3. Flores-Macías, 2014; Flores-Macías, 2022. Building on Gustavo Flores-Macías's work on Colombia, the author sought to test the theory that elite cohesion contributes to positive outcomes for security sector reform, whereas elite fragmentation and divisions between political and business elites inhibit common agenda-setting for security provision. From 2017 to 2018, the author conducted extensive fieldwork in Mexico on this topic, exploring the two subnational case studies of elite taxation presented in this chapter. Flores-Macías's latest monograph, published during the final editing of this book, also tests his theory in Mexico and features complementary subnational analysis that lends support to the conclusion that strong elite linkages and security crises enable elite taxation for improved security provision and, indeed, security sector reform.

4. Flores-Macías, 2022, p. 3.
5. The political science literature on elite theory is substantial and posits that the economic and social composition of political decision makers influences political outcomes (Blondel & Müller-Rommel, 2007). For this book, *economic elite* refers to the minority of citizens who hold a disproportionate amount of a country's wealth and thus have preferential access to political power. They use their economic status, which typically affords them social privilege, to influence policy outcomes through participation in corporations, corporate boards, philanthropic organizations, and agenda-setting institutions such as think tanks. In democratic systems, *political elite*, on the other hand, refers to those elected policymakers who occupy influential positions in the political hierarchy, control access to political power, and play a dominant role in setting policy agendas.
6. Enders et al., 2006; Frey et al., 2007; UNDP, 1994; Keefer & Loayza, 2008; Stewart, 2004.
7. F. Acuña, personal communication, Bogotá, Colombia, October 24, 2017.
8. Rettberg, 2009, p. 193.
9. Sánchez León et al., 2018; Stone, 2016. The literature on corporate complicity with illegal armed groups and human rights abusers is a growing field of academic inquiry (Payne & Pereira, 2016; Reno, 1997; Stanley, 1996; Tófalo, 2006; Verbitsky & Bohoslavsky, 2015; Zabyelina & Thachuk, 2022). On such complicity in the Colombian case, see Duncan, 2006; Grajales, 2017; Gutiérrez Sanín et al., 2007.
10. Senior US development official, personal correspondence, Tegucigalpa, Honduras, August 25, 2016.
11. Rettberg, 2007, pp. 482–483. The security costs of doing business in Colombia were immense. Colombian companies in 2006 spent as much as 10 percent on security-related expenses, and according to the Colombian government, the armed conflict cost the country 2 to 4 GDP points per year between 1991 and 1996 and more than 7 percent of GDP between 1998 and 2003 (Cárdenas et al., 2005; Rettberg, 2007, p. 483).
12. Rettberg, 2007, pp. 485–490.
13. Godoy, 2003, p. 5.
14. Rettberg, 2007, p. 486.
15. Nagle, 2002, p. 22.
16. Rettberg, 2007, p. 489.
17. "Plajian a hija," 2000.
18. "La paz, Sí, pero sin Víctor G. y sin canje," 1999; Rettberg, 2003, p. 199.
19. Colombian business community representative, personal communication, Bogotá, Colombia, December 14, 2017.
20. Even though victimization by paramilitary violence was as fierce as that by guerrilla violence, historical ties between the United Self-Defense Forces of Colombia (Autodefensas Unidas de Colombia, or AUC) and wealthy land and business owners meant that big business was less adversely affected by paramilitary-driven insecurity ("Centro Nacional de Memoria Histórica," n.d.).
21. Nagle, 2002, p. 26.
22. Delgado, 2015.
23. Retired US Army colonel, personal communication, Tegucigalpa, Honduras, September 19, 2016.
24. Richani, 2007, p. 406.
25. DiJohn, 2010.

26. Stone, 2016.
27. Bird, 1992, p. 32; Gracher, 2016, p. 6; Sanchez, 2006, p. 772.
28. Flores-Macías, 2014, p. 486.
29. Gracher, 2016, p. 15.
30. Rodríguez-Franco (2016, pp. 198–199) describes a scenario of elite solidarity with the state in pushing forward with security sector reform in Colombia. Despite the reluctance of elites to pay higher taxes, at the annual conference of bankers in 2002, two-thirds of participants responded that they were willing to pay even more of the wealth tax to fight insecurity. Additionally, 0.4 percent of the security tax revenues collected between 2002 and 2006 were voluntary contributions from people not legally required to pay the wealth tax.
31. Flores-Macías, 2014, pp. 487–488; "Impuesto de seguridad democrática es sólo para eso: Corte Constitucional," 2003. The legality of the special tax by decree was decided by the Constitutional Court in a ruling that favored the Uribe administration and permitted the continued collection of security tax revenue.
32. Flores-Macías, 2014, p. 478.
33. The first tax applied to some 420,000 taxpayers (roughly 1 percent of the population), 120,000 of which were corporations.
34. The figures referenced in this section were originally presented by Flores-Macías (2014).
35. In 2004, the government exempted the wealthiest individual taxpayers from the new imposition of the Democratic Security Tax via juridical stability contracts (*contratos de estabilidad jurídica*), which provided legal certainty for investors by offering them a reduced investment rate based on the legal framework that existed at the time of a substantial investment (Flores-Macías, 2014, p. 491).
36. Flores-Macías, 2022, p. 28. In 2014, the Colombian legislature renewed the wealth tax for the 2015–18 period but no longer earmarked it for public safety expenditures.
37. Marks, 2005, p. 77; Presidencia de la República & Ministerio de Defensa, 2003, p. 14.
38. Brett, 2018, pp. 8–9; Presidencia de la República & Ministerio de Defensa, 2003, p. 8. On the impact of the Democratic Security Policy on state consolidation, see Patiño Villa, 2010, pp. 231–244; Llorente & McDermott, 2014; Mason, 2003; Santader et al., 2012.
39. Flores-Macías, 2014, p. 481.
40. Flores-Macías, 2022, p. 28.
41. Flores-Macías, 2014.
42. Flores-Macías, 2014, p. 489; Flores-Macías, 2022, p. 55.
43. Academic security analyst, personal communication, Bogotá, Colombia, November 20, 2017.
44. Borrero Mansilla, 2006, pp. 132–135; Colombian business community representative, personal communication, Bogotá, Colombia, December 14, 2017.
45. Colombian business community representative, personal communication, Bogotá, Colombia, December 14, 2017.
46. Flores-Macías, 2014, p. 490.
47. Carrasquilla Barrera, 2005.
48. CEIC, 2019; Cerritelli, 2005, p. 180.
49. Avilés, 2001a, p. 166. On elite cohesion in Colombia, see Gutiérrez Sanín et al., 2013, p. 32; Hylton, 2003, p. 68; Lee & Thoumi, 1999; Pearce & Velasco Montoya, 2022; Ocampo, 2015; Stone, 2016.

50. Tobias Franz (2018) describes the reaction of financial elites in Medellín when a political outsider became mayor and imposed policies that harmed local elite interests: they organized politically and sought a greater share of political power by placing business elites in political office.
51. The Colombian economy grew at an average annual rate of 4.8 percent between 2002 and 2009, reassuring elites that their investments in the security sector were well administered (Posada-Carbó, 2011, p. 138). However, elite circles began to fracture during the Santos administration over the issue of the peace negotiations with the FARC, a topic explored in more depth in chapter 8 (Matanock & García-Sánchez, 2017).
52. Gracher, 2016.
53. Flores-Macías, 2014, p. 489.
54. Flores-Macías, 2014; N. Salazar, 2013, p. 489.
55. Fajardo-Heyward, 2015, p. 11; Rettberg, 2007, p. 466.
56. Senior US law enforcement official, personal communication, Tegucigalpa, Honduras, August 23, 2016.
57. The time horizons for elite support for security sector reform through taxation were relatively short, especially as regional elites became more intimately involved in security measures implemented by local governments (Abello Colak & Pearce, 2015; Moncada, 2016). Rettberg (2007, p. 490) notes that attempts to make the wealth tax permanent failed, despite repeated renewals of the Democratic Security Tax, and highlights that tax evasion increased in the successive applications of the security tax.
58. Olson & Baker, 2015.
59. Schedler, 2015, pp. 91–93.
60. Jones, 2016, p. 21; Schedler, 2015, p. 223.
61. Olson et al., 2018.
62. Moncada, 2021, pp. 121–154; Schedler, 2015, pp. 16–17.
63. One of the most common avenues for big business to help address insecurity was the founding of citizens' councils, which aim to generate trust between government actors and the citizenry by channeling information and demands from the citizenry to the state. Financial elites in many parts of the country begrudgingly accepted this role. Luis Wertman, the director of the capital's citizens' council, asserted, "Society should not occupy spaces that are actually of the government. This is how you get mafias. And authorities should not occupy spaces that are actually of the society. This is how you get a citizens' council. We have to find the delicate balance" (Wertman Zaslav, personal communication, Mexico City, February 13, 2018).
64. Government political analyst, personal communication, Mexico City, September 8, 2017.
65. Benítez Manaut, 2014, p. 60.
66. León Hernández, 2011; Calderón administration senior security official, Mexico City, January 26, 2018.
67. Mines 2020, p. 12; Ribano Seelke & Finklea, 2017, p. 13.
68. Calderón administration senior security official, personal communication, Mexico City, January 26, 2018.
69. Santaeulalia, 2014; Calderón administration senior security official, personal communication, Mexico City, January 26, 2018.
70. Government political analyst, personal communication, Mexico City, September 8, 2017.

71. Chapa Koloffon, personal communication, Mexico City, February 9, 2018.
72. J. French, personal communication, Mexico City, August 24, 2017.
73. Private sector security analyst, personal communication, Mexico City, September 8, 2017.
74. Aguilar et al., 2013, pp. 33–35; academic security analyst, personal communication, Mexico City, September 11, 2017. Major taxpayers in Mexico have historically enjoyed broad constitutional protections through a legal mechanism known as the *juicio de amparo*, or writ of protection, which allows the courts to shield taxpayers from taxes believed to violate the constitution (Elizondo & Magaloni, 2009, p. 189).
75. M. Novoa, personal communication, Mexico City, September 13, 2017. Fernández de Castro argues that one of the biggest hurdles to Mexican security sector reform has been a reluctance on part of the country's elites to back the full establishment of the rule of law because, under the status quo, elites continue to benefit from corruption and the flexibility of the law (Olson et al., 2018). Jenny Pearce (2018) explores this theme in her important paper on oligarchies and violence in Latin America.
76. J. French, personal communication, Mexico City, August 24, 2017. This is consistent with the work of Martin and Swank (2012), who argue that large countries like Mexico lack geographically concentrated social networks and thus rely on anonymous methods of coordination (that is, the market) to articulate and protect their interests.
77. Camp, 2012.
78. Camp, 2002, p. 12.
79. P. H. Smith, 2015. Roderic Camp (2012) notes, however, growing interest on part of business elites to pursue political careers at the state and local levels, increasing 140 percent from the pre-democratic era to 2012. President Fox, an influential business professional, appointed eight cabinet-level ministers from the private sector (Camp, 2002, p. 270).
80. Sabet, 2013, pp. 241, 244.
81. Government political analyst, personal communication, Mexico City, January 29, 2018. E. Rendón, personal communication, Mexico City, January 3, 2018.
82. M. Novoa, personal communication, Mexico City, September 13, 2017.
83. Fernández, 2016.
84. Moloeznik, 2013, p. 80; A. Poiré, personal communication, Mexico City, September 14, 2017.
85. Private sector security analyst, personal communication, Mexico City, September 12, 2017.
86. A. Poiré, personal communication, Mexico City, September 14, 2017.
87. A. Poiré, personal communication, Mexico City, September 14, 2017.
88. Schedler, 2015, pp. 14–15.
89. By the end of the Peña Nieto administration, the country's business community became increasingly outspoken over deteriorating security (Saldaña, 2018).
90. Schedler, 2015, p. 15.
91. Flores-Macías (2022, p. 135) explains how the geographic concentration of violence in Mexico attenuated any national elite consensus on increased taxation for public security. However, in some areas of the country, elites took a more proactive role in helping shape security outcomes. In 2007, Tijuana Mayor José Guadalupe Osuna Millán courted the private sector to help revamp the municipal security strategy in the face of rising homicides ("How the private sector," 2015). Big business contributions to this end were considerable and eventually culminated in the introduction of a Business Trust for the state of Baja California, which supports public security and other social investments with 5 percent of total revenues obtained from the collection of personal income tax in the state.

92. Edwards, 2018.
93. Consejo Ciudadano para la Seguridad Pública y la Justicia Penal A.C., 2011.
94. O'Neil, 2013, pp. 1–2.
95. In the decade that followed, some three hundred gangs, working at the behest of the Juárez and Sinaloa cartels, formed and committed between two hundred and three hundred homicides per year until 2008 (Campbell, 2011; Serrano, 2018, p. 60).
96. Durán-Martínez, 2017, p. 204.
97. Conger, 2014, p. 5; Monárrez Fragoso, 2005, p. 279.
98. Quiñones, 2016.
99. The public security strategy was later renamed Joint Operation Chihuahua (Operación Conjunta Chihuahua).
100. Durán-Martínez, 2017, p. 205.
101. Citizen's Observatory for Prevention, Security, and Justice representative, personal communication, Ciudad Juárez, Mexico, January 15, 2018.
102. Valencia & Chacon, 2013.
103. International civil society organization representative, personal communication, Ciudad Juárez, Mexico, January 15, 2018.
104. Citizen's Observatory for Prevention, Security, and Justice representative, personal communication, Ciudad Juárez, Mexico, January 15, 2018. The civil society representative also noted that when federal forces departed the city in 2012, they did so "with their trucks filled with stolen possessions." On federal abuses in Ciudad Juárez, see Meyer, 2010.
105. A. Luján Olivas, personal communication, Ciudad Juárez, Mexico, January 15, 2018.
106. Meyer, 2010, p. 10; international civil society organization representative, personal communication, Ciudad Juárez, Mexico, January 15, 2018.
107. Miroff, 2010.
108. S. Ley, personal communication, Mexico City, January 9, 2018. The US Embassy supported the Mexican government's strategy in Ciudad Juárez, and US Ambassador Carlos Pascual (2009–11) was actively involved in helping shape the city's security strategy (J. Tello Peón, personal communication, Mexico City, February 13, 2018).
109. Flores-Macías, 2022, p. 147. Several senior business representatives and public officials traveled to Colombia in 2009 to learn best practices in reducing violent crime.
110. A. Luján Olivas, personal communication, Ciudad Juárez, Mexico, January 15, 2018.
111. Former senior US diplomat, email correspondence, September 28, 2021.
112. S. Ley, personal communication, Mexico City, January 9, 2018. President Calderón's erroneous public comments accusing the victims of the massacre of belonging to a gang infuriated the Juárez community; between February and March 2010, Calderón visited the city three times in presumed acts of conciliation. The meetings between the president and the parents of the student victims were a critical factor in the massive mobilization of federal, state, and municipal aid to deal with the city's security crisis (S. Ley, personal communication, Mexico City, January 29, 2018).
113. FICOSEC's founders cite Colombia as a successful reference for private sector involvement in security sector reform ("Historia – FICOSEC," 2018).
114. Luján Olivas remarked, "FICOSEC emerged in a very specific context, one in which the private sector of the state had previously addressed a public crisis with the establishment of a trust" (A. Luján Olivas, personal communication, Ciudad Juárez, Mexico, January 15, 2018). FICOSEC was modeled on an earlier trust in the state of Chihuahua. In 1990, the city of Chihuahua, capital of the state, endured historically high levels of flooding after a

torrential rainstorm known as La Tromba (The Downpour), which left ninety-eight people dead, destroyed 275 homes, and rendered thousands of people homeless (Meza Rivera, 2014). The government temporarily relocated the displaced citizens to community gymnasiums and schools, but after months of government inaction to find a permanent solution for these people, the private sector established a trust called the Business Foundation of Chihuahua (Fundación del Empresariado Chihuahuense, A.C., or FECHAC), which applied a payroll tax of 0.1 percent to companies operating in the state. For the people of Chihuahua, the trust helped rebuild homes for thousands of community members and was a resounding success—so much so that the tax remains in place more than twenty years after the completion of the initial projects to finance the construction of community projects, orphanages, and nursing homes.

115. A. Luján Olivas, personal communication, Ciudad Juárez, Mexico, January 15, 2018.
116. A. Luján Olivas, personal communication, Ciudad Juárez, Mexico, January 15, 2018.
117. Quiñones, 2016.
118. Quiñones, 2016. In 2018, Leyzaola became mired in scandals surrounding human rights abuses committed during his tenure as police commissioner (Díaz, 2018).
119. A. Castro, personal communication, Ciudad Juárez, Mexico, January 16, 2018.
120. Valencia & Chacon, 2013.
121. Quiñones, 2016; S. Salazár Gutiérrez, personal communication, Ciudad Juárez, Mexico, January 16, 2018.
122. Ramírez Verdugo & Ruiz González, 2016, p. 11.
123. A. Brillones, personal communication, Ciudad Juárez, Mexico, January 15, 2018; L. Chapa Koloffon, personal communication, Mexico City, February 9, 2018; E. Rendón, personal communication, Mexico City, January 3, 2018. Some analysts discerned that the drop in violence had more to do with a truce between cartels (international civil society organization representative, personal communication, Ciudad Juárez, Mexico, January 15, 2018). Former Chihuahua State Attorney General Jorge González noted, however, that the arrests of the heads of local criminal groups, including the head of the armed wing of the Juárez Cartel, led to a precipitous drop in homicides (Valencia & Chacon, 2013). From October 2010 to January 2013, authorities captured more than four thousand criminals, including 250 kidnappers and two hundred extortionists.
124. The tax arrangement changed in 2013 when the state legislature approved an increase in the payroll tax from 2 to 3 percent, a measure adopted once again in 2015. Security-related expenditures accounted for at least half of the 1 percent increase starting in 2013.
125. A. Luján Olivas, personal communication, Ciudad Juárez, Mexico, January 15, 2018.
126. S. Meza, personal communication, Ciudad Juárez, Mexico, January 17, 2018.
127. The application of the so-called Juárez template in other Mexican municipalities has not been without complications and mostly failures. In Michoacán, a lack of consensus among business elites and a pervasive distrust of government among the business community stunted preliminary discussions about levying a tax similar to the FICOSEC tax (A. Luján Olivas, personal communication, Ciudad Juárez, Mexico, January 15, 2018).
128. The greater metropolitan area of Monterrey includes the municipalities of Apodaca, Cadereyta Jiménez, El Carmen, García, General Escobedo, Guadalupe, Juárez, Monterrey, Salinas Victoria, San Nicolás de los Garza, San Pedro Garza García, Santa Catarina, and Santiago.
129. "Monterrey: The most advanced region," 2019.

130. Dudley, 2012. In 2007, Zetas leaders fractured from the Gulf Cartel and, amid a simultaneous reorganization of the Sinaloa Cartel, seized the opportunity to collaborate with the Beltrán Leyva Cartel in its quest to enlarge its *plaza* quotient by expanding into Monterrey.
131. Conger, 2014, p. 15.
132. Conger, 2014, p. 16.
133. Conger, 2014, p. 16.
134. Mendoza Márquez & Montero Bagatella, 2015, p. 114.
135. S. Ley, personal communication, Mexico City, January 9, 2018.
136. Olson et al., 2018.
137. Olson et al., 2018; A. Poiré, personal communication, Mexico City, September 14, 2017.
138. One researcher noted that financial elites in Monterrey are mostly Catholic, a characteristic that has historically compelled them to participate in community service (G. Fondevila, personal communication, Mexico City, January 9, 2017). Middlebrook, as well, underscores the importance of Catholic social thought and local-level civic engagement to the PAN's ideology (2001, pp. 15–21). However, one civil society member based in Monterrey remarked, "The private sector only gets involved where it is convenient for them. . . . They have been helpful on the security front in Monterrey because it benefits their businesses, but they are less keen to support development and prevention efforts" (regional civil society organization representative, personal communication, Monterrey, Mexico, February 7, 2018).
139. A. A. Fernández Aguilar, personal communication, Monterrey, Mexico, February 7, 2018. The state government of Nuevo León also appealed to federal authorities to remove the Marine Corps from public security roles because the army and navy did not have jurisdiction to fill out the protocol of "first responder," which complicated local authorities' efforts to capture criminals.
140. M. C. Sánchez Bocanegra, personal communication, Monterrey, Mexico, February 7, 2018.
141. S. Ley, personal communication, Mexico City, January 9, 2018.
142. Mendoza Márquez & Montero Bagatella, 2015, p. 111.
143. Peña González, 2016. Luján Olivas noted that the Group of the Ten reached out to FICOSEC to explore the possibility of establishing a trust similar to that in the state of Chihuahua (A. Luján Olivas, personal communication, Ciudad Juárez, Mexico, January 15, 2018). However, unlike in Ciudad Juárez, where most business executives work in similar industries, the Group of the Ten represented a more diverse range of business interests and could not find consensus on the issue of a payroll tax (A. A. Fernández Martínez, personal communication, Monterrey, Mexico, February 7, 2018; Pérez Rolón, personal communication, Monterrey, Mexico, February 7, 2018).
144. Signoret, 2018, pp. 14–16.
145. N. Salazar, 2013.
146. "The new face of Mexican policing," 2013. The Civil Force has a military-style indoctrination and operating orientation, and the philosophy underpinning the institution is one of national security (A. L. Fernández Aguilar, personal communication, Monterrey, Mexico, February 6, 2018).
147. "The new face of Mexican policing," 2013.
148. "Confirman estadísticas crisis de seguridad en Nuevo León," 2018.
149. Carrillo Gamboa & Cantú Escalante, 2018, p. 21; Ramírez Verdugo & Ruiz González, 2016, p. 12.

150. J. Pérez Rolón, personal communication, Monterrey, Mexico, February 7, 2018.
151. US diplomat, personal communication, Mexico City, December 3, 2021.
152. A. L. Fernández Aguilar, personal communication, Mexico City, February 6, 2018.
153. Conger, 2014, p. 19.
154. Castañeda, 2018.
155. Signoret, 2018, p. 16. Pearce stresses that the contingency of elite commitment to violence prevention is the most salient aspect of such interventions because security provision is rarely durable and often generates "its own violences and abuse, with little or no accountability to the rule of law" (Pearce, 2018, p. 20).
156. Fisher et al., 2018.
157. Ramírez Verdugo & Ruiz González, 2016, p. 17.
158. L. Chapa Koloffon, personal communication, Mexico City, February 9, 2018; A. Poiré, personal communication, Mexico City, September 14, 2017.
159. Chantaka, 2019.
160. Ramírez Verdugo & Ruiz González, 2016, p. 2.
161. Cisneros, 2019.
162. Reyes, 2022.

6

Finding Common Ground

Interparty Relations and Continuity in Security Sector Reform

Interparty relations in countries on the receiving end of security assistance are not only a critical indicator of domestic support for security sector reform but also helpful in determining how much leverage Washington can expect to exert through its security assistance. This is true even when the United States holds considerable influence over the recipient government. For instance, despite maintaining constructive relations with the Iraqi executive branch during the US-orchestrated campaign against the Islamic State, opposition parties in the Iraqi parliament rejected the presence of US troops in the country and the US stabilization approach, culminating in a 2020 resolution to expel US forces from the country.[1] In Colombia and Mexico, although Washington negotiated Plan Colombia and the Mérida Initiative with the executive branch directly, setting a reform agenda for the security sector depended on budgets approved by national legislatures and on support for executive-led security strategies from across the partisan spectrum. Legislatures did not stand in the way of financing national contributions to security sector reform in either country, but Colombia benefited from relative convergence among its major parties, resulting in broad interparty support for security sector reform and coherence in the design and application of the government's security strategy. In contrast, polarization among Mexico's political parties contributed to the politicization of the government's security strategy as an electoral issue, undermining consensus on how to improve security in the country. In this view, the characteristics of the party system—especially its tendency toward polarization—are a prominent factor that weighs heavily on whether security assistance can positively affect security outcomes and, more fundamentally, on whether security sector reform even becomes a priority in the recipient country. Continuity in policy over time and from administration to

From Peril to Partnership. Paul J. Angelo, Oxford University Press. © Oxford University Press 2024.
DOI: 10.1093/oso/9780197688106.003.0007

administration is a major facilitator of security sector reform, whereas constantly shifting policies and strategies undermine it.

Party System Institutionalization and Polarization

In some of the few major studies that systematically evaluate the domestic factors that affect the adoption of security sector reform, Louis-Alexandre Berg insists that the diversity and cohesion of the ruling political coalition are especially influential in determining outcomes.[2] He hypothesizes that when a ruling coalition is made up of competing ideological or programmatic platforms and thus tenuous, factions within tend to exert greater influence on policy formulation and often impede an executive's ability to make progress on ambitious reform agendas.[3] Driven by a desire to shore up legitimacy and deliver policy results, executive leaders under these conditions are more likely to turn to international organizations and foreign governments for financing and expertise. This in turn creates greater opportunities for partner governments to condition foreign assistance on democratizing reforms, including in the security sector. Conversely, when a national executive benefits from a cohesive base of support in the legislature, popular support, and the loyalty of the security sector, the governing party is unlikely to invite reforms that might limit its control.

Berg holds that a national commitment to institutional reform reflects internal struggles over political authority, referring specifically to power balances among elites and their access to revenue.[4] Elites who face threats from within their own party and lack resources to carry out their policy agendas are more likely to adopt security sector reform and to use external assistance to this end. Berg supports his hypothesis with the case study of Bosnia and Herzegovina, in which he finds that fragmentation of the ruling coalition and a dependency on international financing created a crucial opening for NATO and the European Union to shape the reform of the country's armed forces.[5] Over time, international security assistance contributed to improved security sector governance. Conversely, in Timor-Leste, largely unconstrained revenue due to rising oil wealth prompted local elites to ignore the conditions, directives, and best practices encouraged by international donors, despite elite network fragmentation. This scenario resulted in the persistence of informal oversight and accountability in the security sector.

Although Berg's case studies feature younger and less established democratic political institutions than those in Colombia and Mexico, his characterization of the political openings that facilitate security sector reform helps clarify the dynamics at play in the case studies of this book. In Colombia, where elite networks were cohesive but had considerable revenue constraints, the political logic was such that security sector reform was in itself advantageous for the governing coalition, and the major parties agreed that international assistance for this reform was essential to resolving the country's myriad problems. The coalition was multipartisan but never shied away from pursuing major reforms in the military and police, largely because of the existential security threat that Colombian elites of all political stripes faced. Moreover, political elites did not perceive significant risks or opportunities in strengthening the security sector because the security forces had not historically been major arbiters of political power.

In Mexico, which featured a fragmented elite network yet a comparatively unconstrained revenue base, political differences within the governing coalition did not obstruct the passage of legislation or the approval of budgets favorable to Calderón's security strategy at the outset of his presidency.[6] But interparty rivalries did eventually impede his ability to deliver on the promise of such reform despite a windfall of resources via the Mérida Initiative, demonstrating the importance of the interparty dynamics for determining security outcomes writ large. The lack of continuity in strategy between administrations, owing to a lack of political consensus on how to deal with insecurity, stunted security sector reform in Mexico.

Thanks to the pioneering work of Scott Mainwaring and Timothy Scully, party system institutionalization (PSI), or the degree to which parties endure and their interactions become predictable, has become a central framework by which to evaluate policy outcomes in modern democracies.[7] Assessing PSI helps identify the nature of relations between parties, illuminating prospects for interparty consensus on policy initiatives such as security sector reform. When the party system is in flux and new parties and political movements appear regularly, the system lacks stability and thus predictability; the converse is true for institutionalized systems.[8]

Polarization is also a striking characteristic of some party systems.[9] Polarization reflects the extent of differentiation of policy preferences among parties in a system.[10] According to Giovanni Sartori, the degree of polarization reveals the patterns of cooperation and opposition at the core of party system analysis.[11] In his seminal work on the topic, he distinguishes between centripetal and centrifugal systems. In centrifugal systems, parties vary more widely by ideology, which reinforces inflexible policy platforms, whereas centripetal systems see party platforms converge on the center in an opportunistic gambit for nonideological voters.[12] Centrifugal orientations that are underpinned by a high degree of PSI, in which parties are entrenched in their policy preferences, render the compromise needed for major reforms especially elusive.[13] Although some degree of polarization among parties may actually indicate the quality of party competition and improve the likelihood that parties provide voters with meaningful alternatives, highly polarized systems tend to be less effective at delivering new policies.[14] Because opposition parties often derive an electoral advantage from obstructing the passage of sweeping reforms initiated by the ruling party, compromise is scarce.[15] In less polarized systems, the stakes of reform initiatives are typically lower given that any potential fallout would affect the parties that make up the governing coalition more or less equally.[16]

The Colombian party system during Plan Colombia exhibited a centripetal tendency, whereas after 2000 Mexico embodied more polarized, centrifugal interparty relations. As these cases demonstrate, polarization had far-reaching implications for how parties formulated policies to deal with crime and violence. In Colombia, although the fluctuating nature of the party system played a practical role in opening political space that permitted a bold security strategy, it was ultimately the long-standing severity of the security threat that inspired convergence and reduced polarization. Given the existential threat posed by nonstate armed groups, the major parties converged on programmatic issues ranging from macroeconomic policy to resolving armed conflict.[17] Because of the homogeneity of security platforms among parties as well as the historical failure of such policies to reduce criminality regardless of the party in power, political elites assumed collective responsibility for the country's security crisis, rather than framing it as a partisan political issue. When the crisis reached its apex during the Pastrana administration (1998–2002), that sense of common ownership created a stable political climate for US investments via Plan Colombia and facilitated interparty cooperation on enhancing security sector governance.

Conversely, in Mexico, the institutionalization of the party system, a product of seven decades of one-party rule, led to entrenched party platforms, fueling polarization and impeding a collaborative approach to security policy. Because the security threat in Mexico was more diffuse and did not necessarily imperil political elites, opposition parties ultimately rejected Calderón's militarized and federally directed response to the crisis. When the executive switched party hands in 2012, President Peña Nieto, who won the election partly by campaigning against Calderón's security strategy, changed course on major security programs, suspended cooperation with the United States, and reoriented the focus of the Mérida Initiative.

In sum, three main factors reinforced interparty consensus on security sector reform and the robust adoption of US security assistance in Colombia: the centripetal orientation of the party system, convergence on

Table 6.1. Factors Affecting Interparty Consensus on Security

	Colombia	Mexico
Party system orientation	centripetal	centrifugal
Interparty response to security crisis	convergence	divergence
Public reaction to security policies	unified	divided
Result	consensus	polarization

Source: Author's tabulation.

security policy to address an existential security crisis, and a public mandate to pursue aggressive security policies. In Mexico, absent a perceived existential threat to the state, programmatically polarized parties offered competing ideas about the security dilemma, which weakened prospects for consensus and consistency on the security strategy. Interparty polarization and the politicization of security as an electoral issue denied Mexico the continuity essential to successful security sector reform.

Colombia: Interparty Consensus and Continuity on Security Strategy

Colombia's two-party system embodied a high degree of institutionalization for much of the country's history, reinforced after 1957 by the National Front pact brokered between the Liberal and Conservative Parties.[18] In exchange for routine political alternation, the traditional parties solidified a closed bipartisan system that persisted formally until 1974.[19] However, as the ruling parties narrowed their ideological offerings in a coordinated effort to forge political stability, brand differentiation between the parties diminished, and Colombian citizens decreasingly identified with one party over the other as the country entered the tumultuous 1980s.[20] Even though some party activists attempted to restore ideological bases for political action, the policy preferences of the two parties remained closely aligned long after the conclusion of the power-sharing period.[21]

Restructuring Party Politics

Throughout the 1980s, Colombia's party establishment quickly became associated with governmental dysfunction because legislators from both traditional parties routinely blocked executive-led initiatives to enhance the provision of public goods in a bid to keep government spending low. The major parties in Colombia were characterized by high levels of party indiscipline. Liberal and Conservative members of Congress often prevented reform proposals from passing, even reforms that originated in their own parties, when policies conflicted with their clientelistic interests.[22] It was not only on matters of policy and in their obstructionism that the Liberal and Conservative Parties became indistinguishable, however. The increasing influence of organized crime groups on political leaders in both parties accelerated popular frustration with the political establishment.[23] It was in this context that the erosion of the traditional parties—and consequently, of PSI—took place. As discussed in chapter 5, political and financial elite circles overlap considerably in Colombia. Given the inability of the Liberal and Conservative Parties to deliver solutions to economic and political problems such as land reform and drug violence, new political movements seized on popular discontent to raise class grievances and challenge the governing establishment—both on the battlefield and at the ballot box. The 1990s in Colombia were a period of guerrilla expansion and a proliferation of political parties, and the resulting fragmentation of political power initiated a protracted transition from an institutionalized party system to a deinstitutionalized one.

Political decentralization (see chapter 7) and electoral reform in the 1980s helped reduce the Liberal and Conservative monopoly of political power outside the major cities because the new changes reduced incentives for mayors and city council members to remain loyal to the established parties.[24] The two leading parties had already lost their programmatic appeal to voters and largely depended on local party machinery to maintain power.[25] When reforms that boosted the political and financial autonomy of local politicians took effect, mayors and city council members abandoned their party allegiances in increasing numbers. Furthermore, the 1991 Constitution altered the terms of political bargaining in Colombia by reducing legal impediments to party formation, establishing special prerogatives such as access to governmental data and guaranteed media attention for opposition parties, and adopting a single national district to elect the senate.[26] The resulting panorama featured high electoral volatility, low levels of partisan attachment, and the emergence of personalism as a defining feature of the political order. By the early 2000s, only 12 percent of respondents in a nationwide survey cited party loyalty as their reason for voting.[27]

Although this reconfiguration of the party system weakened the traditional parties, party fragmentation did not signal the decline of elite rule in Colombia. It instead strengthened centripetal policy convergence. In fact, the

1991 legislative elections resulted in a major victory for the Liberal Party, effectively granting control over the legal mechanisms that governed the implementation of the new constitution to establishment politicians.[28] Additionally, the spirit of compromise at the heart of the Constituent Assembly selected to rewrite the constitution was short-lived in practical terms. The M-19 Democratic Alliance (Alianza Democrática M-19), which sought to disrupt the party system by courting social groups that had been excluded under two-party rule, splintered by the 1994 electoral cycle, ceding electoral terrain back to the traditional parties.[29] And although the policy-negotiating process had grown less predictable with the infusion of new actors, the Liberal and Conservative Parties published the same broad platforms that characterized their governing agenda throughout the 1980s.[30] The elections of President Ernesto Samper of the Liberal Party in 1994 and of President Andrés Pastrana of the Conservative Party in 1998 meant a continuation of market-oriented economic policies, suppressive strategies to combat drug cartels, and renewed interest in finding a negotiated resolution to the country's armed conflict.[31]

Some emerging parties attempted to broaden the ideological spectrum of electoral competition in Colombian politics, especially by incorporating demobilized insurgent groups into the political fray. Yet as ordinary Colombians became less ideological and less politically engaged over time, most new parties adopted administrative discourses. Rather than offering an ambitious ideological vision of a preferred societal order, they campaigned on electoral issues that mattered to the public, such as corruption, bureaucratic inefficiency, clientelism, and governmental negligence.[32] Amid the persistence of insurgent activity in the country, Colombia's socialist movement, which advocated for a major overhaul of the economy, social services administration, and security provision, failed to gain traction among the broader electorate. After the extermination of thousands of members of the Patriotic Union (Unión Patriótica, or UP) party in the 1980s and 1990s, many from the ranks of the radical left returned to subversion or sought exile outside of the country.[33] The Revolutionary Armed Forces of Colombia (Fuerzas Armadas Revolucionarias de Colombia, or FARC) leadership was especially intransigent and refused to abandon its stance on land tenure, property ownership, and foreign trade; FARC commanders routinely criticized the democratic left for pursuing a pragmatic strategy that never really threatened the prevailing order of society.[34] In effect, even as the system became less institutionalized, the absence of leftist parties in Colombian politics resulted in a truncated political space, one that was conducive to greater interparty consensus on policy matters.

The lack of stark ideological differences among parties rendered Colombian politics a competition for the middle ground.[35] Despite the political liberalization granted by the 1991 Constitution, the proliferation of new parties in Colombia did not translate into highly differentiated policy preferences and by the close of the decade merely reinforced the centripetal convergence of party platforms inherited from the previous era.

Security Sector Reform as Crisis Response

By the early 2000s, the corruption of the Samper presidential campaign, the lingering effects of the 1999 recession, and the persistence of insecurity sparked a wave of public frustration with the Liberal-Conservative stewardship of the country. In 2002, a staggering 86 percent of Colombians believed that the country was going in the wrong direction, up 6 percent from 1998.[36] The traditional parties managed to cling to power well beyond the 1991 reforms, but a groundswell of support for nontraditional parties in the 2002 legislative elections signaled the unmistakable breakdown of the party system. Forty-six parties that had never competed in elections, many led by former Liberal and Conservative partisans, won 32.9 percent of the lower congressional chamber. Further, Álvaro Uribe, the first independent candidate to win the presidency, emerged as victor in the 2002 presidential election, which proved to be a referendum on the traditional parties' management of the country.[37] Although most new political movements did not offer the public fundamentally different policy proposals, they appealed to voters nonetheless because they appeared to lack the baggage of establishment politics.[38]

The defining issue of the 2002 presidential race was Colombia's security crisis, and in the run-up to the election, Uribe seized upon the electorate's recent swing in favor of a more militarized strategy for dealing with nonstate armed groups. Following the collapse of Pastrana's peace talks with the FARC, the incumbent Conservative Party had lost credibility to propose new ideas for addressing rising criminal and terrorist activity.[39] Similarly, the Liberal Party failed to produce viable alternatives for curbing violence or putting an end to the armed conflict, as party leaders were hesitant to pursue an aggressive stance that would translate into intensified confrontation and potentially higher death tolls.[40] Meanwhile, the FARC, National Liberation Army (Ejército de Liberación Nacional, or ELN), and United Self-Defense Forces of Colombia (Autodefensas Unidas de Colombia, or AUC) were mounting steadily more audacious attacks against security forces and civilian targets. As much as 40 percent of Colombian territory had fallen under some level of guerrilla control, hundreds of local politicians had been forced out from their jurisdictions due to the threat of violence, and hundreds of thousands of citizens fell victim to forced displacement. Turning a blind eye to the existential threat posed by the country's illegal armed groups was simply not a viable option for the Colombian central government.

The paralysis of the Liberal and Conservative Parties, however, opened the door to bolder voices, and it was Uribe's hard-line position on security that most appealed to voters, including many in the ranks of the traditional parties. In fact, Uribe's candidacy and subsequent victory were consequential for Colombia's party system in the decades to follow, during which personalism and charisma had more to do with national electoral outcomes than party affiliation. Vowing to expand the reforms initiated under Plan Colombia by doubling the size of the military and police and to take the fight to the country's left-wing insurgencies, Uribe won the presidency with 54 percent of the vote during the first electoral round in 2002—an accomplishment he would outdo four years later when he secured reelection with a resounding 62 percent.[41]

Embracing the opening of the party system that had taken hold after 1991, Uribe ran as an independent with a highly personalized campaign called Colombia First (Primero Colombia). Despite his background as the hawkish Liberal governor of Antioquia Department from 1995 to 1997, Uribe presented himself as an antiestablishment outsider, having opted out of the Liberal Party's primary and instead launching his candidacy by collecting signatures from voters to gain ballot access.[42] By 2001, the deinstitutionalization of the party system had already contributed to rising party indiscipline and tenuous party loyalty from politicians nationwide.[43] When Uribe emerged as a strong candidate in the polls thanks to his aggressive antiguerrilla stance, opportunistic politicians from across the political spectrum, inspired by the early achievements of Plan Colombia, rode his wave of popularity and endorsed his agenda.[44] The growing independence of politicians from their parties and the public mandate Uribe enjoyed combined to forge an overwhelming consensus among political elites on the implementation of a more forceful security strategy.[45]

Security sector reform was perceived as necessary and urgent against the backdrop of Colombia's raging armed conflict. To the extent that the country no longer perceived peace negotiations an option, restoring order via a reformed security sector was the only conceivable solution. Uribe's prestige and appeal as an outsider certainly contributed to the public's faith in his candidacy. But he was also the one serious candidate who, from the outset, rejected continuing peace talks with the FARC—a position more politicians adopted as Pastrana's negotiations faltered.[46] Uribe, whose candidacy was strengthened by his relatability to voters, took advantage of growing frustration within the traditional parties to galvanize electoral support against Horacio Serpa, a Samper loyalist and the Liberal Party's 1998 and 2002 presidential candidate, and, later, to form a legislative support base. In fact, the disorder of the party system was so acute that the Conservative Party, which had lost some of its most committed leaders in five successive party secessions, failed to run a candidate in the 2002 and 2006 presidential contests, and President Uribe co-opted a significant portion of the party's membership.[47]

To accomplish his mandate and vision, the new president capitalized on low party unity and the deinstitutionalization of the party system to garner support for his policies. This unprecedented model for coalition formation in Colombia became the key to his interparty success. One analysis highlighted that Uribe could count on "the disciplined conservatives . . . , opinion leaders . . . , career liberals . . . , emerging legislative stars . . . , [and] politicians from the regions with clientelistic tendencies and members of the upper class with a strong presence in the media."[48] Following his election, Uribe received the declared support of Liberal and Conservative legislators representing a combined 58.4 percent of the Senate and 64.0 percent of the House of Representatives.[49] In an attempt to formalize the Uribista movement, some of his top backers eventually formed a new party in 2005 called the Social Party of National Unity (Partido Social de Unidad Nacional), known colloquially as the Party of the U in a flattering reference to the president's surname. Even though Uribe did not formally declare his membership, the party's organization represented the union of politicians who believed in Uribe's policy agenda, possessed the regional party machinery to attract voters, and maintained a majority in Congress.[50]

Uribe's coalition had an impressive legislative approval rate for presidential initiatives of 42.5 percent during his first term, an uncommon feat for Colombian presidents.[51] Despite party system fragmentation and weak party loyalties, Uribe's charisma and popularity helped achieve high governability and discipline within his legislative bloc.[52] Some of the president's most significant victories included the Justice and Peace Law to facilitate the demobilization of the AUC and the legislation governing presidential reelection, which enabled the continuation of his mandate and his security strategy for another four years. Congress also approved Uribe's National Development Plan, successive iterations of the Democratic Security Tax, changes to military conscription, improved benefits for the security forces, and ambitious reintegration programs for demobilized combatants.

Congressional devotion to Uribe's security strategy and the objectives of Plan Colombia led to early and notable improvements in security. Greater freedom of movement during holidays thanks to increased highway security gave an immediate boost to the president's popularity among the middle and upper classes, so much so that even the Liberal Party, the largest opposition bloc in Congress, was reluctant to criticize the administration's record on security and the performance of Colombia's security forces.[53] As Mónica Pachón Buitrago notes, challenging a president with a 75 percent approval rating and whose security policy was wildly popular is a "risky business that does not lead to many votes."[54]

In addition to placing the modernization of Colombia's security forces high on the legislative agenda, Uribe also masterfully used his popularity to consolidate domestic and international buy-in for his framing of the country's security crisis. Rhetorically, he had already rebranded the FARC and ELN as criminals, bandits, and terrorists who were fighting against an open and democratic society.[55] With the passage of Law 782 of 2002 (Ley 782 de 2002), the administration conclusively revoked recognition of the political standing of Colombia's illegal armed groups—a move that closed the door to peace talks while introducing more antagonistic tactics against armed groups.[56] According to Iván Cepeda and Felipe Tascón, Uribe succeeded in implanting a "discourse of fear" throughout Colombia—one that successfully depicted the FARC as public enemy number one. They assert that "[Uribe] rewrote the history of the country, getting rid of the lexicon that referred to an armed conflict, replacing it with terrorism, and increasing the visibility of the war."[57] Following a series of high-profile FARC attacks on civilians in the capital and other heavily populated areas in 2002 and 2003, Colombian citizens broadly accepted Uribe's characterization of Colombia's scourge of violence.[58]

Further, taking advantage of the historical moment presented by Washington's declaration of a global war on terrorism, the Uribe administration affirmed Colombia's status as an unconditional ally of the United States by supporting the 2003 US invasion of Iraq and granting legal immunity under Colombian law for US service members implementing Plan Colombia. These actions endeared the Uribe administration to US policymakers and facilitated the enlargement of Plan Colombia.[59] In August 2002, the US Congress granted the George W. Bush administration expanded authority for a unified campaign in Colombia that targeted drug traffickers and foreign terrorist groups. Months later, President Bush nullified a previous directive limiting intelligence-sharing to counterdrug operations, broadening bilateral cooperation on all manner of security threats in the country.[60] The reform efforts commenced under Plan Colombia garnered strong support among the leading parties in Colombia—and in the United States—throughout the Uribe administration, reinforced by a consensus on security and later counterterrorism as national priorities. Just as important, even though Washington saw Colombia's struggle as part of its own global campaign against terrorism, US officials were careful not to rob Colombia's "leaders of the ability to own the conflict and act as true patriots and nationalists, not stooges of outsiders."[61] That "respectful distance" as much as anything else engendered Colombian ownership of the country's security strategy.

Collective Responsibility for Tackling Insecurity

Elite influence on party priorities further reinforced the consensus on security issues, even long before Uribe's tenure. Starting in the 1980s, representatives of industry, finance, and banking overwhelmingly opposed any negotiated solution to the armed conflict that would jeopardize the neoliberal economic model—a position shared by the military's leadership and prominent currents of the Liberal and Conservative Parties.[62] In 1999, 84 percent of business owners supported the peace process, yet only 24 percent were willing to make economic sacrifices for peace to work.[63] The shared interests of such important constituencies—and their influence within the political establishment—played an essential role in defining the government's strategy for dealing with illegal armed groups. According to this elite agreement, major concessions would only be made to the extent that they did not challenge prevailing economic and political structures, thereby privileging the use of force. In addition, Presidents Gaviria, Samper, and Pastrana all oversaw repressive campaigns against drug cartels.[64] Heavy US diplomatic pressure throughout the 1990s made sure that many of the programmatic elements of the Colombian government's security policy remained the same (for example, coca eradication, drug interdiction, and cartel arrests), even as power passed from one party to another.[65]

As leaders from across the partisan spectrum recognized, polarizing the security debate was not a viable electoral or governing strategy. The fragility of the Colombian state necessitated cooperation to repel the threat posed by insurgents that sought to conquer the state or secede from it, and among the major parties, a spirit of collective responsibility for resolving insecurity took root.[66] As one analyst noted, "The risk became so grave, so the parties aligned their beliefs to save the state. To be the party that politicized security would have been very badly received by the public."[67] The nature of the security threat in Colombia ensured public support for an aggressive security strategy, and partisans from across the political spectrum could all agree that emboldening and professionalizing security forces was central to making it work.[68]

Although support eventually eroded for Pastrana's lumbering management of the peace talks, Colombia's Congress in 2001 still delivered essential legislation that reinforced the importance of the security sector to restoring Colombia's sovereignty over its territory and increased resources to the Ministry of Defense.[69] Despite resistance from civil society organizations concerned about impunity for human rights abuses committed by the military, the law's passage demonstrated considerable cross-party ownership for the fate of the security sector.[70] Ironically, the most controversial aspect of the law—a clause that ostensibly subordinated civilian authorities to the military in zones of military operations—was supported by 69 percent of the public, reflecting both the desperation of the Colombian people and the government's resounding mandate to pursue a militarized security strategy.[71]

Two additional aspects of the Colombian context further explain interparty consensus on security. First, security was a technical realm, and the political class had little related experience, reflected in the low incidence of military or police service among members of the legislature.[72] In the words of one analyst, "there were just too few people who understood security to pose any challenge to whatever the president wanted."[73] This lack of experience among legislators rendered them vulnerable to the lobbying efforts of their contacts in the security forces. One police officer described a national network of departmental police commanders who, armed with an institutional message, worked to persuade their respective legislators to pass laws and budgets favorable to the security forces.[74]

Second, for politicians at the local and national levels, desperation over insecurity became personal as insurgents and criminals stepped up attacks on political elites. The intertwining of political and drug violence rendered politicians from across the spectrum and their families targets for kidnappings, assassinations, and extortion. In 2002, illegal armed groups committed at least 122 politically motivated kidnappings.[75] Under these constraints, the political class knew that it would remain vulnerable until the security sector could restore the state's monopoly of force—a factor that made even the most cautious politicians willing to accept the strengthening of the state's coercive capacity.[76]

Ultimately, these factors combined to generate broad, cross-party support for Uribe's expansion of security sector reform. In turn, this led to continuity in security policies, which set the time horizons for institutional change well into the future. By the 2010 presidential election, all candidates, including progressive Antanus Mockus, supported direct confrontation with insurgent and paramilitary groups and the continuation of force modernization in their security platforms.[77] One Colombian police officer agreed, saying, "The only way to ensure that politicians do not derail our security strategy is to depoliticize security. Security in Colombia has not really had an electoral logic for the past few decades."[78] It was the absence of such an electoral advantage that empowered a reform-minded executive and a unified legislature to embrace US security assistance and make good on the promise of security sector reform.

Mexico: Polarization and Discontinuity

Unlike in Colombia, it was this very "electoral logic" and different interpretations of the nature of the security crisis that engendered polarizing attitudes among the major parties on the issue of security in Mexico, undercutting executive-led strategies to reduce crime and violence. Further, the Mexican party system grew more institutionalized during the transition to democracy, strengthening the centrifugal orientation of the parties in ways that influenced their positions on security, security sector reform, and US security assistance.

The Emergence of an Institutionalized Party System

Mexico's modern party system has its roots in the authoritarian period, when the major party actors of the democratic era emerged as alternatives to the Institutional Revolutionary Party (Partido Revolucionario Institucional, or PRI).[79] To maintain a façade of democracy, the PRI permitted limited pluralism during the hegemonic era, and it was in this context that the National Action Party (Partido Acción National, or PAN)—grounded in the social teachings of the Catholic Church—organized against some of the key tenets of the revolution, including agrarian reform and state-controlled education.[80] The PAN's leadership was fervent in its commitment to electoral politics as the vehicle for national change, but the party's repeated exclusion from power under PRI dominance frustrated meaningful electoral success from the PAN's founding in 1939 until the 1980s.[81] Later in this period, the PAN's oppositionist message began to attract a new class of pro-business adherents, especially following the PRI's controversial nationalization of private banks in September 1982. The *neopanistas*, as the new party militants were called, brought with them abundant resources for electoral campaigns that helped the party secure major victories in legislative and gubernatorial races.[82] As Mexico entered the 1990s, the PAN had already earned a reputation as the leading antiauthoritarian political organization—one that embraced big business, the Church, and pro-democracy constituents in equal measure. The party also represented the regional preferences of the economically dynamic northern states and of the agricultural center-west.[83] The PAN's popularity with the electorate helped it secure a consistently prominent position in Congress starting in 1988 and the first election of a non-PRI president in 2000.

Similarly, the formation of the leftist Democratic Revolutionary Party (Partido de la Revolución Democrática, or PRD) in 1989 further eroded the PRI's hegemony and altered the electoral landscape as the country transitioned to democratic rule. The PRD arose after the presidential succession controversy of 1986, when Cuauhtémoc Cárdenas and other leading PRI officials rejected the selection of Carlos Salinas de Gotari as the 1988 PRI presidential candidate and split from the party. Cárdenas ran for the presidency under a coalition banner of left-leaning organizations, posing a formidable but ultimately unsuccessful challenge to Salinas in an election marred by fraud. The following year, he secured the support of smaller parties and social movements to establish the center-left PRD.[84] Although the PRD embraced social justice and opposed the neoliberalism and austerity programs of the PRI's post-1982 market-led economic opening, factionalism, rife in the party's ranks since its founding, generated an otherwise inconsistent party platform.[85] Partly because of such internal conflict, the PRD struggled to achieve stable victories across electoral cycles, but the party nevertheless ensured leftist representation in national politics.[86] From 1990 to 2012, the PRD held roughly 12 percent of the total municipal elected offices, governed six states and Mexico City, and was consistently the second or third largest party in Congress—a conspicuous placement in the party system.[87]

The rise of these two main opposition parties during the authoritarian period generated a system in which three parties—the PRI, PAN, and PRD—gained approximately 90 percent of the vote, collectively determining policy outcomes at the onset of competitive democracy in 2000.[88] All three parties boasted recognizable candidates and clear programmatic identities among the electorate. In this fashion, when public pressure to address insecurity intensified in the mid-2000s, Mexico was characterized by an institutionalized party system—one that provided voters with "clear and distinct platforms that permit electoral mandates, channel political conflict in system-supporting ways, and facilitate electoral accountability."[89] The three main parties managed to co-opt local politicians under national political umbrellas to deliver remarkable differentiation in the party system—one of the principal challenges faced by the parties in Colombia.[90] Although each party exhibited some programmatic flexibility, political parties in Mexico continued to offer distinct brands to the electorate—a factor that reinforced intraparty cohesion, even if interparty relations tended to vary from election to election.[91]

The PRI did not entirely preclude the political opportunism and alliance-building typically associated with less institutionalized systems, however.[92] Interparty relations evolved in response to perceived electoral opportunities, and opposition parties—despite differing agendas and competitive attitudes toward one another—generally pursued coalitions when they perceived excessive power accumulation or unilateral agenda-setting by the governing party. Consequently, the opposition's use of the legislature as a check on executive power has become one of the defining elements of Mexican democracy, and coalitions of convenience, mostly to block legislation, have become a common measure to undermine the success of the party at the helm of the executive branch.[93] The parties' strategies have adapted to this form of competition. Although parties can tap into their regional and social bases of support, parties in Mexico's institutionalized system, like their counterparts in Colombia's deinstitutionalized system, must compete for swing votes in the center. Each party has thus adopted some widely popular catch-all features to boost their candidates' popularity at the ballot box.[94]

To draw undecided voters to their platform, parties developed increasingly polarized views on specific issues. Government corruption, social topics such as abortion and marriage equality, and security have been recurrent electoral themes and the principal battlegrounds on which parties vie for the median voter. Consensus on security was a self-reinforcing quality of interparty relations in Colombia, whereas polarization became the dominant pattern among the main Mexican parties. Especially following the 2000 presidential victory of the PAN and the concurrent victory of the PRD in Mexico City, bitter interparty conflict has become a persistent feature of Mexico's party system. The Mexican electorate registered as the most politically polarized in Latin America in a 2009 poll, 36 percent of respondents identifying as either extreme left or extreme right.[95]

The 2006 campaign featured striking polarization in what some analysts consider the first truly ideological presidential contest in Mexico.[96] Unlike in previous elections in which the PAN and PRD downplayed their differences to challenge the hegemonic PRI, the two leading candidates in the 2006 contest, Felipe Calderón (PAN) and Andrés Manuel López Obrador (PRD), campaigned on their stark programmatic differences rooted in distinct ideologies and candidate-specific vulnerabilities.[97] From the perspective of the ruling PAN, what was at stake was the neoliberal economic model and free-market policies embraced by the PAN and PRI; the PRD's platform favored state-led economic development and the expansion of the social safety net.[98] PAN leaders futilely attempted in 2004 to implicate López Obrador in a major corruption scandal, and in 2005 sought to block his candidacy altogether by impeaching him as mayor of Mexico City.[99] These efforts proved unsuccessful. In short order, PAN operatives instead turned to time-tested electoral strategies like personal attack ads that characterized the PRD candidate as a threat to democracy and a danger to Mexico.[100]

The vitriol with which conservative voices attacked López Obrador raised the visibility of what was already proving to be a highly consequential political moment. When Calderón won by less than 0.6 percent of the vote, his opponent accused the PAN of fraud and refused to recognize the victory, casting doubt on the outcome and fueling polarization in the postelection period. The PRD's congressional caucus even physically attempted to prevent Calderón from taking office on inauguration day.[101] López Obrador, bereft of further institutional recourse to contest the result, then launched a years-long, nationwide grassroots campaign as the self-proclaimed "legitimate president" to mobilize popular opposition to the Calderón administration, setting the tone for the interparty conflict that intensified during Calderón's term.[102]

Drug Violence as a National Security Crisis, Security Sector Reform as a Way Out

Surprisingly, security was not a central issue of the 2006 presidential race, and Calderón even dubbed himself the "employment president" during his campaign.[103] In his inaugural speech, he did at least ask his political opponents to overcome partisan differences and cooperate on improving citizen security in Mexico.[104] However, the security situation declined drastically just as power transferred from Fox to Calderón, when the mighty Gulf Cartel fractured and contested the Sinaloa Cartel's and La Familia Michoacana's control of smuggling routes.[105] The increasing precariousness of public safety, the expansion of domestic drug consumption, and the co-optation of public officials (such as mayors, municipal police forces, and public prosecutors) by organized crime groups left Calderón few options but to make reforming and modernizing the security forces a top priority. On taking office, the new president swiftly rebranded the criminal threat as a national security crisis. Within days of his inauguration, he declared an all-out war on the drug cartels. Characterizing the menace of organized crime, Calderón said, "They are trying to impose a monopoly by force of arms and are even trying to impose their own laws. Their business is dominating other people."[106] The struggle against organized crime was only one of the many areas Calderón emphasized, but it nonetheless became the administration's signature legacy thanks to the considerable resources expended and, tragically, the number of lives it eventually claimed.[107]

Calderón's predecessor, Vicente Fox, began his presidency with an aspiration of reshaping the country's national security structure.[108] However, infighting among members of Fox's cabinet and obstruction by the PRI-dominated Congress, which blocked legislation aimed at addressing Mexico's security deficiencies, diverted attention away from the issue.[109] Calderón, on the other hand, set the tone for his presidency from his earliest days in office, and in a show of executive force, he launched a major offensive against organized crime, sending more than twenty-five thousand soldiers and federal police officers to border cities and rural regions plagued by cartel and gang violence. This operational strategy, which expanded in the years that followed, entailed the occupation of dangerous municipalities, confrontation with nonstate armed groups, and the arrest of drug kingpins. By the end of Calderón's term, dozens of top cartel operatives had been killed, and more than thirty-five most-wanted drug criminals had been arrested.[110]

Beyond crisis response, the Calderón administration understood that it also needed to lay the groundwork for deeper reforms to eliminate corruption and criminality from the ranks of government institutions. Security sector reform was central to this long-term strategy. From 2007 to 2008, the former director of the Center for Investigation and National Security (Centro de Investigación y Seguridad Nacional, or CISEN), Guillermo Valdés Castellanos, led an initiative known as the National Agreement for Security, Justice, and Legality (Acuerdo Nacional por la Seguridad, la Justicia y la Legalidad), which advocated for strengthening security forces, targeting the perpetrators of financial crimes, and enhancing the professionalism and capacity of the country's Attorney General's Office.[111] Valdés initially spent a year seeking support for the guiding document among opposition legislators and governors. Most demurred, not because they disagreed with it but because they did not yet perceive insecurity to be a critical issue confronting Mexico.[112] However, following the 2008 kidnapping of Fernando Martí, the fourteen-year-old son of one of the country's wealthiest businesspeople, the country's politicians recognized that not signing the agreement could have a political cost and acquiesced to the reform effort.[113]

Buoyed by growing public outrage over insecurity, Calderón pushed major reform measures focused on the security and justice sectors through Congress during his first two years in office. In the 2006 elections, the PAN won the largest share of seats in both houses of Congress but failed to win majorities, forcing the party's leadership to strike deals with minority parties to pass legislation.

At first, a fragile PAN-PRI legislative coalition helped deliver some significant accomplishments, including a new federal police law, a revised criminal code, and the overhaul of the Attorney General's Office (Procuraduría General de la República, or PGR).[114] Furthermore, Calderón succeeded in pushing legislation governing the National System of Public Security and introducing harsher penalties for kidnapping and money laundering.[115] Cooperation with the PRI was possible because electoral stakes were low, with more than two years before midterm elections. Moreover, Calderón's security policies enjoyed support among the public, with roughly 80 percent of respondents endorsing a confrontational approach for dealing with drug traffickers.[116]

Party Differentiation and Polarization on Security

However, by the middle of Calderón's term, legislative realignments and a perceived political opening for the PRI following Mexico's 2008 economic downturn changed the calculus involved in endorsing Calderón's policies, including major security initiatives. The growing controversy over the 2006 presidential race exacerbated the existing polarization, which had already rendered consensus elusive for policy proposals regarding everything from counterterrorism approaches to natural disaster management.[117] But it was a dramatic federal intervention in the state of Michoacán that deepened party polarization on security, and the 2009 midterm legislative and the 2012 presidential elections became referendums on the PAN's security strategy, including security sector reform.

In the 2009 congressional campaign season, the PAN's leadership publicized a narrative that painted the PRI and PRD as complicit with the country's violent actors. When federal forces intervened in Michoacán to extirpate drug criminals in May of that year, they also detained ten mayors and twenty-five other local officials for collusion with organized crime—most of whom were PRI and PRD politicians.[118] The government insisted that this was the first step in dismantling the political protection of cartels in Mexico. However, the timing of the operation in the weeks before subnational and legislative elections raised suspicions that Calderón was intervening to give local advantages to PAN candidates, whose campaigns were managed by Calderón's sister in her role as the head of local PAN operations.[119] Critics soon questioned the motivation behind federal intervention in local security matters and, by extension, the PAN's security policies nationwide.[120]

The PRI and PRD now had a highly visible instance of what they perceived as political persecution through Calderón's securitized anticrime narrative. In a public show of displeasure, opposition members in Congress temporarily withheld the Secretariat of National Defense's (Secretaría de Defensa Nacional, or SEDENA) budget, a rare move that dragged one of the few apolitical state institutions into the partisan battle. This divisiveness in interparty relations was further cemented when the midterm elections delivered a crippling blow to the PAN and thus to the remainder of Calderón's legislative agenda. When the PRI more than doubled its seats in the Chamber of Deputies, securing 37 percent of the vote in the July elections, it formed a temporary alliance with the Green Party (Partido Verde Ecologista de México) and some PRD members to create a working majority and oppose the Calderón administration at every turn. In 2009, only eight of 624 legislative initiatives passed by the close of the year, ushering in a new period of legislative gridlock.[121] As Arturo Franco notes, reform paralysis—the inability of government to pass major reforms due to partisan differences—emerged as the biggest challenge to the new political equilibrium. Party polarization became so acute that by early 2012 critics labeled the legislature the Siesta (Napping) Congress because of its low policy yield.[122]

On a practical level, congressional obstruction did not halt existing security sector reform initiatives but did impede the passage of additional reforms and set the stage for a reversal of Calderón's signature projects when President Peña Nieto came to power. Most significantly, Calderón's push for the adoption of a constitutional amendment to unify command among the country's police bodies, a topic explored in chapter 7, did not muster the requisite support from PRI governors and legislators.[123] In Congress, the PRI and PRD defended their opposition, insisting that the police reform violated the constitutional sovereignty of the municipalities. Yet these legal arguments belied a deeper motive. One observer bemoaned, "The PRI, on the eve of a presidential election, did not necessarily want the PAN to win the issue of security."[124]

In the run-up to the 2012 presidential contest, the PRI and PRD attacked the PAN for its alleged responsibility for the surge in drug-related murders, which exceeded sixty thousand over Calderón's term.[125] Calderón had also linked himself personally with the war on the drug cartels, raising the political costs of backtracking or adjusting the militarized approach.[126] Calderón's ownership of the issue enabled his opposition parties, which were buttressed by social movements that organized tens of thousands of protesters to descend on the capital to push for a new anticrime strategy in 2011. As approval of the PAN's performance on security dropped below 50 percent, opposition candidates seized upon this growing dissatisfaction.[127] One researcher proclaimed, "Security is totally politicized in Mexico. If you want to destroy a party or a candidate, you just 'throw cadavers at them.'"[128] "Calderón's Dead" (*los muertos de Calderón*) became a common rallying cry for those who felt that the PAN had either mismanaged or exacerbated Mexico's security crisis and a compelling image for an electorate that desperately sought change.[129]

New Party, New Policies, No Continuity

The climate of polarization fostered by the 2006 presidential election conditioned a large and vocal element of the PRD to reject the PAN's mandate, and after 2009, the emboldened PRI saw its presidential prospects improve in the run-up to the 2012 election.[130] Mexican voters had grown weary of the toll caused by the drug war violence. Despite some isolated successes in reducing crime at the state level, national homicide rates had surged from 8.8 per hundred thousand inhabitants in 2000 to 23.5 in 2011.[131] Although voters demanded alternatives to Calderón's security strategy, the campaign season did not result in any focused debate on security policy.[132] To the extent that security came up, the PAN's 2012 candidate, Josefina Vásquez Mota, defended her party's record and advocated for an expansion of the Federal Police and the introduction of "military discipline" to the institution.[133] On the other hand, the PRI and PRD candidates, Peña Nieto and López Obrador respectively, emphasized a gradual return of the military to the barracks and economic and social development to tackle the root causes of insecurity.[134] Promising to demilitarize the fight against the cartels, target high-impact crimes such as kidnapping, and create a national crime prevention program, Peña Nieto, whose economic proposals drove additional public support, defeated his competitors with 38.2 percent of the vote.[135]

Peña Nieto entered office with a vision to break with the past, having won the election on a pro-peace platform. The new president denied the existence of a war on drugs and reduced the government's publication of information related to drug trafficking and violence.[136] His initial policy decisions on the security front reflected a rejection of Calderón-era tactics, including deep cooperation with the United States.[137] One former State Department representative reported an unmistakable rebuff by a senior Peña Nieto administration official, who chided that "The PAN lost the election because they were following your strategy. We won't make that mistake."[138] Yet the PRI eventually discovered that the governing conditions in the country had changed after six years of armed confrontation between the state and organized crime. By the second half of his term, President Peña Nieto ended up pursuing strategies similar to those of his predecessor, including militarization and close cooperation with US law enforcement. However, the early reorientation of the government's security strategy unquestionably debilitated several reform initiatives that were only in their incipient stages.

Dramatically, Peña Nieto eliminated the Secretariat of Public Security (Secretaría de Seguridad Pública, or SSP) and transferred the responsibilities of the moribund ministry to the Secretariat of the Interior (Secretaría de Gobernación, or SEGOB).[139] This move was emblematic of the diminished importance of public security and, specifically, of the Federal Police, one of Calderón's signature projects, in the new presidential cabinet.[140] In regard to US-Mexico relations, the president's new secretary of the interior, Miguel Osorio Chong, marketed this change as an effort at improved coordination: the *ventanilla única*, a single coordinating office for matters of security, would relieve US officials from the administrative burden of working with so many federal entities independently.[141] On a practical level, though, this move meant months-long delays in approvals for pending and new Mérida Initiative projects. But it also allowed the incoming president to assert tighter control over the terms of international security cooperation while realigning the security policies and institutions he inherited. Thus when Peña Nieto restructured and renamed the public security body in 2012, opposition parties in Congress reacted with displeasure by stalling the ratification of the new National Security Commission (Comisión Nacional de Seguridad, or CNS).[142]

Although Peña Nieto relied heavily on the Federal Police to reinforce municipal and state police forces after he withdrew the army and navy in some areas of the country, over the course of his presidency he repeatedly cut resources and even reassigned personnel from the Federal Police to fill the ranks of a completely new civilian internal security force, the National Gendarmerie (Gendarmería Nacional).[143] The gendarmerie, which never met its recruiting targets and failed to distinguish its jurisdiction and responsibilities from those belonging to other federal security forces, represented a concerted effort to assuage critics of Calderón's militarization and symbolic evidence that Peña Nieto's security plan was taking the country in a new direction.[144]

Indeed, Calderón's call for greater partnership with the United States on security in 2007 had raised suspicions among opposition leaders and civil society groups from the start. Senior PRI leaders were especially opposed to the Mérida Initiative, viewing Calderón's closeness to the United States as a feeble attempt to shore up legitimacy for his contested mandate. The secrecy of Calderón's executive negotiations with the US government also resulted in distrust within the ranks of the PRI and PRD.[145] Whereas in Colombia's 1998 National Development Plan President Pastrana spelled out his intentions to initiate security sector reform with the support of international partners,

President Calderón made no mention of the Mérida Initiative or of international assistance when he issued his Public Security Strategy in 2007.[146] Unlike Colombia's influential parties, which largely supported Pastrana's overtures to Washington, at the outset of the Mérida Initiative the PRI's leadership categorically rejected US assistance as a matter of national sovereignty and insisted that US prescriptions for solving Mexico's security problems were misguided.[147] Starting in 2012, incoming President Peña Nieto satisfied the PRI's leadership when he unilaterally froze most Mérida Initiative programming.

On taking office, Peña Nieto privately expressed disbelief and outrage over how extensive the US-Mexico relationship had become under Calderón, putting an abrupt halt to bilateral security cooperation until his administration could properly review the nature of Mexico's security ties with Washington.[148] This decision followed on the heels of a widely publicized August 2012 armed attack on Mexican naval officers traveling by road in the company of two US officials, suspected of being CIA operatives. The notion that such granular cross-border and interinstitutional coordination was taking place without centralized control was unfathomable to a party long accustomed to rallying support by rebuffing perceived impingements on Mexican sovereignty.[149] Thus the new president immediately restricted the access of US advisors to Federal Police installations, cut back on US training of SEDENA units, reduced collaboration between the Attorney General's Office and US judicial authorities, and eliminated US Embassy–supported background checks for municipal and state police forces. The new administration also cut funding for the security sector's budding intelligence fusion capability, Platform Mexico, stonewalling information-sharing among Mexico's security forces and with the United States for almost three years.[150] In one controversial incident, the incoming administration requested that US security officials depart a joint intelligence fusion center in Monterrey, where they had worked for years alongside the Mexican military and police in processing drug war intelligence.[151]

As one observer noted, "President Peña Nieto made the US-Mexico relationship rigid when it was already benefiting from a growing closeness and fluidity. It became unnecessarily centralized, which hurt coordination and results."[152] The Mérida Initiative was novel because it was multiyear and evidence based, which committed the Mexican government to building on the same projects from year to year with fixed budget lines. "That consistency is something that you never see in Mexican public policies relating to security," an analyst remarked—and ultimately it was lost in the confusion that accompanied the presidential transition.[153] The resulting lack of certainty even jeopardized Washington's willingness to approve additional Mérida funding.

Senator Patrick Leahy prevented the release of $246 million until the Peña Nieto administration could clarify its intentions and desired relationship with its top international benefactor.[154] The Mexican president eventually did just that when he began to face criticism over rising homicides and thus laid out an assistance request to the United States so as "to be seen doing something" about the violence.[155] Even though Peña Nieto eventually aligned more closely with the United States, especially after the 2014 arrest of the Sinaloa Cartel's leader, the mixed signals that his initial policies sent to the security sector impeded the momentum and consistency of some of the Calderón era's most important programming.

The Politicization of Security

Several factors explain why security became a polarizing theme among Mexican political parties. First, the inconsistency of security policies across administrations was partly a function of the security sector's bureaucratic setup. Mexico's security sector lacks a large, well-trained, and professional civil service, meaning that when a new party assumes power, party leaders staff the bureaucracy with loyalists.[156] This translates into a lack of institutional memory—a feature that has led the government to repeat mistakes from administration to administration.[157] Second, strict one-term limits for political leadership in Mexico's political system ensured a diffusion of responsibility for the country's insecurity. Continuity is important to building on successful policing models, and until a series of electoral reforms took effect in 2018, Mexican voters could not hold legislators or local representatives accountable for their failings on the security front because politicians did not have to prove their records in reelection campaigns.[158] It was instead party representation in the national executive that was responsible for the success or failure of security policy. For the PRI and the PRD, insecurity was one of the PAN's top vulnerabilities going into 2012. When the PRI won the presidency, the party's mandate necessitated differentiation of its security strategy from what voters perceived to be the PAN's costly adherence to US advice and failure to reduce criminal violence.

More broadly, though, Mexico's political class never agreed on the diagnosis of the country's high levels of violence. Whereas in Colombia the threat of political violence helped consolidate political support for security sector reform, Calderón never managed to build a strong interparty coalition around his security policy in general because the parties had different views on how to resolve insecurity. According to analysts familiar with the situations in Colombia and Mexico, the PAN lacked powerful symbols such as "terrorism" and "insurgency" to convince Mexicans of the severity of the security threat.[159] Opposition parties and civil society groups resoundingly rejected a strategy that had "more to do with fighting a war than with law enforcement."[160] Simply put, many political elites did not perceive cartel violence to pose an existential threat to the Mexican political order, especially not one that required military responses. Hence political leaders at the national and subnational levels never overcame the self-reinforcing pattern of polarization in the party system. The election of subnational public officials every three years further exacerbated these sharp partisan divisions given that politicians typically introduced new police leadership and associated strategies every time there was party turnover in municipal and state government. Polarization not only stunted continuity at the federal level but also undermined the continuity and coherence of security strategies and reform efforts implemented by local officeholders.

Growing concern about human rights abuses committed by the military afforded the opposition further grounds to oppose Calderón. According to Patrick Corcoran, Calderón's extraordinary and unabashed deployment of the military as the primary agent to combat drug gangs violated a main security taboo—the involvement of the military in policing operations—which allowed opposition leaders to shift blame for the growing security dilemma to the PAN.[161] Unlike in Colombia, where citizens had long been accustomed to the presence of soldiers in the streets in the context of the armed conflict, Mexican politicians and citizens historically rejected creeping militarization. The PRD and the PRI were therefore largely reticent to express support for the army's deployment in the drug war, even though Calderón initially enjoyed public approval of the measure.[162]

Last, the electoral dynamics of Mexico's federal system incentivized interparty polarization of security across levels of government. The strongest opposition to security reforms came from party leaders in state governments who wanted to protect their institutional prerogatives and refused to purge or reform their police bodies.[163] As Jennifer Bejar and Michael Wilson Becerril note, "that [parties] are so polarized, skirmishing incessantly for power instead of cooperating for the public good, gives [them] an incentive to fail to clamp down on the violence—so that they can use it to discredit opponents."[164] For example, PRI governors in Chihuahua and Michoacán publicly blamed President Calderón for the rise in homicides in their states. In the words of Alejandro Poiré, the administration further "shot itself in the foot" by leveling rhetorical attacks against the PRI and PRD for their supposed complicity with organized crime.[165] This in turn fed the flames of partisan attacks around the issue of Calderón's security strategy.

Some analysts also conclude that the PAN perceived a compelling electoral advantage in sustaining the war on the cartels even though the security situation had improved very little. As Guillermo Trejo and Sandra Ley argue, PAN federal authorities cooperated with local politicians in areas the party controlled "but adopted confrontational strategies [with local governments] in states ruled by leftist subnational authorities," often resulting in the militarization of these regions as a way of profiling the ineptitude of local leadership.[166] In their estimation, these confrontational strategies weakened leftist state and municipal governance, paving the way for cartels to corrupt subnational authorities and police forces. Because of this, despite the Calderón administration's rhetorical commitment to restoring the monopoly of force to the state, partisan polarization across levels of government more likely impeded the president's stated goal.[167]

As the comparison of Colombia and Mexico demonstrates, unique patterns of interparty behavior, rooted in contrasting levels of party institutionalization, resulted in distinct levels of polarization surrounding the issue of security. Whereas the Colombian political establishment achieved consensus to pursue security sector reform as the primary means of containing the country's security crisis, the major parties of Mexico struggled to overcome partisan differences and used insecurity for political advantage in ways that stunted reform. Continuity of funding, strategy, and beneficiary institutions made all the difference in Colombia, and interparty consensus generated the stability necessary to implement security sector reform.

Interparty relations in Colombia and Mexico were so dissimilar that two former Colombian presidents offered candid advice to the Mexican government regarding its implementation of security sector reform. Former President Gaviria urged, "The parties ought to learn how to form political alliances with other ideologies and stop thinking that this undermines their identity."[168] His successor, Samper, insisted, "May the Mexican politicians forgive me, but the very first thing is to construct a state [security] policy. The fight against drugs can't be politicized."[169] However, in the absence of a unified understanding of the causes of insecurity, the Mexican parties offered the electorate contrasting proposals for addressing it. This partisan conflict ended up detouring many of the reform effort's signature programs when the presidency switched party hands. Although greater polarization logically is a boost for accountability, in that opposition parties are conditioned to serve as a check on the policies of the governing party, the Mexican case suggests that polarization may simultaneously hinder efforts to enhance security sector effectiveness. The creation of new federal security agencies following consecutive presidential turnovers diverted resources and distracted attention from ongoing work to address the national tragedy.

These findings are consistent with the literature on public policy and divided government suggesting that highly polarized party systems tend to limit consensus and thus the prospect of reform. Returning to Berg's theory, positive outcomes for security sector reform did not depend on the breadth and fragmentation of the ruling coalition given that the more successful experience occurred in Colombia, where parties represented a narrow political spectrum and exhibited considerable cohesion. Nevertheless, the Mexican case corroborates Berg's contention that executives with weak domestic mandates are more willing to invite international security assistance to help set a domestic security agenda. In both cases, constrained revenue (Colombia) and fragmented political networks (Mexico) created internal challenges for political elites in the recipient countries, thus generating unique opportunities for the US government to facilitate and influence institutional change. Yet as Mexico also demonstrates, external benefactors of security sector reform are successful only to the extent that their activities and prescriptions remain unaffected by partisan competition in the country implementing reform.

Much later in Colombia, the eventual collapse of consensus on security, coinciding with the Santos administration's peace process with the FARC (2012–16), demonstrates that the nature of the security threat was a decisive factor in interparty cooperation. As insurgent activity in Colombia became less visible and as the security sector shifted its focus from an armed conflict to criminal violence, itself a more dispersed threat, interparty relations became more polarized and decidedly more comparable to those in Mexico.[170] By the 2018 presidential election, strong showings for candidates at both extremes of the ideological spectrum reflected a realignment of the electorate—and the emergence of highly differentiated platforms among political movements on the left, right, and center.[171] This outcome suggests that even with a more centripetal party orientation in Mexico, the more dispersed nature of the security threat—and the lack of a public consensus on the prescription for dealing with it—could still have posed a significant barrier to achieving the continuity of policy so essential to security sector reform.

Notes

1. Sowell, 2019; Qiblawi et al., 2020.
2. Berg, 2012, 2022
3. Berg's claim builds on the accepted logic of public policy literature, which understands fragmentation and divided government as principal causes of policy stagnation. See Ames, 2001; Becker & Saalfeld, 2004; Binder et al., 2002; Bueno de Mesquita et al., 2002; Edwards et al., 1997; Hiroi & Renno, 2014; Kernell & Cox, 1991; Mette Kjær & Katusiimeh, 2012.
4. Berg, 2022.
5. Berg, 2014, 2022.
6. Flores-Macías, 2022, p. 126. Mexico's tax revenue was comparatively low and stagnant over the period of analysis, but the country's fiscal pressure was also low by regional standards.
7. Mainwaring & Scully, 1995.
8. Mainwaring, 2018. Substantial literature on the topic covers the links among PSI, party behavior, and party longevity (Dalton & Weldon, 2007; Huntington, 1968; M. P. Jones, 2009, 2010; Levitsky et al., 2016; Lupu, 2015a; Mainwaring, 1999, 2018; Olivares Concha, 2015; Roberts, 2014, 2016; Sartori, 1976; Welfling, 1973).
9. D. R. Jones, 2001. On party polarization, see Curini & Hino, 2012; Dalton, 2008; Maoz & Somer-Topcu, 2010; Morgan, 2018; Sartori, 1976.
10. Barber & McCarty, 2015; Dalton, 2008, p. 900.
11. Sartori, 1976, pp. 131–145.
12. For additional perspectives, see Calvo & Hellwig, 2011; Cox, 1990.
13. In more institutionalized systems, political parties tend to be programmatic—that is, they compete based primarily on policy proposals—and the policy orientations of such parties tend to be more stable because parties are accountable to their partisan voters (M. P. Jones, 2009, p. 16; Levitsky et al., 2016; Mainwaring, 1999).
14. Dalton, 2008; Lupu, 2015a; Yardımcı-Geyikçi, 2013, p. 9.
15. D. R. Jones, 2001; Siaroff, 2000.
16. Alexander, 2002, pp. 8–10.
17. The election of President Belisario Betancur (1982–86), a Conservative Party centrist, signaled an end to the repressive tactics of the Liberal administration of President Julio César Turbay for dealing with guerrilla violence. Betancur called for a democratic opening and offered a truce and amnesty to guerrilla groups (Hanratty & Meditz, 1988). On the consistency of successive administration's National Development Plans and security policies, see López, 2013.
18. On political party development in Colombia, see Dix, 1990; Hartlyn, 2008; Lozano Villegas, 2015.
19. Dix, 1980, p. 317; Palencia Ramos, 2012, pp. 93–94; Peeler, 1976; Stone, 2016.
20. Leal Buitrago, 1989, p. 33.
21. Hoskin, 1979. Hoskin finds that situational factors reduced the likelihood of ideological conflict in the political system, noting that "the coalescent behavior of the traditional party elites when confronted with threats from below" sustained the prevailing structure of power (1979, p. 501).
22. Archer, 1990; Roland & Zapata, 2000, p. 2.
23. Restrepo, 2006, pp. 29–30.
24. Dargent & Muñoz, 2011, pp. 44–45; Lalander, 2003; Ryan, 2004.

25. Gutiérrez Sanín, 2007, p. 258.
26. Gutiérrez Sanín & Dávila Ladrón de Guevara, 2000, pp. 43–44.
27. García & Hoskin, 2003, p. 11.
28. Rampf & Chavarro, 2014, p. 15. Several articles of the 1991 Constitution required implementation legislation, and the Liberal and Conservative Parties, which controlled the Senate with eighty-five of one hundred seats, introduced laws that aimed to restrict some participatory mechanisms decided by the Constituent Assembly.
29. Gutiérrez Sanín & Guataqui, 2009, pp. 42–43.
30. Pizarro, 2002.
31. Wilkinson, 1994.
32. Andrade Terán, 2011, p. 17; Palencia Ramos, 2012, p. 95. Since the 1974 presidential election, voter turnout has not exceeded more than 50 percent of eligible citizens (Giraldo & Muñoz Yi, 2014, p. 384).
33. Gomez-Suarez, 2015. Leftist parties in Colombia struggled to consolidate an attractive oppositionist message in the period following the adoption of the 1991 Constitution, and the lack of a clientelistic base, inexperience in democratic competition, and the rigid and exclusive ideological stances of party leadership all conspired to undermine leftist party organization at the national level (Duque Daza, 2007b, p. 73).
34. Lee, 2012, pp. 29, 33–34; Petras, 2000.
35. Palencia Ramos, 2012, p. 109. According to Moreno's study of party behavior in Colombia, in the congressional sessions of 1986–90 and 1994–98, "virtually no difference among traditional parties and 'new' actors across policy areas" was evident (2005, p. 501). Many new party organizations maintained very close ties to the traditional parties, and some merely represented legalized factions of the larger parties.
36. García & Hoskin, 2003, p. 10.
37. Albarracín et al., 2018, p. 232. Following the 2003 political reform that raised the threshold for party formation, seventy-four parties and political movements formally registered with the government, and between 2002 and 2006, around 40 percent of the members of the lower house of Congress abandoned their previous party affiliation to join new parties (Giraldo & López, 2006; Giraldo & Muñoz Yi, 2014, p. 128). On electoral reforms in Colombia, see Ortiz Ruiz, 2015.
38. Bolaños, 2013.
39. Albarracín et al., 2018, pp. 228, 247.
40. "Álvaro Uribe encabeza las preferencias," 2002.
41. Forero, 2002a; Hoskin et al., 2011.
42. Dargent & Muñoz, 2011, p. 58.
43. Milanese, 2015, p. 80.
44. Dargent & Muñoz, 2011, pp. 62–63; "Uribe y el Partido Conservador," 2006.
45. Rodríguez Raga, 2011.
46. Dargent & Muñoz, 2011, p. 58; Duque Daza, 2007a.
47. Albarracín et al., 2018, p. 230.
48. "Matrimonios por conveniencia," 2003.
49. Ortiz Ruiz, 2015, p. 27.
50. Albarracín et al., 2018, p. 230. In the legislative elections, Uribe's supporters won sixty-five Senate seats and at least ninety of 163 seats in the lower house (Gran Resumen, 2019).
51. Ortiz Ruiz, 2015, pp. 27–28.

52. Milanese, 2015, p. 81.
53. "La oposición Liberal," 2005.
54. Pachón Buitrago, 2009.
55. Lessing, 2017, p. 253.
56. Bailey, 2011b; Leal Buitrago, 2006b. On the national debate over whether to recognize the political nature of Colombia's armed conflict, see Stone, 2011.
57. Cepeda & Tascón, 2015, p. 27.
58. Santader et al., 2012, pp. 30–34.
59. Rojas, 2015, p. 125; Rosen, 2014, p. 49.
60. J. C. Jones, 2009, p. 358; Murillo, 2004, pp. 21–22; Ramírez Lemus et al., 2004, p. 110. Although the FARC and ELN had been on the US list of international terrorist organizations since 1997, the openness with which US policymakers identified these groups as a direct threat to the United States increased (Nagle, 2002, p. 33). Rodrigo Pardo García-Peña (2006) explores the confluence of domestic and international factors in the formulation of security strategy in Colombia.
61. Mines, 2020, p. 19.
62. Avilés, 2001b, p. 37.
63. Tate, 1999.
64. Simpson, 2004.
65. Crandall, 2001; Vargas-Alzate et al., 2015.
66. Lessing, 2017, p. 17.
67. Academic political analyst, personal communication, Bogotá, Colombia, November 8, 2017.
68. Malcolm Deas adopts a slightly different perspective: "Most Colombian violence today is neither revolutionary nor political" (1997, p. 365). Although much of Colombia's violence is criminal, it still occurs against the backdrop of historical political violence and involves nonstate armed groups who make historical claims to political exclusion. As Roddy Brett notes, the conceptualization of violence in Colombia as political has a "bearing on the strategic mechanisms employed to transform violence [and] to calibrate interventions aimed to mitigate it" (2018, p. 9).
69. Ley de Seguridad y Defensa Nacional, 2001; Montaña & Criado, 2001.
70. The law was controversial from its inception because it granted extraordinary judicial power to the armed forces; it even jeopardized Plan Colombia assistance due to US congressional objections ("Aprobada Ley de Defensa y Seguridad," 2001; "E.U. respalda Ley de Seguridad," 2001; Gómez Maseri, 2001). However, in May 2002, the law was nullified in a ruling by the Constitutional Court ("La polémica ley," 2001). Uribe issued Executive Decree 2002, which reiterated most of the elements of the previous law while removing the elements declared unconstitutional.
71. Pardo, 2002.
72. Because political elites had all but renounced civilian oversight in matters relating to citizen security in the National Front era, politicians historically failed to resource the Ministry of Defense adequately, and through the 1990s, the size of the military grew lethargically despite the magnitude of the country's security challenges (Deas, 2017, p. 41).
73. Academic political analyst, personal communication, Bogotá, Colombia, November 8, 2017.

74. Colombian National Police captain, personal communication, Bogotá, Colombia, November 24, 2017. The Ministry of Defense runs a permanent congressional affairs office, which is co-located with the offices of the national legislature. This office ensures that the Ministry of Defense can vet legislation that affects the security forces and preempt any foreseen opposition to the passage of budgets or favorable legislation (Colombian Army colonel, personal communication, Bogotá, Colombia, October 27, 2017).
75. "Centro Nacional de Memoria Histórica," n.d.
76. M. Gomis, correspondence, Bogotá, Colombia, October 30, 2017.
77. C. Nasi, correspondence, Bogotá, Colombia, October 30, 2017; "Principales propuestas de Antanas Mockus," 2010.
78. Colombian National Police captain, personal communication, Bogotá, Colombia, November 24, 2017; Rodríguez Pinzón, 2016. The first major partisan fissures on the security front occurred after Plan Colombia. Santos, who secured an endorsement from Uribe for his electoral bid, was expected to usher in a period of reformism due to his coalition's control of more than 90 percent of Congress (Posada-Carbó, 2011; Shifter, 2014). However, when Santos put himself at odds with his predecessor on the issue of peace talks with the FARC in 2012, polarization among political parties ensued.
79. Before 1989, the PRI had not lost a presidential, gubernatorial, or federal senatorial race since 1929, and opposition parties only occasionally won municipal elections and federal congressional seats. Mexico represented a hegemonic party system for much of the twentieth century—one in which opposition parties existed but posed no real challenge to the PRI (Klesner, 2001, p. 6).
80. Loaeza, 2003, pp. 200–201.
81. Barraza & Bizberg, 1991.
82. Loaeza, 2003, p. 223. On the political opening that permitted greater electoral competition, see Middlebrook, 1986; on declining cohesion among political elites in the 1980s, see Ronfeldt, 1988.
83. Camp, 2007, p. 99; Klesner, 2005, p. 115.
84. Garrido, 1993.
85. Langston, 2004; Mossige, 2013, p. 9. The PRD's ideological orientation was diverse given that it drew from social democrats, socialists, Stalinists, ex-guerrilla fighters, and other left-wing elements (Camp, 2007, p. 63). The umbrella-like nature posed a challenge for the party's programmatic coherence and eventually contributed to its formal fragmentation with the 2014 secession of López Obrador.
86. The PRD's erratic track record on elections is partly attributable to its inability to construct a realistic alternative to neoliberal economic policies and its inability to contain cults of personality that developed around some of its most prominent yet controversial leaders (Bruhn, 2012).
87. Bruhn, 2012.
88. Loaeza, 2003, p. 238.
89. Greene & Sánchez-Talanquer, 2018a, pp. 201–202. The 2018 Mexican election delivered victories to President López Obrador, founder of the National Regeneration Movement Party (Movimiento de Regeneración Nacional, or MORENA), and a majority legislative coalition favorable to the president elect's policy agenda. The defeat of Mexico's most institutionalized parties—the PRI, PAN, and PRD—suggests a potential reversal of PSI (Greene & Sánchez-Talanquer, 2018b).

90. Albarracín et al., 2018.
91. Knight, 2018; Langston, 2007.
92. Eisenstadt, 2004, p. 166. For much of Mexico's postrevolutionary history, the legislative branch and state governors worked largely "in tune" with presidential and party directives administered by the PRI in Mexico City (Bolaños, 2016, p. 99). When the PRI lost its congressional majority in 1997, though, the executive and Congress faced the constitutional and procedural demands of democratic checks and balances that ultimately produced gridlock.
93. Langston, 2007; Zamora & Cossío, 2006, p. 415.
94. Greene, 2015; Greene & Sánchez-Talanquer, 2018a, p. 213; Klesner, 2001, p. 2; Reyes-Heroles, 2005, p. 43.
95. Cárdenas, 2009; Trejo & Ley, 2016, p. 20.
96. Mossige, 2013, p. 30.
97. Bruhn & Greene, 2007.
98. Moreno, 2007.
99. Authers, 2005; Ortega Ortiz, 2017, pp. 101–102.
100. Wolf & Celorio Morayta, 2011, p. 685.
101. Klesner, 2007, p. 5.
102. A 2007 survey of national and local party elites indicated widespread differences between the PAN and PRD on most major issues (Bruhn & Greene, 2007). The survey also indicated that party elites were markedly more polarized than voters were.
103. Guerrero, 2013, p. 113.
104. Bolaños, 2016, p. 102.
105. Santa Cruz, 2013, p. 547.
106. "Mexico: Cartels move beyond drugs," 2010.
107. Santa Cruz, 2013, p. 538.
108. Rodríguez Sumano, 2007, p. 2.
109. Schaefer et al., 2009b, pp. 13–14; Watt & Zepeda, 2012, pp. 142, 150.
110. Aglionby, 2013.
111. Secretaría de Gobernación, 2008.
112. Valdés Castellanos, 2013.
113. Calderón administration senior security official, personal communication, Mexico City, January 26, 2018.
114. López Portillo, 2012, p. 109; "Mexico: Taxes, Pemex and Calderón's Reforms," 2007. The contested elections of 2006 further fractured the opposition, as López Obrador continued to reject Calderón's legitimacy and created a set of extraparty organizations on the sidelines of the PRD (Mossige, 2013, p. 4). This internal discord meant that the party did not vote in Congress as a bloc, and the two factions expressed different views on issues ranging from electoral reforms to petroleum policy. This worked to the advantage of Calderón, who could count on some PRD legislators to overcome legislative gridlock.
115. Guerrero, 2013, p. 114.
116. Camp, 2010, p. 293; *Mexicans back military campaign*, 2012.
117. Rodríguez Sumano, 2007, p. 1.
118. Ferreyra, 2015. Within two years, all those arrested were released due to a lack of evidence.
119. "Federal crackdown on corruption in Michoacán," 2009.
120. Kenny et al., 2012, pp. 205–206.

121. Since 2000, the strengthening of legislative opposition has limited presidential authority, and the president only retains veto power, unlike in Colombia where the president can also decree new legislation (Camp, 2016, p. 225).
122. Franco 2013, pp. 40, 46. From 2003 to 2013, legislation originating in the executive branch plummeted to below 20 percent (Franco, 2013, p. 45). Ironically, in 2010, party cooperation shifted again when the PAN and the PRD formed alliances in some states to thwart the resurgence of the PRI (Vale & Guerrero Vásquez, 2010).
123. Verduzco Chávez, 2012.
124. Calderón administration senior security official, personal communication, Mexico City, January 26, 2018.
125. Bailey, 2014a, p. 2.
126. Lessing, 2017, p. 264.
127. "Felipe Calderón reviews," 2010; Miller Llana, 2011; Rozental, 2013, pp. 180–181. Kate Putnam (2014, p. 2) finds that perceptions of crime were a significant predictor of vote choice in both the 2006 and 2012 elections.
128. K. Ansolabehere, personal communication, Mexico City, September 4, 2017.
129. "Los muertos de Calderón," 2010.
130. Insecurity and the weak economy hurt the PAN's electability. Even though Mexico's gross domestic product (GDP) grew by 5.3 percent in 2010, a 6.0 percent fall in GDP in 2009 due to global economic downturn devastated Calderón's record (Ortega Ortiz, 2017, p. 158).
131. Heinle et al., 2015, p. 3.
132. Olson, 2017, p. 10.
133. E. Méndez, 2012.
134. Romero, 2012.
135. "México: El plan de Peña Nieto contra el narcotráfico," 2012. When President Peña Nieto entered office in 2012, his first major victory was overcoming political gridlock to forge the Pact for Mexico, which elicited resounding support from the PAN and PRD. The badly defeated PAN sought to make a comeback by demonstrating its usefulness to the electorate, whereas the PRD proved eager to "dispel its image as a naysayer" (Heredia, 2013). However, Peña Nieto's early successes eventually gave way to a string of frustrating defeats in implementing the pact's agenda and public security debacles that undermined citizen confidence in his administration (Flores-Macías, 2016).
136. Benítez Manaut, 2014, p. 55.
137. Felbab-Brown, 2013; private sector security analyst, personal communication, Mexico City, September 12, 2017.
138. Former senior US diplomat, email correspondence, September 28, 2021.
139. Zepeda, 2013.
140. According to Fernández de Castro, the Peña Nieto administration paid a high price for subordinating the SSP to the SEGOB; the president no longer had a cabinet-level official focused 100 percent of the time on the country's security dilemma (Olson et al., 2018). Nevertheless, the move resulted in a 235 percent budget increase for SEGOB from 2012 to 2014, placing substantial resources and discretion in the hands of the president's top cabinet advisor (Sánchez Lara, 2017, p. 86).
141. Olson, 2017, p. 11.
142. Sánchez Lara, 2017, p. 67.

143. Muedano, 2019.
144. Archibold, 2013. The creation of the gendarmerie diverted resources from the Federal Police, which had received considerable training and equipment under Calderón; according to one observer, the Peña Nieto administration outright refused to capitalize on a Calderón-era legacy institution (academic security analyst, personal communication, Mexico City, September 11, 2017). One analyst noted that the gendarmerie was an attempt to install a PRI-oriented body in the Federal Police, which President Peña Nieto perceived as a vestige of an oppositionist government (S. Ley, personal communication, Mexico City, January 9, 2018).
145. Chanona, 2009, pp. 59–60; Constitución Política de los Estados Unidos Mexicanos, 1917, sec. 76.
146. Calderón, 2007; Pastrana, 1998.
147. León Hernández, 2011; Wolf & Celorio Morayta, 2011, p. 678. In 2009, Mexican citizens overwhelmingly supported US assistance in the form of money and equipment to confront drug trafficking but were split on whether US agents or soldiers should be operationally deployed in the country (Camp, 2010, p. 317).
148. Political security analyst, telephone conversation, October 25, 2017.
149. Olson, 2017, p. 11.
150. A. Poiré, personal communication, Mexico City, September 14, 2017.
151. Archibold et al., 2013.
152. J. Tello Peón, personal communication, Mexico City, February 13, 2018.
153. L. Chapa Koloffon, personal communication, Mexico City, February 9, 2018.
154. Archibold et al., 2013.
155. Former senior US diplomat, email correspondence, September 28, 2021.
156. S. Ley, personal communication, Mexico City, January 9, 2018.
157. Private sector security analyst, personal communication, Mexico City, September 12, 2017.
158. Olson et al., 2018. One of President Peña Nieto's signature accomplishments was the overhaul of the electoral system, and starting with the 2018 elections, legislators could run for up to four consecutive terms in office for the Chamber of Deputies and up to two terms for the Senate.
159. Bailey, 2014b, p. 101; Benítez Manaut, 2013, p. 156.
160. Benítez Manaut, 2013, p. 154; Escalante, 2012, p. 104.
161. Corcoran, 2008.
162. Rath, 2016, pp. 19–21. The opposition's distaste for the military's use domestically may be more rhetorical than actual. The army's use in maintaining public order was a consistent yet discrete feature of the hegemonic period, reinforcing the PRI's predominance by providing elections security, capturing political intelligence, and containing popular discontent (Ronfeldt, 1975). Even though some PRI officials worried about the military's growing political influence throughout the decades, there was never a serious risk of coup activity, which has consistently reassured the political establishment. Despite the PRD's and MORENA's historical rejection of militarized responses, President López Obrador's most recent reform to the security sector, the creation of the National Guard (Guardia Nacional de México), was paradoxically conceived as subordinate to SEDENA, but at least initially, opposition voices successfully pressed for the new force to be assigned to the SSPC (Ferri, 2019).

163. A. Poiré, personal communication, Mexico City, September 14, 2017.
164. Bejar & Becerril, 2017.
165. A. Poiré, personal communication, Mexico City, September 14, 2017.
166. Trejo & Ley, 2016, pp. 12–13.
167. Trejo & Ley, 2016, p. 47.
168. Bailey, 2014b, p. 95.
169. Bailey, 2014b, p. 95.
170. Duncan, 2014.
171. Posada-Carbó, 2018.

7

Building a Monopoly of Force

The Effect of Security Sector Centralization on Security Sector Reform

The degree of centralization in a recipient country's security sector bureaucracy also helps explain differing outcomes for US security assistance. Whereas a high level of centralization among Colombia's security institutions facilitated US-Colombian dialogue and enabled the top-down implementation of reforms, the dispersal of authority and responsibility for security in Mexico hindered bilateral cooperation on implementing reforms across Mexico's security forces. In fact, bureaucratic divisions among security providers at the federal level and the decentralization of policing authority not only complicated the adoption of US security assistance, but also provided criminals with more avenues to suborn and subvert the Mexican government. Rather than improving its security, Mexico became more violent over the years of the Mérida Initiative's implementation, and the very organization of the security sector played an unmistakable role in this devastating outcome.

The Centralization Debate

The security sector reform literature and the broader literature on democratic decentralization have traditionally emphasized a correlation between a security sector's legitimacy in the eyes of citizens and its linkages to the communities it is charged to protect.[1] Decentralized security sector governance therefore has multiple advantages, according to scholars in this camp. In principle, decentralization helps alleviate the administrative congestion that usually burdens centralized government institutions, permitting the center to act more strategically rather than focus on day-to-day operations.[2] Additionally, a security sector that is "close" to the citizenry—one drawn from and co-located with communities and familiar with local customs and concerns—better

From Peril to Partnership. Paul J. Angelo, Oxford University Press. © Oxford University Press 2024.
DOI: 10.1093/oso/9780197688106.003.0008

represents the population.[3] Local security providers are especially well suited to respond to crises more rapidly and in ways that account for local nuances.[4] Thus devolving security provision to subnational governments is believed to enhance the coverage, quality, and efficiency of security services and to give citizens a greater say in matters of accountability.[5] A growing number of scholars and practitioners stress that governments undertaking security sector reform today should prioritize "avenues for operationalizing ownership at the local level in order to avoid an overly centralized focus."[6]

Despite the importance of local ownership of security sector reform, decentralization in the security sector carries risks, which were consequential in both Colombia and Mexico.[7] Chiefly, decentralization of security provision, which disperses decision-making authority across multiple organizations and across levels of government, has often been associated with the undesirable prospect of corruption and even state capture, especially when organized crime competes against the state for economic space and political influence.[8] Kent Eaton posits that "decentralization in the pursuit of security can be a particularly dangerous option where the state's most important identifying feature—its monopoly over the use of force—is absent."[9]

Grichawat Lowatcharin finds that, practically speaking, decentralization of policing is more effective in preventing property crimes than violent crimes and actually has little impact on levels of citizen trust in the police.[10] In fact, efforts to bring democracy "closer to the people" have tended to strengthen clientelism at the local level.[11] After a period of political decentralization, some popularly elected mayors in Colombia and Mexico used their newfound powers to strike mutually beneficial bargains with organized crime groups.[12] In exchange for judicial protection and political cover from elected political leaders, nonstate armed groups contributed to political campaigns by intimidating voters and financing election activities.[13] Where subnational authorities were vulnerable to inducement or coercion, they predictably stood in the way of security sector reform.

Contrasting Colombia and Mexico

One of the major distinctions between Colombia and Mexico that tends to weigh heavily on many political outcomes, including security sector reform, is that of Colombia's unitary governance structures versus Mexico's federal ones.

Colombia, a country divided by treacherous mountain terrain and an extensive Amazon River network, historically featured centralized political institutions and a powerful national executive. These political conditions prevailed because of an early consensus among Bogotá's political elites to build nationwide infrastructure to connect the country's topographically varied regions while containing civil unrest among geographically dispersed populations.[14] In this type of constitutional order, "the prerogatives for determining and enforcing the rules are vested in a single decision structure that has an ultimate monopoly over the legitimate exercise of coercive capabilities."[15] Although Colombia underwent an important process of devolution of political authority to subnational offices in 1991 and ultimately became a decentralized unitary system, the coercive power of the state to this day rests exclusively in the hands of the president.

The Mexican state, on the other hand, is constitutionally a federal system—a political structure in which "deliberation, bargaining, and compromise-seeking are the main modi operandi in governance networks."[16] During the rule of the Institutional Revolutionary Party (Partido Revolucionario Institucional, or PRI), the state monopolized the use of force through a centralized military apparatus and a national network of municipal police forces and rural defense forces whose loyalty to the regime was cemented by party-centered political alliances.[17] However, following a period of decentralization and democratization in the 1980s and 1990s, policymakers at the national, state, and municipal levels began to exhibit real interdependence.[18] In this context, the president, governors, and mayors and their associated executive bureaucracies all have a say in policy formulation, and each has formal authority over elements of the security sector in their geographic jurisdictions.

In Mexico, the absence of a single chain of command and the lack of coordination mechanisms between security sector actors contributed to crippling inefficiency and a lack of accountability for security sector agencies. Federal, state, and municipal actors could not agree on a whole-of-government approach throughout more than a decade of security sector reform, rendering strategies for improvement both incomplete and easily sidestepped by non-compliant subnational authorities. This lack of commitment eventually led both to suboptimal agreements on strategy and abundant finger-pointing among political elites in the capital and those in the regions. Successive Mexican presidents found that once security provision was decentralized, it was extremely difficult to recentralize to improve the security sector's performance.

The resulting chaos of decentralized environments underscores the value of having a single node of coordination to manage and monopolize security.[19] In Mexico, corrupt security forces and opportunistic political rivals customarily doubled down on their opposition to institutional reforms led by the national executive.[20] This chapter argues that the challenges confronted in Mexico are

Table 7.1. Evolution of Political Organization in Colombia and Mexico

	Colombia	Mexico
Historically	centralized unitary state	centralized federal state
Post-1980s	decentralized unitary state	decentralized federal state
Security sector governance	centralized	decentralized

Source: Author's tabulation.

not the fault of the federal system itself but instead linked to the degree of security decentralization, which provided insufficient coordination mechanisms among security institutions and introduced more opportunities for corruption. Decentralized systems require the active participation of civil society at the local level to shape security interventions and hold actors accountable, as well as constitutional mechanisms that define the competencies of each level of government and are respected by all security sector institutions.[21] In the absence of such vigilance and in contexts plagued by high levels of corruption, parochialism takes center stage, the number of veto players increases, and policy stagnation is highly likely.[22]

Conversely, in centralized security bureaucracies, security sector reform does not necessarily require such active buy-in from multiple levels of government, reducing the bureaucratic burden carried by reform-minded leadership. As this book demonstrates, Colombia's 1991 Constitution, which was signed at a time of intensifying violence, prevented any major devolution of authority in the realm of security. The preservation of national executive control over the security sector and its concentration in a single ministry minimized the interference of subnational spoilers that derailed federal-led security sector reform in Mexico.[23]

Colombia: Centralized Security Provision in a Decentralized Unitary State

Colombia underwent one of the most radical episodes of political decentralization in recent Latin American history.[24] Starting in the late nineteenth century, it featured a unitary constitutional model in which the centralized political authority wielded the legal powers and state institutions necessary to mediate regional politics.[25] The 1886 Constitution denied Colombia's departments the authority to set fiscal policy, print money, and maintain militias.[26] From 1886 until 1991, the only significant representation of departments in political decision-making was via the national legislature.

However, persistent indifference to outlying regions among Bogotá's political class granted de facto autonomy to regional elites, who equally resented the interference of national authorities in local matters.[27] Regional elites also contested the centralized power of the purse, which limited the ability of resource-strapped local governments to administer public services. In 1983, encouraged by multilateral lending agencies such as the World Bank, the Colombian Congress approved Law 14 (Ley 14 de 1983) in a bid to strengthen the ability of municipalities to levy taxes and distribute their own fiscal resources. Impelled by domestic political strife over a lack of local representation in national politics, Congress went one step further in 1986 by introducing measures (Law 12, Ley 12 de 1986) to relieve the tax burden on smaller municipalities and to improve fiscal administration in subnational government.[28] Structural adjustment linked to neoliberal economic reforms, a wave of civic activism, and a period of political crisis collectively advanced the devolution of political power to departments and municipalities. And starting with the popular election of mayors in 1988 (Ley 11 de 1986), the Colombian political system conclusively shifted to decentralized unitary governance.[29]

The 1991 Constitution expanded the popular election of subnational authorities to governorships, and the following year witnessed the first popular elections for all subnational political offices.[30] By the early 1990s, political power solidly rested in the hands of officeholders at three levels of government, and the revamped constitutional order formally established political, administrative, and fiscal decentralization in Colombia. Despite the retention of important rights for the national executive, governors and mayors enjoyed more fiscal resources, managed more social services, and were better organized to represent collective local interests than at any point in the preceding century.[31]

The architects of the 1991 Constitution conceived of political decentralization as a definitive solution to a crisis of representation in the political system. Decentralization against the backdrop of Colombia's armed conflict, however, further contributed to a decline in security as guerrilla and paramilitary networks expanded—in part by chipping away at the integrity of subnational authorities.[32] The constitutional reforms fractured political power, which increased opportunities for organized crime to access the political system through subnational officeholders. The fragmentation of political power and the diffusion of political representation ultimately made state protection of organized crime at the various levels of government unpredictable. Nonstate armed groups, keen to secure stable arrangements with corrupt officials, aggressively used bribes and violence to infiltrate state institutions from the municipality upward.[33] Decentralization and the concurrent process of party system deinstitutionalization also empowered new parties and political movements that were willing to challenge the growing influence of the cartels openly—and to suffer the fatal consequences that such opposition entailed. Luis Carlos Galán, for instance, founded a political current of the Liberal Party known as New Liberalism (Nuevo Liberalismo). In his 1990 bid for the presidency, Galán railed against the government's passivity regarding organized crime, declared himself at odds with the drug cartels, and favored an extradition treaty with the United States—a position unpopular among drug traffickers that ultimately led to the candidate's assassination in 1989.

The cartel's intimidation campaign had plunged Colombian society into a devastating security crisis that featured a multifront drug war, renewed fighting between the state and leftist insurgencies, and the rapid growth of right-wing paramilitary groups. The state's monopoly of force was in no uncertain terms nonexistent, and regional political figures, now subject to popular election rather than appointment by the central government, were compelled to negotiate with illegal armed power brokers as they campaigned for votes. Some found themselves at the mercy of insurgents and paramilitaries in areas of the country bereft of the security sector's permanent presence; others capitalized on opportunities to make money and consolidate votes by quietly cooperating with organized crime.[34]

This scenario resulted in the dynamic by which the central Ministry of Finance (Ministerio de Hacienda) transferred revenue to popularly elected local governments that were sometimes controlled by armed groups engaged in outright war against the Colombian state.[35] What emerged was a new type of corruption at the local level: armed clientelism, or the private capture of public services, contracts, and resources through armed threats.[36] The *parapolítica* scandal, which entailed widely publicized investigations into political collusion with the United Self-Defense Forces of Colombia (Autodefensas Unidas de Colombia, or AUC) paramilitary group beginning in 2006, demonstrated just how deeply state capture ran at the local level in some parts of Colombia.[37] In the decade that followed, the Attorney General's Office opened more than five hundred disciplinary processes against public servants for ties to the AUC and BACRIM (*bandas criminales*), implicating at least 109 mayors, thirty-seven governors, and seventy-three members of Congress.[38] Other high-profile cases, such as that of accused AUC kingpin Guillermo León Acevedo Giraldo (alias Memo Fantasma), revealed how some paramilitary leaders hid in plain sight for many years, continuing to launder money and infiltrate elite social and political circles before facing justice.[39]

Although decentralization was perceived as necessary from a political standpoint, the elected delegates of the Constituent Assembly sought to hedge against the security risks that decentralization posed by retaining centralized security institutions in the new constitution. Despite the tendency to devolve powers from Bogotá to subnational governments, the provision of security remained firmly a responsibility of the central government. Recognizing the risk of state capture that the decentralizing reforms of the 1980s were already beginning to pose, the Constituent Assembly stopped short of turning over command of Colombia's police force to subnational entities, who were uniquely situated to succumb to the pressures of illegal armed groups or to abuse their authority to consolidate local power.[40] Moreover, in Colombia, a historical legacy of the security forces' institutional autonomy and apolitical identity influenced the preservation of the status quo. The prospect of subordinating the police forces to governors and mayors and thus partisan designs was inconceivable following La Violencia, when the Liberal and Conservative Parties recruited members of the police to create their own praetorian guards, with disastrous consequences.[41] The reassignment of the police as subordinate to the Ministry of Defense in 1953 and reforms adopted during the National Front period to nationalize the police's chain of command had been successful at depoliticizing the institution—even though these measures also gave it a more militarized orientation.[42]

The 1991 Constitution reiterated the president's operational control of the public forces (*fuerza pública*) to include the four services of the Ministry of Defense (Army, Navy, Air Force, and National Police). The new constitution also extended shared responsibility for the management of public order to governors and mayors for the first time since the 1950s by giving them a say on security policy, but the president retained agenda-setting and veto authority over subnational security initiatives.[43] This historical moment—one in which the mounting forces of decentralization were halted—was a critical juncture that reaffirmed the central government's aspirational commitment to monopolizing the legitimate use of force. It also precluded any legal proliferation of competing security sector actors without the explicit consent of the national executive.[44]

A brief but instructive experiment with the limited devolution of security provision via a network of self-defense cooperatives confirmed the central government's worst fears and demonstrated the wisdom of the new constitution's prescriptions for security. In 1994, the Ministry of Defense issued a decree, approved by President Gaviria and later ratified by the Colombian Congress, that authorized the creation of neighborhood watch groups in communities where guerrilla activity was on the rise and central state presence was weak. Known as the CONVIVIR (to coexist) and armed by the central government, the self-defense groups, which numbered more than four hundred, quickly earned a reputation for their brutality against civilians and for their own role in perpetrating violence and insecurity.[45] In the absence of any meaningful governmental oversight, many of the CONVIVIR extorted the communities they were charged to protect and openly collaborated with paramilitary groups like the AUC, which had come to monopolize some of Colombia's most profitable drug routes.[46] Criticizing the government's lack of accountability over the CONVIVIR, the Colombian Constitutional Court imposed severe restrictions on them in 1997, reducing the caliber of weaponry they were legally permitted to use and requiring greater supervision by the central government. When dozens of the groups refused to comply with the new measures, the national executive completely disbanded the program and disarmed the CONVIVIR in 1998, pushing units that refused to demobilize underground and often into the ranks of the AUC.

Cooperation across Levels of Government

In the wake of the CONVIVIR debacle, the Pastrana administration confirmed the constitution's structural vision of the security sector in 2001 with the passage of the National Security and Defense Law, which, although ultimately struck down by the Constitutional Court for text unrelated to the security sector's centralization (see chapter 6), reiterated the preeminence of the national executive in the political and administrative management of security.[47] Significantly, the new legislation asserted the existence of a centralized security bureaucracy that was above the partisan fray. In Colombia, although the security forces take their orders from the president, the military and police profess loyalty to the state, not their political bosses.[48]

Nevertheless, mayors and governors are constitutionally empowered to design, implement, and oversee local public security strategies in coordination with the National Police. Historically, some have exercised considerable autonomy to implement citizen security initiatives.[49] Although the coercive capacity of the police force remains in the hands of the president, subnational political authorities are responsible for municipal and departmental crime and violence prevention initiatives. To the extent that mayors' and governors' security strategies do not contravene those of the president, subnational politicians are lawfully permitted to issue orders to National Police units administratively assigned to their territories. In Colombia's major cities, intrepid and innovative politicians have been especially involved in crime prevention.[50] Citizen Culture (Cultura Ciudadana) in Bogotá and Social Urbanism (Urbanismo Social) in Medellín are two prominent examples of municipal-led security initiatives—both of which entailed reconceptualizing urban space in ways that encourage coexistence among city dwellers.[51] These policies understood urban criminality as a consequence of the disorder and deterioration of poorly maintained public spaces, and they prioritized infrastructural improvements and community conflict resolution mechanisms as keys to reducing violence.[52] In pursuing more preventive security strategies, local politicians avoided impinging on the central government's security prerogatives or appearing insubordinate to presidential authority, all while carving out noteworthy space to shape outcomes and take credit for advances in citizen security. Some municipalities and departments have even levied their own security taxes to finance everything from public works aimed at reducing exposure to crime to educational campaigns targeting youth at risk of gang recruitment.[53]

Subnational security strategies in Colombia were broadly compatible with President Uribe's Democratic Security Policy and security sector reform.[54] Horacio Serpa, the former governor of Santander Department, described the delicate dance expected of subnational authorities:

> I have been a critic of President Uribe's Democratic Security, and as governor I am strictly compliant with the Democratic Security policies because that is what the Constitution says. In a matter as important as security you cannot have a president ordering one thing, the governor doing whatever he wants, and the mayors going off in another direction. There are some things that have to be national, and we all have to respect them.[55]

The constitutional prohibition on the development of subnational armed security providers further facilitated the coherence of Colombian security strategies and reforms. Municipal authorities have occasionally raised local police forces to address specific public order concerns, but to avoid duplicating mandates of the National Police, their functions have been limited to the enforcement of municipal transit laws or to provide logistical support during large public events.[56]

One of the strengths of the Colombian security model has been the development of complementary preventive and coercive strategies at different levels of government—and the reliance of mayors and governors on national forces to endorse and implement their subnational security initiatives.[57] The 1991 Constitution explicitly states that the National Police will comply with orders issued by mayors—a declaration supported by Law 4 of 1991 (Ley 4 del 1991) and

Law 62 of 1993 (Ley 62 del 1993)—but in practice, the relationship tends to be less hierarchical and more cooperative than the statutes prescribe.[58] Although the president retains veto power over the decisions of mayors and governors with the police actively helping politicians design their policies, the day-to-day operations of the National Police in municipal areas necessitate close collaboration between local political authorities and the security forces.

In some parts of the country, though, mayors and governors have demonstrated indifference and a lack of vision in fulfilling their assigned security duties.[59] Elsewhere, local governance reforms, including improved services provision, brought local politicians increasingly into direct contact with organized crime groups and gangs, creating opportunities for criminals to co-opt officials or take credit for their activities.[60] To encourage greater interest in prevention and control at the subnational level, the central government—via the National Police and Ministry of the Interior and with support from the US Embassy—inaugurated the Safe Departments and Municipalities Program (Programa Departamentos y Municipios Seguros) as a component of a broader territorial consolidation strategy.[61] Starting in March 2004, President Uribe employed the ministries of the central government to host workshops with all subnational authorities about their rights, responsibilities, and tools in the protection of citizen security.[62] The government then paired departmental and municipal police commanders with their political counterparts to devise security strategies that accounted for regional security conditions and priorities. This tactic, which became police doctrine, ensured that security sector reform took on a certain local character while eliciting buy-in from subnational elected officials—many of whom were eager to collaborate with Uribe, who had a proven track record on security and invited unusually close relations with mayors throughout the country.[63] This innovation, which has served as a model for other countries in Latin America, improved coordination and long-range implementation of security strategies while giving police nationwide a preventive rather than an exclusively reactive footing.

Additionally, Uribe and his cabinet ministers increased the frequency of municipal and departmental security consultations with subnational authorities and community members, who aired grievances and offered suggestions in ways that directly and publicly took the central government to task for insecurity. Under this arrangement, the national government became increasingly responsive to local needs and demands without having to outsource security provision to local actors.[64] For example, in the conflict-ridden Chocó Department, the minister of defense and leadership of the Colombian Navy convened a series of security consultations with local authorities and community members following the tragic massacre of more than one hundred civilians during AUC-FARC (Fuerzas Armadas Revolucionarias de Colombia, or Revolutionary Armed Forces of Colombia) combat in the town of Bojayá in 2002.[65] In light of requests made during such consultations, the central government organized a series of civic action projects through the Ministries of Defense and Health, constructed homes for families displaced by violence, and reinforced the military's presence on waterways vital to the local economy. In El Chocó as elsewhere, the central government made efforts to tailor its responses to local conditions and preferences, especially given that helping communities rebound from tragedy and prevent additional violence typically translated into votes for the ruling party.[66] Although the scale of investments made following security consultations varied across Colombia's regions, presidential and cabinet-level interest in local security crises represented a symbolic pivot in a national executive that for too much of history had neglected the country's geographic periphery.

In Colombia, the benefits of centralized security provision, informed by subnational participation, have been numerous. First, centralization helped streamline the Colombian government's relationship with its main external enabler of security sector reform, the United States. From a logistical standpoint, new equipment acquisitions from the United States, channeled principally to the Ministry of Defense, reached their ultimate beneficiaries according to a standardized procedure and timeline. The US Embassy supported security sector reform programming with all four services of the Ministry of Defense, and the interpersonal links between bureaucrats on both sides of the relationship—which took place at the level of the ministry's professional civil service with inputs from the individual armed services—made the Colombian security sector a predictable partner.[67] One US representative engaged in Plan Colombia and later in security sector reform programs in Mexico and Central America noted that having a single node through which to "plug US resources" was essential to the success of Colombia's reform: "No matter how much SOUTHCOM would like to export the mentality elsewhere, we can't build up both the military and police in Honduras and Mexico as seamlessly as we did in Colombia because they are separate and divided institutions plagued by onerous bureaucracies."[68]

The US military's goal was not to work with every unit in the Colombian security sector. Instead, strategic planners anticipated the diffusion of US-exported processes and doctrine throughout the Ministry of Defense via personnel and leadership rotations. Central to this strategy was the invitation of hundreds of Colombian military officers, from all three services and the National Police, to attend US military schools, which created a common experience for the Colombian security forces, cultivated ties between the two countries, and standardized administrative and operational practices ministry-wide.[69] Although this approach was not necessarily new in the hemisphere, Plan Colombia ensured that Colombians were the top beneficiaries of such training: in 2012, Colombian students made up 53 percent of Latin American students in resident courses in the United States and 70 percent of students participating in regional mobile training teams.[70] Similarly, SOUTHCOM helped the Colombian military establish a noncommissioned officer school in a bid to professionalize the enlisted corps.[71] From the vantage of multiple US defense officials, one of the most vital US contributions to the homogenization of the services was the establishment of the Colombian Army's counternarcotics units in 1998 in that it gave the US government a clean slate to set up a new staff structure and decision-making hierarchy. The new brigade served as a template for later structural reforms in the military and police that reorganized the security forces according to the US-NATO continental staff system.[72]

Second, centralization reduced bureaucratic resistance to the introduction of new reforms, disempowering would-be spoilers of security sector reform. Centralization and a single hierarchy established a respected system of accountability. In light of the prominent role afforded US advisors in the security sector reform endeavor, Colombia's military and police leadership, energized by the prospect of sustained engagement with the US government, seldom pushed back against recommendations for organizational modifications.[73] According to one former Colombian advisor to the Mexican Federal Police, security sector reform in Colombia was so successful because the chain of command was clear and everyone respected it. Domestic political authorities and international partners lodged their praise, concerns, and complaints about the military and police in the front office of the minister of defense.[74] Civilian control of the military permitted the minister and the president to remove officers whose behavior betrayed the principles of security sector reform while rewarding those who embraced reforms with promotions and desirable commands. In this way, the executive prevented the erosion of support for security sector reform from within the forces undergoing reform—an essential feat.[75]

Furthermore, the constitutional declaration that the country's security agencies would remain national in character prevented them from being drawn into partisan competition for votes and, especially, corrupt local pacts between subnational officials and organized crime. As one Colombian police officer observed,

> There is a lack of trust in subnational governments. If the state begins to look at what it spends on the National Police, it will find motives to decentralize the force

> [to cut costs], but this would expose subnational police to corruption at departmental and municipal levels—something Congress does not want to risk.[76]

That is not to say that the security forces are immune to corruption or clientelistic arrangements. A recent series of investigations within the military exposed sixteen generals and more than one hundred lower-ranking officials for corrupt practices ranging from the sale of arms permits to graft.[77] In one instance, a general formed an alliance with influential drug traffickers and later claimed that these links contributed to his work combating the FARC.[78] Systemic corruption by drug gangs, which minimize detection by infiltrating at as low a level of government as possible, has nonetheless proved more difficult thanks to the security sector's hierarchical structure. Ministry-wide policies that enforce the routine rotations of soldiers and police officers at variable intervals have helped deter unit infiltration by local criminals, a feature absent in Mexico's geographically bound municipal police forces. In addition, an organizational and social rift between officers and their subordinate soldiers or beat cops has meant that this brand of corruption, when it does occur, typically takes place in clusters (such as among peers at the unit level) instead of across the organization at large.[79] Broad public approval of police performance during Plan Colombia and zero-tolerance policies enacted by successive governments to dismiss venal officers suggest that links to organized crime were the exception during Plan Colombia, not the norm.[80]

A third major benefit of centralized security bureaucracy, specifically the concentration of forces in the Ministry of Defense, is that it helped limit redundancies and inefficiencies among security sector institutions. The legal separation of the faculties ascribed to the Colombian Armed Forces and those of the National Police clarified responsibilities in responding to criminality and enabled civilian leadership to determine the strategic direction of each service in an integrated way, including doctrinal reforms, capability enhancements, and some equipment acquisitions. For example, all the national forces have a role in counternarcotics missions, but their mandates differ from service to service. Whereas the Colombian Army's counternarcotics responsibilities include combating armed groups in areas of the country flush with drug crops to prepare these territories for eradication missions, the National Police's JUNGLA Commandos (Compañía Jungla Antinarcóticos) follow up the actions of the army with specialized interdiction missions targeting processing labs, narcotics caches, and precursor chemicals.[81]

Moreover, the uniformed leadership of each security force have used their positions within the Ministry of Defense to help shape security sector reform goals.[82] The incorporation of the services' institutional preferences has facilitated useful innovation. In the early 2000s, the Colombian military's seizure of laptops, thumb drives, and mobile phones during raids on insurgent camps often rendered evidence inadmissible in trials because the military did not have the legal right to secure criminal evidence. In response, the National Police began embedding specialized police officers in operational military units, thereby fusing military operations and judicial investigations in the same task force.[83] In some operations, the government dispatches civilian prosecutors alongside military units to expedite judicial procedures for high-profile captures or arrests. This brand of interagency integration and interoperability, which saves resources and makes the delivery of justice easier, would be unlikely were it not for the high degree of bureaucratic centralization and trust among Colombia's executive agencies and departments.

The preservation of a centralized security bureaucracy, despite the decentralizing impulses of the Colombian government in the late twentieth century, proved to be an important facilitator of security sector reform. The Colombian security sector managed to maintain a centralized administration and hierarchy, which streamlined the adoption of reforms and neutralized spoilers, all while instituting programs to bring the security forces closer to local concerns. Although the drug business and its associated corruption continue to pose challenges for Colombian institutions across the board, security sector reform entailed the implementation of organizational policies and operational strategies that minimized the risk of institution-wide infiltration of the security forces. The Colombian example encourages scholars to reconsider the efficacy of decentralizing security provision as a component of security sector reform. It also validates arguments that favor the conservation of existing centralized security provision, especially in societies plagued by corruption and pervasive nonstate security threats.

Mexico: Multinodal Security Provision in a Decentralized Federal State

Mexico has a decentralized and deconcentrated model of security provision that complicated the adoption of security sector reform and, in fact, undermined security sector governance, contributing to worsening insecurity. One Mexican government official concluded, "Mexico is a fragmented system, which works for everything except for security. Decentralizing security has been the wrong approach. Two things always need to be controlled centrally: macroeconomic growth and security, which requires the monopoly of the legitimate use of force."[84] It would appear that, at least in this latter regard, the contrasting experiences of Colombia and Mexico powerfully validate this point.

From the mid-1930s until the 1990s, Mexican federalism existed only in name, as the political system exhibited solidly centralized tendencies.[85] Presidential power rooted in PRI predominance was the arbiter of national, state, and municipal politics for decades, and the ruling party often manipulated elections to ensure its continued occupation of power.[86] During this period, law enforcement, which per Article 115 of the Mexican Constitution is a responsibility of municipal government, was not a party priority because the PRI governing coalition often resorted to bargaining and pact-making to neutralize security challenges. As a consequence, the federal government historically failed to allocate enough resources to municipal governments, which depended on the federal government for revenue to professionalize and properly equip local police.[87] According to Alejandra Gómez Céspedes, police forces were principally instruments of political control, granted enough autonomy to repress and extort citizens as long as the police expressed loyalty to state-level PRI authorities.[88] Although the administration of public security was decentralized as far back as 1917, the use of the police as an extension of national political authority was a persistent practice that aligned police forces with the PRI.

However, like Colombia, the Mexican government acquiesced to the prodding of international lending bodies in the 1980s following the regional debt crisis and implemented major decentralizing reforms, both economic and political.[89] This push also helped the PRI meet its own domestic challenges. Indeed, the Mexican government's decentralization efforts were a coordinated strategy to regain legitimacy and credibility that the PRI began to lose as rival parties criticized the authoritarian system for Mexico's growing economic troubles.[90] President Miguel de la Madrid's Municipal Reform of 1983 strengthened subnational autonomy with the allocation of federal funds to municipalities via state governments, which empowered governors to determine the federal monies each municipality received. Additionally, the reform affirmed the municipal government's responsibility for public safety and eventually extended a greater share of revenue to subnational authorities for citizen security, traffic enforcement, and fire and emergency medical services. From this point forward, municipalities began lobbying for and expending considerable resources to develop and maintain municipal police services, at once forces of public order and agents of party clientelism. Yet investment in public security remained minimal throughout the 1990s, estimated at 0.008 percent of GDP.[91]

The de la Madrid administration's reforms extended to the electoral realm as well. Under his watch, the government enforced a greater commitment to electoral integrity, permitting for the first time the popular election of non-PRI candidates to subnational offices on a wide scale. When the 1983 elections resulted in opposition victories in five state capitals and more than a dozen smaller cities, the PRI recognized its growing unpopularity and its electoral vulnerability. This in turn stalled further political liberalization—and opposition victories—until the contested and fraudulent electoral cycle of 1988.[92] After that year, party system reorganization and popular mobilization combined to make subnational elections increasingly competitive.[93]

In the mid-1990s, President Ernesto Zedillo's New Federalism project took decentralization one step further. His sweeping reforms provided a major boost to the autonomy of subnational governments, increased the transparency of administrative functions at all levels of government, and strengthened the administrative and taxation capacity of the municipalities.[94] Likewise, electoral and judicial reforms gave more privileges to state governments, and a 1995 fiscal overhaul afforded subnational governments an increasing share of national expenditures devolved from the federal government—a modification that emboldened the political ambitions of mayors and governors, who could extract more resources for their political platforms. In 1999, transfers made up 39 percent of the federal budget, up from just 21.2 percent in the period preceding the reform.[95] As the PRI's reign began to crack, decentralization intersected with democratization, strengthening the clout of subnational actors in defining the extent of governmental reforms.[96]

Decentralization Creates Additional Nodes for State Capture

Mexico's process of decentralization had, in just over a decade, both formalized an important role for subnational authorities in providing citizen security and at last permitted the free election of subnational officeholders.[97] Not unlike the politicization of security issues at the national level (see chapter 6), this confluence of factors ensured that security would eventually become a top electoral and partisan issue at the subnational level, too, particularly after cartel activity and intimidation of local politicians ballooned by the late 1990s. Even though decentralization increased electoral accountability, its effect on security provision was negative given that police forces often became conduits for the transmission of partisan preferences and favors. Zedillo's reforms to the Attorney General's Office and the creation of new subnational and judicial police forces increased institutional fragmentation in Mexico, inadvertently multiplying corruption channels and reducing the central government's ability to regulate the drug market and security threats.[98] State and municipal police forces possessed a partisan identity dating to the PRI's hegemonic period; even after democratization, though, mayors and governors often continued to appoint their local police commissioners in exchange for campaign contributions and political loyalty.[99] As Ernesto López Portillo explains, "The basis of police behavior—and of the regime as a whole—has been political, not legal. The police were excluded from the modernization policies of the state and were consolidated as a privileged resource of repression and corruption."[100] Most state constitutions do not specify the qualifications necessary for the appointment of police leadership, and in practice, one need not have experience in the realm of public security to become a municipal police chief.[101] In addition, changes in subnational political leadership often put a halt to the continuity of police reforms undertaken by previous municipal and state administrations, especially when subnational political power changed party hands.[102]

The design of Mexican federalism bestows inordinate power on state governors, in turn creating a competition to attain or influence regional political offices at all costs.[103] In the democratic era, governors exercise a de facto veto power by refusing to cooperate with federal strategies—a rare occurrence during the PRI's hegemony given the president's ability to remove governors from office. State governments similarly tend to use Public Security Support Fund (Fondo de Aportaciones para la Seguridad Pública, or FASP) monies to enhance their coercive capacity, leaving little for municipal police forces in many states.[104] In much of Mexico, state police forces were better funded but at the expense of municipal police forces and local crime and violence prevention efforts.

In this context, the ruling party at the federal level could "no longer reach down into the territories," where opposition parties—or unaligned mayors or governors—held the reins of local government and, at times, actively undermined federal strategies for resolving criminality.[105] In some regions, municipal and state police forces, alongside mayors and governors, engaged in underhanded arrangements with organized crime, functioning as important points of entry for state capture.[106] These circumstances put them in direct competition with the federal forces of law and order, which were charged with confronting criminal groups but also colluded with different organized crime groups on occasion themselves. In 2005, in a high-profile instance of blue-on-blue crime, municipal police forces fired on unarmed federal police officers in Nuevo Laredo, which resulted in the detention of the seven-hundred-member municipal force and subsequent dismissal of more than half of them over ties to drug gangs.[107] For this reason, the Mexican Army's leadership was long insistent on the passage of an interior security law to expand the military's autonomy in the whole of the national territory in a bid to counter the prerogatives of subnational authorities reluctant to cooperate with federal security mandates.[108]

The politicization of subnational police forces—and their use in the clientelistic practices of corrupt mayors and governors or as agents of organized crime—has rendered them particularly effective spoilers of security sector reform.[109] The decentralization of Mexico's federal system facilitated multinodal cover for illegality and violence as nonstate armed actors carved out influence among municipal and state authorities. A human rights defender noted that in some municipalities organized crime groups strong-arm mayors to handpick members of the municipal police forces, thereafter demanding that the officers extort the local populace at their behest.[110] Under these circumstances, civil society faces risks far too fatal to be an effective check on local state power.[111] Furthermore, from the 1990s through the early 2000s, the simultaneous fragmentation in the national, subnational, and criminal spheres generated instability and opportunities for corruption for the political world and organized crime alike.[112] Corrupt agreements at one level of government sometimes inhibited law enforcement operations conducted by another, as documented in the chapter 5 case study of Ciudad Juárez.[113] As Wil Pansters explains, "Democratization . . . was not accompanied by diminishing violence and coercion, but rather by their displacement, or even democratization and decentralization," underscoring the increasingly localized expression of violent behavior in Mexico.[114]

Political liberalization during the 1990s represented a shift in Mexico's security panorama because the prerogatives of newly empowered subnational authorities over citizen security made it difficult for the federal government to maintain a monopoly of force following the decline of the PRI's hegemonic rule.[115] Even when President Calderón, frustrated by his inability to nationalize security provision, attempted to entice municipal governments to professionalize their police by providing Municipal Public Security Subsidies (Subsidio de Seguridad Pública Municipal, or SUBSEMUN) to forces that met certain minimum requirements, the program provided "perverse incentives for municipalities to implement window dressing reform."[116] Although SUBSEMUN continued to operate after Calderón's presidency, little evidence suggests that even after a decade this top-down, centralizing approach had managed to standardize security provision in ways that had a demonstrable impact on crime rates or perceptions of insecurity.[117] Additionally, the revelation of major acts of corruption committed by senior public officials in states such as Tamaulipas, Coahuila, Nayarit, and Veracruz was a reminder of the hidden interests at stake and the pervasiveness of state capture across Mexico.[118]

Deconcentration of the Security Sector

In addition to decentralization, divisions between the federal security forces themselves further complicate the state's ability to monopolize and coordinate armed power. In the 1930s and 1940s, Presidents Lázaro Cárdenas and Miguel Alemán oversaw the reorganization of the national-level security and defense apparatus to protect the presidency against political interference or coups from within the security sector. To prevent such meddling, the government divided the security sector's corporate power to act as a single entity and split the Secretariat of War into two separate cabinet-level ministries, the Secretariat of National Defense (Secretaría de Defensa Nacional, or SEDENA) and the Secretariat of the Navy (Secretaría de Marina, or SEMAR). For good measure, PRI presidents thereafter founded two additional security forces, the Presidential Chiefs of Staff (Estado Mayor Presidencial) and the Mexico City Police Force.[119] In doing so, the political establishment definitively diffused the federal forces of law and order. Yet government officials often went one step further by playing to the rivalries among the services and using whichever one appeared most convenient to the government's immediate political ends.[120] In exchange for loyalty, PRI leaders implicitly ceded organizational self-governance to the security sector's top commanders, bestowing on the most loyal forces considerable autonomy that persisted from the 1940s to the present.[121] During the hegemonic era, the PRI was largely successful at managing the various federal forces and their interinstitutional relations. However, as SEDENA, SEMAR, and federal law enforcement forces grew less susceptible to partisan manipulation in the 2000s, their institutional autonomies and a lack of tradition of working together contributed to a general hesitation to coordinate with one another on matters of citizen security.

As a result, hybrid policing models—those that include multiple actors and stakeholders of different origins participating in the provision of public security—have contributed to the perpetuation of insecurity.[122] As Alejandro Poiré, the secretary of public security during the Calderón administration, remarked,

> Centralization is an important factor because it contributes to efficiency. You can reproduce reform at every level because the standards are the same . . . but the Mexican government possesses an institutional resilience, which prevents our institutions from being more adaptable, flexible, and innovative—and even honest.[123]

Platform Mexico, as highlighted in chapter 3, was a well-financed effort to consolidate intelligence operations and promote information-sharing across security sector agencies laterally and vertically. According to one observer, though, the program was dead on arrival because there was no accountability at the local level. Where poorly trained municipal police lacked the technical capacity to use the system or helped criminal actors to infiltrate it, security interventions (by federal forces) stalled or failed because of incomplete and misleading data.[124]

Other attempts to centralize coordination among federal security forces faced a similar fate. There were repeated efforts to streamline an interagency process in Mexico, including the 1995 National Public Security System (Sistema Nacional de Seguridad Pública), the 2005 National Security Council (Consejo de Seguridad Nacional), and the reorganization of the SSP during the Peña Nieto administration. However, the federal security institutions all retained special exemptions from legal restrictions placed on other government agencies, making intergovernmental strategies difficult to coordinate. The protection of classified information, undisclosed budgets, separate judicial systems, and specialized recruitment and entry requirements point to the privileged legal status of the federal forces.[125] Moreover, SEDENA and SEMAR are both led by uniformed military officers, not civilian ministers, as in Colombia's Ministry of Defense. The institutional autonomy is, in that regard, notably greater than in Colombia, where subordination to civilian control is unquestioned.

Successive Mexican presidents have attempted to consolidate security decision-making and coordinate interinstitutional activities in civilian hands. The Technical Secretary of the National Security Council (Secretariado Técnico del Consejo de Seguridad Nacional, or STCSN), a senior-level executive advisory position created by the National Security Law in 2005 (Ley de Seguridad Nacional), was intended to be a single node through which the executive's various security dependencies could fuse information and collectively make decisions. Still, the leadership of the STCSN, SEDENA, and CISEN (Centro de Investigación y Seguridad Nacional, or Investigation and National Security Center) competed for the attention and support of President Calderón.[126] The lack of real institutional enforcement power, budget restrictions, and personnel limitations prevented the STCSN from realizing its intended potential as a useful coordinating body.[127]

As this suggests, one of the most significant problems with Mexico's decentralized and deconcentrated federal security model is layering, or adding new practices or institutions without eliminating old ones.[128] At the federal, state, and municipal levels, the leaders of the country's security institutions still lack clarity about their jurisdictions and responsibilities.[129] In instances of homicide or kidnapping, it is sometimes unclear whether these crimes should be treated as activities associated with organized crime and thus fall under federal jurisdiction or as common crimes processed by state authorities.[130] This leads to ambiguity surrounding the level of authority under which investigations and judicial procedures should proceed, as well as what the working relationship with state and local security forces should look like. Judicial investigations have also increased tension at the federal level in cases brought against federal security forces. For instance, when President Fox reorganized federal investigative bodies under the Federal Investigative Agency (Agencia Federal de Investigación, or AFI), he empowered them to investigate cases of military and federal police corruption.[131] However, SEDENA and SEMAR retained their investigative arms, and military leaders often refused to cooperate with AFI investigations on national security grounds. During the highly publicized investigations into the disappearance of the students at Ayotzinapa in 2014, SEDENA repeatedly denied access to federal investigators who proffered a warrant to inspect an army base thought to have been used in the commission of the crime.[132]

The layering of investigative authority has unmistakably contributed to bureaucratic inefficiency, but deconcentration in the federal security sector has also produced a redundancy in operational areas of responsibility.[133] Drug interdiction operations are the responsibility of the navy, army, Secretariat of the Interior, Federal Police, and state and local police forces. Similarly, drug investigations fall under the purview of the municipal police, the AFI/PFM (Policía Federal Ministerial, or PFM), and in some instances the army.[134] President Peña Nieto even instituted his signature security effort, the National Gendarmerie, without empowering it with a differentiated mission from other federal forces. The initial premise was that it would complement other federal forces in combating organized crime. But Peña Nieto's inordinate focus on quantity of agents over quality recruiting rendered the gendarmerie no more successful than the countless federal reorganizations that preceded it.[135] Critics claim that the gendarmerie "took the wind out of local responses that were gaining steam," such as the performance of background checks and the certification of municipal police forces.[136] At the very least, its creation provoked tension among the top ranks of SEDENA, who saw the military's budget and prominent role in domestic security threatened by the new federal force.

Accounting for Local Preferences

Federal forces faced further criticism in the performance of their duties in some regions over their inability to account for the complexity of community relations at the local level, exposing citizens to retaliation by criminal groups for cooperation with federal authorities or to predatory behavior by corrupt federal agents.[137] The failure on this front was especially evident in Ciudad Juárez, as noted in chapter 5. One researcher explained:

> The strategy needs to focus on dealing with infrastructure and social problems, and municipal presidents need to be at the heart of any solution because they are the only ones who know how to produce order. Calderón sent forty-two thousand troops into the countryside, but none of them knew how to integrate into local power relations.[138]

Recent federal approaches to insecurity and reform that embraced local knowledge have been the exception, not the norm. Instead, federal forces often dismissed local institutions as corrupt and effectively disbanded municipal police forces in regions to which they deployed. Former Secretary of Public Security Genaro García Luna at one point proposed eliminating municipal police forces altogether. Yet, as one researcher highlighted, municipal police officers "serve a social function. They have sustained contact with the communities and are from the communities they represent. Small towns would resent losing their local representatives."[139] Not only that, but such a drastic measure would also betray the municipal autonomy at the heart of de la Madrid's 1983 reform.

In regard to overcoming institutional division, Benjamin Lessing points to the necessity of either cohesion among political and security force leaders or centralized control of security—both of which were absent in the overall development of security sector reform in Mexico.[140] He contrasts this with that of Brazil from 2009 to 2014, where political forces aligned at the national, state, and municipal levels in Rio de Janeiro, overlaying municipal resources and a commitment to violence reduction on top of an existing national strategy. The Mexican case exhibits "endemic horizontal and vertical fragmentation" of the country's security institutions, and any successful coordination between security agencies and political actors at every level of government typically came down to personal or partisan relationships among officials.[141] Strikingly, this issue revealed the true limits of presidential power in modern democratic Mexico.[142] In 2009, Mexican authorities reported at least 1,661 independent police forces and some 350,000 federal, state, and municipal police officers. However, roughly 90 percent of the police force remained under state or municipal control, reducing those police at the disposal of the executive to only thirty-three thousand officers in a country of nearly 130 million citizens.[143]

Decentralization and deconcentration of the security bureaucracy also complicated Washington's ability to facilitate security sector reform. US authorities, themselves overseen by a large and cumbersome bureaucracy, found working with the Mexican security sector to be laborious and slow moving, a sharp contrast to the ease they found in working with Colombia's centralized security sector. One former US Embassy representative described Colombia as "a user-friendly country," but in Mexico, US officials had to write a memorandum of request merely to speak to their counterparts in the security ministries—perhaps as much a consequence of ingrained Mexican nationalism as of bureaucratic inefficiency.[144] This phenomenon has not abated over time: under an amendment to the National Security Law passed in December 2020, any Mexican official seeking to meet with a foreign agent must first seek approval through an oversight panel and then report on the contents of the meeting after the fact.

US officials responsible for implementing the Mérida Initiative also complained that the dispersion of federal policing authority was debilitating because US diplomats had to readjust programming to accommodate shifting operational control among SEDENA, SEMAR, and the SSP over the geographic theaters of operation.[145] But one US official noted that it was hard for the United States to criticize "a system that mimics US-style federalism."[146] The inefficiencies posed by decentralization unquestionably slowed the pace of bilateral coordination and thus the rollout of security sector reform programs, but Mexico was hardly the only culprit in this regard. Also, even though Washington's objective was to focus on the Mexican states most seriously affected by organized criminal activity, the Mérida Initiative, at the request of the Mexican national executive, remained almost exclusively a federal-to-federal program that skirted around the problems associated with subnational police forces in the most crime-ridden regions.[147]

Mando Único: A Compromise Solution

During the Calderón and Peña Nieto administrations, the national debate over whether to standardize police recruitment requirements, responsibilities, and chain of command across all levels nationwide via a federal effort known as the Unified Command (Mando Único) exemplified the overall challenges that decentralizing Mexico's security bureaucracy posed. The entry and training standards for Mexican police forces at each level of government vary dramatically and remain remarkably low in many places because recruitment for such dangerous and thankless work is difficult.[148] Despite some improvements in recruitment, police forces still lack standardized promotion schemes and pay scales, leading to disparate levels of aptitude, trust, and success across the country. The Unified Command model was originally conceived as an initiative to reverse this disorder by enforcing the same qualifications, training, and benefits for all municipal and state police forces. Former Baja California State Governor José Guadalupe Osuna Millán became the first to implement the program in his state in early 2011, and the experiment was at least partially credited with a subsequent reduction in crime in the state's largest city, Tijuana.[149] From 2008 to 2011, homicides in Tijuana halved, and the homicide rate plateaued at a much lower rate than that of other border cities, such as Ciudad Juárez.[150] Although crime rates in Tijuana surged once again from 2017 to 2021, the early empirical success of the Unified Command in Baja California helped build momentum for President Calderón's proposal to extend the plan nationwide. The proposal even won the backing of the National Governors Conference and prominent civil society organizations.[151] For the final two years of his mandate, Calderón persistently argued for Congress to adopt a single chain of command and standard of performance for all police in Mexico. Having lost some credibility on security issues and in the face of legislative obstructionism, though, Calderón proved unable to deliver the reform by the end of his term.

Even so, in a 2016 poll, only two-fifths of Mexicans believed that local police were best equipped to protect their communities, indicating the need to improve municipal security provision. Yet the Unified Command model—later endorsed by President Peña Nieto as well—failed to pass congressional muster after more than seven years of deliberation.[152] Critics pointed to the simplicity of unifying command of the police forces in a state such as Baja California, with only five municipalities and the concentration of 85 percent of the forces in a single municipality, and the challenge that said unification would pose across more than 2,400 municipalities nationally.[153]

Understandably, some feared that major structural changes would reveal the extent of local corruption, and other politicians opposed the move because it would effectively undo the partisan ties between local political elites and municipal police forces.[154] However, some states and congressional districts with highly professional and effective subnational police forces simply resented having to conform to a national standard when local responses appeared to be working just fine. A handful of well-positioned and vocal subnational politicians, including Osuna's successor in Baja California, rejected the federal imposition on subnational governance as a violation of the constitutional right to municipal autonomy.[155]

Ultimately, in 2017, national and local political forces decided that the Unified Command would not originate at the federal level but instead would be determined state by state.[156] The reform became a matter of cooperation between mayors and governors alone, ignoring federal involvement altogether. The plan therefore placed greater responsibility for citizen security squarely on the shoulders of governors while ensuring that the security sector accounted for local preferences. By 2018, 1,757 mayors had relinquished their control of municipal police to state governments, and twenty-eight of thirty-two state governments had subscribed to the Unified Command with all the municipalities in their territories.[157] The benefits of this new system had yet to be seen, however, given that many of Mexico's crime indicators crept up to record levels from 2017 to 2020.

As one researcher so aptly summarized, "the fractured nature of power in Mexico puts the Mexican state at great risk. There are too many interests to be protected."[158] Decentralization and deconcentration of security provision in Mexico enabled confusion, corruption, and criminality, even as the federal government attempted major reforms to the country's security institutions. In the absence of a single responder or single node of authority, responsibility fell to multiple actors, with competing and overlapping roles and objectives. Interviewed subjects often placed the blame for local violence on the inability of a single level of government—municipal, state, or federal—to fulfill its obligations to the citizenry. However, vast disparities in perceived culpability among the three levels of government, even among voices in the same city, epitomize the outright confusion that resulted from Mexico's decentralized security architecture. It further serves as a telling example of just how heavily the degree of centralization weighs on the citizenry's perceptions of insecurity. Speaking from violence-ridden Acapulco shortly before taking office in 2018, President-elect López Obrador proclaimed to his audience,

> We are going to unify all the forces: the navy, the army, the Federal Police, the ministerial police, the state and municipal police. We are going to create coordination in all of Guerrero territory and in the whole county, and each coordination will be done jointly and respecting the Unified Command.[159]

Although his centralizing instincts have not yet reduced violent crime in Mexico, the president has made abundantly clear one thing that PAN, PRI, and MORENA (Movimiento de Regeneración Nacional, or National Regeneration Movement Party) presidents all agree on: some degree of security sector centralization is a necessary step to resolve Mexico's grave security challenges.

The cases of Colombia and Mexico exhibit contrasting frameworks for the organization of security bureaucracy that contributed to disparate experiences of security sector reform. Because a security crisis coincided with decentralizing reforms in Colombia, national political leaders rejected the possibility of devolving responsibility for security to subnational actors in the 1991 Constitution, a critical juncture that ensured a highly centralized security sector for the duration of security sector reform. Centralization made the support infrastructure provided by the US government more effective, minimized the impact of spoilers within the security sector, and reduced inefficiencies that could have delayed the delivery of reforms. Just as important, the Colombian security sector, though centralized, tailored its approaches by creating coordination mechanisms between central security providers and local actors, thereby boosting the accountability and legitimacy of state forces at a time when nonstate armed actors violently contested state power.

Conversely, in Mexico the long-standing decentralization of security responsibility and the growing power of subnational authorities rendered officials within the security sector agents of local political and often criminal power. This relationship permitted subnational elements of the security sector to undermine federal-led interventions and reforms, complicating everything from the enforcement of anticrime policies to relations with Washington. Despite repeated efforts by federal politicians to centralize security provision or improve coordination across levels of government, for more than three decades the executive proved unable to establish a clear, consolidated chain of command and scheme of interagency coordination throughout the security system. These federal efforts were exacerbated by an existing organizational fragmentation at the national level, where security institutions also staked claims to overlapping authorities. This in turn weakened strategies to reduce crime and violence across the national territory, detracting noticeably from the executive's ability to implement security sector reform.

Notwithstanding these conclusions, complete centralization should not necessarily be the goal in Mexico or any country, no matter how much it has contributed to security sector reform in Colombia. Respecting the constitutional prerogatives of subnational governments remains an important source of legitimacy in Mexico's federal system. A coalition of local actors, including civil society, can successfully coalesce to professionalize and reform local security sector actors and practices, as was partially accomplished in Ciudad Juárez. In fact, bureaucratic centralization is not necessarily entirely advantageous: both centralized and federal models of governance—and even of security sector governance—can work well if corruption is not a prevailing feature of the political order.[160] The experiences of other federal systems such as Germany, Australia, Canada, and Argentina powerfully validate this point. To this end, Jorge Tello Peón remarked, "You direct from top to bottom. You build from the bottom to the top."[161] A lasting solution thus lies in striking a balance between monopolizing the use of force and encouraging local civic participation to develop effective and accountable security institutions.

Notes

1. Bangura, 2017; Bevir, 2016; Castro, 1998; Hayek, 1948; Hermansson, 2019; Lawrence, 2012; Moderan, 2015.
2. Grindle, 2009; Rodríguez, 1997, pp. 3–4; T. Smith, 1989.
3. Litvack et al., 1998.
4. Acero Velásquez, 2004, p. 177; Piattoni, 2009, p. 174.
5. Ostrom & Whitaker, 1973; Shah et al., 2001, p. 11; Smoke, 2015, p. 220.
6. Keane & Downes, 2012, pp. 3–4.
7. Philip Oxhorn (2009, pp. 3–4) describes three ways in which the central state transfers power to regional and/or local authorities: deconcentration (decentralization of policy administration, while policy is made centrally), delegation (transfer of some decision-making authority, while the center reserves control over key aspects of policy), and devolution (transfer of maximum authority to subnational government).
8. Gambetta, 1996; Garay Salamanca et al., 2008. Decentralized, or polycentric, political systems entail multiple centers of decision-making, which are formally independent of one another (Ostrom et al., 1961, p. 831). In purely decentralized systems, no single entity can claim the ultimate monopoly of the government's coercive capabilities.
9. Eaton, 2006, p. 534.
10. Lowatcharin, 2016.
11. Faletti, 2010, pp. 3–5.
12. Moncada, 2016, pp. 7–8, 34; Trejo & Ley, 2020.

13. Gay, 2012; Gallego, 2018.
14. Borja, 1989; Graham, 1990. From 1863 to 1886, the Colombian constitutional order was briefly federalist after radical Liberals, who had won a partisan civil war in 1862, introduced a new constitution and renamed the country as the United States of Colombia (Estados Unidos de Colombia) (Paredes, 2014). On executive power and constraints, see Bonvecchi & Scartascini, 2014; Cox & Morgenstern, 2001; Ginsburg et al., 2010; Mainwaring, 1990; Pérez-Liñán et al., 2019; Posner & Vermeule, 2011.
15. Aligica & Boettke, 2009, p. 21.
16. Papadopoulos, 2014, pp. 273–274.
17. Camp, 2005; Knight, 2010; Müller, 2012. Articles 21 and 115 of the Constitution of 1917 establish the rights of municipal governments in Mexico, including autonomy over the political and administrative organizations deemed necessary for the delivery of public services such as local public safety (Cienfuegos Salgado & Jiménez Dorantes, n.d.; López Portillo, 2000). However, following the revolution, national political leaders made a concerted effort to "patch together a rough and tumble police force comprised of personnel whom they thought they could trust to help keep the local peace" (Davis, 2007, p. 8). The creation of municipal police forces, known as preventive police, was inconsistent across national territory, though, and their jurisdictions and prerogatives were limited to those tasks not assumed by the judicial police, who were agents of the national executive and represented the policing arm of the Public Ministry. The Municipal Reform of 1983 and a subsequent reform in 1999 both further clarified the duties and rights of municipal governments in the administration of local policing.
18. Haber et al., 2008, 123–160.
19. Groenewegen, 2010, pp. 108–110.
20. Lessing, 2017, p. 6.
21. Oxhorn et al., 2004.
22. Schiavon, 2006; Tsebelis, 2002, pp. 136–137.
23. In systems that feature high levels of corruption at the top of a centralized security bureaucracy, senior actors in the executive branch also have the potential to enfeeble security sector reform. However, this study's scope is limited to those cases that exhibit presidential commitment to security sector reform—a feature common to both Colombia and Mexico at the outset of Plan Colombia and the Mérida Initiative, respectively.
24. Fundación Konrad Adenauer, 2010, p. 7.
25. Acosta & Bird, 2003.
26. Rivera Salazar, 2001, p. 102.
27. de la Fuente, 2018; Guerrero Rincón, 1996; Mauceri, 2001; Mazzuca & Robinson, 2009; Palacios, 2016; Romero, 2000.
28. Eaton, 2006; Schultze-Kraft et al., 2016.
29. Gutiérrez Sanín, 2010.
30. Artículo 260, Constitución Política de Colombia, 1991; Fiszbein, 1997.
31. Falleti, 2010, p. 9.
32. Eaton, 2006.
33. Duncan, 2015; Durán-Martínez, 2017, p. 76.
34. On the Colombian government's efforts to regulate party collusion with illegal actors, see Perdomo & Uribe Burcher, 2016.
35. Eaton, 2006, p. 537.

36. Reitano & Hunter, 2016, p. 36.
37. Álvaro, 2007.
38. "El informe que indica," 2016.
39. "Colombian Prosecutors Dismiss," 2021.
40. Gutiérrez Sanín, 2010, pp. 16, 38.
41. Ruiz Vásquez, 2004a, p. 128; Ruiz Vásquez et al., 2006, p. 249.
42. de Francisco Z., 2006, p. 95; Ruiz, 2016. George Berkley (1970) argues that centralized police forces, should they as a corporate entity not pose a threat to democratic government, may actually facilitate democratic consolidation because they enhance equal and impartial treatment across geographic space and are subjected to increased control and oversight. Howard Kurtz (1995) also contends that in societies undergoing democratic change and demographic transition, maintaining centralized policing structures makes sense.
43. Acero Velásquez, 2004, p. 181.
44. In the 1990s and 2000s, there was even a push toward recentralizing some elements of decision-making over fiscal affairs and gaining territorial control through centralized security strategies like the National Territorial Consolidation Plan (Schultze-Kraft et al., 2016).
45. Bargent, 2015.
46. Grajales, 2017.
47. Bell Lemus, 2001; Libreros, 2001, p. 203.
48. The Colombian security forces have expressed occasional displeasure with executive political decision-making by resigning en masse or stalling policy implementation (Deas, 2001). For instance, Minister of Defense Rodrigo Lloreda and ten generals resigned in 1999 based on their perception that President Pastrana had granted too many concessions to the FARC in the conduct of peace talks.
49. Subnational authorities can also participate in security initiatives as part of "territorial development plans" adopted by city councils and departmental assemblies (Artículos 300, 313 and 315, Constitución Política de Colombia, 1991). On this division of responsibility, see Osorio Rendón, 2010.
50. Libreros, 2001, p. 208.
51. Abello Colak & Pearce, 2015; Gutiérrez Sanín et al., 2013.
52. Osorio Rendón, 2010, pp. 54–60.
53. Chamorro Córdoba, 2020.
54. Osorio Rendón, 2010, p. 13.
55. Barberena Nisimblat, 2010, p. 74.
56. Colombian National Police captain, personal communication, Bogotá, Colombia, October 27, 2017; Polémica por policía municipal, 1996.
57. Ospina Restrepo, 2010, p. 145.
58. Marmolejo et al., 2016. Law 4 states that mayors can override decisions taken by municipal police chiefs, and Law 62 outlines the obligations of mayors and governors in commanding the National Police.
59. Acero Velásquez, 2004, pp. 181–185.
60. Abello Colak & Guarneros-Meza, 2014.
61. This effort "represents a positive break with previous practice," as it has improved coordination between security forces and civilian government and helped addressed some government agency limitations at the local and regional level (Schultze-Kraft et al., 2016). However, some critics maintain that the program in practice merely strengthened the

influence of the police over subnational civilian authorities in matters of security policy (Casas Dupuy, 2005, p. 71).

62. Acero Velásquez, 2004, pp. 226–229.
63. "Presidente Uribe realizó su consejo comunal," 2008.
64. General Salgado remarked, "Colombia is a regionalist country. What works in Antioquia does not necessarily work in Tumaco, and we learned a long time ago that our responses have to be local. Our military is adaptable like this" (J. A. Salgado Restrepo, personal communication, Medellín, Colombia, November 7, 2017).
65. Consejo de Seguridad en Bojayá, 2004.
66. Plan Colombia, as well, sought to strengthen subnational governance through economic and social development projects, but they did not figure as the central component of security sector reform policies (Ramírez, 2002). According to Antonio Navarro Wolff, who was a mayor, governor, and congressional representative during the years of Plan Colombia, the bilateral security sector reform initiative was "militarily a success, but [Plan Colombia] also had a social development component . . . that failed" (Wynne, 2016).
67. The high level of cooperation and trust between Colombian and US personnel even led to Washington's decision to embed its personnel in Colombian units during the conduct of some operations ("Run through the jungle," 2018).
68. Retired US Army colonel, personal communication, Tegucigalpa, Honduras, May 20, 2016.
69. Retired US Army colonel, personal communication, Tegucigalpa, Honduras, May 20, 2016.
70. Office of the Secretary of Defense, 2012.
71. Rhem, 2005.
72. Retired US Army colonel, personal communication, Washington, DC, October 12, 2017; US defense official, personal communication, Washington, DC, October 12, 2017. The continental staff system refers to the division of labor among staff specialties in the military according to functions such as manpower, intelligence, operations, logistics, and plans.
73. One major exception was human rights vetting, which generated heated discussions between diplomats and military officers on both sides of the bilateral relationship (Tate, 2011).
74. Colombian defense contractor, personal communication, Tegucigalpa, Honduras, September 13, 2016.
75. According to two analysts, Santos had been orchestrating the promotion of more open-minded, apolitical officers for more than a decade. The "false positives" scandal resulted in the firing of many unsavory and corrupt officers by then Minister of Defense Santos, who was able to purge several senior officers loyal to Uribe. This action permitted Santos to modify the composition of the high command so that it would support his peace overtures to the FARC during his presidency (V. Barrera, personal communication, Bogotá, Colombia, October 27, 2017; F. González, personal communication, Bogotá, Colombia, October 27, 2017).
76. Colombian National Police captain, personal communication, Bogotá, Colombia, November 24, 2017.
77. Laverde Palma, 2022; Publicaciones Semana S. A., 2020.
78. Gómez, 2022.
79. Ruiz Vásquez, 2013.
80. Francisco Z., 2006, p. 110. The author is not suggesting that the military and police have handled venality within their ranks perfectly. Illicit enrichment, criminal links, and abuse

of authority remain problems, suggesting that incentives to engage in illegal behavior persist. During the past two decades, the Ministry of Defense has uncovered major contracting irregularities among all the services (Nagle, 2002, pp. 16–20). However, when scandal has hit the Ministry of Defense, it has typically resulted in sweeping dismissals of implicated personnel. This has permitted the forces to retain the trust of the Colombian public, who recurrently demand the presence of police officers in their neighborhoods (Ruiz Vásquez, 2013).

81. "Run through the jungle," 2018.
82. R. García, personal communication, Bogotá, Colombia, October 24, 2017.
83. Colombian National Police captain, personal communication, Bogotá, Colombia, November 24, 2017; senior US law enforcement official, personal communication, Tegucigalpa, Honduras, August 23, 2016. The leadership of the armed forces initially lobbied to secure judicial prerogatives such as the right to arrest for military units involved in counterinsurgency in Colombia's most remote regions, but when the National Police's leadership demanded that police personnel fulfill this function, the military ceased pressing for an expanded role (Colombian National Police captain, personal communication, Bogotá, Colombia, November 24, 2017).
84. Former Mexican ambassador to the United States, personal communication, Mexico City, August 25, 2017.
85. Schiavon, 2006.
86. Acosta Romero, 1982. On election rigging and how the PRI used social relief to expand its clientelistic network of electoral support, see Diaz-Cayeros et al., 2016; Molinar & Weldon, 1994.
87. López Portillo, 2002, p. 114.
88. Gómez Céspedes, 1998.
89. The debt crisis in Latin America, during which the region's foreign debt exceeded countries' repayment capacities, prompted political leadership in the region to reconsider the centralized management of governance. Fiscal stress exposed the vulnerability of large central governments, encouraged greater efficiency, and created incentives for politicians to delegate responsibilities to lower levels of government (Willis et al., 1999, p. 16). Additionally, de la Madrid viewed decentralization as a means of managing growing opposition to the PRI (Cook et al., 1994; Santín del Río, 2004).
90. Haber et al., 2008; Rodríguez, 1997; Selee, 2011.
91. Sabet, 2011, p. 254.
92. Cornelius, 1985, p. 102.
93. Camp, 2015.
94. Rodríguez, 1997, p. 84.
95. Camacho-Gutiérrez, 2003, p. 136; Courchene & Díaz-Cayeros, 2000, p. 206.
96. Falleti, 2010, p. 229. Decentralization in Mexico reinforced clientelistic networks because actual authority and the bulk of resources remained at the state level, where governments utilized them to consolidate regional electoral advantages (Oxhorn, 2009, p. 5).
97. Whereas in Colombia subnational officeholders became popularly elected with the 1991 Constitution, in Mexico they had always been elected, although the PRI severely limited opposition victories.
98. Durán-Martínez, 2017, p. 94.
99. López Portillo, 2002; Sabet, 2012, pp. 62–94.

100. López Portillo, 2002, p. 116.
101. Gamboa Montejano, 2005.
102. Sabet, 2012.
103. Valadés, 2017. Mexico's states are often seen as "bastions of the old regime," making it difficult for the federal government to impose top-down initiatives (Vale & Guerrero Vásquez, 2010, pp. 13, 41–70). Edward Gibson (2013) and Agustina Giraudy (2015) explore how federal systems can preserve the position of subnational autocrats despite democratization.
104. Sabet, 2011, p. 256.
105. Former Mexican Ambassador to the United States, personal communication, Mexico City, August 25, 2017; Guzmán-Sánchez & Espriu-Gura, 2014; Rodríguez, 1997.
106. Although seldom have governors and mayors been convicted on collusion charges, there is no shortage of allegations of political collusion with organized crime and widespread tolerance of such corruption (Sabet, 2011, p. 266).
107. Althaus & Grillo, 2005.
108. The Interior Security Law, which was passed in 2017 but overturned by the Supreme Court in 2018, removed the onus on state governments to be proactive about security because governors knew that a "federal bail-out will always be an option" (L. Chapa Koloffon, personal communication, Mexico City, February 9, 2018).
109. Bailey, 2011a, p. 332; Powell, 2012; Sabet, 2012, pp. 105–109.
110. L. D. Vázquez Valencia, personal communication, Mexico City, September 5, 2017.
111. Civil society in Mexico suffers from other challenges, including limited access to information to monitor public security, indifference from political authorities, and a lack of legal oversight authority (Sabet, 2013).
112. Chindea, 2014.
113. Rios Contreras, 2012, p. iii. Davis (2006, p. 60) asserted as early as 2006 that an environment of obsessive partisan competition, combined with the fragmentation of the state's coercive apparatus, impeded the government from reforming Mexico's policing model.
114. Pansters, 2012, p. 6.
115. Bailey, 2014a, p. 117.
116. Sabet, 2011, p. 261.
117. Orpozeda-Rodríguez, 2015.
118. Goi, 2017.
119. The Mexico City Municipal Police was under the command of the Mexican presidency until 2014, when the force underwent a sweeping reform. Following the creation of the SSP in 2000 and its strengthening during the Calderón administration, the Peña Nieto administration devolved authority over the capital's police force to the mayor's office.
120. Rath, 2016, p. 16.
121. J. J. Romero, personal communication, Mexico City, December 21, 2017.
122. Laurency, 2017, pp. 7–8.
123. A. Poiré, personal communication, Mexico City, September 14, 2017.
124. J. Furszyfer, personal communication, Mexico City, September 5, 2017.
125. Sánchez Lara, 2017, p. 21.
126. Sánchez Lara, 2017, pp. 60–62.
127. Academic security analyst, personal communication, Bogotá, Colombia, November 20, 2017.

128. Lessing, 2017, p. 257.
129. Laurency, 2017, pp. 10–11; Paul et al., 2014, pp. 38–39.
130. For a description of the role that conflicting laws at the state and federal level play in producing impunity, see Cossío et al. in Aguayo et al., 2021.
131. In 2009, Calderón eliminated the AFI, one of Fox's achievements, due to corruption, and he replaced it in 2012 with the PFM. However, Calderón, constrained by partisan resistance, largely neglected the role of the municipal and state police in the restructuring, which was ultimately counterproductive because local police forces are typically first responders at crime scenes and the first link in the chain of justice delivery (Schaefer et al., 2009, pp. 31–44).
132. Turati, 2014.
133. Chabat, 2012, p. 153; Watt & Zepeda, 2012, p. 188.
134. Paul et al., 2014, p. 39.
135. J. French, personal communication, Mexico City, August 24, 2017.
136. S. Ley, personal communication, Mexico City, January 9, 2018. López Obrador's opponents have leveled similar criticism against his initiative to establish a civilian-controlled National Guard (Washington Office on Latin America, 2019).
137. Anaya Muñoz, 2012, p. 135.
138. F. Escalante, personal communication, Mexico City, September 13, 2017. One civil society representative bemoaned, "The National Development Plan is issued by the federal government and informs policies implemented at the state level. This is unfortunate because the policies do not account for the singularity, the uniqueness of each state. For instance, police forces are not seen as members of the community or as allies to the citizenry but rather a temporary imposition from the outside" (A. Brillones, personal communication, Ciudad Juárez, Mexico, January 15, 2018).
139. G. Fondevila, personal communication, Mexico City, September 6, 2017.
140. Lessing, 2017, pp. 256–257.
141. Trejo & Ley, 2016.
142. According to one analyst, local elites tend to hold immense influence over governors, and presidential power has always hinged on the central government's respect for local agreements between municipal governments and social and financial elites, even organized crime (F. Escalante, personal communication, Mexico City, September 13, 2017).
143. Schaefer et al., 2009, p. 18.
144. Retired US Army colonel, personal communication, Tegucigalpa, Honduras, May 20, 2016. Mexican sensitivities were not necessarily unfounded. In 2009, the US Bureau of Alcohol, Tobacco, Firearms, and Explosives oversaw "Operation Fast and Furious," in which it let people purchase weapons it knew would end up in the hands of criminals in Mexico to track the weapons and then build a case against the criminals. At least sixty-nine of these firearms were linked to killings (Dunagan, 2016; Epatko, 2011).
145. Retired US Army colonel, personal communication, Tegucigalpa, Honduras, May 20, 2016; US defense official, personal communication, Mexico City, September 19, 2017.
146. Former senior US diplomat, personal communication, Mexico City, December 3, 2021.
147. D. V. Negroponte, 2013, p. 157.
148. Sabet, 2012.
149. Diaz, 2011.
150. Pachico, 2011b.

151. Naimark-Rowse & Markowitz, 2018, p. 7.
152. Camp, 2016, p. 229.
153. Former Mexican ambassador to the United States, Mexico City, August 25, 2017.
154. Laurency, 2017, pp. 24–25.
155. Lamas, 2015; Padilla, 2016; Ramírez Baena, 2019.
156. At the national level, this means that municipal and state police qualifications, training, and chains of command are determined by state governments.
157. López, 2018.
158. M. Novoa, personal communication, Mexico City, September 13, 2017.
159. "AMLO propone coordinación y Mando Único," 2018.
160. J. Tello Peón, personal communication, Mexico City, February 13, 2018.
161. J. Tello Peón, personal communication, Mexico City, February 13, 2018.

8

Sustaining Progress

A Retrospective of Plan Colombia and the Mérida Initiative

As discussed in chapters 1 through 7, domestic political and institutional factors shaped the degree to which Colombia and Mexico were able to implement US security assistance and deliver sweeping reforms. However, changing conditions and attitudes in the recipient countries and in the United States ultimately contributed to Washington's pullback from Plan Colombia and the Mérida Initiative. Colombia's pivot toward a negotiated solution with the Revolutionary Armed Forces of Colombia (Fuerzas Armadas Revolucionarias de Colombia, or FARC) in 2012 heralded a new approach to ending violence, and the Colombian security forces' ability to conduct police and military operations without US-led planning or intelligence meant that the focus of US support for Colombia needed to evolve. At a minimum there was strong bilateral consensus that Colombia was no longer at risk of state failure, and sustained drug crop eradication had led to record reductions in annual coca yield in the country. Positive gross domestic product (GDP) growth and the expansion of social services helped lift millions out of poverty. By the close of the 2010s, Colombia's newfound prosperity led to its admission as the thirty-seventh member of the Organization for Economic Co-operation and Development. Against this backdrop, *Plan Colombia* no longer appeared in the presidential budget request starting in 2011, even though security cooperation between Washington and Bogotá persisted beyond this date.

The same year, the US and Mexican governments unfurled the Beyond Mérida strategy, which broadened the terms of bilateral cooperation to include synchronizing border protocols and creating economic opportunities in border communities. The Obama administration continued to implement much of the Mérida Initiative programming it had inherited from its predecessor and never strayed from the broader goal of US security assistance: building the capacity of Mexican security and justice institutions to serve the Mexican people. However, insecurity and violence were once again on the rise by the end of the Peña Nieto administration; the delays in the rollout of the country's new justice system and the Federal Police's disempowerment

From Peril to Partnership. Paul J. Angelo, Oxford University Press. © Oxford University Press 2024.
DOI: 10.1093/oso/9780197688106.003.0009

after major investments in its professionalization made many Mexican and US officials alike question the Mexican federal government's plans for security provision looking ahead. The United States remained committed to a security partnership with Mexico but expected a clearer vision for reducing criminality than the militarized path that Peña Nieto haphazardly ended up pursuing.

When the Trump administration took office in 2017, the new president publicly scrutinized US-Mexican security cooperation, which led to a recalibration of the relationship. Following an electoral campaign that repeatedly demonized Mexicans and disparaged cooperation with Mexico on a host of bilateral issues, Trump abandoned the language of "shared responsibility" and in 2018 deployed US National Guard troops to the southern border in a contentious move to militarize responses to cross-border crime and irregular migration. Similarly, in Mexico, the election of President López Obrador in 2018 marked a break with the past. Shortly after entering office, López Obrador ordered a review of Mexican security policies, including cooperation with the United States; inaugurated a new public security approach and federal policing force; and publicly rebuffed the Mérida Initiative. He also disbanded the Investigation and National Security Center (Centro de Investigación y Seguridad Nacional, or CISEN) and the Presidential Security Staff (Estado Mayor Presidential), removing two institutional counterbalances to the army and setting the stage for further militarization of the federal government's public security strategy.[1]

This chapter explores developments on the security front in Colombia and Mexico in the years following a drawdown of US security assistance, focusing on how changing political dynamics in the two countries affected the sustainability of programming associated with security sector reform. In Colombia, interparty consensus on security, which was so critical to the accomplishment of Plan Colombia's security sector reform objectives, deteriorated as President Juan Manuel Santos and former President Álvaro Uribe clashed over peace negotiations with the FARC. Yet, regardless of growing political divisions in Colombia surrounding the issue of security, which increasingly resembled those that undermined progress on security sector reform in Mexico, the security forces did not experience major reversals in professionalization thanks to the institutionalization of reforms through bureaucratic processes and doctrine documentation. In Mexico, despite successive attempts to centralize security provision, the federal government failed to learn from its mistakes, refusing to build on existing security sector architecture and to institutionalize reforms. As Mexico entered the 2020s, the country's crime rates suggested that it was more insecure than ever, with more than thirty-four thousand homicides a year and a homicide rate of 26.6 deaths per hundred thousand people.[2] The country's security sector remained a bureaucratic labyrinth marred by redundancy, inefficiency, and corruption. Given the relative resilience of Colombia's security institutions and the Mexican security sector's disappointment, the analysis that follows reinforces the overarching conclusions of the preceding chapters while revealing the opportunities and challenges the United States and partner governments are apt to confront after the most pressing incentives for security sector reform have subsided.

Sustaining Reform and Cooperation through Institutionalization in Colombia

The executive branch in Colombia changed hands in August 2010, when President Uribe's eight-year term came to an end, and his former defense minister, Juan Manuel Santos, took his place. Santos benefited from his close association with Uribe and the Democratic Security Policy, especially after leading the Colombian security forces during their most consequential operations against the FARC and National Liberation Army (Ejército de Liberación Nacional, or ELN). His anointment as the candidate to carry Uribe's mantle, however, reportedly occurred only after Santos vowed to protect and expand on his predecessor's legacy, which Uribe referenced in terms of *tres huevitos*, or three small and fragile eggs: investor confidence, social advancements and prosperity, and security. During Santos's inauguration speech, he praised the former administration's work on all three fronts and promised to sustain successful and popular programs. He parted with Uribe on one major issue, though: making peace with the FARC, which later served as the grounds for his public break with Uribismo after reminding the country's insurgent groups that the "door to dialogue is not closed under lock and key."[3] Uribe understood this act as a betrayal of his legacy, and the divisions that ensued came to define Santos's presidency and emerged as the principal fault line around which interparty consensus on Colombia's security strategy eventually collapsed.

A False Dichotomy: Peace or Security

From his earliest days in office, Santos struck a pragmatic tone when it came to preserving the hard-won gains from the previous administration. He continued major offensives against the FARC's leadership, including aerial bombardments that killed secretariat members "Mono Jojoy" in 2010 and "Alfonso Cano" in 2011. He even transformed Uribe's popular Social Action initiative from a presidential agency to a standing cabinet-level department called the Department for Social Prosperity (Departamento de la Prosperidad Social), which continued to foster socioeconomic inclusion among vulnerable populations and implemented programs associated with the 2011 law governing reparations for victims of the country's conflict. Investor confidence was high, and Santos claimed credit for a notable rebound in foreign direct investment from 2010 to 2011.

However, it was on the diplomatic front where Santos began to chart his own course.[4] Just days after taking office, Santos met face to face with Venezuelan President Hugo Chávez in a successful bid to end an existing diplomatic row over evidence presented by Uribe's delegation to the Organization of American States that Chávez was protecting Colombian rebels in Venezuelan territory. Uribe insisted that resuming ties with Venezuela would enfeeble Colombia's military campaign against the FARC and ELN; Santos, on the other hand, stressed the economic ramifications of shuttered borders, with an eye toward long-term peacebuilding in the Andean region as well. In December 2010, with Venezuela's facilitation, Santos restored diplomatic relations with the government of Ecuador under leftist President Rafael Correa after a thirty-three-month impasse that resulted from a Colombian military raid on a FARC camp inside Ecuadoran territory. And it was ultimately through Venezuela's Chávez, Cuban leader Fidel Castro, and the Norwegian government that Santos was able to offer the FARC the assurances needed to commence peace talks in 2012.[5]

Although Uribe himself had repeatedly attempted to entice the FARC and ELN into dialogue through secret contacts during his eight-year term, the former president outright rejected the overtures his successor made to Colombia's nonstate armed groups.[6] In 2011, after consultations with the armed forces and his own party's leadership, Santos publicly conceded the state's recognition of a political armed conflict in Colombia for the first time since the beginning of the Uribe administration, which had rebuffed the FARC's and ELN's political ambitions and characterized the insurgent groups as mere bandits and terrorists. The official denial of the armed conflict had long been an obstacle to exacting accountability for the victims of Colombia's armed groups and for making peace. Santos's recognition enabled the government's administration of reparations to Colombians who had suffered state, insurgent, and paramilitary abuses and built confidence between state officials and the FARC's leadership. But this reversal in state policy was equally consequential for Colombia's party system: as Santos advanced on his peace objectives with the FARC, Uribe launched a new conservative party called the Democratic Center (Centro Democrático) as "a crusade against terrorism"—one that would turn the 2014 electoral cycle into a referendum on Santos's security and peace policies.[7]

Santos nevertheless proved victorious. Despite the appeal of Uribe's hard-line message to many Colombians, 51 percent of voters opted for Santos in a runoff election, which saw him go toe to toe with Democratic Center candidate Óscar Iván Zuluaga, who vowed to end the peace negotiations. Santos's first four years in office saw sustained economic growth and an unprecedented agreement between the government and the FARC on three of the five planks of the peace agenda being negotiated in Havana. In 2014, a majority of Colombians were still willing to give peace a chance. Although Santos's reelection was a setback for the Democratic Center's antipeace campaign, Uribe's consolation was his own election as a senator to the Colombian Congress. In the years that followed, he used his new platform—and his Twitter account—to rally legislative opposition to the executive branch and to grandstand against the peace negotiations with the FARC.

When the Colombian government and the FARC finally reached a comprehensive agreement in August 2016 and commenced a bilateral ceasefire, Santos put the terms of the accord, meticulously hashed out over four years with significant international support, to a simple Yes-No national plebiscite scheduled for October 2, 2016. But it was Uribe, waging a massive public campaign to reject the accord, who had the final say; in a surprise result the No vote narrowly defeated the 49.7 percent of the population that backed the peace settlement. Uribe had leveraged popular aversion to the FARC to the No campaign's advantage. He insisted that the accord granted impunity for former FARC insurgents and, thereby, condoned drug trafficking and other criminal activities, and he outright rejected the stipulation that awarded ten uncompetitive congressional seats to individuals he considered narco-terrorists. For Uribe and for many Colombians, it was unconscionable that former guerilla fighters responsible for grave human rights abuses would have such access to political power, no matter the precedent set by previous insurgent demobilizations in the 1980s and 1990s. Uribe further sowed doubt and fear among Colombians by insisting that the participation of a revolutionary leftist party in politics would make Colombia vulnerable to the "Castrochavismo" that had converted neighboring Venezuela from the wealthiest country in South America into one of the world's largest humanitarian disasters.[8]

Despite a nonparticipation rate of more than 60 percent in the plebiscite, the binary nature of the question posed to Colombians had major implications for the polarization in Colombian society. For Santos and his allies, those who voted No rejected the best and only chance in a generation to put an end to one of the world's longest-running armed conflicts. A vote for No was seen as a vote for war. Yet for Uribe, his adherents, and some others, a Yes vote was tantamount to overlooking the FARC's crimes. For many Colombians, their opposition centered on specific line items contained in a 297-page document, not the idea of peace wholesale. Those who still believed in a military solution to the conflict were a small minority, meaning that many people who voted No were not opposed to peace in theory but instead were opposed to the peace stipulations as negotiated.[9]

In the days following the plebiscite, Santos and Uribe met and agreed to form a commission to oversee adjustments to the accord that would satisfy the former president and his followers. By November, the government's peace negotiators secured additional concessions from the FARC to hand over their assets to fund reparations for victims of the conflict, to release exhaustive information about their involvement in drug trafficking, and to restrict the operation of the transitional justice system governing crimes committed during the conflict to a maximum of ten years. When the new version of the peace agreement was put to a definitive vote in Congress, Santos's governing coalition ensured the approval of the document in the legislature's two houses. But Uribe, who denounced the changes made to the accord as "cosmetic" and continued to press for harsher judicial sentences for the former rebels, led the Democratic Center's total opposition to ratification.

Although the Colombian Constitutional Court ruled in an 8–1 decision in December 2016 that Santos could seek expedited approval for laws and constitutional changes needed for the implementation of the peace accord, Uribe's persistent antagonism of the deal and his continued popularity among the electorate shrouded the peace deal and its subsequent implementation in an air of perfidy. By 2018, a mere one-third of Colombians in a national poll supported the continued application of the accord without additional modifications.[10] This lack of consensus led to a concurrent breakdown in consensus on security. The Santos administration failed to make the case to the Colombian people that their personal security was enhanced by peace with the FARC, enabling its opponents to frame the debate in terms of one principal false dichotomy: peace versus security.[11] Even though Colombia reported its lowest homicide rate ever in the first year of peace implementation and the most conflict-ridden regions of the country had largely come out in favor of peace, citizen security was a top concern among voters going into the 2018 electoral cycle, reflecting how emotionally charged the security debate remained.[12] Not even a neutral, international observer in the form of a United Nations special political mission, launched in 2016 to verify the bilateral ceasefire and implementation of the final peace agreement, could build societal trust in a way that tempered Colombia's flaring polarization.

When Democratic Center presidential nominee Iván Duque (2018–22) launched his presidential campaign in 2017, his conservative proposals centered primarily on security, justice, and anticorruption.[13] Duque, yet another disciple of Uribe, pledged to go back to the drawing board to refashion elements of the peace accord and to constitutionally ban amnesty for drug trafficking going forward. He also advocated for expanding the size and response capacity of the National Police. When he found himself competing in a second-round runoff against a former M-19 insurgent fighter-cum-politician, Gustavo Petro, who promised to protect the FARC peace accord, Colombian voters were left with a choice between two starkly different candidates and visions for the future of their country.[14] In what many consider to be the first true ideological contest in modern Colombian history, a deeply divided Colombian public went to the polls, with some 54 percent of voters putting their faith in the "firm hand, big heart" vision of Duque and the Democratic Center.[15] Just as Colombia's party system realigned two decades prior, the societal fissures that percolated out of elite disagreements on peace and security policies had a defining effect on interparty competition during the 2018 electoral cycle and beyond.

Legacy of US Security Assistance and Security Sector Reform: Local Ownership

Naturally, Colombia's security sector experienced its own reorientation during this period of shifting state policy toward the FARC and other sources of insecurity in the country. With the drawdown of Plan Colombia and the negotiation of peace with the FARC, the Santos administration pivoted toward a human security–centric approach to resolving Colombia's ongoing crime and violence challenges. Although the armed forces remained a vital part of the government's strategy, the expansion of the National Police and other civilian agencies responsible for services provision and rural development facilitated greater citizen inclusion in Colombia's most remote departments, where insurgent and drug-trafficking groups historically found ready recruits and safe havens from combat.[16]

As the Colombian government prepared for peace, Santos and his legislative coalition sought to redirect funds for peace implementation, drawing closer scrutiny of the military's activities and spending habits. After more than a decade of professionalization and transformation, however, military leaders recognized that the institution's published doctrine—its internal manuals and public-facing materials—had not kept pace with the rapid adoption of new warfighting practices and techniques.[17] This in turn constrained military leaders from communicating their budgetary and acquisitions needs to those outside the institution.[18] For instance, the integration of the Colombian Air Force's geospatial intelligence on insurgent and criminal hideouts into Colombian Army and Navy targeting missions did not have a pre–Plan Colombia precedent. Although the services had developed joint procedures to govern these kinds of missions in the field, the procedures had never been codified at the headquarters level. The Colombian security forces—better equipped and better trained than ever before—had not devoted enough attention to creating a paper record.

What followed was a concerted effort to do so by expanding the ministry's internal bureaucracy to sustain newly adopted processes and by enshrining practice in doctrine, which informed everything from budgets and long-range planning to recruitment and the adoption of new missions. The Colombian Ministry of Defense had become a "learning institution," one that draws from its organizational memory to adapt in the face of new and recurrent challenges, but only through institutionalization could the ministry ensure that lessons learned would underpin decision-making long into the future.[19] In Colombia, the often-cited need for local ownership in the security sector reform literature was more than an ambition: through bureaucracy and doctrine, it became a reality.

By the late 2000s, the US government was already nudging the Colombian military and police to assume greater financial ownership of US-introduced programs, especially equipment maintenance. Washington had seldom extended such generous security assistance over so many years to a Latin American country, and in 2008, Congress reduced the proportion of assistance designated for militarized initiatives and boosted funding for economic and social aid. This shift coincided with Uribe's and then Santos's National Consolidation Plan, for which the US interagency strategy increasingly focused on helping "fill gaps" in Colombian government efforts to stabilize areas of the country where the state's influence and authority remained weak.[20] Furthermore, the Obama administration's support for the FARC peace process eventually culminated in $450 million in assistance directed at protecting human rights, promoting economic opportunity, and facilitating postconflict reconstruction under the banner of a program called Peace Colombia. As Washington stepped up its nonmilitary assistance and turned over operational and financial responsibility for Plan Colombia programs to its Colombian counterparts, Bogotá "nationalized" training, equipment, and continuity budgets for the army's counterdrug units, air bridge denial, rotary maintenance and operation, and maritime interception assets.[21] These technologies and even some of these missions constituted the advent of Plan Colombia, and once Colombian taxpayers had to start funding them, the Ministry of Defense had to make the case more explicitly for why they were necessary for national security.

By the 2010s, Washington was also undergoing its own endogenous process of transformation with respect to security assistance, positioning defense institution-building (DIB) as the cornerstone of all US military relations with partner security forces worldwide.[22] DIB describes US efforts to help ministries of defense establish or reorient personnel, rules, norms, values, and planning processes; enhance accountability to civilian authorities, where appropriate; and design the foundations on which effective and legitimate democratic defense sectors can absorb future US security assistance.[23] In response to the 2010 Quadrennial Defense Review, which highlighted shortcomings in the sustainability of security assistance in places such as Afghanistan and Iraq, the Department of Defense established the Defense Institution Reform Initiative (DIRI) and the Ministry of Defense Advisors Program. This shift eventually was codified in the 2017 National Defense Authorization Act (NDAA), which mandated DIB as a requirement for all Department of Defense foreign capacity-building. The NDAA also required more rigorous and routine assessments of US security assistance implementation and its effects on the value, relevance, and sustainability of cooperation.[24]

Given its close security partnership with the United States, Colombia was among the initial beneficiaries of DIB programming, which ushered in the first of many bureaucratic shifts that helped institutionalize the gains generated through US security assistance. In 2009, the Colombian Ministry of Defense requested US Department of Defense support in designing budgets in accordance with national strategic objectives via the Defense Resource Management Reform program, facilitating long-range capabilities-based planning for force structure, readiness, personnel recruitment and benefits, and sustainment. The program also helped institutionalize three critical operating processes to ensure continuity of Plan Colombia objectives: estimating future defense costs, ensuring that future costs align with expected appropriations, and improving planning for the acquisition of new and emerging technologies.[25] In 2012, the Ministry of Defense's strategy and planning directorate further stood up new offices focused on future capabilities projections, logistics, and human capital development in a bid to prioritize and staff the security forces' reorganization and modernization processes.

Moreover, the DIB mission encouraged each of the security services, including the National Police, to contextualize its budget according to ministry-wide priorities and to develop budget requests in coordination with the other services—a departure from previous practice in which individual services developed their strategic and spending plans in relative isolation. By 2013, the Colombian Ministry of Defense had published its first integrated long-term plan, detailing anticipated threats and operational concepts for the country's security forces as far in the future as 2030, and released the first budget estimate that accounted for annual requirements to sustain Plan Colombia–era programs through 2040.

In addition to adopting new bureaucratic processes at the level of the ministry, creating new organizational bodies devoted to developing and documenting service doctrine reflected a significant degree of local ownership of the security sector reform process.[26] The Defense Resource Management Reform program facilitated interoperability among the services by adopting a common language for describing missions and capabilities across the security sector. As the FARC retreated to more remote corners of the country, strategists within the ministry drew on the notion of integrated campaigns across the services to confront the new battlefield reality. In the army, this gave rise in 2011 to the establishment of the first iteration of the Committee for Strategic Review and Innovation (Comité de Revisión Estratégica e Innovación, or CREI), an internal council focused on conceptualizing the nature of Colombia's present and future security threats and helping define the institution's responsibilities for confronting them. In subsequent years, the army's leadership launched additional initiatives—the Strategic Committee for Transformation and Innovation (Comité Estratégico de Transformación e Innovación, or CETI) and the Committee for the Design of the Army of the Future (Comité de Diseño del Ejército del Futuro, or CEDEF)—to regularize internal review processes and to foster an institutional culture of adaptability. As the peace process with the FARC evolved, these institutionalization efforts ultimately culminated in the inauguration of the Command for the Transformation of the Army of the Future (Comando de Transformación del Ejército del Futuro, or COTEF) to oversee the reorientation of the army from an institution focused on fighting the FARC into one prepared to deliver security in a postconflict setting.[27] The spirit of adaptability in COTEF reappeared in the Strategic Transformation Plan for an Army of the Future (Plan Estratégico de Transformación Ejército del Futuro, or PETEF), a framework designed to streamline the army's planning for a more professionalized force.[28]

One of the most important accomplishments in sustaining budgets and institutionalizing progress that evolved from the establishment of COTEF was the publication of doctrine under the auspices of the Damascus Plan (doctrina de Damasco), coordinated out of the Military Doctrine Center.[29] Starting with its first release in 2016, the Damascus Plan enshrined in the guiding principles and practices of the army long-standing missions such as counterinsurgency and conventional warfare, emphasizing Colombia's respect for International Humanitarian Law and the military's role as guarantors of the human rights of the Colombian population.[30] The human rights commitment was central to the professionalization undertaken during Plan Colombia and thus became a core aspect of the military's responsibilities as it prepared for the postconflict era. The institution had even become the guarantor of the safety of its former adversaries—demobilizing FARC militants—as they concentrated in reintegration camps as a condition of the peace process, all with zero reported incidents of abuse or violence.

The Damascus Plan also highlighted the military's unprecedented international presence in training missions and the prospect of deeper involvement in global peacekeeping, symbolic of the army's multidimensional aspirations. According to one Colombian military officer, the armed forces' growing participation abroad even had the effect of strengthening the institution's convictions about aspects of its doctrine.[31] As Colombian security forces introduced their lessons learned, tactics, and procedures to other military and police forces through the US-Colombia Action Plan (USCAP), their pedagogical role encouraged them to question and assess their practices in the context of other legal frameworks while learning from other partners confronting similar threats to security.[32] This interaction in turn enabled those who had participated in international deployments, some of whom were later posted to the Military Doctrine Center, to help refine the ministry's policies.

The Damascus Plan did more than address those issues for which the Colombian military had already developed expertise. The army's doctrine experts went one step further in defining the military's utility in responding to future and contingent threats, laying out the implicit argument that the armed forces have a role to play in addressing everything from climate change and food insecurity to natural disasters and pandemics.[33] One doctrine manual states,

> In the future, the National Army will be a force distinguished for its high standards of effectiveness and competitiveness in the missions and roles assigned to it . . . [embracing technological innovation] to combat new threats, take on emerging challenges, preserve peace and the environment, and contribute to the State's wellbeing.[34]

Such an ambitious realignment of the Colombian military's doctrine prompted some within the ranks of the military to brand the Damascus Plan as the "second major reform" of the army, nearly a hundred years after the nation's first major reform in response to the painful experience of the Thousand Day's War.[35]

The publication of existing doctrine and the adoption of new doctrine created additional incentives to revamp military education curricula. As detailed in chapter 4, the military had already made significant strides in recruiting and retaining talent by offering better benefits and enhancing the capacity and prestige of the professional career track. In 2007, the Ministry of Defense, advised by the Pentagon, made additional strides in professionalization by launching the Armed Services Education Plan (Plan de Educación de las Fuerzas Armadas, or PEFA), which for the first time brandished a long-range vision for human resources and personnel development within the institution. Some of the initiative's top priorities included establishing continuing education programs, certifying academic curricula, promoting international educational opportunities and language learning, and developing technological and communications expertise.[36] Thereafter, the CETI and the Minerva Plan (Plan Minerva), launched in 2015, carried on the work of developing projects to facilitate a human resources transformation, especially in the military sciences, military history, and historical memory. As the Santos administration negotiated peace with the FARC, the Colombian military and police even worked with civilian academic institutions to produce a definitive narrative of the conflict told through the eyes of the state's security forces, which it featured in a permanent exhibition in Bogotá's military museum.[37] The testimonies collected in support of that project also informed the work of the truth commission and special justice tribunal that emerged from the peace negotiations.

The institutionalization of Plan Colombia's most successful reforms through bureaucratic processes and doctrine publication has ensured that the ministry's readiness and posture remain constant despite changes in political leadership. Bogotá's early and continuous investment in the personnel of its security forces, though, has perhaps been the most critical factor in sustaining reforms and in exacting local ownership of the security sector reform process. Santos in particular was focused on recruiting, retaining, and promoting the best leaders for the security forces. As defense minister, he cultivated a generation of reform-minded field-grade officers, whom he later promoted as top service leaders during his presidency. Army General Alberto José Mejía Ferrero, for instance, directed the CREI, became the commander of the army, and then took the reins as the commander of the armed forces in 2017, permitting him to oversee the military's role in providing security during the earliest stages of peace implementation. In this vein, one Colombian officer remarked, "When I joined the army, I signed up for more than a job: it was a profession. And as the service branch transforms to address new challenges, I continue to acquire and integrate new knowledge, reinventing myself to better serve the Colombian people."[38] This brand of adaptability, undergirded by a commitment to service to nation, is no doubt a long-standing Colombian trait—but one institutionalized thanks in no small part to the country's collaboration with the United States.

An Uncertain Future

The Colombian military has continued to build from the DIB legacy of the 2010s, and the US Department of Defense remains a critical facilitator of joint planning, logistics, and some maintenance processes in Colombia. However, the 2016 election of President Trump and the 2018 election of President Duque led to changes in the Colombian security sector's operational focus. Despite great strides made previously in diversifying the US-Colombia partnership with a focus on building economic prosperity and peace, the Trump administration returned to rhetoric that emphasized repressive counterdrug strategies and security cooperation focused on dismantling trafficking networks, especially those exploited by the Nicolás Maduro administration in neighboring Venezuela. Likewise, President Duque, whose opposition to the peace deal had underpinned his electoral victory, implemented the accord in a piecemeal fashion while rhetorically undermining the transitional justice body that represents the peace agreement's cornerstone.[39] Although homicides remained low by historical standards, criminal activity increased both in cities and in the countryside. Former FARC combatants, peace and land activists, and social leaders found themselves especially vulnerable to this new wave of intimidation by organized crime and insurgent groups. Despite broad FARC compliance with the reintegration process, dissident FARC groups, the ELN, and the BACRIM (*bandas criminales*) took advantage of power vacuums left by demobilized FARC units in remote areas to expand their own spheres of influence. As Adam Isacson predicted in 2010, Colombia's security gains ran the risk of being "partial [and] possibly reversible, and weighed down by [human rights concerns]" unless Colombian authorities started to pay attention to the rule of law and the country's stark social inequalities—a concern that resurfaced during President Duque's term.[40]

Duque relieved Santos's security sector leaders from their roles in late 2018 and installed service commanders who were decidedly less aligned with Santos's reformism. Worryingly for those seeking to exact justice for military abuses, some of the new commanders were even suspected of close ties to the false positives scandal.[41] Colombia's security forces had spent two decades earning the trust of the Colombian people, which the institution's leadership understood as critical to restoring the state's monopoly of force.[42] Duque's promotion of individuals associated with human rights violations committed during the conflict, though, raised doubts about the direction of the Ministry of Defense.

As Colombia's security forces complied with orders to reduce coca cultivation through forced eradication and to increase offensive attacks on illegal armed groups, security analysts and civil society organizations denounced the operational strategy for failing to build on the opportunities and spirit of the peace process.[43] For a war-weary Colombian public, the Duque administration's security footing represented a return to the relentless fighting of the Uribe era. The military and police, few doubted, could kill and capture to great effect, but many Colombians were left asking themselves whether such an offensive posture would have been necessary had President Duque more forcefully supported peace implementation from the outset. What is more, the Ministry of Defense confronted mounting scandals that jeopardized public confidence in the effectiveness and conduct of the security forces. The National Police force was dealt a major blow when its top commander resigned in 2016 over successive personnel and corruption scandals.[44] Following protests in urban areas from 2019 to 2021, human rights groups denounced the police's overreliance on arbitrary detentions and excessive force.[45] The judicial process overseeing the investigations into those abuses, including the death of eighteen-year-old Dilan Cruz during an attempt to disperse protestors, was widely criticized for having fallen under the jurisdiction of the military courts, not the ordinary justice system, further eroding public trust. In May 2021, following dozens of protestor deaths at the hands of the Mobile Antiriot Squad (Esquadrón Móvil Antidisturbios, or ESMAD), calls for major reform of the National Police gained even more traction, and civil society representatives and politicians from across the political spectrum vowed to seek a reckoning with the institution as the country geared up for 2022 elections.[46]

In June 2021, President Duque announced his intention to modernize the Ministry of Defense and reinitiate police reform. His proposal called for rebranding the institution as the Ministry of National Defense and Citizen Security (Ministerio de Defensa Nacional y Seguridad Ciudadana) and for standing up a new human rights directorate led by an outside expert, echoing a similar measure adopted during the 1990s. The proposed legislation also called for improvements to processing citizen complaints, changes to disciplinary standards, and the installation of body cameras on police uniforms. Although these new requirements were a step in the right direction for many Colombians, some civil society organizations insisted that they did not go far enough. Instead, they and opposition legislators advocated for the complete removal of the National Police from the Ministry of Defense, accountability for police abuses in the civilian justice system, and additional reforms to the military, especially in relation to its use for domestic security operations. For its part, the US Embassy noted in its annual human rights report, "The government generally took steps to investigate, prosecute, and punish officials who committed human rights abuses, although some cases continued to experience long delays. The government generally implemented effectively laws criminalizing official corruption."[47]

In December 2021, Colombia's Senate approved a law intended to professionalize the police force through better access to education and benefits programs for officers. Just weeks later, the Senate passed another bill codifying the citizenry's right to record police interactions with the public and forbidding officers from hiding their identities. The legislative package would, in theory, increase the quality of Colombia's police force and stamp out misconduct, both issues of great concern to Colombians whose trust in the institution had plummeted. In 2021, only 55 percent of Colombians reported having confidence in the police, and their demands matched those misgivings.[48]

The repressive response to the 2021 protest movement gave rise to these proposed changes, but the need for additional reforms in the security sector was evident for years. Starting in 2012, the military's approval ratings dropped below 70 percent for the first time in a decade, declining further after recordings surfaced implicating the institution's leadership in attempts to interfere with investigations into false positives.[49] Accusations of sexual violence and the military's participation in illegal surveillance operations additionally shrouded the institution in suspicion and raised questions about the military's accountability. Further, as the peace process divided the country, the broader polarization in Colombian society likely affected attitudes toward the military, which, despite honoring the terms of the peace accord, had become associated with President Duque's refusal to embrace fully the negotiated peace after 2018. As Juanita Léon relates, during the peace process many soldiers and police objected to the feeling that they were being treated not as defenders of the constitutional order or as victims of the conflict but as somehow on par with the FARC insurgents.[50] Even though Santos appointed two retired police and army generals to defend the security sector's interests and reputation during the negotiations, the victory of the No vote in the referendum and the Democratic Center's rhetorical break with Santos over peace and security helped politicize elements of the security forces.[51] As the truth commission and special justice tribunal advanced investigations into conflict abuses perpetrated by military members, the number of alleged false positive murders crept above six thousand—about half the total number of combat killings reported between 2002 and 2008—leading to unprecedented judicial testimony from active-duty army generals about their alleged involvement in the abuses.[52] More than 3,300 members of the armed forces, including some very high-ranking officials, admitted to participating in the killings and orchestrating the subsequent masquerade.[53] For the first time since the beginning of Plan Colombia, popular approval of the armed forces and the National Police both simultaneously dropped below 50 percent in 2020.[54] In addition, from 2012 to 2020, the percentage of Colombians who believed that the armed forces respected human rights dropped from 55.1 percent to 37.1 percent.[55] For some, Colombia has approached its security strategy from far too militarized a position, and whether the PETEF, PEFA, or other modernization and education initiatives can catalyze a definitive shift toward a human-centric model of security provision remains to be seen.

Although a spirit of reformism, innovation, and versatility runs deep within the security forces, empowering individuals who embody these values remains squarely in the hands of political leaders. This tension was evident in the wake of a 2021 military bombing of a FARC dissident camp where underage fighters were known to be present—an operation that resulted in the deaths of at least twelve minors that Minister of Defense Diego Molano polemically defended by arguing that the children, albeit forcibly recruited, were "war machines."[56] Likewise, attempts to resume the unpopular aerial spraying of coca crops and the militarization of antiriot activities in Cali in 2021—decisions made at the political level but implemented by security forces—fueled controversy over the function and accountability of the security sector.[57] As Alejandra Ortiz Ayala notes, "civil authorities are complicit in enabling that feeling of immunity among security forces when they minimize state responsibility."[58] For his part, President Gustavo Petro (2022-present), who came to office in August 2022, signaled his desire to enforce greater accountability of soldiers and police. In his first month, the former guerilla fighter dismissed nearly fifty admirals and generals from across the armed forces and National Police and announced his intentions to prosecute human rights violations vehemently, root out corruption in the ranks, and eventually separate the National Police from the Ministry of Defense.

No matter the reorientation of security policy at the political level, the institutionalization of security sector reform has ensured that major reversals in professionalism across most of the security sector's rank and file are uncommon, especially against the backdrop of continued security cooperation with the United States. As of 2022, the US-Colombia security relationship still centered on tackling transnational organized crime, territorial control through peace implementation, and—significantly—DIB. From this perspective, one analyst contends that among the most important processes of institutionalization is the bilateral relationship itself—and the ability of the US government to steer it in ways that promote an unrelenting commitment to the objectives of Plan Colombia, including accountability.[59] President Joe Biden's (2021–present) decision to designate Colombia a major non-NATO ally of the United States in 2022, making it even easier for the country to purchase US military equipment and collaborate on security issues, was not only a recognition of the trust in the bilateral relationship but also a symbol of the continued influence Washington wields vis-à-vis its top strategic partner in Latin America and the Caribbean. In this vein, the Colombian Ministry of Defense knows all too well that partnership with the United States is not a given—that it depends on a recognition of the two countries' shared responsibility to take on common threats and a commitment to uphold shared values. For this reason, US support—and the legitimacy it has bestowed since the start of Plan Colombia—will continue to be an important lever for preserving and advancing Colombia's security sector reform.

Criminality, Corruption, and Complacency: Unfulfilled Promise and the Reorientation of Cooperation in Mexico

Given the overall inability of the Mexican government to deliver security sector reform over the years of Mérida Initiative assistance, it is unsurprising that the country's security forces remained only partially effective and largely unaccountable as of 2022. Whereas the Colombian government assumed ownership of the reforms, innovations, and doctrine adopted during Plan Colombia, the Mexican government failed to institutionalize the most significant reforms associated with the Mérida Initiative. In fact, successive Mexican presidents reoriented the security sector in both cosmetic and fundamental ways, stunting the institutional momentum of the Calderón presidency and failing to consolidate institutional reforms during a dip in violence when the Peña Nieto administration took office.

The election of President Trump in 2016 also accelerated a reduction in the unprecedented security assistance ushered in by the Mérida Initiative, diminishing Washington's ability to leverage security assistance in ways that reinforced professionalization and reform. Delivering on a campaign promise, Trump announced during his first week in office the construction of a wall along the US-Mexico border to keep out migrants, drugs, and spill-over crime and violence. President Peña Nieto had already spent the months before the US presidential inauguration encouraging unity and continued bi-lateral cooperation on border and regional security. But when Trump went ahead with his border wall plans and doubled down on rhetoric suggesting that Mexico would pay for the wall's construction, his Mexican counterpart took offense and canceled a scheduled meeting between them at the White House, leading to "perhaps the worst period in Mexican-American relations since President Calvin Coolidge."[60] As Azam Ahmed noted in the *New York Times*, Peña Nieto faced a decision between two bad options: defending Mexico's honor as most Mexicans expected or accepting Trump's unilateral approach to border security to preserve other aspects of the bilateral relation-ship, including free trade. Facing low approval ratings already and a Mexican presidential election in 2018, the Institutional Revolutionary Party's (Partido Revolucionario Institucional, or PRI) standard-bearer opted to unify the Mexican public against President Trump and his unpopular and seemingly racist border policy.

The remaining years of the Peña Nieto administration were characterized by initial public sparring between the US and Mexican presidents, including threats of US tariffs of Mexican goods and even of the United States' unilat-eral withdrawal from the North American Free Trade Agreement (NAFTA), which eventually gave way to limited cooperation. The renegotiation of NAFTA as the United States–Mexico–Canada Agreement (USMCA) in 2018 was a hallmark of this more collaborative stage, as was the continuation of bi-lateral law enforcement and intelligence sharing.[61] Significantly, the Mexican government continued to extradite drug kingpins to the United States, in-cluding Joaquín "El Chapo" Guzmán in 2017.[62] But a spate of executive or-ders from President Trump governing US border and counterdrug policies refocused the Mérida Initiative away from the institutional reform aspects that had been the centerpiece of the Bush and Obama administrations. President Trump instead emphasized tackling money laundering, stem-ming irregular migration through the construction of a border wall, and improving drug interdiction at the border.[63] The Trump administration's for-eign assistance requests reflected this shift—and an overall reduction in US aid to Mexico.

A New President, a New Era

Mexico's 2018 presidential election, which marked the worst electoral defeat that any incumbent government in Mexico's constitutional history had suffered, led to even more constrained US-Mexico security ties and a diminished focus on security sector reform. The landslide victory of the left-wing populist National Regeneration Movement (Movimiento de Regeneración Nacional, or MORENA) party's Andrés Manuel López Obrador signaled a major shift in foreign policy, with the new president favoring noninterventionism over the more outward-looking administrations of Calderón and Peña Nieto. Notably, the new president—who campaigned on populist messages that focused on the PRI's corruption, the National Action Party's (Partido Acción Nacional, or PAN) mismanagement of security, and the failure of both parties to invest in the social welfare of the Mexican people—promised to restore Mexico's dignity with respect to the country's relationship with the United States. Yet even though López Obrador, the candidate, struck an indignant and even combative tone when referring to President Trump's policies toward Mexico, López Obrador, the president, eventually carved out a more cordial working relationship with Washington, preserving the spirit of the USMCA and agreeing to enforce migration and asylum cooperation agreements with the United States.

In large part, he complied with US preferences on these fronts, especially because free trade and migration control were equally popular among the Mexican electorate. López Obrador's decision to deploy the military to conduct border control activities diverted the security forces from their other missions and ironically relieved some of the pressure on organized crime groups. But the seriousness with which the Mexican president appeared to be taking the migration issue satisfied Trump, who remained largely indifferent to López Obrador's domestic agenda even when the Mexican president's conduct undermined other US interests, like democratic governance.[64] Yet on the security front, López Obrador's message to the United States was clear.[65] In November 2020, López Obrador's foreign minister stated emphatically that "the Mérida Initiative is null and void, in what it seeks to do or in what it does to the Mexican government."[66]

Consistent with the new administration's rhetoric, López Obrador's strategy for combating violence in Mexico initially focused on social programs to prevent recruitment by gangs and criminal organizations, an initiative he branded as Hugs, Not Bullets (Abrazos, No Balazos). The new Mexican president decried the previous administration's focus on going after drug kingpins and instead targeted the rank-and-file recruits to reduce Mexico's soaring homicide rate. However, scholarship and internship programs for at-risk youth were no match for the wave of violence that had already beset Mexico as intercartel competition raged during the early years of López Obrador's *sexenio*, thanks in part to an emboldened Jalisco New Generation Cartel (Cartel de Jalisco Nueva Generación).[67] From 2015 to 2019, Mexico's homicide rate surged by more than 80 percent, reaching a historical record in 2019 and almost equaling that record in 2020, despite homicide reductions elsewhere in Latin America during the coronavirus pandemic. Likewise, femicides and forced disappearances increased markedly, and in the run-up to 2021 legislative and local elections, at least ninety-one politicians or candidates were murdered.[68]

All the while, Mexico's security forces faced mounting scandals. In December 2019 in Texas, the FBI arrested Genaro García Luna, President Calderón's former secretary of public security and the head of the effort to stand up the Federal Police, on charges of accepting millions of dollars in bribes from the Sinaloa Cartel in exchange for access to sensitive information and safe passage for the cartel's drug shipments.[69] The announcement of the arrest sent shockwaves across Mexico for revealing the true extent of organized crime's penetration of the security sector. The downfall of someone so closely associated with the PAN's security strategy, though, was an opportunity for López Obrador. Despite promising not to politicize the detention of Calderón's top security official, López Obrador could not help himself, moments later describing the arrest as "a defeat to an authoritarian, corrupt regime, an element of proof that [Calderón's] model failed."[70]

The association of the Federal Police with García Luna, who a US federal jury found guilty of all charges in early 2023, afforded López Obrador the powerful imagery he desired to further justify his decision to disband the Federal Police altogether. From the outset of his presidency, López Obrador decried the endemic corruption in the ranks of the Federal Police and, reneging on his long-standing promise to demilitarize Mexico's war on the cartels, replaced Federal Police officers on the streets with soldiers and marines. He also formed yet another national-level civilian force with a mandate to gradually assume policing duties from the military. Article 21 of the Mexican Constitution establishes that public security institutions be civilian in nature, and to this end, the National Guard (Guardia Nacional), as it is known, was approved by Mexico's Congress and entered into force by the early summer of 2019.

The creation of the National Guard was symbolic of the now-habitual practice of new Mexican presidents to engage in layering in the security sector, as explored in chapter 7. Rather than building on the considerable albeit imperfect experience, training, and momentum of the professionalization of the Federal Police, President López Obrador discontinued the existing national police force on December 31, 2019—and did so without introducing enough incentives for former federal officers to join the new force. In fact, more than nine thousand Federal Police officers, many of whom had received training and been vetted under the Mérida Initiative, opted for a buy-out from the government rather than the opportunity to serve in the National Guard, in part because of the president's denigration of the Federal Police as corrupt and complicit with organized crime. But even among the twenty-five thousand who accepted a transfer despite a reduction in their salaries and benefits, many eventually left the ranks of the National Guard due to its militarized organization and an aggressive approach to public security at odds with civilian policing practices for which they trained during the previous administrations.[71] One US observer remarked, "We work with the National Guard because they are the police force, but they lack discipline and an investigative mandate."[72]

Roughly 75 percent of the National Guard in 2020 were transfer personnel from the ranks of the army and navy, most of whom never received adequate law enforcement training. By 2021, National Guard membership almost tripled that of the defunct Federal Police, boasting nearly a hundred thousand officers in service. That same year López Obrador publicly contemplated a constitutional amendment to transfer the National Guard from the Secretariat of Security and Civilian Protection (Secretaría de Seguridad y Protección Ciudadana, or SSPC) to the Secretariat of National Defense (Secretaría de Defensa Nacional, or SEDENA), effectively eliminating civilian control of the country's premier federal law enforcement body. SEDENA leaders appeared supportive of this move given that leaked documents detailed a plan to substitute all remaining civilians within the National Guard with SEDENA personnel.[73] By September 2022, the formal transfer of the National Guard's operational and administrative control to SEDENA was complete after a reform to the National Guard and Public Security Law garnered resounding majorities in both houses of Congress. However, in 2023, the Mexican Supreme Court declared this transfer unconstitutional, throwing the status of the National Guard into legal limbo. Further, although 75 percent of Mexicans expressed at least some trust in the country's newest security institution, human rights abuses had not abated, and illegal detentions, abuse, and extrajudicial murders perpetrated by National Guard personnel revealed a lack of training, standardization, and professionalization within the rapidly growing security institution.[74]

Many Mexicans remained concerned about the militarization of public security provision. This became especially troubling given President López Obrador's willingness to task the National Guard and, by extension, the army with missions of political patronage, including assigning service members to provide security for the distribution of pensions for the elderly and differently abled, scholarships for secondary school students, and aid to children of single mothers.[75] National Guard members also "provide security assistance" for the distribution of fertilizer to farmers in the state of Guerrero, a government program in place since 1994, which has been plagued in recent years by supply failures in corn cultivation and is often abused by growers to increase production of opium poppy.[76] Meanwhile, as the military's and National Guard's budgets and share of responsibility for security increased, municipal security subsidies and federal funding to nearly all other security and justice institutions, including the Attorney General's Office and intelligence services, declined.

Back to Square One: A Security Sector in Crisis

López Obrador's excessive reliance on the military was not only a setback for institutionalizing a civilian federal police force but also presented challenges for the armed forces' own processes of professionalization. The 2019 Law on the Use of Force (Ley de Uso de la Fuerza) spelled out the types of authorized weapons, methods, and reporting requirements for security forces in policing roles. Despite the increased contact between the civilian population and SEDENA and SEMAR (Secretaría de Marina, or Secretariat of the Navy), accusations of human rights abuse actually decreased by 49.5 percent in comparison with the first years of the Peña Nieto administration.[77] Impunity for suspected crimes involving members of the military remained alarmingly high, however, even after the limited advances in the previous decade to transfer some crimes from military courts to civilian ones. Between 2015 and 2019, fewer than 1 percent of the cases of torture or forced disappearance brought against soldiers ended up in court.[78] Accountability of the security sector faced further erosion in May 2020, when the president issued a decree extending the deployment of the military in policing duties through 2024, a measure later extended until 2028 by the Mexican Congress. Unlike the constitutional reform that created the National Guard and specified civilian oversight of armed forces units operating in public security roles, stipulations reiterating civilian control were noticeably absent in this new strategic formulation. What is worse, in one of the few public instances in which the president asserted his authority over the military in the conduct of operations, his request to military commanders was, in fact, a betrayal of their professionalism and broader societal justice. In October 2019, security forces detained the son of Sinaloa Cartel leader El Chapo. Even though the United States requested the extradition of the detained suspect, López Obrador ordered his release in a bid to save civilian lives, prompting concern and even discontent among the military's high command.[79]

Meanwhile, the military faced added scrutiny over mounting accusations of corruption. In late 2020, US authorities blindsided the Mexican government when they arrested in Los Angeles Mexico's former SEDENA head General Salvador Cienfuegos Zepeda on charges of taking bribes in exchange for protecting the H-2 Cartel between 2015 and 2017. Cienfuegos, whom US officials had long treated as an ally in the war on drugs and who previously led the institution that had become central to López Obrador's governing strategy, outright denied the accusations, but Washington's decision was not taken lightly. The Department of Justice maintained extensive files of evidence on the general, which it shared with the Mexican government, only to see some of those confidential files made public by President López Obrador. When the case against Cienfuegos was dismissed in November 2020 and the retired general was transferred back to Mexico due to "sensitive and important foreign policy considerations" that outweighed Washington's interest in prosecuting him, US authorities nonetheless expected the Mexican government to independently adjudicate the matter.[80] In early 2021, however, the Mexican Attorney General's Office cleared Cienfuegos of all charges and closed the investigation into his suspected protection of the cartel. Making matters worse, López Obrador insisted that the US Drug Enforcement Administration (DEA) had fabricated evidence against Cienfuegos, presenting a new nadir in bilateral relations. The publication of sensitive information obtained by US intelligence, a violation of the US-Mexico Mutual Legal Assistance Treaty, and the outright refusal of the Mexican president to investigate Cienfuegos in good faith symbolized just how far US-Mexico security ties had deteriorated and were a clear indication of the military's growing influence over political decision-making in Mexico.

As the Cienfuegos debacle suggests, the military was no less susceptible to major corruption than Mexico's myriad police forces.[81] President López Obrador, who campaigned on a security platform that promised to return the army to the barracks, nonetheless continued to lean heavily on SEDENA and SEMAR—both to provide security and to resolve several governance tasks not typically associated with democratic militaries. Reversing a tradition of relative discretion in domestic affairs dating back decades, under López Obrador "the armed forces [became] omnipresent in the daily life of Mexico."[82] Facing record homicides, the infiltration of police forces by organized crime, and a polarized political context, the new president not only reasserted the military's role in policing missions but also expanded the scope of the military's responsibilities by rendering SEDENA "the president's go-to force for tasks previously managed by civilian agencies."[83] Under López Obrador, the military acquired a more enduring role in the administration of public services, running the risk of politicizing the institutions due to their increased budgetary and economic prerogatives.[84] According to Mary Beth Sheridan, "Mexico's armed forces have assumed a broader role in the country's affairs than at any point since the end of military-led government in the 1940s."[85] López Obrador repeatedly lauded the army and navy for their efficiency and relative transparency, but civil society groups in Mexico and abroad warned of the creeping militarization of governance and the possible disruption of the long-standing equilibrium between civilian and military power.[86]

Nowhere has this worrying trend been more evident than in the procurement of major infrastructure projects, which have exposed the institution to new opportunities for graft.[87] Most prominently, the Peña Nieto administration assigned SEDENA responsibility for the renovation of Mexico City's civilian airport, and from 2015 to 2018, the army reportedly paid nearly $100 million to shell companies to which it awarded fraudulent supply contracts.[88] Despite this clear violation of trust, López Obrador launched a completely different Mexico City airport project only to administer the funding directly via SEDENA's budget and to delegate the construction of the airport in its entirety to the military. The president went one step further and brought the military into additional infrastructure and services provision roles. By deeming megaprojects in the southeastern part of Mexico a matter of national security, the Mexican government turned ownership, including the finances, construction, and operation, of a major tourist train network over to SEDENA, bypassing the civilian finance ministry's accountability mechanisms.[89] The military also installed more than 2,700 automated teller machine sites to deliver government benefits to civilians. Likewise, SEDENA and SEMAR assumed responsibility for migration enforcement at Mexico's borders and for customs at border crossings and seaports in 2020 in a supposed bid to cut down on bribery. In 2020, when the coronavirus pandemic struck Mexico, the number of soldiers in domestic operations ranging from public security to public health measures increased by 20 percent, and the number of navy personnel deployed internally increased by 75 percent. In 2021, more than ninety thousand military personnel participated in domestic operations in Mexico to supplement some hundred thousand members of the National Guard, most of whom were transferred from the ranks of the military to begin with.[90]

The rapid expansion and the long-term contracting associated with many of these new roles suggest that they are more than mere stop-gap measures, disrupting the armed forces' modernization efforts.[91] Raúl Benítez Manaut and Sergio Aguayo both warn that if "today's trends persist, Mexico runs the risk of converting renewed militarization into militarism, plunging the country back into the nineteenth and early twentieth centuries."[92] The armed forces will continue to have an outsized role in public life for the foreseeable future—an overreliance that has not only enfeebled civilian agencies but also sidelined efforts to develop professional civilian police forces. López Obrador's favoritism toward the army has also had lethal consequences. In the first three years of his term, the army fought armed civilians more than 640 times. In those conflicts, 515 civilians and twenty-one members of the military perished. As critics argue, the excessive use of the military fosters the conditions for further clashes, and moving forward without meaningful reform is apt to result in additional misconduct and a tendency toward lethal force among Mexico's federal security institutions.[93]

Craig Deare contends that "the continued reliance of successive Mexican presidents on the armed forces to perform a wide range of missions for which they are not trained represents an indictment of the Mexican political system across all parties."[94] The creation of the National Guard and the extension of the military's public security mandate through 2028 sidelined ongoing efforts to reform and professionalize subnational police forces. Although the Municipal Public Security Subsidy (Subsidio de Seguridad Pública Municipal, or SUBSEMUN) program was restructured in 2016 and continued to provide financial incentives to municipalities under a new initiative, the Subsidy for the Strengthening of Performance in Public Security (Fortalecimiento del Desempeño en Materia de Seguridad Pública, or FORTASEG), the national-level strategy to unify subnational police command structures all but disappeared from public discourse in Mexico.[95] Further, the abrupt rise in insecurity in the state of Guanajuato, which was among the earliest adopters of the Unified Command, shed doubt on the merits of the policing model that had been in the works for more than a decade and was intended to be a solution to Mexico's runaway criminality.

No matter López Obrador's centralizing instincts, municipal police forces still retain important advantages for reducing crime and violence across Mexico's national territory, which is why federal security strategies in Mexico cannot simply ignore subnational security forces.[96] For starters, municipal jurisdictions have responsibility for the everyday crimes that most affect citizen perceptions of insecurity, including burglary, assaults, and carjacking. At least 95 percent of crimes committed in Mexico in 2019 fell outside federal jurisdiction, meaning that responsibility for investigating, interviewing witnesses, and administering justice in these cases requires subnational leadership. As Ernesto López Portillo and Claudia Rodón Fonte highlight, municipal police forces are best poised to implement crime prevention strategies.[97] Yet, although the military and National Guard enjoy inflated budgets and enhanced personnel benefits, Mexico's municipal police often lack salaries commensurate with the costs of living and raising a family, health insurance coverage, or even state-supplied uniforms. As of 2021, roughly 650 municipalities of the 2,457 in the country lacked a local police force.[98] In addition, in cities and towns that enjoyed a local police presence, the Mexican government failed to vet and certify 46 percent of the country's municipal law enforcement agents by a 2021 deadline set by the country's National Security Council in 2019—signaling a lapse that left nearly half of the country's municipal police operating in violation of federal security regulations.[99]

All the while, subnational police forces in many parts of the country continue to be some of the main perpetrators of abuse against the civilian population. Although bribery, extortion, and unlawful detention remain the leading concerns in much of the national territory, some police forces terrorize the population through death threats, torture, and murder. This reality was driven home in early 2021 by headlines that a special forces unit of the Tamaulipas State Police had massacred sixteen Guatemalan and three Mexican migrants near the Texas border.[100] Although media on both sides of the border picked up on what was one of the worst such atrocities in Mexico in years, the event had a particular resonance in the United States because members of the police unit had been trained by the US government through Mérida Initiative programs. In the absence of sustained cross-border cooperation and in the face of the Mexican federal government's relative indifference to the professionalization of the subnational police, Mexico's security sector was as ineffective and unaccountable as ever.

As if to add injury to insult, in January 2021, President López Obrador approved a new foreign agents law requiring US authorities to report any interactions with Mexican security forces to the Mexican federal government. Following Cienfuegos's arrest, López Obrador sought to prevent future affronts or violations of Mexican sovereignty, but the decision to push through the controversial legislation just days before President Biden took office came across to US authorities as both truculent and inflexible. Although the final language in the law was adjusted to "lower the volume and tone," it nonetheless introduced new bureaucratic processes for US law enforcement officers to carry firearms in Mexico and required US officials to report all intelligence obtained within the country to their Mexican counterparts.[101] Fearing retaliation against sources of information or the infiltration of criminal investigations by unscrupulous Mexican officials, agents on both sides paused intelligence-sharing, canceled jointly planned raids on cartel properties, and ceased joint tracking of US-bound drug shipments from South and

Central America.[102] In 2022, Mexican officials rescinded the DEA's aircraft parking space at the Toluca airport outside Mexico City, a privilege the United States had held since the 1990s to facilitate US law enforcement operations in the country, and shut down a DEA intelligence unit the Mexican president alleged had been infiltrated by criminals.[103] In effect, López Obrador's move put an immediate halt of unspecified length to all US-Mexican security cooperation on dismantling drug cartels—a disappointing denouement to what was hailed a little more than a decade earlier as "a new era" of crime-fighting, capacity-building, and partnership.[104]

In September 2021, President Biden's top Western Hemisphere advisor acknowledged that the Mérida Initiative as a framework had outlived its utility, seeking to "turn the page" and chart a new course in the bilateral security relationship.[105] Soon afterward, the two countries renewed efforts at cooperation under the banner of the US-Mexico Bicentennial Framework for Security, Public Health, and Safe Communities. The agreement underscored shared concerns over homicides and drug trafficking, especially in fentanyl and methamphetamines, and prioritized a public health approach to reducing drug use and drug-related violence. It also stressed the importance of interdiction of precursor chemicals and firearms being transported into Mexico and of illicit drugs and trafficked people crossing into the United States. However, short of strengthening forensics cooperation to solve crimes and the introduction of policing programs to prevent high-impact crimes in vulnerable communities, the framework lacked references to the reform or reorientation of Mexico's security institutions. The new approach focused on specific crimes that fuel insecurity on both sides of the border, but it rather conspicuously avoided programming aimed at curbing the Mexican security sector's own responsibility for some of the country's crime and violence.[106]

In both Colombia and Mexico, despite the implementation of major security sector reform initiatives and the infusion of US security assistance to that end, insecurity remains a formidable governance challenge, central electoral issue, and principal concern in bilateral relations with the United States. Although many Colombians grew frustrated over the growing sense of insecurity during the Duque administration, most harbored little doubt that the security forces could and would enforce the directives of the president—a far cry from the operational blows endured by the Ministry of Defense only two decades prior. Although corruption and human rights abuses had not fully disappeared from the ranks of Colombia's security forces, the security sector, government, and civil society institutionalized mechanisms and processes—some, thanks to the FARC peace process—that helped unearth misconduct and hold individuals accountable. Just as important, continued partnership with the US government helped reinforce many of the gains made during Plan Colombia while positioning Colombia as a major exporter of security expertise globally.

In contrast, Mexico's security sector failed to overcome the partisan politics, bureaucratic inertia, and distrust in the US government that have long constrained bona fide security sector reform. Although the Mérida Initiative represented only a fraction of the Mexican government's total spending on security from 2007 to 2021, the bilateral effort was significant in terms of providing Mexico access to new technologies and in setting an apolitical security agenda that could endure across US and Mexican administrations. Yet successive Mexican presidents neglected to institutionalize the practices, procedures, and even organizational bodies that were the focus of US assistance. When US-Mexican relations experienced an overall realignment first following the election of President Trump and then with the election of President López Obrador, the Mérida Initiative ceased to function as a framework for bilateral security cooperation, putting an end as well to cross-border programs aimed at cultivating effectiveness and accountability in Mexico's security sector.

Notes

1. Deare, 2021, p. 9.
2. Vision of Humanity, 2022.
3. Hofstetter, 2018.
4. Santos also demonstrated early independence when he mended ties between the Social Party of National Unity and the Liberal Party, to which he had belonged and which had become a leading force among Uribe's opposition in Congress. When Santos invited the Liberal Party to join his governing coalition and then nominated Liberal Party member Viviane Morales as Attorney General of Colombia, Uribe felt betrayed that his former acolyte had extended such influence to his political adversaries. Morales would eventually oversee investigations into Uribe's ministers and presidential advisors, suspected wiretapping of members of the Supreme Court, and the irregular administration of agricultural subsidies.
5. Beaumont, 2012.
6. Rodríguez, 2014.
7. Peña, 2012; Davis et al., 2016, p. 183.
8. León, 2016.
9. "Apoyo a los diálogos," 2016.
10. Gaviria Dugand et al., 2019, p. 45.
11. Burnyeat, 2020, 2021.
12. Beittel & Gracia, 2018, p. 1.

13. "Lucha anticorrupción, seguridad y justicia," 2018.
14. Symmes Cobb & Murphy, 2018; Liendo, 2018.
15. Tamayo Gaviria, 2018.
16. Davis et al., 2016, p. 181.
17. For perspectives on Colombian military doctrine prior to Plan Colombia, see Cardona-Angarita, 2020.
18. Colombian Army captain, personal communication, Bogotá, Colombia, November 20, 2017.
19. Nagl, 2005, p. xxii. For instance, in 2010, when crime rates increased unexpectedly, then Defense Minister Juan Carlos Pinzón led an internal review of the overall strategy and thereafter oversaw the Sword of Honor (Espada de Honor) and Green Heart (Corazón Verde) campaigns that helped once again reduce crime and violence. The Colombian armed forces then conducted routine comprehensive reviews of service campaign strategies, taking into account political guidance, public perception, and operational results—a planning process that shows "a clear lineage from Plan Colombia" (Davis et al., 2016, p. 183).
20. Beittel, 2019, p. 30.
21. Beittel, 2019, p. 29. US investments in developing Colombia's noncommissioned officer corps proved critical to maintaining and sustaining new technologies, especially in aviation.
22. *Defense institution capacity-building* is also used interchangeably with DIB.
23. Kerr, 2018, pp. 23, 31.
24. NDAA, 2016, pp. 506–508.
25. Miklaucic & Pinzón, 2017, pp. 280–281.
26. For a detailed look at the structural transformation of the Colombian Army and future planning, see Ciro Gómez & Correa Henao, 2014.
27. González Martínez & Betancourt Montoya, 2018.
28. "El Plan de Transformación del Ejército de Colombia," 2017.
29. In 2020, the Army's Military Doctrine Center director publicly resigned from his position, declaring to President Duque that he had lost complete faith in the army's senior leadership, who had purportedly sought to dismantle the Damascus Plan due to its association with President Santos and the FARC peace process ("Fuentes del Ejército," 2020).
30. González Martínez & Betancourt Montoya, 2018.
31. Retired Colombian Army colonel, personal communication, Bogotá, Colombia, September 25, 2017.
32. Tickner, 2014.
33. For information on the desecuritization of military doctrine in Colombia in the wake of the FARC peace deal, see Niño González, 2016.
34. *Manual fundamental del Ejército*, 2017, p. 16.
35. Rojas Guevara, 2017.
36. Ministerio de Defensa Nacional, 2008.
37. Pérez Coronado, 2021. For publications and interactive media related to the Ministry of Defense's work on historical memory, see the "Dirección de Memoria Histórica y Contexto" website, 2021.
38. Colombian Army captain, personal communication, Bogotá, Colombia, October 27, 2017.
39. Angelo, 2019.
40. Isacson, 2010.
41. Human Rights Watch, 2019.

42. *Manual fundamental de referencia de Ejército*, 2017, pp. 3.1–13.
43. Ávila, 2019.
44. "Los escándalos," 2018.
45. "Colombia: Abusos policiales," 2020.
46. Casas Ramírez, 2019, p. 77. As Malcolm Deas notes in response to civil society demands to dismantle the ESMAD, "governments everywhere in the world need an ESMAD with the right preparation so as not to depend on police without the right training or the army [for crowd control and antiriot missions]. It doesn't make sense to request the ESMAD's abolition. The request should be one of improving the institution" (Deas, 2021).
47. US Department of State, 2021a, p. 1.
48. "Colombia, uno de los países del mundo que menos confía en la policía," 2021.
49. Angelo & Illera, 2020, pp. 35–38. Absolute values for public approval of the Colombian security forces vary depending on the agency conducting the poll, explaining why these figures differ from those presented in table 4.A.1. Even so, data trendlines remain fairly consistent regardless of the polling source.
50. Léon, 2021.
51. Juanita Léon (2021) cautions, "The growing ideologization of the armed forces, that is increasingly replacing the military doctrine for which they were being trained until recently and a very serious effort at building good intelligence, has not been mediated by a civilian control," given the military leadership's alignment with the Democratic Center Party. Other observers noted President Duque's deference to uniformed leadership on all matters of security. Héctor Riveros (2022) suggests that Duque's deference was so extreme that the president was guilty of totally abandoning his responsibility to assert civilian control over the armed forces, leaving them instead to their "own devices."
52. Isacson, 2021; León, 2021.
53. Jurisdicción Especial para la Paz, 2021.
54. Invamer, 2020.
55. Ortiz Ayala, 2021.
56. Maihold, 2021.
57. For an overview of the major controversies confronting the military and police in 2021, see Dávila, 2021.
58. Ortiz Ayala, 2021. In 2022, presidential candidate Gustavo Petro reignited debate surrounding the role of the military in Colombian politics. The controversy arose after the former guerrilla fighter claimed that military generals were in the pockets of corrupt politicians and drug traffickers. Army Commander General Eduardo Zapateiro issued a defense of the army, a rebuke of Petro's remarks, and a criticism of the presidential candidate on social media, but in doing so, he purportedly violated Article 219 of the Constitution, which prescribes security forces that are apolitical ("Art. 219: La Fuerza Pública," 2022). This unprecedented involvement of the armed forces in political sparring symbolized for many the increasing partisanship of military leaders, especially as anonymous interviews with security force personnel published in early 2022 indicated pervasive consternation within the Ministry of Defense over Petro's possible election ("Malestar en los cuarteles," 2022).
59. Academic political analyst, personal communication, Bogotá, Colombia, November 8, 2017. The election of President Biden in 2020 and the resumption of Democratic majorities in both houses of the US Congress signaled a subtle but important shift in US policy in Colombia.

Early rhetoric from leading Democratic voices and US diplomats favored the implementation of the peace accord and support for the special justice tribunal as a way of advancing reconciliation and reducing drug trafficking from Colombia (Gómez Maseri, 2021).
60. Ahmed, 2017.
61. Cárdenas, 2018.
62. Critics have questioned the efficacy of the kingpin strategy, a tactic that focuses on reducing organized crime by extracting group leadership. Although the removal of a kingpin such as El Chapo can temporarily weaken criminal groups, it leads to group fragmentation, allows new groups to expand into previously controlled areas, and creates power vacuums that are quickly filled or result in succession battles. Between 2010 and 2020, the number of criminal organizations in Mexico increased from seventy-six to 205. Diversification of illicit revenue streams and expansion into new territories have been linked to the removal of kingpins. The Peña Nieto administration criticized the kingpin strategy, claiming that it makes criminal groups "more violent and much more dangerous." Yet Mexican authorities continued to focus on arresting leaders of crime organizations throughout his presidency (Crisis Group, 2022).
63. US Department of State, 2021b, pp. 75, 90.
64. Kitroeff, 2021.
65. Sheridan, 2019.
66. Domínguez, 2020.
67. One analyst noted that some organized crime groups sought to avoid confrontation with SEDENA and SEMAR starting in 2018, even going as far as publishing dated warnings to soldiers saying, "To those of you in green, please do not show up." During López Obrador's tenure, SEDENA and SEMAR operational deaths have dropped (E. Guerrero, personal communication, Mexico City, December 8, 2021).
68. Etellekt Consultores, 2021. For a summary of legislative action to reduce femicides in Mexico, see Kánter Coronel (pp. 105–113) in Aguayo et al., 2021.
69. For a comprehensive exploration of the implications of García Luna's criminality, see Cruz, 2020. For a summary of high-level corruption and its effect on security, see Hernández and Vargas (pp. 221–232) in Aguayo et al., 2021.
70. Semple & Villegas, 2019.
71. Lambertucci & Guillén, 2020.
72. US diplomat, personal communication, Mexico City, December 3, 2021.
73. Rincón & Ángel, 2022.
74. Meyer, 2020; Lambertucci & Guillén, 2020. In April 2023, Mexico's Supreme Court ruled that the transfer of the National Guard from civilian to military control was unconstitutional, casting doubt on the future of the force and its formal relationship with civilian and military leaders.
75. Rodríguez Bucio, 2021.
76. Cortez Bacilio, 2021.
77. Vicenteño, 2021.
78. Pradilla, 2021. In April 2021, SEMAR turned thirty special forces marines over to the Attorney General's Office in support of an investigation into forty-seven forced disappearances in Tamaulipas in 2014. The case is emblematic of just how ill-suited Mexico's military—even its best trained and most trusted units—is for the performance of public order missions.

79. Sheridan, 2021. López Obrador has faced accusations of providing the Sinaloa Cartel political cover that he has not extended to other organized crime groups. In addition to authorizing the release of El Chapo's son, Ovidio, he also offered a handshake to the imprisoned kingpin's mother on a visit to Sinaloa. Some believe the Mexican president is sympathetic to the Sinaloa Cartel's work as a "significant social benefactor" responsible for social welfare initiatives that are popular in many parts of the Mexican Pacific coast (E. Guerrero, personal communication, Mexico City, December 8, 2021). In January 2022, Ovidio Guzmán López was eventually recaptured just days before President Biden was due to visit Mexico for a North American Leader's Summit, the first such trip for a US president in nine years.
80. Grant, 2020.
81. Antúnez Estrada, 2021.
82. Fonseca, 2021.
83. Sheridan, 2020.
84. Croda, 2021.
85. Sheridan, 2020.
86. Carrasco & Meza, 2020; Vivanco, 2020.
87. Stevenson, 2020.
88. "1.7 bn pesos in airport contracts," 2020.
89. Flores, 2021.
90. Sheridan, 2020.
91. Guevara Moyano, 2022.
92. Aguayo et al., 2021, p. 27.
93. Ángel, 2021; Gottesdiener, 2021.
94. Deare, 2021, pp. 18–19.
95. The López Obrador administration established 266 regional coordination security roundtables to bring together the authorities from all three levels of government to form public security policies with local preferences in mind. One observer noted, "These roundtables are not merely rhetorical. Real dialogue is taking place among the levels of government, and local authorities are being involved and heard" (E. Guerrero, personal communication, Mexico City, December 8, 2021).
96. Chapa Koloffon, 2020.
97. Aguayo et al., 2021, pp. 151–160.
98. Aguayo et al., 2021, p. 152.
99. Ángel, 2021.
100. Lindsay-Poland, 2021.
101. "Mexico softens rules for controversial new foreign agents law," 2021.
102. Shiffman et al., 2021.
103. Reina, 2022.
104. J. D. Negroponte, 2007. Notwithstanding diplomatic and law enforcement tensions, a US representative reported high levels of coordination between the United States and SEDENA and SEMAR during this period, hailing a spirit of cooperation that would suggest "the United States' best relationship with the [Mexican] armed forces in history" (US defense official, personal communication, Mexico City, December 3, 2021).
105. Esquivel, 2021, p. 21.
106. Brewer, 2021.

Conclusion: Security Assistance and Local Preferences and Power Relations

As demonstrated in this paired comparison, US security assistance is only successful to the extent that it accounts for the local dynamics in recipient countries. This book underscores the importance of private sector support, interparty consensus, and the centralization of security bureaucracy in shaping outcomes for security sector reform and, by extension, security assistance. Indeed, business elites, party leadership, and the security bureaucracy itself offer the best opportunities (or risks) for political leadership seeking to usher in major institutional reforms. Armed with this knowledge, policymakers negotiating and administering US security assistance should address these factors using incentives, disincentives, and safeguards where possible.

First, security sector reform should occur in consultation with a country's private sector, and security assistance deliberations should involve a recipient country's business community in ways that encourage increased participation in and contributions to the reform effort. Donors should help provide guarantees to a recipient country's national investors to protect their contributions to the security sector from corruption when viable. In Colombia and in the two Mexican subnational cases of Ciudad Juárez and Monterrey, it was not until the private sector staked its resources in security sector reform—and benefited from oversight mechanisms through the imposition of security taxes—that real progress on effectiveness and accountability began to show. The Mexican private sector's reluctance to back the professionalization of federal security institutions more directly was principally based on the fear that corrupt federal authorities would misuse the money or steal it outright. To build confidence in the process, Washington could leverage its influence in regional organizations and among multinational corporations to push for public-private trusts that pool resources to address public security problems while also ensuring stakeholder oversight, akin to the Ciudad Juárez model.

From Peril to Partnership. Paul J. Angelo, Oxford University Press. © Oxford University Press 2024.
DOI: 10.1093/oso/9780197688106.003.0010

The US government could condition some of its security assistance on improved transparency in the security sector. President Biden's intention to condition US foreign assistance to the governments of Central America on anticorruption progress could be a compelling proof of concept in this regard. However, as of 2022, the Biden administration's plan to address the root causes of migration in Central America focused more on attracting multinational investment to the region than on linking big business to strategies for improving state security provision. Likewise, the largest and most prominent companies in Guatemala, El Salvador, and Honduras continued to pay some of the lowest effective tax rates in the world, leaving few national resources to finance the overhaul of security forces, especially following the COVID-19 pandemic.[1]

Even so, US conditions for human rights were controversial in both Colombia and Mexico, revealing the limits of external accountability tools. Colombia complied with annual human rights certification because it sorely needed US resources and the legitimacy that international partnership bestowed. But Mexico, much wealthier than Colombia, had more relative leverage to shape the terms of US-imposed human rights conditions. In the same way that human rights defenders informed annual certification in Colombia and participated in the routine security dialogues with the US Embassy and Mexican authorities, US anticorruption conditionality could benefit from cooperation with the private sector, the resources of which are indispensable to the policy initiatives of the political class. US assurances will not necessarily overcome decades of distrust between economic and political elites where they are divided and run the risk of encumbering already slow and labyrinthine security assistance approval processes. Yet Washington could facilitate spaces for cooperation between these sectors on specific issues and, if necessary, serve as an external guarantor of expenditures and programs that use private sector contributions and US security assistance funds jointly.

Second, partisan polarization is likely to derail the objectives of security assistance when security is an electoral issue and when parties outside the governing coalition have formal or de facto veto power over security outcomes—either via the legislature, the courts, or subnational executive authorities. To hedge against spoilers from within a country's party system, Washington should seek to negotiate security assistance with a national executive in ways that preempt opposition from other parties, especially within the legislature. Plan Colombia and all the international security assistance it entailed were articulated to Colombia's Congress in President Pastrana's National Development Plan in 1998, meaning that opposition parties were on the record for supporting a more robust relationship with international donors to deliver security sector reform—a process replicated during the Uribe administration on the signature projects associated with the security sector's transformation. Starting with the negotiating phase of Plan Colombia but continuing throughout its implementation, US legislators and representatives from the White House met repeatedly not just with the Colombian president but also with members of the Colombian legislature.

Conversely, in Mexico, the US government and the Calderón administration brokered the Mérida Initiative confidentially, and opposition leaders within the Mexican Congress found out about the security assistance package only after it had been fully negotiated. The reluctance to include opposition parties was likely a result of the highly polarized climate in the country and a fear that the aid would have somehow been thwarted had Calderón's opponents been able to hijack the public narrative by appealing to the Mexican public's sovereignty concerns. Nevertheless, had legislative review of the Mérida Initiative been a part of the negotiation process, it likely would have been more difficult for subsequent administrations to interrupt the continuity of US-Mexican collaboration on the signature projects of security sector reform.

Although depoliticizing security strategies may not always be possible in highly contentious political contexts, a professional civilian bureaucracy in the security sector can ensure programmatic continuity and serve as the institutional memory of a security institution even when there is an alternation in power in the national executive. The Colombian Ministry of Defense's civil service remained modest in size and professional capacity throughout Plan Colombia but significantly more capable than its Mexican counterpart in defending and building on successful programs. Mexico's security institutions—almost entirely staffed by uniformed personnel—lacked internal continuity at the headquarters level, thanks to changes in service leadership and operational rotations that dispersed employees geographically across the country, limiting the degree to which planners and strategists were able to guard against repeating mistakes of the past.

In this vein, US security assistance, especially programs associated with defense institution-building, should prioritize the professionalization of a civilian bureaucracy within the security sector if politically acceptable in a recipient country. Civil servants, legislators, and civil society representatives are well situated to provide both historical memory and oversight of the security sector, but US assistance has seldom prioritized these beneficiaries. Moreover, because long-term donor commitment to security sector reform is just as important as continuity on the recipient government's side, Washington, especially Congress, should take its cues from the success of

Plan Colombia and commit to multiyear security cooperation programs that are not subject to annual reprogramming. And it should allow executive departments and agencies enough flexibility to respond to rapidly changing security environments when necessary.[2] All too often, politicians invoke citizen security strategies, especially tough-on-crime ones, to deal with crises, knowing full well that the real solutions are in long-term reforms to address deep-seated structural problems. To the extent that the US government can help set longer time horizons for such strategies through its security assistance, it should.

Third, although the United States will often not have the luxury of choosing where it intervenes with security assistance based on its own national security determinations, it stands a better chance of meeting success when security provision is centralized or when cohesion among recipient security institutions is strong. To this end, Washington should prioritize support for security sector reform in countries with these more favorable conditions and limit its expectations—and investments—to meet minimum stabilization goals where decentralized security sector governance poses major challenges. Relevant human rights vetting and conditionality still apply to beneficiary institutions in decentralized security sectors, but achieving sector-wide reform is unlikely against a backdrop of prominent and diverse political and criminal interests. The US government should also continue to channel its resources and training into select institutions in which it sees progress as possible or where it sees value in building relationships to preserve spheres of influence vis-à-vis competition with other global powers. Building broad partner government legitimacy and advancing democratic consolidation through these more limited efforts should be seen as a welcome but not inevitable outcome, however.

On a practical level, centralization in a recipient security bureaucracy reduces the number of interlocutors with whom Washington must negotiate its assistance, boosting efficiency. Centralization also helps enforce sector-wide accountability. The proliferation of security forces across levels of government in Mexico not only diffused responsibility for security in ways that impeded greater effectiveness but also provided organized crime groups with more points of entry for state capture. In a contested security environment where the rule of law is weak, such decentralization runs the risk of further eroding an already fragile government's legitimacy. The centralizing instincts of successive Mexican presidents reflect this wisdom, but the early devolution of authority to local officials for raising and maintaining subnational security forces made it exceedingly difficult to dismantle the partisan and criminal incentives these officials had to derail security sector reform.

Centralized security bureaucracies, although more efficient from a donor-driven perspective, still pose several challenges. For one, if the security sector's leadership is already corrupt, then it is probable that the entire sector is compromised or at least complicit in criminality. Donor governments would struggle to encourage progress under these circumstances until civilian leaders in the recipient government addressed the most egregious acts of corruption in the ranks. In Colombia, the Pastrana administration, encouraged by the US government's conditions on assistance, made clear from the outset of Plan Colombia that state forces' collusion with paramilitary groups and drug cartels would not be tolerated. Although old habits persisted into the early years of the Uribe administration in some police and military units, accountability to the law and the US refusal to bankroll units that sustained ties to paramilitary groups or committed gross violations of human rights proved a sector-wide deterrent. Further, because the United States did not negotiate its security assistance at the subnational level in Colombia, it averted complicity with the warlordism and local corruption common in places such as Afghanistan and the Middle East.

Across the board, donor governments should determine from the outset of their security interventions what level of corruption among partner security forces is acceptable in the interim. As the Cienfuegos debacle highlighted, Washington should administer security assistance with its eyes wide open through early and continuous collection of financial intelligence, while signaling to political leaders in recipient countries that corruption undermines government credibility and thus effectiveness. The Uribe administration's early efforts to dismantle a corrupt contracting ring led to the dismissal of senior military leaders and their replacement by less compromised officers. Such displays of political resolve in a recipient government reflect the local ownership so fundamental to the success of security sector reform. On this point, as well, centralized security bureaucracies often lack the attention to subnational dynamics or preferences that often fuel conflict to begin with. Colombia, though, makes a convincing case for complementing the centralized coercive power of the state with preventive security policies devised in consultations involving the National Police, other national ministries, municipal and departmental elected officials, civic organizations, and affected communities.

A final factor that underpinned a favorable result in Colombia—and affected outcomes for three independent variables discussed in this book—was the whole-of-government approach. Colombia's executive departments—starting with the Ministry of Defense but including the Ministries of the Interior, Justice, and Health—had "real skin in the game" to bring the government back from the brink through an integrated state-building strategy.[3]

Mexico, on the other hand, tended to treat insecurity in isolation from other ills such as corruption, impunity, underdevelopment, poverty, and social exclusion. The federal government's crime and violence prevention work and the military's civic action projects were severely underfunded throughout the Mérida Initiative and lacked systematic coordination with the other government ministries. The major difference between Colombia and Mexico in this regard was a perception in Colombia of the state's vulnerability to revolutionary violence. The threat posed by the Revolutionary Armed Forces of Colombia (Fuerzas Armadas Revolucionarias de Colombia, or FARC) to subvert the political and economic order by overthrowing the state concentrated the minds of elites—in the business sector, across the party spectrum, and in the ranks of the Ministry of Defense. A counterinsurgency and counterterrorism strategy that had the needs of the civilian population at its core necessitated broad cooperation across the Colombian government. In Mexico, on the other hand, different perceptions of risk—understood as partial state capture instead of revolution—were mediated by relatively few institutions that were focused on what they considered a law enforcement matter. Whereas in Colombia the nature, ambition, and reach of the principal enemy—insurgent forces—were clear, Mexico lacked a consensus diagnosis on the source of the country's security crisis and the motivations of its most pernicious offenders.

From a US policy perspective, Plan Colombia was a counterdrug, counterinsurgent, counterterror, stabilization, and state-building mission all at once—in large part because the Colombian government also understood its challenges through those same lenses. For the Mexican government, however, the Mérida Initiative was primarily an opportunity to gain access to new equipment, technology, and intelligence, and Mexican authorities siloed their law enforcement strategies in rigid institutions that seldom cooperated with one another, let alone with the United States.[4] US and Mexican ambitions via the Mérida Initiative were mismatched: whereas Washington sought to stabilize Mexico by dismantling criminal groups through deeper cross-border cooperation and improved security sector governance, Mexico City preferred the less disruptive train-and-equip model. The incongruity of strategic vision between the US and Mexican governments led to disappointments on both sides of the bilateral relationship; the Mérida Initiative began and ended as a mismatched partnership. Given the overall failure of the Mexican security sector to improve its effectiveness and accountability, the principal accomplishments of the Mérida Initiative related not to stabilization concerns but to the maintenance of the US-Mexico security relationship, including the expansion of the US defense industry into the Mexican market. In clarifying the strategic assumptions of security assistance across the donor-recipient relationship from the outset, Washington can prioritize and better fund interventions that feature a commitment to both effectiveness and accountability in the security sector among recipient government leaders.

Theoretical Implications

In addition to the practical application of lessons learned during Plan Colombia and the Mérida Initiative, the comparison of these two cases advances the theory on security assistance and security sector reform. First, as the case of Colombia exhibits, security sector reform is possible in countries characterized by highly adverse social conditions. Economic crisis, poverty, rampant unemployment, the widespread availability of small arms, and ubiquitous land disputes made Colombia a dubious prospect for genuine institutional reform at the beginning of the Pastrana administration. Nevertheless, improvements in the effectiveness and accountability of the security sector played a definitive role in reducing insecurity and enhancing state legitimacy. Thanks to an increasing monopoly of force, the Colombian government even showed considerable progress over the same time frame on several other issues that undermined human security, including a reduction in poverty, the passage of a land reform law, and the introduction of new criminal codes—an outcome that would suggest that security sector reform can stimulate other needed reforms.

Second, as the literature holds, clientelistic and authoritarian traditions present significant challenges for security sector reform, but it is often in these contexts that such interventions and security assistance are most needed.[5] For this reason, making a deliberate effort to overcome, or in some cases even accommodate, these attitudes is a primary task for donor governments. A critical difference between Colombia and Mexico is that the Colombian government advanced programs to extend responsibility for citizen security to regional politicians by empowering them and allowing them to take some credit for successes, whereas in Mexico federally imposed security strategies threatened the constitutionally enshrined rights and clientelistic arrangements of subnational civil authorities, oftentimes driving their resistance to reform.[6] The Democratic Security Policy in Colombia encouraged communities to join the government's fight against insecurity through efforts such as the Safe Departments and Municipalities Program and local security consultations. These initiatives linked the citizenry to a centralized state-building project that was anchored in the transformation of the security sector, and the Uribe administration incentivized local participation and buy-in, to great effect, by offering access to resources for the most supportive and engaged communities.[7] In Colombia, clientelism did not stand in the way of security sector reform, but instead, national authorities created incentives for subnational authorities to embrace Bogotá's policies and associated funding, helping advance a winning security strategy and, consequentially, local electoral agendas.

Despite the authoritarian legacy in Mexico, a degree of accountability of the security sector was possible even in the absence of civilian control of the military. Thanks to external pressure exerted by the Inter-American Court of Human Rights and foreign governments, the country's courts and legislature led the reform of Mexico's code of military justice, formally limiting its jurisdiction in cases of egregious human rights abuses. Also, even though the party control that contributed to civilian oversight of the security sector during the hegemonic period had dissolved, the legacy of interservice rivalries, formalized by the separation of the Secretariat of National Defense (Secretaría de Defensa Nacional, or SEDENA) and the Secretariat of the Navy (Secretaría de Marina, or SEMAR) as distinct ministries, forced the main organizations within the security sector to compete for resources and operational taskings based on the institution's perceived competence and trustworthiness. During the Mérida Initiative, Mexican officials and the US Embassy achieved broad, informal accountability by partnering with SEMAR, sidelining both SEDENA and the Federal Police in conducting the most sensitive citizen security operations. However, looking ahead, the absence of civilian control of the armed forces secretariats—the lack of any civilian ministers—stands out as the principal accountability challenge for the military, especially at a time when President López Obrador has expanded the military's mandate and increased its autonomy.

Third, the outcomes of this book's two case studies support the hypothesis that international security assistance has the best chance of improving security sector governance and stabilizing a fragile environment when it avoids disrupting existing balances of power, even if doing so impedes more robust democratic reform.[8] To facilitate security sector reform, external actors tend to embrace elite-centric consultations, sometimes neglecting the preferences of nonelite interlocutors.[9] This propensity leads to the establishment of hybrid security regimes, or those that combine elements of domestic and external security sector governance prescriptions, in which local reformers accept only those reform items that do not undermine their power relative to other sectors of the population and to donors.[10] Such tactics ensured that the US government avoided becoming part of the struggle for power and influence within the countries undergoing reform and facilitated local ownership of the effort, even though this approach tended to curtail the delivery of more sweeping reforms.[11]

Although these compromises suggest that security assistance will rarely deliver security sector governance that aligns perfectly with a liberal democratic ideal, hybrid security regimes can be a desirable result in their own right.[12] For one, they can reinvigorate the legitimacy of the security sector, both internationally and domestically. Abroad, even marginally improved security sector governance can alleviate diplomatic censure, thereby generating new opportunities for international actors to engage in reforming security sectors and to shape outcomes. The removal of the military *fuero* in Mexico enabled Washington to release funds previously withheld at the request of Congress and civil society over the armed forces' continued impunity for human rights abuses. Similarly, in Colombia, drops in most indicators of insecurity and a perceived improvement of human rights protections meant that Bogotá's global reputation had rebounded after the scandal-ridden 1990s. By 2012, these advances were enough to convince US legislators to reward the Colombian government with a long-delayed bilateral free-trade agreement. Changes in the relationship between the US and Colombian governments were incremental, but they culminated in a diversification of bilateral objectives that extended well beyond the drug war. Improved security and economic liberalization eventually resulted in high levels of foreign investment, further engendering cooperative agreements between the Colombian government and the European Union and the North Atlantic Treaty Organization that provided additional incentives to sustain and even institutionalize the gains of the Plan Colombia period.

Simply placing security sector reform on the national agenda created new spaces for dialogue between the Colombian and Mexican governments and civil society. In both countries, reform inspired long-needed national conversations about resolving insecurity and consolidating weak democratic institutions, and conditioning US security assistance on progress on human rights exposed the security sector to public scrutiny as never before. Civil society activism was critical to improving accountability and security sector governance in Colombia and Mexico. Just as decisively, the security sectors of both countries became attuned to popular opinion and have incorporated into their doctrine the importance of public trust to accomplishing their operational objectives. In this way, the security policies implemented became more human-centric (for example, humanitarian and civil affairs activities implemented in vulnerable communities during the later years of the Uribe administration), even though the overall objective of reform remained the state-centric monopoly of the legitimate use of force. Neither Colombia nor Mexico established a full monopoly of security provision; few governments do. However, improvements in the security sector's effectiveness and accountability in Colombia engendered a newfound legitimacy for state actors and an expansion of the rule of law across much of the national territory. Plan Colombia even set a precedent for reformism in a security sector culture in which reform was historically contentious. Indeed, from 2012 to 2017, the Colombian military underwent the fourth major institutional reform in its history, a process that originated not in the civilian ruling class but from among the ranks of the military leadership itself.[13]

Fourth, the three independent variables examined in this study, taken individually, had differentiated effects on the two components of security sector governance, effectiveness and accountability. Private sector support in Colombia, for instance, resulted in improvements for both elements of the dependent variable thanks to the application of a security tax, which enabled professionalization and improved the transparency of government spending on the security sector. However, interparty consensus in Colombia, although a boost for efficiency and, consequently, effectiveness, did little to introduce more robust accountability mechanisms, especially given the deference of the legislature to the national executive on matters of security. Finally, even though the centralization of the security sector reduced bureaucratic inefficiency and resistance to reform, it also risked a reduction of accountability at the local level. The introduction of programs specifically designed to ensure that security strategies were compatible with the preferences and needs of subnational political authorities and citizens was an essential component of enhancing security sector governance among the agencies of a highly centralized security sector in Colombia. The Mexican case, though, also shows that accountability is not necessarily improved in decentralized contexts given that decentralized security provision frequently enabled state capture by organized crime groups in some regions of the country.

In relation to the dependent variable, the explanatory value of each independent variable differs. The degree of continuity, related to partisan polarization, appears to have the greatest effect on security sector governance in that low polarization tends to facilitate the long time horizons necessary to deliver institutional reform. Similarly, as demonstrated in Mexico, the politicization of security as an electoral issue was the principal impediment to the implementation of security sector reform. Mexico could have likely overcome the private sector's detachment or spoilers within the decentralized security bureaucracy had it not been for the latter's protection by unaligned partisans, demonstrating the supreme importance of the polarization variable. Colombia's experience in the wake of the 2016 peace accord with the FARC corroborates this contention. Growing polarization in the party system and among the electorate contributed to a slowdown in the implementation of meaningful reforms and a reversal in security gains; meanwhile, security increasingly became a divisive electoral issue. Continuity of strategy, enabled by interparty consensus or a strong national executive capable of sidelining opponents, thus appears to be a necessary condition for improved security sector governance in a democratic context.

However, such consensus is not a sufficient condition, and interaction effects among independent variables were clearly present in both Colombia and Mexico. The politicization of security took place in a hyperpartisan environment in Mexico and against a backdrop of decentralized security provision, which multiplied the influence of spoilers across three levels of government. In Colombia, on the other hand, low polarization combined with a highly centralized security bureaucracy helped minimize obstacles to the implementation of reforms, especially sector-wide corruption. Likewise, parties in Colombia may have been less susceptible to polarization in the context of significant support from the private sector, a constituency with outsized influence in Colombian politics. Whereas the Colombian private sector made resources available to the national budget in such a way that prioritized security sector reform, the Mexican private sector did not routinely raise the security sector as a priority investment in consultations or lobbying with federal authorities. Private sector support and centralization are certainly not sufficient conditions for improved security sector governance, but resource-strapped national governments facing high levels of corruption, particularly at subnational levels, would find them necessary conditions for any meaningful enactment of security sector reform.

From this perspective, the cases examined here draw attention to the agency of governments receiving security assistance and undertaking reform. By shifting the discussion away from the influence of enablers such as the US government (but not ignoring their relevance to the outcomes), this book centers the debate on the beneficiaries of security assistance—their internal deliberations and political features—and underscores the prominence of domestic conditions in facilitating or impeding reforms. Although the conclusions drawn identify the strengths of the Colombian experience, the discussion in chapter 8 reflects just how far Colombia still needs to go in preserving and advancing the gains of the Plan Colombia period. Colombia remains an incomplete, or hybrid, instance of security sector reform. Yet the case still provides compelling lessons for researchers attempting to reformulate theory on security assistance and security sector reform. As second-generation security sector reform comes into focus, scholars should necessarily envision a larger role for the private sector, detect ways to enshrine reforms as a policy of state rather than as a policy of a particular administration, and resolve the tension between centralized and local security provision that may undermine the state's monopoly of force.[14] Theorists should also accept compromise as inevitable in the negotiation of security assistance and sector reform, reevaluating the ambition of such efforts to accommodate hybrid security regimes that reflect certain aspects of the liberal democratic model without achieving it absolutely. Acknowledging that democratic consolidation is unlikely to occur unless the state can get a handle on insecurity—even in ways that may betray the rigid prescriptions of traditional security sector reform—is an essential lesson given that even the modest provision of security by the state is central to its claims of legitimacy in the eyes of its citizens.

Final Reflections on Citizen Security

The analysis of the Colombian and Mexican cases also reveals notable trends in the realm of citizen security and government security strategies. First, conducting security sector reform while confronting violent nonstate actors tends to exacerbate the burden for the security sector and may lead to reversals in security provision, at least initially. Both cases reveal that upticks in violence and insecurity occurred shortly after security assistance was introduced and initial reforms were enacted, and insecurity in Colombia worsened before indicators of crime and violence steadied at much-reduced levels. Changes in criminal behaviors appear to have some link to these peaks and troughs (for example, fewer kidnappings contributed to more extortion) given that the Colombia case features a drop in violent crimes despite consistent figures for victimization over the period of analysis. Remarkably, public trust in the security sector reached its peak during the most conflictive years, when violence was also most visible. Visibility, which refers to instances in which criminals publicly expose violence or claim responsibility for attacks, tends to peak just before a shift toward criminal participation in less visible illicit activities.[15] The invisibility of crime—which Colombians opaquely ascribe to "the dark hand" (*la mano negra*)—does not make it less menacing, and a wholly effective security sector is one that demonstrates a certain adaptability to counter even less perceptible manifestations of violence, an unresolved challenge for both Colombia and Mexico.[16]

Second, the security sector—itself often a major source of citizen insecurity—runs the risk of reproducing the violence it seeks to uproot unless reform initiatives include robust democratic accountability mechanisms. The security forces in both countries began to take human rights accountability seriously only in the face of major scandals that the media and human rights community unearthed. It was primarily the resulting loss of public confidence, specifically for institutions that previously enjoyed broad public support, that seems to have encouraged security sector leaders to address and curtail abusive conduct. The false positives tragedy in Colombia and the mystery surrounding the Ayotzinapa massacre in Mexico generated enough public outrage and international attention to provoke a newfound sensitivity to human rights among security sector leaders. Although US diplomatic pressure and funding conditionality are an important gauge of performance on this front, national checks on the security sector—both among government entities and from civil society—contributed to the adoption of new attitudes, practices, and doctrine concerning human rights. Further, security assistance should also entail a program of robust protections for vulnerable journalists and human rights defenders, whose vigilance, in the absence of rigorous governmental oversight of the security sector, bestows on police and military forces the credibility to act on behalf of the citizenry.

Third, improved security for the majority does not mean improved security for all, and public opinion polls do not necessarily reflect the lived experience of insecurity. Because the Colombian government prioritized addressing those crimes that most fueled a sense of insecurity, like kidnappings and terrorist attacks in cities, most urban residents of Colombia reported an improved perception of security during the middle years of the Uribe administration, even as armed conflict raged in more remote regions of Colombia. Drops in violent organized crime activity were notable, but homicide rates appear to have been largely unaffected several years into the implementation of Plan Colombia.[17] Similarly, in Mexico, a reduction in cartel violence in the country's border cities after 2012 coincided with an explosion of violence in smaller cities and the countryside. Security is fluid, and improvements in the provision of citizen security are likely not sustainable unless they target the systemic roots of crime and violence across national territory and build on progress in ways that account for the geographic displacement of violent actors in the face of successful government-led strategies. To this end, as Eduardo Moncada advocates, governments should develop more granular data on criminal victimization to capture subnational variation and thus structure security interventions with differences across the national territory in mind.[18]

Fourth, as security forces improve their operational effectiveness, the state should simultaneously expand its judicial capacity. In Mexico, the federal government addressed comprehensive penal reform only after enhancing the security sector's capacity to pursue organized crime. What resulted was profound confusion about how to process and punish record numbers of criminal suspects under a new system that was poorly understood by judicial professionals, let alone the public. For this reason, judges and prosecutors continued to rely on unhelpful habits from the old judicial regime, especially an overreliance on testimony rather than evidence-based cases, and Mexican politicians and citizens placed imbalanced blame for surges in criminal activity on the justice sector, which released pretrial suspects back into society under the legal procedures of the new accusatorial system. In addition, penitentiary capacity lagged behind even the judiciary's ability to curb impunity, and a lack of attention to and resources for prisons in Colombia and Mexico rendered the facilities largely ineffective at deterring corruption and crime, with massive prison breaks sometimes even exacerbating violent crime. These consequences point to the importance of sequencing the implementation of reforms. In Colombia and Mexico, government efforts to satisfy public demands for results in the form of captures, kills, and extraditions occluded a bona fide, long-term commitment to the legal system in the early years of Plan Colombia and the Mérida Initiative. Comprehensive justice reform came too long after the emphasis on crime suppression, and such short time horizons at the outset ultimately help explain the persistence of insecurity well beyond the heavy-lifting phase of security sector reform. As Raúl Benítez Manaut and Sergio Aguayo contend, insecurity is a multidimensional issue that necessitates real attention to addressing everything from judicial impunity to environmental justice, and security sector reform will only be successful to the extent that governments address these broader drivers of criminality.[19]

Last, shifts in criminal dynamics unquestionably played an important role in some of the changes mentioned. Benjamin Lessing argues that policy approaches to organized crime that do not necessarily require the repressive apparatus of the state may be enough to stop the violent behavior of criminal groups and thereby reduce the overall incidence of insecurity.[20] Unrestricted crackdowns against cartels, for instance, tend to lead to an increase in antistate violence, whereas approaches that exert conditional repression against organized crime—that is, only resorting to repressive strategies when a criminal group commits violence—may have the overall effect of reducing public violence.

For Colombia and Mexico, it is difficult given the available data to determine whether dramatic reductions in violent crime were the direct result of security sector reform, a change in the state-criminal dynamic, or a combination of factors, but Lessing's argument warrants consideration, especially given public statements made by President López Obrador in 2019: "Kingpins haven't been detained because this is not our principal function; the function of the government is to guarantee public security. Our strategy is not one of operations to detain kingpins."[21] Criminal dynamics are a vague and largely unexplored field of inquiry that undoubtedly has ramifications for the success of any given governmental response to violence. Moreover, the small number of cases and large number of variables in this book result in a degrees-of-freedom problem that no amount of rigorous process tracing can eliminate. That criminal activity in some areas of Colombia in 2022 looked remarkably like the brand of nonideological violent criminality that has plagued Mexico for years raises the question of why certain types of illicit activity are more resilient than others. As one observer noted, Colombian organized crime groups are increasingly diversifying their revenue flows, driving a shift in their priorities and behavior in relation to the government.[22] This analysis, then, should be seen as an invitation for other researchers to test the findings of this study in different contexts and with different methodologies. In both Colombia and Mexico, the opacity of state-criminal ties—and the corruption that they engender—renders the determination of causality a Sisyphean task, but acknowledging this limitation underscores the messy and at times unsavory reality of administering security assistance and conducting security sector reform in less consolidated democracies.

The conclusions outlined in this study can ultimately help practitioners structure security assistance in ways that attract local ownership of the desired reforms. If the hurried expansion of security cooperation across the globe following the 9/11 attacks is any indication, security assistance as a tool of democracy promotion and citizen security provision is here to stay, but the one-size-fits-all model has failed. More nuanced, tailored designs that permit the accommodation of local preferences and power relations present a sustainable direction for security assistance and, in the end, a more palatable and natural model for security sector leaders in recipient countries.

Scholarship on the topic must evolve to reflect these insights, for the operating environment has come to demand it. Citizen security is one of the defining political issues of this century, in Latin America and beyond. In the absence of effective, responsible remedies to reduce criminality and violence while bolstering democratic governance, government strategies are apt to draw from historically entrenched and categorically illiberal measures that jeopardize human rights and transparency. Security assistance can be an important lever in changing the trajectory of a security sector. Ultimately, though, whether police and military forces in democratic countries embrace democratic practices is still a function of the security sector's local context, and their success depends on the degree to which public officials, business leaders, and civil society organizations rally around institutional reform. First acknowledging and then accounting for such complexity is at the heart of rendering US security assistance and the partnership it confers stabilizing influences.

Notes

1. Narea, 2021.
2. Marczak et al., 2022, p. 61.
3. Retired US Army colonel, personal communication, Tegucigalpa, Honduras, May 20, 2016.
4. Even in Colombia, the US government provided years of training before large-scale joint operations across the security sector became commonplace, suggesting that a capacity for intragovernmental coordination can be learned.
5. Hanlon & Shultz, 2016.
6. Gordon, 2014, p. 128.
7. In Colombia's coca regions, the government rewarded communities that voluntarily and manually eradicated coca from their territory with Integrated Action social development projects (US Army lieutenant colonel, personal communication, Mexico City, September 19, 2017). In Mexico, on the other hand, the electoral calculations of the ruling party ensured that resources designated for violence prevention initiatives were dispersed across many beneficiary communities nationwide instead of directly to those most with the most pressing security challenges. On the relationship between civilian loyalty to state security forces and levels of governmental repression, see Moreno León, 2017.
8. Wolff, 2015.
9. Ghimire, 2016, p. 273.
10. Schröder et al., 2014.
11. Leininger, 2010. Nicole Jenne and Rafael Martínez (2021) examine the use of security forces to address domestic problems in Latin American countries and conclude that such expanded mandates subvert the development of functioning, legitimate democracies. They argue that the utilization of the security sector in this capacity undermines the legitimacy of civil leaders, prevents the development of civilian mechanisms to address domestic problems, erodes public confidence in democracy, and hinders military reform—particularly size reduction.
12. Schröder et al., 2014.
13. Colombian Navy lieutenant, personal communication, Bogotá, Colombia, October 31, 2017.
14. Jackson, 2018; Muggah & de Boer, 2019; Sedra, 2010.
15. Durán-Martínez, 2017, p. 2.
16. The absence of violence does not necessarily signify the absence of criminality (Durán-Martínez, 2017, p. 71). Although violence dropped off dramatically in Colombia and the security sector's effectiveness improved, criminality remained elevated despite security sector reform.
17. Pérez V., 2014.

18. Moncada, 2021, p. 195.
19. Aguayo et al., 2021, p. 28.
20. Lessing 2017, p. 9.
21. Aguayo et al., 2021, p. 31.
22. US defense official, personal communication, Mexico City, December 3, 2021.

Appendix

Source: UNODC, 2016; UNODC, 2019; Rosen & Ribando Seelke, 2020; Frissard, 2020; México Unido Contra La Delinuencia, 2021; Nácar, 2019.

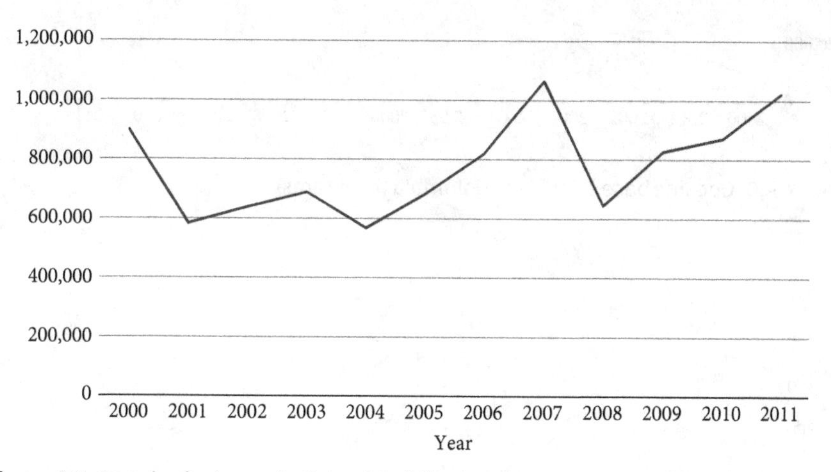

Figure A.1 Coca leaf seizures in Colombia (kilograms)

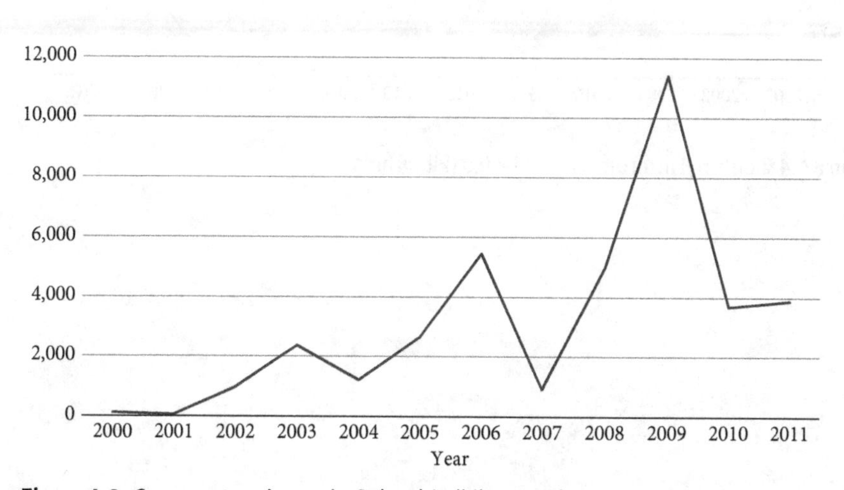

Figure A.2 Coca paste seizures in Colombia (kilograms)

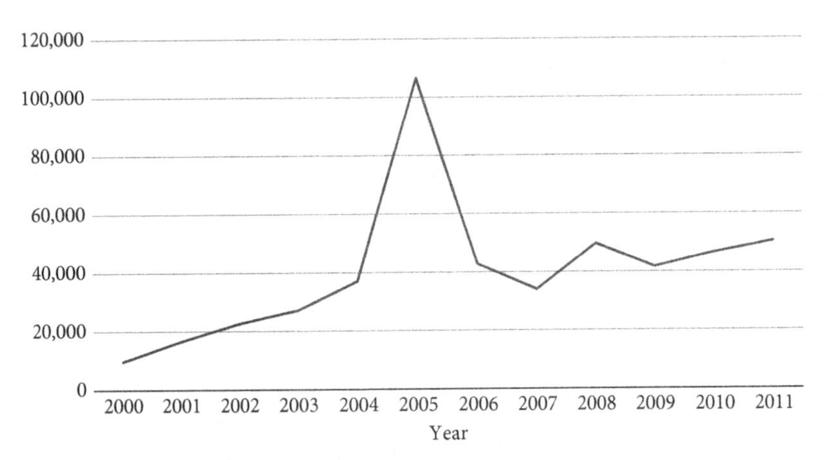

Figure A.3 Cocaine base seizures in Colombia (kilograms)

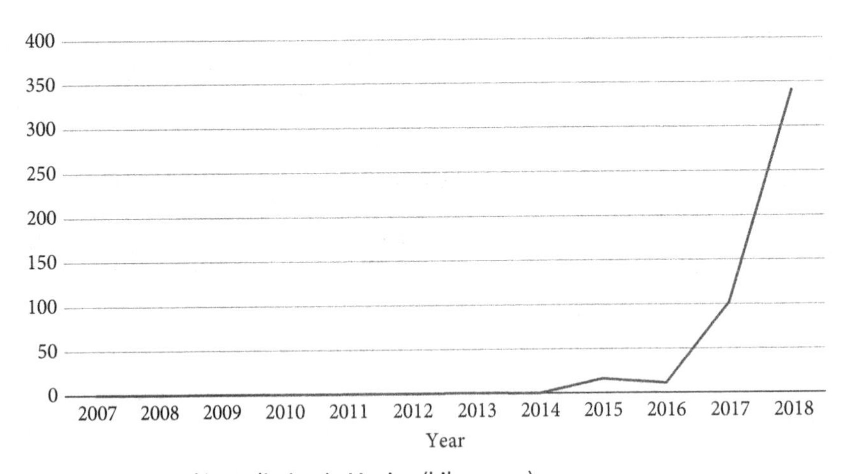

Figure A.4 Fentanyl interdiction in Mexico (kilograms)

Bibliography

1.7bn pesos in airport contracts reportedly issued to shell companies. (2020, February 25). *Mexico News Daily*. https://mexiconewsdaily.com/news/national-defense-issued-1-7bn-pesos-in-airport-contracts-to-shell-companies/

Abello Colak, A., & Guarneros-Meza, V. (2014). The role of criminal actors in local governance. *Urban Studies, 51*(15), 3268–3289. https://doi.org/10.1177/0042098013519831

Abello Colak, A., & Pearce, J. (2015). Securing the global city? An analysis of the "Medellín model" through participatory research. *Conflict, Security & Development, 15*, 197–228. https://doi.org/10.1080/14678802.2015.1055136

Acero Velásquez, H. (2004). Los gobiernos locales y la seguridad ciudadana. In Casas Dupuy, P. et al. (Eds.), *Seguridad urbana y policía en Colombia* (pp. 169–234). Fundación Seguridad y Democracia. https://pdba.georgetown.edu/Security/citizensecurity/Colombia/evaluaciones/gobiernoslocales.pdf

Acosta, O. L., & Bird, R. M. (2003). The dilemma of decentralization in colombia. *International Tax Program Paper 0404*. Joseph L. Rotman School of Management, University of Toronto. https://www.researchgate.net/publication/24137641_The_Dilemma_of_Decentralization_in_Colombia

Acosta Romero, M. (1982). Mexican federalism: Conception and reality. *Public Administration Review, 45*, 399–404. https://www.jstor.org/stable/975641?seq=1#metadata_info_tab_contents

Aglionby, J. (2013). Timeline: Mexico's crackdown on organized crime. *Financial Times*. https://www.ft.com/content/e650694e-edee-11e2-a325-00144feabdc0

Agné, H. (2012). Is successful democracy promotion possible? The conceptual problem. *Democratization, 21*, 49–71. https://doi.org/10.1080/13510347.2012.709240

Aguayo, S. (2009). Mexico, Living with Insecurity. openDemocracy. http://www.opendemocracy.net/article/mexico-living-with-insecurity

Aguayo, S., & Treviño Rangel, J. (2010). El 'piadoso olvido': el PAN y los derechos humanos. In Alvarado, A., & Serrano, M. (Eds.), Seguridad nacional y seguridad interior (pp. 331–361). El Colegio de México. https://2010.colmex.mx/16tomos/XV.pdf

Aguayo, S., Benítez Manaut, R., Le Clerq, J. A., Sánchez Lara, G. R., & Vargas, K. (Eds.). (2021). *Atlas de la seguridad y la defensa de México 2020*. Instituto Belisario Domínguez del Senado de la República, Fundación Universidad de las Américas–Puebla, and Colectivo de Análisis de la Seguridad con Democracia, A.C.

Agüero, F. (1992). The military and the limits of democratization in South America. In Mainwaring, S., O'Donnell, G., & Valenzuela, & J. S. (Eds.), *Issues in democratic Consolidation: new South American democracies in comparative perspective* (pp. 153–198). University of Notre Dame Press.

Aguilar, M., Archundia, E., & Regalado, R. (2013). The security crisis in Mexico and its impact on business management. *Review of Business and Finance Studies, 4*, 29–47. https://papers.ssrn.com/sol3/papers.cfm?abstract_id=2263289

Ahmed, A. (2017, January 26). In a corner, President Enrique Peña Nieto of Mexico punches back. *The New York Times*. https://www.nytimes.com/2017/01/26/world/americas/mexico-pena-nieto-donald-trump.html

AJ+. (2015). It's still dangerous to do journalism in Colombia. *Medium*. https://medium.com/aj-news/it-s-still-dangerous-to-do-journalism-in-colombia-221252341fe1

Albarracín, J., Gamboa, L., & Mainwaring, S. (2018). Deinstitutionalization without collapse: Colombia's party system. In Mainwaring, S. (Ed.), *Party systems in Latin America: Institutionalization, decay, and collapse* (pp. 227–254). Cambridge University Press. https://doi.org/10.1017/9781316798553

Alexander, G. (2002). *The sources of democratic consolidation*. Cornell University Press.

Aligica, P. D., & Boettke, P. J. (2009). *Challenging institutional analysis and development: The Bloomington School*. Routledge.

Alquila Lawrence, D. (1997, March 25). "Faceless" justice in drug war faces scrutiny in Colombia. *Christian Science Monitor*. https://www.csmonitor.com/1997/0325/032597.intl.intl.1.html

Althaus, D., & Grillo, I. (2005, June 14). Nuevo Laredo Police detained for drug testing. *Houston Chronicle*. https:// www.chron.com/news/nation-world/article/Nuevo-Laredo-police-detained-for-drug-testing-1947411.php

Alvarado Mendoza, A., & Zaverucha, J. (2010). La actuación de las fuerzas armadas en la seguridad pública en México y Brasil: Una visión comparada. In Alvarado, A., & Serrano, M. (Eds.), *Seguridad nacional y seguridad interior* (pp. 227–268). El Colegio de México.

Álvaro, M. (2007, April 11–14). La parapolítica: La infiltración paramilitar en la clase política colombiana. Paper presented at *Nuevo Mundo Mundos Nuevos. Nouveaux mondes mondes nouveaux—Novo Mundo Mundos Novos—New World New Worlds*, Brussels. http://journals.openedition.org/nuevomundo/4636

Álvaro Uribe encabeza las preferencias presidenciales en Colombia. (2002, January 31). *VOA*. https://www.vozdeamerica.com/amp/a-2002-01-31-6-1/15266.html

Ames, B. (2001). *The deadlock of democracy in Brazil*. University of Michigan Press. https://muse.jhu.edu/book/6260

AMLO propone coordinación y Mando Único para fuerzas armadas y de seguridad. (2018, October 3). *Etcétera*. https://www.etcetera.com.mx/nacional/coordinacion-mando-unico-fuerzas-armadas-seguridad/

Anaya Muñoz, A. (2012). Security versus human rights: The case of contemporary Mexico. In Kenny, P., Serrano, M., & Sotomayor, A. (Eds.), *Mexico's security failure, collapse into criminal violence* (pp. 122–140). Routledge. https://www.taylorfrancis.com/chapters/edit/10.4324/9780203805787-8/security-versus-human-rights-alejandro-anaya-mu%C3%B1oz

Anckar, C. (2008). On the applicability of the most similar systems design and the most different systems design in comparative research. *International Journal of Social Research Methodology, 11*, 389–401. https://doi.org/10.1080/13645570701401552

Anderson, B., & Cockcroft, J. D. (1965). *Control and co-optation in Mexican politics*. Stanford University Technical Report. Stanford University. https://stacks.stanford.edu/file/druid:yn042rv7128/TR16%20Control%20and%20Cooptation%20in%20Mexican%20Politics.pdf

Andrade Terán, R. (2011). *La crisis de los partidos políticos en Colombia*. Fevira.

Ángel, A. (2019). 2018, el año más violento con más de 34 mil homicidios. *Animal Político*. https://www.animalpolitico.com/2019/01/2018-violencia-homicidios-delitos-mexico/

Ángel, A. (2021). México incumple con certificación de policías: Más del 40% no están evaluados. *Animal Político*. https://www.animalpolitico.com/2021/03/mexico-incumple-con-certificacion-de-policias-mas-del-40-no-estan-evaluados/

Angelo, P. (2019, October 11). Peace is slipping away in Colombia. *Foreign Affairs*. https://www.foreignaffairs.com/articles/united-states/2019-10-11/peace-slipping-away-colombia

Angelo, P., & Illera Correal, O. (2020). *Colombian military culture 2020*. Florida International University. https://gordoninstitute.fiu.edu/publications/military-culture-series/colombian-military-culture1.pdf

Antúnez Estrada, M. (2021, December 25). García Luna, Cárdenas Palomino, Reyes Arzate. De emblemas de Guerra a presos. SinEmbargo.mx. https:// www.sinembargo.mx/25-12-2021/4084851

Apoyo a los diálogos. (2016). Fundación ideas para La paz. https://www.ideaspaz.org/especiales/termometro/#p1

Aprobada ley de defensa y seguridad. (2001, June 15). *El Tiempo*. https://www.eltiempo.com/archivo/documento/MAM-489858

Aranda, J. (2016, August 1). La Sedena ha realizado obras para terceros por más de $5 mil 508 millones. *La Jornada*. https://www.jornada.com.mx/2016/08/01/politica/011n1pol

Archer, R. P. (1990). *The transition from traditional to broker clientelism in Colombia: Political stability and social unrest*. Working Paper #140, Kellogg Institute, University of Notre Dame, Notre Dame, IN. https://kellogg.nd.edu/sites/default/files/old_files/documents/140_0.pdf

Archibold, R. C. (2013, February 19). Mexico anticrime plan challenged by unabated violence. *The New York Times*. https://www.nytimes.com/2013/02/19/world/americas/mexico-anticrime-plan-challenged-by-unabated-violence.html

Archibold, R. C., Cave, D., & Thompson, G. (2013, May 1). Friction between US and Mexico threatens efforts on drugs. *The New York Times*. https://www.nytimes.com/2013/05/01/world/americas/friction-between-us-and-mexico-threatens-efforts-on-drugs.html

Arias, E. D., & Goldstein, D. M. (Eds.). (2010). *Violent democracies in Latin America*. Duke University Press. https://www.dukeupress.edu/violent-democracies-in-latin-america

Arnson, C., Olson, E., & Zaino, C. (Eds.). (2014). *One goal, two struggles: Confronting crime and violence in Mexico and Colombia*. Woodrow Wilson Center Press. https://www.wilsoncenter.org/publication/one-goal-two-struggles-confronting-crime-and-violence-mexico-and-colombia-no-32

"Art. 219: La Fuerza Pública no es deliberante . . . " (2022, April 24). *El Espectador*. https://www.elespectador.com/opinion/editorial/art-219-la-fuerza-publica-no-es-deliberante/

Arteaga, B. Nelson. (2009). The Merida Initiative: Security-surveillance harmonization in Latin America. *European Review of Latin American and Caribbean Studies / Revista Europea de Estudios Latinoamericanos y del Caribe, 87*, 103–110. https://www.jstor.org/stable/25676378

Ashby, P. (2014). *NAFTA-Land Security: The Mérida Initiative, transnational threats, and US security projection in Mexico*. PhD dissertation. University of Kent. https://kar.kent.ac.uk/48367/

Ashby, P. (2015). *Is the Mérida Initiative working?* https://www.americas.org/is-merida-working/

Astorga, L. (2005). *El siglo de las drogas*. Plaza & Janes.

Atwell, K., & Bailey, P. (2021). Wanna fight? Pushing partners aside in Afghanistan. *War on the Rocks*. https://warontherocks.com/2021/10/we-wanted-to-fight-incentivizing-advising-over-fighting-in-afghanistan-and-beyond/

Authers, J. (2005). Confusion widens over López Obrador impeachment. *Financial Times*. https://www.ft.com/content/579182e6-ad2f-11d9-ad92-00000e2511c8

Ávila, A. (2019, February 12). La política de seguridad de Duque, una copia para repetir errores. *El País*. https:// elpais.com/internacional/2019/02/12/colombia/1549974290_288112.html

Ávila, A., & Valencia, L. (2018, August 18). Grupos posFarc y la posible reactivación de la guerra. *El Espectador*. https:// www.elespectador.com/noticias/politica/grupos-posfarc-y-la-posible-reactivacion-de-la-guerra-articulo-807019

Avila Ceballos, C. A. (2015, September 22). Better access to justice services in Colombia. *The World Bank*. http://www.worldbank.org/en/results/2015/09/22/better-access-to-justice-services-in-colombia

Avilés, W. (2001a). Assessing Colombia's political system: review of Colombia: The politics of reforming the state. *Latin American Perspectives, 28*, 165–174. https://doi.org/10.1177/0094582X0102800110

Avilés, W. (2001b). Institutions, military policy, and human rights in Colombia. *Latin American Perspectives, 28*, 31–55. https://www.jstor.org/stable/3185091

Baginski, T. R., Donovan, F., Lacquement, R. A., & Roach, S. D. (2009). *A comprehensive approach to improving US security force assistance efforts*. US Army War College. https://press.armywarcollege.edu/cgi/viewcontent.cgi?article=1353&context=monographs

Bailey, J. (2011a). Combating organized crime and drug trafficking in Mexico: What are Mexican and US strategies? Are they working? In Olson, E. L., Selee, A., & Shirk, D. (Eds.), *Shared responsibility* (pp. 327–349). Woodrow Wilson Center Press. https://www.wilsoncenter.org/publication/shared-responsibility

Bailey, J. (2011b). The US Homeland Security role in the Mexican war against drug cartels, House Committee on Homeland Security, Subcomittee on Oversight, Investigations, and Management, March 31. https://www.govinfo.gov/content/pkg/CHRG-112hhrg72224/html/CHRG-112hhrg72224.htm

Bailey, J. (2014a). *The politics of crime in Mexico: Democratic governance in a security trap*. Lynne Rienner.

Bailey, J. (2014b). What can Mexico learn from Colombia to combat organized crime? In Arnson, C., Olson, E., & Zaino, C. (Eds.), *One goal, two struggles: Confronting crime and violence in Mexico and Colombia* (pp. 95–108). Woodrow Wilson Center Press. https://www.wilsoncenter.org/publication/one-goal-two-struggles-confronting-crime-and-violence-mexico-and-colombia-no-32

Bailey, J., & Dammert, L. (2006). Public security and police reform in the Americas. In Bailey, J., & Dammert, L. (Eds.), *Public security and police reform in the Americas* (pp. 1–23). University of Pittsburgh Press.

Baires, L. (2017). USCAP, a regional strategy against transnational threats. Dialogo Americas. https://dialogo-americas.com/articles/uscap-regional-strategy-against-transnational-threats

Bajraktari, Y., et al. (2006, January 3). The PRIME system: Measuring the success of post-conflict police reform. Paper presented at Woodrow Wilson School of Public & International Affairs, Princeton University. https://www.dmeforpeace.org/sites/default/files/Princeton%20University_%20The%20Prime%20System%20Measuring%20the%20Success%20of%20Post%20Conflict%20Police%20Reform.pdf

Ball, N., Bouta, T., & van de Goor, L. (2003). *Enhancing democratic governance of the security sector: An institutional assessment framework*. Clingendael Institute for the Netherlands Ministry of Foreign Affairs. https://www.clingendael.org/publication/enhancing-democratic-governance-security-sector-institutional-assessment-framework

Bangura, I. (2017). *The gradual emergence of second generation security sector reform in Sierra Leone*. Centre for Security Governance. https://reliefweb.int/report/sierra-leone/gradual-emergence-second-generation-security-sector-reform-sierra-leone

Barber, M. J., & McCarty, N. (2015). Causes and consequences of polarization. In Persily, N. (Ed.). *Solutions to political polarization in America* (chap. 3). Cambridge University Press. https://www.cambridge.org/core/books/abs/solutions-to-political-polarization-in-america/causes-and-consequences-of-polarization/B252678122CA8906210AF544181123E4

Barberena Nisimblat, V. (2010). Las preguntas sin resupesta de la descentralisación: la encrucijada y los nuevos caminos. In *25 años de la descentralización en Colombia* (pp. 55–87). Fundación Konrad Adenauer Stiftung. https://www.kas.de/c/document_library/get_file?uuid=46399884-9718-2b22-5e2e-f6aaaf99bdf3&groupId=287914

Barbosa Castillo, G. (2016). Justicia, justicia transicional y fuerzas armadas, un análisis desde la perspectiva del derecho penal. In Bernal Pulido, C., Barbosa Castillo, G., & Ciro Gómez, A. R. (Eds.), *Justicia transicional: el papel de las fuerzas armadas* (pp. 29–98). Universidad Externado de Colombia.

Bargent, J. (2015, May 25). The legacy of Colombia's vigilante security: The convivir. *InSight Crime*. https://www.insightcrime.org/news/analysis/the-legacy-of-colombia-vigilante-security-the-convivir/

Barraza, L., & Bizberg, I. (1991). El Partido Acción Nacional y el règimen político méxicano. *Foro Internacional, 31*, 418–445. https://www.jstor.org/stable/27738373

Beaumont, P. (2012, October 13). Fidel Castro and Hugo Chávez played role in Colombia's peace talks with Farc. *The Guardian*. https://www.theguardian.com/world/2012/oct/13/fidel-castro-hugo-chavez-colombia-farc-talks

Becker, R., & Saalfeld, T. (2004). The life and times of bills. In Döring, H., & Hallerberg, M. (Eds.), *Patterns of parliamentary behaviour* (pp. 57–90). Ashgate Publishing. https://kar.kent.ac.uk/955/

Beckhusen, R. (2015, March 31). Mexico is arming itself with US military hardware. *Medium*. https://medium.com/war-is-boring/mexico-is-arming-itself-with-u-s-military-hardware-a57c91b8283a

Beittel, J. S. (2012). *Colombia, background, US relations, and congressional interest*. Congressional Research Service. https://www.refworld.org/pdfid/50d1eff82.pdf

Beittel, J. S. (2019). *Colombia, background, US Relations, and congressional interest*. Congressional Research Service. https://fas.org/sgp/crs/row/R43813.pdf

Beittel, J. S., & Gracia, E. Y. (2018). *Colombia's 2018 elections*. Congressional Research Service. https://crsreports.congress.gov/product/pdf/IF/IF10817/7

Bejar, J., & Wilson Becerril, M. (2017, September 29). Violent crime in Mexico is at a 20-year high. This is why Mexico's political parties don't fix it. *The Washington Post*. https://www.washingtonpost.com/news/monkey-cage/wp/2017/09/29/violent-crime-in-mexico-is-at-a-20-year-high-this-is-why-mexicos-political-parties-dont-fix-it/

Bell Lemus, G. (2001, August 21). *¿Qué es la Ley de Defensa y Seguridad Nacional? El Tiempo*. http:// www.eltiempo.com/archivo/documento/MAM-466426

Benítez Manaut, R. (2009). La Iniciativa Mérida: nuevo paradigma en la relación de seguridad México-Estados Unidos-Centroamérica. *Revista Mexicana de Política Exterior, 87*, 215–242. https://revistadigital.sre.gob.mx/images/stories/numeros/n87/benitez.pdf

Benítez Manaut, R. (2013). Organized crime as the highest threat to Mexican national security and democracy. In Payan, T., Staudt, K., & Kruszewski, Z. A. (Eds.), *A war that can't be won: Binational perspectives on the war on drugs* (2nd ed., pp. 149–173). University of Arizona Press.

Benítez Manaut, R. (2014). Mexico-Colombia: US assistance and the fight against organized crime. In Arnson, C., Olson, E., & Zaino, C. (Eds.), *One goal, two struggles: Confronting crime and violence in Mexico and Colombia* (pp. 47–70). Woodrow Wilson Center Press. https://www.wilsoncenter.org/publication/one-goal-two-struggles-confronting-crime-and-violence-mexico-and-colombia-no-32

Benítez Manaut, R., & Deare, C. A. (2021). Mexican military culture 2021. Gordon Institute. https://gordoninstitute.fiu.edu/publications/military-culture-series/mexican-military-culture_2021.pdf

Berg, L.-A. (2012). Guns, laws and politics: The political foundations of rule of law and security sector reform. *Hague Journal on the Rule of Law, 4*, 4–30. https://www.cambridge.org/core/journals/hague-journal-on-the-rule-of-law/article/guns-laws-and-politics-the-political-foundations-of-rule-of-law-and-security-sector-reform/8B027967943502BFF7D9156E2824CC91

Berg, L.-A. (2014). From weakness to strength: The political roots of security sector reform in Bosnia and Herzegovina. *International Peacekeeping, 21*, 149–164. https://doi.org/10.1080/13533312.2014.910397

Berg, L.-A. (2022). *Governing security after war: The Politics of institutional change in the security sector*. Oxford University Press. https://global.oup.com/academic/product/governing-security-after-war-9780197572382?cc=us&lang=en&

Bergmann, M. (2022, March 6). Thread on US security assistance to Ukraine. It's working. Ukraine might be one of the biggest successes of US sec assistance. And the reason is b/c US aid didn't focus on some high-end shiny objects but on core mil tasks. That focus s/d remain. *Twitter*. https://twitter.com/maxbergmann/status/1500634443232563203

Bergmann, M., & Schmitt, A. (2021). A plan to reform US security assistance. Center for American Progress. https://www.americanprogress.org/issues/security/reports/2021/03/09/496788/plan-reform-u-s-security-assistance/

Berkley, G. E. (1970). Centralization, democracy, and the police. *Journal of Criminal Law, Criminology and Police Science, 61*, 309–312. https://scholarlycommons.law.northwestern.edu/cgi/viewcontent.cgi?article=5663&context=jclc

Bermúdez Liévano, A. (2013, June 20). *País Libre tenía razón: el secuestro no desapareció durante la Seguridad Democrática*. https://www.lasillavacia.com/historias/silla-nacional/pais-libre-tenia-razon-el-secuestro-no-desaparecio-durante-la-seguridad-democratica

Bermúdez Liévano, A. (2022, September 1). Colombia: New challenges for the military who don't admit to their crimes. JusticeInfo.net, Foundation Hirondelle. https://www.justiceinfo.net/en/105798-colombia-new-challenges-military-dont-admit-crimes.html

Bernal Pulido, C., Barbosa Castillo, G., & Ciro Gómez, A. R. (Eds.). (2016). *Justicia transicional: El papel de las Fuerzas Armadas*. Vol. 3. Universidad Externado de Colombia.

Bernal Pulido, C., & Correa Henao, M. (2016). Justicia, justicia transicional y fuerzas armadas: un análisis desde la perspectiva del derecho constitucional. In Bernal Pulido, C., Barbosa Castillo, G., & Ciro Gómez, A. R. (Eds.), *Justicia transicional: El papel de las Fuerzas Armadas* (pp. 99–252). Universidad Externado de Colombia.

Bevir, M. (2016). Decentring security governance. *Global Crime, 17*, 227–239. https://doi.org/10.1080/17440572.2016.1197509

Binder, S. A., Lawrence, E. D., & Smith, S. S. (2002). Tracking the filibuster, 1917 to 1996. *American Politics Research, 30*, 406–422. https://doi.org/10.1177/1532673X02030004003

Bird, R. (1992). Tax reform in Latin America: A review of some recent experiences. *Latin American Research Review, 27*, 7–36. https://www.jstor.org/stable/i322708

Blair, D. (2017). Attributes of a democratic and competent defense partner. In Kerr, A., & Miklaucic, M. (Eds.), *Effective, legitimate, secure, insights for defense institution building* (pp. 47–58). National Defense University. https://cco.ndu.edu/LinkClick.aspx?fileticket=9YCCggKpP6s%3D&portalid=96

Bleiker, C., & Krupanski, M. (2012). *The rule of law and security sector reform: Conceptualising a complex relationship*. Geneva Centre for the Democratic Control of Armed Forces. https://www.jstor.org/stable/j.ctv6zdbqh

Blondel, J., & Müller-Rommel, F. (2007) . Political elites. In Dalton, R. J., & Klingemann, H. D. (Eds.), *The Oxford handbook of political behavior* (pp. 813–832). Oxford University Press. https://www.oxfordhandbooks.com/view/10.1093/oxfordhb/9780199270125.001.0001/oxfordhb-9780199270125-e-044?q=Life

Bolaños, A. (2016). SSR in Mexico: A case of organized crime and democratic transition. In Hanlon, Q., & Shultz, Jr., R. H. (Eds.), *Prioritizing security sector reform: A new US approach* (pp. 97–134). United States Institute of Peace.

Bolaños Bolaños, L. del C. (2013). Las coaliciones políticas como una expresión de los partidos políticos en Colombia desde 1991. *Criterio Libre Jurídico, 19*, 35–45. https://revistas.unilibre.edu.co/index.php/criteriojuridico/article/view/708

Bonvecchi, A., & Scartascini, C. (2014). The organization of the executive branch in Latin America: What we know and what we need to know. *Latin American Politics and Society, 56*, 144–165. https://doi.org/10.1111/j.1548-2456.2014.00222.x

Borja, J. (1989). *Estado, descentralización y democracia*. Ediciones Foro Nacional por Colombia.
Borrero Mansilla, A. (2006). Los militares: los dolores del crecimiento. In Leal Buitrago, F. (Ed.), *En la encrucijada, Colombia en el siglo XXI* (pp. 113–146). Editorial Norma.
Botero Suárez, María Isabel, ed. (2017). *Análisis de coyuntura*. Centro de Análisis Estratégico Ejército del Futuro.
Bowden, M. (2015). *Killing Pablo, The Hunt for the World's Greatest Outlaw*. Grove Press.
Boyle, M. J. (2010). Do counterterrorism and counterinsurgency go together? *International Affairs, 86*, 333–353. https://doi.org/10.1111/j.1468-2346.2010.00885.x
Breslow, J. M. (2015, July 27). *The staggering death toll of Mexico's drug war*. http://www.pbs.org/wgbh/frontline/article/the-staggering-death-toll-of-mexicos-drug-war/
Brett, R. (2018). *Elite bargains and political deals Project: Colombia case study*. Stabilisation Unit. https://assets.publishing.service.gov.uk/government/uploads/system/uploads/attachment_data/file/766016/Colombia_case_study.pdf
Brewer, S. (2021, December 3). The bicentennial framework: Opportunities and challenges as US-Mexico security cooperation begins a new chapter. Washington Office on Latin America. https://www.wola.org/analysis/the-bicentennial-framework-opportunities-and-challenges-as-u-s-mexico-security-cooperation-begins-a-new-chapter/
Briscoe, C. (2006). Plan Lazo: Evaluation and execution. *Veritas, 2*, 38–46. https://arsof-history.org/articles/v2n4_plan_lazo_page_1.html
Brooks, R. A., & Stanley, A. S. (Eds.). (2007). *Creating military power: The sources of effectiveness*. Stanford University Press.
Bruhn, K. (2012). PRD and the Mexican Left. In Camp, R. A. (Ed.), *The Oxford handbook of Mexican politics* (pp. 187–209). Oxford University Press. http://www.oxfordhandbooks.com/view/10.1093/oxfordhb/9780195377385.001.0001/oxfordhb-9780195377385-e-9
Bruhn, K., & Greene, K. F. (2007). Elite polarization meets mass moderation in Mexico's 2006 elections. *PS, Political Science & Politics, 40*, 33–38. https://doi.org/10.1017/S1049096507070060
Bueno de Mesquita, B., Morrow, J. D., Siverson, R. M., & Smith, A. (2002). Political institutions, policy choice and the survival of leaders. *British Journal of Political Science, 32*, 559–590. https://doi.org/10.1017/S0007123402000236
Burnyeat, G. (2020). *The face of peace, pedagogy and politics among government officials in Colombia's peace process with the FARC-EP*. PhD dissertation. University College London.
Burnyeat, G. (2021, April 13). Government peace pedagogy in Colombia. *Anthropology News*. https:// www.anthropology-news.org/articles/government-peace-pedagogy-in-colombia/
Burnyeat, G. (2022). *The face of peace: Government pedagogy amid disinformation in Colombia*. The University of Chicago Press. https://press.uchicago.edu/ucp/books/book/chicago/F/bo180167952.html
Buzan, B., Wæver, O., & de Wilde, J. (1998). *Security: A new framework for analysis*. Lynne Rienner.
Cadavid, E. S. (2017). Para el 2030 Colombia deberá ser un líder regional en defensa y seguridad. *Tecnología Militar, 3*, 8–10
Calderón, F. de J. (2007). Decreto por el que se aprueba el Programa Sectorial de Seguridad Pública 2007–2012. https://catalogonacional.gob.mx/FichaRegulacion?regulacionId=47968.
Calvo, E., & Hellwig, T. (2011). Centripetal and centrifugal incentives under different electoral systems. *American Journal of Political Science, 55*, 27–41. https://www.jstor.org/stable/25766252
Camacho-Gutiérrez, P. (2003). Fiscal federalism in Mexico: Analysis first, then reform. *Annual Conference on Taxation and Minutes of the Annual Meeting of the National Tax Association, 96*, 136–143. https://www.jstor.org/stable/41954402?seq=1#metadata_info_tab_contents

Cammett, M. (2007). *Globalization, business politics and development, North Africa in comparative perspective*. Cambridge University Press. https://www.ssrc.org/publications/view/globalization-business-politics-and-development-north-africa-in-comparative-perspective/

Camp, R. A. (1992). *Generals in the palacio: The military in modern Mexico*. Oxford University Press.

Camp, R. A. (2002). *Mexico's mandarins: Crafting a power elite for the twenty-first century*. Berkeley: University of California Press. https://muse.jhu.edu/book/26114

Camp, R. A. (2005). *Mexico's military on the democratic stage*. Greenwood Publishing Group.

Camp, R. A. (2007). *Politics in Mexico: The democratic consolidation*. Oxford University Press.

Camp, R. A. (2010). Armed forces and drugs: Public perceptions and institutional challenges. In Olson, E. L., Shirk, D. A., & Seelee, A (Eds.), *Shared responsibility: US-Mexico policy options for confronting organized crime* (pp. 291–326). Woodrow Wilson Center Press. https://www.wilsoncenter.org/event/shared-responsibility-us-mexico-policy-options-for-confronting-organized-crime

Camp, R. A. (2012). Mexican political elites in a democratic setting. In Camp, R. A. (Ed.), *The Oxford handbook of Mexican politics*. Oxford University Press. http://www.oxfordhandbooks.com/view/10.1093/oxfordhb/9780195377385.001.0001/oxfordhb-9780195377385-e-13

Camp, R. A. (2015). Democratizing Mexican politics, 1982–2012. *Oxford research encyclopedia of Latin American history*. http://oxfordre.com/view/10.1093/acrefore/9780199366439.001.0001/acrefore-9780199366439-e-12

Camp, R. A. (2016). A democratic paradox: More governability, less trust. In Foweraker, J., & Trevizo, D. (Eds.), *Democracy and its discontents in Latin America* (pp. 223–239). Lynne Rienner.

Campbell, H. (2011). No end in sight: Violence in Ciudad Juárez. *North Atlantic Council on Latin America*. https://nacla.org/article/no-end-sight-violence-ciudad-ju%C3%A1rez

Caracol Radio. (2005, April 8). Mancuso: 'el 35 por ciento del Congreso fue elegido en zona de influencia de las AUC'. *Caracol Radio*. http://caracol.com.co/radio/2005/08/04/judicial/1123166760_191922.html

Cárdenas, J. R. (2018). The US-Mexico relationship has survived and thrived under Trump. *Foreign Policy*. https://foreignpolicy.com/2018/03/22/the-u-s-mexico-relationship-has-survived-and-thrived-under-trump

Cárdenas, M. (2009, November 6). Political polarization in Latin America. *Up Front*. https://www.brookings.edu/blog/up-front/2009/11/06/political-polarization-in-latin-america/

Cárdenas, M., Cadena, X., & Cabellero, C. (2005, June). Análisis del incremento en el gasto en defensa y seguridad: resultados y sostenibilidad de la estrategia. In *Análisis Coyuntural Para Coyuntura Económica XXXV No. 1*, Fedesarrollo. https://www.repository.fedesarrollo.org.co/bitstream/handle/11445/964/Co_Eco_Junio_2005_Fedesarrollo_I.pdf?sequence=2&isAllowed=y

Cardona-Angarita, J. M. (2020). Colombian military doctrine in officer's practices during the internal armed conflict (1995–1998). *Revista Científica General José María Córdova 18*, 607–625. https://revistacientificaesmic.com/index.php/esmic/article/download/606/704/

Carlsen, L. (2010, September 15). A "Plan Colombia" for Mexico? *Huffington Post*. https://www.huffingtonpost.com/laura-carlsen/a-plan-colombia-for-mexic_b_717688.html

Carlsen, L. (2018). Effects of militarization in the name of counter-narcotics efforts and consequences for human rights. In Pansters, W. G., Smith, B. T., & Watt, P. (Eds.), *Beyond the drug war in Mexico: Human rights, the public sphere, and justice* (pp. 76–94). Routledge.

Carrasco, G., & Meza, M. A. (2020). La inconstitucionalidad del acuerdo AMLO que militariza la seguridad ciudadana. *Mexicanos contra la Corrupción y la Impunidad*. https://contralacorrupcion.mx/amlo-militarizacion-seguridad-publica/

Carrasquilla Barrera, A. (2005). La sostenibilidad fiscal del esfuerzo en seguridad. In Rangel, A. (Ed.), *Sostenibilidad de la Seguridad Democrática* (pp. 113–138). Fundación Seguridad y Democracia.

Carrillo Gamboa, O., & Cantú Escalante, J. (2018). *Indicadores de la percepción ciudadana de seguridad.* Tecnológico de Monterrey. Monterrey, Mexico. https://consejocivico.org.mx/admin/uploads/projects/downloads/59-pulso-metropolitano-de-seguridad-abril-2018.pdf

Casas Dupuy, P. (2005, April 5). Reformas y contrarreformas en la policía Colombiana. *Fundación Seguridad y Democracia.* https://pdba.georgetown.edu/Security/citizensecurity/Colombia/evaluaciones/reformasycontrarreformas.pdf

Casas Ramírez, D. A. (2019). Esmad, seguridad y posacuerdo: Perspectivas sobre la protesta en Colombia. Ciencias Sociales y Educación. https://revistas.udem.edu.co/index.php/Cienci as_Sociales/article/view/3352

Casas-Zamora, K., & Cárdenas, M. (2010). The "Colombianization" of Mexico. Brookings Institution. https://www.brookings.edu/opinions/the-colombianization-of-mexico/

Castañeda, J. G. (1994). *Utopia unarmed: The Latin American Left after the Cold War.* Vintage Books.

Castañeda, J. G. (2018, January 12). Fuerza civil en Nuevo León, ¿modelo para armar? *El Financiero.* http://www.elfinanciero.com.mx/opinion/jorge-g-castaneda/fuerza-civil-en-nuevo-leon-mod elo-para-armar

Castellanos, R. (2006). Operación Libertad Uno: La política de Seguridad Democrática en acción. In Martínez Osorio, G. (Ed.), *Hablan los generales. Grandes batallas del conflicto colombiano, relatos de los protagonistas* (pp. 37–72). Editorial Norma.

Castillo Castañeda, A., & Niño González, C. A. (2016). La Doctrina de Acción Integral como política de seguridad en el postconflicto armado en Colombia. In Niño González, C. A. (Ed.), *Perspectivas y prospectivas de la seguridad en Colombia* (pp. 121–148). Universidad de Santo Tomás.

Castro, J. (1998). *Descentralizar para pacificar.* Editorial Ariel.

CEIC. (2019). *Colombia foreign direct investment (FDI) [1996–2019].* https://www.ceicdata.com/en/indicator/colombia/foreign-direct-investment

Center for Democracy and Governance. (1998). *Handbook of democracy and governance program indicators.* Technical Publication Series. US Agency for International Development. https://pdfusaid.gov/pdf_docs/PNACC390.pdf

Centro de Investigación y Educación Popular. (2011). *Colombia, deuda con la humanidad 2, 23 años de falsos positivos (1988–2011).* CINEP.

Centro Miguel Agustín Pro Juárez de Derechos Humanos. (2015). *Informe sobre patrones de violaciones de derechos humanos en el marco de las políticas de seguridad y del sistema de justicia penal en México.* Centro Prodh. https://centroprodh.org.mx/2015/06/09/informe-sobre-patrones-de-violaciones-a-derechos-humanos/

Centro Nacional de Memoria Histórica. (n.d.). http://www.centrodememoriahistorica.gov.co/informes

Cepeda, I., & Tascón, F. (2015). *Uribe y la derecha transnacional.* Editorial Gemenis.

Cerritelli, J. (2005). La inversión extranjera y la Seguridad Democrática: Percepciones. In Rangel, A. (Ed.), *Sostenibilidad de la Seguridad Democrática* (pp. 177–188). Fundación Seguridad y Democracia.

Chabat, J. (2010). La respuesta del gobierno de Calderón al desafío del narcotráfico: entre lo malo y lo peor. In Alvarado, A., & Serrano, M. (Eds.), *Seguridad nacional y seguridad interior* (pp. 21–40). El Colegio de México.

Chabat, J. (2012). Drug trafficking and United States-Mexico relations. In Kenny, P., Serrano, M., & Sotomayor, A. (Eds.), *Mexico's security failure, collapse into criminal violence* (pp. 143–160). Routledge.

Chamorro Córdoba, Á. M. (2020). *La "Tasa de Seguridad y Convivencia Ciudadana."* Maestría en derecho del estado con énfasis en derecho tributario, Universidad Externado de Colombia. https://bdigital.uexternado.edu.co/bitstream/handle/001/3615/GLAAA-spa-2020-La_tasa_de_seguridad_y_convivencia_ciudadana_un_reflejo_de_la_necesidad_de_delimitar_el_poder

Chanona, A. (2009). La Iniciativa Mérida y el Congreso Mexicano. In Velásquez, R., & Prado, J. P. (Eds.), *La Iniciativa Mérida, ¿nuevo paradigma de cooperación entre México y Estados Unidos en seguridad?* (pp. 55–75). UNAM/BUAP.

Chantaka, A. (2019, December 3). Plantea el legislador Samuel García refundar Fuerza Civil en Nuevo León. *Vanguardia*. https://vanguardia.com.mx/articulo/plantea-el-legislador-samuel-garcia-refundar-fuerza-civil-en-nuevo-leon

Chapa Koloffon, L. (2020, February 1). La solución es municipal. *Nexos*. https://www.nexos.com.mx/?p=46668

Childs, S. J. (2019). Granting security? US security assistance programs and political stability in the greater Middle East and Africa. *Journal of the Middle East and Africa*, *10*(2), 157–182. https://doi.org/10.1080/21520844.2019.1596649

Chindea, I. A. (2014, June 16). Coordination failures among Mexican security forces. *Small Wars Journal*. https://smallwarsjournal.com/jrnl/art/coordination-failures-among-mexican-security-forces

Cienfuegos Salgado, D., and Jiménez Dorantes, M. El municipio mexicano: una introducción. *Instituto de Investigaciones Jurídicas de la UNAM*. https://archivos.juridicas.unam.mx/www/bjv/libros/7/3077/3.pdf

Ciro Gómez, A. R., & Correa Henao, M. (2014). Transformación estructural del ejército colombiano: construcción de escenarios futuros. *Revista Científica 'General José María Córdova'*, *12*, 19–88. https://doi.org/10.21830/19006586.155

Cisneros, F. (2019, December 2). No hay depuración de corporaciones desde el 2008: FICOSEC. El Diario de Parral y la Región Sur. https://eldiariodeparral.mx/local/amp/no-hay-depuracion-de-corporaciones-desde-el-2008-ficosec-20191202-1595016.html

Clavijo, S. (2011). *Costos y eficiencia de la rama judicial en Colombia, políticas de choque-operativo*. Asociación Nacional de Instituciones Financieras.

Clinton, W. J. (2000). A national security strategy for a global age. The White House. https://history.defense.gov/Portals/70/Documents/nss/nss2000.pdf?ver=2014-06-25-121312-560

Cole, B., Hsu, E., Brineman, E., Caan, C., Chabalowski, M., Flavin, M., O'Connor, V., & Rusin, C. (2009). *Guiding principles for stabilization and reconstruction*. United States Institute of Peace. https://www.usip.org/sites/default/files/guiding_principles_full.pdf

Coleman, B. (2008). *Colombia and the United States, the making of an Inter-American alliance*. Kent State University Press. https://digitalcommons.kent.edu/new_foreign_relations/4/

Colombia: Abusos policiales en el contexto de manifestaciones multitudinarias. (2020, March 10). Human Rights Watch. https://www.hrw.org/news/2020/03/10/colombia-abuses-amid-massive-demonstrations

Colombia: JEP cita a Marcos Pinto y a Édgar Rodríguez por "falsos positivos." (2021, April 13). *Deutsche Welle*. https://www.dw.com/es/colombia-jep-cita-a-marcos-pinto-y-a-%C3%A9dgar-rodr%C3%ADguez-por-falsos-positivos/a-57177276

Colombia Reports. (2017). Colombia's false positives: Fact sheet. https://colombiareports.com/false-positives/

Colombia, uno de los países del mundo que menos confía en la policía. (2021, November 22). *Infobae*. https:// www.infobae.com/america/colombia/2021/11/22/colombia-uno-de-los-paises-del-mundo-que-menos-confia-en-la-policia/

Colombian prosecutors dismiss memo fantasma libel case against InSight Crime director. (2021, December 14). *InsightCrime*. https://insightcrime.org/news/colombia-dismiss-libel-case-insight-crime-director/

Comisión legal de seguimiento a las actividades de inteligencia y contrainteligencia. (2014). http://www.senado.gov.co/comision-de-etica/itemlist/category/642-comision-legal-de-seguimiento-a-las-actividades-de-inteligencia-y-contrainteligencia

Comité Cerezo México. (2017). 6° Informe VDH. Defender los DH en México, la ejecución extrajudicial como respuesta del estado. (Junio de 2016 a Mayo de 2017). Comité Cerezo

México. https://www.comitecerezo.org/spip.php?article2867&lang=es#Sexto-informe-de-violaciones-de-derechos-humanos-contra-personas-defensoras-nbsp

Confirman estadísticas crisis de seguridad en Nuevo León. (2018, January 12). *El Horizonte.* http://www.elhorizonte.mx/local/confirman-estadisticas-crisis-de-seguridad-en-nuevo-leon/2062997

Conger, L. (2014). The private sector and public security: The cases of Ciudad Juárez and Monterrey. Working Paper Series on Civic Engagement and Public Security in Mexico, Wilson Center, Mexico Institute. https://www.wilsoncenter.org/sites/default/files/media/documents/publication/Resilient_Communities_Mexico.pdf

Consejo de Seguridad en Bojayá. (2004). *Armada Nacional de Colombia.* https://www.armada.mil.co/eng/node/6953

Consolidated Appropriations Act, 2008. (2007). https://www.gpo.gov/fdsys/pkg/PLAW-110publ161/html/PLAW-110publ161.htm

Constitución Política de Colombia. (1991).

Constitución Política de los Estados Unidos Mexicanos. (1917).

Cook, C. W. (2007). *Mexico's drug cartels.* Congressional Research Service. https://sgp.fas.org/crs/row/RL34215.pdf

Cook, C. W., & Ribando Seelke, C. (2008). *Merida Initiative: Proposed US anticrime and counterdrug assistance to Mexico and Central America.* Congressional Research Service. https://digital.library.unt.edu/ark:/67531/metacrs10730/m1/1/high_res_d/RS22837_2008Jun03.pdf

Cook, M. L., Middlebrook, K. J., & Molinar Horcasitas, J. (Eds.) (1994). The politics of economic restructuring in Mexico: Actors, sequencing, and coalition change. In *The politics of economic restructuring: State-society relations and regime change in Mexico* (pp. 3–52). Center for US Mexican Studies, University of California-San Diego. https://ecommons.cornell.edu/bitstream/handle/1813/75064/Cook28_The_politics_of_economic_restructuring015.pdf

Coordinación Colombia-Europa-Estados Unidos. (2012). *Ejecuciones extrajudiciales en Colombia 2002–2010, crímenes de lesa humanidad bajo el mandato de la Seguridad Democrática.* CCEEU.

Coppedge, M. (2012). *Democratization and research methods.* Cambridge University Press. https://doi.org/10.1017/CBO9781139016179

Corcoran, P. (2008, December 12). Mexico's Calderón faces more obstacles ahead. *World Politics Review.* https://www.worldpoliticsreview.com/articles/3035/mexicos-calderon-faces-more-obstacles-ahead

Córdoba, J. de, Montes, J., & Martínez V., Y. (2018, November 14). "It's a crisis of civilization in Mexico." 250,000 dead. 37,400 missing. *Wall Street Journal.* https://www.wsj.com/articles/its-a-crisis-of-civilization-in-mexico-250-000-dead-37-400-missing-1542213374

Cornelius, W. A. (1985). The political economy of Mexico under de la Madrid: Austerity, routinized crisis, and nascent recovery. *Mexican Studies/Estudios Mexicanos, 1,* 83–124. https://www.jstor.org/stable/1051981?seq=1#metadata_info_tab_contents

Corporación Observatorio para la Paz. (2009). *Guerras inútiles, una historia de las FARC.* Intermedio Editores.

Correa Castañeda, H. (2006). Operación Colombia: La toma de Casa Verde. In Martínez Osorio, G. (Ed.), *Hablan los generales. Grandes batallas del conflicto colombiano, relatos de los protagonistas* (pp. 37–72). Editorial Norma.

Corrupción y seguridad, temas de López Obrador, Anaya y Meade; ya son candidatos presidenciales. (2018, February 19). *El Sur de Acapulco.* https://suracapulco.mx/impreso/grafico/corrupcion-y-seguridad-temas-de-lopez-obrador-anaya-y-meade-ya-son-candidatos-presidenciales/

Cortés, D., Vargas, J. F., & Hincapié, L. (2012). The democratic security policy, police presence and conflict in Colombia. *Desarrollo y Sociedad, 69,* 11–33.

Cortez Bacilio, M. (2021). Programa de fertilizantes en Guerrero: Costumbre o idiosincrasia. *ADN Cultura*. https://www.adncultura.org/programa-de-fertilizantes-en-guerrero-costumbre-o-idiosincrasia

Cosgrove, J. (2017, December 21). Outside of war zones, Mexico is the most dangerous place for journalists. *Los Angeles Times*. http://www.latimes.com/world/mexico-americas/la-fg-mexican-journalists-20171221-htmlstory.html

Courchene, T., & Díaz-Cayeros, A. (2000). Transfers and the nature of the Mexican Federation. In Webb, S. B., & Giugale, M. (Eds.), *Achievements and challenges of fiscal decentralization, lessons from Mexico* (pp. 200–236). World Bank. http://www1.worldbank.org/publicsector/decentralization/March2004Course/achievementsandchallengesCH5.pdf

Cox, G. W. (1990). Centripetal and centrifugal incentives in electoral systems. *American Journal of Political Science, 34*, 903–935. https://doi.org/10.2307/2111465

Cox, G. W., & Morgenstern, S. (2001). Latin America's reactive assemblies and proactive presidents. *Comparative Politics, 33*, 171–189. https://doi.org/10.2307/422377

Crandall, R. (2001). Explicit narcotization: US Policy toward Colombia during the Samper administration. *Latin American Politics and Society, 43*, 95–120. https://www.jstor.org/stable/3177145

Crandall, R. (2002). *Driven by drugs, US policy toward Colombia*. Lynne Rienner.

Crandall, R. (2020). *Drugs and thugs: The history and future of America's war on drugs*. Yale University Press.

Cristo, J. S. (2016). *El país que se hizo posible*. Planeta.

Croda, R. (2021, March 29). Militarización en la 4T: El espejo venezolano. *Proceso*. https://www.proceso.com.mx/reportajes/2021/3/29/militarizacion-en-la-4t-el-espejo-venezolano-260943.html

Cruz, F. (2020). *García Luna, El señor de la Muerte*. Editorial Planeta.

Curini, L., & Hino, A. (2012). Missing links in party-system polarization: How institutions and voters matter. *Journal of Politics, 74*, 460–473. https://doi.org/10.1017/S0022381611001721

Dalton, R. J. (2008). The quantity and the quality of party systems: Party system polarization, its measurement, and its consequences. *Comparative Political Studies, 41*, 899–920. https://doi.org/10.1177/0010414008315860

Dalton, R. J., & Weldon, S. (2007). Partisanship and party system institutionalization. *Party Politics, 13*, 179–196. https://doi.org/10.1177/1354068807073856

Dammert, L. (2013). Security challenges for Latin American democratic governance. In Domínguez, J. I., & Shifter, M. (Eds.), *Constructing democratic governance in Latin America* (4th ed., pp. 78–101). Johns Hopkins University Press.

Dargent, E., & Muñoz, P. (2011). Democracy against parties? Party system deinstitutionalization in Colombia. *Journal of Politics in Latin America, 3*, 43–71. https://journals.sagepub.com/doi/pdf/10.1177/1866802X1100300202

Darling, J. (2000, May 3). To Colombians, he is the war on drugs. *Los Angeles Times*. https://www.latimes.com/archives/la-xpm-2000-may-03-mn-25970-story.html

Davis, D., Kilcullen, D., & Mills, G. (2016). Conclusion: Prospects for peace and wider implications. In Davis, D., Kilcullen, K., Mills, G., and Spencer, D. (Eds.), *A great perhaps? Colombia, conflict and divergence* (pp. 179–190). Hurst Publishers.

Davis, D. E. (2006). Undermining the rule of law: Democratization and the dark side of police reform in Mexico. *Latin American Politics & Society, 48*, 55–86. https://www.jstor.org/stable/4490449?seq=1#metadata_info_tab_contents

Davis, D. E. (2007). *Policing, regime change and democracy: Reflections from the case of Mexico*. Crisis States Working Paper no. 2, London School of Economics, Destin Development Studies Institute. https://citeseerx.ist.psu.edu/viewdoc/download?doi=10.1.1.631.2535&rep=rep1&type=pdf

Deare, C. A. (2017). *A tale of two eagles: The US-Mexico bilateral defense relationship post* Cold War. Rowman & Littlefield.

Deare, C. A. (2021). *Militarization a la AMLO: How bad can it get?* Wilson Center. https://www.wilsoncenter.org/publication/militarization-la-amlo-how-bad-can-it-get

Deas, M. (1997). Violent exchanges: Reflections on political violence in Colombia. In Apter, D. (Ed.), *The legitimisation of violence* (pp. 350–404). Palgrave MacMillan.

Deas, M. (2001). Plan Colombia. *London Review of Books, 23*(7), 34–36. https://www.lrb.co.uk/the-paper/v23/n07/malcolm-deas/plan-colombia

Deas, M. (2017). *Las fuerzas del orden y once ensayos de historia de Colombia y las Américas.* Penguin Random House.

Deas, M. (2021, May 13). En Colombia no habrá revolución, pero toca hacer reformas. *Contexto.* https://contextomedia.com/en-colombia-no-habra-revolucion-pero-toca-hacer-reformas-malcolm-deas/

Defense Intelligence Agency. (1977). *Latin America: Regional and political analysis.* Defense Intelligence Agency. https://www.cia.gov/readingroom/document/06628219

Defense Manpower Data Center. (2015). *Active duty military strength by service.* https://dwp.dmdc.osd.mil/dwp/app/dod-data-reports/workforce-reports

Delgado, J. E. (2015). Colombian military thinking and the fight against the FARC-EP insurgency, 2002–2014. *Journal of Strategic Studies, 38*, 826–851. https://10.1080/01402390.2015.1005610

DeShazo, P., Mendelson Forman, J., & McLean, P. (2009). *Countering threats to security and stability in a failing state: Lessons from Colombia.* Center for Strategic and International Studies.

Detzner, S. (2017). Modern post-conflict security sector reform in Africa: Patterns of success and failure. *African Security Review, 26*, 116–142. https://doi.org/10.1080/10246029.2017.1302706

DeYoung, K. (2016, February 3). Colombian president Arrives in

DC as a peace accord appears imminent, but some grumble at the cost. *The Washington Post.* https://www.washingtonpost.com/world/national-security/colombian-president-arrives-in-dc-as-a-peace-accord-appears-imminent-but-some-grumble-at-the-cost/2016/02/03/01709f8a-ca9e-11e5-88ff-e2d1b4289c2f_story.html

Diaz, F. A., & Jiménez, M. (2018, April 6). Colombia's murder rate is at an all-time low but its activists keep getting killed. http://theconversation.com/colombias-murder-rate-is-at-an-all-time-low-but-its-activists-keep-getting-killed-91602

Díaz, G. L. (2018, May 2). Leyzaola Pérez, acusado de tortura en Tijuana, candidato a diputado del PES. *Proceso.* https://www.proceso.com.mx/reportajes/2018/5/2/leyzaola-perez-acusado-de-tortura-en-tijuana-candidato-diputado-del-pes-204271.html

Diaz, L. (2022, March 28) Mexican armed forces knew about attack on 43 students, report says. *Reuters.* https://www.reuters.com/world/americas/mexican-armed-forces-knew-about-attack-43-students-report-says-2022-03-28/

Diaz, L. (2011, September 5). Tijuana violence slows as one cartel takes control. *Reuters.* https://www.reuters.com/article/us-mexico-drugs-tijuana-idUSTRE7844EX20110905

Diaz-Cayeros, A., Estévez, F., & Magaloni, B. (2016). *The political logic of poverty relief, electoral strategies and social policy in Mexico.* Cambridge University Press. https://www.cambridge.org/core/books/political-logic-of-poverty-relief/clientelism-and- the-political-manipulation-of-pronasol/DA8B1917B7A5F965143B962408848D94/core-reader

DiJohn, J. (2010). *Taxation, resource mobilisation and state performance.* Working Paper Series on Development as State-Making, GSDRC Applied Knowledge Services.

Dix, R. H. (1980). Consociational democracy: The case of Colombia. *Comparative Politics, 12*, 303–321. https://www.jstor.org/stable/421928

Dix, R. H. (1990). Social change and party system stability in Colombia. *Government and Opposition, 25*, 98–114. https://www.jstor.org/stable/44482489?seq=1#metadata_info_tab_contents

Domínguez, J. I., & Fernández de Castro, R. (2013). *The United States and Mexico: Between partnership and conflict*. Routledge.

Domínguez, P. (2020, November 18). Iniciativa Mérida ya quedó sin efecto: SRE. *Milenio*. https://www.milenio.com/politica/sre-iniciativa-merida-ya-quedo-sin-efecto

Donadio, M., & Kussrow, S. (2016). *A comparative atlas of defence in Latin America and Caribbean*. RESDAL. https://www.resdal.org/ing/atlas-2016.html

Donais, T. (2017). Engaging nonstate security providers: Whither the rule of law? *Stability, International Journal of Security and Development, 6*, 1–13. http://doi.org/10.5334/sta.553

Donais, T. (2018). Security sector reform and the challenge of vertical integration. *Journal of Intervention and Statebuilding, 12*, 31–47. https://doi.org/10.1080/17502977.2018.1426681

Downes, A. B. (2021). *Catastrophic success: Why foreign-imposed regime change goes wrong*. Cornell University Press. https://www.cornellpress.cornell.edu/book/9781501761157/catastrophic-success/

Dudley, S. (2012). The Zetas and the battle for Monterrey. *InSight Crime*. https://www.insightcrime.org/investigations/the-zetas-and-the-battle-for-monterrey/

Dunagan, S. A. (2016, May 25). *Justice Department documents reveal widespread use of fast and furious weapons by major Mexican drug cartels—Linked to at least 69 killings*. [Press release]. Judicial Watch. https://www.judicialwatch.org/press-room/press-releases/judicial-watch-justice-department-documents-reveal-widespread-use-fast-furious-weapons-major-mexican-drug-cartels-linked-least-69-killings/

Duncan, G. (2006). *Los senores de la guerra, de paramilitares, mafiosos y autodefensas en Colombia*. Planeta.

Duncan, G. (2014). Colombia: Toward a Mexicanization of the war. *Per la Pau Magazine, 20*. http://www.icip-perlapau.cat/numero20/

Duncan, G. (2015). *Más que plata o plomo, el poder político del marcotráfico en Colombia y México*. Debate Editorial.

Dunlap, C. (2019, January 17). The Golsteyn case and civilian oversight in military justice. *Lawfare*. https://www.lawfareblog.com/golsteyn-case-and-civilian-oversight-military-justice

Duque Daza, J. (2007a). Institucionalización organizativa y procesos de selección de candidatos presidenciales en los partidos Liberal y Conservador Colombianos 1974–2006. In *Estudios Políticos, 31*. https://www.redalyc.org/articulo.oa?id=16429059008

Duque Daza, J. (2007b). *Los partidos políticos colombianos, 1974–2006, subinstitutcionalización de los partidos tradicionales y emergencia de organizaciones políticas alternativas*. Consejo Latinoamericano de Ciencias Sociales. http://bibliotecavirtual.clacso.org.ar/ar/libros/becas/semi/2004/partidos/duque.pdf

Durán-Martínez, A. (2017). *The politics of drug violence, criminals, cops and politicians in Colombia and Mexico*. Oxford University Press.

Dursun-Özkanca, O. (2021). *The nexus between security sector governance/reform and sustainable development goal-16: An examination of conceptual linkages and policy recommendations*. Ubiquity Press. https://www.ubiquitypress.com/site/books/m/10.5334/bcm/

Eaton, K. (2006). The downside of decentralization: Armed clientelism in Colombia. *Security Studies, 15*, 533–562. https://escholarship.org/content/qt1jp0454c/qt1jp0454c.pdf

Edwards, G. C., Barrett, A., & Peake, J. (1997). The legislative impact of divided government. *American Journal of Political Science, 41*, 545–563. https://doi.org/10.2307/2111776

Edwards, R. (2018). 10 safest & most dangerous metro cities of 2018. *SafeWise*. https://www.safewise.com/blog/safest-metro-cities/

Egnell, R., & Haldén, P. (2009). Laudable, ahistorical and overambitious: Security sector reform meets state formation theory. *Conflict, Security & Development, 9*, 27–54. https://doi.org/10.1080/14678800802704903

Eijking, J. (2019, June 3–4). Why does Colombia export security expertise? Presented at the Security and Criminality in the Americas Conference, Latin American Centre, University of Oxford

Eisenstadt, T. A. (2004). *Courting democracy in Mexico: Party strategies and electoral institutions*. Cambridge University Press.

El ICESI, una "respuesta al dramático problema de la inseguridad": De la Barreda. (2002). *Proceso*. https://www.proceso.com.mx/nacional/2002/5/14/el-icesi-una-respuesta-al-dramatico-problema-de-la-inseguridad-de-la-barreda-66303.html

Elizondo, C., & Magaloni, A. L. (2009). The rule of law in Mexico: Challenges for the Obama administration. In Lowenthal, A. F., Piccone, T. J., & Whitehead, L. (Eds.), *The Obama administration and the Americas: Agenda for change* (pp. 183–202). Brookings Institution Press.

Elliott, C. (2016). *Democracy promotion as foreign policy: Temporal othering in international relations*. Routledge.

El informe que indica que la parapolítica no es cosa del pasado. (2016, April 17). *Semana*. https://www.semana.com/nacion/articulo/procuraduria-adelanta-519-investicaciones-por-parapolitica-y-bacrimpolitica/470010

El plan de transformación del ejército de Colombia. (2017). *Defensa.com*. https://www.defensa.com/colombia/plan-transformacion-ejercito-colombia

Enders, W., Sachsida, A., & Sandler, T. (2006). The impact of transnational terrorism on US foreign direct investment. *Political Research Quarterly, 59*, 517–531. https://doi.org/10.1177/106591290605900402

Epatko, Larisa. (2011, July 15). "Fast and furious" gun operation provokes outrage in Mexico. *PBS News Hour*. https://www.pbs.org/newshour/world/fast-and-furious

Epstein, S. B., & Rosen, L. W. (2018). *US security assistance and security cooperation programs, overview of funding trends*. Congressional Research Service. https://crsreports.congress.gov/product/pdf/R/R45091/3

Erazo, C. (2012). *Impunity: Has implementation of the accusatory legal system been an effective response to the fight against impunity in Colombia?* US Office on Colombia. https://reliefweb.int/sites/reliefweb.int/files/resources/Impunity-in-Colombia-web-FINAL.pdf

Escalante, F. (2012). *El crimen como realidad y representación*. El Colegio de México.

Esquivel, J. (2021). Narcotráfico, migración, violencia. . . "omos parte del problema": Juan González, asesor de Biden. *Proceso*. https://www.proceso.com.mx/reportajes/2021/9/14/narcotrafico-migracion-violencia-somos-parte-del-problema-juan-gonzalez-asesor-de-biden-271901.html

Etellekt Consultores. (2021). Sexto informe de violencia política en México 2021. https://www.etellekt.com/informe-de-violencia-politica-en-mexico-2021-J5-etellekt.html

E.U. respalda Ley de Seguridad. (2001, August 19). *El Tiempo*. https://www.eltiempo.com/archivo/documento/MAM-465421

Evans, M. (2005). *Paramilitaries as proxies: Declassified evidence on the Colombian army's anti guerrilla "allies."* https://nsarchive2.gwu.edu/NSAEBB/NSAEBB166/index.htm

Exploring the transition from first to second generation SSR in conflict-affected societies. (2016). *Centre for Security Governance*. https://www.ssrresourcecentre.org/2016/09/30/exploring-the-transition-from-first-to-second-generation-ssr-in-conflict-affected-societies/

Fabian, S. (2021, February 12). US-educated foreign soldiers learn "democratic values," study shows—though America also trains future dictator. *The Conversation*. https://theconversation.com/us-educated-foreign-soldiers-learn-democratic-values-study-shows-though-america-also-trains-future-dictators-143885

Fajardo-Heyward, P. (2015). Understanding the effect of security assistance on human rights: The case of Plan Colombia. The Latin Americanist, 59(2), 3–27. https://doi.org/10.1111/tla.12052

Falco, M. (1996). US drug policy: Addicted to failure. *Foreign Policy, 102*, 120–133. https://www.jstor.org/stable/1149263

Falleti, T. G. (2010). *Decentralization and subnational politics in Latin America*. Cambridge University Press. https://www.cambridge.org/core/books/decentralization-and-subnational-politics-in-latin-america/78FED9C495B2B6A4139983BA012DA527

Federal crackdown on corruption in Michoacán: Nearly 30 local officials arrested. (2009). Justice in Mexico. https://justiceinmexico.org/simultaneous-arrests-made-to-fight-organized-crime-in-michocan/

Feeley, J. (2013b). *US-Mexico security cooperation: An overview of the Merida Initiative 2008–present*. Foreign Affairs Western Hemisphere Subcommittee, US House of Representatives, May 23. Serial No. 113-3. https://docs.house.gov/meetings/FA/FA07/20130523/100907/HHRG-113-FA07-20130523-SD001.pdf

Feeley, J., & Nealon, J. D. (2022, November 22). Diplomats frustrated by the DEA's dark side. Univision. https://www-univision-com.cdn.ampproject.org/c/s/www.univision.com/amp/univision-news/opinion/oped-foreign-policy-and-the-role-of-dea

Felbab-Brown, V. (2013). *Peña Nieto's piñata: The promise and pitfalls of Mexico's new security policy against organized crime*. Latin America Initiative. Brookings Institution. https://www.brookings.edu/research/pena-nietos-pinata-the-promise-and-pitfalls-of-mexicos-new-security-policy-against-organized-crime/

Felbab-Brown, V. (2020). *The problem with militias in Somalia: Almost everyone wants them despite their dangers*. Brookings Institution. https://www.brookings.edu/research/the-problem-with-militias-in-somalia-almost-everyone-wants-them-despite-their-dangers/

Felipe Calderón reviews Mexico's drug-war strategy after scathing criticism. (2010, August 11). *The Guardian*. http://www.theguardian.com/world/2010/aug/11/felipe-calderon-drugs-strategy-mexico

Fellowship for Reconciliation and US Office on Colombia. (2010). *Military assistance and human rights: Colombia, US accountability, and global implications*. Fellowship of Reconciliation. https://forpeacepresencearchive.kent.edu/items/show/899

Fernández, H. (2016, May 13). Firman convenio para construcción de cuartel militar en Coahuila. *El Universal*. https://www.eluniversal.com.mx/articulo/estados/2016/05/13/firman-convenio-para-construccion-de-cuartel-militar-en-coahuila

Ferreyra, G. (2015). The Michoacanazo: A case-study of wrongdoing in the Mexican federal judiciary. *Mexican Law Review, 8*, 3–31. https://www.elsevier.es/en-revista-mexican-law-review-123-articulo-the-michoacanazo-a-case-study-wrongdoing-S1870057815000025

Ferri, P. (2019, April 11). El nombramiento de un general al frente de la Guardia Nacional evidencia el poder del Ejército en México. *El País*. https://elpais.com/internacional/2019/04/11/mexico/1555002830_590391.html

Finkenbusch, P. (2016). Expansive intervention as neo-institutional learning: Root causes in the Mérida Initiative. *Journal of Intervention and Statebuilding, 10*, 168–180. https://doi.org/10.1080/17502977.2016.1146503

Finkenbusch, P. (2017). Governing through critique: Post-conditionality and bottom-up governance in the Merida Initiative. *Globalizations, 14*, 1–15. https://doi.org/10.1080/14747731.2017.1287449

Finkenbusch, P. (2017). The demise of the intervention paradigm—Resilience thinking in the Merida Initiative. *Conflict, Security & Development, 17*, 313–332. https://doi.org/10.1080/14678802.2017.1337419

Fisher, M., Taub, A., & Martínez, D. (2018, January 7). Losing faith in the state, some Mexican towns quietly break away. *The New York Times*. https://www.nytimes.com/2018/01/07/world/americas/mexico-state-corruption.html

Fiszbein, A. (1997). The emergence of local capacity: Lessons from Colombia. *World Development, 25*, 1029–1043. https://doi.org/10.1016/S0305-750X(97)00020-X

Flores, H. (2021). What military control of the Mayan Train means for Mexico. *Medium*. https://huizarflores.medium.com/what-military-control-of-the-mayan-train-means-for-mexico-f5bd3b228566

Flores-Macías, G. A. (2014). Financing security through elite taxation: The case of Colombia's "democratic security taxes." *Studies in Comparative International Development, 49*, 477–500. https://link.springer.com/article/10.1007/s12116-013-9146-7

Flores-Macías, G. A. (2016). Mexico's stalled reforms. *Journal of Democracy, 27*, 66–78. https://www.journalofdemocracy.org/articles/latin-americas-new-turbulence-mexicos-stalled-reforms/

Flores-Macías, G. A. (2022). *Contemporary state building: Elite taxation and public safety in Latin America*. Cambridge University Press. https://www.cambridge.org/core/books/contemporary-state-building/027726BF6F3995C94222E7BCB769F7CD

Flores-Macías, G. A., & Zarkin, J. (2019). The militarization of law enforcement: Evidence from Latin America. *Perspectives on Politics, 19*(2), 519–538. https://doi.org/10.1017/S1537592719003906

Fonseca, B. (2016, May 22). In Mexico it's institutions, stupid. *Huffington Post*. https://www.huffingtonpost.com/brian-fonseca/in-mexico-its-institution_b_9523684.html

Fonseca, D. (2021, April 1). La guardia pretoriana de AMLO. *The New York Times*. https://www.nytimes.com/es/2021/04/01/espanol/opinion/amlo-ejercito.html

Forero Ángel, A. M. (2017). *El coronel no tiene quien le escuche, una aproximación antropológica a las narrativas militares*. Universidad de los Andes.

Forero, J. (2002a, May 17). Hard-liner elected in Colombia with a mandate to crush rebels. *The New York Times*. https://www.nytimes.com/2002/05/27/world/hard-liner-elected-in-colombia-with-a-mandate-to-crush-rebels.html

Forero, J. (2002b, October 4). New role for US in Colombia: Protecting a vital oil pipeline. *The New York Times*. https://www.nytimes.com/2002/10/04/world/new-role-for-us-in-colombia-protecting-a-vital-oil-pipeline.html

de Francisco Z., G. (2006). Armed conflict and public security in Colombia. In Bailey, J., & Dammert, L. (Eds.), *Public security and police reform in the Americas* (pp. 94–110). University of Pittsburgh Press.

Franco, A. (2013). Unlocking Mexico's political gridlock. In Negroponte, D. V. (Ed.), *The end of nostalgia: Mexico Confronts the challenges of global competition* (pp. 40–56). Brookings Institution Press.

Franz, T. (2018). Power balances, transnational elites, and local economic governance: The political economy of development in Medellín. *Local Economy, 33*, 85–109. https://doi.org/10.1177/0269094218755560

Freeman, L., & Sierra, J. L. (2004). Mexico: The militarization trap. In Youngers, C. A., & Rosin, E. (Eds.), *Drugs and democracy in Latin America: The impact of US policy* (pp. 263–302). Lynne Rienner.

Frey, B. S., Luechinger, S., & Stutzer, A. (2007). Calculating tragedy: Assessing the costs of terrorism. *Journal of Economic Surveys, 21*, 1–24. https://doi.org/10.1111/j.1467-6419.2007.00505.x

Friedman, G. (2008). *Mexico: On the road to a failed state?* https://worldview.stratfor.com/article/mexico-road-failed-state

Frissard, P. (2020, November 9). Estancados en la erradicación de cultivos ilícitos. *Nexos*. https://seguridad.nexos.com.mx/estancados-en-la-erradicacion-de-cultivos-ilicitos/

Fuentes del Ejército le confirman a medios que continúa el Centro de Doctrina y la doctrina Damasco. (2020, December 2). *Infobae*. https://www.infobae.com/america/colombia/2020/12/02/fuentes-del-ejercito-le-confirman-a-medios-que-continua-el-centro-de-doctrina-y-la-doctrina-damasco/

de la Fuente, D. M. (2018). *Radiografía del poder en Colombia, élites y vínculos de parentesco. Cambios y continuidades desde la teoría de redes*. Master's thesis. University of Salamanca. https://gredos.usal.es/handle/10366/138058

Fulo Regilme Jr., S. S. (2018). A human rights tragedy: Strategic localization of US foreign policy in Colombia. *International Relations, 32*(3) 343–365. https://doi.org/10.1177/0047117818777830

Fundación Konrad Adenauer. (2010). *25 años de la descentralización en Colombia*. Fundación Konrad Adenauer Stiftung. https://www.kas.de/c/document_library/get_file?uuid=46399884-9718-2b22-5e2e-f6aaaf99bdf3&groupId=287914

Gallego, J. (2018). *A theory of armed clientelism*. Serie Documentos de Trabajo No. 214. Universidad del Rosario. https://repository.urosario.edu.co/bitstream/handle/10336/17833/dt214.pdf?sequence=4

Gambetta, D. (1996). *The Sicilian mafia: The business of private protection*. Harvard University Press.

Gamboa Montejano, C. (2005). *La seguridad pública en los 31 estados y el Distrito Federal, estudio comparativo de la legislación en la materia*. Comisión Bicameral del Sistema de Bibliotecas. http://www.diputados.gob.mx/sedia/sia/spi/DPI-ISS-02-05.pdf

Garay Salamanca, L. J., Salcedo-Albarán, E., de León-Beltrán, I., & Guerrero, B. (2008). *La captura y reconfiguración cooptada del estado en Colombia*. Grupo Método. https://www.cels.org.ar/web/wp-content/uploads/2018/01/Captura-y-Reconfiguracion-Cooptada-del-Estado-en-Colombia.pdf

García Castillo, T. (2015). La reforma constitucional mexicana de 2011 en materia de derechos humanos: Una lectura desde el derecho internacional. *Boletín mexicano de derecho comparado, 48*, 645–696. http://dx.doi.org/10.22201/iij.24484873e.2015.143.4942

García Covarrubias, J. (2007). Los tres pilares de una transformación militar. *Military Review, 87*, 16–24. https://www.academia.edu/42573327/LOS_TRES_PILARES_DE_LA_TRANSFORMACI%C3%93N_MILITAR

García, J. F., Mejía, D., & Ortega, D. (2013). *Police reform, training and crime: Experimental evidence from Colombia's Plan Cuadrantes*. CAF Working Paper No. 1-2013, CAF. https://10.2139/ssrn.2229368

García, M., & Hoskin, G. (2003). *Political participation and war in Colombia: An analysis of the 2002 elections*. Crisis States Programme Working Papers Series No. 1, London School of Economics. https://www.lse.ac.uk/international-development/Assets/Documents/PDFs/csrc-working-papers-phase-one/wp38-political-participation-and-war-in-colombia.pdf

García Sánchez, M. (2014). Cultivos ilícitos y confianza institucional en Colombia. *Política y gobierno, XXI*, 95–126. http://mobile.repositorio-digital.cide.edu/bitstream/handle/11651/1571/20-971-1-PB.pdf

García Villegas, M. (2006). Reformismo introvertido: las transformaciones de la justicia en Colombia durante los últimos treinta años. In Leal Buitrago, F. (Ed.), *En la encrucijada, Colombia en el siglo XXI* (pp. 451–478). Editorial Norma. https://10.15332/s1909-0528.2010.0002.06

Garrido, A. (2001). *Guerrilla y Plan Colombia*. Producciones Karol C.A.

Garrido, L. J. (1993). *La ruptura, la corriente democrática del PRI*. Grijalbo. https://www.researchgate.net/publication/31644458_La_ruptura_La_Corriente_Democratica_del_PRI_LJ_Garrido

Gates, R. M. (2010). Helping others defend themselves: The future of US security assistance. *Foreign Affairs, 89*(3), 2–6. https://www.foreignaffairs.com/articles/2010-05-01/helping-others-defend-themselves

Gaviria Dugand, A., Ávila Garcia, C. A., & García Sánchez, M. (2019). *Barómetro de las Américas Colombia 2018, Paz, posconflicto y reconciliación*. Universidad de los Andes. https://www.vanderbilt.edu/lapop/colombia/Colombia_2018_Informe_Paz_conflicto_y_reconciliacion_W_11.07.19.pdf

Gay, R. (2012). Clientelism, democracy, and violence in Rio de Janeiro. In Hilgers, T. (Ed.), *Clientelism in everyday Latin American politics* (pp. 81–98). Palgrave Macmillan. https://doi.org/10.1057/9781137275998_5

Ghimire, S. (2016). Making security sector reform organic: Infrastructures for peace as an entry point? *Peacebuilding, 4*, 262–281. https://doi.org/10.1080/21647259.2016.1156813

Gibson, E. (2013). *Boundary control, subnational authoritarianism in federal democracies*. Cambridge University Press. https://doi.org/10.1017/CBO9781139017992

Gill, S. (2017, January 25). Extortion in Colombia: Crime groups filling FARC void. *Colombia Reports*. https://colombiareports.com/extortion-colombia-crime-groups-filling-farc-void/

Ginsburg, T., Cheibub, J. A., & Elkins, Z. (2010). Latin American presidentialism in comparative and historical perspective. *Texas Law Review, 89*, 1707–1740. https://chicagounbound.uchicago.edu/cgi/viewcontent.cgi?article=1176&context=public_law_and_legal_theory

Giraldo, F., & López, J. D. (2006). El comportamiento electoral y de partidos en los comicios para Cámara de Representantes de 2002 a 2006: un estudio comparado desde la Reforma Política. *Colombia International, 64*, 122–153. https://10.7440/colombiaint64.2006.06

Giraldo, F., & Muñoz Yi, P. (2014). *Partidos políticos en Colombia. Evolución y prospectiva*. Fundación Konrad Adenauer Stiftung. https://www.kas.de/c/document_library/get_file?uuid=696741a6-8eb3-0558-d773-1e7859ca898e&groupId=252038

Giraldo, J. (2017). Assessment and program design. In Kerr, A., & Miklaucic, M. (Eds.), *Effective, legitimate, secure, insights for defense institution building* (pp. 75–93). National Defense University. https://cco.ndu.edu/LinkClick.aspx?fileticket=9YCCggKpP6s%3D&portalid=96

Giraudy, A. (2015). *Democrats and autocrats: Pathways of subnational undemocratic regime continuity within democratic countries*. Oxford University Press. https://10.1093/acprof:oso/9780198706861.001.0001

Global Impunity Index Mexico. (2016). Fundación Universidad de las Américas Puebla. https://www.casede.org/BibliotecaCasede/IGI_MEX_2016.pdf

Gobierno presenta 15 medidas contra impunidad en violación de DD.HH. (2011, June 13). http://www.eluniversal.com.co/cartagena/nacional/gobierno-presenta-15-medidas-contra-impunidad-en-violacion-de-ddhh-29097

Godoy, H. (2003, March 27–29). Plan Colombia's strategic weakness. Presented at the Annual Congress of the Latin American Studies Association, Dallas. https://www.academia.edu/5972417/Plan_Colombias_Strategic_Weaknesses

Goi, L. (2017, April 10). Mexico ex-governor captured as PRI tries to clean up before elections. *InsightCrime*. https://insightcrime.org/news/brief/fmr-mexican-governor-captured-pri-clean-before-elections/

Golden, T. (2022, December 8). The Cienfuegos affair: Inside the case that upended the drug war in Mexico. *The New York Times*. https://www.nytimes.com/2022/12/08/magazine/mexico-general-cienfuegos.html

Goldenberg, I., Friend, A. H., Tankel, S., & Heras, N. (2016). *Remodeling partner capacity, maximizing the effectiveness of US counterterrorism security assistance*. Centre for New American Security. https://www.cnas.org/publications/reports/remodeling-partner-capacity

Gómez Céspedes, A. (1998). *The dynamics of organised crime in Mexico*. PhD dissertation. University of Cardiff.

Gómez, I. (2022, February 11). "Esta es la puta Guerra": General reconoce alianza con narcotraficantes para enfrentar disidencias de las Farc. *Cambio*. https://cambiocolombia.com/articulo/conflicto/esta-es-la-puta-guerra-general-reconoce-alianza-con-narcotraficantes-para

Gómez, G. I. (2020). Las disputas por la Jurisdicción Especial para la Paz (JEP): Una reflexión crítica sobre su sentido político y jurídico. *Vniversitas, 69*, 1–16. DOI https://doi.org/10.11144/Javeriana.vj69.djep

Gómez Maseri, S. (2001, May 19). Legislación de guerra complicaría Plan Colombia. *El Tiempo*. https://www.eltiempo.com/archivo/documento/MAM-509402

Gómez Maseri, S. (2021, March 14). "EE. UU. ve una relación directa entre la paz y erradicar narcocultivos." *El Tiempo*. https://www.eltiempo.com/mundo/eeuu-y-canada/paz-y-narcotrafico-la-estrategia-que-tiene-ee-uu-para-colombia-573223

Gómez-Suárez, A. (2015). *Genocide, geopolitics and transnational networks: Contextualising the destruction of the Unión Patriótica in Colombia*. Routledge. https://www.crcpress.com/Genocide-Geopolitics-and-Transnational-Networks-Con-textualising-the-destruction/Gomez-Suarez/p/book/9780815377429

González, S. (2014). *The making of narco-terrorism: Constructing the US war on drugs in Colombia*. MSc thesis. Leiden University. https://studenttheses.universiteitleiden.nl/access/item%3A2663483/view

González Martínez, M. A., & Betancourt Montoya, M. A. (2018). La transformación del Ejército Nacional de Colombia: Una interpretación teórica. *Revista Latinoamericana de Estudios de Seguridad, 22*, 70–84. https://doi.org/10.17141/urvio.22.2018.3093

Gordon, E. (2014). Security sector reform, statebuilding and local ownership: Securing the state or its people? *Journal of Intervention and Statebuilding, 8*, 126–148. https://doi.org/10.1080/17502977.2014.930219

Gottesdiener, L. (2021, July 13). Mexican navy offers rare apology over missing people in border town. *Reuters*. https://www.reuters.com/world/americas/mexican-navy-offers-rare-apology-over-missing-people-border-town-2021-07-13/

Gould, J. (2022, April 11). For America's security aid programs, who will run the show? *Defense News*. https://www.defensenews.com/global/the-americas/2022/04/11/for-americas-security-aid-programs-who-will-run-the-show/

Gracher, H. (2016, March 23). Elites and taxation: The case of the Colombian democratic security tax. Presented at the 66th Annual International Conference, Political Studies Association, Brighton, UK. https://www.psa.ac.uk/sites/default/files/conference/papers/2016/PSA%20Paper%20-%20Elites%20and%20taxation.pdf

Graham, L. S. (1990). *The state and policy outcomes in Latin America*. Praeger.

Graham, R. (2011, September 16). US congressman demands counterinsurgency strategy for Mexico. *InSight Crime*. http://www.insightcrime.org/news-briefs/us-congressman-demands-counterinsurgency-strategy-for-mexico

Grajales, J. (2017). Private security and paramilitarism in Colombia: Governing in the midst of violence. *Journal of Politics in Latin America, 9*, 27–48. https://doi.org/10.1177/1866802X1700900302

Gran Resumen de las Elecciones Parlimentarias 2006 (2019). https://www.colombia.com/noticias/autonoticias/2006/DetalleNoticia26786.asp

Grant, W. (2020, November 21). Salvador Cienfuegos: From "godfather" on trial to free man. *BBC News*. https://www.bbc.com/news/world-latin-america-55015207

Greene, K. F. (2015). Campaign effects since Mexico's democratization. In Domínguez, J. I., Greene, K. F., Lawson, C. H., & Moreno, A. (Eds.), *Mexico's evolving democracy: A comparative study of the 2012 elections* (pp. 128–152). Johns Hopkins University Press. https://doi.org/10.1017/S1537592716003790

Greene, K. F., & Sánchez-Talanquer, M. (2018a). Authoritarian legacies and party system stability in Mexico. In Mainwaring, S. (Ed.), *Party systems in Latin America: Institutionalization, decay, and collapse* (pp. 201–226). Cambridge University Press. https://doi.org/10.1017/9781316798553

Greene, K. F., & Sánchez-Talanquer, M. (2018b). Latin America's shifting politics: Mexico's party system under stress. *Journal of Democracy, 29*, 31–42. https://www.journalofdemocracy.org/articles/latin-americas-shifting-politics-mexicos-party-system-under-stress/

Grimm, S., & Leininger, J. (2012). Not all good things go together: Conflicting objectives in democracy promotion. *Democratization, 19*, 391–414. https://doi.org/10.1080/13510347.2012.674355

Grindle, M. S. (2009). *Going local, decentralization, democratization, and the promise of good governance*. Princeton University Press.

Groenewegen, J. (2010). Review of Paul Dragos Algica and Peter J. Boettke's challenging insitutional analysis and development: The Bloomington School. *Erasumus Journal for Philosophy and Economics, 3*, 108–113. https://citeseerx.ist.psu.edu/viewdoc/download?doi=10.1.1.192.5659&rep=rep1&type=pdf

Grugel, J. (Ed.). (2002). *Democracy without borders: Transnationalisation and conditionality in new democracies*. Routledge.

Guerrero, E. (2013). Security policy and the crisis of violence in Mexico. In Negroponte, D. V. (Ed.), *The end of nostalgia: Mexico confronts the challenges of global competition* (pp. 112–151). Brookings Institution Press.

Guerrero Rincón, A. A. (1996). El poder político local y la conformación de las elites regionales en la sociedad colonial: el caso de la gobernación de Girón en los siglos XVII y XVIII. *Historia y sociedad, 3*, 60–82. https://revistas.unal.edu.co/index.php/hisysoc/article/view/20242

Guevara Moyano, I. (2011). *Adapting, transforming, and modernizing under fire: The Mexican military 2006–11*. Strategic Studies Institute. US Army War College.

Guevara Moyano, I. (2022). *From a modernizing fighting force to national development stewards: Mexico's armed forces under AMLO*. Wilson Center and Mexico Institute. https://gbv.wilsoncenter.org/sites/default/files/media/uploads/documents/22.04.12%20-%20Guevara%20-%20Mexico%27s%20Armed%20Forces%20Under%20AMLO_0.pdf

Gurney, K. (2015, January 13). Behind Colombia's dramatic fall in kidnappings. *InSight Crime*. https://insightcrime.org/news/analysis/behind-colombia-dramatic-fall-in-kidnappings/

Gutiérrez Sanín, F. (2007). *Lo que el viento se llevó, los partidos políticos y la democracia en Colombia (1958–2006)*. Editorial Norma.

Gutiérrez Sanín, F. (2010). Instituciones y territorio: la descentralización en Colombia. In *25 años de la descentralización en Colombia*. Fundación Konrad Adenauer Stiftung (pp. 11–54). https://www.kas.de/c/document_library/get_file?uuid=46399884-9718-2b22-5e2e-f6aaaf99bdf3&groupId=287914

Gutiérrez Sanín, F., et al. (2013). The importance of political coalitions in the successful reduction of violence in Colombian cities. *Urban Studies, 50*, 3134–3151. https://www.researchgate.net/publication/275504786_The_Importance_of_Political_Coalitions_in_the_Successful_Reduction_of_Violence_in_Colombian_Cities

Gutiérrez Sanín, F., & Dávila Ladrón de Guevara, A. (2000). Paleontólogos o politólogos: ¿Qué podemos decir hoy sobre los Dinosaurios? *Revista de Estudios Sociales, 6*, 39–49. https://doi.org/10.7440/res6.2000.04

Gutiérrez Sanín, F., & Guataqui, J. C. (2009, December 9–11). The Colombian case: Peacemaking and power sharing; the National Front (1958–1974) and new constitution (1991–2002) Experiences. Presented at the Peace and Development Dissemination Conference, Washington, DC. http://web.worldbank.org/archive/website01241/WEB/IMAGES/COLOMBIA.PDF

Guzmán-Sánchez, R., & Espriu-Guerra, A. (2014). External police oversight in Mexico: Experiences, challenges, and lessons learn(ed). *Stability, International Journal of Security and Development, 3*(1). http://www.stabilityjournal.org/articles/10.5334/sta.ek/

Gwinn, J. (2022, April). Sweeter carrots and harder sticks: Rethinking US security assistance. *War on the Rocks*. https://warontherocks.com/2022/04/sweeter-carrots-and-harder-sticks-rethinking-u-s-security-assistance/

Haber, S., Klein, H. S., Maurer, N., & Middlebrook, K. J. (2008). *Mexico since 1980*. Cambridge University Press. https://www.cambridge.org/core/books/mexico-since-1980/53819855A1D1605AC697122B5D3F23A0

Hanlon, Q., & Shultz Jr., R. H. (Eds.). (2016). *Prioritizing security sector reform: A New US approach*. United States Institute of Peace.

Hanratty, D. M., & Meditz, S. W. (Eds.). (1988). *Colombia: A country study*. Library of Congress. http://countrystudies.us/colombia/

Hanson Bond, J. (2016, February 4). Plan Colombia: A geopolitical and bipartisan triumph. *The Hill*. http://thehill.com/blogs/congress-blog/foreign-policy/267969-plan-colombia-a-geopolitical-and-bipartisan-triumph

Hartlyn, J. (2008). *The politics of coalition rule in Colombia*. Cambridge University Press.

Hayek, F., von. (1948). *Individualism and the economic order*. University of Chicago Press. http://www.library.fa.ru/files/Hayek-Individualism.pdf

Heiduk, F. (Ed.). (2014). *Security sector reform in Southeast Asia: From policy to practice*. Palgrave Macmillan. http://www.palgrave.com/us/book/9781137365484

Heinle, K., Molzahn, C., & Shirk, D. A. (2015). *Drug violence in Mexico*. Justice in Mexico Project. University of San Diego. https://justiceinmexico.org/drug-violence-in-mexico-2015-special-report/

Heredia, C. (2013, October 17). To fix Washington, look to Mexico. *Christian Science Monitor*. https://www.csmonitor.com/Commentary/Common-Ground/2013/1017/To-fix-Washington-look-to-Mexico

Hermansson, H. (2019). Challenges to decentralization of disaster management in Turkey: The role of political-administrative context. *International Journal of Public Administration, 42*, 417–431. https://www.diva-portal.org/smash/get/diva2:1096422/FULLTEXT02.pdf

Hernandez, D. (2012, December 1). Calderon's war on drug cartels: A legacy of blood and tragedy. *Los Angeles Times*. https://www.latimes.com/world/la-xpm-2012-dec-01-la-fg-wn-mexico-calderon-cartels-20121130-story.html

Herrera-Lasso, M. L. (2010). Inteligencia y seguridad nacional: apuntes y reflexiones. In Alvarado, A., & Serrano, M. (Eds.), *Seguridad nacional y seguridad interior* (pp. 191–226). El Colegio de México.

Heyns, C. (2016). *Report of the special rapporteur on extrajudicial, summary or arbitrary executions in follow-up to his mission to Mexico*. United Nations. https://reliefweb.int/sites/reliefweb.int/files/resources/G1609208-1.pdf

Higgins, K. M. (2022). Plan Colombia and the US Army's 7th Special Forces Group. In Sheehan, M.A., Marquardt, E., and Collins, M. (Eds). *Routledge handbook of US counterterrorism and irregular warfare operations* (pp. 190–202). Routledge.

Hiroi, T., & Renno, L. (2014). Dimensions of legislative conflict: Coalitions, obstructionism, and lawmaking in multiparty presidential regimes. *Legislative Studies Quarterly, 34*, 357–386. https://doi.org/10.1111/lsq.12049

Historia - FICOSEC. (2018). http://ficosec.org/fideicomiso/historia/

Hobbes, T. (2012). *Leviathan*. Malcolm, N. (Ed.). Clarendon Press. (Original work published 1651).

Hofstetter, M. (2018, June 20). La historia de los tres huevitos. *La Silla Vacía*. https://lasillavacia.com/silla-llena/blogoeconomia/historia/la-historia-de-tres-huevitos-66661

Hoskin, G. (1979). Belief systems of Colombian political party activists. *Journal of Interamerican Studies and World Affairs, 21*, 481–504. https://doi.org/10.2307/165682

Hoskin, G., Masías Núñez, R., & García Sánchez, M. (2011). La decisión de voto en las elecciones presidenciales del 2002. In Botero, F. (Ed.), *Partidos y elecciones en Colombia* (pp. 385–446). Universidad de los Andes. http://www.jstor.org/stable/10.7440/j.ctt18d83jk

How the private sector helped make Tijuana safe again. (2015). *Center for International Private Enterprise*. https://www.cipe.org/blog/2015/11/12/how-the-privatesector-helped-make-tijuana-safe-again/

Human Rights Watch. (2019). Colombia: New army commanders linked to killings. https://www.hrw.org/video-photos/video/2019/02/20/327646

Human Rights Watch. (1993). *Human Rights Watch world report 1993: Colombia*. https://www.hrw.org/reports/1993/WR93/Amw-02.htm

Human Rights Watch. (2018). *World report 2018: Rights trends in Mexico*. https://www.hrw.org/world-report/2018/country-chapters/mexico

Huntington, S. P. (1968). *Political order in changing societies*. Yale University Press.

Hurst, R. L. (2002). Plan Colombia: A strategy for continued failure in America's fight against drugs. Thesis. National War College, National Defense University. https://apps.dtic.mil/sti/pdfs/ADA441716.pdf

Hylton, F. (2003). Colombia: An evil hour. *New Left Review, 23*, 51–93. https://newleftreview.org/issues/ii23/articles/forrest-hylton-colombia-an-evil-hour

Hylton, F. (2010). Plan Colombia: The measure of success. *Brown Journal of World Affairs, 17*, 99–116. https://www.jstor.org/stable/24590760/

Idler, A. (2019). *Borderland battles, violence, crime, and governance at the edges of Colombia's war*. Oxford University Press. https://10.1093/oso/9780190849146.001.0001

Igarapé Institute. (2021). Homicide monitor. https://igarape.org.br/en/apps/homicide-monitor/

Impuesto de seguridad democrática es sólo para eso: Corte Constitucional. (2003, February 27). *Caracol Radio*. https://caracol.com.co/radio/2003/02/27/nacional/1046300400_035435.html

Índice Global de la Impunidad. (2017). https://www.udlap.mx/cesij/Default.aspx

Informes Anuales. (2008). http://www.latinobarometro.org/latContents.jsp.

Ingram, M. C., & Shirk, D. A. (2012). Building institutional capacity in Mexico's criminal justice system. In Philip, G., & Berruecos, S. (Eds.), *Mexico's struggle for public security* (pp. 119–145). Palgrave Macmillan.

Instituto Nacional de Estadística y Geografía. (2011). *Encuesta nacional de victimización y percepción sobre seguridad pública 2011*. Instituto Nacional de Estadística y Geografía. http://internet.contenidos.inegi.org.mx/contenidos/Productos/prod_serv/contenidos/espanol/bvinegi/productos/metodologias/est/ENVIPE2011_Informe_operativo.pdf

Instituto Nacional de Estadística y Geografía. (2016a). *Censo nacional de gobierno, seguridad pública y sistema penitenciario estatales 2016*. Instituto Nacional de Estadística y Geografía. http://www.beta.inegi.org.mx/proyectos/censosgobierno/estatal/cngspspe/2016/

Instituto Nacional de Estadística y Geografía. (2016b). *Encuesta Nacional de victimización y percepción sobre seguridad pública 2016*. Instituto Nacional de Estadística y Geografía. http://www.beta.inegi.org.mx/contenidos/proyectos/enchogares/regulares/envipe/2016/doc/envipe2016_presentacion_nacional.pdf

IInternational Crisis Group. (2002). Crime in pieces: The effects of Mexico's "war on drugs," explained. https://www.crisisgroup.org/content/crime-pieces-effects-mexicos-%E2%80%9Cwar-drugs%E2%80%9D-explained

Invamer. (2020). *#137: Colombia, 25 años del poll*. Invamer. https://www.valoraanalitik.com/wp-content/uploads/2020/06/Resultados-Poll-137.pdf

Invamer. (2021). *#140: Colombia, enero de 2021*. Invamer. https://imgcdn.larepublica.co/cms/2021/01/27171049/Informe_022900200000_Poll-140.pdf

Isacson, A. (2007. September 25). Washington's "new war" in Colombia: The war on drugs meets the war on terror. *North Atlantic Council on Latin America*. https://nacla.org/article/washington%27s-%27new-war%27-colombia-war-drugs-meets-war-terror

Isacson, A. (2010). Colombia: Don't call it a model. Washington Office on Latin America. https://www.wola.org/2010/07/colombia-dont-call-it-a-model/

Isacson, A. (2011). *A cautionary tale: Plan Colombia's lessons for Mexico and beyond*. WOLA Report. Washington Office on Latin America. https://www.wola.org/2011/11/new-report-on-mistakes-of-plan-colombia-and-lessons-for-latin-america/

Isacson, A. (2021, October 28). A periodic reminder: Nearly half of #Colombia's security forces claimed combat killings between 2002 and 2008 may have been faked. The JEP's estimate of 6,402 "false positive" killings of civilians is 49.6% of the 12,908 combatants that the Defense Ministry's reporting claimed. *Twitter*. https://twitter.com/adam_wola/status/1453754336488603651?s=20&t=Nu8gn4Tr6oJfEj4j1C-FTQ

Isacson, A., Haugaard, L., Poe, A., Kinosian, S., & Withers, G. (2013). *Time to listen: Trends in US security assistance to Latin America and the Caribbean*. Security Assistance Monitor. https://securityassistance.org/publications/time-to-listen-trends-in-u-s-security-assistance-to-latin-america-and-the-caribbean/

ISSAT. (2015). *Mexico country profile - International Security Sector Advisory Team (ISSAT)*.

ISSAT. (2017). *Colombia SSR background note - International Security Sector Advisory Team (ISSAT)*.

Jackson, P. (2011). Security sector reform and state building. *Third World Quarterly, 32*, 1803–1822. https://doi.org/10.1080/01436597.2011.610577

Jackson, P. (2018). Introduction: Second-generation security sector reform. *Journal of Intervention and Statebuilding, 12*, 1–10. https://doi.org/10.1080/17502977.2018.1426384

Jackson, P., & Bakrania, S. (2018). Is the future of SSR non-linear? *Journal of Intervention and Statebuilding, 12*, 11–30. https://doi.org/10.1080/17502977.2018.1426548

Jayamaha, D., Brady, S., Fitzgerald, B., & Fritz, J. (2010). *Lessons learned from US government law enforcement in international operations* (pp. 45–88). US Army War College, Strategic Studies Institute.

Jenne, N., & Martínez, R. (2021). Domestic military missions in Latin America: Civil-military relations and the perpetuation of democratic deficits. *European Journal of International Security, 7*(1), 58–83. https://doi.org/10.1017/eis.2021.25

Jones, C. L. (1939). The good neighbor policy and Mexican relations. *World Affairs, 102*, 44–48. https://www.jstor.org/stable/20663217

Jones, D. R. (2001). Party polarization and legislative gridlock. *Political Research Quarterly, 54*, 125–141. https://doi.org/10.1177/106591290105400107

Jones, J. C. (2009) . US Policy and peace in Colombia: Lost in a tangle of wars. In Bouvier, V. M. (Ed.), *Colombia, building peace in a time of war* (pp. 353–370). US Institute of Peace.

Jones, M. P. (2009). Democracy in the LAC region, challenges and solutions: Political party and party system institutionalization and women's legislative representation. In Lomborg, B. (Ed.), *Latin American development priorities* (pp. 13–44). Cambridge University Press.

Jones, M. P. (Ed.). (2010). How democracy works: Political institutions, actors, and arenas in Latin American policymaking. In *Beyond the Electoral connection: The effect of political parties on the policymaking process* (pp. 19–46). Inter-American Development Bank/David Rockefeller Center for Latin American Studies, Harvard University.

Jones, N. P. (2016). *Mexico's illicit drug networks and the state reaction*. Georgetown University Press.

Jurisdicción Especial para la Paz. (2021). Caso 3: Asesinatos y desapariciones forzadas presentados como bajas en combate por agentes del Estado. https://www.jep.gov.co/especiales1/macrocasos/03.html

Kahn, C. (2013, September 28). *Mexican state's anti-corruption plan: Hire female traffic cops.* https://www.npr.org/2013/09/28/226903227/mexican-state-s-anti-corruption-plan-hire-women-traffic-cops

Karl, R. A. (2017). *Forgotten peace: Reform, violence, and the making of contemporary Colombia.* University of California Press. http://www.jstor.org/stable/10.1525/j.ctt1m3p0x8

Kaufman, R. R., & Trejo, G. (1997). Regionalism, regime transformation, and PRONASOL: The politics of the national solidarity programme in four Mexican states. *Journal of Latin American Studies, 29*, 717–745. https://www.jstor.org/stable/158357

Keane, R., & Downes, M. (2012). *Security-sector reform applied: Nine ways to move from policy to implementation.* International Peace Institute. https://www.jstor.org/stable/resrep09500

Keefe, P. R. (2012, June 17). Cocaine incorporated: How a Mexican drug cartel makes its billions. *The New York Times.* https://www.nytimes.com/2012/06/17/magazine/how-a-mexican-drug-cartel-makes-its-billions.html

Keefer, P., & Loayza, N. (Eds.). (2008). *Terrorism, economic development, and political openness.* Cambridge University Press. https://www.cambridge.org/core/books/terrorism-economic-development-and-political-openness/B85CF1E3818EC683069CD03839583E1A.

Kelly, T. K., Marquis, J. P., Thurston, C. Q., Moroney, J., & Lynch, C. (2010). *Security cooperation organizations in the country team: Options for success.* RAND Corporation. https://www.rand.org/pubs/technical_reports/TR734.html

Kenny, P., Serrano, M., & Sotomayor, A. (Eds.). (2012). *Mexico's security failure: Collapse into criminal violence.* Routledge.

Kernell, S., & Cox, G. W. (Eds.). (1991). *The politics of divided government.* Westview Press. https://trove.nla.gov.au/version/24058601

Kerr, A. (2018). Defense institution building in the US context. *Connections, 17*, 23–38. https://www.jstor.org/stable/26934688?seq=1#metadata_info_tab_contents

Kerry, J. (2016, January 30). Herald exclusive: John Kerry: Getting the endgame right in Colombia. *Miami Herald.* http://www.miamiherald.com/opinion/op-ed/article57352418.html

Kinzelbach, K., & Cole, E. (Eds.). (2007). *Monitoring and investigating the security sector: Recommendations for ombudsman institutions to promote and protect human rights for public security.* United Nations Development Programme. Geneva Centre for the Democratic Control of Armed Forces. https://gsdrc.org/document-library/monitoring-and-investigating-the-security-sector-recommendations-for-ombudsman-institutions-to-promote-and-protect-human-rights-for-public-security/

Kitroeff, N. (2021, January 18). Once a Trump-basher, Mexico's leader misses him already. *The New York Times.* https://www.nytimes.com/2021/01/18/world/americas/mexico-trump-amlo.html

Kleinfeld, R. (2016). *Fragility and security sector reform.* United States Institute of Peace. https://www.usip.org/publications/2016/09/fragility-and-security-sector-reform

Kleinfeld, R. (2018). *A savage order: How the world's deadliest countries can forge a path to security.* Pantheon.

Klesner, J. L. (2001, September 6–8). Electoral competition and the new party system in Mexico. Presented at the Annual Conference of the Latin American Studies Association, Washington, DC. http://biblioteca.clacso.edu.ar/ar/libros/lasa98/Klesner.pdf

Klesner, J. L. (2005). Electoral competition and the new party system in Mexico. *Latin American Politics and Society, 47*, 103–142. https://www.jstor.org/stable/4490405

Klesner, J. L. (2007). The July 2006 presidential and congressional elections in Mexico. *Electoral Studies, 26*, 1–6. https://www2.kenyon.edu/Depts/PSci/Fac/klesner/KlesnerES2006.pdf

Knight, A. (2010). The myth of the Mexican revolution. *Past & Present, 209*, 223–273. https://academic.oup.com/past/article/209/1/223/1536627

Knight, R. D. (2018). Strategic coalitions and agenda-setting in fragmented congresses: How the PRI sets the legislative agenda in Mexico. *Brazilian Political Science Review, 12*, 1–33. https://10.1590/1981-3821201800020001

Kocak, D., & Kode, J. (2014). Impediments to security sector reform in Thailand. In Heiduk, F. (Ed.), *Security sector reform in Southeast Asia: From policy to practice* (pp. 83–101). Palgrave Macmillan. http://www.palgrave.com/us/book/9781137365484

Kruijt, D., & Koonings, K. (2013). The military and their shadowy brothers-in-arms. In Koonings, K., & Kruijt, D. (Eds.), *Armed actors, organized violence and state failure in Latin America* (pp. 16–30). Zed Books.

Kurtenbach, S. (2018). Judicial reform – A neglected dimension of SSR in El Salvador. *Journal of Intervention and Statebuilding, 13*, 1–18. https://doi.org/10.1080/17502977.2018.1517112

Kurtz, H. A. (1995). Criminal justice centralization versus decentralization in the Republic of China. *Journal of the Oklahoma Criminal Justice Research Consortium, 2*, 90–96. https://www.scribd.com/document/473139819/Criminal-Justice-Centralization-versus-Decentralization-in-the-Republic-of-China-doc

Kyle, B. J., & Reiter, A. G. (2013). Militarized justice in new democracies: Explaining the process of military court reform in Latin America. *Law and Society Review, 47*, 375–407. https://www.jstor.org/stable/43670331

Lakhani, N., & Tirado, E. (2016, December 8). Mexico's war on drugs: What has it achieved and how is the US involved? *The Guardian*. https://www.theguardian.com/news/2016/dec/08/mexico-war-on-drugs-cost-achievements-us-billions

Lucha anticorrupción, seguridad y justicia, principales ejes de Duque. (2018, June 17). *El Tiempo*. https://www.eltiempo.com/elecciones-colombia-2018/presidenciales/lucha-anticorrupcion-seguridad-y-justicia-principales-ejes-de-duque-231964

La oposición Liberal. (2005, June 19). *El Tiempo*. https://www.eltiempo.com/archivo/documento/MAM-1956387

La paz, Sí, pero sin Víctor G. y sin canje. (1999, October 24). *El Tiempo*. http://www.eltiempo.com/archivo/documento/MAM-959451

La polémica ley. (2001, September 16). *Semana*. https://www.semana.com/nacion/articulo/la-polemica-ley/47319-3

Lalander, R. (2003). Decentralization and the party system in Venezuela. *Iberoamericana: Nordic Journal of Latin American and Caribbean Studies, 33*, 97–121. http://doi.org/10.16993/ibero.165

Lamas, L. (2015, February 10). Gobernador de Baja California rechaza Mando Único policial. *La Jornada Baja California*. http://jornadabc.mx/tijuana/10-02-2015/gobernador-de-baja-california-rechaza-mando-unico-policial

Lambertucci, C., & Guillén, B. (2020, September 25). ¿Por qué no soy guardia nacional? *El País*. https://elpais.com/mexico/2020-09-25/por-que-no-soy-guardia-nacional.html

Langston, J. (2007). Strong parties in a struggling party system: Mexico in the democratic era. In Webb, P., & White, S. (Eds.), *Party Politics in New Democracies* (ch. 9). Oxford University Press. http://www.oxfordscholarship.com/view/10.1093/acprof:oso/9780199289653.001.0001/acprof-9780199289653-chapter-9

Langston, J. (2004). Legislative recruitment in Mexico. In Siavelis, P., & Morgenstern, S. (Eds.), *Pathways to power, political recruitment and candidate selection in Latin America* (pp. 143–163). University Park: Pennsylvania State Press.

Larson, C. (2021). Mexico's navy is small, but it shouldn't be underestimated. *The National Interest*. https://nationalinterest.org/blog/reboot/mexicos-navy-small-it-shouldnt-be-underestimated-182438

Lastiri, D. (2016, October 31). All state governments in Mexico manipulate crime data: México evalúa. *El Universal*. http://www.eluniversal.com.mx/articulo/english/2016/10/31/all-state-governments-mexico-manipulate-crime-data-mexico-evalua

Latin American Public Opinion Project. (n.d.). https://www.vanderbilt.edu/lapop

La tecnología supervigilancia garantiza la seguridad de los ciudadanos. (2018). https://www.colombia.com/tecnologia/emprendimiento/la-tecnologia-supervigilancia-garantiza-la-seguridad-de-los-ciudadanos-187794

Latinobarómetro. (2017). https://www.latinobarometro.org/lat.jsp

Laurency, P. (2017). *Hybrid police work and insecurity in the Mexican federal state*. Centre for Security Governance Report No. 17. Centre for Security Governance. http://docplayer.net/180299538-Csg-papers-hybrid-police-work-and-insecurity-in-the-mexican-federal-state-patrick-laurency.html

Laverde Palma, J. D. (2022, January 8). Las pruebas que salpican a cinco oficiales del Ejército en escándalo de corrupción en la Cuarta Brigada. *El Espectador*. https://www.elespectador.com/judicial/las-pruebas-que-salpican-a-cinco-oficiales-del-ejercito-en-escandalo-de-cor rupcion-en-la-cuarta-brigada/

Lawrence, M. (2012). *Towards a nonstate security sector reform strategy*. SSR Issue Papers. Waterloo, Ontario: The Centre for International Governance Innovation. https://www.cigionline.org/static/documents/ssr_no_8_0.pdf

Leal Buitrago, F. (1989). Structural crisis and the current situation in Colombia. *Canadian Journal of Latin American and Caribbean Studies / Revue canadienne des études latino-américaines et caraïbes, 14*, 31–49. https://doi.org/10.1080/08263663.1989.10816624

Leal Buitrago, F. (1994). Defensa y seguridad nacional en Colombia, 1958–1993. In Leal Buitrago, F., & Tokatlian, J. G. (Eds.), *Orden mundial y seguridad, nuevos desafíos para Colombia y América Latina* (pp. 131–172). Tercer Mundo S. A.

Leal Buitrago, F. (2006a). *La inseguridad de la seguridad, Colombia 1958–2005*. Editorial Planeta.

Leal Buitrago, F. (2006b). La política de seguridad democrática 2002–2005. *Análisis Político, 57*, 3–30. http://www.scielo.org.co/pdf/anpol/v19n57/v19n57a01.pdf

Lee, C. (2012). The FARC and the Colombian Left: Time for a political solution? *Latin American Perspectives, 39*, 28–42. https://www.jstor.org/stable/23238966

Lee, R. W., & Thoumi, F. E. (1999). The political-criminal nexus in Colombia. *Trends in Organized Crime, 5*, 59–84

Leininger, J. (2010). "Bringing the outside in": Illustrations from Haiti and Mali for the re-conceptualization of democracy promotion. *Contemporary Politics, 16*, 63–80. https://10.1080/13569771003593888

Lemay-Hébert, N. (2013). Everyday legitimacy and international administration: Global governance and local legitimacy in Kosovo. *Journal of Intervention and Statebuilding, 7*(1), 87–104. https://doi.org/10.1080/17502977.2012.655622

León Hernández, A. I. (2011). When cooperation and intervention meet: Sovereignty in the Mexico-United States relationship. *Amsterdam Law Forum, 3*(5), 4–73. https://10.37974/ALF.202

León, J. (2016, September 29). Los temores del No: 4. El castrochavismo. *La Silla Vacía*. https://lasillavacia.com/historia/los-temores-del-no-4-el-castrochavismo-58133

Léon, J. (2021, February 25). Así llegó la JEP a la cifra de 6.402 víctimas de falsos positivos. *La Silla Vacía*. https://lasillavacia.com/asi-llego-jep-cifra-6402-victimas-falsos-positivos-80319

Lessing, B. (2017). *Making peace in drug wars: Crackdowns and cartels in Latin America*. Cambridge University Press. https://www.cambridge.org/core/books/making-peace-in-drug-wars/7D2A0D9F3E1347973813DC1AF102801F

Lettieri, M. (2018, January 30). Why are Mexico's elections likely to generate violence? *Latin America Bureau*. https://lab.org.uk/why-are-mexicos-elections-likely-to-generate-violence/

Levi, M. (1988). *Of rule and revenue*. University of California Press.

Levine, M. (2000). *Deep cover: The inside story of how DEA infighting, incompetence and subterfuge lost us the biggest battle of the drug war*. iUniverse.

Levitsky, S., Loxton, J., & Van Dyck, B. (2016). *Challenges of party-building in Latin America* (pp. 1–50). Cambridge University Press.

Ley de Seguridad y Defensa Nacional de la República de Colombia. (2001). https://dialnet.unirioja.es/descarga/articulo/174875.pdf

Libreros, J. (2001). Descentralización y orden público en Colombia. *Opera, 1*, 199–212. https://revistas.uexternado.edu.co/index.php/opera/article/view/1274

Liddy, G. (1991). *Will: The autobiography of G. Gordon Liddy*. St. Martin's Press.

Liendo, N. (2018, May 30). ¿Iván Duque o Gustavo Petro?: Dos modelos de país. *El Espectador*. https://www.elespectador.com/noticias/politica/ivan-duque-o-gustavo-petro-dos-modelos-de-pais/

Lijphart, A. (1971). Comparative politics and the comparative method. *American Political Science Review, 65*, 682–693. https://doi.org/10.2307/1955513

Lindsay-Poland, J. (2015, March 23). The Mexican military's buying binge. *North Atlantic Council on Latin America*. https://nacla.org/news/2015/03/23/mexican-military%27s-buying-binge-0

Lindsay-Poland, J. (2018). *Plan Colombia: US ally atrocities and community activism*. Duke University Press. https://doi.org/10.1215/9781478002611

Lindsay-Poland, J. (2021, March 28). Mexican police who massacred Guatemalan migrants get their guns from the US North Atlantic Council on Latin America. https://nacla.org/news/2021/03/29/mexican-police-massacre-guns-tamaulipas

Latinobarómetro. (n.d.). https://www.latinobarometro.org/lat.jsp

Linz, J. J., & Stepan, A. (1996). *Problems of democratic transition and consolidation, southern Europe, South America, and post-communist Europe*. Johns Hopkins University Press.

Litvack, J., Ahmad, J., & Bird, R. (1998). *Rethinking decentralization in developing countries*. The World Bank. https://doi.org/10.1596/0-8213-4350-5

Llorente, M. V. (2006). Demilitarization in a war zone. In Bailey, J., & Dammert, L. (Eds.), *Public security and police reform in the Americas* (pp. 111–131). University of Pittsburgh Press. https://doi.org/10.2307/j.ctt7zw885

Llorente, M. V., & McDermott, J. (2014). Colombia's Lessons for Mexico. In Arnson, C., Olson, E., & Zaino, C. (Eds.), *One goal, two struggles: Confronting crime and violence in Mexico and Colombia* (pp. 1–46). Woodrow Wilson Center Press. https://www.wilsoncenter.org/publication/one-goal-two-struggles-confronting-crime-and-violence-mexico-and-colombia-no-32

Loaeza, S. (2003). The National Action Party (PAN): From the fringes of the political system to the heart of change. In Mainwaring, S. (Ed.), *Christian democracy in Latin America: Electoral competition and regime conflicts* (pp. 196–246). Stanford University Press.

Loaeza, S. (2013). Estados Unidos y la contención del comunismo en América Latina y en México. *Foro Internacional, 53*, 5–56. https://www.redalyc.org/pdf/599/59931080001.pdf

Locke, J. (1980). *Second treatise of government*. Indianapolis: Hackett Publishing. (Original work published 1690.)

Loeza Reyes, L., & Pérez-Levesque, M. (2010). La sociedad civil frente a la militarización de la seguridad pública en México. *Nueva Sociedad, 227*, 136–152. https://nuso.org/articulo/la-sociedad-civil-frente-a-la-militarizacion-de-la-seguridad-publica-en-mexico/

Logros de la Política de Consolidación de la Seguridad Democrática. (2008). Ministerio de Defensa Nacional. https://www.mindefensa.gov.co/irj/go/km/docs/Mindefensa/Documentos/descargas/Resultados_Operacionales_2/resultadosenero-marzo.pdf

López, C. (2013). *¡Adiós a las FARC! ¿y ahora qué?, construir ciudadanía, estado y mercado para unir las tres Colombias*. Debate Editorial. https://www.crolar.org/index.php/crolar/article/view/368/pdf

López, L. (2018, September 30). Con mando único, siete de cada 10 municipios del país. *Milenio*. https://www.milenio.com/policia/con-mando-unico-siete-de-cada-10-municipios-del-pais

López Portillo, E. (2000). La policía en México: Función política y reforma. *Inseguridad pública y gobernabilidad democrática: retos para México y Estados Unidos* (pp. 3–43). Smith Richardson Foundation. https://pdba.georgetown.edu/Security/citizensecurity/mexico/evaluaciones/policia.pdf

López Portillo, E. (2002). The police in Mexico: Political functions and needed reforms. In Bailey, J., & Chabat, J. (Eds.), *Transnational crime and public security: Challenges to Mexico and the United States* (pp. 109–136). Center for US Mexican Studies, University of California-San Diego.

López Portillo, E. (2012). Accounting for the unaccountable: The police in Mexico. In Kenny, P., Serrano, M., & Sotomayor, A. (Eds.), *Mexico's security failure: Collapse into criminal violence* (pp. 107–121). Routledge.

Los escándalos que han salpicado a la Policía en la última década. (2018, February 20). *El Tiempo*. https://www.eltiempo.com/colombia/otras-ciudades/los-escandalos-en-la-policia-nacional-en-los-ultimos-anos-184988

Los muertos de Calderón. (2010, October 30). *Proceso*. https://www.proceso.com.mx/reportajes/2010/10/30/los-muertos-de-calderon-3189.html

Lowatcharin, G. (2016). *Centralized and decentralized police systems: A cross-national mixed-methods study of the effects of policing structures with lessons for Thailand*. MA thesis. University of Missouri-Columbia. https://mospace.umsystem.edu/xmlui/handle/10355/56543

Lozano Vázquez, A. (2016). *The Mérida Initiative: Perceptions, interests and security cooperation in the Mexico US relationship*. PhD dissertation. University of Miami. https://scholarship.miami.edu/discovery/fulldisplay/alma991031447471002976/01UOML_INST:ResearchRepository

Lozano Villegas, G. (2015). Historia de los partidos políticos en Colombia. *Revista Virtual Via Inveniendi et Iudicandi, 10*, 11–42. https://www.redalyc.org/pdf/5602/560258677002.pdf

Lupu, N. (2015a). *Party brands in crisis: Partinsanship, brand dilution, and the breakdown of political parties in Latin America*. Cambridge University Press. https://www.cambridge.org/core/books/party-brands-in-crisis/FF3A9C59D329AE74A5712254DF2C5BAF

Maihold, G. (2021, March 11). "Máquinas de guerra": Los menores de edad en el conflicto armado de Colombia. *Deutsche Welle*. https://www.dw.com/es/máquinas-de-guerra-los-menores-de-edad-en-el-conflicto-armado-de-colombia/a-56844094#:~:text=Las%20declaraciones%20del%20ministro%20de,métodos%20de%20combate%20utilizados%20por

Mainwaring, S. (1990). Presidentialism in Latin America. *Latin American Research Review, 25*, 157–179. https://www.jstor.org/stable/2503565

Mainwaring, S. (1999). *Rethinking party systems after the third wave: The case of Brazil*. Stanford University Press.

Mainwaring, S. (2003). Introduction: Democratic accountability in Latin America. In Mainwaring, S., & Welna, C. (Eds.), *Democratic accountability in Latin America* (pp. 3–30). Oxford University Press. https://10.1093/0199256373.001.0001

Mainwaring, S. (Ed.). (2018). *Party systems in Latin America: Institutionalization, decay, and collapse*. Cambridge University Press. https://doi.org/10.1017/9781316798553

Mainwaring, S., & Scully, T. (Eds.). (1995). *Building democratic institutions: Party systems in Latin America*. Stanford University Press.

Malestar en los cuarteles: Generales, coroneles y soldados se destapan con SEMANA y cuestionan a Gustavo Petro. (2022, January 5). *Semana*. https://www.semana.com/nacion/articulo/malestar-en-los-cuarteles-generales-coroneles-y-soldados-se-destapan-con-semana-y-cuestionan-a-gustavo-petro/202254/

Malkin, E., & Ahmed, A. (2017, October 20). US withholds $5 million in antidrug aid to Mexico as human rights rebuke. *The New York Times*. https://www.nytimes.com/2015/10/20/world/americas/us-withholds-5-million-in-antidrug-aid-to-mexico-over-human-rights.html

Manetto, F. (2019, June 6). El Senado de Colombia aprueba el ascenso del cuestionado jefe del Ejército. *El País*. https://elpais.com/internacional/2019/06/06/colombia/1559781218_699138.html

Mani, K. (2011). *Democratization and Military transformation in Argentina and Chile: Rethinking rivalry*. Lynne Reinner.

Manual fundamental del Ejército, MFE 1.0 El Ejército. (2017). Imprenta Militar del Ejército.

Manual fundamental de referencia de Ejército, MFRE 1.0 Nuestra Profesión. (2017). Imprenta Militar del Ejército.

Maoz, Z., & Somer-Topcu, Z. (2010). Political polarization and cabinet stability in multiparty systems: A social networks analysis of European parliaments, 1945–98. *British Journal of Political Science, 40*, 805–833. https://10.1017/S0007123410000220

Marcella, G. (1982). Security assistance revisited: How to win friends and not lose influence. The US *Army War College Quarterly, Parameters, 12*(1), 43–52. https://press.armywarcollege.edu/cgi/viewcontent.cgi?article=1299&context=parameters

Marczak, J., Hernández, C., & Arnson, C. J. (Eds.). (2022). *Allies: Twenty-seven bold ideas to reimagine the US-Colombia relationship*. Atlantic Council, Wilson Center. https://www.atlanticcouncil.org/category/content-series/allies-us-colombia-book/

Markovits, M. (2016, October 4). *Private security businesses boom in Mexico's drug war*. GGTN America. https://america.cgtn.com/2016/10/04/private-security-businesses-boom-in-mexicos-drug-war

Marks, T. A. (2005). La sostenibilidad del apoyo estratégico-miliar a la seguridad democrática. In Rangel, A. (Ed.), *Sostenibilidad de la seguridad democrática* (pp. 67–112). Fundación Seguridad y Democracia.

Marmolejo, L., Alvarado, N., & Muggah, R. (2016). Por qué el Plan Cuadrante ayudó a reducir los homicidios en Colombia. *Sin miedos, seguridad ciudadana*. https://blogs.iadb.org/seguridad-ciudadana/es/3022/

Martin, C. J., & Swank, D. (2012). *The Political construction of business interests*. Cambridge University Press. https://www.cambridge.org/core/books/political-construction-of-business-interests/25D26DD1004E42AA19BB9BFCC2649D4F

Martin, W. C. (2013). Cartels, corruption, carnage, and cooperation. In Payan, T., Staudt, K., & Kruszewski, Z. A. (Eds.), *A war that can't be won: Binational perspectives on the war on drugs* (2nd ed., pp. 33–64). University of Arizona Press.

Martínez Álvarez, C., & Garza Elizondo, H. (2013). La geopolítica de México y sus efectos en la seguridad nacional, 1820–2012. *Foro Internacional, 53*, 57–106. https://forointernacional.colmex.mx/index.php/fi/article/download/2146/2136/2136n

Martínez Cárdenas, E. E., Ramírez Mora, J. M., & Pico García, H. D. (2015). *25 años: Elección popular de Alcaldes*. Escuela Superior de Administración Pública. https://www.esap.edu.co/portal/index.php/Descargas/109/publicaciones-no-seriadas/1874/eleccion-de-alcaldes_28_03_16_2.pdf

Mason, A. (2001, April 10–14). Colombian state failure: The global context of eroding domestic authority. Paper presented at the Conference on Failed Sates, Florence, Italy.

Mason, A. (2003). Colombia's democratic security agenda: Public order in the security tripod. *Security Dialogue, 34*, 391–409. https://doi.org/10.1177/0967010603344002

Matanock, A. M., & García-Sánchez, M. (2017). The Colombian paradox: Peace processes, elite divisions & popular plebiscites. *Daedalus, 146*, 152–166. https://www.amacad.org/publication/colombian-paradox-peace-processes-elite-divisions-popular-plebiscites

Matisek, J., & Reno, W. (2019). Getting American security force assistance right: Political context matters. *Joint Force Quarterly, 92*, 65–73. https://ndupress.ndu.edu/Portals/68/Documents/jfq/jfq-92/jfq-92_65-73_Matisek-Reno.pdf

Matrimonios por conveniencia. (2003, July 4). *Semana*. https://www.semana.com/nacion/articulo/matrimonios-conveniencia/59156-3/

Mauceri, P. (2001). Estado, élites y contrainsurgencia: una comparación preliminar entre Colombia y Perú. *Colombia Internacional, 52*, 44–64. https://revistas.uniandes.edu.co/doi/abs/10.7440/colombiaint52.2001.02

Maullin, R. L. (1973). *Soldiers, guerrillas, and politics in Colombia*. Lexington Books.

Maxfield, S., & Schneider, B. R. (Eds.). (1997). *Business and the state in developing countries*. Cornell Studies in Political Economy. Cornell University Press.

Mazzetti, M., & Bergman, R. (2021, July 17). Israeli companies aided saudi spying despite Khashoggi killing. *The New York Times*. https://www.nytimes.com/2021/07/17/world/middleeast/israel-saudi-khashoggi-hacking-nso.html

Mazzuca, S., & Robinson, J. (2009). Political conflict and power sharing in the origins of modern Colombia. *Hispanic American Historical Review, 89*, 285–321. https://scholar.harvard.edu/files/jrobinson/files/jr_colombia.pdf

McCallister, E. B., et al. (Eds.). (2020). *Security cooperation management*. Defense Security Cooperation University.

McCormick, G. I. (2016). *The logic of compromise in Mexico: How the countryside was key to the emergence of authoritarianism*. University of North Carolina Press. http://www.jstor.org/stable/10.5149/9781469627755_mccormick

McDermott, J. (2014, May 2). The BACRIM and Their Position in Colombia's Underworld. *InSight Crime*. https://insightcrime.org/investigations/bacrim-and-their-position-in-colombia-underworld/

McDougall, A. (2009). State power and its implications for civil war Colombia. *Studies in Conflict & Terrorism, 32*, 322–345. https://doi.org/10.1080/10576100902743815

McInnis, K. J., & Lucas, N. J. (2015). What is "building partner capacity?" *Congressional Research Service*. https://sgp.fas.org/crs/natsec/R44313.pdf

Meharg, S., & Arnusch, A. (2012). *Security sector reform: A case study approach to transition and capacity building*. Lulu.

Mehta, A. (2016). Future of global security contingency fund unclear. https://www.defensenews.com/pentagon/2016/09/05/future-of-global-security-contingency-fund-unclear/

Mejía, D. (2016). Plan Colombia: An analysis of effectiveness and costs. Improving Global Drug Policy: Comparative Perspectives and UNGASS 2016. Brookings Institution. https://www.brookings.edu/wp-content/uploads/2016/07/mejia-colombia-final-2.pdf

Mejia, P. R. (2010, May 13). The gap between polls and election results: Mocku's greatest fear. *Colombia Reports*. https://colombiareports.com/polls-and-election-results-what-mockus-is-afraid-of/

Méndez, Á. (2017). *Colombian agency and the making of US foreign policy: Intervention by invitation*. Taylor & Francis.

Méndez, E. (2012, May 7). Los ataques personales opacan las propuestas en materia de seguridad. *La Jornada*. https://www.jornada.com.mx/2012/05/07/politica/002n1pol

Méndez, J. L. S. (2015, October 14). How Colombia is improving access to justice services. *Governance for Development*. http://blogs.worldbank.org/governance/how-colombia-improving-access-justice-services

Mendoza Márquez, H. E., & Montero Bagatella, J. C. (2015). Gobernanza para la gobernabilidad. La construcción de "Fuerza Civil", la nueva policía de Nuevo León. *Revista Mexicana de Análisis Político y Administración Pública, IV*: 103–128. http://www.remap.ugto.mx/index.php/remap/article/view/110

Mertens, D. M., & Wilson, A. T. (2012). *Program evaluation theory and practice: A comprehensive guide*. Guilford Press.

Mette Kjær, A., & Katusiimeh, M. (2012). Growing but not transforming: Fragmented ruling coalitions and economic developments in Uganda. DIIS Working Paper Sub-Series on Elites, Production, and Poverty. Danish Institute for International Studies. https://www.jstor.org/stable/resrep15666.1

Mexicans back military campaign against cartels. (2012). Pew Research Center, Global Attitudes and Trends. https://www.pewglobal.org/2012/06/20/mexicans-back-military-campaign-against-cartels/

Mexico: Cartels move beyond drugs, seek domination. (2010, August 4). Newsmax. https://www.newsmax.com/newsfront/lt-drug-war-mexico/2010/08/04/id/366631/

México: El plan de Peña Nieto contra el narcotráfico. (2012, December 18). BBC News Mundo. https://www.bbc.com/mundo/noticias/2012/12/121218_mexico_pena_nieto_estrategia_seguridad_narcotrafico_jg

México Unido Contra la Delincuencia. (2021). Datos abiertos sobre acciones antidrogas. https://www.mucd.org.mx/datos-abiertos-sobre-acciones-antidrogas/

México Evalúa. (2017). *Hallazgos 2016: Evaluación de la operación del sistema de justicia penal acusatorio en México.* Centro de Análisis de Políticas Públicas. http://cidac.org/wp-content/uploads/2017/06/DOCUMENTO-HALLAZGOS-2016_COMPLETO-digital.pdf

Mexico sees fentanyl seizures up 465%, denies making the drug. (2020, September 18). *AP News.* https://apnews.com/article/virus-outbreak-synthetic-opioids-opioids-mexico-archive-d52284f90b89939ff6c4b3bfa655733f

Mexico softens rules for controversial new foreign agents law. (2021, January 24). *Reuters.* https://www.reuters.com/article/us-mexico-usa-security/mexico-softens-rules-for-controversial-new-foreign-agents-law-idUSKBN29J24M

Mexico: Taxes, Pemex and Calderon's reforms. (2007, July 5). Stratfor. https://worldview.stratfor.com/article/mexico-taxes-pemex-and-calderons-reforms

Meyer, M. (2010). *Abused and afraid in Ciudad Juárez: An analysis of human rights violations by the military in Mexico.* Washington Office on Latin America. https://www.casede.org/BibliotecaCasede/wola_prodh_juarez%20_report_oct2010.pdf

Meyer, M. (2020). *One year after National Guard's creation, Mexico is far from demilitarizing public security.* Washington Office on Latin America. https://www.wola.org/sites/default/files/downloadable/Mexico/2010/WOLA_RPT_Juarez_FNL2-color.pdf

Meyer, P. J. (2019). *US strategy for engagement in Central America: Policy issues for Congress.* Congressional Research Service. https://sgp.fas.org/crs/row/R44812.pdf

Meza Rivera, F. (2014). La tromba en Chihuahua, el día en que se cayó el cielo. https://www.cronicadechihuahua.com/Cronicas-de-mi-tierra-Chihuahua,30877.html

Middlebrook, K. J. (1986). Political liberalization in an authoritarian regime: The case of Mexico. In O'Donnell, G., Schmitter, P. C., & Whitehead, L. (Eds.), *Transitions from authoritarian rule: Latin America* (pp. 123–147). Johns Hopkins University Press.

Middlebrook, K. J. (Ed.). (2001). *Party Politics and the struggle for democracy in Mexico: National and state-level analyses of the Partido Acción Nacional.* US-Mexico Contemporary Perspectives Series, 17. Center for US Mexican Studies, University of California-San Diego.

Miklaucic, M., & Pinzón, J. C. (2017). Partnership: The Colombia-US experience. In Kerr, A., & Miklaucic, M. (Eds.), *Effective, legitimate, secure, insights for defense institution building* (pp. 273–286). National Defense University. https://cco.ndu.edu/LinkClick.aspx?fileticket=9YCCggKpP6s%3D&portalid=96

Milanese, J. P. (2015). The relationships between the executive and legislative branches of power. In Bagley, B. M., & Rosen, J. D. (Eds.), *Colombia's political economy at the outset of the twenty-first century: From Uribe to Santos and beyond* (pp. 71–87). Lexington Books.

Mill, J. S. (1843 [1882]). *A system of logic, ratiocinative and inductive: Being a connected view of the principles of evidence and the methods of scientific investigation*, 8th ed. Harper and Brothers.

Miller Llana, S. (2011, May 9). Mexico's Calderón popular, despite massive protests about his drug strategy. *Christian Science Monitor.* https://www.csmonitor.com/World/Americas/2011/0509/Mexico-s-Calderon-popular-despite-massive-protests-about-his-drug-strategy

Mines, K. W. (2020). *Why nation-building matters: Political consolidation, building security forces, and economic development in failed and fragile states*. University of Nebraska Press.

Ministerio de Justicia. (2018). http://www.minjusticia.gov.co

Miroff, N. (2010, August 11). Mexico hopes $270 million in social spending will help end Juarez drug violence. *The Washington Post*. http://www.washingtonpost.com/wp-dyn/content/article/2010/08/11/AR2010081106253.html

Mitchell, P. R. (2018). *Understanding Latino history: Excavating the past, examining the present*. ABC-CLIO.

Moderan, O. (2015). *Political leadership and national ownership of security sector reform processes*. Toolkit for Security Sector Reform and Governance in West Africa. Geneva Centre for the Democratic Control of Armed Forces. https://www.dcaf.ch/tool-1-political-leadership-and-national-ownership-security-sector-reform-processes

Molinar, J., & Weldon, J. (1994). Electoral determinants and consequences of national solidarity. In Cornelius, W., Craig, A., & Fox, J. (Eds.), *Transforming state-society relations in Mexico: The national solidarity strategy* (pp. 123–141). Center for US Mexican Studies, University of California-San Diego.

Moloeznik, M. P. (2006). Public security and police reform in Mexico. In Bailey, J., & Dammert, L. (Eds.), *Public security and police reform in the Americas* (pp. 169–186). University of Pittsburgh Press.

Moloeznik, M. P. (2013). President Felipe Calderón's strategy to combat organised crime. In Payan, T., Staudt, K., & Kruszewski, Z. A. (Eds.), *A war that can't be won: Binational perspectives on the war on drugs* (2nd ed., pp. 65–92). University of Arizona Press.

Monárrez Fragoso, J. (2005). Violencia e (in)seguridad ciudadana en Ciudad Juárez. In Cervera Gómez, L. E. (Ed.), *Diagnóstico geo-socioeconómico de Ciudad Juárez y su sociedad* (pp. 273–314). Ciudad Juárez: Instituto Nacional de las Mujeres.

Moncada, E. (2016). *Cities, business, and the politics of urban violence in Latin America*. Stanford University Press.

Moncada, E. (2021). *Resisting extortion*. Cambridge University Press.

Montaña, J., & Criado, M. (2001). La ley colombiana de seguridad y defensa nacional: constitucionalidad y significación dentro del "Plan Colombia." *Jueces para la Democracia, 42*, 80–87.

Montenegro, A. (2017, August 4). Robo de celulares en el país ha crecido un 79 por ciento. *El Tiempo*. http://www.eltiempo.com/justicia/delitos/robo-de-celulares-en-colombia-ha-crecido-un-79-por-ciento-116800

Monterrey: The most advanced region in Mexico. (2019, November 24). Cities Driving Trade, GrantThornton. https://www.grantthornton.mx/en/insights/articles/cities-driving-trade/cities---chennai2/

Moreno, A. (2007). The 2006 Mexican presidential election: The economy, oil revenues, and ideology. *PS: Political Science & Politics, 40*, 15–19. https://www.jstor.org/stable/20451885

Moreno, E. (2005). Whither the Colombian two-party system? An assessment of political reforms and their limits. *Electoral Studies, 24*, 485–509. https://doi.org/10.1016/j.electstud.2004.08.001

Moreno León, C. E. (2017). Chronicle of a survival foretold: How protest behavior against armed actors influenced violence in the Colombian civil war, 1988–2005. *Latin American Politics and Society, 59*, 3–25. https://doi.org/10.1111/laps.12031

Morgan, J. (2018). Deterioration and polarization of party politics in Venezuela. In Scott Mainwaring (Ed.), *Party systems in latin america: Institutionalization, decay, and collapse* (pp. 291–325). Cambridge University Press. https://www.cambridge.org/core/books/party-systems-in-latin-america/A62FA6AE29245CAB328B2AEB45DD4D1A

Morin, R. (1990, February 9). Americans, Colombians disagree over drug War, survey says. *The Washington Post*. https://www.washingtonpost.com/archive/politics/1990/02/09/americans-colombians-disagree-over-drug-war-survey-shows/e0662b42-6d7b-4b68-814a-54131d40bc68/

Mossige, D. (2013). *Mexico's Left: The paradox of the PRD*. Lynne Rienner.

Muedano, M. (2019, May 2). Peña Nieto disminuyó estado de fuerza de la Policía Federal. *La Silla Rota*. https://lasillarota.com/nacion/pena-nieto-disminuyo-estado-de-fuerza-de-la-policia-federal-epn-policia-seguridad-delincuencia/269836

Muggah, R., & de Boer, J. (2019). *Security sector reform and citizen security: Experiences from urban Latin America in global perspective*. Ubiquity Press. https://www.jstor.org/stable/j.ctv11cvx6v

Muggah, R., & Szabo de Carvalho, I. (2014). *Changes in the neighborhood: Reviewing citizen security cooperation in Latin America*. Rio de Janeiro: Igarapé Institute. https://igarape.org.br/en/changes-in-the-neighborhood-reviewing-citizen-security-cooperation-in-latin-america/

Müller, M.-M. (2012). *Public security in the negotiated state: Policing in Latin America and beyond*. Palgrave MacMillan. https://www.palgrave.com/gp/book/9780230295414

Murillo, M. A. (2004). *Colombia and the United States: War, unrest, and destabilization*. Seven Stories Press.

Murphy, K. (1988, August 3). Mexico security agents aided murder figures, DEA official testifies. *Los Angeles Times*. https://www.latimes.com/archives/la-xpm-1988-08-03-me-6846-story.html

Myrttinen, H. (2019). *Security sector governance, security sector reform and gender*. Geneva Centre for Security Sector Governance. https://www.osce.org/files/f/documents/1/1/440834_0.pdf

Nadelmann, E. (1987). The DEA in Latin America: Dealing with institutionalized corruption. *Journal of Interamerican Studies and World Affairs, 29*, 1–39. https://doi.org/10.2307/165816

Nagle, L. E. (2002). *Plan Colombia: Reality of the Colombian crisis and implications for hemispheric security*. Strategic Studies Institute. US Army War College. https://www.jstor.org/stable/resrep11578?seq=33#metadata_info_tab_contents

Nagle, L. E. (2012). Process issues of Colombia's new accusatory system. *Southwestern Journal of Law and Trade in the Americas, 14*, 223–286. https://ssrn.com/abstract=1815643

Nagl, J. (2005). *Learning to eat soup with a knife: Counterinsurgency lessons from Malaya and Vietnam*. University of Chicago Press.

Naimark-Rowse, B. R., & Markowitz, A. (2018). *Refashioning the Federal Police Service: Mexico, 2006–2012*. Innovations for Successful Societies, Princeton University. https://successfulsocieties.princeton.edu/sites/successfulsocieties/files/Mexico%20Federal%20Police%2012_13_19.pdf

Narea, N. (2021, June 18). US investment alone won't solve Central America's migrant crisis. *Vox*. https://www.vox.com/policy-and-politics/2021/6/18/22534859/harris-investment-central-america-migrant

National Center for Health Statistics. (2022). US overdose deaths in 2021 increased half as much as in 2020—but are still up 15%. Centers for Disease Control and Prevention. https://www.cdc.gov/nchs/pressroom/nchs_press_releases/2022/202205.htm

National Defense Authorization Act for Fiscal Year 2017 (NDAA). (2016). https://www.congress.gov/114/plaws/publ328/PLAW-114publ328.pdf

Navarro, A. W. (2010). *Political intelligence and the creation of modern Mexico, 1938–1954*. Penn State University Press. http://www.psupress.org/books/titles/978-0-271-03705-9.html

Negroponte, D. V. (2013). The Mérida Initiative: A mechanism for bilateral cooperation. In Negroponte, D. V. (Ed.), *The end of nostalgia: Mexico confronts the challenges of global competition* (pp. 152–169). Brookings Institution Press. https://www.jstor.org/stable/10.7864/j.ctt4cg7r1

Negroponte, J. D. (2007). Borders and law enforcement: Remarks at the Monterrey conference dinner. US Department of State. https://2001-2009.state.gov/s/d/2007/94526.htm

Neild, R. (1999). *From national security to citizen security: Civil society and the evolution of public order debates*. International Centre for Human Rights and Democratic Development. https://www.umass.edu/legal/Benavides/Fall2005/397U/Readings%20Legal%20397U/9%20Richard%20Neild.pdf

The new face of Mexican policing. (2013, June 15). *The Economist*. https://www.economist.com/the-americas/2013/06/15/the-new-face-of-mexican-policing

Niño González, C. A. (Ed.). (2016). *Perspectivas y prospectivas de la seguridad en Colombia*. Universidad de Santo Tomás.

Nuñez, J. R. (2002). *A 21st century security architecture for the Americas: Multilateral cooperation, liberal peace, and soft power*. Strategic Studies Institute. US Army War College. https://press.armywarcollege.edu/cgi/viewcontent.cgi?article=1816&context=monographs

Ocampomi. (2021). The Mérida Initiative. US Embassy & Consulates in Mexico. https://mx.usembassy.gov/the-merida-initiative/

Ocampo, G. I. (2015). *Poderes regionales, clientelismo y estado, etnografías del poder y la política en Córdoba, Colombia*. Odecofi-CINEP.

OECD. (2010). *Security sector reform: What have we learned?* Organisation for Economic Co-operation and Development. https://www.oecd-ilibrary.org/development/the-oecd-dac-handbook-on-security-system-reform/security-system-reform-what-have-we-learned_9789264027862-11-en

OECD. (2011). *The OECD Development Assistance Committee handbook on security sector reform, supporting security and justice*. 2nd ed. Organisation for Economic Co-operation and Development. https://issat.dcaf.ch/Learn/Resource-Library/Policy-and-Research-Papers/OECD-DAC-Handbook-on-Security-Sector-Reform

Oehme, C. G. (2010). Plan Colombia: Reassessing the strategic framework. *Democracy and Security, 6*, 221–236. https://doi.org/10.1080/17419166.2010.521055

Office of National Drug Control Policy. (2016). *Strengthen International Partnerships*. The White House. https://obamawhitehouse.archives.gov/ondcp/strengthen-international-partnerships

Office of the Secretary of Defense. (2012). *Report to Congress on the Western Hemisphere Institute for Security Cooperation*. US Department of Defense.

Ojeda, M. (1976). *Alcances y límites de la política exterior de México*. El Colegio de México.

Olivares Concha, E. (2015). *Party system institutionalisation in new democracies of Latin America, Europe and Asia*. PhD dissertation University of Manchester. https://www.research.manchester.ac.uk/portal/files/54575749/FULL_TEXT.PDF

Olson, E. L. (2017, Winter). The Mérida Initiative and shared responsibility in US-Mexico security relations. *The Wilson Quarterly*. https://wilsonquarterly.com/quarterly/after-the-storm-in-u-s-mexico-relations/the-m-rida-initiative-and-shared-responsibility-in-u-s-mexico-security-relations/

Olson, E. L., & Baker, G. (2015). Violent crime plagues businesses in Mexico. Wilson Center. https://www.wilsoncenter.org/article/violent-crime-plagues-businesses-mexico

Olson, E. L. et al. (2018, May 7). Soaring homicide rates in Mexico: Understanding the crisis and proposing solutions. Event. Woodrow Wilson Center, Mexico Institute. https://www.wilsoncenter.org/event/soaring-homicide-rates-mexico-understanding-the-crisis-and-proposing-solutions

Omelicheva, M. (2017). Military aid and human rights: Assessing the impact of US security assistance programs. *Political Science Quarterly, 132*, 119–144. https://doi.org/10.1002/polq.12575

O'Neil, S. (2013). Mexico: Democratic Advances and Limitations. In Domínguez, J. I., & Shifter, M. (Eds.), *Constructing Democratic Governance in Latin America* (4th ed., pp. 255–281). Johns Hopkins University Press.

Orpozeda-Rodríguez, L. E. (2015). *Efectos del subsidio para la seguridad en los municipios (SUBSEMUN), en los ayuntamientos de Jalisco*. Master's thesis. Universidad Tecnológico y de Estudios Superiores de Occidente. https://core.ac.uk/reader/47249590

Ortega Ortiz, R. Y. (2017). *Presidential elections in Mexico: From hegemony to pluralism*. Palgrave MacMillan.

Ortiz Ayala, A. (2021). Moral licensing and impunity: Reflections on Colombian security sector narratives. Center for Latin American Studies, *UC Berkeley*. https://clasberkeley.wpcomstaging.com/2021/04/27/moral-licensing-and-impunity-reflections-on-colombian-security-sector-narratives/

Ortiz Ruiz, M. A. (2015). *La organización interna de los partidos políticos como determinante del grado de polarización del sistema partidario en Colombia (2002–2014)*. Undergraduate thesis. Universidad Colegio Mayor de Nuestra Señora del Rosario. https://repository.urosario.edu.co/bitstream/handle/10336/11331/1020786855-2015.pdf?sequence=1

Osorio Rendón, L. C. (2010). *Seguridad democrática vs. seguridad ciudadana. Un estudio de caso, Sumapaz*. Master's thesis. Pontífica Universidad Javeriana. https://repository.javeriana.edu.co/handle/10554/868

Ospina Restrepo, L. J. (2010). Seguridad ciudadana y gobernabilidad democrática de la ciudad: reflexiones a propósito de Bogotá. In *25 años de la descentralización en Colombia* (pp. 139–174). Fundación Konrad Adenauer Stiftung. https://www.kas.de/c/document_library/get_file?uuid=46399884-9718-2b22-5e2e-f6aaaf99bdf3&groupId=287914

Ostrom, E., & Whitaker, G. (1973). Does local community control of police make a difference? Some preliminary findings. *American Journal of Political Science, 17*, 48–76. https://www.jstor.org/stable/2110474

Ostrom, V., Tiebout, C. M., & Warren, R. (1961). The organization of government in metropolitan areas: A theoretical inquiry. *American Political Science Review, 55*, 831–842. https://doi.org/10.1017/S0003055400125973

Otis, J. (2014). *The FARC and Colombia's illegal drug trade*. Woodrow Wilson Center. http://fileserver.idpc.net/library/Otis_FARCDrugTrade2014-ENGLISH%20(1).pdf

Oxhorn, P. (2009). *Clientelism or empowerment? The dilemma of state decentralization for securing peace and development*. World Bank. http://web.worldbank.org/archive/website01241/WEB/IMAGES/OXHORNCL.PDF

Oxhorn, P., Tulchin, J. S., & Selee, A. (Eds.). (2004). *Decentralization, democratic governance, and civil society in comparative perspective, Africa, Asia, and Latin America*. Woodrow Wilson Center Press. https://www.wilsoncenter.org/book/decentralization-democratic-governance-and-civil-society-comparative-perspective-africa-asia

Ozer, M., & Lee, S.-H. (2009). When do firms prefer individual action to collective action in the pursuit of corporate political strategy? A new perspective on industry concentration. *Business and Politics, 11*, 1–21. https://doi.org/10.2202/1469-3569.1234

Pachico, E. (2011a, March 11). Can Tijuana's top cop clean up Juárez? *InSight Crime*. https://www.insightcrime.org/news/analysis/insight-can-tijuanas-top-cop-clean-up-juarez/

Pachico, E. (2011b, August 17). Time to privatize Colombia's prisons? *InSight Crime*. https://www.insightcrime.org/news/analysis/time-to-privatize-colombias-prisons/

Pachón Buitrago, M. (2009). Colombia 2008: éxitos, peligros y desaciertos de la política de Seguridad Democrática de la administración Uribe. *Revista de Ciencia Política, 29*, 327–353. https://doi.org/10.4067/S0718-090X2009000200005

Pachón Buitrago, M. (2020). *Seguimiento legislativo y control político al sector de seguridad y defensa en Colombia. Estudio de referencia*. DCAF. https://www.dcaf.ch/sites/default/files/publications/documents/DCAF_Estudio%20Legislativo-ONLINE_Revisado_FINAL.pdf

Padilla, J. R. (2016, March 1). Procedencia constitucional del Mando Único de Policía Estatal. *Foro Jurídico*. https://issuu.com/forojuridico/docs/fj_150_marzo_2016

Palacios, C. (2016). *Perdonar lo imperdonable*. Planeta.

Palencia Ramos, E. A. (2012). La coalición de los partidos políticos en Colombia como elemento estratégico para mantener su legitimación. *Jurídicas CUC, 8*, 91–114. https://revistascientificas.cuc.edu.co/juridicascuc/article/view/434

Palma, O. (2019, June 3–4). A model for counterinsurgency success? Balancing achievements and failures in the struggles against the Revolutionary Armed Forces of Colombia (2003–2012). Presented at the Security and Criminality in the Americas Conference, Latin American Centre, University of Oxford. https://doi.org/10.1080/1057610X.2020.1780007

Pansters, W. G. (2012). Zones of state-making: Violence, coercion, and hegemony in twentieth-century Mexico. In Pansters, W. G. (Ed.), *Violence, coercion, and hegemony in twentieth-century Mexico: The other half of the centaur* (pp. 3–42). Stanford University Press. https://10.11126/stanford/9780804781589.001.0001

Papadopoulos, Y. (2014). Accountability and multi-level governance. In Bovens, M., Goodin, R. E., & Schillemans, T. (Eds.), *The Oxford handbook of public accountability* (pp. 1–30). Oxford University Press.

Pardo García-Peña, R. (2006). Un país problema en un mundo intervencionista. In Leal Buitrago, F. (Ed.), *En la encrucijada, Colombia en el siglo XXI* (pp. 545–574). Editorial Norma.

Pardo, R. (2002, September 15). Panacea o golpe sicológico. *El Tiempo*. https://www.eltiempo.com/archivo/documento/MAM-1349273

Paredes, C. S. (2014). Federalismo y centralismo en los orígenes de la Colombia contemporánea. *História (São Paulo), 33*, 330–345. https://www.scielo.br/j/his/a/RYLczWCKhjNCWYFkgkpMwvp/?format=pdf&lang=es

Paris, R. (2001). Human security: Paradigm shift or hot air? *International Security, 26(2)*, 87–102. https://doi.org/10.1162/016228801753191141

Partlow, J. (2015, June 15). What's behind Mexico's military buying binge? *The Washington Post*. https://www.washingtonpost.com/news/worldviews/wp/2015/06/15/whats-behind-mexicos-military-buying-binge/?utm_term=.3ebe4337608e

Pastrana Arango, A. (1998). *Plan nacional de desarrollo, 1998–2002. Cambio para construir la paz*. https://colaboracion.dnp.gov.co/cdt/pnd/pastrana2_contexto_cambio.pdf

Pastrana Arango, A. (2005). *La palabra bajo fuego*. Planeta.

Patiño Villa, C. A. (2010). *Guerra y construcción del estado En Colombia, 1810–2010*. Random House.

Paterson, P. (2022). Civil-military relations: Guidelines in politically charged societies. *The US Army War College Quarterly, Parameters*. https://press.armywarcollege.edu/cgi/viewcontent.cgi?article=3126&context=parameters

Paul, C., Clarke, C. P., & Serena, C. C. (2014). *Mexico is not Colombia: Alternative historical analogies for responding to the challenge of violent drug-trafficking organizations*. RAND Corporation. https://www.jstor.org/stable/10.7249/j.ctt7zvzdn

Paul, C., et al. (2015). *A building partner capacity assessment framework, tracking inputs, outputs, outcomes, disrupters, and workarounds*. RAND Corporation. https://www.rand.org/pubs/research_reports/RR935.html

Payne, L., & Pereira, G. (2016). Corporate complicity in international human rights violations. *Annual Review of Law and Social Science, 12*, 63. https://doi.org/10.1146/annurev-lawsocsci-110615-085100

Paz, J. G. (2014). *El fenómeno actual de la seguridad privada en América Latina y su impacto sobre la seguridad pública*. INSYDE Ideas. INSYDE.

Paz, M. E. (1997). *Strategy, security, and spies: Mexico and the US as allies in World War II*. Pennsylvania State University Press.

Peace and Security Sectors. (2021). http://foreignassistance.gov/

Pearce, J. (2018). *Elites and violence in Latin America: Logics of the fragmented security state*. Violence, Security, and Peace Working Papers, Latin America and Caribbean Centre, LSE. https://doi.org/10.13140/RG.2.2.34352.92161

Pearce, J., and Velasco Montoya, J. D. (2022). Élites, poder y principios de dominación en Colombia (1991-2022: Orígenes, perfiles y recuento histórico. CAPAZ and London School of Economics. https://www.lse.ac.uk/lacc/assets/documents/PEARCE-VELASCO-ELITES-Y-PODER-EN-COLOMBIA-1991-2022.pdf

Pécaut, D. (2008). *Las FARC, ¿una guerrilla sin fin o sin fines?* Editorial Norma.

Peeler, J. A. (1976). Colombian parties and political development: A reassessment. *Journal of Interamerican Studies and World Affairs, 18*, 203–224. https://doi.org/10.2307/174775

Peña, A. (2012, July 19). Fight between Uribe and Santos splits Colombia's conservatives. *El País*. https://english.elpais.com/elpais/2012/07/19/inenglish/1342701887_912483.html

Peña González, R. (2016). La cultura de la legalidad en contextos de violencia. El fenómeno de Hagámoslo Bien en Monterrey. *Revista Mexicana de Opinión Pública, 20*, 107–128. https://doi.org/10.1016/j.rmop.2015.12.006

Perdomo, C., & Uribe Burcher, C. (2016). *Protecting politics, deterring the influence of organized crime on local democracy*. Global Initiative Against Transnational Organized Crime. https://globalinitiative.net/wp-content/uploads/2016/09/TGIATOC-IDEA-Protecting-Politics-Deterring-the-Influence-of-Organized-Crime-on-Local-Democracy-web.pdf

Pérez Coronado, A. (2021, April 13). Crónicas de una historia poco conocida. *La Silla Vacía*. https://www.lasillavacia.com/historias/historias-silla-llena/cronicas-de-una-historia-poco-conocida/

Pérez V., G. J. (2014). Plan Colombia's onset: Effects on homicides and violent deaths. *Revista de Economía del Rosario, 17*, 119–156. https://www.redalyc.org/pdf/5095/509555098001.pdf

Pérez-Liñán, A., Schmidt, N., & Vairo, D. (2019). Presidential hegemony and democratic backsliding in Latin America, 1925–2016. *Democratization, 26*, 606–625. https://doi.org/10.1080/13510347.2019.1566321

Pérez Ricart, C. A. (2017). US pressure and Mexican anti-drugs efforts from 1940 to 1980: Importing the war on drugs? In Pansters, W. G., Smith, B. T., & Watt, P. (Eds.), *Beyond the drug war in Mexico: Human rights, the public sphere, and justice* (pp. 33–52). Routledge.

Pérez Ricart, C. A. (2020). Taking the war on drugs down south: The Drug Enforcement Agency in Mexico (1973–1980). *The Social History of Alcohol and Drugs, 34*, 82–113. https://doi.org/10.1086/707645

Petraeus, D., & O'Hanlon, M. E. (2013). The success story in Colombia. Brookings Institution. https://www.brookings.edu/opinions/the-success-story-in-colombia/

Petras, J. (2000). The FARC faces the empire. *Latin American Perspectives, 27*, 134–142. https://doi.org/10.1177/0094582X0002700508

Pew Research Center. (2001). Interdiction and incarceration still top remedies. https://www.pewresearch.org/politics/2001/03/21/interdiction-and-incarceration-still-top-remedies/

Piattoni, S. (2009). Multi-level governance: A historical and conceptual analysis. *Journal of European Integration, 11*, 163–180. https://doi.org/10.1080/07036330802642755

Pickering, T. R. (2009, November 1). Anatomy of Plan Colombia. *The American Interest*. https://www.the-american-interest.com/2009/11/01/anatomy-of-plan-colombia/

Piñyero, J. L. (2001, September 6–8). Gobernabilidad democrática y Fuerzas Armadas en México con Fox. Presented at the Annual Conference of the Latin American Studies Association, Washington, DC.

Piñyero, J. L. (2010). Las Fuerzas Armadas Mexicanas en la seguridad pública y la seguridad nacional. In Alvarado, A., & Serrano, M. (Eds.), *Seguridad nacional y seguridad interior* (pp. 155–190). El Colegio de México.

Pinzón, V. G. (2015). *Cooperación y seguridad en la guerra contra las drogas, el Plan Colombia y la Iniciativa Mérida*. Instituto Unidad de Investigaciones Jurídico-Sociales "Gerardo

Molina," Universidad Nacional de Colombia. http://www.academia.edu/11973406/Cooper aci%C3%B3n_y_seguridad_en_la_guerra_contra_las_drogas_el_Plan_Colombia_y_la_I niciativa_M%C3%A9rida

Pizarro, E. (2002). *La atomización partidista en Colombia, el fenómeno de las micro-empresas electorales*. Kellogg Institute. https://kellogg.nd.edu/sites/default/files/old_files/documents/292_0.pdf

Polémica por policía municipal. (1996, July 30). *El Tiempo*. http://www.eltiempo.com/archivo/documento/MAM-419513

Popovic, N. (2008). *Security sector reform assessment: Monitoring & evaluation and gender*. Geneva Centre for the Democratic Control of Armed Forces. https://www.dcaf.ch/security-sector-reform-assessment-monitoring-evaluation-and-gender-tool-11

Porch, D. (2008). Preserving autonomy in conflict: Civil-military relations in Colombia. In Bruneau, T., & Trinkunas, H. (Eds.), *Global politics of defense reform* (pp. 127–154). Palgrave Macmillan. https://10.1057/9780230611054_6

Posada-Carbó, E. (2011). Colombia after Uribe. *Journal of Democracy, 22*, 137–151. https://www.journalofdemocracy.org/articles/latin-america-colombia-after-uribe/

Posada-Carbó, E. (2018, June 20). The most surprising aspect of Colombia's election. *Time*. http://time.com/5316992/colombia-elections-duque-political-divide/

Posner, E. A., & Vermeule, A. (2011). *The executive unbound: after the Madisonian republic*. Oxford University Press. https://www.oxfordscholarship.com/view/10.1093/acprof:osobl/9780199765331.001.0001/acprof-9780199765331

Powell, J., Faulkner, C., Dean, W., & Romano, K. (2018). Give them toys? Military allocations and regime stability in transitional democracies. *Democratization*: 1–20. https://doi.org/10.1080/13510347.2018.1450389

Powell, K. (2012). Political practice, everyday political violence, and electoral processes during the neoliberal period in Mexico. In Pansters, W. G. (Ed.), *Violence, coercion, and hegemony in twentieth-century Mexico: The other half of the centaur* (pp. 212–232). Stanford University Press.

Pradilla, A. (2021). Menos del 1% de los casos por tortura y desaparición contra el Ejército llegó a un juez entre 2015 y 2019. *Animal Político*. https://www.animalpolitico.com/2021/01/casos-tortura-desaparicion-forzada-ejercito-juez/

Presidencia de la República & Ministerio de Defensa Nacional. (2003). *Política de defensa y seguridad democrática*. República de Colombia. https://www.oas.org/csh/spanish/documentos/colombia.pdf

Presidente Uribe realizó su consejo comunal número 200, estilo de gobierno que ha provocado polémica. (2008, June 3). *El Tiempo*. https://www.eltiempo.com/archivo/documento/CMS-4232292

Preston, J. (1997, February 23). Mexico's drug czar: Busted. *The New York Times*. https://www.nytimes.com/1997/02/23/weekinreview/mexico-s-drug-czar-bust(Ed.)html

Pridham, G. (1994). The international dimension of democratisation: Theory, practice, and inter-regional comparisons. In Pridham, G., Herring, E., & Sanford, G. (Eds.), *Building democracy? The international dimension of democratisation in eastern Europe* (pp. 7–31). Leicester University Press.

Pridham, G., & Vanhanen, T. (2002). Conclusion. In Pridham, G., & Vanhanen, T. (Eds.), *Democratisation in eastern Europe* (pp. 255–263). Routledge.

Principales propuestas de Antanas Mockus. (2010, June 19). *Caracol Radio*. http://caracol.com.co/radio/2010/06/19/nacional/1276959240_315419.html

Przeworski, A., & Teune, H. (1970). *The logic of comparative social inquiry*. John Wiley & Sons.

Publicaciones Semana S. A. (2020, May 16). Operación Bastón. *Semana*. https://www.semana.com/operacion-baston-los-secretos-de-las-redes-de-corrupcion-en-el-ejercito/671835/

Putnam, K. M. (2014). *Voting behavior in violence-plagued new democracies: Crime voting in Mexico's recent presidential elections*. Master's thesis. University of Texas-Austin. https://repositories.lib.utexas.edu/handle/2152/26383

Qiblawi, T., Karadsheh, J., & Damon, A. (2020, January 6). *Iraq has voted to expel US troops. Whether they'll actually be kicked out is far from clear*. https://www.cnn.com/2020/01/06/middleeast/iraq-us-troops-explainer-intl/index.html

Quiñones, S. (2016, June). Once the world's most dangerous city, Juárez returns to life. *National Geographic*. https://www.nationalgeographic.com/magazine/2016/06/juarez-mexico-border-city-drug-cartels-murder-revival/

Rabasa, A., & Chalk, P. (2001). *Colombian labyrinth: The synergy of drugs and insurgency and its implications for regional stability*. RAND Corporation. https://www.rand.org/content/dam/rand/pubs/monograph_reports/MR1339/RAND_MR1339.pdf

Ramírez Baena, R. (2019). *La iniciativa de Mando Único Policial trastoca el pacto federal, la autonomía municipal y la democracia*. http://www.prt.org.mx/node/213

Ramírez de Rincón, M. L. (2014). Drug trafficking: A national security threat—similarities between Colombia and Mexico. In Arnson, C., Olson, E., & Zaino, C. (Eds.), *One goal, two struggles: Confronting crime and violence in Mexico and Colombia* (pp. 71–94). Woodrow Wilson Center Press. https://www.wilsoncenter.org/publication/one-goal-two-struggles-confronting-crime-and-violence-mexico-and-colombia-no-32

Ramírez Lemus, M. C., Stanton, K., & Walsh, J. (2004). Colombia: A vicious circle of drugs and war. In Youngers, C. A., & Rosin, E. (Eds.), *Drugs and democracy in Latin America: The impact of US Policy* (pp. 99–141). Lynne Rienner Publishers.

Ramírez, M. C. (2002). *Balance sobre el componente social del Plan Colombia*. Del Plan Colombia a la Iniciativa Regional Andina. Mamá Coca. http://www.mamacoca.org/separata_nov_2002/art_ramirez_balanc_%20social__plan_colombia.htm

Ramírez Verdugo, A., & Ruiz González, R. (2016). *Security strategies: Experiences of the Mexican states of Chihuahua and Nuevo León*. Hoover Institution Press. https://www.hoover.org/sites/default/files/research/docs/hoover_2016_mexicosecuritystrategies.pdf

Rampf, D., & Chavarro, D. (2014). *The 1991 Colombian National Constituent Assembly: Turning exclusion into inclusion, or a vain endeavour?* Berghof Foundation. https://berghof-foundation.org/library/the-1991-colombian-national-constituent-assembly-turning-exclusion-into-inclusion-or-a-vain-endeavour

Randall, S. (1992). *Colombia and the United States: Hegemony and interdependence*. University of Georgia Press.

Rangel, A. (2005). La sostenibilidad miliar de la seguridad. In Rangel, A. (Ed.), *Sostenibilidad de la seguridad democrática* (pp. 51–66). Fundación Seguridad y Democracia.

Rath, T. (2013). *Myths of demilitarization in postrevolutionary Mexico, 1920–1960*. University of North Carolina Press.

Rath, T. (2016). From spent cartridges to militarization: The military and the political right in modern Mexico. *Nuevo Mundo Mundos Nuevos. Colloques*. http://journals.openedition.org/nuevomundo/68869

Rath, T. (2018). Modernizing military patriarchy: Gender and state-building in postrevolutionary Mexico, 1920–1960. *Journal of Social History*. https://academic.oup.com/jsh/advance-article/doi/10.1093/jsh/shx118/4804308

Reagan, R. (1986). National Security Decision Directive 221: Narcotics and national security. https://www.hsdl.org/?abstract&did=463177

Reding, A. (1995, November 26). Mexico's new experiment: More power to states and cities. *The Los Angeles Times*. https://www.latimes.com/archives/la-xpm-1995-11-26-op-7467-story.html

Reding, A., & Whalen, C. (1993). The perfect dictatorship: Repression and one-party rule in Mexico. *Multinational Monitor, 15*. https://www.multinationalmonitor.org/hyper/issues/1993/10/mm1093_05.html

Reich, S., & Aspinwall, M. (2013). The paradox of unilateralism: Institutionalizing failure in US Mexican drug strategies. *Norteamérica, 8*, 12–39. http://www.scielo.org.mx/scielo.php?script=sci_arttext&pid=S1870-35502013000200001

Reina, E. (2022, April 21). López Obrador defiende el cierre de una unidad de la DEA: "Ese grupo estaba infiltrado por la delincuencia." *El País*. https://elpais.com/mexico/2022-04-21/lopez-obrador-defiende-el-cierre-de-una-unidad-de-la-dea-ese-grupo-estaba-infiltrado-por-la-delincuencia.html

Reitano, T., & Hunter, M. (2016). *Protecting politics, deterring the influence of organized crime on public service delivery*. Global Initiative Against Transnational Organized Crime. https://www.idea.int/sites/default/files/publications/protecting-politics-deterring-the-influence-of-organized-crime-on-public-service-delivery.pdf

Rennemo, A. (2020, January 20). Mexico's strategic confusion. *Journal of International Affairs*. https://jia.sipa.columbia.edu/online-articles/mexico%E2%80%99s-strategic-confusion

Reno, W. (1997). African weak states and commercial alliances. *African Affairs, 96*, 165–185. https://www.jstor.org/stable/723857

Restrepo, E. M. (2009). The pursuit of efficiency and the Colombian criminal justice system. In Bergman, M., & Whitehead, L. (Eds.), *Criminality, public security, and the challenge to democracy in Latin America* (pp. 176–202). University of Notre Dame Press.

Restrepo, L. A. (2006). ¿Hacia el reino de los "caudillos ilustrados"?: los gobiernos colombianos como actores políticos. In Leal Buitrago, F. (Ed.), *En la encrucijada, Colombia en el siglo XXI* (pp. 27–50). Editorial Norma.

Rettberg, A. (2003). Is peace your business? The private sector and peace talks in Colombia. *Iberoamericana, 3*, 196–201. https://doi.org/10.18441/ibam.3.2003.11.196-201

Rettberg, A. (2007). The private sector and peace in El Salvador, Guatemala, and Colombia. *Journal of Latin American Studies, 39*, 463–494. https://doi.org/10.1017/S0022216X07002817

Rettberg, A. (2009). Business and peace in Colombia: Responses, challenges, and achievements. In Bouvier, V. M. (Ed.), *Colombia, building peace in a time of war* (pp. 191–206). US Institute of Peace.

Reveron, D. S. (2010). Weak states and security assistance. *PRISM, 1*(3), 27–42. https://cco.ndu.edu/Portals/96/Documents/prism/prism_1-3/Prism_27-42_Reveron.pdf

Reyes, A. (2022, September 19). El nuevo modelo de seguridad reducirá la violencia, necesitamos más elementos en Fuerza Civil. La Política Online. https://www.lapoliticaonline.com/mexico/entrevista-mx/el-nuevo-modelo-de-seguridad-reducira-la-violencia-a-todos-nos-conviene-que-fuerza-civil-se-mas-numerosa-en-el-combate-del-crimen-organizado-4050/

Reyes-Heroles, F. (2005). Mexico's changing social and political landscape. In Crandall, R., Paz, G., & Roett, R. (Eds.), *Mexico's democracy at work, political and economic dynamics* (pp. 39–60). Lynne Rienner.

Reyna García, V. H. (2018). State of denial: Reporting and political communication in Sonora. In Pansters, W. G., Smith, B. T., & Watt, P. (Eds.), *Beyond the drug war in Mexico: Human rights, the public sphere, and justice* (pp. 111–125). Routledge.

Rhem, K. T. (2005, November 29). US helping colombian military cope with drug war's legacy. *US Department of Defense News*. https://www.globalsecurity.org/military//library/news/2005/11/mil-051129-afps05.htm

Ribando Seelke, C., & Finklea, K. (2017). *US Mexican Security Cooperation: The Merida Initiative and Beyond*. Congressional Research Service. https://sgp.fas.org/crs/row/R41349.pdf

Richani, N. (2007). Caudillos and the crisis of the Colombian State: Fragmented sovereignty, the war system and the privatisation of counterinsurgency in Colombia. *Third World Quarterly, 28*, 403–417. https://doi.org/10.1080/01436590601153937

Rincón, S., & Ángel, A. (2022). Para 2023, la Guardia Nacional no quiere tener elementos civiles, revela plan de Sedena; militares advierten falta de capacitación. *Animal Político*. https://www.animalpolitico.com/2022/05/guardia-nacional-2023-plan-sin-elementos-civiles/

Rios Contreras, V. (2012). *How government structure encourages criminal violence: The causes of Mexico's drug war*. PhD dissertation. Harvard University. http://scholar.harvard.edu/files/vrios/files/rios_phddissertation.pdf

Riesenfeld, L. (2015, February 10). Why are Mexico's cocaine seizures falling? *Insight Crime*. https://insightcrime.org/news/brief/why-are-mexico-cocaine-seizures-falling/

Rivera, Astrid. (2017, May 12). Drug use in Mexico. *El Universal*. https://www.eluniversal.com.mx/english/drug-use-mexico

Rivera Salazar, R. (2001). *Hacia un nuevo federalismo para Colombia*. Editorial La Oveja Negra.

Riveros, M. (2022, April 23). Sin comandante. *La Silla Vacía*. https://www.lasillavacia.com/la-silla-vacia/opinion/articulos-columna/sin-comandante/

Roberts, J. M., & Walser, R. (2007). *The US and Mexico: taking the "Mérida Initiative" against narco-terror*. Heritage Foundation. https://www.heritage.org/crime-and-justice/report/the-us-and-mexico-taking-the-merida-initiative-against-narco-terror

Roberts, K. M. (2014). *Changing course in Latin America: Party systems in the neoliberal era*. Cambridge University Press. https://www.cambridge.org/core/books/changing-course-in-latin-america/EA7A9EAAACBDD8A069A3ABB9FB708572

Roberts, K. M. (2016). Historical timing, political cleavages, and party-building in Latin America. In Levitsky, S., et al. (Eds.), *Challenges of party-building in Latin America* (pp. 51–75). Cambridge University Press.

Rochlin, J. F. (2007). *Social forces and the revolution in military affairs: The cases of Colombia and Mexico*. Palgrave Macmillan.

Rodríguez Bucio, L. (2021, April 21). Versión estenográfica de la conferencia de prensa matutina del presidente Andrés Manuel López Obrador. https://presidente.gob.mx/21-04-21-version-estenografica-de-la-conferencia-de-prensa-matutina-del-presidente-andres-manuel-lopez-obrador/

Rodríguez, G. P. (2014). Álvaro Uribe y Juan Manuel Santos: ¿una misma derecha? *Nueva Sociedad, 254*, 84–99. https://www.liderazgos-sxxi.com.ar/bibliografia/rodriguez.pdfRodríguez Hernández, S. M. (2005). La influencia de los Estados Unidos en el Ejército Colombiano, 1951–1959. La Carreta Editores.

Rodríguez, N. (2013, June 22). Las cifras del secuestro y sus lecturas. *El Espectador*. https://www.elespectador.com/colombia/mas-regiones/las-cifras-del-secuestro-y-sus-lecturas-article-429463/

Rodríguez Pinzón, E. (2016). Discurso, representaciones y significados del conflicto armado en Colombia: un análisis prospectivo. In Niño González, C. A. (Ed.), *Perspectivas y prospectivas de la seguridad en Colombia* (pp. 15–31). Universidad de Santo Tomás.

Rodríguez Raga, J. C. (2011). Voto preferente y cohesión partidista. Entre el voto personal y el voto de partido. In Botero, F. (Ed.), *Partidos y elecciones en Colombia* (pp. 447–476). Universidad de los Andes. http://www.jstor.org/stable/10.7440/j.ctt18d83jk

Rodríguez Sumano, A. (2007). Mexico's insecurity in North America. *Homeland Security Affairs Journal*, Suppl. no. 1, 1–14. https://www.hsaj.org/articles/139

Rodríguez, V. (1993). The politics of decentralization in Mexico: From Municipio Libre to Solidaridad. *Bulletin of Latin American Research, 12*, 133–145. https://doi.org/10.2307/3338144

Rodríguez, V. (1997). *Decentralization in Mexico: From Reforma Municipal to Solidaridad to Nuevo Federalismo*. Westview Press.

Rodríguez-Franco, D. (2016). Internal wars, taxation, and state building. *American Sociological Review, 81*, 190–213. http://asr.sagepub.com/cgi/content/abstract/81/1/190

Rohter, L. (1999, December 5). Armed forces in Colombia hoping to get fighting fit. *The New York Times*. https://www.nytimes.com/1999/12/05/world/armed-forces-in-colombia-hoping-to-get-fighting-fit.html

Rojas Betancourth, D. (2005). *Balance crítico de la Unidad de Derechos Humanos y DIH de la Fiscalía General de La Nación*. Centro de Estudios Derecho, Justicia y Sociedad (DJS). https://www.dejusticia.org/wp-content/uploads/2017/04/fi_name_recurso_27.pdf

Rojas, D. M. (2015). *El Plan Colombia, la intervención de Estados Unidos en el conflicto armado colombiano (1998–2012)*. Penguin Random House.

Rojas Guevara, P. J. (2017). Doctrina Damasco: Eje articulador de la segunda gran reforma del Ejército Nacional de Colombia. *Revista Científica General José María Córdova, 15*(19), 95–119. https://revistacientificaesmic.com/index.php/esmic/article/view/78/372

Rojas, O. E., & Benavides, F. L. (2017). *Ejecuciones extrajudiciales en Colombia, 2002–2010, obediencia ciega en campos de batalla ficticios*. Universidad de Santo Tomás

Roland, G., & Zapata, J. G. (2000). Colombia's Electoral and party system: Proposals for reforms. In Alesina, A. (Ed.), *Institutional reforms in Colombia*. MIT Press. https://eml.berkeley.edu/~groland/pubs/columbia.pdf

Romero, H. (2012, May 25). Mexico presidential front-runner vows to cut violence: Critics call plan a deal with cartels. *National Post*. https://nationalpost.com/news/world/mexico-presidential-front-runner-vows-to-put-an-end-to-gruesome-violence

Romero, J. E. (2004). El Plan Colombia: Nueva definición de sujetos hegemónicos en Latinoamérica y su impacto sobre el proceso venezolano. *Revista de Ciencias Sociales, 10*, 51–69

Romero, M. (2000). Changing identities and contested settings: Regional elites and the paramilitaries in Colombia. *International Journal of Politics, Culture, and Society, 14*, 51–69. https://www.jstor.org/stable/20020064

Ronfeldt, D. (1975). *The Mexican army and political order since 1940*. RAND Corporation. https://www.rand.org/pubs/papers/P5089-1.html

Ronfeldt, D. (1988). *Whither elite cohesion in Mexico: A comment*. RAND Corporation. https://www.rand.org/pubs/papers/P7509.html

Roosevelt, T. (1904). *Annual message to Congress*. December 6, 1904, Washington, DC. https://millercenter.org/the-presidency/presidential-speeches/december-6-1904-fourth-annual-message

Rosen, J. D. (2014). *The losing war: Plan Colombia and beyond*. State University of New York Press.

Rosen, L. W., & Ribando Seelke, C. (2020). *Trends in Mexican opioid trafficking and implications for US-Mexico Security Cooperation*. Congressional Research Service. https://sgp.fas.org/crs/row/IF10400.pdf

Rosenberg, T. (1992). *Children of Cain: Violence and the violent in Latin America*. Penguin Random House. https://www.jstor.org/stable/45290199?seq=1#metadata_info_tab_contents

Ross, P. (2015, September 23). *The pre-trial services experience in Mexico. Penal Reform International*. https://www.penalreform.org/blog/the-pre-trial-services-experience-in-mexico/

Ross, T., & Dalton, M. (2020, January). A roadmap for better choices from security partners. *War on the Rocks*. https://warontherocks.com/2020/01/a-roadmap-for-better-choices-from-security-partners/

Rozental, A. (2013). Mexico and the United States: Where are we and where should we be? In Negroponte, D. V. (Ed.), *The end of nostalgia: Mexico confronts the challenges of global competition* (pp. 170–188). Brookings Institution Press.

Ruiz, J. C. (2016, February 29). La Policía Nacional: ¿por qué es tan difícil reformarla? *Razón Pública*. https://razonpublica.com/la-policia-nacional-por-que-es-tan-dificil-reformarla

Ruiz Pérez, A. (2011). Los factores internos de la política exterior mexicana: los sexenios de Carlos Salinas y Vicente Fox. *Foro Internacional, 51*, 304–335. https://www.jstor.org/stable/23035040

Ruiz Vásquez, J. C. (2004a). La encrucijada de la seguridad ciudadana en América Latina: Entre la tentación autoritaria y la participación comunitaria. In Cardona C., et al. (Ed.), *Encrucijadas de la seguridad en Europa y las Américas* (pp. 123–146). CEPI-Universidad del Rosario. https://www.urosario.edu.co/urosario_files/PortalUrosario/c9/c919a37d-16ba-401e-bbf5-7f6084996e41.pdf

Ruiz Vásquez, J. C. (2013). Colombian police under fire: Image, corruption and controls. *Policing: An International Journal, 36*, 399–420. https://www.emerald.com/insight/content/doi/10.1108/13639511311329769/full/html

Ruiz Vásquez, J. C., Illera Correal, O., & Manrique Zuluaga, V. (2006). *La tenue línea de la tranquilidad, estudio comparado sobre seguridad ciudadana y policía*. Universidad del Rosario.

Run through the jungle: Colombia's JUNGLA commandos. (2018, November 22). *Small Wars Journal*. https://smallwarsjournal.com/blog/run-through-the-jungle-colombia%E2%80%99s-jungla-commandos

Ryan, J. J. (2004). Decentralization and democratic instability: The case of Costa Rica. *Public Administration Review, 64*, 81–91. https://www.jstor.org/stable/3542628

Sabet, D. M. (2011). Police reform in Mexico: Advances and persistent obstacles. In Olson, E. L., Selee, A., & Shirk, D. (Eds.), *Shared responsibility* (pp. 247–269). Woodrow Wilson Center Press. https://www.wilsoncenter.org/sites/default/files/media/documents/publication/Chapter%208-Police%20Reform%20in%20Mexico%2C%20Advances%20and%20PErsistent%20Obstacles.pdf

Sabet, D. M. (2012). *Police reform in Mexico: Informal politics and the challenge of institutional change*. Stanford University Press. http://www.sup.org/books/title/?id=21512

Sabet, D. M. (2013). The role of citizens and civil society in Mexico's security crisis. In Payan, T., Staudt, K., & Kruszewski, Z. A. (Eds.), *A war that can't be won: Binational perspectives on the war on drugs*. 2nd ed. University of Arizona Press (pp. 239–257). https://www.jstor.org/stable/j.ctt16xwbq2

Salazar, H. (2011, March 24). Desmovilizaciones en Colombia: polémica por las cifras. *BBC News Mundo*. https://www.bbc.co.uk/mundo/noticias/2011/03/110324_colombia_paramilitares_desmovilizados_en

Salazar, H. (2013). *Fuerza Civil, la fuerza de todos*. Gobierno del Estado de Nuevo León.

Salazar, N. (2013). *Political economy of tax reforms: The case of Colombia*. Update on the Americas. Woodrow Wilson Center. https://www.wilsoncenter.org/sites/default/files/media/documents/publication/SalazarTaxReformColombia.pdf

Saldaña, I. (2018, May 29). Businessmen urge the government to fight insecurity in Mexico. *El Universal*. https://www.eluniversal.com.mx/english/businessmen-urge-govermnent-fight-insecurity-mexico/

Sánchez Lara, G. R. (2017). *Seguridad nacional en México y sus problemas estructurales*. Fundación Universidad de las Américas. https://www.casede.org/index.php/biblioteca-casede-2-0/autores-casede/gerardo-rodriguez-sanchez-lara/548-seguridad-nacional-en-mexico-y-sus-problemas-estructurales

Sánchez León, N. C., et al. (2018). *Cuentas claras, el papel de la Comisión de la Verdad en la develación de la responsabilidad de empresas en el conflicto armado colombiano*. Dejusticia. https://www.dejusticia.org/wp-content/uploads/2018/02/Cuentas-Claras.pdf

Sanchez, O. (2006). Tax system reform in Latin America: Domestic and international causes. *Review of International Political Economy, 13*, 772–801. https://www.jstor.org/stable/25124102

Santa Cruz, A. (2013). La política exterior de Felipe Calderón hacia América del Norte: crisis interna y redefinición de fronteras. *Foro Internacional, 53*, 537–571. https://www.jstor.org/stable/23608715

Santader, J., et al. (2012). *El proceso de formación de agenda de la política pública de Seguridad Democrática*. Universidad de los Andes.

Santaeulalia, I. (2014, January 24). El General Naranjo deja México para regresar a Colombia. *El País*. https://elpais.com/internacional/2014/01/24/actualidad/1390602323_372282.html

Santín del Río, L. (2004). Decentralization and democratic governance in Mexico. In Tulchin, J. S., & Selee, A. (Eds.), *Decentralization and democratic governance in Latin America* (pp. 167–186). Woodrow Wilson Center Press.

Santos, J. M. (2009). *Jaque al terror, los años horribles de las FARC*. Editorial Planeta.

Sartori, G. (1976). *Parties and party systems: A framework for analysis*. Cambridge University Press.

Schaefer, A. G., Bahney, B., & Riley, K. J. (2009). *Security in Mexico: Implications for US policy options*. Implications for US Policy Options. RAND Corporation. http://www.jstor.org/stable/10.7249/mg876rc.10

Schedler, A. (2015). *En la niebla de la guerra, los ciudadanos ante la violencia criminal organizada*. Investigación e Ideas. Centro de Investigación y Docencia Económicas. https://doi.org/10.14201/rlop.22326

Scheina, R. L. (2003). *Latin America's wars Volume II: The age of the professional soldier, 1900–2001*. Brassey's.

Schemo, D. J. (1997, October 25). US is to help army in Colombia fight drugs but skeptics abound. *The New York Times*. https://www.nytimes.com/1997/10/25/world/us-is-to-help-army-in-colombia-fight-drugs-but-skeptics-abound.html

Schiavon, J. A. (2006). The central-local division of power in the Americas and renewed Mexican federalism: Old institutions, new political realities. *International Journal of Constitutional Law, 4*, 392–410. https://academic.oup.com/icon/article/4/2/392/722129

Schmitt, E., & Ahmed, A. (2016, May 26). En México, la letalidad desproporcionada de sus fuerzas armadas genera preocupación. *The New York Times*. https://www.nytimes.com/es/2016/05/26/la-letalidad-desproporcionada-de-las-fuerzas-armadas-genera-preocupacion-en-mexico/

Schnabel, A. (2010). Ideal requirements versus real environments in SSR. In Born, D. H., & Schnabel, A. (Eds.), *Security sector reform in challenging environments* (pp. 3–36). Lit Verlag. https://www.dcaf.ch/sites/default/files/publications/documents/YEARBOOK_2009.pdf

Schröder, U. C. (2010). *Measuring security sector governance: A guide to relevant indicators*. Occasional Paper no. 10. Geneva Centre for the Democratic Control of Armed Forces. https://www.dcaf.ch/sites/default/files/publications/documents/OP_20_SCHROEDER_FORM.pdf

Schröder, U. C., & Chappuis, F. (2014). New perspectives on security sector reform: The role of local agency and domestic politics. *International Peacekeeping, 21*, 133–148. https://doi.org/10.1080/13533312.2014.910401

Schröder, U. C., Chappuis, F., & Kocak, D. (2014). Security sector reform and the emergence of hybrid security governance. *International Peacekeeping, 21*, 214–230. https://doi.org/10.1080/13533312.2014.910405

Schultze-Kraft, M., Valencia, O., & Alzate, D. (2016). Decentralisation, security consolidation and territorial peacebuilding: Is Colombia about to close the loop? *Third World Thematics: A TWQ Journal, 1*, 837–856. https://www.researchgate.net/publication/320107659_Decentralisation_security_consolidation_and_territorial_peacebuilding_is_Colombia_about_to_close_the_loop

Secretaría de Gobernación. (2008). *Acuerdo Nacional por la Seguridad, la Justicia y la Legalidad*. http://www.oas.org/juridico/spanish/mesicic3_mex_anexo24.pdf

Secretaría de la Defensa Nacional. (n.d.). https://www.gob.mx/sedena.

Sedra, M. (2010). Towards second generation security sector reform. In Sedra, M. (Ed.), *The future of security sector reform* (pp. 16–27). Centre for International Governance Innovation. https://www.cigionline.org/sites/default/files/the_future_of_security_sector_reform.pdf

Sedra, M. (2016). *Security sector reform in conflict-affected countries: The evolution of a model.* Taylor & Francis.

Selee, A. (2011). *Decentralization, democratization, and informal power in Mexico.* Penn State University Press. http://www.jstor.org/stable/10.5325/j.ctt7v376

Selim, G. M. (2015). *The international dimensions of democratization in Egypt: The limits of externally induced change.* Cham: Springer.

Semple, K., & Villegas, P. (2019, December 11). Arrest of top crime fighter stuns Mexico, where corruption is all too routine. *The New York Times.* https://www.nytimes.com/2019/12/11/world/americas/mexico-garcia-luna-indictment.html

Serafino, N. M., Beittel, J. S., & Ploch Blanchard, L. (2014). *"Leahy Law" human rights provisions and security assistance, issue overview*, 7-5700. Congressional Research Service. https://sgp.fas.org/crs/row/R43361.pdf

Serrano, M. (2018). Mexico: A humanitarian crisis in the making. In Pansters, W. G., Smith, B. T., & Watt, P. (Eds.), *Beyond the drug war in Mexico: Human rights, the public sphere, and justice* (pp. 53–75). Routledge.

Shah, A., Thompson, T., & Zou, H. (2001). *The impact of decentralization on service delivery, corruption, fiscal management and growth in developing and emerging market economics: A Synthesis of empirical evidence.* China Economics and Management Academy, Central University of Finance and Economics. https://www.ifo.de/DocDL/dicereport104-forum2.pdf

Shaw, C. M. (2007). The United States: Rhetoric and reality. In Legler, T., Lean, S. F., and Boniface, D. S. (Eds.), *Promoting democracy in the Americas* (pp. 63–84). Johns Hopkins University Press.

Sheridan, M. B. (2019, May 9). Mexico's president just says no to US cash to fight drugs and crime. *The Washington Post.* https://www.washingtonpost.com/world/the_americas/amlo-rejects-us-crime-fighting-funds-injecting-new-uncertainty-into-relationship/2019/05/09/f9e368fe-71c2-11e9-9331-30bc5836f48e_story.html

Sheridan, M. B. (2020, December 17). As Mexico's security deteriorates, the power of the military grows. *The Washington Post.* https://www.washingtonpost.com/graphics/2020/world/mexico-losing-control/mexico-military-security-drug-war/

Sheridan, M. B. (2021, October 8). Facing stunning levels of deaths, US and Mexico revamp strained security cooperation. *The Washington Post.* https://www.washingtonpost.com/world/2021/10/08/mexico-merida-initiative-security/

Sheridan, M. B., & Sief, K. (2021, July 29). Mexico declares $3 billion US security deal "dead," seeks revamp. *The Washington Post.* https://www.washingtonpost.com/world/2021/07/29/mexico-merida-initiative-violence/

Shiffman, J., Health, B., & Oré, D. (2021, March 30). Exclusive: US investigations into cartels paralyzed by standoff with Mexico. Reuters. https://www.reuters.com/world/americas/exclusive-us-investigations-into-cartels-paralyzed-by-standoff-with-mexico-2021-03-30/

Shifter, M. (2009). Seven steps to improve US-Colombia relations. In Lowenthal, A. F., Piccone, T. J., & Whitehead, L. (Eds.), *The Obama administration and the Americas: Agenda for change* (pp. 69–82). Brookings Institution Press.

Shifter, M. (2014, May 28). The brawl in Bogota. *Foreign Policy.* https://foreignpolicy.com/2014/05/28/the-brawl-in-bogota/

Shirk, D. A. (2010). *Justice reform in Mexico: Change and challenges in the judicial sector.* Mexico Institute, Woodrow Wilson International Center for Scholars and Trans-Border Institute, University of San Diego. https://www.wilsoncenter.org/sites/default/files/media/

documents/publication/Chapter%207-%20Justice%20Reform%20in%20Mexico%2C%20Change%20and%20Challenges%20in%20the%20Judicial%20Sector.pdf

Shirk, D. A., Wood, D., & Olson, E. L. (Eds.). (2014). *Building resilient communities in Mexico: Civic responses to crime and violence*. Woodrow Wilson Center Press. https://www.wilsoncenter.org/sites/default/files/media/documents/publication/Resilient_Communities_Mexico.pdf

Siaroff, A. (2000). The fate of centrifugal democracies: Lessons from consociational theory and system performance. *Comparative Politics, 32*, 317–332. https://doi.org/10.2307/422369

Sieff, K. (2018, May 20). 36 Local candidates have been assassinated in Mexico. And the election is still 2 months away. *The Washington Post*. https://www.washingtonpost.com/news/worldviews/wp/2018/05/20/36-local-candidates-have-been-assassinated-in-mexico-and-the-election-is-still-2-months-away/

Signoret, P. (2018). *A force for change: Nuevo León bolsters police capacity in tough times, 2011–2015*. Woodrow Wilson School of Public & International Affairs, Princeton University. https://successfulsocieties.princeton.edu/sites/successfulsocieties/files/PS_Mexico_NL%20Police_Formatted_ToU_962018.pdf

Simpson, E. M. (2004, August 20–21). Explaining variation in Colombian counterinsurgency strategy, 1982–2002. Presented at the conference on the Techniques of Violence in Civil War, International Peace Research Institute, Oslo.

Smith, K. E. (2001). Western actors and the promotion of democracy. In Zielonka, J., & Pravda, A. (Eds.), *Democratic consolidation in eastern Europe Volume 2: International and transnational factors*. Oxford Studies in Democratization (pp. 31–57). Oxford University Press. https://10.1093/019924409X.001.0001

Smith, P. H. (2015). *Labyrinths of power: Political recruitment in twentieth-century Mexico*. Princeton University Press. https://press.princeton.edu/titles/1947.html

Smith, P. H., & Ziegler, M. R. (2008). Liberal and illiberal democracy in Latin America. *Latin American Politics and Society, 50*, 31–57. https://doi.org/10.1111/j.1548-2456.2008.00003.x

Smith, S. (2003). National security liberalism and American foreign policy. In Cox, M., Ikenberry, G. J., & Inoguchi, T. (Eds.), *American democracy promotion, impulses, strategies, and impacts* (pp. 85–10). Oxford University Press. https://doi.org/10.1093/0199240973.001.0001

Smith, T. (1989). Literature review: Decentralization and community. *The British Journal of Social Work, 19*, 137–148.

Smoke, P. (2015). Accountability and service delivery in decentralising environments: Understanding context and strategically advancing reform. In *A governance practitioner's notebook: Alternative ideas and approaches* (pp. 219–232). Organisation for Economic Co-operation and Development. https://www.oecd.org/dac/accountable-effective-institutions/Governance%20Notebook.pdf

Sotomayor, A. C. (2014). *The myth of the democratic peacekeeper: Civil-military relations and the United Nations*. Johns Hopkins University Press.

Sowell, K. H. (2019). The stalled effort to expel US troops from Iraq. https://carnegieendowment.org/sada/78782

Stanley, W. (1996). *The protection racket state, elite politics, military extortion, and civil war in El Salvador*. Temple University Press.

Steele, A. (2017). *Democracy and displacement in Colombia's civil war*. Cornell University Press. http://www.jstor.org/stable/10.7591/j.ctt1w1vjrv

Stevenson, M. (2020, July 17). Mexico puts military in charge of customs operations. *AP News*. https://apnews.com/article/109267cdfae007002429bdeae1cb4f8c

Stevenson, M. (2022, October 2). Report: Mexico continued to use spyware against activists. *AP News*. https://apnews.com/article/technology-mexico-caribbean-hacking-cd4e4a0bcf13705072af19b2d97bbf63

Stewart, F. (2004, January 25). Working Paper 3: Development and Security. Presented at the Security and Development Workshop, Fifth Annual Global Development Conference, Queen Elizabeth House, University of Oxford. https://assets.publishing.service.gov.uk/media/57a08cd140f0b652dd00159c/wp3.pdf

Stokes, D. (2004). *America's other war*. University of Chicago Press.

Stone, H. (2011, May 9). The war of words over Colombia's conflict. *InSight Crime*. https://www.insightcrime.org/news/analysis/the-war-of-words-over-colombias-conflict/

Stone, H. (2016, August 6). Colombia elites and organized crime: Introduction. *InSight Crime*. https://www.insightcrime.org/investigations/colombia-elites-and-organized-crime-intro duction/

Suárez-Enríquez, X., & Indacochea, Ú. (2018). *A fiscalía that works in Mexico: The path to ending pacts of impunity and corruption in the country*. Washington Office on Latin America; Due Process of Law Foundation. https://www.wola.org/wp-content/uploads/2018/04/Rep ort-Fiscalia-ENG.pdf

Swedish contact group security sector reform assessment framework. (2010). Folke Bernadotte Academy.

Symmes Cobb, J., & Murphy, H. (2018, May 24). Colombia's election could mark the start of a resurgent left. Reuters. https://www.reuters.com/article/us-colombia-election-left-analysis/colombias-election-could-mark-the-start-of-a-resurgent-left-idUSKCN1IP2TY

Tamayo Gaviria, N. (2018, November 24). La marca de Uribe en la imagen de Duque. *El Espectador*. https://www.elespectador.com/noticias/politica/la-marca-de-uribe-en-la-ima gen-de-duque/

Tate, W. (1999). *Negotiations update: From paramilitary offensives to earthquakes, Colombia peace talks face a number of obstacles*. Colombia Bulletin.

Tate, W. (2011). Human rights law and military aid delivery: A case study of the Leahy Law. *PoLAR: Political and Legal Anthropology Review, 34*, 337–354. https://www.jstor.org/stable/24497312

Tate, W. (2013). Congressional "drug warriors" and US Policy towards Colombia. *Critique of Anthropology, 33*, 214–233. https://doi.org/10.1177/0308275X13478225

Tate, W. (2015). *Drugs, thugs, and diplomats: US policymaking in Colombia*. Stanford University Press.

Testimonio, Sobreviviente de la masacre a estudiantes de Ayotzinapa. (2014, September 28). *Vanguardia/MX*. https://vanguardia.com.mxtestimoniosobrevivientedelamasacrea estudiantesdeayotzinapa-2185573.html

Thies, C. (2005). War, rivalry, and state building in Latin America. *American Journal of Political Science, 49*, 451–465. https://doi.org/10.2307/3647725

Tickner, A. B. (2014). Colombia, the United States, and security cooperation by proxy. *Insight Crime*. https://insightcrime.org/news/analysis/colombia-the-united-states-and-security-cooperation-by-proxy/

Tickner, A. B., & Morales Callejas, M. (2015). Narrating success: Colombian security expertise and foreign policy. In Bagley, B. M., & Rosen, J. D. (Eds.), *Colombia's political economy at the outset of the twenty-first century: From Uribe to Santos and beyond* (pp. 241–262). Lexington Books.

Tilly, C. (1975). *The formation of national states in western Europe*. Princeton University Press.

Tófalo, I. (2006). Overt and hidden accomplices: Transnational corporation's range of complicity for human rights violations. In de Schutter, O. (Ed.), *Transnational corporations and human rights* (pp. 335–358). Hart Publishing. https://www.bloomsburyprofessional.com/uk/transnational-corporations-and-human-rights-9781847312761/

Tokatlian, J. G. (1994). Seguridad y drogas: una cruzada militar prohibicionista. In Leal Buitrago, F., & Tokatlian, J. G. (Eds.), *Orden mundial y seguridad, nuevos desafíos para Colombia y América Latina* (pp. 77–117). Tercer Mundo S.A.

Tokatlian, J. G. (2000). La mirada de la política exterior de Colombia ante un nuevo milenio: ¿ceguera, miopía o estrabismo? *Colombia International, 48.* https://doi.org/10.7440/colombiaint48.2000.01

Tomesani, A. M. (2018). International Assistance and security sector reform in Latin America: A profile of donors, recipients and programs. *Brazilian Political Science Review, 12.* http://www.scielo.br/scielo.php?script=sci_abstract&pid=S1981-38212018000200202&lng=en&nrm=iso&tlng=en

Toro, M. C. (1999). The internationalization of police: The DEA in Mexico. *Journal of American History, 86,* 623–640.

Torres Velasco, J. (1994). La ciudadanía pacta con su policía: el proceso de modernización de la Policía Nacional de Colombia. In Leal Buitrago, F., & Tokatlian, J. G. (Eds.), *Orden mundial y seguridad, nuevos desafíos para Colombia y Améri* (pp. 173–205). Alfaomega.

Traficant, J. (1998). *On Mexico.* US House of Representatives, February 12. Congressional Record. https://www.congress.gov/117/crec/2021/02/12/CREC-2021-02-12.pdf

Trejo, G., & Ley, S. (2016). Federalismo, drogas y violencia: Por qué el conflicto partidista intergubernamental estimuló la violencia del narcotráfico en México. *Política y gobierno, 23,* 11–56. http://www.politicaygobierno.cide.edu/index.php/pyg/article/view/741

Trejo, G., & Ley, S. (2020) *Votes, drugs, and violence: The political logic of criminal wars in Mexico.* Cambridge University Press. https://doi.org/10.1017/9781108894807

Tsebelis, G. (2002). *Veto players: How political institutions work.* Princeton University Press. http://www.jstor.org/stable/j.ctt7rvv7

Turati, M. (2014, December 23). Ayotzinapa: las huellas de los militares. *Proceso.* https://www.proceso.com.mx/reportajes/2014/12/23/ayotzinapa-las-huellas-de-los-militares-141397.html

Turbiville Jr., G. H. (2010). *US military engagement with Mexico: Uneasy past and challenging future.* Joint Special Operations University. https://www.globalsecurity.org/military/library/report/2010/1003_jsou-report-10-2.pdf

Ucko, D. H. (2013). Beyond clear-hold-build: Rethinking Local-level counterinsurgency after Afghanistan. *Contemporary Security Policy, 34,* 526–551.

United Nations Development Programme (UNDP). (1994). *Human development report.* Oxford University Press.

United Nations Office on Drugs and Crime (UNODC). (2005). *Colombia: Coca cultivation survey.* https://www.unodc.org/pdf/andean/Part3_Colombia.pdf

United Nations Office on Drugs and Crime (UNODC). (2012). *Colombia: Coca cultivation survey 2011.* https://www.unodc.org/documents/crop-monitoring/Colombia/Colombia_Coca_cultivation_survey_2011.pdf

United Nations Office on Drugs and Crime (UNODC). (2016). *Cultivation of opium poppy in selected countries, 1998–2015 (hectares).* https://www.unodc.org/doc/wdr2016/8.2_Opium_cultivation_production_eradication.pdf

United Nations Office on Drugs and Crime (UNODC). (2019). *E4J university module series: Crime prevention and criminal justice.* https://www.unodc.org/e4j/en/crime-prevention-criminal-justice/module-11/key-issues/4--collecting-victim-data.html

Un texto para comprender qué es la "Comunidad del Anillo." (2016, February 17). *El Espectador.* https://www.elespectador.com/noticias/judicial/un-texto-comprender-comunidad-del-anillo-articulo-617228

Uribe y el Partido Conservador. (2006). https://www.portafolio.co/economia/finanzas/uribe-partido-conservador-316392

US Agency for International Development (USAID), US Department of Defense, and US Department of State. (2009). *Security sector reform.* Washington, DC. https://www.usaid.gov/sites/default/files/documents/1866/State-USAID-Defense%20Policy%20Statement%20on%20Security%20Sector%20Reform.pdf

US Agency for International Development (USAID). (2018a). Our work: Mexico. https://www.usaid.gov/mexico/our-work

US Agency for International Development (USAID). (2018b) . USAID in Mexico: Rule of Law. https://2017-2020.usaid.gov/mexico/rule-of-law

US Army Intelligence and Threat Analysis Center. (1993). *Army country profile—Mexico, part I*. Department of the Army.

US Department of Defense. (2001). *Quadrennial defense review report*. Government Printing Office. https://www.comw.org/qdr/qdr2001.pdf

US Department of State. (1995). *The Mexican army: Still passive, isolated, and above the fray?* National Security Archive. https://nsarchive2.gwu.edu/NSAEBB/NSAEBB120/doc2.pdf

US Department of State. (1998). *Colombian military: Our judiciary requires no reform, and police have responsibility for combatting paramilitaries*. National Security Archive. https://nsarchive.gwu.edu/document/25107-document-5-colombian-military-our-judiciary-requires-no-reform-and-police-have

US Department of State. (2009). Mérida Initiative: Myth vs. fact. https://2009-2017.state.gov/j/inl/rls/fs/122395.htm

US Department of State. (2016a). *Plan Colombia*. https://bogota.usembassy.gov/plancolombia.html

US Department of State. (2016b). Congressional budget justification for foreign operations. https://2009-2017.state.gov/documents/organization/236395.pdf

US Department of State. (2018a). Justice sector reform. https://co.usembassy.gov/embassy/bogota/sections-offices/department-of-justice/justice-sector/

US Department of State. (2018b). The Merida Initiative. https://mx.usembassy.gov/our-relationship/policy-history/the-merida-initiative/

US Department of State. (2020). United States strategy to prevent conflict and promote stability. https://www.state.gov/wp-content/uploads/2021/01/2020-US-Strategy-to-Prevent-Conflict-and-Promote-Stabilit-508c-508.pdf

US Department of State. (2021a). Colombia 2021 human rights report. https://www.state.gov/wp-content/uploads/2022/03/313615_COLOMBIA-2021-HUMAN-RIGHTS-REPORT.pdf

US Department of State. (2021b). FY2021 Congressional budget justification: Department of State, foreign operations, and related programs. https://www.usaid.gov/sites/default/files/documents/9276/FY-2021-CBJ-Final.pdf

US Drug Enforcement Administration. (2009). Department of Justice announces resources for fight against Mexican drug cartels. https://www.dea.gov/sites/default/files/divisions/hq/2009/pr032409p.html

US General Accounting Office (GAO). (1998). *US Counternarcotics efforts in Colombia face continuing challenges*. https://www.gao.gov/assets/t-nsiad-98-103.pdf

US Government Accountability Office (GAO). (2008). Plan Colombia: Drug reduction goals were not fully met, but security has improved; US agencies need more detailed plans for reducing assistance. https://www.gao.gov/products/GAO-09-71

US Government Accountability Office (GAO). (2010). Mérida Initiative: The United States has provided counternarcotics and anticrime support but needs better performance measures. https://www.gao.gov/assets/310/307523.pdf

US Government Accountability Office (GAO). (2019a). *US assistance to Mexico: State and USAID allocate over $700 million to support criminal justice, border security, and related efforts from fiscal year 2014 through 2018*. GAO-19-647. https://www.gao.gov/assets/gao-19-647.pdf

US Government Accountability Office (GAO). (2019b). Colombia: US counternarcotics assistance achieved some positive results, but state needs to review the overall US approach. GAO-19-106. https://www.gao.gov/assets/gao-19-106.pdf

US House of Representatives. (2002). *Committee on Appropriations. Foreign Operations, Export Financing, and Related Programs Appropriations Bill, 2003, (to Accompany H. R. 5410) together with additional views. 107 H. Rpt. 663.* https://www.congress.gov/107/crpt/hrpt663/CRPT-107hrpt663.pdf

US House of Representatives. (2007). *The Merida Initiative, Assessing plans to step up our security cooperation with Mexico and Central America.* Committee on Foreign Affairs, 110th Congr., 1st sess. Serial No. 110-135. https://www.gpo.gov/fdsys/pkg/CHRG-110hhrg38938/pdf/CHRG-110hhrg38938.pdf

US Office on Colombia. (2012). *Impunity: Has implementation of the accusatory legal system been an effective response to the fight against impunity in Colombia?* https://reliefweb.int/sites/reliefweb.int/files/resources/Impunity-in-Colombia-web-FINAL.pdf

Vaicius, I., & Isacson, A. (2000). Policy brief: "Plan Colombia," *The debate in Congress, 2000.* http://ciponline.org/colombia/1200ipr.htm

Vaicius, I. (2003). *CIP memorandum:* The US military presence in Colombia. *Center for International Policy.* http://ciponline.org/colombia/03022601.htm

Valadés, D. (2017, June 6). El federalismo como coartada. *Reforma.* https://vlex.com.mx/vid/diego-valades-federalismo-coartada-682117633

Valdés Castellanos, G. (2013). *Historia del narcotráfico en México.* Aguilar. https://www.redalyc.org/pdf/633/63332506008.pdf

Vale, T., & Guerrero Vásquez, J. (2010). *¿Todos contra el PRI?, la construcción de las alianzas en 2010.* Miguel Ángel Porrúa.

Valencia, N., & Chacon, A. (2013, January 5). *Juárez shedding violent image, statistics show.* https://www.cnn.com/2013/01/05/world/americas/mexico-juarez-killings-drop/index.html

Valencia Tovar, A. (2006). Tulio Bayer y la primera guerrilla comunista. In Martínez Osorio, G. (Ed.), *Hablan los generales. Grandes batallas del conflicto colombiano, relatos de los protagonistas* (pp. 37–72). Editorial Norma.

Vallejo, K., Tapias, J., and Arroyave, I. (2018). Trends of rural/urban homicide in Colombia, 1992–2015: Internal armed conflict and hints for postconflict. *BioMed Research International, 2018,* Article ID 6120909. https://www.hindawi.com/journals/bmri/2018/6120909/

Valora Analitik. (2022). Ocupación hotelera en Colombia llegaría al 55 % en 2022. https://www.valoraanalitik.com/2022/01/13/ocupacion-hotelera-colombia-llegaria-55-2022/

Vargas, A. (2002). *Las Fuerzas Armadas en el conflicto colombiano, antecedentes y perspectivas.* Intermedio Editores.

Vargas-Alzate, L. F., Sosa Noreña, S., & Galeano David, H. J. (2015). The evolution of security in South America: A comparative analysis between Colombia and Brazil. *Revista de Relaciones Internacionales, Estrategia y Seguridad, 10,* 41–63. https://doi.org/10.18359/ries.350

Veillette, C. (2005). *Plan Colombia: A progress report.* Congressional Research Service. https://sgp.fas.org/crs/row/RL32774.pdf

Velásquez, R., & Schiavon, J. (2009). La Iniciativa Mérida en el marco de la política exterior de Felipe Calderón y la relación México-EU. In Velásquez, R., & Prado, J. P. (Eds.), *La Iniciativa Mérida, ¿nuevo paradigma de cooperación entre México y Estados Unidos en seguridad?* (pp. 77–98). Universidad Nacional Autónoma de México; Benemérita Universidad Autónoma de Puebla.

Verbitsky, H., & Bohoslavsky, J. P. (2015). *The economic accomplices to the Argentine dictatorship: Outstanding debts*. Cambridge University Press. https://www.amazon.com/Economic-Accomplices-Argentine-Dictatorship-Outstanding/dp/1107114195

Verduzco Chávez, B. (2012). La geopolítica de la protección contra el crimen en México: El debate sobre la propuesta del mando único policial. *Espacialidades*, *2*(1). https://www.redalyc.org/pdf/4195/419545117001.pdf.

Vicenteño, D. (2021, March 15). Sedena registra baja en quejas por Derechos Humanos. *Excelsior*. https://www.excelsior.com.mx/nacional/sedena-registra-baja-en-quejas-por-derechos-humanos/1437963

Víctimas de falsos positivos reiteran su rechazo a la declaración del general Mario Montoya ante la JEP. (2021, April 6). *Infobae*. https://www.infobae.com/america/colombia/2021/04/06/victimas-de-falsos-positivos-reiteran-su-rechazo-a-la-declaracion-del-general-mario-montoya-ante-la-jep/

Villegas, M. G., & Revelo, E. (2010). *Estado alterado clientelismo, mafias y debilidad institucional en Colombia*. Centro de Estudios de Derecho, Justicia y Sociedad.

Villegas, P. (2018a, September 1). As violence soared in Mexico, this town bucked the trend. *The New York Times*. https://www.nytimes.com/2018/09/01/world/americas/mexico-violence-police.html

Villegas, P. (2018b, April 30). Missing Mexican's Case Shines Light on Military's Role in Drug War. *The New York Times*. https://www.nytimes.com/2018/04/30/world/americas/mexico-missing-military-drugs.html

Vision of Humanity. (2017). *Mexico peace index*. https://www.visionofhumanity.org/resources/mexico-peace-index-2017/mexico-peace-index-2017_english/

Vision of Humanity. (2022). *Mexico peace index 2022: Identifying and measuring the factors that drive peace*. https://www.visionofhumanity.org/wp-content/uploads/2022/05/ENG-MPI-2022-web.pdf

Vivanco, J. M. (2020, August 3). Militarization: Colossal error. Human Rights Watch. https://www.hrw.org/news/2020/08/03/militarization-colossal-error.

Votel, J. L., & Keravuori, E. R. (2018). The by-with-through operational approach. *Joint Forces Quarterly 89*, 40–47. https://ndupress.ndu.edu/Portals/68/Documents/jfq/jfq-89/jfq-89_40-47_Votel-Keravuori.pdf?ver=2018-04-11-125441-307

Waldman, T. (2014). The use of statebuilding research in fragile contexts: Evidence from British policymaking in Afghanistan, Nepal and Sierra Leone. *Journal of Intervention and Statebuilding*, *8*, 149–172. https://doi.org/10.1080/17502977.2014.885675

Walton, J. (1977). *Elites and economic development comparative studies on the political economy of Latin American Cities*. University of Texas Press. https://utpress.utexas.edu/books/waleli

Washington Office on Latin America. (2019). Mexico Must Consider Human Rights Concerns when Implementing Its New National Guard. https://www.wola.org/2019/02/mexico-national-guard-human-rights-accountability/

Watt, P., & Zepeda, R. (2012). *Drug war Mexico: politics, neoliberalism, and violence in the new narcoeconomy*. Zed Books.

Webb, M. (2005). *Rethinking democratic consolidation and civilian control of the military: Toward a conceptual model*. PhD dissertation. University of California-Riverside.

Weber, M. (2004). *The vocation lectures: "Science as a Vocation" and "Politics as a Vocation."* Edited by Owen, D., & Strong, T. B. Hackett Publishing.

Weintraub, S. (2010). *Unequal partners; The United States and Mexico*. University of Pittsburgh Press. http://www.jstor.org/stable/j.ctt5hjsrw

Welfling, M. B. (1973). Political institutionalization: Comparative analyses of African party systems. *Sage Professional Papers in Comparative Politics*, *4*, 1–63.

The White House. (2002). The national security strategy of the United States of America. https://2009-2017.state.gov/documents/organization/63562.pdf

The White House. (2013). The United States and Colombia –Strategic partners. Fact Sheet. *National Archives and Records Administration*. https://obamawhitehouse.archives.gov/the-press-office/2013/12/03/fact-sheet-united-states-and-colombia-strategic-partners

Whitehead, L. (Ed.) (2001). *The International dimensions of democratisation: Europe and the Americas*. Oxford University Press. https://doi.org/10.1093/0199243751.001.0001

Whitehead, L. (2002). *Democratisation: Theory and experience*. Oxford University Press. https://doi.org/10.1093/0199253285.001.0001

Whitlock, C. (2021, August 15). Afghan security forces' wholesale collapse was years in the making. *The Washington Post*. https://www.washingtonpost.com/investigations/afghan-security-forces-capabilities/2021/08/15/052a45e2-fdc7-11eb-a664-4f6de3e17ff0_story.html

Why Mexico's murder rate is soaring. (2018, May 9). *The Economist*. https://www.economist.com/the-economist-explains/2018/05/09/why-mexicos-murder-rate-is-soaring

Wilkinson, D. (2018, October 17). Mexico: Violence and opacity. *Human Rights Watch*. https://www.hrw.org/news/2018/10/17/mexico-violence-and-opacity

Wilkinson, T. (1994, June 20). Economist elected Colombian president. *Los Angeles Times*. https://www.latimes.com/archives/la-xpm-1994-06-20-mn-6364-story.html

Willis, E., Garman, C. da C. B., & Haggard, S. (1999). The Politics of decentralization in Latin America. *Latin American Research Review, 34*, 7–56. https://www.jstor.org/stable/2503925

Wilson, S., & Kornblut, A. E. (2010, September 9). Obama, Clinton split on drug war parallels. *The Washington Post*. http://www.washingtonpost.com/wp-dyn/content/article/2010/09/09/AR2010090906741.html

Wolf, S., & Celorio Morayta, G. (2011). La guerra de México contra el narcotráfico y la Iniciativa Mérida: piedras angulares en la búsqueda de legitimidad. *Foro Internacional, 51*, 669–714. https://www.jstor.org/stable/41337568

Wolff, J. (2015). Power in democracy promotion. *Alternatives, 40*, 219–236. https://www.jstor.org/stable/24569459

Wollack, K. (2010). Retaining the human dimension. In Diamond, L., Plattner, M. F., & Costopoulos, P. J. (Eds.), *Debates on democratization* (pp. 108–113). Johns Hopkins University Press. https://www.journalofdemocracy.org/articles/debating-the-transition-paradigm-retaining-the-human-dimension/

Woody, C. (2017, May 16). The US and Mexico may be teaming up to fight heroin, but the enemy is tougher than it appears. *Business Insider*. https://uk.businessinsider.com/us-mexico-heroin-eradication-efforts-problems-2017-5?op=1

Woody, C. (2019, September 10). 400 murders a aay: 10 reasons why Latin America is the world's most violent place. *Business Insider*. https://www.businessinsider.com/latin-america-is-the-worlds-most-violent-region-crime-2019-9#high-impunity-4

World Bank Open Data. (2018). https://data.worldbank.org/

World Economic Outlook Database. (2016). http://www.imf.org/external/pubs/ft/weo/2016/02/weodata/index.aspx

Wynne, P. L. (2016, February 4). El Plan Colombia: "un éxito militar y un fracaso social." *Sputnik Mundo*. https://mundo.sputniknews.com/entrevistas/201602041056401732-plan-colombia-exito-militar-fracaso-social/

Yardımcı-Geyikçi, Ş. (2013, March 11–16). The stability in the quality of party systems and its impact on the level of democracy. Presented at Party System Dynamics: New Tools for the Study of Party System Change and Party Transformation, 41st ECPR Joint Sessions of Workshops, Mainz, Germany. https://ecpr.eu/Events/Event/PaperDetails/1163

Yashar, D. J. (2018) *Homicidal ecologies: Illicit economies and complicit states in Latin America*. Cambridge University Press.

Yayboke, E., et al. (2021). A policymaker's guide to the Global Fragility Act. *Center for International and Strategic Studies*. https://www.csis.org/analysis/policymakers-guide-global-fragility-act

Zabyelina, Y., & K. L. Thachuk (2022). The private sector and organized crime: Criminal entrepreneurship, illicit profits, and private sector security governance. Routledge.

Zamora, S., & Cossío, J. R. (2006). Mexican constitutionalism after presidencialismo. *International Journal of Constitutional Law, 4*, 411–437. https://doi.org/10.1093/icon/mol011

Zepeda, M. (2013, January). 30 días con la estrategia de seguridad de EPN. *Animal Político*. https://www.animalpolitico.com/2013/01/30-dias-con-la-estrategia-de-seguridad-de-epn/

Zepeda, R., & Rosen, J. D. (Eds.). (2014). *Cooperation and drug policies in the Americas*. Lexington Books.

Reading Bibliography

A model to end Washington gridlock: Mexico. (2013, March 24). *Christian Science Monitor*. https://www.csmonitor.com/Commentary/the-monitors-view/2013/0324/A-model-to-end-Washington-gridlock-Mexico

Abad, H. (2014, February 13). Colombia's warning for Mexico. *The New York Times*. https://www.nytimes.com/2014/02/14/opinion/mexicos-illusory-cure.html

Abrahamsen, R. (2016). Exporting decentered security governance: The tensions of security sector reform. *Global Crime, 17*, 281–295. https://doi.org/10.1080/17440572.2016.1197507

Abrahamsen, R., & Williams, M. C. (2006). Security sector reform: Bringing the private in. *Conflict, Security & Development, 6*, 1–23. https://doi.org/10.1080/14678800600590595

Acosta, H. (2017). *El hombre clave*. Aguilar.

Acusan a policías de élite de Coahuila de ser un cartel. (2021, December 9). *El Universal*. https://www.eluniversal.com.mx/nacion/acusan-policias-de-elite-de-coahuila-de-ser-un-cartel

Aguayo, S. (2009) . *Mexico, living with insecurity*. openDemocracy

Aguayo, S., & Treviño Rangel, J. (2010). El 'piadoso olvido': el PAN y los derechos humanos. In Alvarado, A., & Serrano, M. (Eds.), *Seguridad nacional y seguridad interior* (pp. 331–361). El Colegio de México. https://2010.colmex.mx/16tomos/XV.pdf

Adcock, R., & Collier, D. (2001). Measurement validity: A shared standard for qualitative and quantitative research. *American Political Science Review, 95*, 529–546. https://www.jstor.org/stable/3118231

Agüero, F. (1995). *Soldiers, civilians, and democracy: post-Franco Spain in comparative perspective*. Johns Hopkins University Press.

Alemán, A. J. (2017). Transforming defense in Guatemala. In Kerr, A., & Miklaucic, M. (Eds.), *Effective, legitimate, secure, insights for defense institution building* (pp. 287–308). National Defense University. https://cco.ndu.edu/LinkClick.aspx?fileticket=9YCCggKpP6s%3D&portalid=96

Alesina, A., Carrasquilla, A., & Steiner, R. (2000). *Decentralization in Colombia*. Inter-American Development Bank. https://publications.iadb.org/publications/english/document/Decentralization-in-Colombia.pdf

Almond, G. A., & Verba, S. (1989 [1963]). *The civic culture: Political attitudes and democracy in five nations*. Princeton University Press.

Alsema, A. (2015). Is Colombia's justice system really that rotten? Yes, it is. *Colombia Reports*. https://colombiareports.com/is-colombias-justice-system-really-that-rotten-yes-it-is/

Alvarez, M., Cheibub. J., Limongi, F. & Przeworski, A. (1996). Classifying political regimes. *Studies in Comparative International Development, 31*, 3–36. https://link.springer.com/content/pdf/10.1007/BF02719326.pdf

Álvarez Icaza Longorio, E. (2021). La izquierda abandonó sus luchas democratizadoras para someterse a la militarización impulsada por @lopezobrador_, sin importar que incluso haya militares violadores de #DDHH cómo el titular de @Birmex vinculado con la desaparición de personas. @CorteIDH. Twitter, 5:06 p.m. December 14, 2021. https://twitter.com/emilioalvarezi/status/1470877845513715721?s=11

Análisis integral del secuestro en México: Cómo entender esta problemática. (2014). Observatorio Nacional Ciudadano: Seguridad, Justicia y Legalidad. https://lasillarota.com/opinion/columnas/2014/8/26/analisis-integral-del-secuestro-en-mexico-326048.html

Anderson Hudson, L., & Ozanne, J. L. (1988). Alternative ways of seeking knowledge in consumer research. *Journal of Consumer Research, 14*, 508–521. https://www.jstor.org/stable/2489157

Ángel, A. (2016, June 15). La iniciativa de Mando Único cumple 6 años sin aprobarse; mil 200 municipios siguen sin policías. *Animal Político*. https://mirror.animalpolitico.com/2016/06/mando-unico-cumple-6-anos-sin-aprobarse-mil-200-municipios-siguen-sin-policias/

Ángel, A. (2021). Crece letalidad con AMLO: Ejército mata en enfrentamientos a más de 500 civiles y lesiona a 89. *Animal Político*. https://mirror.animalpolitico.com/2021/11/crece-letalidad-ejercito-amlo-enfrentamientos/

Ángel, A. (2022, January 13). 2021 cerró con casi 10 mil personas más en prisión; van tres años con crecimiento de población penitenciaria. *Animal Politico*. https://headtopics.com/mx/2021-cerr-con-casi-10-mil-personas-m-s-en-prisi-n-van-tres-anos-con-crecimiento-de-poblaci-n-penit-23401991

Angelo, P., & Munde, L. (2021, March 25). More than a few good women: Improving hemispheric security by advancing gender inclusivity in military and police. Council on Foreign Relations. https://www.cfr.org/article/more-few-good-women-improving-hemispheric-security-advancing-gender-inclusivity-military

Archibold, R. C. (2014a, August 22). Elite Mexican Police corps targets persistent violence, but many are skeptical. *The New York Times*. https://www.nytimes.com/2014/08/23/world/americas/familiar-flaws-seen-in-mexicos-new-elite-police-force.html

Archibold, R. C. (2014b, November 27). Mexican leader, facing protests, promises to overhaul policing. *The New York Times*. https://www.nytimes.com/2014/11/28/world/americas/mexican-leader-facing-protests-promises-to-overhaul-policing.html

Arellano Trejo, E. (2008). *Instituciones policiales: Situación y perspectivas de reforma*. Centro de Estudios Sociales y de Opinión Pública. http://insyde.org.mx/pdf/seguridad-y-reforma/arellano-instituciones-policiales.pdf

Arias, E. D. (2017). *Criminal enterprises and governance in Latin America and the Caribbean*. Cambridge University Press. /core/books/criminal-enterprises-and-governance-in-latin-america-and-the-caribbean/9010435C967FFD890CF1EDF40D99DA47

Army Doctrine Reference Publication (ADRP) 3-07 Stability Operations. (2011). Headquarters, Department of the Army. https://www.jcs.mil/Portals/36/Documents/Doctrine/pubs/jp3_07.pdf

Arrarás, A., et al. (2017). *Culture and national security in the Americas*. Fonseca, B., & Gamarra, E. A. (Eds.). Lexington Books.

Asch, B. J., Burger, N., & Fu, M. M. (2011). *Mitigating corruption in government security forces: The role of institutions, incentives, and personnel management in Mexico*. RAND Corporation. http://www.jstor.org/stable/10.7249/tr906rc.11

Atkins, G. P. (2018). *Latin America in the international political system*. Taylor & Francis. https://doi.org/10.4324/9780429036781

Atkinson, R., & Flint, J. (2001). Accessing hidden and hard-to-reach populations: Snowball research strategies. *Social Research Update*, 33. https://sru.soc.surrey.ac.uk/SRU33.html

Bagley, B. M., & Rosen, J. D. (Eds.). (2015). *Colombia's political economy at the outset of the twenty-first century: From Uribe to Santos and Beyond*. Lexington Books.

Bailey, J. (2008, November 21–22). Plan Colombia and the Mérida Initiative: Policy Twins or distant cousins? Presented at Politique Etrangere Dans Les Ameriques: Entre Crises et Alliances, Institut des Ameriques, VI Colloque International. Paris. http://www.univ-paris3.fr/politique-etrangere-dans-les-ameriques-entre-crises-et-alliances--9431.kjsp

Bakrania, S. (2014). *Topic guide: Safety, security and justice*. GSDRC Applied Knowledge Services. http://www.gsdrc.org/docs/open/gsdrc_ssj.pdf

Ball, N. (2005a). Promoting security sector reform in fragile states. Bureau for Policy and program Coordination paper, 11. US Agency for International Development.

Ball, N. (2005b). Strengthening democratic governance of the security sector in conflict-affected countries. *Public Administration and Development, 25*, 25–38. https://gsdrc.org/document-library/strengthening-democratic-governance-of-the-security-sector-in-conflict-affected-countries/

Ball, N. (2014). Strengthening democratic governance in the security sector: The unfulfilled promise of security sector reform. In Kaldor, M., & Rangelov, I. (Eds.), *The handbook of global security policy* (pp. 282–299). Wiley-Blackwell.

Baranyi, S. (2019). Second-generation SSR or unending violence in Haiti? *Stability, International Journal of Security and Development, 8*, 1–19. http://doi.org/10.5334/sta.668

Bargent, J. (2016, November 29). Report slams Colombia's failure to control prison overcrowding. *InSight Crime*. https://www.insightcrime.org/news/brief/report-slams-colombia-failure-to-control-prison-overcrowding/

Bargent, J. (2017, July 27). Sentenced without conviction: A tale of pre-trial detention in Colombia. *InSight Crime*. https://www.insightcrime.org/news/analysis/sentenced-without-conviction-pretrial-detention-colombia/

Barkawi, T., & Laffey, M. (2006). The postcolonial moment in security studies. *Review of International Studies, 32*, 329–352. https://doi.org/10.1017/S0260210506007054

Barrenechea, R., Gibson, E. L., & Terrie, L. (2016). Historical institutionalism and democratisation studies. In Fioretos, O., Falleti, T. G., & Sheingate, A. (Eds.), *The Oxford handbook of historical institutionalism* (ch. 11). Oxford University Press. http://www.oxfordhandbooks.com/view/10.1093/oxfordhb/9780199662814.001.0001/oxfordhb-9780199662814-e-11#oxfordhb-9780199662814-e-11-div2-58

Bartman, J. M. (2018). Murder in Mexico: Are journalists victims of general violence or targeted political violence? *Democratization, 25*, 1–21. https://doi.org/10.1080/13510347.2018.1445998

Bates, R. H. (2009). From case studies to social science: A strategy for political research. In Boix, C., & Stokes, S. C. (Eds.), *The Oxford handbook of comparative politics* (ch. 7). Oxford University Press. http://www.oxfordhandbooks.com/view/10.1093/oxfordhb/9780199566020.001.0001/oxfordhb-9780199566020-e-7

Baumgartner, F. R., et al. (2009). *Lobbying and policy change*. University of Chicago Press. https://www.press.uchicago.edu/ucp/books/book/chicago/L/bo6683614.html

Beate, J. (2012). Rethinking democracy promotion. *Review of International Studies, 38*, 685–705.

Bedoya Lima, J. (2008). *En las trincheras del Plan Patriota*. Intermedio Editores.

Beer, C. C. (2003). *Electoral competition and institutional change in Mexico*. University of Notre Dame Press.

Beetham, D. (Ed.). (1994). *Defining and measuring democracy*. Sage Publications.

Beichelt, T., Hahn-Fuhr, I., Schimmelfennig, F., & Worschech, S. (Eds.). (2014). *Civil society and democracy promotion*. Palgrave Macmillan.

Beichelt, T., & Merkel, W. (2014). Democracy promotion and civil society: Regime types, transitions modes and effects. In Beichelt, T., Hahn-Fuhr, I., Schimmelfennig, F., & Worschech, S. (Eds.), *Civil society and democracy promotion* (pp. 42–64). Palgrave Macmillan.

Beith, M. (2011). A broken Mexico: Allegations of collusion between the Sinaloa Cartel and Mexican political parties. *Small Wars & Insurgencies, 22*, 787–806. https://doi.org/10.1080/09592318.2011.620813

Beith, M. (2020, September 20). A long fall from grace: The trial of Genaro Garcia Luna, Mexico's former security chief. *CrimeReads*. https://crimereads.com/a-long-fall-from-grace-the-trial-of-genaro-garcia-luna-mexicos-former-security-chief/

Bennett, A., & Elman, C. (2006a). Complex causal relations and case study methods: The example of path dependence. *Political Analysis, 14*, 250–267. https://www.jstor.org/stable/25791852

Bennett, A., & Elman, C. (2006b). Qualitative research: Recent developments in case study methods. *Annual Review of Political Science, 9*, 455–476. https://www.annualreviews.org/doi/pdf/10.1146/annurev.polisci.8.082103.104918

Bernal-Meza, R. (2013). Heterodox autonomy doctrine: Realism and purposes and its relevance. *Revista Brasileira de Política Internacional, 56*, 45–62. https://10.1590/S0034-73292013000200003

Bernhard, M. (2009). Review: Methodological disputes in comparative politics. *Comparative Politics, 41*, 495–515. https://www.jstor.org/stable/40599220

Besançon, M. (2003). *Good governance rankings: The art of measurement*. World Peace Foundation. https://www.researchgate.net/publication/242287099_Good_Governance_Rankings_The_Art_of_Measurement

Biddle, S., Macdonald, J., & Baker, R. (2017). Small footprint, small payoff: The military effectiveness of security force assistance. *Journal of Strategic Studies, 40*, 1–54. https://cpb-us-e1.wpmucdn.com/blogs.gwu.edu/dist/b/1590/files/2018/08/Small-footprint-small-payoff-The-military-effectiveness-of-security-force-assistance-2lzetou.pdf

Biden, J. R., Jr. (2015, January 30). Joe Biden: A plan for Central America. *The New York Times*. https://www.nytimes.com/2015/01/30/opinion/joe-biden-a-plan-for-central-america.html

Boies, J. L. (1989). Money, business, and the state: Material interests, Fortune 500 Corporations, and the size of political action committees. *American Sociological Review, 54*, 821–833. https://www.jstor.org/stable/pdf/2117756.pdf

Boix, C., & Stokes, S. C. (Eds.). (2009). *The Oxford handbook of comparative politics*. Oxford University Press.

Bollen, K. A. (1980). Issues in the comparative measurement of political democracy. *American Sociological Review, 45*, 370–390. https://www.jstor.org/stable/pdf/2095172.pdf

Bollen, K. A. (1990). Political democracy: Conceptual and measurement traps. *Studies in Comparative International Development, 25*, 7–24. https://www.researchgate.net/publication/225467406_Political_Democracy_and_Measurement_Traps

Boniface, D. S. (2007). The OAS's mixed record. In Legler, T., Lean, S. F., & Boniface, D. S. (Eds.), *Promoting democracy in the Americas* (pp. 40–62). Johns Hopkins University Press.

Bonilla, A. (2006). US Andean policy, the Colombian conflict, and security in Ecuador. In Loveman, B. (Ed.), *Addicted to failure, US security policy in Latin America and the Andean region* (pp. 103–129). Rowman & Littlefield.

Bonilla, L. (2014). ELN y el narcotráfico: una relación peligrosa. *El Espectador*. http://www.elespectador.com/noticias/paz/eln-y-el-narcotrafico-una-relacion-peligrosa-articulo-502301

Boone, P. (1996). Politics and the effectiveness of foreign aid. *European Economic Review, 40*, 289–329.

Born, H., & Schnabel, A. (2009). *Security sector reform in challenging environments*. Geneva Centre for Security Sector Governance. http://www.dcaf.ch/security-sector-reform-in-challenging-environments

Brady, H. E., & Collier, D. (Eds.). (2010). *Rethinking social inquiry: Diverse tools, shared standards*. 2nd ed. Rowman & Littlefield.

Breña, C. M., & Manetto, F. (2021, December 5). López Obrador se abraza a la buena imagen del Ejército. *El Pais*. https://elpais.com/mexico/2021-12-06/lopez-obrador-se-abraza-a-la-buena-imagen-del-ejercito.html

Brubaker, R. (1996). *Nationalism reframed: Nationhood and the national question in the new Europe*. Cambridge University Press. https://doi.org/10.1017/CBO9780511558764

Bruneau, A. (2006). The military in post-conflict societies: Lessons from Central America and prospects for Colombia. In Schnabel, A., & Ehrhart, H.-G. (Eds.), *Security sector reform and post-conflict peacebuilding* (pp. 225–242). United Nations University Press. https://collections.unu.edu/eserv/UNU:2552/pdf9280811096.pdf

Bruneau, T., & Giraldo, J. (2003, March 27–29). Domestic roles of the Colombian armed forces: Implications for civil-military relations. Presented at Annual Congress of the Latin American Studies Association, Dallas, TX.

Bryman, A. (2012). *Social research methods*. 4th ed. Oxford University Press.

Brzoska, M. (2006). Introduction: Criteria for evaluating post-conflict reconstruction and security sector reform in peace support operations. *International Peacekeeping, 13*, 1–13. https://doi.org/10.1080/13533310500424603

Buen, N. de, & Solís, L. (2012, October 4). Lo que INEGI no preguntó. *Animal Político*. https://www.animalpolitico.com/analisis/organizaciones/lo-que-mexico-evalua/lo-que-inegi-no-pregunto/

Bueno de Mesquita, B., Morrow, J., Siverson, R., & Smith, A. (2004). Testing novel implications from the selectorate theory of war. *World Politics, 56*, 363–388. https://www.jstor.org/stable/25054264

Bull, B. (2014). Towards a political economy of weak institutions and strong elites in Central America. *European Review of Latin American and Caribbean Studies / Revista Europea de Estudios Latinoamericanos y del Caribe, 97*, 117–128. https://www.jstor.org/stable/23972443

Burnell, P. J. (2000). Democracy assistance: The state of the discourse. In P. Burnell, (Ed.), *Democracy assistance, international co-operation for democratization* (pp. 3–33). Frank Cass Publishers.

Burnyeat, G. (2018). *Chocolate, politics and peace-building: An ethnography of the peace community of San José de Apartadó, Colombia*. Palgrave MacMillan. https://www.palgrave.com/gb/book/9783319514772

Burt, G. (2016). *Security Sector reform, legitimate politics, and SDG 16*. SSR 2.0 Brief. Centre for Security Governance.

Bushnell, D. (1993). *The making of modern Colombia: A nation in spite of itself*. University of California Press. https://www.ucpress.edu/book/9780520082892/the-making-of-modern-colombia

Busse, M., & Gröning, S. (2009). Does foreign aid improve governance? *Economics Letters*, 104, 76–78. https://doi.org/10.1016/j.econlet.2009.04.002

Buzan, B. (1991). New patterns of global security in the twenty-first century. *International Affairs, 67*, 431–451. https://www.jstor.org/stable/2621945

Cadena Montenegro, J. L. (2011). Nuevos actores de la geopolítica, Plan Colombia y Plan Mérida: dos guerras ajenas. *Revista CIFE, 17*, 167–186. https://doi.org/10.15332/s2248-4914.2010.0017.08

Cámara de Diputados. (2017). *Congreso de la cultura de seguridad nacional*. Conmutador General. http://www5.diputados.gob.mx/index.php/camara/Comision-Bicamaral-de-Seguridad-Nacional/Congreso-de-la-Cultura-de-la-Seguridad-Nacional

Camp, R. A. (1980). *Mexico's leaders, their education and recruitment*. University of Arizona Press. https://www.amazon.com/Mexicos-Leaders-Their-Education-Recruitment/dp/0816506604

Camp, R. A. (1985). *The making of a government, political leaders in modern Mexico*. University of Arizona Press.

Campbell, D. T. (1975). "Degrees of freedom" and the case study. *Comparative Political Studies, 8*, 178–193. https://doi.org/10.1177/001041407500800204

Cancino, M. (2018, January 31–February 1). Justicia Cívica y Jóvenes en Riesgo. Presented at First International Summit on Citizen Security, Tijuana, Mexico.

Cantú, F., & Desposato, S. (2012). The new federalism of Mexico's party system. *Journal of Politics in Latin America, 4*, 3–38. https://journals.sagepub.com/doi/pdf/10.1177/1866802X1200400201

Caparini, M. (2010). Civil society and the future of security sector reform. In Sedra, M. (Ed.), *The future of security sector reform* (pp. 244–262). Centre for International Governance Innovation. https://www.cigionline.org/sites/default/files/the_future_of_security_sector_reform.pdf

Capoccia, G. (2016). When do institutions "bite"? Historical institutionalism and the politics of institutional change. *Comparative Political Studies, 49*, 1095–1127. https://doi.org/10.1177/0010414015626449

Carlson, J. D., et al. (2013, March 28–30). The rebirth of the PRI and party realignment in Mexico: The import of (negative) party identification, 1996–2006. Presented at the Annual Meeting of the Western Political Science Association, Hollywood, CA3.

Carothers, T. (1998). The rule of law revival. *Foreign Affairs, 77*, 95–106. https://www.foreignaffairs.com/articles/1998-03-01/rule-law-revival.

Carothers, T., et al. (2014). *Non-western roots of international democracy support*. http://carnegieendowment.org/2014/06/03/non-western-roots-of-international-democracy-support-pub-55765

Carranza, V. (2018, January 31–February 1). Justicia Cívica y Jóvenes en Riesgo. Presented at the First International Summit on Citizen Security, Tijuana, Mexico.

Carroll, R., & L. A. Correspondent. (2010, September 9). Hillary Clinton: Mexican drugs war is Colombia-style Insurgency. *The Guardian*. https://www.theguardian.com/world/2010/sep/09/hillary-clinton-mexican-drug-war-insurgency

Casas-Zamora, K. (2013). *The besieged polis, citizen insecurity in Latin America*. Brookings Institution. https://www.brookings.edu/research/the-besieged-polis-citizen-insecurity-in-latin-america/

Casey, N. (2019, May 18). Colombia army's new kill orders send chills down ranks. *The New York Times*. https://www.nytimes.com/2019/05/18/world/americas/colombian-army-killings.html

Castillo Castañeda, A. (2020). El proceso de desecuritización de la doctrina militar en Colombia. *América Latina Hoy, 84*, 31–47. https://doi.org/10.14201/alh.21021

Castrillón, G., & Moreno Barreto, J. D. (2018, April 24). "Los militares le pondremos la cara y el pecho a la JEP": general Mejía. *El Espectador*. https://www.elespectador.com/colombia-20/jep-y-desaparecidos/los-militares-le-pondremos-la-cara-y-el-pecho-a-la-jep-general-mejia-article/

Causa en Común. (2020). Presupuesto 2021: ¿cuánto para seguridad? *Animal Político*. https://www.animalpolitico.com/el-blog-de-causa-en-comun/presupuesto-2021-cuanto-para-seguridad/#_ftn8

Celorio Mancera, M. (2018). The Local Context. Presented at the First International Summit on Citizen Security, Tijuana, Mexico, January 31–February 1, 2018.

Centro de Estudios de Finanzas Públicas. (2018). https://cefp.gob.mx/cefpnew/index.php

Centro de Investigación en Conflicto y Memoria Histórica Militar. (2018). https://americamilitar.com/museos-militares/2425-centro-de-investigacion-en-conflicto-y-memoria-historica-militar.html

Centro de Investigación y Educación Popular, CINEP / Programa Por La Paz. (2018). http://www.cinep.org.co/

Ch, R., Shapiro, J., Steele, A., & Vargas, J. R. (2019, January 29). Death and taxes: Political violence shapes local fiscal institutions and state building. *VoxEU.org*. https://voxeu.org/article/political-violence-shapes-local-fiscal-institutions-and-state-building.

Chabat, J. (2010a). La iniciativa y la relación México-Estados Unidos: En busca de la confianza perdida. Working paper #195. *CIDE*. http://repositorio-digital.cide.edu/handle/11651/898

Chabat, J. (2013). La seguridad en la política exterior de Calderón. *Foro Internacional, 53*, 729–749. https://www.redalyc.org/pdf/599/59931907010.pdf

Chalfin, J. E., & Thomas-Greenfield, L. (2017). The Security governance initiative. In Kerr, A., & Miklaucic, M. (Eds.), *Effective, legitimate, secure, insights for defense institution building* (pp. 183–199). National Defense University. https://cco.ndu.edu/LinkClick.aspx?fileticket=9YCCggKpP6s%3D&portalid=96

Chalmers, M. (2000). *Security sector reform in developing countries: An EU perspective.* Saferworld.

Chambers, P. (2014). Superficial consolidation: Security sector governance and the executive branch in the Philippines today. In Heiduk, F. (Ed.), *Security sector reform in Southeast Asia, from policy to practice* (pp. 102–130). Palgrave Macmillan. http://www.palgrave.com/us/book/9781137365484

Chandler, D. (2013). Peacebuilding and the politics of non-linearity: Rethinking "hidden" agency and "resistance." *Peacebuilding, 1*, 17–32. https://doi.org/10.1080/21647259.2013.756256

Chandler, D. (2018). Intervention and statebuilding beyond the human: From the "black box" to the "great outdoors." *Journal of Intervention and Statebuilding, 12*, 80–97. https://doi.org/10.1080/17502977.2017.1412108

Chappuis, F., & Hänggi, H. (2009). The interplay between security and legitimacy: Security sector reform and state-building. In Raue, J., & Sutter, P. (Eds.), *Facets and practices of state-building* (pp. 31–52). Martinus Nijhoff.

Chávez Castillo, J. A. (2011, June 8). El sistema penitenciario en México. *Revista Replicante.* http://revistareplicante.com/el-sistema-penitenciario-en-mexico/

Checkel, J. T. (2012). Theoretical pluralism in IR: Possibilities and limits. In Carlsnaes, W., Risse, T., & Simmons, B. A. (Eds.), *Handbook of international relations* (2nd ed., pp. 220–242). Sage Publications.

Cheema, G. S., & Rondinelli, D. A. (2007). *Decentralizing governance, emerging concepts and practices.* Brookings Institution Press. http://www.jstor.org/stable/10.7864/j.ctt1261v1

Cifras de secuestros en Colombia en el 2016. (2016, December 27). *El Tiempo.* http://www.eltiempo.com/justicia/cortes/cifras-de-secuestros-en-colombia-en-el-2016-42728

Civic, M. A., & Miklaucic, M. (2011). The State and the use of force: Monopoly and legitimacy. In Civic, M. A., & Miklaucic, M. (Eds.), *Monopoly of force, the nexus of DDR and SSR* (pp. xv–xxv). National Defense University. https://cco.ndu.edu/Portals/96/Documents/books/monopoly-of-force/monopoly-of-force.pdf

Clark, T. D. (2002). *Beyond post-communist studies, political science and the new democracies of Europe.* M. E. Sharpe. http://link.law.upenn.edu/portal/Beyond-post-communist-studies--political-science/XStN6qguLE0/

Coca-growing in Colombia is at an all-time high. (2017, May 23). *The Economist.* https://www.economist.com/news/americas/21719468-government-hopes-former-farc-guerrillas-will-persuade-villagers-switch

Cohen, N., & Arieli, T. (2011). Field research in conflict environments: Methodological challenges and snowball sampling. *Journal of Peace Research, 48* (4): 423–435. https://doi.org/10.1177/0022343311405698

Colacrai, M. (2009). Los aportes de la Teoría de la Autonomía, genuina contribución sudamericana. ¿La autonomía es hoy una categoría en desuso o se enfrenta al desafío de una renovación en un contexto interdependiente y más complejo? In Lechini, G., Klagsburnn, V., & Goncalves, W. (Eds.), *Argentina e Brasil, vencendo os preconceitos. As varias arestas de uma concepcao estratégica* (pp. 33–50). REVAN.Collier, D. (1993). The comparative method. In Finifter, A. W. (Ed.), *Political science: The state of the discipline II* (pp. 105–117). American Political Science Association.

Collier, D. (2011). Understanding process tracing. *PS, Political Science & Politics, 44*, 823–830. https://polisci.berkeley.edu/sites/default/files/people/u3827/Understanding%20Process%20Tracing.pdf

Collier, D., & Adcock, R. (1999). Democracy and dichotomies: A pragmatic approach to choices about concepts. *Annual Review of Political Science, 2*, 537–565. https://www.annualreviews.org/doi/10.1146/annurev.polisci.2.1.537

Collier, D., Brady, H. E., & Seawright, J. (2010). Introduction to the second edition: A sea change in political methodology. In Brady, H. E., & Collier, D. (Eds.), *Rethinking social inquiry, diverse tools, shared standards* (2nd ed., pp. 1–10). Rowman & Littlefield.

Collier, D., Brady, H. E., & Seawright, J. (2010). Refocusing the discussion of methodology. In Brady, H. E., & Collier, D. (Eds.), *Rethinking social inquiry, diverse tools, shared standards* (2nd ed., pp. 15–32). Rowman & Littlefield.

Collier, D., & Mahoney, J. (1996). Insights and pitfalls: Selection bias in qualitative research. *World Politics, 49*, 56–91. https://www.jstor.org/stable/25053989

Collier, P. (2006). *Democracy, development, and governance*. New School of Athens.

Colombia: Monitoreo de territorios afectados por cultivos ilícitos 2020 (2021). Oficina de las Naciones Unidas contra la Droga y el Delito. https://www.unodc.org/documents/crop-monitoring/Colombia/Colombia_Monitoreo_de_territorios_afectados_por_cultivos_ilicitos_2020.pdf

Colombia, Uribe Popular with Voters. (2004, December 21). https://worldview.stratfor.com/situation-report/colombia-uribe-popular-voters

Comisión Interamericana de Derechos Humanos. (1998). *Informe Anual 1998*. Comisión Interamericana de Derechos Humanos. https://corteidh.or.cr/docs/informes/info_98.pdf

Comisión Nacional de los Derechos Humanos. (2015). *La sobrepoblación en los centros penitenciarios de la República Mexicana, análisis y pronunciamento*. Comisión Nacional de Derechos Humanos. http://www.cndh.org.mx/sites/all/doc/Informes/Especiales/Pronunciamiento_20151014.pdf

¿Cómo se juzga en el Estado de México? una radiografía de la operación del sistema de justicia penal acusatorio. (2016). Centro de Investigación para el Desarrollo, A. C. https://law.ucla.edu/sites/default/files/PDFs/Academics/Como_Juzga_Edomex%20-%20Latin%20American%20Dossier%20Report%20in%20Spanish.pdf

Consejo de Seguridad Nacional. (2014). *Programa para la Seguridad Nacional 2014–2018, una política multidimensional para México en el Siglo XXI*. Presidencia de la República. https://www.resdal.org/caeef-resdal/assets/mexico----programa-para-la-seguridad-nacional.pdf

Contreras López, R. E. (2014). *La reforma constitucional de seguridad y justicia*. Letras Jurídicas. Universidad Nacional Autónoma de México.

Control Risks. (2017). The peace dividend, mitigating challenges and seizing opportunities in Colombia's Post-Conflict Period. Control Risks, Cotton Center. https://www.controlrisks.com/-/media/corporate/files/our-thinking/insights/reports/colombia-the-peace-dividend/control-risks-colombia-the-peace-dividend.pdf

Cooper, A., & Legler, T. (2006). *Intervention without intervening? The OAS defense and promotion of democracy in the Americas*. Palgrave Macmillan.

Coordinación Colombia-Europa-Estados Unidos. (2018). http://coeuropa.org.co/

Coppedge, M., et al. (2011). Conceptualizing and measuring democracy: A new approach. *Perspectives on Politics, 9*, 247–267. https://doi.org/10.1017/S1537592711000880

Corrales, J. (2016). Radical claims to accountability. In Foweraker, J., & Trevizo, D. (Eds.), *Democracy and its discontents in Latin America* (pp. 115–131). Lynne Rienner.

Cortés, N. G., Rodríguez Ferreira, O., & Shirk, D. A. (2016, April 13). *Perspectives on Mexico's criminal justice system, what do its operators think?* Justiciabarómetro. University of San Diego. https://justiceinmexico.org/justicebarometer-2016/

Costa, G. (2012). Citizen security and transnational organized crime in the Americas: Current situation and challenges in the inter-American arena. *Sur International Journal on Human Rights, 9*, 127–149. https://sur.conectas.org/en/citizen-security-transnational-organized-crime-americas/

Cox, M., Ikenberry, G. J., & Inoguchi, T. (Eds.). (2003). *American democracy promotion, impulses, strategies, and impacts*. Oxford University Press. https://10.1093/0199240973.001.0001

Craig, A. L., & Cornelius, W. A. (1995). Houses divided: Parties and political reform in Mexico. In Mainwaring, S., & Scully, T. (Eds.), *Building democratic institutions, party systems in Latin America* (pp. 249–297). Stanford University Press.

Crandall, R. (2002b). Clinton, Bush, and Plan Colombia. Survival, *44*, 159–172. https://doi.org/10.1080/00396338.2002.9688545

Crece presencia de mujeres en el ejército mexicano. (2015, February 19). https://lopezdoriga.com/sin-categoria/crece-presencia-de-mujeres-en-el-ejercito-mexicano/

Crespo, J. A. (2004). The party system and democratic governance in Mexico. *Policy Papers on the Americas*, vol. XV, Study 2. Center for Strategic and International Studies. https://csis-website-prod.s3.amazonaws.com/s3fs-public/legacy_files/files/media/csis/pubs/ppcrespo%5B1%5D.pdf

Cronología de los secuestros políticos de las FARC. (2008, July 2). *Libertad Digital*. http://www.libertaddigital.com/mundo/cronologia-de-los-secuestros-politicos-de-las-farc-1276334001/

Cuauhtémoc Blanco abre la posibilidad de trabajar con el modelo policial del Mando Único en Morelos. (2018, July 7). *El universal*. http://www.eluniversal.com.mx/estados/cuauhtemoc-blanco-abre-la-posibilidad-de-trabajar-con-mando-unico-en-morelos

Cutright, P. (1963). National political development: Measurement and analysis. *American Sociological Review, 28*, 254–264. https://doi.org/10.2307/2090612

Cyrenne, C. (2006). Is thick description social science? *Anthropological Quarterly, 79*, 531–540. https://10.1353/anq.2006.0019

Dahl, R. A. (1973). *Polyarchy: Participation and opposition*. Yale University Press.

Datos Abiertos, Gobierno de Colombia. (2022). Sistema de información de eventos de violencia del conflicto armado, gobierno de Colombia. https://www.datos.gov.co/Inclusi-n-Social-y-Reconciliaci-n/Sistema-de-Informaci-n-de-Eventos-de-Violencia-del/c59y-p4sz/data

Davies, T., & Loveman, B. (Eds.). (1997). *The politics of antipolitics: The military in Latin America*. Rowman & Littlefield.

Dávila, V. (2021, April 1). Exclusivo: el comandante del Ejército y el director de la Policía responden a todo. *Semana*. https://www.semana.com/nacion/articulo/el-destape-de-los-generales/202156/

Davis, D. E. (2012). Policing and regime transition: From postauthoritarianism to populism to neoliberalism. In Panters, W. G. (Ed.), *Violence, coercion, and hegemony in twentieth-century Mexico, The other half of the centaur* (pp. 68–90). Stanford University Press.

Deas, M. (2015). The Colombian conflict: A historical perspective. In Bagley, B. M., & Rosen, J. D. (Eds.), *Colombia's political economy at the outset of the twenty-first century, from Uribe to Santos and beyond* (pp. 91–106). Lexington Books.

Delgado, J. E. (2021). Time to rethink Colombia's militarised national security approach. *University of Oxford, The Changing Character of Conflict Platform*. https://conflictplatform.ox.ac.uk/cccp/research/time-to-rethink-colombias-militarised-national-security-approach

Delgado-Ramos, G. C., & Romano, S. M. (2011). Political-economic factors in US foreign policy: The Colombia Plan, the Mérida Initiative, and the Obama administration. *Latin American Perspectives, 38*, 93–108. https://www.jstor.org/stable/23060192

Democracy Index. (2017). http://www.eiu.com/public/thankyou_download.aspx?activity=download&campaignid=DemocracyIndex2017

Departamento Administrativo Nacional de Estadística. (2017). *Encuesta de Convivencia y Seguridad Ciudadana*. DANE Información para Todos. https://formularios.dane.gov.co/Anda_4_1/index.php/catalog/532/overview

Departamento Administrativo Nacional de Estadística, Gobierno de Colombia. (2021). *Encuesta de Convivencia y Seguridad Ciudadana (ECSC)*. DANE Información para Todos. https://www.dane.gov.co/files/investigaciones/poblacion/convivencia/2020/Bol_ECSC_2020.pdf

Department for International Development. (2004). *Appendix 3, Understanding "Political Will."* Politiking for the Poor: Senior Leader's Political Management of Pro-Poor Initiatives in an Era of Centrists. Department for International Development. https://www.gov.uk/research-for-development-outputs/appendix-3-understanding-political-will

Derdzinski, A. (2016). Measuring security: Homicide as an indicator of state capacity in oil-producing states. *Centre for Security Governance Insights, No. 11*.

Derwich, K. (2019, June 3–4). State DI kn Mexico. Presented at the Security and Criminality in the Americas Conference, Latin American Centre, University of Oxford. Oxford.

Destituidos 34 policías por desvío de ayuda para luca antinarcóticos. (2005, April 19). *El Tiempo*. https://www.eltiempo.com/archivo/documento/MAM-1637422

Deutsche Welle. (2018, June 7). *Ayotzinapa, CIDH insta a determinar participación policial y militar*. http://www.dw.com/es/ayotzinapa-cidh-insta-a-determinar-participaci%C3%B3n-policial-y-militar/a-44104757

Dexter, L.A (Ed.). (1970). *Elite and specialized interviewing*. Northwestern University Press. https://doi.org/10.1177/106591297002300422

Diamond, L., Linz, J.J., & Lipset, S. M. (1995). *Politics in developing countries: Comparing experiences with democracy*. Lynne Rienner.

Díaz Briseño, J. (2021). Valoraremos impacto de militarización en México-EU. *Reforma*. https://www.reforma.com/valoraremos-impacto-de-militarizacion-en-mexico-eu/ar2308500

Dion, M. L., & Russler, C. (2008). Eradication efforts, the state, displacement and poverty: Explaining coca cultivation in Colombia during Plan Colombia. *Journal of Latin America Studies, 40*, 399–421. https://10.1017/S0022216X08004380

Dirección de investigación criminal e Interpol - Policía nacional. (2018). https://www.policia.gov.co/dijin

Djankov, S., Montalvo, J. G., & Reynal-Querol, M. (2008). The curse of aid. *Journal of Economic Growth, 13*, 169–194. https://www.jstor.org/stable/41219212

Domínguez, S. (2016, April 7–9). Unlocking the decision-making process: An analysis of US Counter-narcotic policy making towards Mexico and Colombia. Presented at the National Conference on Undergraduate Research. Asheville, NC.

Dowding, K. (2015). *The philosophy and methods of political science*. Palgrave.

Doyle, D. (2016). State capacity and democratic quality. In Foweraker, J., & Trevizo, D. (Eds.), *Democracy and its discontents in Latin America* (pp. 33–50). Lynne Rienner.

Doyle, M. (1983). Kant, liberal legacies, and foreign affairs. *Philosophy and Public Affairs, 12*, 205–235. https://www.jstor.org/stable/2265298

Drug Enforcement Administration. (2006). *2007 National threat assessment*. US Department of Justice. https://www.justice.gov/archive/ndic/pubs21/21137/21137p.pdf

Drug Enforcement Administration. (2010). *2010 National threat assessment*. US Department of Justice. https://www.justice.gov/archive/ndic/pubs38/38661/38661p.pdf

Drug Enforcement Administration. (2015). *2015 National threat assessment*. US Department of Justice. https://www.dea.gov/sites/default/files/2018-07/2015%20NDTA%20Report.pdf

Drug Enforcement Administration. (2021). *2020 National threat assessment*. US Department of Justice. https://www.dea.gov/sites/default/files/2021-02/DIR-008-21%202020%20National%20Drug%20Threat%20Assessment_WEB.pdf

Dudley, S. (2006). *Walking ghosts, murder and guerrilla politics in Colombia*. Routledge.

Duverger, M. (2010). *Los partidos políticos*. Fondo de Cultura Económica. https://mcrcalicante.files.wordpress.com/2014/06/los-partidos-politicos-maurice-diverger.pdf

Duzán, M. J. (2018). *Santos, paradojas de la paz y del poder*. Penguin Random House.

Eaton, K. (2018). Federalism vs. decentralization in Latin America. *50 Shades of Federalism*. http://50shadesoffederalism.com/case-studies/federalism-vs-decentralization-latin-america/

Echavarría, J. A. (2013). *In/security in Colombia: Writing political identities in the democratic security policy*. Manchester University Press.

Eckhard, S. (2016). *The challenges and lessons learned in supporting security sector reform*. Friedrich-Ebert-Stiftung and the Global Public Policy Institute. https://library.fes.de/pdf-files/iez/12630.pdf

Edmunds, T. (2003). Security sector reform: Concepts and implementation. In Edmunds, T., & Germann, W. N. (Eds.), *Towards security sector reform in post Cold War Europe: A framework for assessment* (pp. 15–30). Nomos Verlagsgesellschaft.

Ejército Nacional de Colombia. (2021). Lanzamiento del plan estratégico de transformación ejército del futuro PETEF, 6 December 2021. YouTube video, 1:12:09. https://www.youtube.com/watch?v=8bzr3Tiq1Hs

El costo de la violencia en Colombia llega al 30% del PIB. (2016, June 8). *El Espectador*. https://www.elespectador.com/noticias/economia/el-costo-de-violencia-colombia-llega-al-30-del-pib-articulo-636599

El liberalismo y sus crisis históricas. (2017, November 17). *El Espectador*. https://www.elespectador.com/noticias/politica/el-liberalismo-y-sus-crisis-historicas-articulo-723660

Ellis, R. E. (2016). Transformación militar en el contexto del crimen organizado transnacional en América Latina: los casos de México, El Salvador, Honduras y Perú. *Transformación Militar, 1*, 76–84. https://econvue.com/sites/default/files/Transformacion%20Militar%20en%20el%20Contexto%20del%20Crimen%20Organizado%20Transnacional%20en%20America%20Latina%20-%20R%20Evan%20Ellis%20-%20bw.pdf

Ellis, R. E. (2019). The US military in support of strategic objectives in Latin America and the Caribbean. *PRISM, 8*, 26–39. https://cco.ndu.edu/News/Article/1761014/the-us-military-in-support-of-strategic-objectives-in-latin-america-and-the-car/

En el 2012 fueron secuestradas 305 personas en Colombia, según la Fundación País Libre. (2013, February 19). *El País*. http://www.elpais.com.co/judicial/en-el-2012-fueron-secuestradas-305-personas-en-colombia-segun-la-fundacion-pais-libre.html

Encuesta Medición #142, abril y mayo de 2021 (2021). *Invamer, investigación y asesoría de mercadeo*. https://www.valoraanalitik.com/wp-content/uploads/2021/05/2021-05-Invamer-Poll.pdf

Enyedi, Z. (2016). Populist polarization and party system institutionalization. *Problems of Post-Communism, 63*, 210–220. https://doi.org/10.1080/10758216.2015.1113883

Escalante, F. (2009). *El homicidio en México entre 1990 y 2007*. El Colegio de México.

Escudé, C. (2015). Realism in the periphery. In Dominguez, J. I., & Covarrubias, A. (Eds.), *Routledge handbook of Latin America in the world* (pp. 45–57). Routledge.

Espejo, G. (2022, February 6). La Gran Encuesta: asunto del país que más le preocupa a los colombianos. *La FM*. https://www.lafm.com.co/colombia/la-gran-encuesta-asunto-del-pais-que-mas-le-preocupa-los-colombianos

Espinosa, V., & Rubin, D. B. (2015). Did the military interventions in the Mexican drug war increase violence? *The American Statistician, 69*, 17–27. https://doi.org/10.1080/00031305.2014.965796

Estadísticas de Asistencia Integral a las Víctimas de MAP y MUSE. (2022). Gobierno de Colombia. http://www.accioncontraminas.gov.co/Estadisticas/estadisticas-de-victimas

Estatuto antiterrorista. (2004, October 16). *Semana*. https://www.semana.com/on-line/articulo/estatuto-antiterrorista/67905-Este fue el discurso del presidente Juan M. Santos sobre los 15 años del Plan Colombia. (2016, February 4). *El Espectador*. http://www.elespectador.com/noticias/politica/fue-el-discurso-del-presidente-juan-m-santos-sobre-los-articulo-614779

Evans, M. (2002). *War in Colombia: Guerrillas, Drugs and human rights in US-Colombia policy, 1988–2002*. The National Security Archive. https://nsarchive2.gwu.edu/NSAEBB/NSAEBB69/part3.html

Feeley, J. (2013a). An overview of the Merida Initiative, 2008–Present. *Hampton Roads International Security Quarterly*. https://docs.house.gov/meetings/FA/FA07/20130523/100907/HHRG-113-FA07-20130523-SD001.pdf

Ferri, P. (2019b, February 21). Morena cede ante la oposición para crear la Guardia Nacional. *El País*. https://elpais.com/internacional/2019/02/21/mexico/1550778798_311422.html

Fioretos, O., Falleti, T. G., & Sheingate, A. (2016a). Historical institutionalism in political science. In Fioretos, O., Falleti, T. G., & Sheingate, A. (Eds.), *The Oxford handbook of historical institutionalism* (pp. 3–28). Oxford University Press. http://www.oxfordhandbooks.com/view/10.1093/oxfordhb/9780199662814.001.0001/oxfordhb-9780199662814-e-1

Fioretos, O., Falleti, T. G., & Sheingate, A. (Eds.). (2016b). *The Oxford handbook of historical institutionalism*. Oxford University Press.

Fisher, M., & Taub, A. (2019, January 10). When corporate elites won partial control of a Mexican city—and then lost it. *The New York Times*. https://www.nytimes.com/2018/01/10/world/americas/interpreter-monterrey-when-corporate-elites-won-partial-control-of-a-mexican-city-and-then-lost-it.html

Flores, E. (2017, December 20). *La lista de periodistas caídos en 64 años, el sexenio de Calderón es el más letal, le sigue el de EPN*. http://www.sinembargo.mx/20-12-2017/3360109

Flores-Macías, G. A. (2015). The political economy of Colombia's 2012 and 2014 fiscal reforms. In Mahon Jr., J. E., Bergman, M., & Arnson, C. (Eds.), *Progressive tax reform and equality in Latin America* (pp. 101–126). Woodrow Wilson Center Press. https://www.wilsoncenter.org/sites/default/files/media/documents/publication/ProgressiveTaxReform_Equality.pdf

Flores-Macías, G. A. (2016). *Building support for taxation in developing countries, experimental evidence from Mexico*. ICTD Working Paper #51, International Centre for Tax and Development. https://www.ictd.ac/publication/building-support-for-taxation-in-developing-countries-experimental-evidence-from-mexico/

Flores-Macías, G. (2018). The consequences of militarizing anti-drug efforts for state capacity in Latin America: Evidence from Mexico. *Comparative Politics, 51*, 1–20. http://flores-macias.government.cornell.edu/pdfs/GFM%20_%20Militarization%20and%20State%20Capacity%20Latin%20America.pdf

Flores-Macías, G. A., & Kreps, S. E. (2017). Borrowing support for war: The effect of war finance on public attitudes toward conflict. *Journal of Conflict Resolution, 61*, 997–1020.

Forero, J. E. (2016). State, illegality, and territorial control: Colombian armed groups in Ecuador under the Correa government. *Latin American Perspectives, 43*, 238–251.

Four Mexican military officials accused of organized crime ties. (2012, August 1). CNN. https://www.cnn.com/2012/08/01/world/americas/mexico-military-corruption/index.html

Foweraker, J., & Trevizo, D. (Eds.). (2016). *Democracy and its discontents in Latin America*. Lynne Rienner.

Fowler, M. W. (2015). A brief survey of democracy promotion in US foreign policy. *Democracy and Security, 11*, 227–247. https://doi.org/10.1080/17419166.2015.1045974

Franzese, Jr., R. J. (2009). Multicausality, context-conditionality, and endogeneity. In Boix, C., & Stokes, S. C. (Eds.), *The Oxford handbook of comparative politics* (ch. 2). Oxford University Press. http://www.oxfordhandbooks.com/view/10.1093/oxfordhb/9780199566020.001.0001/oxfordhb-9780199566020-e-2

Friman, H. R. (2009). Drug markets and the selective use of violence. *Crime Law and Social Change, 53*, 285–295. https://link.springer.com/article/10.1007/s10611-009-9202-4

Frühling, H., Tulchin, J. S., & Golding, Heather (Eds.). (2003). *Crime and violence in Latin America, citizen security, democracy, and the state*. Woodrow Wilson Center Press.

Fuentes, C. (2009). Political Dimensions of Security Transformation in Latin America. *IDS Bulletin, 40*, 79–87. https://gsdrc.org/document-library/political-dimensions-of-security-transformation-in-latin-america/

Fuentes, C. (2011). *La gran novela latinoamericana*. Alfagura. https://www.academia.edu/26812003/Carlos_Fuentes_-_La_gran_novela_latinoamericana

Fukuyama, F. (1995). The primacy of culture. *Journal of Democracy, 6*, 7–14. https://www.journalofdemocracy.org/articles/democracys-future-the-primacy-of-culture/

Fundación Ideas Para La Paz. (2018). http://www.ideaspaz.org/

Galen Carpenter, T. (2014, July 21). The child migrant crisis is just the latest disastrous consequence of America's drug war. *The Washington Post*. https://www.washingtonpost.com/news/the-watch/wp/2014/07/21/the-child-migrant-crisis-is-just-the-latest-disastrous-consequence-of-americas-drug-war/?utm_term=.74911036ed22

Garay Salamanca, L. J., & Salcedo-Albarán, E. (2010). Crimen, captura y reconfiguración cooptada del Estado: cuando la descentralización no contribuye a profundizar la democracia. In *25 años de la descentralización en Colombia* (pp. 89–137). Fundación Konrad Adenauer Stiftung. https://www.kas.de/es/web/kolumbien/einzeltitel/-/content/25-jahre-dezentralisierung-in-kolumbien2

García Durán, M. (2006). De Turbay a Uribe: sin política de paz pero con un conflicto armado. In Leal Buitrago, F. (Ed.), *En la encrucijada, Colombia en el siglo XXI* (pp. 479–512). Editorial Norma.

García Soto, S. (2016, February 4). Luz verde a Mando Único; crean Sistema Nacional de Policías. *El Universal*. http://www.eluniversal.com.mx/entrada-de-opinion/columna/salvador-garcia-soto/nacion/2016/04/2/luz-verde-mando-unico-crean-sistema

Gargarella, R. (2013). *Latin American constitutionalism, 1810–2010. The engine room of the constitution*. Oxford University Press. https://academic.oup.com/icon/article/12/1/256/628632

Gasper, D., & Gómez, O. A. (2015). Human security thinking in practice: "Personal security," "citizen security," and comprehensive mappings. *Contemporary Politics, 21*, 100–116. https://doi.org/10.1080/13569775.2014.993906

Gasto militar (% del PIB)—Mexico. (2021). Banco Mundial. https://datos.bancomundial.org/indicador/ms.mil.xpnd.gd.zs?locations=MX

Geddes, B. (1990). How the cases you choose affect the answers you get: Selection bias in comparative politics. *Political Analysis, 2*, 131–150. https://doi.org/10.1093/pan/2.1.131

George, A. L., & Bennett, A. (2005). *Case studies and theory development in the social sciences*. MIT Press.

Gerdes, C. (2015). The best quotes from "Narcos." *Bustle*. https://www.bustle.com/articles/112331-13-narcos-quotes-that-will-really-make-you-think

Gerring, J. (2004). What is a case study and what is it good for? *American Political Science Review, 98*, 341–354. https://doi.org/10.1017/S0003055404001182

Gibb III, A. (2010). *Arms for reforms: The effectiveness of US military assistance at encouraging human rights reforms*. PhD dissertation, University of North Carolina-Chapel Hill. https://cdr.lib.unc.edu/indexablecontent/uuid:912177fc-2287-4727-9f5c-977e26dd7cd7

Gibson, E. (Ed.). (2004). *Federalism and democracy in Latin America*. Johns Hopkins University Press. https://jhupbooks.press.jhu.edu/title/federalism-and-democracy-latin-america.

Girod, D. M., Krasner, S. D., & Stoner-Weiss, K. (2009a). Governance and foreign assistance: The imperfect translation of ideas into outcomes. In Magen, A., Risse, T., & McFaul, M. A. (Eds.), *Promoting democracy and the rule of law, American and European strategies* (pp. 61–92). Basingstoke, UK: Palgrave Macmillan.

Goldsmith, A. A. (2001). Foreign aid and statehood in Africa. *International Organization, 55*, 123–148. https://doi.org/10.1162/002081801551432

Goldstone, J. A., et al. (2010). A global model for forecasting political instability. *American Journal of Political Science, 54*, 190–208. https://doi.org/10.1111/j.1540-5907.2009.00426.x

Gómez Buendía, H. (2009, March 2). Álvaro Uribe y los partidos políticos. *Razón Pública*. https://razonpublica.com/index.php/politica-y-gobierno-temas-27/336-alvaro-uribe-y-los-partidos-politicos.html

Gompert, D., Oliker, O., & Timilsina, A. (2004). *Clean, lean, and able: A strategy for defense development*. RAND Corporation. https://www.rand.org/pubs/occasional_papers/OP101.html

González, C. E. (2018, July 10). Si piensa contratar servicios de seguridad privada, le pueden salir hasta por $7,2 millones al mes. La República. https://www.asuntoslegales.com.co/actualidad/si-piensa-contratar-servicios-de-seguridad-privada-le-pueden-salir-hasta-por-72-millones-al-mes-2523910

González, D. (2019, June 3–4). Injustice and lack of punishment: Torture and state capacity to prosecute crime, 2006–2018. Presented at the Security and Criminality in the Americas Conference, Latin American Centre, University of Oxford.

González, G. G., & Flores, R. V. (2013). La política exterior de México hacia América Latina en el sexenio de Felipe Calderón (2006–2012): Entre la prudencia política y el pragmatismo económico. *Foro Internacional, 53*, 572–618.

González, R. P. (2016). La cultura de la legalidad en contextos de violencia: El fenómeno de Hagámoslo Bien en Monterrey. In *Revista Mexicana de Opinión Pública* 20, Universidad Nacional Autónoma de México. http://revistas.unam.mx/index.php/rmop/article/view/50916

González González, G. (2008). Democratización y política exterior: ¿El fin del predominio presidencial? In Arturo C. Sotomayor Velázqiez & Gustavo Vega Cánovas (Eds.), *El mundo desde México. Ensayos de política internacional. Homenaje a Olga Pellicer* (pp. 47–90). El Colegio de México, CIDE, ITAM.

González González, G., & Tienda, M. (Eds.). (1989). *México y Estados Unidos en la cadena internacional del narcotráfico*. Fondo de Cultura Económica. https://biblioteca.ufm.edu/library/index.php?title=29635&query=@title=Special:GSMSearchPage@process=@field1=clasificacion@value1=363.45@mode=advanced&recnum=8

Grabendorff, W. (2009). Limited security sector reform in Colombia. In *Security Sector Reform in Challenging Environments*. Irénées. http://www.irenees.net/bdf_fiche-analyse-935_en.html

Grant, R. W., & Keohane, R. O. (2003). Accountability and abuses of power in world politics. *American Political Science Review, 99*, 29–43. https://doi.org/10.1017/S0003055405051476

Gratius, S., & Legler, T. (2009). Latin America is different: Transatlantic discord on how to promote democracy in "problematic" countries. In Magen, A., Risse, T., & McFaul, M. A. (Eds.), *Promoting Democracy and the rule of law, American and European strategies* (pp. 185–215). Basingstoke, UK: Palgrave Macmillan.

Grupo de Economistas y Asociados. (2018). http://structura.com.mx/gea/

Grzymala-Busse, A. (2011). Time will tell? Temporality and the analysis of causal mechanisms and processes. *Comparative Political Studies, 44*, 1267–1297. https://doi.org/10.1177/0010414010390653

Guiding principles for stabilization and reconstruction. (2009). US Institute of Peace. https://www.usip.org/sites/default/files/guiding_principles_full.pdf

Guillén, G. (2014, January 3). *Las2Orillas*. Cuñada de Álvaro Uribe extraditada a EE.UU. fue operaria del "Chapo" Guzmán. https://www.las2orillas.co/cunada-de-alvaro-uribe-extraditada-ee-uu-fue-operaria-del-chapo-guzman/

Guillén, G. (2017). Colombianización de México y mexicanización de Colombia. *Semana*. http://www.semana.com/opinion/articulo/asesinato-de-periodista-mexicano-javier-valdez/526378

Gurney, K. (2014, May 19). Los riesgos de trasladar a la policía de Colombia a un nuevo ministerio. *InSight Crime*. https://es.insightcrime.org/noticias/analisis/riesgos-trasladar-policia-colombia-nuevo-ministerio/

Gutiérrez Sanín, F. (2003). *Hyper-fragmentation and traditional politics in Colombia: discussing alternative explanations*. Crisis States Programme Working Papers Series No. 1, London School of Economics. https://www.gov.uk/research-for-development-outputs/working-paper-no-24-hyper-fragmentation-and-traditional-politics-in-colombia-discussing-alternative-explanations

Gutiérrez Sanín, F., Acevedo, T., & Viatela, J. M. (2007). *Violent liberalism? State, conflict, and political regime in Colombia, 1930–2006: An analytical narrative on state-making*. Crisis States Working Papers Series No. 2, London School of Economics. https://www.lse.ac.uk/international-development/Assets/Documents/PDFs/csrc-working-papers-phase-two/WP19.2-state-conflict-and-political-regime-in-colombia.pdf

Guzmán, A. (2013). Un mando policial, dos presidentes. *Reporte Indigo*.

Habeeb, W. M. (1988). *Power and tactics in international negotiation: How weak nations bargain with strong nations*. Johns Hopkins University Press. https://doi.org/10.2307/1962473

Halfpenny, P. (1987). Laws, causality and statistics: Positivism, interpretivism and realism. *Sociological Theory, 5*, 33–36. https://doi.org/10.2307/201992

Hall, P. (2003). Aligning ontology and methodology in comparative research. In Mahoney, J., & Rueschemeyer, D. (Eds.), *Comparative historical analysis in the social sciences* (pp. 373–404). Cambridge University Press. https://doi.org/10.1017/CBO9780511803963

Hall, P. (2004). Beyond the comparative method. *Newsletter of the Organized Section in Comparative Politics of the American Political Science Association, 15*, 1–4.

Hammersley, M., & Gomm, R. (1997). Bias in social research. *Sociological Research Online* 2. https://journals.sagepub.com/doi/10.5153/sro.55

Hänggi, H. (2004). Making sense of security sector governance. In Hänggi, H., & Winkler, T. H. (Eds.), *Challenges of security sector governance* (pp. 3–23). Geneva Centre for the Democratic Control of Armed Forces.

Harbers, I. (2010). Decentralization and the development of nationalized party systems in new democracies: Evidence from Latin America. *Comparative Political Studies, 43*, 606–627. https://doi.org/10.1177/0010414008330285

Hartford, T., & Klien, M. (2005). Aid and the resource curse. *Public Policy Journal* 291. https://openknowledge.worldbank.org/handle/10986/11223

Hay, C. (2002). *Political analysis: A critical introduction*. Palgrave Macmillan.

Heer, J. (2018, March 6). Trump's disdain for democracy promotion. *The New Republic*. https://newrepublic.com/article/147290/trumps-disdain-democracy-promotion

Heiduk, F. (2014b). Introduction: Security sector reform in Southeast Asia. In Heiduk, F. (Ed.), *Security Sector reform in Southeast Asia: From policy to practice* (pp. 1–22). Palgrave Macmillan. http://www.palgrave.com/us/book/9781137365484

Heine, J., & Weiffen, B. (2014). *21st century democracy promotion in the Americas: Standing up for the polity*. Routledge. https://www.taylorfrancis.com/books/9781317626206

Hernandez, C. G. (2014). Security sector reform in Southeast Asia: From policy to practice. In Heiduk, F. (Ed.), *Security sector reform in Southeast Asia: From Policy to practice* (pp. 23–53). Palgrave Macmillan. http://www.palgrave.com/us/book/9781137365484

Heupel, M. (2012). Rule of law promotion and security sector reform: Common principles, common challenges. *Hague Journal on the Rule of Law, 4*, 158–175. https://doi.org/10.1017/S1876404512000097

Higley, J., & Burton, M. (2006). *Elite foundations of liberal democracy*. Rowman & Littlefield.

Hochschild, J. L. (2009). Conducting intensive interviews and elite interviews. In Lamont, M., & White, P. (Eds), *Workshop on interdisciplinary standards for systematic qualitative research* (pp. 124–128). National Science Foundation. https://www.nsf.gov/sbe/ses/soc/ISSQR_workshop_rpt.pdf

Holmes, L. (2001). Crime, corruption, and politics: Transnational factors. In Zielonka, J., & Pravda, A. (Eds.), *Democratic consolidation in Eastern Europe*. Vol. 2: *International and transnational factors* (pp. 192–230). Oxford University Press. https://10.1093/019924409X.003.0008

Hopkin, J. (2010). The comparative method. In Marsh, D., & Stoker, G. (Eds.), *Theory and methods in political science* (3rd ed., pp. 285–307). Palgrave Macmillan.

Hough, D. (2017). *Analysing corruption*. Agenda Publishing.

Hristoulas, A. (2012). Mexico's war on terrorism: Rhetoric and reality. In Kenny, P., Serrano, M., & Sotomayor, A. (Eds.), *Mexico's security failure, collapse into criminal violence* (pp. 161–182). Routledge.

Huber, D. (2015). *Democracy promotion and foreign policy: Identity and interests in US EU and non-western democracies*. Palgrave Macmillan. https://doi.org/10.1111/1468-2346.12563

Hughes, M. C. (2013). *Mérida Initiative and effectiveness: An analysis of supply-side policy*. Master's thesis. Naval Postgraduate School. https://calhoun.nps.edu/bitstream/handle/10945/34680/13Jun_Hughes_Michael.pdf

Human Rights Watch. (2015). *On their watch: Evidence of senior army officer's responsibility for false positive killings in Colombia*. Human Rights Watch. https://www.hrw.org/report/2015/06/24/their-watch/evidence-senior-army-officers-responsibility-false-positive-killings#

Human Rights Watch. (2020, March 10). Colombia: Abuses amid massive demonstrations. https://www.hrw.org/news/2020/03/10/colombia-abuses-amid-massive-demonstrations

Huntington, S. P. (1957). *The soldier and the state*. Harvard University Press.

Huntington, S. P. (1993). *The third wave: Democratization in the late twentieth century*. University of Oklahoma Press.

Hyman, G. (2010). Tilting at straw men. In Diamond, L., Plattner, M. F., & Costopoulos, P. J. (Eds.), *Debates on democratization* (pp. 114–120). Johns Hopkins University Press.

Índice de Paz México 2022. (2022). Instituto para la Economía y la Paz. https://www.visionofhumanity.org/wp-content/uploads/2022/05/ESP-MPI-2022-web.pdf

InSight Crime's 2016 homicide round-up. (2016, January 16). *InSight Crime*. https://www.insightcrime.org/news/analysis/insight-crime-2016-homicide-round-up/

Instituto Ciudadano de Estudios sobre la Inseguridad. (2008). *Quinta encuesta nacional sobre inseguridad, ENSI-5 2008*. Instituto Ciudadano de Estudios sobre la Inseguridad. https://drcureces.files.wordpress.com/2009/12/icesi-5a-encuesta-nacional-sobre-inseguridad.pdf

Instituto Ciudadano de Estudios sobre la Inseguridad. (2009). *Sexta encuesta nacional sobre inseguridad, ENSI-6 2009*. Instituto Ciudadano de Estudios sobre la Inseguridad. http://internet.contenidos.inegi.org.mx/contenidos/Productos/prod_serv/contenidos/espanol/bvinegi/productos/metodologias/est/io_ENSI-6_2009.pdf

Instituto Nacional de Estadística y Geografía. (2012). *Encuesta nacional de victimización y percepión sobre seguridad pública 2012*. Instituto Nacional de Estadística y Geografía.

Instituto Nacional de Estadística y Geografía. (2017a). *Encuesta Nacional de Victimización y Percepción Sobre Seguridad Pública 2017*. Instituto Nacional de Estadística y Geografía.

Instituto Nacional de Estadística y Geografía. (2017b). *INEGI*.

Instituto Nacional de Estadística y Geografía. (2021a). *Encuesta Nacional de Victimización y Percepción sobre Seguridad Pública (ENVIPE) 2021*. INEGI. https://www.inegi.org.mx/contenidos/programas/envipe/2021/doc/envipe2021_presentacion_nacional.pdf

Instituto Nacional de Estadística y Geografía. (2021b). *Censo Nacional de Gobierno, Seguridad Pública y Sistema Penitenciario Estatales 2020*. INEGI. https://www.inegi.org.mx/contenidos/programas/cngspspe/2020/doc/cngspspe_2020_resultados.pdf

Instituto Nacional de Estadística y Geografía. (2022). *Censo Nacional de Seguridad Pública Federal 2021*. INEGI. https://www.inegi.org.mx/programas/cnspf/2021/

Inter-American Commission on Human Rights. (2013). *Truth, justice, and reparation*. Organization of American States.

Inter-American Commission on Human Rights. (2018). *Informe de balance, seguimiento al asunto Ayotzinapa realizado por el Mecanismo Especial de Seguimiento de La CIDH*. Organization of American States. http://www.oas.org/es/cidh/docs/mesa/informebalanceayotzinapa.pdf

IPI Death Watch. (2021). *The IPA database of killed journalists*. International Press Institute. https://ipi.media/deaths/?topic=0&country=mexico&years=2021&

Jacomet, D. (2005). The collective aspect of corporate political strategies: The case of US and European business participation in textile international trade negotiations. *International Studies of Management & Organization, 35*, 78–93. https://doi.org/10.1080/00208825.2005.11043731

Jaitman, L., & Torre, I. (2017). A systematic approach to measuring the costs of crime in 17 Latin American and Caribbean countries. In Jaitman, L. (Ed.), *The costs of crime and violence, new evidence and insights in Latin America and the Caribbean* (pp. 19–29). Inter-American Development Bank. http://dx.doi.org/10.18235/0000615

Janda, K. (2012). Governance in democracies and non-democracies. In Bissessar, A. M. (Ed.), *Governance: Is It for everyone?* (UK ed., pp. 171–159)Nova Science Publishers. https://www.janda.org/bio/parties/articles/Janda%202012.pdf

Jarvis, M. D. (2014). Hierarchy. In Bovens, M., Goodin, R. E., & Schillemans, T. (Eds.), *The Oxford handbook of public accountability* (pp. 405–420). Oxford University Press.

Joaquín 'El Chapo' Guzmán's trial: From shocking to bizarre. (2019, February 4). BBC News. https://www.bbc.com/news/world-us-canada-46282173

Johnson, S. (2001). Helping Colombia fix its plan to curb drug trafficking, violence, and insurgency. The Heritage Foundation. https://www.heritage.org/americas/report/helping-colombia-fix-its-plan-curb-drug-trafficking-violence-and-insurgency

Jones, S. G., et al. (2006). *Securing tyrants or fostering reform? US internal security assistance to repressive and transitioning regimes*. RAND Corporation. https://www.rand.org/content/dam/rand/pubs/monographs/2006/RAND_MG550.pdf

Jorgic, D. (2022). Exclusive: US Anti-drugs agency pulls plane from Mexico in fresh cooperation blow. Reuters. https://www.reuters.com/world/americas/exclusive-us-anti-drugs-agency-pulls-plane-mexico-fresh-cooperation-blow-2022-05-11/

Joshi, M., Melander, E., & Quinn, J. M. (2017). Sequencing the peace: How the order of peace agreement implementation can reduce the destabilizing effects of post-accord elections. *Journal of Conflict Resolution, 61*, 4–28. https://doi.org/10.1177/0022002715576573

Kaldor, M., & Rangelov, I. (Eds.). (2014). *The handbook of global security policy*. Wiley-Blackwell.

Karime Grajales Cardona, L. (2022, January 24). Colombia podría explorar usos lícitos de la amapola como lo ha hecho Europa: expertos ven en la industria farmaceútica y gastronómica la clave para avanzar. *Semana*. https://www.semana.com/mejor-colombia/articulo/en-la-gastronomia-y-la-industria-nacional-de-farmacos-estarian-las-oportunidades-para-explorar-usos-licitos-de-la-amapola-como-lo-han-hecho-paises-europeos/202104/

Karlin, M. E. (2017). *Building militaries in fragile states*. University of Pennsylvania Press.

Kennan, G. F. (1985). Morality and foreign policy. *Foreign Affairs, 64*, 205–218. https://www.foreignaffairs.com/articles/united-states/1985-12-01/morality-and-foreign-policy

Kerr, A., & Miklaucic, M. (2017). Partnership: The Colombia-US experience. In Kerr, A., & Miklaucic, M. (Eds.), *Effective, legitimate, secure, insights for defense institution building* (pp. 273–286). National Defense University. https://cco.ndu.edu/LinkClick.aspx?fileticket=9YCCggKpP6s%3D&portalid=96

Kim, D. (2014). Democracy promotion and American's support for troop use. *Trames: A Journal of the Humanities and Social Sciences; Tallinn, 18*, 135–157. https://kirj.ee/trames-publications/?filter[year]=2014&filter[issue]=238&filter[publication]=1791

King, G., Keohane, R. O., & Verba, S. (1994). *Designing social inquiry: Scientific inference in qualitative research*. Princeton University Press.

Kirchherr, J., & Charles, K. (2018). Enhancing the sample diversity of snowball samples: Recommendations from a research project on anti-dam movements in Southeast Asia. *PLos One, 13* (8). https://doi.org/10.1371/journal.pone.0201710

Kissinger, H. (1999). Reality and illusion about the Chinese. *Independent.*

Kitschelt, H., et al. (2010). *Latin American party systems.* Cambridge University Press. https://doi.org/10.1017/CBO9780511750311

Knack, S. (2004). Does foreign aid promote democracy? *International Studies Quarterly, 48,* 251–266. https://www.jstor.org/stable/3693571

Knight, A. (1992). Mexico's elite settlement: Conjuncture and consequences. In Higley, J., & Gunther, R. (Eds.), *Elites and democratic consolidation in Latin America and southern Europe* (pp. 113–145). Cambridge University Press.

Knight, M. (2009). Security sector reform, democracy and the social contract: From implicit to explicit. *Journal of Security Sector Management, 7,* 1–20. https://ciaotest.cc.columbia.edu/journals/jssm/v7i1/f_0022143_18211.pdf

Krauze, E. (2013, November 28). The danger in Mexico's divided house. *The New York Times.* https://www.nytimes.com/2013/11/29/opinion/krauze-the-danger-in-mexicos-divided-house.html

Krempel, J. (2014). Eurocentric or ahistorical? Concept of SSR and its limits. In Heiduk, F. (Ed.), *Security sector reform in Southeast Asia: From policy to practice* (pp. 54–82). Palgrave Macmillan. http://www.palgrave.com/us/book/9781137365484

Kreuzer, M., & Pettai, V. (2003). Patterns of political instability: Affiliation patterns of politicians and voters in post-communist Estonia, Latvia, and Lithuania. *Studies in Comparative International Development, 38,* 76–98. https://link.springer.com/article/10.1007/BF02686269

Kümmel, G. (2003). Why engage in security sector reform abroad? International Norms, external democratisation and the role of DCAF. In Edmunds, T., & Germann, W. N. (Eds.), *Towards security sector reform in post Cold War Europe: A framework for assessment* (pp. 56–86). Nomos Verlagsgesellschaf.

La depuración de la policía. (2016). *El Colombiano.* https://www.elcolombiano.com/opinion/editoriales/la-depuracion-de-la-policia-GC4127549

Laitin, D. D. (2000, September). Comparative politics: The state of the subdiscipline. Presented at the Annual Meeting of the American Political Science Association. Washington, DC. https://web.stanford.edu/group/laitin_research/cgi-bin/wordpress/wp-content/uploads/2013/10/Cpapsa.pdf

Lantis, J. S., & Fonseca, B. (2017). Culture and the formation of national security. In Fonseca, B., & Gamarra, E. A. (Eds.), *Culture and national security in the Americas* (pp. 1–14). Lexington Books.

LaRosa, M. J., & Mejía, G. R. (2012). *Colombia: A concise contemporary history.* Rowman & Littlefield.

La Rota, M. (2019, June 3–4). Urban policing and policy responses. Presented at the Security and Criminality in the Americas Conference, Latin American Centre, University of Oxford.

Las propuestas de los presidenciales. (2002, May 26). *El Tiempo.* https://www.eltiempo.com/archivo/documento/MAM-1317379

Latin America Public Opinion Project. (2010). *The Political Culture of Democracy, 2010.* Vanderbilt University. https://www.vanderbilt.edu/lapop/ab2010/2010-comparative-en-revised.pdf

Lawson, M. L., & Epstein, S. B. (2017). *Democracy promotion: An objective of US foreign assistance.* Congressional Research Service. https://sgp.fas.org/crs/row/R44858.pdf

Leal Buitrago, F. (2006c). Políticas de seguridad: De improvisación en improvisación. In Leal Buitrago, F. (Ed.), *En la encrucijada, Colombia en el siglo XXI* (pp. 513–544). Editorial Norma. https://doi.org/10.7440/res25.2006.13

Lee, F. E. (2009). *Beyond ideology*. University of Chicago Press. https://www.press.uchicago.edu/ucp/books/book/chicago/B/bo8158910.html

Legler, T., Lean, S. F., & Boniface, D. S. (Eds.). (2007). *Promoting democracy in the Americas*. Johns Hopkins University Press.

Lessons from Mexico: "Our sugar tax hasn't worked," says beverage association. (2018, April 4). *FoodBev Media*. https://www.foodbev.com/news/lessons-mexico-sugar-tax-hasnt-worked-says-beverage-association/

Levitsky, S., & Way, L. (2010). *Competitive authoritarianism: Hybrid regimes after the Cold War*. Problems of International Politics. Cambridge University Press.

Lieberson, S. (1991). Small *N*'s and big conclusions: An examination of the reasoning in comparative studies based on a small number of cases. *Social Forces, 70*, 307–320. https://doi.org/10.2307/2580241

Lieuwen, E. (1968). *Mexican militarism: The political rise and fall of the Revolutionary Army, 1910–1940*. University of New Mexico Press. https://www.questia.com/library/120082382/mexican-militarism-the-political-rise-and-fall-of

Lijphart, A. (1999). *Patterns of democracy: Government forms and performance in thirty-six countries*. Yale University Press. https://www.amazon.com/Patterns-Democracy-Government-Performance-Thirty-Six/dp/0300078935

Linz, J. J., & Stepan, A. (1996b). Toward consolidated democracies. *Journal of Democracy, 7*, 14–33. https://doi.org/10.1353/jod.1996.0031

Lipset, S. M. (1959). Some social requisites of democracy: economic development and political legitimacy. *American Political Science Review, 53*, 69–105. https://doi.org/10.2307/1951731

Loada, A., & Moderan, O. (2015). *Civil society involvement in security sector reform and governance*. Geneva Centre for the Democratic Control of Armed Forces. https://www.dcaf.ch/sites/default/files/publications/documents/SSR_toolkit-T6-EN-FINAL.pdf

Locke, R. (2018, January 31–Feburary 1). Violence prevention. Presented at the First International Summit on Citizen Security, Tijuana.

Long, T. (2015). *Latin America confronts the United States: Asymmetry and influence*. Cambridge University Press. https://www.cambridge.org/core/books/latin-america-confronts-the-united-states/asymmetry-influence-and-uslatin-american-relations/A33598A08A6BC1686FB98C4D2B7B3372/core-reader

Loveman, B. (Ed.). (2006). *Addicted to failure: US security policy in Latin America and the Andean region*. Rowman & Littlefield.

Lowenthal, A. F. (2009). Renewing cooperation in the Americas. In Lowenthal, A. F., Piccone, T. J., & Whitehead, L. (Eds.), *The Obama administration and the Americas: Agenda for change* (pp. 1–21). Brookings Institution Press. https://www.jstor.org/stable/10.7864/j.ctt127zfr

Luckham, R. (2009). Introduction: Transforming security and development in an unequal world. *Institute of Development Studies Bulletin*, 40. https://doi.org/10.1111/j.1759-5436.2009.00016.x

Lugo, L. A., & Goodman, J. (2016, December 20). *Rights group: Testimony links Colombia general to killings*. https://apnews.com/c84da7a07dd34751932ea7258cfe12c7/rights-group-testimony-links-colombia-general-killings

Lupu, N. (2015b). Party polarization and mass partisanship: A Comparative perspective. *Political Behavior, 37*, 331–356. https://link.springer.com/article/10.1007/s11109-014-9279-z

MacGinty, R. (2010). Hybrid peace: The interaction between top-down and bottom-up peace. *Security Dialogue, 41*, 391–412. https://doi.org/10.1177/0967010610374312

MacGinty, R., & Richmond, O. (2016). The fallacy of constructing hybrid political orders: A reappraisal of the hybrid turn in peacebuilding. *International Peacekeeping, 23*, 219–239. https://doi.org/10.1080/13533312.2015.1099440

MacCoun, R. J., & Reuter, P. (2001). *Drug war heresies*. Cambridge University Press. https://www.cambridge.org/core/books/drug-war-heresies/B61DD8A502D0B7C80F181AB2EE8C77AE

Magen, A. A., & McFaul, M. A. (2009). Introduction: American and European strategies to promote democracy—shared values, common challenges, divergent tools? In Magen, A. A., Risse, T., & McFaul, M. A. (Eds.), *Promoting democracy and the rule of law: American and European strategies* (pp. 1–33). Palgrave Macmillan.

Magen, A. A., & Morlino, L. (Eds.). (2008). *International actors, democratization and the rule of law: Anchoring democracy?* Routledge/UACES Contemporary European Studies Series 8. Routledge.

Mahoney, J. (2000). Path dependence in historical sociology. *Theory and Society, 29*, 507–548. https://www.jstor.org/stable/3108585

Mahoney, J. (2004). Comparative-historical methodology. *Annual Review of Sociology, 30*, 81–101. https://doi.org/10.1146/annurev.soc.30.012703.110507

Mahoney, J. (2007). Qualitative methodology and comparative politics. *Comparative Political Studies, 40*, 122–144. https://doi.org/10.1177/0010414006296345

Mahoney, J., Mohamedali, K., & Nguyen, C. (2009). Causality and time in historical institutionalism. In Boix, C., & Stokes, S. C. (Eds.), *The Oxford handbook of comparative politics* (ch. 4). Oxford University Press. http://www.oxfordhandbooks.com/view/10.1093/oxfordhb/9780199662814.001.0001/oxfordhb-9780199662814-e-4

Mahoney, J., & Thelen, K. (2010). A theory of gradual institutional change. In Mahoney, J., & Thelen, K. (Eds.), *Explaining institutional change: Ambiguity, agency, and power* (pp. 1–37). Cambridge University Press.

Mahoney, J., & Villegas, C. M. (2009). Historical enquiry and comparative politics. In Boix, C., & Stokes, S. C. (Eds.), *The Oxford Handbook of Comparative Politics* (ch. 3). Oxford University Press. http://www.oxfordhandbooks.com/view/10.1093/oxfordhb/9780199566020.001.0001/oxfordhb-9780199566020-e-3

Mainwaring, S., & Pérez-Liñán, A. (2014). *Democracies and dictatorships in Latin America: Emergence, survival, and fall*. Cambridge University Press.

Mainwaring, S., & Welna, C. (Eds.). (2002). *Democratic accountability in Latin America*. Oxford University Press. https://10.1093/0199256373.001.0001

Mair, P. (1998). Comparative politics: An overview. In Goodin, R. E., & Klingemann, H.-D. (Eds.), *A new handbook of political science* (pp. 309–335). Oxford University Press. https://doi.org/10.1093/0198294719.003.0012

Mancini, F. (2005). *In Good company? The role of business in security sector reform*. Demos. https://www.jstor.org/stable/resrep09527.1

Manor, J. (1999). *The political economy of democratic decentralization*. The World Bank. https://doi.org/10.1596/0-8213-4470-6

Mansbridge, J., & Martin, C. (2013). *Negotiating agreement in politics*. American Political Science Association. https://www.apsanet.org/Portals/54/files/Task%20Force%20Reports/Negotiating%20Agreement%20in%20Politics.pdf

Mares, D. R., & Martínez, R. (Eds.). (2013). *Debating civil-military relations in Latin America*. Sussex Academic Press.

Marks, T. A. (2003). Colombian Army counterinsurgency. *Crime, Law and Social Change, 40*, 77–105. https://doi.org/10.1023/A:1024989802910

Martínez, P. (2015). Reforma al fuero militar en México no cumple la norma internacional: Corte Interamericana de DH. *Animal Político*.

Martínez Rodríguez, A. (1998). Parliamentary Elites and the polarisation of the party system in Mexico. In Serrano, M. (Ed.), *Governing Mexico: Political parties and elections* (pp. 58–70). Institute of Latin American Studies.

Mateus, J. (2017, February 20). Estrategia de seguridad para reducir delitos en Medellín en 5 claves. *El Tiempo*. https://www.eltiempo.com/colombia/medellin/5-claves-de-la-estrategia-de-seguridad-para-reducir-delitos-en-medellin-60665

Maxwell, D., et al. (2018). Trajectories of international engagement with state and local actors: Evidence from South Sudan. *Journal of Intervention and Statebuilding, 12*, 98–119. https://doi.org/10.1080/17502977.2017.1371876

Mcintosh, J. (2017, August 27). Mexico creates new federal police division to protect cultural heritage. *Deutsche Welle*. https://www.dw.com/en/mexico-creates-new-federal-police-division-to-protect-cultural-heritage/a-40255182

McNerney, M. J., et al. (2014). *Assessing security cooperation as a preventive tool*. RAND Corporation. https://www.rand.org/content/dam/rand/pubs/research_reports/RR300/RR350/RAND_RR350.pdf

Mejía, D., & Restrepo, P. (2008). The war on illegal drug production and trafficking: An economic evaluation of Plan Colombia. Documento CEDE no. 2008-19. https://papers.ssrn.com/sol3/papers.cfm?abstract_id=1485690

Méndez, Á. (2012). *Negotiating intervention by invitation: How the Colombians shaped US participation in the genesis of Plan Colombia*. PhD dissertation, London School of Economics and Political Science (LSE). http://etheses.lse.ac.uk/519/

Mendieta, E. (2014, September 13). Fuerza Civil, a tres años, es un modelo a seguir. *Milenio*. http://www.milenio.com/estados/fuerza-civil-a-tres-anos-es-un-modelo-a-seguir

Mexico army gives drug cartels free rein as critics claim "non-aggression pact." (2021, November 8). *The Guardian*. https://www.theguardian.com/world/2021/nov/08/mexico-army-drug-cartels-michoacan

México Evalúa. (2012). *Seguridad y justicia penal en los estados: 25 indicadores de nuestra debilidad institucional*. Centro de Análisis de Póliticas Públicas. http://mexicoevalua.org/2012/03/01/seguridad-y-justicia-penal-en-los-estados-25-indicadores-de-nuestra-debilidad-institucional/

Mexico News Daily staff. (2020, February 25). 1.7bn pesos in airport contracts reportedly issued to shell companies. *Mexico News Daily*. https://mexiconewsdaily.com/news/national-defense-issued-1-7bn-pesos-in-airport-contracts-to-shell-companies/

México: Monitoreo de Plantíos de Amapola, 2018–2019. (2021). Oficina de las Naciones Unidas contra la Droga y el Delito. https://www.un-ilibrary.org/content/books/9789214030508

México Unido Contra La Delincuencia. (2018). http://www.mucd.org.mx/

México Unido Contra la Delincuencia & Consulta Mitofsky. (2016). *Décimo quinta encuesta nacional sobre percepción de inseguridad ciudadana en México*. MUCD. http://www.mucd.org.mx/recursos/Noticias/XVEncuestaNacionalSobrePercepcindeInseguridadCiudadanaenMxico/documentos2/BoletinMitofsky2016VTL.pdf

Meyer, P. J., & Ribando Seelke, C. (2015). *Central America regional security initiative: Background and policy issues for Congress*. Congressional Research Service. https://sgp.fas.org/crs/row/R41731.pdf

Middlebrook, K. J. (1995). *The paradox of revolution: Labor, the state, and authoritarianism in Mexico*. Johns Hopkins University Press.

Middlebrook, K. J. (Ed.). (2000). *Conservative parties, the right, and democracy in Latin America*. Johns Hopkins University Press. http://search.ebscohost.com/login.aspx?direct=true&AuthType=ip,shib&db=nlebk&AN=75734&site=ehost-live&scope=site

Middlebrook, K. J., & Rico, C. (Eds.). (1986). *The United States and Latin America in the 1980s: Contending perspectives on a decade of crisis*. Pitt Latin American Series. University of Pittsburgh Press.

Miller, B. (2010). Democracy promotion: Offensive liberalism versus the rest (of IR theory). *Millennium, 38*, 561–591. https://doi.org/10.1177/0305829810366475

Millett, R. L. (2002). *Colombia's conflicts: The spillover effects of a wider war*. Strategic Studies Institute. US Army War College. https://www.jstor.org/stable/resrep11296

Mira González, C. M. (2016). Los estados de excepción en Colombia y aplicación del principio de proporcionalidad: un análisis de seis casos representativos. *Revista Opinión Jurídica, 15*, 141–163. https://doi.org/10.22395/ojum.v15n29a7

Miroff, N. (2019, February 7). Mexicans want security, but candidates to succeed Calderon vague on drug war policy. *Washington Post*. https://www.washingtonpost.com/world/the_americas/mexicans-want-security-but-candidates-to-succeed-calderon-vague-on-drug-war-policy/2012/02/07/gIQALzhhJR_story.html

Mitchell, N.J., Hansen, W. L., & Jepsen, E. M. (1997). The determinants of domestic and foreign corporate political activity. *Journal of Politics, 59*, 1096–1113. https://doi.org/10.2307/2998594

Mobekk, E. (2010). Security sector reform and the challenges of ownership. In Sedra, M. (Ed.), *The future of security sector reform* (pp. 230–243). Centre for International Governance Innovation. https://www.cigionline.org/sites/default/files/the_future_of_security_sector_reform.pdf

Molano Aponte, D. A. (2021). Memorias al Congreso, 2020–2021. Ministrerio de Defensa Nacional, Gobierno de Colombia. https://www.mindefensa.gov.co/irj/go/km/docs/pccshr content/Recursos%20MDN/Plantillas%20Documentos/Ministerio/CentroDocumentos/InformesAlCongreso/Recursos/memorias2020-2021.pdf

Monsalve, R. (2022, March 23). Colombia: Vivir a la sombra de los conflictos armados. *Comité Internacional de la Cruz Roja*. https://www.icrc.org/es/document/balance-humanitario-colombia-2022-dih

Moreno, A. (1998). Party competition and the issue of democracy: Ideological space in Mexican elections. In Serrano, M. (Ed.), *Governing Mexico: Political parties and elections* (pp. 38–57). Institute of Latin American Studies.

Moreno, J. D. (2014). Relaciones cívico-militares en Colombia: supremacía y control de los partidos políticos sobre la organización militar. *Revista Científica "General José María Córdova," 12*, 333–355. https://doi.org/10.21830/19006586.166

Moreno, L. A. (2014, August 12). Plan Colombia work(ed). Why not try something similar in Central America? *Miami Herald*. https://www.miamiherald.com/opinion/op-ed/article 1979415.html

Moreno Torres, A. (2012). Seguridad democrática y militarización en Colombia: Más allá del conflicto armado. *Revista Latinoamericana de Seguridad Ciudadana, 12*, 41–56. https://www.redalyc.org/pdf/5526/552656545004.pdf

Morin, R. (1990, February 9). Americans, Colombians disagree over drug war, survey says. *The Washington Post*. https://www.washingtonpost.com/archive/politics/1990/02/09/americans-colombians-disagree-over-drug-war-survey-shows/e0662b42-6d7b-4b68-814a-54131d40bc68/

Morlino, L. (2012). *Changes for democracy: Actors, structures, processes*. Oxford University Press. https://10.1093/acprof:oso/9780199572533.001.0001

Moroney, J. D. P. et al. (2011). *How successful are US efforts to build capacity in developing countries? A framework to assess the Global Train and Equip "1206" Program*. RAND Corporation. http://www.rand.org/content/dam/rand/pubs/technical_reports/2011/RAND_TR1121.pdf

Moroney, J. D. P., Thaler, D. E., & Hogler, J. (2013). *Review of security cooperation mechanisms combatant commands utilize to build partner capacity*. RAND Corporation. http://www.rand.org/content/dam/rand/pubs/research_reports/RR400/RR413/RAND_RR413.pdf

Morris, S. D. (2013). Drug trafficking, corruption, and violence in Mexico: Mapping the linkages. *Trends in Organized Crime, 16*, 195–220. https://link.springer.com/article/10.1007/s12117-013-9191-7

Moyano, I. G. (2022). From a modernizing fighting force to national development stewards: Mexico's armed forces under ALMO. Wilson Center. https://www.wilsoncenter.org/sites/default/files/media/uploads/documents/22.04.12%20-%20Guevara%20-%20Mexico%27s%20Armed%20Forces%20Under%20AMLO_0.pdf

Muggah, R. (2017). The rise of citizen security in Latin America and the Caribbean. *International Development Policy, 9*, 291–322. https://doi.org/10.4000/poldev.2377

Muggah, R., & Aguirre Tobón, K. (2018). *Citizen security in Latin America, facts and figures*. Igarapé Institute. https://igarape.org.br/en/citizen-security-in-latin-america-facts-and-figures/

Müller, H. (2012). Security cooperation. In Carlsnaes, W., Risse, T., & Simmons, B. A. (Eds.), *Handbook of international relations* (2nd ed., pp. 607–634). SAGE Publications.

Muñoz, P., & Dargent, E. (2016). Patronage, Subnational linkages, and party-building: The cases of Colombia and Peru. In Levitsky, S., et al. (Eds.), *Challenges of party-building in Latin America* (pp. 187–216). Cambridge University Press.

Murders, corruption and crime: The hell of Mexican prisons. (2017, March 19). http://www.thejournal.ie/mexican-prisons-3418092-Jun2017/

Nácar, J. (2019). Fentanilo tiene sus epicentros en BC y CDMX. *Eje Central*. https://www.ejecentral.com.mx/fentanilo-epicentros-bc-cdmx/

Nájar, A. (2013, October 2). México, el país de los 100.000 secuestros. BBC News Mundo. http://www.bbc.com/mundo/noticias/2013/10/131002_mexico_pais_secuestros_inegi_garcia_valseca_narcotrafico_an

Nardo, M., et al. (2005). *Tools for composite indicators building*. Joint Research Centre, European Commission. http://publications.jrc.ec.europa.eu/repository/bitstream/JRC31473/EUR%2021682%20EN.pdf

National Institute on Drug Abuse. (2021). Overdose death rates. https://www.drugabuse.gov/drug-topics/trends-statistics/overdose-death-rates

Nau, H. R. (2010). Scholarship and policy-making: Who speaks truth to whom? In Reus-Smit, C., & Snidal, D. (Eds.), *The Oxford handbook of international relations* (pp. 635–647). Oxford University Press. https://10.1093/oxfordhb/9780199219322.001.0001

Nealon, J. (2018). The "place-based strategy" in Honduras. The Foreign Service Journal (October 2018). http://www.afsa.org/place-based-strategy-honduras

Neuman, W. (2017, April 16). Killing of 10 soldiers deals a setback to Colombian peace talks with FARC rebels. *The New York Times*. https://www.nytimes.com/2015/04/16/world/americas/colombia-attack-attributed-to-farc-threatens-peace-talks.html

Observatorio de Derechos Humanos y Derecho Internacional Humanitario. (2018). http://www.derechoshumanos.gov.co/observatorio/Paginas/Observatorio.aspx

O'Donnell, G. (Ed.). (1986). *Transitions from authoritarian rule: Latin America*, vol. 2. Johns Hopkins University Press.

O'Donnell, G. (1992). Transitions, continuities, and paradoxes. In Mainwaring, S., O'Donnell, G., & Valenzuela, J. S. (Eds.), *Issues in democratic consolidation: New South American democracies in comparative perspective* (pp. 17–56). University of Notre Dame Press.

O'Donnell, G. (1996). Illusions about consolidation. *Journal of Democracy, 7*, 34–51. https://muse.jhu.edu/article/16748

O'Donnell, G. (1998). Horizontal accountability in new democracies. *Journal of Democracy, 9*, 112–126.

O'Donnell, G. (1999). Delegative Democracy. *Journal of Democracy, 5*, 57–64.

O'Donnell, G. (2002). Horizontal accountability: The legal institutionalization of mistrust. In Mainwaring, S., & Welna, C. (Eds.), *Democratic accountability in Latin America* (pp. 34–55). Oxford University Press. https://10.1093/0199256373.001.0001

O'Donnell, G. (2004). Why rule of law matters. *Journal of Democracy, 15*, 31–46. https://www.journalofdemocracy.org/articles/the-quality-of-democracy-why-the-rule-of-law-matters/

Office of Rule of Law and Security Institutions. (2012). *The United Nations SSR Perspective*. United Nations. http://www.un.org/en/events/peacekeepersday/pdf/securityreform.pdf

Office of the Press Secretary. (2013, April 5). Fact Sheet: US security sector assistance policy. The White House. https://www.hsdl.org/?abstract&did=747214

OHCHR, Informes anuales. (2018). https://www.ohchr.org/en/countries/colombia

Olson, Jr., M. (1971). *The logic of collective action.* Harvard University Press.

Oosterveld, W., & Galand, R. (2012). Justice reform, security sector reform and local ownership. *Hague Journal on the Rule of Law, 4*, 194–209. https://doi.org/10.1017/S1876404512000115

Osborne, M. (2014). More than a Mexican problem: How the US can adapt Plan Colombia to Mexico. *Small Wars Journal.* https://smallwarsjournal.com/jrnl/art/more-than-a-mexican-problem-how-the-us-can-adapt-plan-colombia-to-mexico#_ednref17

Ospina, C. A. (2005). El Plan Patriota como estrategia militar. In Rangel, A. (Ed.), *Sostenibilidad de la seguridad democrática* (pp. 41–50). Fundación Seguridad y Democracia.

Palacios, M. (1986). *Estado y clases sociales en Colombia.* Procultura.

Palacios, M., & Safford, F. (2001). *Colombia: Fragmented land, divided society.* Oxford University Press.

Palacios, M., & Serrano, M. (2010). Colombia y México: las violencias del narcotráfico. In Alvarado, A., & Serrano, M. (Eds.), *Seguridad nacional y seguridad interior* (pp. 105–154). El Colegio de México. https://2010.colmex.mx/16tomos/XV.pdf

Pansters, W. G., Smith, B. T., & Watt, P. (2018). Introduction: Beyond the drug war: The United States, the public sphere, and human rights. In Pansters, W. G., Smith, B. T., & Watt, P. (Eds.), *Beyond the drug war in Mexico, human rights, the public sphere, and justice* (pp. 1–30). Routledge.

Parás, P., Moreno, A., & Seligson, M. A. (2008). *Cultura política de la democracia en México, 2008, el impacto de la gobernabilidad.* Latin American Public Opinion Project. http://www.vanderbilt.edu/lapop/mexico/2008-impactodegobernabilidad.pdf

Parás, P., Pizzolitto, G., & Romero, V. (2021). Cultura política de la democracia en México y en las Américas 2021: Tomándole el pulso a la democracia. *Latin American Public Opinion Project.* Vanderbilt University. https://www.vanderbilt.edu/lapop/mexico/AB2021MEX_Country_Report_Spanish_Final_220510.pdf

Paras exigen cuotas a alcaldes. (2004, April 27). *El Tiempo.* https://www.eltiempo.com/archivo/documento/MAM-1535451

Paris, R. (2009). Understanding the coordination problem in postwar statebuilding. In Paris, R., & Siske, T. D. (Eds.), *The dilemmas of statebuilding: Confronting the contradictions of postwar peacebuilding operations* (pp. 53–78). Routledge.

Parish Flannery, N. (2013). Calderón's war. *Journal of International Affairs, 66*, 181–196. https://www.jstor.org/stable/24388296

Partido Liberal arrecia crítica a Seguridad Democrática de Álvaro Uribe. (2011, June 22). *El Espectador.* https://www.elespectador.com/content/partido-liberal-arrecia-cr%C3%ADtica-seguridad-democr%C3%A1tica-de-%C3%A1lvaro-uribe

Partido Liberal Colombiano. (2019). https://congresovisible.uniandes.edu.co/partidos/perfil/liberal-colombiano/2/

Partidos y elecciones en Colombia. (2011). Universidad de los Andes. http://www.jstor.org/stable/10.7440/j.ctt18d83jk

Pastrana Arango, A. (2005). Antecedentes y perspectivas de la seguridad democrática. In Rangel, A. (Ed.) *Sostenibilidad de la Seguridad Democrática* (pp. 225–238). Fundación Seguridad y Democracia.

Patton, M. (1990). *Qualitative evaluation and research methods.* SAGE Publications.

Paul, C., et al. (2013). *What works best when building partner capacity and under what circumstances?* RAND Corporation. https://www.rand.org/pubs/monographs/MG1253z1.html

Paul, C., Schaefer, A. G., & Clarke, C. P. (2011). *The challenge of violent drug-trafficking organizations: An assessment of Mexican security based on existing RAND research on urban unrest, insurgency, and defense-sector reform.* RAND Corporation.

Payan, T., Staudt, K., & Kruszewski, Z. A. (Eds.). (2013). *A war that can't be won: Binational Perspectives on the war on drugs*, 2nd ed. University of Arizona Press.

Paz: Sí a la interlocución con el Partido Liberal. (2000, March 25). *El Tiempo*. https://www.eltiempo.com/archivo/documento/MAM-1257987

Pearce, J. (2010). Perverse state formation and securitized democracy in Latin America. *Democratization, 17*, 286–306. https://doi.org/10.1080/13510341003588716

Pearce, J. (2016). The "violence turn" in peace studies and practice. In Barbara Unger, Véronique Dudouet, Matteo Dressler, & Beatrix Austin (Eds.), *"Undeclared wars" - Exploring a peacebuilding approach to armed social violence* (pp. 31–40). Berghof Foundation. https://berghof-foundation.org/library/undeclared-wars-exploring-a-peacebuilding-approach-to-armed-social-violence

Pearce, J. (2017). The demonic genius of politics? Social action and the decoupling of politics from violence. *International Journal of Conflict and Violence (IJCV), 11*, 624. https://doi.org/10.4119/ijcv-3093

Pérez-Esparza, D., & Hemenway, D. (2018). We can reduce gun violence in Mexico, but we have to be smart about it. *RUSI*. https://shoc.rusi.org/informer/we-can-reduce-gun-violence-mexico-we-have-be-smart-about-it

Perito, R. M. (2009). *The private sector in security sector reform: Essential but not yet optimiz(ed)*. Peace Brief. United States Institute of Peace. https://www.usip.org/publications/2009/01/privatesector-security-sector-reform-essential-not-yet-optimized

Perito, R. M., & Kraut, J. (2016). SSR in Libya: A case of reform in a postconflict environment. In Hanlon, Q., & Shultz, Jr., R. H. (Eds.), *Prioritizing security sector reform: A new US approach* (pp. 39–68). United States Institute of Peace.

Peschard-Sverdrup, A. B. (2005). Foreword. In Roderick Ai Camp, *Mexico's military on the democratic stage*, pp. ix–xv. Greenwood Publishing.

PESE, Plan Estratégico del Sistema Educativo de las Fuerzas Armadas, 2007–2019 (2008). Ministerio de Defensa. https://www.mindefensa.gov.co/irj/go/km/docs/Mindefensa/Documentos/descargas/estrategia_planeacion/desa_capital/Pagina/PESE_FINAL.pdf

Phippen, J. W. (2021, May 5). Mexico just took an important step toward ending military impunity. *Politico*. https://www.politico.com/news/magazine/2021/05/05/mexico-marines-arrested-kidnappings-485250

Piccone, T. J. (2009). Supporting democracy in the Americas: The case for multilateral action. In Lowenthal, A. F., Piccone, T. J., & Whitehead, L. (Eds.), *The Obama administration and the Americas: Agenda for change* (pp. 47–68). Brookings Institution. https://www.jstor.org/stable/10.7864/j.ctt127zfr

Pierson, P. (2000). Increasing returns, path dependence, and the study of politics. *American Political Science Review, 94*, 251–267.

Pierson, P. (2004). *Politics in time, history, institutions, and social analysis*. Princeton University Press.

Pierson, P., & Skocpol, T. (2002). Historical institutionalism in contemporary political science. In Katznelson, I., & Milner, H. V. (Eds.), *Political science, state of the discipline* (pp. 693–721). American Political Science Association.

Pion-Berlin, D. (Ed.) (2001). *Civil-military relations in Latin America: New analytical perspectives*. University of North Carolina Press.

Pion-Berlin, D. (2016). Making the military accountable. In Foweraker, J., & Trevizo, D. (Eds.), *Democracy and its discontents in Latin America* (pp. 75–92). Lynne Rienner.

Plajian a hija del presidente de la ANDI. (2000, November 29). *El Tiempo*. http://www.eltiempo.com/archivo/documento/MAM-1287794

Policía Nacional de Colombia. (2017). *Escritos generales*. Policía Nacional de Colombia.

Popularity of Mexico's Calderon edges down—Poll. (2008, August 11). Reuters. https://www.reuters.com/article/us-mexico-calderon-idUSN1141807220080811

Posada-Carbó, E. (2013). Colombia: Democratic governance amidst an armed Conflict. In Domínguez, J. I., & Shifter, M. (Eds.), *Constructing democratic governance in Latin America* (4th ed., pp. 233–254). Johns Hopkins University Press. https://10.1353/jod.2011.0016

Post, L. A., Raile, A. N. W., & Raile, E. D. (2010). Defining political will. *Politics & Policy, 38*, 653–676. https://doi.org/10.1111/j.1747-1346.2010.00253.x

Pravda, A. (2001). Introduction. In Zielonka, J., & Pravda, A. (Eds.), *Democratic consolidation in Eastern Europe. Vol. 2, International and transnational factors.* Oxford Studies in Democratization (pp. 1–29). Oxford University Press. https://doi.org/10.1093/019924409X.001.0001

Preston, J. (1999, November 5). Mexican candidate plays the bad boy. *New York Times*. https://www.nytimes.com/1999/11/05/world/mexican-candidate-plays-the-bad-boy.html

Prevost, G., et al. (Eds.). (2014). *US national security concerns in Latin America and the Caribbean: The concept of ungoverned spaces and failed states.* Palgrave Macmillan. https://doi.org/10.1057/9781137379528_1

Przeworski, A. (1991). *Democracy and the market, political and economic reforms in Eastern Europe and Latin America.* Cambridge University Press. https://doi.org/10.1017/CBO9781139172493

Przeworski, A. (2009). Is the science of comparative politics possible? In Boix, C., & Stokes, S. C. (Eds.), *The Oxford handbook of comparative politics* (ch. 6). Oxford University Press. http://www.oxfordhandbooks.com/view/10.1093/oxfordhb/9780199566020.001.0001/oxfordhb-9780199566020-e-6

Przeworski, A., Stokes, S. C., & Manin, B. (Eds.). (1999). *Democracy, accountability, and representation.* Cambridge University Press. https://doi.org/10.1017/CBO9781139175104

Puck, L. (2017). Uneasy partners against crime: The ambivalent relationship between the police and the private security industry in Mexico. *Latin American Politics & Society, 59*, 74–95. https://doi.org/10.1111/laps.12011

Puig, J. C. (1984). *Doctrinas internacionales y autonomía latinoamericana.* Instituto de Altos Estudios de América Latina, Universidad Simón Bolívar.

Putnam, K. M. (2013). Campaigns, issue voting, and crime in developing democracies: evidence from Mexico's recent elections. APSA 2013 Annual Meeting Paper. https://papers.ssrn.com/abstract=2301390

Putnam, R. D. (1988). Diplomacy and domestic politics: The logic of two-level games. *International Organization, 42*, 427–460. https://www.jstor.org/stable/2706785

¿Qué es el fuero y por qué se inventó? (2017, March 29). http://tiempo.com.mx/noticia/77614-fuero_que_es_y_por_que_se_invento_mexico_politica_fuero_universitario/1

Ragin, C. C. (1989). *The comparative method: Moving beyond qualitative and quantitative strategies.* University of California Press.

Ramos, J. M. (2018, January 31–February 1). The local context. Presented at the First International Summit on Citizen Security, Tijuana, Mexico.

Ramos García, J. M. (2006). *Inseguridad pública en México, una propuesta de gestión de política estratégica en gobiernos locales.* UABC.

Renon, E. (2021). *Bringing the firm back in state and business relations in Latin America.* PhD dissertation. University College London.

Restrepo, E. M., & Martínez Cuéllar, M. (2004a, October 22). Algunas verdades sobre la impunidad penal en el sistema colombiano. *El Tiempo*. http://www.eltiempo.com/archivo/documento/MAM-1535599

Reyes Garmendia, E. S. (2008). Los partidos políticos frente a la reforma del estado en México. *Política y Cultura, 29*, 41–69. http://www.scielo.org.mx/scielo.php?script=sci_arttext&pid=S0188-77422008000100003

Ribando Seelke, C. (2018). *Mexico: Background and US relations.* Congressional Research Service. https://crsreports.congress.gov/product/pdf/R/R42917/43

Richani, N. (2002). *Systems of violence: The political economy of war and peace in Colombia.* State University of New York Press.

Richmond, O. P. (2010). Resistance and the post-liberal peace. *Millennium, 38*, 665–692.

Rico, D. M. (2013). *La dimensión internacional del crimen organizado en Colombia, las Bacrim, sus rutas y refugios.* Wilson Center. https://www.wilsoncenter.org/sites/default/files/media/documents/misc/Daniel%20Rico.pdf

Rivard Piché, G. (2017). *Building states, undermining public order? Security sector reform in pluralist public order regimes.* PhD thesis. Carleton University. https://curve.carleton.ca/d83efc31-4579-4cf5-9d6c-79239b3d4197

Robinson, W. I. (1996). Globalization, the world system, and "democracy promotion" in US foreign policy. *Theory and Society, 25*, 615–665. https://www.jstor.org/stable/658078

Rochlin, J. F. (1997). *Redefining Mexican "security": Society, state, & region under NAFTA.* Lynne Rienner.

Rochlin, J. F. (2011). Plan Colombia and the revolution in military affairs: The demise of the FARC. *Review of International Studies, 37*, 715–740. https://doi.org/10.1017/S0260210510000914

Rodríguez Cuadrado, J. F. (2008). La historia y el presente de las cifras delictivas y contravencionales en Colombia: Un nuevo conocimiento. *Revista Criminalidad, 50*, 109–318. http://www.scielo.org.co/scielo.php?script=sci_arttext&pid=S1794-31082008000100008

Rodríguez Luna, A. (2018). Violence, co-optation, and corruption: Risks for the exercise of journalism and freedom of expression in Mexico. In Pansters, W. G., Smith, B. T., & Watt, P. (Eds.), *Beyond the drug war in Mexico, human rights, the public sphere, and justice* (pp. 97–110). Routledge.

Rodríguez Pellecer, M. (2013, August 21). *Los militares y la élite, la alianza que ganó la Guerra 1982/1983. Plaza Pública* (Guatemala). https://www.plazapublica.com.gt/content/los-militares-y-la-elite-la-alianza-que-gano-la-guerra

Rodríguez Sánchez Lara, G. (2017). *Seguridad nacional en México y sus problemas estructurales.* Universidad de las Américas Puebla.

Ronfeldt, D. (1985). *The modern Mexican military.* RAND Corporation. https://www.rand.org/pubs/notes/N2288.html

Rosen, J. D., & Zepeda, R. (2016). Una década de narcoviolencia en México: 2006–2016. *Atlas de la seguridad y la defensa de México, 59*, 55–65. https://www.casede.org/PublicacionesCasede/Atlas2016/JonathanD_Rozen_Roberto_Zepeda.pdf

Rosenberg, T. (2014, November 20). Colombia's data-driven fight against crime. *The New York Times, Opinionator.* https://opinionator.blogs.nytimes.com/2014/11/20/colombias-data-driven-fight-against-crime/

Rothstein, B., & Varraich, A. (2017). *Making sense of corruption.* Cambridge University Press. https://www.cambridge.org/core/books/making-sense-of-corruption/15628A762B21D7189DB3D09D1AC9BE37

Ruiz, J. C. (2013, July 15). La policía nacional bajo presión. *Razón Pública.* https://razonpublica.com/la-policia-nacional-bajo-presion

Ruiz Vásquez, J. C. (2004b). Reinventando la seguridad en Colombia: reformas fallidas y modernización inconclusa de la policía colombiana. *Ensayos sobre seguridad y defensa, 1*(1), 18–29.

Ruiz Vásquez, J. C. (2012). Community police in Colombia: An idle process. *Policing and Society, 22*, 43–56. https://doi.org/10.1080/10439463.2011.597855

Russell, R., & Tokatlian, J. (2002). De la autonomía antagónica a la autonomía relacional: una mirada teórica desde el Cono Sur. *POSTData, Revista de Reflexión y Análisis Político, 21*, 159–194.

Russett, B. (1993). *Grasping the democratic peace: Principles for a post Cold War world.* Princeton University Press.

Sánchez, G. (2011, April 5). "Narconovelas" play out drama of Mexican drug war. *NPR*. https://www.npr.org/2011/04/06/135148342/narco-novelas-play-out-drama-of-mexican-drug-war

Sánchez David, R., & Rodríguez Morales, F. A. (2007). *Seguridad, democracia y Seguridad Democrática*. Editorial Universidad del Rosario.

Sandoval Perea, S. (2016). Assessing attitudes toward municipal police in Mexico during democratic times: A case study. *Mexican Law Review, 8*, 57–92. https://doi.org/10.1016/j.mexlaw.2016.07.003

Santos, J. M. (2005). El apoyo político a la seguridad democrática. In Rangel, A. (Ed.), *Sostenibilidad de la Seguridad Democrática* (pp. 201–210). Fundación Seguridad y Democracia.

Sartori, G. (1970). Concept misformation in comparative politics. *American Political Science Review, 64*, 1033–1053. https://doi.org/10.2307/1958356

Sartori, G. (1987). *The theory of democracy revisited - Part One, The contemporary debate*. CQ Press.

Savona, E. U., Dugato, M., & Garofalo, L. (2012). *A framework for the quantification of organized crime and assessment of availability and quality of relevant data in three selected countries of Latin America and the Caribbean*. Joint Research Centre on Transnational Crime; Centre of Excellence for Statistical Information on Governance, Public Security, Victimization, and Justice. http://www.transcrime.it/wp-content/uploads/2014/05/CoE_MOC-in-Latin-America-and-the-Caribbean-Sept-2012.pdf

Scharpf, F. W. (1988). The joint-decision trap: Lessons from German federalism and European integration. *Public Administration, 66*, 239–278. https://doi.org/10.1111/j.1467-9299.1988.tb00694.x

Schedler, A. (2010). What is democratic consolidation? In Diamond, L., Plattner, M. F., & Costopoulos, P. J. (Eds.), *Debates on democratization* (pp. 59–75). Johns Hopkins University Press.

Schimmelfennig, F. (2014). Democracy promotion and civil society in eastern Europe. In Beichelt, T., et al. (Eds.), *Civil society and democracy promotion* (pp. 217–233). Palgrave Macmillan.

Schmitter, P. (2001). The influence of the international context upon the choice of national institutions and policies in neo-democracies. In Whitehead, L. (Ed.), *The international dimensions of democratisation, Europe and the Americas* (pp. 26–54). Oxford University Press. https://10.1093/0199243751.001.0001

Schmitter, P., & Karl, T. L. (1991). What democracy is . . . and is not. *Journal of Democracy, 2*, 3–16. https://www.journalofdemocracy.org/articles/what-democracy-is-and-is-not/

Schnabel, A., & Ehrhart, H. G. (Eds.). (2005). *Security sector reform and post-conflict peacebuilding*. United Nations University Press. https://collections.unu.edu/eserv/UNU:2552/pdf9280811096.pdf/

Schönrock-Martínez, P. (2006). The European Union and security and defense policy in the Andean region. In Loveman, B. (Ed.), *Addicted to failure, US security policy in Latin America and the Andean region* (pp. 224–238). Rowman & Littlefield.

Schröder, U. C., & Kode, J. (2012). Rule of law and security sector reform in international statebuilding: Dilemmas of converging agendas. *Hague Journal on the Rule of Law, 4*, 31–53. https://doi.org/10.1017/S1876404512000036

Schumpeter, J. A. (1976). *Capitalism, socialism, and democracy*. 5th ed. George Allen and Unwin. https://periferiaactiva.files.wordpress.com/2015/08/joseph-schumpeter-capitalism-socialism-and-democracy-2006.pdf

Seawright, J., & Gerring, J. (2008). Case selection techniques in case study research: A menu of qualitative and quantitative options. *Political Research Quarterly, 61*, 294–308. https://doi.org/10.1177/1065912907313077

Se cayó el Plan de Desarrollo. (2000, May 17). El Tiempo. https://www.eltiempo.com/archivo/documento/MAM-1255358

Secretaría de Hacienda y Crédito Público. (2017). https://www.gob.mx/hacienda

Secretariado Ejecutivo del Sistema Nacional de Seguridad Pública. (2017). *Cifras de homicidio doloso, secuestro, extorsión y robo de vehículos, 1997–2017*. Secretaría de Gobernación. http://secretariadoejecutivo.gob.mx/docs/pdfs/cifras%20de%20homicidio%20doloso%20secuestro%20etc/HDSECEXTRV_062017.pdf

Secretariado Ejecutivo del Sistema Nacional de Seguridad Pública. (2019). *Reporte de incidencia delictiva del fuero federal por entidad federativa, 2012–2019*. Secretaría de Seguridad y Protección Ciudadana.

Security sector reform. (2015). SSR backgrounder series. Geneva Centre for the Democratic Control of Armed Forces. https://www.dcaf.ch/sites/default/files/publications/documents/DCAF_BG_2_Security%20Sector%20Reform_1.pdf

Security sector reform in post-conflict peacebuilding. (2009). DCAF Backgrounder. Geneva Centre for the Democratic Control of Armed Forces. https://www.files.ethz.ch/isn/100125/19_SSR_in_PCP.pdf

Sedra, M. (2018). Adapting security sector reform to ground-level realities: The transition to a second-generation model. *Journal of Intervention and Statebuilding, 12*, 48–63. https://doi.org/10.1080/17502977.2018.1426383

Sedra, M., & Burt, G. (2010). *Integrating SSR and SALW programming*. Occasional Paper no. 16, Geneva Centre for the Democratic Control of Armed Forces.

Sedra, M., & Burt, G. (2011). *Security sector reform (SSR) and the domestic-international security nexus: The role of public safety Canada*. Centre for International Governance Innovation. https://www.cigionline.org/publications/security-sector-reform-ssr-and-domestic-international-security-nexus/

Seidelmann, R. (2001). International security and democracy building. In Zielonka, J., & Pravda, A. (Eds.), *Democratic consolidation in Eastern Europe, vol. 2: International and transnational factors*. Oxford Studies in Democratization (pp. 112–138). Oxford University Press. DOI:10.1093/019924409X.001.0001

Selee, A., & Putnam, K. (2009). *Mexico's 2009 midterm elections: Winners and losers*. Woodrow Wilson Center. https://www.wilsoncenter.org/sites/default/files/media/documents/publication/Mexico%2527s%20Midterm%20Elections%20F.pdf

Serbin, A., & Fontana, A. (2006). Civil-military relations in Latin America: The post-9/11 scenario and the civil society dimension. In Schnabel, A., and Ehrhart, H.-G. (Eds.), *Security sector reform and post-conflict peacebuilding* (pp. 207–224). United Nations University Press.

Serna de la Garza, J. M. (1999). Constitutional federalism in Latin America. *California Western International Law Journal, 30*, 277–301. https://scholarlycommons.law.cwsl.edu/cgi/viewcontent.cgi?article=1270&context=cwilj

Sheridan, M. B. (2019, November 3). López Obrador and Mexico's military in rare public spat after El Chapo son is free. *The Washington Post*. https://www.washingtonpost.com/world/lopez-obrador-and-mexicos-military-in-rare-public-spat-after-el-chapos-son-is-freed/2019/11/03/c5d572f2-fda7-11e9-9e02-1d45cb3dfa8f_story.html

Shifter, M. (2012, July 18). Plan Colombia: A retrospective. *Americas Quarterly*. http://www.americasquarterly.org/node/3787

Shultz, R., et al. (2011). The sources of instability in the twenty-first century: Weak states, armed groups, and irregular conflict. *Strategic Studies Quarterly, 5*, 73–94. https://www.jstor.org/stable/26270558

Sikkink, K. (2001). The effectiveness of US human rights policy, 1973–1980. In Whitehead, L. (Ed.), *The international dimensions of democratisation, Europe and the Americas* (pp. 93–124). Oxford University Press. https://10.1093/0199243751.001.0001

Simangan, D. (2018). Domino effect of negative hybrid peace in Kosovo's peacebuilding. *Journal of Intervention and Statebuilding, 12*, 120–141. https://doi.org/10.1080/17502977.2018.1423772

Sisk, T. D. (2001). *Democracy at the local level: The international IDEA handbook on participation, representation, conflict management and governance*. International IDEA. https://www.idea.int/publications/catalogue/democracy-local-level

Skocpol, T., & Somers, M. (1980). The uses of comparative history in macrosocial inquiry. *Comparative Studies in Society and History, 22*, 174–197. https://www.jstor.org/stable/178404

Smith, C. E. (2000). *Inevitable partnership: Understanding Mexico-US relations*. Lynne Rienner.

Smith, M. A. (2000). *American business and political power*. University of Chicago Press. https://www.press.uchicago.edu/ucp/books/book/chicago/A/bo3630093.html

Smith, S. (2003b). US democracy promotion: Critical questions. In Cox, M., Ikenberry, G. J., & Inoguchi, T. (Eds.), *American democracy promotion, impulses, strategies, and impacts* (pp. 63–83). Oxford University Press. https://10.1093/0199240973.001.0001

Snyder, J. (2001). *From voting to violence: Democratization and nationalist conflict*. W. W. Norton.

Sohnen, E. (2012). *Paying for crime: A Review of the relationships between insecurity and development in Mexico and Central America*. Migration Policy Institute. https://www.migrationpolicy.org/pubs/RMSG-PayingforCrime.pdf

Soifer, H. D. (2012). The causal logic of critical junctures. *Comparative Political Studies, 45*, 1572–1597. https://doi.org/10.1177/0010414012463902

Soifer, H. D. (2016). The development of state capacity. In Fioretos, O., Falleti, T. G., & Sheingate, A. (Eds.), *The Oxford handbook of historical institutionalism* (ch. 10). Oxford University Press. http://www.oxfordhandbooks.com/view/10.1093/oxfordhb/9780199662814.001.0001/oxfordhb-9780199662814-e-10

Solicita ONU a Senado eliminar figuras de arraigo y prisión preventiva. (2018, November 15). https://www.uniradioinforma.com/noticias/politica/546974/solicita-onu-a-senado-eliminar-figuras-de-arraigo-y-prision-preventiva.html

Solingen, E., & Wan, W. (2016). Critical junctures, developmental pathways, and incremental change in security institutions. In Fioretos, O., Falleti, T. G., & Sheingate, A. (Eds.), *The Oxford handbook of historical institutionalism* (ch. 33). Oxford University Press. http://www.oxfordhandbooks.com/view/10.1093/oxfordhb/9780199662814.001.0001/oxfordhb-9780199662814-e-33

Sonnel, H. K. (2017, August 30). *Weekly chart, oil and remittances in Mexico's GDP*. https://www.as-coa.org/articles/weekly-chart-oil-and-remittances-mexicos-gdp

Sotomayor, M. A. (2018, January 31–February 1). The local context. Presented at the First International Summit on Citizen Security, Tijuana, Mexico.

Steinmo, S. (2008). What is historical institutionalism? In Porta, D. D., & Keating, M. (Eds.), *Approaches and methodologies in the social sciences: A pluralist perspective* (pp. 162–176). Cambridge University Press. https://doi.org/10.1017/CBO9780511801938

Stepan, A. C. (1988). *Rethinking Military politics: Brazil and the Southern Cone*. Princeton University Press.

Stipić, I. (2016). Conceptualizing autonomy in Latin American foreign policy: Case study of Brazil under the PT government (2003–2016). *Encuentro Latinoamericano, 3*, 68–88.

Stockholm International Peace Research Institute. (2021). *Data for all countries from 1988–2020 in Constant (2019) USD*. SIPRI Military Expenditure Database. https://www.sipri.org/databases/milex

Stojanović, S. (2012). An approach to mapping and measuring security sector reform. In Hadžić, M., et al. (Eds.), *Yearbook of security sector reform in Serbia* (pp. 69–102). Belgrade

Centre for Security Policy. https://bezbednost.org/wp-content/uploads/2020/07/6_stojanovic.pdf

Stokes, S. C. (2001). *Mandates and democracy: Neoliberalism by surprise in Latin America*. Cambridge University Press. https://www.amazon.co.uk/Mandates-Democracy-Neoliberalism-Cambridge-Comparative/dp/0521805112

Suárez Díaz, E., & Velasco Chaves, E. (2016). Consideraciones frente a la omisión impropia o comisión por omisión: posición de garante y Fuerzas Armadas. In Bernal Pulido, C., Barbosa Castillo, G., & Ciro Gómez, A. R. (Eds.), *Justicia transicional, el papel de las Fuerzas Armadas* (pp. 253–370). Universidad Externado de Colombia.

Suárez-Enríquez, X., & Meyer, M. (2017, February 8). La Ley de Seguridad Interior de México, pasando por alto los abusos militares en operaciones de seguridad pública. https://www.wola.org/es/analisis/la-ley-de-seguridad-interior-de-mexico-pasando-por-alto-los-abusos-militares-en-operaciones-de-seguridad-publica/

Sullivan, P. L. (2021, November 15). Does security assistance work? Why it may or may not be the answer for fragile states. Modern War Institute at West Point. https://mwi.usma.edu/does-security-assistance-work-why-it-may-not-be-the-answer-for-fragile-states/

Sullivan, P. L., Tessman, B. F., & Li, X. (2011). US military aid and recipient state cooperation. *Foreign Policy Analysis, 7*, 275–294. https://doi.org/10.1111/j.1743-8594.2011.00138.x

Talbot, O., & Wilde, N. (2011). Modeling security sector reform activities in the context of stabilization operations. *Journal of Defense Modeling and Simulation, 8*, 113–121. https://doi.org/10.1177/1548512910388202

Tansey, O. (2009). *Regime-building: Democratization and international administration*. Oxford University Press.

Tarrow, S. (1995). Review: Bridging the quantitative-qualitative divide in political science. *The American Political Science Review, 89*, 471–474. https://doi.org/10.2307/2082444

Teixeira, N. S. (2008). *The international politics of democratization: Comparative perspectives*. Routledge.

Tekin, Y. (2015). US and Mexican cooperation: The Merida Initiative and drug trafficking. *Pepperdine Policy Review, 8*. https://digitalcommons.pepperdine.edu/cgi/viewcontent.cgi?article=1111&context=ppr

Thelen, K. (1999). Historical institutionalism in comparative politics. *Annual Review of Political Science, 2*, 369–404. https://doi.org/10.1146/annurev.polisci.2.1.369

Thelen, K. (2003). How institutions evolve. In Mahoney, J., & Rueschemeyer, D. (Eds.), *Comparative historical analysis in the social sciences* (pp. 208–240). Cambridge University Press. https://www.cambridge.org/core/books/comparative-historical-analysis-in-the-social-sciences/how-institutions-evolve/B458636706123692DA1DA365A047489E

Thelen, K., & Conran, J. (2016). Institutional change. In Fioretos, O., Falleti, T. G., & Sheingate, A. (Eds.), *The Oxford handbook of historical institutionalism* (ch. 3). Oxford University Press. http://www.oxfordhandbooks.com/view/10.1093/oxfordhb/9780199662814.001.0001/oxfordhb-9780199662814-e-3

Thelen, K., & Steinmo, S. (1992). Historical institutionalism in comparative politics. In Thelen, K., Steinmo, S., & Longstreth, F. (Eds.), *Structuring politics: Historical institutionalism in comparative analysis* (pp. 1–32). Cambridge University Press.

Tilly, C. (1985). War making and state making as organized crime. In Evans, P. B., Reuschemeyer, D., & Skocpol, T. (Eds.), *Bringing the state back in* (pp. 169–191). Cambridge University Press. https://www.cambridge.org/core/books/bringing-the-state-back-in/war-making-and-state-making-as-organized-crime/7A7B3B6577A060D76224F54A4DD0DA4C

Tilly, C. (1992). *Coercion, capital, and European states, AD 1990–1992*. Blackwell.

Toledo, D. (2017). Reporte ethos: Descifrando el gasto público en seguridad. *ETHOS, Laboratorio de Políticas Públicas*. https://www.ethos.org.mx/finanzas-publicas/publicaciones/reporte_ethos_descifrando_el_gasto_publico_en_seguridad

The Tormented isthmus. (2011, April 14). *The Economist.* http://www.economist.com/node/18558254

Torres, R. (2011). Encuesta del INEGI, irresponsable: ICESI. *El Economista.* http://eleconomista.com.mx/sociedad/2011/09/30/encuesta-inegi-irresponsable-icesi

Torres, R. (2012). De la Barreda deja el ICESI. *El Economista.* http://eleconomista.com.mx/sociedad/2012/01/25/barreda-deja-icesi

Transparency International. (2018, February 21). *Corruption perceptions index 2017.* https://www.transparency.org/news/feature/corruption_perceptions_index_2017

Trejo, G., & Ley, S. (2018). Why did drug cartels go to war in Mexico? Subnational party alternation, the breakdown of criminal prosecution, and the onset of large-scale violence. *Comparative Political Studies, 51*, 900–937. https://doi.org/10.1177/0010414017720703

Trevizo, D. (2016). Counting the costs of political repression. In Foweraker, J., & Trevizo, D. (Eds.), *Democracy and its discontents in Latin America* (pp. 241–259). Lynne Rienner.

Tulchin, J. S., & Selee, A. (Eds.). (2004). *Decentralization and democratic governance in Latin America.* Woodrow Wilson Center Press.

Turkewitz, J. (2021a). 21 members of the Colombian military accept responsibility for the extrajudicial killings of at least 247 civilians in Colombia's "false positives" scandal, announces the country's special peace court. Next step: a tribunal and the determination of penalties. Twitter, December 10, 2021, 1:37 p.m. https://twitter.com/julieturkewitz/status/1469375856896364548?s=11

Turkewitz, J. (2021b, July 6). Colombian military leaders accused of assassinating civilians in civil war. *The New York Times.* https://www.nytimes.com/2021/07/06/world/americas/colombia-false-positives.html

U for Uribe. (2006, May 16). *The Economist.* https://www.economist.com/the-americas/2006/03/16/u-for-uribe

Ungar Bleier, E., & Cardona Cárdenas, J. F. (2006). El Congreso en la encrucijada. In Leal Buitrago, F. (Ed.), *En la encrucijada, Colombia en el siglo XXI* (pp. 51–80). Editorial Norma.

United Nations Department of Peacekeeping Operations and Office of the United Nations High Commissioner for Human Rights. (2011). *The United Nations rule of law indicators, implementation guide and project tools.* United Nations. https://www.un.org/ruleoflaw/blog/document/the-united-nations-rule-of-law-indicators-implementation-guide-and-project-tools/

United Nations Office for the Coordination of Humanitarian Affairs. (2022). Colombia: Impacto y tendencias humanitarias entre enero diciembre de 2021 a 8 de febrero de 2022. *ReliefWeb.* https://reliefweb.int/report/colombia/colombia-impacto-y-tendencias-humanitarias-entre-enero-diciembre-de-2021-08-de

United Nations Office on Drugs and Crime. (2014). *Global study on homicide 2013: Trends, contexts, data.* United Nations.

United Nations Office on Drugs and Crime. (2016). *World drug report 2016.* https://www.unodc.org/doc/wdr2016/WORLD_DRUG_REPORT_2016_web.pdf

United Nations Peacekeeping. (2017). Security sector reform. https://peacekeeping.un.org/en/security-sector-reform

United Nations Security Council. (2004). *The rule of law and transnational justice in conflict and post-conflict societies.* Report of the Secretary General. United Nations. https://digitallibrary.un.org/record/527647?ln=en

UNODC Statistics Online (2000–2015). (2017). https://data.unodc.org/#state:0

Uribe, V. (2017). Colombia: Ungoverned territory and the proliferation of nonstate actors. In Fonseca, B., & Gamarra, E. A. (Eds.), *Culture and national security in the Americas* (pp. 33–60). Lexington Books.

Uribe encabezó consejo de seguridad. (2004, April 27). *El Tiempo.* https://www.eltiempo.com/archivo/documento/MAM-1594744

Uribe vs. Serpa (bis). (2006, May 12). *Semana*. https://www.semana.com/nacion/articulo/uribe-vs-serpa-bis/78857-3

US Agency for International Development. (2010). *Guide to rule of law country analysis: The rule of law strategic framework*. https://pdfusaid.gov/pdf_docs/PNADT593.pdf

US Department of the Army. (2008). *Field manual (FM) 3-07 stability operations*. https://irp.fas.org/doddir/army/fm3-07.pdf

US Department of State. (2006). FY2007 congressional budget justification for foreign operations. https://2009-2017.state.gov/documents/organization/60641.pdf

US Department of State. (2008, December 19). Joint press conference on the Merida Initiative high-level consultative group. https://2001-2009.state.gov/secretary/rm/2008/12/113401.htm

US Department of State. (2018). *International narcotics control strategy report*. Vol. 1: Drug and chemical control. https://www.state.gov/wp-content/uploads/2019/04/2018-INCSR-Vol.-I.pdf

US House of Representatives. (2008). Congressional record. *Congressional Record* 154. https://www.govinfo.gov/app/collection/crecb/154_crecb

US Joint Chiefs of Staff. (1945). State-War-Navy Coordinating Committee, joint statement, records of the US-Mexico Military Defense Commission 5400

Vaicius, I. (2003). The US military presence in Colombia. *Center for International Policy*. http://ciponline.org/colombia/03022601.htm

Valenzuela, J. S. (1992). Democratic consolidation in post-transitional settings: Notion, process, and facilitating conditions. In Mainwaring, S., O'Donnell, G., & Valenzuela, J. S. (Eds.), *Issues in democratic consolidation, new South American democracies in comparative perspective* (pp. 57–104). University of Notre Dame Press.

Vandemoortele, A. (2015). Learning from failure? British and European approaches to security and justice programming. *Centre for Security Governance Insights, No. 6*. https://www.ssrresourcecentre.org/files/-justice-programming_kn3y2p5huigkn5hqzhmxb2/

Vanhanen, T. (1997). *Prospects of democracy: A study of 172 Countries*. Routledge.

Vela, D. S. (2016, May 12). Policías no tienen derecho a sindicato ni a huelga: SCJN. *El Financiero*. http://www.elfinanciero.com.mx/nacional/policias-no-tienen-derecho-a-sindicato-ni-a-huelga-scjn.html

Velásquez, R., & Prado Lallande, J. P. (Eds.). (2009). *La Iniciativa Mérida, ¿nuevo paradigma de cooperación entre México y Estados Unidos en seguridad?* Benemérita Universidad Autónoma de Puebla; Universidad Nacional Autónoma de México.

Veljko, J., Zoran, R., & Marina, D. (2016). *Emerging trends in the development and application of composite indicators*. IGI Global. https://www.igi-global.com/book/emerging-trends-development-application-composite/148514

Vidal, D. X. M., et al. (2010). Partisan attachment and democracy in Mexico: Some cautionary observations. *Latin American Politics and Society, 52*, 63–87. https://doi.org/10.1111/j.1548-2456.2010.00074.x

Villalobos, J. D. (2013). A federalist George W. Bush and an anti-federalist Barack Obama? In Payan, T., Staudt, K., & Kruszewski, Z. A. (Eds.), *A war that can't be won: Binational perspectives on the war on drugs* (2nd ed., pp. 174–194). University of Arizona Press.

Vision of Humanity. (2017). *Global peace index*. http://maps.visionofhumanity.org/#/page/indexes/global-peace-index

Visualización periodistas asesinados. (2015). *Semana*. http://especiales.semana.com/periodistas-asesinados/

Vivanco, J. M. (2021a). Celebro el anuncio de @FiscaliaCol sobre la imputación al Gen. Mario Montoya, excomandante del Ejército de Colombia, por su presunto rol en ejecuciones extrajudiciales conocidas como "falsos positivos." Se trata de un paso importante para el

derecho a la verdad de las víctimas. Twitter, July 31, 2021, 10:36 a.m. https://twitter.com/VivancoJM/status/1421479818621853697?s=11
Vivanco, J. M. (2021b). Colombia: Celebro que @FiscaliaCol haya imputado a tres miembros de la Policía (incluyendo un coronel) por su presunta responsabilidad en homicidios cometidos durante el paro nacional. Es necesario terminar con la impunidad de los abusos policiales en Colombia. Twitter, December 3, 2022, 11:50 a.m. https://twitter.com/VivancoJM/status/1466812050861137923?s=11
Vivanco, J. M. (2021c). Excelentes noticias del Congreso de EEUU! El subcomité de apropiaciones de la Cámara aprobó un proyecto para condicionar la asistencia de EEUU a la Policía de Colombia a mejorías en DDHH. Hoy esa exigencia sólo existe para fondos destinados al Ejército. Twitter, July 1, 2021, 6:51 p.m. https://twitter.com/VivancoJM/status/1410732876669329409?s=21
Vogel, D. (1989). *Fluctuating fortunes: The political power of business in America*. Basic Books.
Von Bredow, W. (2003). Assessing success and failure: Practical needs and theoretical answers. In Edmunds, T., & Germann, W. N. (Eds.), *Towards security sector reform in post Cold War Europe: A framework for assessment* (pp. 175–188). Nomos Verlagsgesellschaft.
Wager, S. J. (1984). Basic characteristics of the modern Mexican military. In Ronfeldt, D. (Ed.), *The modern Mexican military: A reassessment* (pp. 87–105). Center for US Mexican Studies, University of California-San Diego.
Waldmann, P. (2005). El impacto del terrorismo sobre la opinión pública y la política. In Rangel, A. (Ed.), *Sostenibilidad de la Seguridad Democrática* (pp. 211–224). Fundación Seguridad y Democracia. http://www.realinstitutoelcano.org/wps/portal/rielcano_es/contenido/!ut/p/a1/04_Sj9CPykssy0xPLMnMz0vMAfGjzOKNQ1zcA73dDQ38_YKNDRwtfN1cnf2cDf1DjfULsh0VAepxmvs!/?WCM_GLOBAL_CONTEXT=/elcano/Elcano_es/Zonas_es/ARI%2076-2006
Walker, S., Bridoux, J., & Zanotti, L. (2015). The contingent nature of democracy promotion. *Political Studies Review, 13*, 2–10. https://doi.org/10.1111/1478-9302.12032
Wallis, D. (2003). Democratizing a hegemonic regime: From institutionalized party to institutionalized party system in Mexico? *Democratization, 10*, 15–38. https://doi.org/10.1080/13510340312331293917
The White House. (2013). Fact sheet, US Security sector assistance policy. https://obamawhitehouse.archives.gov/the-press-office/2013/04/05/fact-sheet-us-security-sector-assistance-policy
Whitehead, L. (1986). International aspects of democratisation. In O'Donnell, G., Schmitter, P., & Whitehead, L. (Eds.), *Transitions from authoritarian rule, comparative perspectives, prospects for democracy* (vol. 3, pp. 3–46). Johns Hopkins University Press.
Wilén, N. (2018). Examining the links between security sector reform and peacekeeping troop contribution in post-conflict States. *Journal of Intervention and Statebuilding, 12*, 64–79. https://doi.org/10.1080/17502977.2018.1426680
The World Economic Forum. (2018). https://www.weforum.org/
W Radio Colombia. (2021). Los uniformados tendrán varios beneficios, entre ellos un puntaje adicional para acceso de vivienda, la priorización para el ingreso a jardines de sus hijos, y se creará el Centro de Estándares. Twitter, December 14, 2021, 3:31 a.m. https://twitter.com/wradiocolombia/status/1470672687395745792?s=11
Wuhs, S. T. (2001). Barbarians, bureaucrats, and bluebloods: fractional change in the National Action Party. In Middlebrook, K. J. (Ed.), *Party politics and the struggle for democracy in Mexico, National and state-level analyses of the Partido Acción Nacional* (pp. 129–155). Center for US Mexican Studies, University of California.
WVS Database. (2018). http://www.worldvaluessurvey.org/WVSDocumentationWV6.jsp
Yashar, D. J. (1997). *Demanding democracy: Reform and reaction in Costa Rica and Guatemala, 1870s–1950s*. Stanford University Press.

Youngers, C. A., & Rosin, E. (Eds.). (2004). *Drugs and democracy in Latin America: The impact of US policy*. Lynne Rienner.

Youngs, R. (2004). *International democracy and the West: The role of governments, civil society, and multinational business*. Oxford University Press. https://10.1093/0199274460.001.0001

Zanotti, L. (2011). *Governing disorder: UN peace operations, international security, and democratization in the postCold War era*. Pennsylvania State University Press.

Zartman, W. (1997). *The structuralist dilemma in negotiation*. Research Group in International Security.

Zepeda Lecuona, G. (2010). *La policía mexicana dentro del proceso de reforma del sistema penal*. Centro de Investigación para el Desarrollo, A.C.

Zepeda Patterson, J. (2009). Entrevista a Felipe Calderón. *El Universal*. http://www.eluniversal.com.mx/

Ziegler Rogers, M. (2016). Inequality and democratic representation. In Foweraker, J., & Trevizo, D. (Eds.), *Democracy and its discontents in Latin America* (pp. 51–73). Lynne Rienner.

Index

For the benefit of digital users, indexed terms that span two pages (e.g., 52–53) may, on occasion, appear on only one of those pages.

Tables and figures are indicated by *t* and *f* following the page number.